THE BERGDOLL BOYS

OTHER BOOKS BY THE AUTHOR

Hang on and Fly: A Post-War Story of
Plane Crash Tragedies, Heroism, and Survival
Association Island: General Electric's Vacation Paradise
Henderson Harbor: Fishing, Boating, and Summer Recreation

www.TimLakeBooks.com

THE BERGDOLL BOYS

America's Most Notorious Millionaire Draft Dodgers

TIMOTHY W. LAKE

BROOKLINE
books
Havertown, Pennsylvania

Brookline Books is an imprint of Casemate Publishers

Published in the United States of America and Great Britain in 2023 by
CASEMATE PUBLISHERS
1950 Lawrence Road, Havertown, PA 19083, USA
and
The Old Music Hall, 106–108 Cowley Road, Oxford OX4 1JE, UK

Copyright 2023 © Timothy W. Lake

Hardcover Edition: ISBN 978-1-955041-08-9
Digital Edition: ISBN 978-1-955041-09-6

A CIP record for this book is available from the British Library

Printed and bound in the United Kingdom by CPI Group (UK) Ltd, Croydon, CR0 4YY
Typeset in India by DiTech Publishing Services

For a complete list of Brookline Books titles, please contact:

CASEMATE PUBLISHERS (US)
Telephone (610) 853-9131
Fax (610) 853-9146
Email: casemate@casematepublishers.com
www.casematepublishers.com

CASEMATE PUBLISHERS (UK)
Telephone (0)1226 734350
Email: casemate-uk@casematepublishers.co.uk
www.casematepublishers.co.uk

Cover images: Grover Bergdoll fingerprints (U.S. Department of Justice); wanted poster (U.S. Department of Justice); Berta Bergdoll (Temple University Urban Archives); Emma Bergdoll (postcard); Bergdoll Brewery logo and trademark (Bergdoll Family Collection); 1950 Protective goggles (Wikipedia); Peccary driving gloves (Wikipedia); Sauer gun used by Bergdoll to kill a kidnapper in 1923 (Bergdoll Family Collection); Grover and Erwin Bergdoll sitting on an airplane (Chester County Historical Society/Roger Grigson)

To Polly Holmes Davis, whose love, encouragement, advice, and support inspired me to complete this incredibly challenging project.

Contents

Foreword

My father was Erwin R. Bergdoll. I was born in 1955 when he was 65. I never heard anything of his history, exploits, or family matters when I was growing up. It's hard to believe, but he never spoke of his 1911 racing win at the Fairmount Park Motor Race in Philadelphia, Pennsylvania. Nor did he speak of building the many Erwin Special race cars and racing them throughout the country. He died when I was ten years old. At a young age, I can understand why nobody spoke of my family's infamy. What could a child make of such things? On a couple of occasions, I did get to hear about my uncle Grover crashing one of my father's handmade racecars, destroying it when it burned. My father never let that go and would bring it up on occasion, very quietly, and like it was just to himself. There would be a couple of choice expletives thrown in.

While I never met my uncles Louis and Charles, or my aunt Betty, I did meet Uncle Grover a couple of times. He lived with my family for a short period in the early 1960s. I also never heard a word about past family history from him either. Neither directly nor from overhearing the adults talk.

It would have been great to be regaled with racing stories and talk of early flight. My sister, Mercedes, thought Grover was a menace and did not care for him at all. I thought of him as kind of amusing. In one of the only times Mercedes and I ever had what you would call a babysitter, it was Grover. My parents went out alone for an unknown reason. Uncle Grover took us out and about in the woods on our farm in Honey Brook, Pennsylvania, and we picked mushrooms with his directions. We went back to the house where he cooked them, and we ate them. I have to say they were quite good, and I remember the taste to this day. When my mother returned and heard about this, even though she didn't show it, I think she was quite livid. I believe, although I don't know, Uncle Grover may have become persona non grata over this, right then and there. I never saw him again.

I've always been relieved that my father didn't join his brother, Grover, and make a career out of evading the draft. Thinking about it, my father's draft evasion could very well be how I can write this. I discovered in this book that Grover was somewhat brilliant and he'd studied several different subjects. Just this year a friend contacted me about books of my uncle's that he had acquired in a collectibles purchase. He wanted someone in the family to have them, so I reimbursed him. I wanted to help offset his expenses but he wouldn't hear of it. Some of Uncle Grover's writings in the books had obvious use to an aviator, like navigation. Others are more of a mystery, such as toxicology. The notes are handwritten and very meticulous. They contain hand-drawn sketches that show some decent amount of skill. Oddly enough one book contained the Manual for Noncommissioned Officers and Privates of Infantry of the Army of the United States, of which Uncle Grover proudly claims ownership with his name stamped inside the cover, *GROVER C. BERGDOLL*. A rather ironic collector's item!

Uncle Grover, it seems, was always looking for a way to make a splash and gain notoriety. Often his zeal got him into trouble, like flying his Wright B Flyer around City Hall in Philadelphia, racing his many cars around the streets recklessly, and eventually running from the draft. His taunting of various authorities has always been a mystery to me. I've never been able to reconcile why he would insult his pursuers, and if nothing else, further motivate them. The Pot of Gold story and his subsequent escape are hard for me to understand. Why anyone would be released to recover buried treasure leads me to believe his draft evasion was not that big of a deal with the authorities who held him. This happened, regardless of the anger of the public concerning his actions. His exploits became so much that they created a rift in the family that was never reconciled to this day.

When my cousins, Louis and Wilbur Bergdoll's place at 22nd and Green Street in Philadelphia suffered a fire in the 1980s I thought I could try to mend the rift, but it was not to be. I knew they were up in their years, and looking at the place I figured they could use some help. I offered my services to Wilbur and helped out a bit. One day I stopped in and Wilbur had some coins out to go to a show. I came to realize that day that he didn't trust me because he wouldn't invite me in. I decided to no longer darken his doorstep with my visits. My father had a hand in that rift, but I think to a much lesser degree than Uncle Grover. I believe my father was forgiven in the family even if I'm fairly certain he never forgave himself. He lived out the rest of his life on the farm in Honey Brook in self-imposed seclusion. He didn't want to talk to anyone about these affairs, and suspected anyone who tried to see him was looking for a sensational story.

In light of my grandmother Emma's involvement in the legal affairs of my father and Uncle Grover, I've come to the belief that she was overindulgent with them as young men. Her involvement was such that she and Uncle Charles, and their cohorts, were tried and convicted of conspiracy in the draft evasion affairs. I can't put myself in her situation in that time, so while I'm inclined to frown upon their actions, I have to withhold judgment. That my uncle was living in virtual exile for 20 years, while he was married, is just one more oddity to me. His jail term was roughly a quarter of his self-imposed imprisonment.

The various machines of the boys disappeared over time from their storage at the Bergdoll family farm in Broomall, Pennsylvania. Uncle Grover's Wright B Flyer

Louis Erwin Bergdoll in front of his uncle Louis J. Bergdoll Bergson's magnificent Philadelphia Italianate mansion, 2019. Long legs and short torsos are physical traits for the Bergdoll men, except for Grover. (Timothy W. Lake)

is now in the Franklin Institute in Philadelphia. Uncle Louis' Bleriot, a French aircraft, is now at a museum in New York. My father's championship Benz race car is missing. I thought it was in the Mercedes Benz museum in Stuttgart, Germany, but the research in this book indicates they have an earlier model. In an act of revisionist history, the Wright B Flyer was restored to factory specifications rather than how it was flown over Philadelphia and the surrounding areas with BERGDOLL painted across the bottom of the lower wing. They were all taken under questionable circumstances.

My father's racing trophies—I saw three of them—were no doubt to me stolen and sold by my brother, Erwin, Jr. I pieced this together from reading a newspaper article about my brother and his subsequent jailing for stealing from my father. It's only circumstantial, but the trophies disappeared, my brother was jailed, and one of the trophies appeared somewhere else.

This book tied together many things that I had already thought about. It gave me additional insights into things that were news to me. Throughout my life, I have encountered people who either loved my family or reviled them. Many times, when someone authored a story about some aspect of my family history, be it aviation, beer brewing, automobile manufacturing, or auto racing, the family infamy always is mentioned. As the Don Henley song states, "We love dirty laundry!" This book is the fairest treatment of my family history that I have ever read.

Louis Erwin Bergdoll, 2023

The Bergdoll boys of Philadelphia and their sister. Top to bottom, left to right, Louis Bergdoll Bergson, Charles Bergdoll Brawn, Elizabeth Bergdoll Hall, Grover Bergdoll, and Erwin Bergdoll. Each inherited fortunes from the Bergdoll Brewery leading to the decades-long drama that is *The Bergdoll Boys*. (Bergdoll Family Collection)

Introduction

Philadelphia, Pennsylvania, 1994

Exploring the Franklin Institute science museum one day in 1994, I entered the Hall of Aviation to find the exhibit of a 1911 Wright B Flyer, the 13th airplane mass-produced by the famous Wright Brothers with a design in which they deviated from their original glider by installing the elevator in the tail.

There was scant information to satisfy my curiosity about why the plane was in Philadelphia, not the Smithsonian National Air and Space Museum in Washington. It also appeared shabby. The fuselage fabric was discolored with brown stains, and a large flat aluminum pan sat beneath the engine catching dirty oil drippings. A small plaque said the plane last flew in the 1930s. I didn't give it much attention, and neither did anyone else.

Several years later, while delivering the news on Philadelphia's WCAU-TV, I received a press release from the museum that explained how their Wright B Flyer was being dismantled and sent to Ohio for restoration. Again, there was very little information about the origin of the airplane, except that it was the most intact example of a Wright Brothers airplane, containing more original parts than the famous Kitty Hawk glider on display at the Smithsonian. I grew determined to explore the real story behind this airplane. Who owned it? Who flew it? And why was it in Philadelphia at the Franklin Institute?

What I discovered about the original owner who purchased the plane from the Wright Brothers in 1912, shipped it to Philadelphia on a rail car, and flew it from his private grass strip in the Pennsylvania countryside is one of the most dramatic and captivating stories I've encountered in my long career as a newspaper and broadcast journalist.

This rare and rudimentary airplane performed 748 successful flights around eastern Pennsylvania and New Jersey, astonishing people in their farm fields, rowhouse windows, churches, and on the beach. Some of these flights set early aviation records, while others raced steam locomotives on Pennsylvania's Main Line railroad and scattered spectators and horses at the prestigious Devon Horse Show.

On and on, it flew through virgin airspace with a daring pilot who could have been nicknamed Glorious Grover long before Lucky Lindy if not for one inglorious

Grover Bergdoll's 1911, most original Wright B Flyer has been displayed at the Franklin Institute Hall of Aviation in Philadelphia, Pennsylvania since it was last flown in 1934. Whether sitting on the floor or hanging from the ceiling, its provenance has always been ascribed to the Wright Brothers, with scant information about Bergdoll. (Franklin Institute)

Since 1933, Grover Bergdoll's Wright B Flyer has undergone three restorations, most recently in 2002–2003. (Timothy W. Lake)

mistake. Instead, the original owner and pilot of this now million-dollar one-of-a-kind airplane flew it for less than two years and then stashed it in a garage on his family's Pennsylvania country estate.

Then, as a millionaire brewery-heir celebrity, he converted his cash to gold and fled the country as the most notorious draft dodger in American history.

For many years I've been researching the incredible life of Grover Cleveland Bergdoll, the man who bought the airplane from the Wright Brothers in 1912 and was trained partly by Orville Wright to fly it. I read Roberta Dell's 1977 book, *The United States against Bergdoll*. (A.S. Barnes and Company). I determined that while Dell told a good story, she did not have access in the 1970s to the wealth of materials available from around the world in the Internet research age that I could gather from the United States, Canada, France, and Germany on the Bergdoll story.

However, I put the project on hold to write and publish three other books already on my agenda: *Henderson Harbor* (2012), *Association Island* (2013), and *Hang on and Fly* (2015).

During my research, I discovered that the late Alfred Bergdoll, Grover's eldest son, wrote a 645-page manuscript that he annotated into a diary of the Bergdoll family. His margin and full-page longhand notes are nearly illegible. Still, after many hours studying his script and understanding the family foibles, I could piece together his positive and negative comments about his father's ignominious life. Alfred wished to publish the story, but I found it in less than first draft form, nowhere near publication-ready, and missing key parts of the story.

Within the diary-manuscript, the personal, intimate, and emotional elements of the story of Grover Bergdoll and his dedicated wife and gun-waving, check-writing mother are all there. It includes a delicious tale of how Grover and his mother withdrew thousands of dollars in gold coins from the U.S. Treasury to fund his escape. Today, people still hunt for Bergdoll's gold, said to be buried in the hills of Maryland, West Virginia, or Pennsylvania, or maybe nowhere.

Some of Alfred Bergdoll's recollections and figures in the diary-manuscript are conjecture, and challenging to prove. However, of the many items in this story up for discussion, one thing is sure. Like his son, Alfred, Grover Bergdoll was a meticulous record keeper who put everything on paper, usually with his typewriter. Grover was also a knowledgeable man who studied and kept diaries on mathematics, physics, engineering, chemical components of explosives, ballistics on German rifles, formulas for light and bullet refraction, meteorology and astrology, ancient Egyptian history, celestial navigation, and wind impacts on aerial navigation. He even recorded much of his life with his own cameras and produced photographs in his own studio and darkroom. He was a highly intelligent man but, at the same time, his intellect hovered near the edge of insanity.

And, while his life unraveled for public display of his personal tragedy, a long-time family friend told Congress, Grover had too much money at a young, unsupervised age, enabling his unwise decisions.

Later in life, it appears that Grover's poor decisions were influenced by mental illness and a lifetime of being pursued and denigrated, leading to selfishness, paranoia, destructive and abusive behavior, and abandonment.

With Bergdoll's family's permission and support, I have utilized portions of Alfred's diary in this story, adding to my deep research. As the oldest of nine surviving children to Grover and Berta Franck Bergdoll, Alfred was able to witness most of the tragic events of his father's adult life.

Alfred's richly scandalous story was virtually hidden away from view by all but a few who were determined to read it. I am glad I found it filed away in a Philadelphia archive, and I'm grateful that Alfred wrote and saved his diary-manuscript, the *Curse of the Bergdoll Gold*. I also appreciate that Alfred's sister and executor of his estate, Katharina Bergdoll, permitted me to utilize the narrative for this book. Without it, the Bergdoll story could have been told, but it would not have been complete.

Additionally, other members of the Bergdoll family reached out to me with approval and encouragement to go ahead with the story. They have been incredibly patient while I was stymied by research roadblocks for years, waiting for the entire story to come out.

***

Grover Cleveland Bergdoll was initially an American hero who became an absolute scoundrel. His story is that of a rising national celebrity in the days before modern mass media.

Philadelphia women loved him. Racing fans gathered around the Bergdoll race cars in Philadelphia's Fairmount Park to glimpse the daring Grover or his equally famous brother and championship driver, Erwin. Crowds of spectators would gather at the Bergdolls' private airfield just in case Grover might be in a flying mood. Orville Wright called him one of his most accomplished pilots. Grover's many court appearances for speeding in his luxury cars guaranteed a packed gallery and press coverage. He cultivated the adulation.

He had his name, Bergdoll, painted in large letters on the underside of his airplane just in case there was any doubt about who was flying one of the few Wright B planes in the Mid-Atlantic region in 1912 and 1913.

And when Grover sullied the Bergdoll name, his brothers chose new ones.

ARREST THIS MAN

GROVER CLEVELAND BERGDOLL, convicted for violation of the 58th Article of War (Draft Evader). Sentenced to five years' imprisonment. Escaped from military guard at Philadelphia, Pa., on May 21, 1920. Was a fugitive from Justice from August 8, 1917, to January 7, 1920.

DESCRIPTION.—White; 28 years old; 5 feet 4 inches tall; 175 pounds; heavy build; broad, square shoulders; dark brown hair, brushed back from forehead; dark brown eyes; good teeth, but stained from tobacco; scar on neck and throat; is a member of a wealthy Philadelphia family and has traveled extensively. Constantly on the move and probably accompanied by a male companion. Expert automobile driver and traveler, and delights in exploiting his ability. Flashy and dramatic. Liberal spender and well supplied with money. When last seen was in a Hudson Super Six Automobile, Pennsylvania License No. 85478, accompanied by chauffeur.

If located, arrest and notify nearest Military Post, Agent of the Department of Justice, or local Police authorities and the Military Intelligence Division, General Staff, War Department, Washington, D. C.

Grover Cleveland Bergdoll was a millionaire and the most wanted draft dodger in America between 1917 and 1939. Initially, he snubbed his nose at the law, and was annoyed at the Army's description of him as 5′4″ tall (he was 5′6″) and with tobacco-stained teeth. However, it's correct that he was flashy, dramatic, and well-supplied with money. (United States Department of Justice)

Grover Bergdoll built and cultivated his fame by inheriting massive wealth from his family's Philadelphia brewery fortune, racing cars on the first speed tracks of America, and then becoming a daring aviation pioneer long before Lindbergh.

But, in one foolish move, he threw it all away. By dodging the military draft when America entered the Great War, Bergdoll destroyed his hero status and celebrity. He would forever be known as America's most notorious millionaire playboy draft dodger.

When Grover Bergdoll ran from the draft, Americans were fervently loyal to the millions of soldiers sent to fight against the Germans in World War I. As Americans were whipped into a frenzy of European war support, a wealthy celebrity and first-generation German-American like Grover never stood a chance with the patriotic public.

Even though the government and press ignored hundreds of thousands of other draft dodgers, Grover was vilified primarily because of his wealth and fame, and because he openly taunted his adversaries with his unique ability to remain free.

Digging deep, I found more insidious and petty motives for Bergdoll's vilification. An arch-rival to the Bergdolls was simultaneously a highly patriotic Philadelphia newspaper editor and war draft official tasked with choosing the names of young men to join the fight. He held a long vendetta against the rich Bergdolls and exacted his revenge. And when presented with specific allegations of targeting Grover, he didn't deny them.

Not to say the Bergdolls were innocent. It is a fact that four Bergdoll men in three generations ran from their military duty. But so did hundreds of thousands of other men who were never persecuted like the Bergdolls.

Wealth, celebrity, notoriety, and taunting will paint a bullseye on one's back. In the dawn of modern media, that's precisely what happened with Grover and Erwin Bergdoll.

I researched and wrote this story for entertainment and for readers to experience the great sense of adventure the Bergdoll boys experienced with their lives—and the destruction it caused for many other lives. It's not meant to be educational or instructional, but a portrayal of their incredible and dramatic lives, good and bad. Within these pages, I've presented dialogue for the characters based entirely on their own words and edited, in some instances, only for grammar and spelling.

Some of this story comes from Alfred Bergdoll's lengthy diary-manuscript. Other parts are from personal letters and documents written by members of the Bergdoll family, friends, and associates, interviews compiled by newspaper and magazine reporters, investigative reports, and sworn testimony from the many court appearances and Congressional hearings involving the Bergdolls, including Grover's children.

The Bergdoll draft-dodging story was so popular in 1920–1921 that press syndicates featured full-page synopses in newspapers worldwide. This one featured, clockwise from top left, Erwin, the Wynnefield mansion, Grover, Emma, Louis, Russell Gross, and Grover's Army defense attorney Major Bruce Campbell. (Newspaper Feature Service, 1921, Hearst Co.)

Sometimes, the dialogue (testimony) is from another period and inserted into a relevant descriptive scene. If it's in quotation marks, it's dialogue from the source, but in some cases, it's the source's recollection of a previous time.

Throughout the decades of Bergdoll drama—the racing, flying, running from the law, hidden gold, and legal wrangling with the courts and Congress—the Bergdoll family was hounded by the public and press. Their notoriety became part and parcel of their persecution.

Undoubtedly, Grover Cleveland Bergdoll disgraced himself and his family by his actions as America's greatest draft dodger. How new generations of Bergdoll family members and others express anger, sorrow, or forgiveness is their difficult choice.

However, all these years later, the question remains: Should the Bergdolls' draft-evading actions still be considered the overriding story of their lives, or should there be more recognition of their early achievements in aviation and automobile racing? For years, Grover's plane has been displayed in a prestigious museum with little information about its owner's accomplishments. And now, there is scant information about how the museum acquired the airplane in the first place with its long-claimed written agreement reduced to an oral gift through a third-party museum volunteer who may have simply taken the airplane from a Bergdoll property without a record of permission to save it from ruin. Their once-mighty brewery has been reduced to a graveyard tour, and most people mistake the only surviving Bergdoll mansion for Grover's house of gold, secrets, and escape.

Today's population views World War I, and the Korean and Vietnam conflicts, differently than prior generations. Perhaps after a deep examination of *The Bergdoll Boys,* the much-maligned family will be viewed differently one day, despite their foibles.

Bergdoll Family Tree

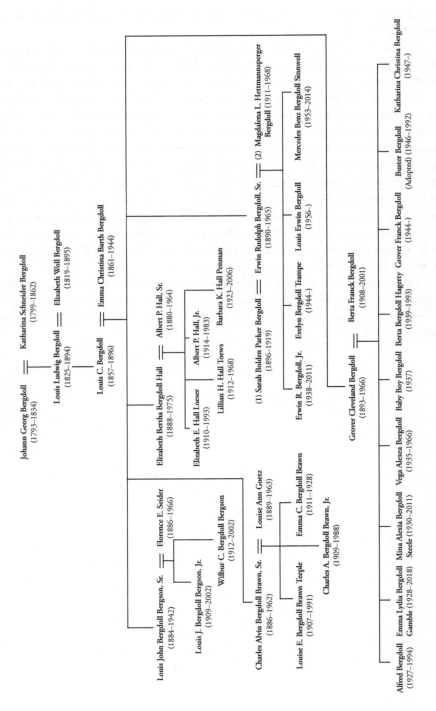

Prologue: A Milk Can Full of Gold

Washington, D.C., May 1920

America's most wanted millionaire draft dodger arrived in Washington with an empty milk can to be filled with gold. He wanted thousands of shiny gold coins to pay for secrecy and bribes while running away. Gold coins commanded attention after the Treasury discontinued their use in favor of the dollar.

Currency and gold certificates wouldn't do. Not where he was going. He needed precious gold coins and lots of them for his new life away from home. And, with a bounty on his head as America's number one slacker, he and his driver were about to enter the financial nest of the United States government to get them.

Slowing their mud-spattered touring car to a stop at the curb of the North Wing of the Treasury building, the driver, Eugene Andrew (Ike) Stecher, felt his heart racing as he pulled the brake. It marked the end of a week-long journey for the German-born chauffeur-mechanic driving with his wealthy American patron next to him in their 1917 Hudson Super Six Series J sedan, license plate number *85-478 Penna* 1920.[1] They were federal fugitives, traveling nonstop at significant risk through cities and towns in Mid-Atlantic states, arriving at the Treasury with one aim: to fill their luxury car with gold.

While pushing a button with his thumb to release an electrical current, Stecher, as most people called the bull of a man at the wheel, with a hard K for his surname, simultaneously engaged the clutch by gradually releasing his foot from the rubber-covered steel pedal. The car lurched forward, shuddered, and coughed, halting the high-powered gasoline engine. Stecher's passenger climbed to stand on the long, flat running board. Stretching and feeling sore after a short night of sleep following the muscle-jarring eastward excursion in the open-style sedan across Indiana, Ohio, Pennsylvania, and Maryland, Grover Cleveland Bergdoll surveyed the early morning scene outside the Treasury building.

At 26, he was a short figure, about five feet six, with broad square shoulders, wearing a thick and heavy brown wool suit and with his dark brown hair brushed back into a pompadour, a rapidly fading style among young men following the war.

---

[1] The Super Six designation for several Hudson models indicates a straight six-cylinder engine.

A thick scar curved upward from his neck and throat to the right side of his face. Another scar on his chin formed an inverted horse-shoe, matching his bristly mustache, and he displayed tobacco-stained teeth from his sweet Beech-Nut chew and burned cigar nubs. Flashy and dramatic, Grover Bergdoll was a free spender and an expert automobile driver and traveler. It said so on his federal WANTED posters. He was a well-known celebrity millionaire at home in Philadelphia, but Bergdoll was merely a man on the run this spring morning in Washington.

Grover Bergdoll, center, at the wheel of Big Red, his powerful Benz touring car in Germany in the early 1920s. Eugene "Ike" Stecher is behind Grover, at left. The third man is unidentified but appears to be magazine journalist Leighton Blood. (Bergdoll Family Collection)

Scanning the macadam street and the concrete walkway leading to the neoclassical Treasury building's tall columns, Bergdoll feared he and Stecher would be recognized. The Super Six was his car, and in the heart of the nation's capital, a coin's throw from the Executive Mansion and the Bureau of Investigation, he had reason to be wary that such a stylish machine would attract attention.

At the approach of summer in 1920, Grover Bergdoll was a famous beer brewery heir, record-setting airplane pilot, and champion racing car driver. He was also the most wanted man in America, a notorious draft dodger from the war whose spectacular escape from his military guards in his opulent Philadelphia stone mansion made national headlines and was the nation's talk. He defied the notoriety, exuding confidence with paper banknotes neatly folded in a canvas bag under his arm, inside his coat.

Grover was intent on tendering the cash, filling the milk can with gold, and disappearing.

Workers who had recently completed construction of the beaux-arts Treasury annex along Lafayette Park across Pennsylvania Avenue at Madison Place had much of the street torn up to install new rails for trolley cars. They ignored the man standing on the parked Hudson's running board. The Greek Ionic columns of the Treasury building towered above federal employees hurrying along the sidewalk to and from their offices. They had a laborious walk. The building was 468 feet long and 264 feet wide. Despite the work activity in the rapidly developing capital following the

Grover and Stecher used this 1917 Hudson Super Six touring car to escape across the upper Midwestern United States to the border with Canada. (Temple University Urban Archives)

war, the dark-suited man didn't see much to alarm him as he stood for a moment on the side of the Hudson. Despite the prominence of the Super Six, their appearance on 15th Street in Washington was nothing extraordinary, but their mission caused both men to be alert to anything unusual. Recognition from a federal worker could land them both in the guardhouse. They hurried to get off the street.

The Hudson was a fast car with a big engine and three-speed transmission. It displayed sleek, gentle curves on a blue-black body and a fully retractable fabric roof. Near the top-of-the-line with wire wheels, a spare tire, and bumpers, it was one of the most reliable automobiles on the market. The seven-passenger Phaeton body style, ample floor space, and full rear leather bench seat were ideal for their job. It had plenty of room to carry a can heavy with gold.

The Hudson was such a prestigious car that the wealthy man scanning the sidewalk owned more than a few. Bergdoll frequently traveled in the touring vehicle he and Stecher motored across the heartland of America. He kept a more luxurious hardtop limousine model in his 12-dormer garage topped by a dome behind his four-story Gothic stone mansion in an affluent section of Philadelphia. He also kept a fleet of stylish roadsters used for racing.

Several days earlier, the two men fled in the Super Six from Bergdoll's Army guards in Philadelphia in a nearly unbelievable stunt. They drove south to Bel Air, Maryland, and westward to Pittsburgh, Columbus, and Indianapolis. And then, realizing they needed an instant influx of gold coins for a journey over the northern border and across the Atlantic to Europe, they motored back to Washington to fetch them. Back home in the garage, the limousine would have been much more comfortable, but it attracted more attention and was slower. He didn't want to scratch the limo with the heavy gold and "knock it all to pieces," either.

Stepping down to the sidewalk, Bergdoll scanned again for signs of people watching, anyone who may have been following them. He saw none.

Both men were dressed in four-button lapel coats over vests, wearing stiff and snug chalk-white Murray Hill celluloid shirt collars, matching button-down long-sleeved shirts with linked cuffs, ties, dark slacks, and thick black high-top leather boot-shoes with tight laces around their ankles, German-style.

Bergdoll wore the high collar to hide part of a vicious scar across his neck from a disastrous race car crash when he'd driven into a barbed-wire fence installed to keep livestock off the track. Stecher just wore his formal collar to appear more substantial for their mission. Bergdoll's steep heels were to boost his short stature to match his enormous wealth and oppressive demeanor. Checked in under aliases, each man shaved that morning at their pricey Washington hotel and expertly coiffed his hair to present a professional appearance in a departure from their routine. They could have passed for Washington bankers except for the unusual bulge under Bergdoll's coat.

On the short drive from their hotel to the Treasury, the men motored in front of the Executive Mansion, the State, War, and Navy Building, and the offices housing the Department of Justice several times while assessing the streets of Washington and the spirit of their mission.[2]

At the curb of the Treasury building around the corner from Washington's famous Pennsylvania Avenue, calming his nerves with a deep breath, Stecher reached into the rear floorboard section of the car and, with a loud clanging noise, banged open the lid of the milk can they had picked up in Pennsylvania.[3] Shiny and polished smooth inside, the big empty can would appear as if gleaming in the first rays of the morning sun. Grabbing it by a handle and quickly darting across the sidewalk and through a gate in the spiked iron fencing, Stecher and Bergdoll ducked into the Treasury building's nearest door. They headed for small wooden signs directing them to the stately Cash Room on the North Wing's second floor. They moved with the stealth of burglars. For Stecher, the weight of the can would tug on his hand like a long-barreled revolver. However, neither man carried a gun. They were left in the car.

The riskiest part of their mission lay ahead.

A tall, stout German man with a round face, wide-set brown eyes, thick walrus mustache under his pointy nose, and smooth black receding hair tamped with waxy cream over his ample forehead, Ike Stecher was a long-trusted motor mechanic for his younger companion, Grover. At 33, Stecher had known Bergdoll since they were kids on the streets of one of America's most industrial cities, Philadelphia. Stecher's father had worked for Bergdoll's father in his enormous Philadelphia brewery that generated immense wealth, some of which they would fetch from the Treasury.

---

[2] Many years after its name was first used in 1901, the president's home was referred to as the White House and the Executive Mansion. The State, War, and Navy building became the Old Executive Office Building.

[3] Before World War I, German-born Eugene Stecher spelled his name with a K. He was alternately called Gene and Ike. However, his most used nickname was Stecker.

As boys, they developed their trust and dependence from playing in the streets of the Fairmount and Brewerytown neighborhoods of Philadelphia. As young adults, they raced cars around a long track in the city's renowned Fairmount Park. Together, they rode in races all over the country, winning some and becoming celebrities with photographs of their dirt and carbon-blackened faces on the pages of newspapers on more than a few occasions. Their access to wealth and their racing notoriety gave them a sense of celebrity, and confidence that they were consistently recognized wherever they traveled. They weren't.

Stecher knew his way around internal combustion engines and behind the wheel of a fast car, and he was so loyal to the Bergdolls that he left his wife at home to run with Grover from the law. In doing so, Stecher disregarded his decade of service in the Pennsylvania National Guard. He drove the car, racing away from the security of a Philadelphia mansion and two Army guards with the convicted draft dodger. Now, he was a fugitive too.

***

Months earlier, Stecher waited behind the Hudson's wheel while Bergdoll entered a Camden, New Jersey bank and returned with a canvas bag filled with Federal Reserve notes.[4] They were primarily tens, with a few twenties, fifties, and hundreds, in packs of 500 dollars neatly arranged with glued and labeled paper straps and rubber bands. The wealthy man specifically demanded lower denomination federal gold notes from the teller instead of accepting local banknotes. He withdrew cash until the thick paper bricks filled a large canvas bag. He hung it from his shoulder inside his jacket, partially concealing the underarm lump when he hauled on his long woolen overcoat. Some bill straps displayed a printed mark from the *Camden Safe Deposit and Trust Company*. Others were stamped *First National Bank of Philadelphia* and *Drexel and Company*. It was cash instantly redeemable for gold to feed their days and nights on the run, pay bribes, buy silence, and fund bigger, faster, get-a-way automobiles. Flashing gold was more impressive than straight cash, and it would produce immediate results if the fugitives had to flee the country and pay for their freedom or their lives.

Bergdoll and Stecher entered the grand Treasury atrium conspicuously carrying the milk can but appearing like bankers on a routine visit. Above the teller's counting tables in the Cash Room, enormous brass chandeliers hung from the lofty ceiling of gold leaf accents. The large room was wrapped with balconies separating tall stacked windows peering out to the portico columns. Natural light flooded the vast expanse, joined by a soft yellow glow from dozens of electrified round globes scattered about the three grand chandeliers. The Cash Room was typically a Washington banker's

---

[4] Federal Reserve notes represented legal tender currency, typically enabling the bearer to exchange notes for gold coins, bullion, or certificates.

bank to exchange old stacks of currency for new gold certificates and coins or bullion in relatively small amounts. At this early morning hour, the thick Virginia Aquia freestone and Dix Island, Maine granite of the Treasury's exterior walls made the cash room as quiet as a library. It was nearly empty except for the counter clerks and supervisors.

Stecher stood his distance on the polished Carrara marble floor and allowed Bergdoll to approach the counting tables. From his position Stecher wondered about the ruddy-complected and tobacco teeth-stained man dressed as a banker approaching a counting table. Would the teller recognize him? Bergdoll's photograph appeared on every newspaper's front page from the District of Columbia to California, especially in Washington, a city with multiple newspapers. Because of the press reports, an alert teller would suspect a man lacking bankers' credentials requesting vast quantities of gold coins. Bergdoll was sure to be recognized and revealed, Stecher believed, appearing somewhat suspect, holding onto a farmer's milk can inside the U.S. Treasury cash room.

Moreover, the Treasury had all but stopped handing out gold coins. Since the Federal Reserve Bank's establishment seven years earlier, they no longer handed out bullion, gradually moving to a greenback dollar system. No one had ever waltzed into the cash room to fill a milk can with gold until Philadelphia's notorious Grover Bergdoll. But, in 1920, the Treasury still needed to fully migrate from gold to cash. And Bergdoll knew the Treasury must honor the promise on each gold certificate issued. After all, they were demand notes, and he knew the tellers would have no choice but to fulfill his demand for gold coins. Opening his coat and removing the canvas bag, Bergdoll extended his arm across the counter and handed the teller the first thick wad of neatly wrapped green and gold embossed certificates.

The teller could have been more alert to his customer's appearance, but, turning over his hands and looking into the notes, he was startled at the amount. It was too much! Even though the Treasury hauled in thousands of pounds of gold coins, bullion, and cash daily, it did not routinely hand over this much gold to a stranger walking in from the street with certificates, no matter how businesslike and gentlemanly he appeared.

"Why do you want all this gold?" the teller demanded.

"That's my business," Bergdoll shot back.

"There's a rule that we never change more than $2,000 at one time," the teller countered.

Bergdoll calmly pointed to the message on the notes declaring that each would be redeemed in gold at the U.S. Treasury upon presentation.

"How do you plan to carry away $40,000 in gold?" the teller asked in the first sign of defeat.[5]

---

[5] The value of the cash tendered for gold was about $525,000 in 2023. However, new federal banking regulations should have barred the conversion of notes to gold coins.

Bergdoll turned and motioned toward Stecher, holding the shiny milk can.

The teller excused himself to consult his boss, the head clerk, in a room behind the counting table aisle. When he returned, he said, "It's against the rules, but I'll do it this time."[6]

For whatever reason, in the heart of Washington following the Great War and days after the escape of an infamous draft dodger, the teller did not realize the significance of a $40,000 withdrawal of gold coins from the Treasury. Nor did he recognize convicted federal prison escapee and fugitive Grover Cleveland Bergdoll, America's most notorious celebrity millionaire draft dodger. Instead, he quietly began counting Bergdoll's notes and ordering gold on a cart into the cash room from the Treasury's massive fire-proof steel, iron, and masonry vaults. Incredibly, Bergdoll and Stecher's bold plan was working. The two lifelong friends and their milk can full of gold would be back on the run in their speedy Hudson in minutes.

The Treasury honored its obligation printed on the face of Bergdoll's many gold certificates. When the counting was complete, the fugitive got his gold. It rattled and clanged as the ties on bags of coins were loosened into the mouth of the milk can. The Treasury kept its heavy gray canvas bags. Curious clerks turned toward the unexpected clattering noise to witness the spectacle. When filled, Bergdoll and Stecher carried the milk can on the wheeled cart out of the cash room, down the hydraulic elevator, out onto the 15th Street sidewalk, and together grasping a looped steel handle, hoisted the can into the back seat floor of the parked Hudson. The car's leaf springs sank.

"The can was so heavy we were afraid the floorboards would give," Bergdoll said. "Because of this, we had to drive slowly through the principal streets of Washington, past the Department of Justice again, the headquarters of the hunt for me." Then, Stecher began motoring the Hudson out of Washington, heading north into Maryland bound for Pennsylvania and the Lincoln Highway. They drew a line on a folding filling station paper map westward for the Minnesota boundary with Canada.

Notwithstanding the elaborate mission Bergdoll and Stecher bragged about pulling off that morning in May 1920 to obtain the gold, it was too incredible for most rational people to comprehend and believe, except for those anxious with greed and the gullible American public awash with sensational Bergdoll press. And they swallowed it. The sparkling coins jingling in the shiny milk can and weighing down the stylish automobile would instigate one of American military history's most incredible legal cases. The infamous Bergdoll gold would be pursued for decades by

---

[6] Bergdoll's verbatim exchange with the teller was provided to Leighton H. Blood, a journalist hired by the American Legion to track down Bergdoll in Germany and write an article for *Hearst's International* magazine in April 1924. It was also gleaned from the teller's sworn testimony to a Congressional investigating committee. Treasury records, Blood, Stecher, and the teller confirmed that Bergdoll withdrew $40,000 in gold coins, but Bergdoll greatly embellished the story for the magazine, making up most of the details.

federal officials up to the White House, but it would never be seen again by anyone other than Grover Cleveland Bergdoll.

Stecher pressed his foot on the gas pedal at the wheel beside him.

Their long incredible journey was beginning.[7]

---

[7] This is a narrative nonfiction book, meaning everything in it is accurate or based on events presented as factual when they were happening. But sometimes, people lie. Therefore, I should explain that this prologue is a story by Grover Cleveland Bergdoll, who had a penchant for lying. While he traveled to the United States Treasury in Washington to withdraw gold coins, separately from Emma and Judge Romig's trips, the events surrounding were highly embellished by Grover and recited to magazine journalist Leighton Blood to support Grover's fictional story about needing to get out of jail to hunt for buried gold in the Maryland mountains. This is the only fiction chapter because Grover made up most of the story and stuck with it for decades. The portion made up by Grover pertains to doubling back to Washington in the Hudson Super Six and filling a milk can with gold. Otherwise, Grover's story is accurate about driving to the upper Midwest and across the border into Canada. It's an example of how Grover lied and spun his dramatic life to fit his needs, disregarding anyone in his path. The Hearst Corporation provided a full copy of the 1924 *Hearst's International* magazine. The description of Washington in 1920 came from a private photograph album purchased in an antique store in Pennsylvania with multiple 1920-era photographs of key Washington government buildings, including the Treasury, the White House, the Capitol, and the Army and Navy Building.

CHAPTER ONE

Bergdoll Beer

Philadelphia, Pennsylvania, 1871–1890

On Saturday morning, November 18, 1871, workers at the massive Bergdoll and Psotta Brewery in Philadelphia were busy lining hogsheads with rosin, using generous squirts of steam to expand the wooden staves of the barrels to prevent leaking when filled with the brewery's crisp lager beer. Entering the brew house with his father, Louis, as they usually did on a Saturday morning, ten-year-old George Bergdoll was standing too closely when intense pressure blew out the head from a beer barrel, and it flew into George's skull, killing him on the spot. The Philadelphia coroner ruled it an accidental instant death. It was a tremendous blow to the Bergdoll family and it upset the chain of succession that had been as carefully planned as the Deutscher Kaisers of the Bergdoll's homeland in Baden, Germany.

In fact, Louis Ludwig Bergdoll and his wife, Elizabeth, had planned for George to join his brothers, Charles and (another) Louis, when all three would take over the brewery one day. With a strong stable of sons, Bergdoll beer would be assured well into the future, they believed. With young George's death, beer production continued, but the family and the brewery complex were cast into a long mourning period. Then, just over a decade after the death of George, Charles Bergdoll died from an unknown cause at 29 on October 7, 1883. And days later, on October 22, the Bergdoll's daughter Elizabeth "Lizzie" Bergdoll Schoening died following childbirth at 30. By then, Louis and Elizabeth were sole owners of the renamed and rapidly growing Bergdoll Brewery. They focused on their only surviving son, Louis, whose singular role in continuing the Bergdoll beer tradition rested solely upon the untimely fate of his brothers. And, soon enough, Louis' untimely fate would also determine the future of the brewery and the Bergdoll family.

***

"Gib-me a Bergdoll" was a common phrase among the working-class men in Philadelphia saloons in the early 20th century. Factory and mill workers would walk or ride a trolley to their jobs and dip into the saloons before and after work, many of which were owned by the city's brewers and part of their daily lives. Workers had

The Bergdoll Brewery in Philadelphia in the late 1870s, before the devastating fire at the malt house, bottom left. Oak barrels can be seen at the bottom, near the long two-story office building, later topped with a decorative Victorian third floor. The brew house's inlaid Bergdoll & Psotta 1875 sign is at the bottom right. The 1830s Greek Revival Founder's Hall of Girard College is at the top background. (Library Company of Philadelphia)

numerous beer options, depending upon the saloon in their neighborhood. Still, they often chose inexpensive Bergdoll Beer, one of the most popular brands in the city before the Great War.

Even when drunk, the beer's name, Bergdoll, rolls off the tongue, and refill demands could easily be heard in a loud, crowded saloon. A barkeeper could even recognize the brand being ordered by reading lips. The beer was trusted for taste and price in several Mid-Atlantic states.

Everyone knew that Louis Bergdoll made a good beer. The smooth and cold yellow lagers (dark for the holidays) quickly satisfied the thirst of Philadelphia's working men and women.

The year 1887 was a prosperous one for the Bergdoll Brewery, approaching its fourth decade producing beer for a vast region surrounding its Philadelphia home. Profits exceeded $300,000, split between five shareholders, all members of the Bergdoll family.

The brewery's daily operations were overseen by the founder's youngest son, Louis Bergdoll, the accidental heir to the beer operations because of the untimely deaths of his older brothers. Young Louis' father, also Louis, with his thick German accent and deteriorating health, spent much of his time at his country estate southwest of

The Bergdoll Brewery in 1887, after redesign but before the fire in the malt house, left. Otto Wolf's 1880s architecture changed the buildings dramatically. The office building, center, includes the Victorian third floor, and Parrish Street, center, takes on a more urban appearance. Large oak beer barrels lay in a storage yard across North 29th Street from the office building. (Hagley Museum)

Philadelphia in a region named Upland by the first European settlers who navigated up the mouth of the Delaware River.

The wooded and rich farmlands had been part of the vast acreage granted to William Penn by King Charles II of England to pay debts England owed to Penn's father. Louis Bergdoll's farmhands milked a few cows for milk, butter, and cheese, and they also grew hops on the property, befitting a wealthy Philadelphia brewer. From his farm, Louis the elder could monitor daily reports from the brewery, tracking production and inventory, prices, and shipments of barrels and boxed bottles of Bergdoll Beer to saloons the brewery owned or controlled in Eastern Pennsylvania, New Jersey, Maryland, and Delaware.

Despite personal and business setbacks, the Bergdoll Brewery was on track to celebrate its 40th anniversary in 1889 as one of the "best in the country," according to a business profile in the *Philadelphia Inquirer*. "Manufacturing beer exclusively, [it is] made from the best Canada malt and finest Bohemian hops. The Bergdoll Beer possesses superior strength, flavor, aroma, and color." Like Pabst beer in Milwaukee and Carling Black and White lager in London, Canada, Bergdoll Beer was for the Philadelphia-area men who toiled with their hands.

***

The American Bergdoll family patriarch, Ludwig (Louis) Bergdoll, was born on July 25, 1825, in the small town of Sinsheim, Baden, in the German Confederation of states and kingdoms.[1] Ludwig's parents, Johann Georg and Katharina Schneider Bergdoll, produced seven children in their two-story stone house with a vaulted cellar along Sinsheim's main commercial street across from the town hall.[2]

Johann Georg was a foundry master and blacksmith and a respected citizen of Sinsheim. However, just before Ludwig's ninth birthday, Johann Georg died on May 5, 1834, leaving Katharina pregnant to care for the family. As was customary, the Sinsheim council appointed citizens as an assistant to Katharina and the children's supervisors. To help Katharina with her finances, the *stadt* fathers ordered her late husband's debtors to pay their bills. When some didn't, the board seized possessions and assets until the debts were satisfied.

Nearly 10 at the time, Ludwig was mature enough to understand his family's severe difficulties. It would leave a long-lasting impact on his life and cause him to strive for economic security.

Katharina Bergdoll's financial stress didn't last long, however. She remarried in 1836 to a widowed wagonmaker, Heinrich Stein, who brought his children into the family before the new couple produced more children.

Death struck the family again on September 25, 1843, when Stein died, leaving Katharina to care for seven children at home. Ludwig was 18 and already under apprentice to Jacob Schneider, a Steinsfurt brewer. Stein had paid the three-year apprenticeship contract of 60 gulden in 1842 through the Cooper and Brewer's Guild. Still, Ludwig was released early for outstanding work and ethical behavior and was awarded his apprenticeship certificate within two years.

Such a rapid procession through learning the trade was standard and contributed to economic strife in the German states of the 1840s. Workers advancing too quickly caused more labor supply than demand. Not enough jobs were available, even among the masters of their trades—the system pushed Ludwig out.

In 1844, Ludwig attended a business school, Gewerbeschule, at Sinsheim, where he trained in arithmetic, economics, earth science, and technical drawing. Ludwig appeared to become an artisan among other merchants of the German Confederation formed after Napoleon's defeat. Feeling restless, Ludwig also applied for travel to seek his vocation as a journeyman brewer. But he ran into trouble.

---

[1] Ludwig (Louis) Bergdoll wrote his birthdate as "on or about July 21" on an 1886 passport application. He was baptized on July 27, 1825. A witness to his christening was his uncle, Steinsfurt, Germany beer brewer Jacob Schneider. Therefore, the beer brewing trade was in Ludwig Bergdoll's family since birth.

[2] In genealogy records, Katharina/Catharina and Katherine/Catherine are indicated. This story uses Katharina with a K for continuity with her American usage and that of a successive generation. It's pronounced *cotta-reena*.

Under the laws of the military affairs of the German Empire in 1845, men capable of bearing arms were required to serve military duty for seven years, the first three as an active soldier, the remaining four as a reserve.

In 1845, Ludwig was called up to join the military or feared his time was approaching. A Bergdoll family story of successive generations suggests that Ludwig paid a close friend 300 Gulden to serve his military duty despite military affairs law stating that "no substitute [could] be accepted." This indiscretion caught the attention of the authorities, and more trouble followed. Ludwig and his brother, Georg, an artisan baker, were cited for slander and other minor street offenses, including scandal and staying in beer halls after curfew, for which they were ordered to pay fines.

During this time, farmers and artisans of the Confederation were openly rebelling against the poor economic conditions. Oral history passed down through the Bergdoll family suggests that Ludwig participated in these often violent rebellions, leading to his ultimate decision to emigrate to America to seek a better life.

Or, more likely, to flee imminent arrest and conscription. In simple terms, Ludwig Bergdoll may have run from the military draft.

According to a diary written in the 1960s by Ludwig Bergdoll's great-grandson, Alfred Bergdoll, Ludwig learned that he would be arrested in his room at the Crocodile Inn of Sinsheim for his political activities and possibly for failing to report for military duty.[3] But, when a policeman arrived to apprehend him, Ludwig bit the officer's finger and fled with his sister, Christine Luise, to the United States.[4]

Alfred Bergdoll's diary lists Johann Friedrich Steinman as Ludwig's close friend and the man paid to serve as Ludwig's substitute in the German military. Steinman's granddaughter, Alma Metzger, told a researcher for Alfred, "[Ludwig] came back later to visit in Sinsheim after he had acquired a considerable fortune, and gave gifts to my grandfather [Steinman] in a very generous amount."

There are no records available to confirm this story. If true, Ludwig Bergdoll was the first of four men in the Bergdoll family to shirk his military duty.

On June 27, 1846, having changed his first name, 20-year-old Louis (Ludwig) Bergdoll arrived in New York aboard the Duke of Mecklenburg's 399-ton sailing bark, *Doris*, from Antwerp, Belgium. A few years later, his mother, Katharina, siblings, and half-siblings sold the Bergdoll and Stein homes in Sinsheim and arrived in 1850 and 1851.[5] How and why they chose Philadelphia for their new home is

---

[3] Alfred Bergdoll contracted the services of an American genealogist to research his great-grandfather's activities.

[4] The finger-biting incident would reappear in family lore many years later with Grover Bergdoll biting off a kidnapper's thumb.

[5] German immigrants of this period were known as "Forty-Eighters." They fled the political unrest and poor economic conditions that led to the Revolution of 1848, when citizens of many kingdoms, empires, duchies, grand duchies, and principalities unsuccessfully fought for a unified German parliament.

unknown. However, Philadelphia and Pennsylvania contained the largest German populations in America in the 19th century, to which shiploads of new immigrants were joined monthly.[6]

Family history suggests that Louis shipped out from the United States for several months in the late 1840s on a whaling vessel to earn some cash. If he did, it would explain how he rapidly accumulated assets to open his first brewery by 1849 in Philadelphia. Louis first worked at established breweries such as Engel and Wolf and Muller's, and then, with fellow brewer Peter Schemm, he opened the first Bergdoll Brewery and a beer hall along Vine Street in Philadelphia.[7] Within months, he married Elizabeth C. Woll, who had also fled Germany for the United States.

Starting in 1850, Louis and Elizabeth produced eight children, but their first son, also named Louis, died in 1851. Louisa (Louise) came next, followed by Elizabeth (Lizzie). Charles followed, and then, with the birth of their third son in Philadelphia on March 8, 1857, they returned to the paternal family forename with Louis C. Bergdoll. His middle initial was different, but they called him junior.[8] Two other children followed: Caroline and George.

The Bergdoll Brewery partnership with Schemm continued until 1851 when Louis, the elder, joined his brother-in-law, Charles Psotta, who emigrated from St. Wendel, Saarland, Germany.[9] Bergdoll and Psotta became brewery partners the same year Louis became a naturalized citizen tending to the brewing, while Psotta handled the business affairs.

By 1856, they produced lager beer, which was quickly becoming popular among American beer drinkers, especially Germans. Louis also invested heavily in Philadelphia residential and commercial real estate, owning or holding mortgages

---

[6] Louis' brother, Georg, arrived to become the keeper of a Bergdoll saloon in Philadelphia and, later, a dairy farmer near Boothwyn, Delaware County, Pennsylvania. His son, Georg, and Anna Whelan Bergdoll ran the farm for many years, passing it on to their son, John C., and Mary Jane Bergdoll, who ran the highly reputable Bergdoll Dairy until 1965. Their son, John C. Bergdoll, Jr., was a U.S. Army veteran of World War II. The farm was on 94 acres between Bethel Road and Chichester Avenue, across from Chichester High School. It's now the Willowbrook Shopping Center and apartments.

[7] Peter Schemm independently developed a substantial Philadelphia brewery and created a North American sensation by committing suicide in 1898. Having developed cataracts in his eyes, Schemm mysteriously disappeared from Philadelphia by taking a train to Niagara Falls, where he climbed down from his rented carriage on the bridge to Goat Island, jumped into the rapids of the Niagara River, and while tourists watched in disbelief, was swept over the American Falls to his death. His body was never found.

[8] German custom provided that the name of a deceased son would be given to a future son in the family to honor the departed. Louisa Brocker Bergdoll eventually became Louise, probably through many misspelled federal documents.

[9] Charles (Johann Carl) Psotta married Louis Bergdoll's sister, Louisa Christine Bergdoll, who died soon after giving birth in 1854. Psotta then married Louis' other sister, Elizabeth Magdalena Bergdoll. Future business partners included Bergdoll's sons-in-law, John J. Alter and Charles F. Schoening.

Left: Ludwig Bergdoll, later known as Louis Bergdoll (1825–1894), founded the Bergdoll Brewery in Philadelphia, Pennsylvania, in 1849. For years his portrait hung in Philadelphia City Hall, a scene of later Bergdoll family court appearances. *Right:* Louis C. Bergdoll (1857–1896), heir to the Bergdoll Brewery fortune, husband of Emma Barth Bergdoll, and father of Louis, Charles, Elizabeth, Erwin, and Grover Bergdoll. (Augustus Kollner photos, William L. Clements Library, University of Michigan)

on many rowhouses and saloons. He and Elizabeth purchased a 120-acre farm in Chester Township, Delaware County, Pennsylvania, an hour-long buggy ride from the apartment where they lived on the grounds of the rapidly expanding brewery. Chester Creek bordered the northeastern farm portion, and the Philadelphia and Baltimore Central Railroad ran along the creek. Louis and the family could board a Baltimore and Ohio Railroad train in Philadelphia, disembark minutes later at the Upland station near Chester, Pennsylvania, and, if connections were timely, hop on a Philadelphia and Baltimore train to be dropped nearly at their farmhouse doorstep via the Bridgewater station.[10]

In his book *Philadelphia Beer*, historian Rich Wagner chronicled the history of lager beer among German brewers of the 19th century. Lager beer begins with

---

[10] Today, the former 120-acre Louis Bergdoll farm in Chester Township, Pennsylvania, is suburban housing surrounded by Chester Creek, Bridgewater Road, Park Lane, and Baldwin Run. The farm would pass into the possession of Louis, and then his wife, Emma, who sold it to focus on the Bergdoll country estate along West Chester Pike in Broomall, Pennsylvania.

special Bavarian yeast brought to America by John Wagner in 1840 and brewed at his Philadelphia home in the Northern Liberties section of the city.[11]

From John Wagner, the lager yeast was obtained by the brewers Charles Engel and Charles Wolf, who initially made several barrels of lager just for their friends. Their market beer in the 1840s was fruity and bitter ale, which packed a punch in alcohol and was brewed and served at room temperature.

Rich Wagner explains that lager beer requires cold fermentation and aging; therefore, caves were excavated in the earth along the Schuylkill for cold storage. Later, with tons of ice and refrigeration, lager beer was kept cold until sold. With its smoother taste and lower alcohol content, lager quickly became Philadelphia's most popular beer variety.

Realizing that their German friends and many customers were drinking their lager beer first, Engel and Wolf moved their operations to farmlands along the Schuylkill in Philadelphia, known as Fountain Green. Here they could harvest ice, utilize caves for cold storage, tap into artesian wells, and access the Philadelphia and Reading Railroad to receive hops and barley, coal for electricity, and ship their barrels of lager. Wagner describes the Engel and Wolf Brewery as the first large-scale lager brewery in the United States.[12] Engel and Wolf became the beer kings of Philadelphia. Bergdoll and Psotta would soon follow.

Brewed in copper kettles with water from artesian wells along the Schuylkill, Bergdoll Beer was stored and aged in cypress lagering tanks.[13] In time, the beer was shipped out in oak barrels, with the Louis Bergdoll Brewing Company trademark burned into the barrel staves. Also available in clear glass bottles with raised vertical lettering spelling *B-e-r-g-d-o-l-l B-e-e-r*, the liquid gold lager generously filled the Bergdoll family coffers until it grew into a fortune.

Workers from the city's knitting mills and saw blade factories often drank Bergdoll lagers in Bergdoll-sponsored saloons at the end of their overnight shifts at 7 am and again at 7 pm, seven days a week.

In Philadelphia, Bergdoll Beer flowed in a circle, from the Schuylkill water pumped into the brewing kettles with Bergdoll hops and Bergdoll barley to the fermentation tanks to the Peerless barrel taps, to the mugs, to the men lining the bars, to the tobacco-spitting and floor-mopping waste trough at their feet, to the open gutters in the streets, and then back into the Schuylkill.

---

[11] Rich Wagner, no relation to John Wagner, is responsible for encouraging the *Pennsylvania Historical Commission* to place a marker in front of John Wagner's (American Street, 2018) home denoting the American origin of lager beer. John Wagner smuggled the yeast out of Bavaria and from the Bohemian monks who first brewed the bottom-fermenting beer in the 1300s. Rich Wagner's book is titled *Philadelphia Beer, A Heady History of Brewing in the Cradle of Liberty. By The History Press.*

[12] Engel and Wolf later became the brewing giant Bergner and Engel.

[13] Philadelphia beer historian Rich Wagner graciously met with me to discuss the great breweries of Philadelphia and the origin of lager beer.

These saloons were so crowded that the men often urinated into the shallow trough below the bar to avoid losing their place if they stepped into the toilet room. Embarrassing and insulting women by peeing in an open saloon in the heyday of Bergdoll Beer was not an issue. They were relegated to the back rooms with an exterior door marked "Women's Entrance."

Raising a Bergdoll old-style lager beer was part of life in the factory neighborhoods of Philadelphia. Everyone knew the brand, the taste, and the Bergdoll name. Bergdoll wasn't the only beer in town, however. Before the war, the 33 large production breweries in Philadelphia were famous brands and German family names such as brewing giant Bergner and Engel and others like Poth, Ortlieb, Schemm, Baltz, Betz, and Schmidt. They produced millions of gallons of beer annually.

They sent leather and canvas bags of cash and checks to the Brewers Bank and other financial institutions in Philadelphia. Many of these breweries, saloons, stables, warehouses and supporting businesses like Spaeter and Sons Cooperage formed the community in Philadelphia known as Brewerytown.[14] There was an eclectic mix of family neighborhoods, but with gritty streets of cobblestone, brick, or oil-packed gravel and piles of dirty coal and horse manure (often stiff dead horses) scattered about the streets and alleys.

The Bergdolls were an integral part of the community. They lived for many years in a large multi-story apartment at the brewery, and later in a three-story German Northern Gothic brick mansion at 29th and Cambridge Streets in the heart of Brewerytown.

They inhaled the thick, sweet banana-bread aroma from at least 10 breweries in the community, walked to their sprawling facility at 29th and Parrish Streets, crossed the street to shop for Bratwurst at a German butcher shop, and stood for fittings for elegant suits at the neighborhood tailor and dressmaker on the corner. It was their German home away from their German homeland.

***

From 1866 to 1894, the insurance survey company operated by Ernest Hexamer created schematic drawings of the breweries in Brewerytown. The Hexamer illustrations were colorful and descriptive and provided documentation for insurance companies of the brewery construction materials, firefighting apparatus, and safety procedures designed to prevent costly fires and accidents.

The Bergdoll and Psotta Brewery drawings and descriptions detail the number of night guards and the purpose of their inspection rounds. The brewers located their primary business convenient to the Engel spur of the Philadelphia and Reading,

---

[14] Brewerytown was and still is an eclectic mix of nationalities northwest of Center City, Philadelphia. The Bergdoll German genealogy has been researched by German and American genealogists and is available online through genealogical websites. Biographer Wiltrud Flothow, who shared it with me, has expertly researched the German Bergdoll family origins.

The Bergdoll Brewery logo and trademark. Featuring a griffin spouting the phrase "Old Style Lager Beer," and with its talons wrapped around a barrel of beer, the Bergdoll logo was widely recognized. Bergdoll lager was made for working men and women to drink at home and in the many saloons of the Mid-Atlantic region. Charles Barth, Emma Bergdoll's brother, is listed as general manager. (Bergdoll Family Collection)

which was already named for the Engel and Wolf Brewery. The Bergdoll and Psotta Brewery grew to encompass more than three city blocks.

Designed by the renowned Philadelphia brewery architect Otto C. Wolf, the multi-story brick and steel buildings with ornate archways and cornices included stables, a brewery house, a malt house, a cooper shop, a bottling plant, beer storage house, offices, and a grain elevator.[15] There was also a dwelling house for Louis and Elizabeth Bergdoll, among many residential buildings for employees.[16]

Brewery workers were allowed all the beer they could drink while on the job. The beer was believed to make workers more content and less apt to complain about the grueling and dangerous conditions of 14-to 16-hour days, seven days a week. The primarily immigrant (German) laborers earned $15 per week, and often, a portion (or all) of that was spent drinking more beer in Bergdoll saloons.

The bottling plant, brewery house, cooperage, administrative offices, and beer storage house were built and updated over many years as the brewing methods advanced in technology.[17] A 1979 nomination to the Register of Historic Places describes the one-story, 75 feet by 145 feet brick bottling plant of 1882 as

---

[15] The Philadelphia Library and the National Archives have plenty of information and renderings of architect Otto Wolf's magnificent brewery and residential designs.

[16] Otto C. Wolf was the son of Charles C. Wolf, co-founder of Engel and Wolf Brewery in Philadelphia, with Charles Engel in 1844. Trained at the University of Pennsylvania as an architect and engineer, Wolf's practice at Broad and Arch streets in Philadelphia also provided the Germanic Gothic designs for the Poth, Betz, Schmidt, Germania, Bergner and Engel, and Welder and Thomas breweries. Wolf's firm also designed breweries in Pittsburgh, Trenton, Baltimore, New York, Boston, Washington, Florida, California, Cuba, and Norway. U.S. Department of Interior, National Register of Historic Places Inventory Nomination.

[17] The buildings are used today as condominiums.

"excellent workmanship with arched openings (which) impart a strong rhythm to the street façade."

The 1856 brewery house contained Louis and Elizabeth Bergdoll's residence and was eventually enlarged to six floors for "fermenting, cooling, malt milling, storing, cleaning, and mashing." The nomination form describes it as "an eclectic mixture of rich detail and exuberant vitality… reminiscent of Italian Renaissance urban architecture."

Embedded in the exterior brick wall of "a quality of design and workmanship, which is uncommon in today's industrial structures," between the third and fourth-floor elevation, is a brick and concrete nameplate, Bergdoll & Psotta 1875. The sign remains there today.

The brewery's Victorian administrative office building stands three stories with tall arched windows and is capped with a mansard-style roof with many dormer windows facing North 29th Street at Parrish.[18] Matching halves of the 24 by 90 feet building are split by "a four-story square tower topped by a pyramidal crown dominating the center of the building and well-crafted Corinthian capitals anchoring the building's corners. The workmanship is a level that is today irreproducible."

Cast iron fencing of at least 15 feet surrounded the various structures with elaborate gates across the cobblestone streets. Buttonwood trees lined North 29th Street with their arching canopies providing shade over the brick sidewalk. A railroad track was embedded in the center of Parrish Street—a spur from the Philadelphia and Reading main line along the river—to offload the raw materials and load the barrels of beer for shipment to several East Coast cities. The buildings were initially lit by gas and warmed by the natural heat from the coal-fired kiln and furnaces. Later, steam boilers to generate electricity were encased in brick walls 4 feet thick in case of an explosion. Stables, the cooperage, and elaborate gardens surrounded the brewery.

In the early stages, oak barrels were stored in a large open lot across North 29th Street. Large fermenting barrels were about the width of a flatbed train car, but most were the 54-gallon hogsheads that could be easily rolled and drained off while excess yeast settled to the bottom.

The tallest brewery building was a grain elevator along the main railroad tracks, attached to the brewhouse by an elevated conveyor. The conveyer's steel bracing cast an eerie shadow with the setting sun across the building.[19] The top of the bin structure bore a massive sign with Bergdoll Beer spelled in cursive lettering and

[18] Architect Angus S. Wade designed the brewery office building in 1888. It was the reconstruction of a nondescript two-story brick building adjacent to North 29th Street overlooking a massive yard of oak beer barrels. He also designed 44 pressed brick rowhouses built for the elder Louis Bergdoll at 28th and Brown Streets, just a few blocks from the brewery. Wade also designed the Gimble Bros. department store, the Rittenhouse Hotel, and the Hotel Hanover in Philadelphia.

[19] A large iron walkway over the main railroad tracks and Pennsylvania Avenue at North 29th Street was still utilized in 2023 with long cast beams stamped *Pencoyd Iron Works*, a manufacturer formerly located across and upstream along the Schuylkill in Lower Merion Township, Pennsylvania. The elevated walkway appears in photographs from 1888.

facing southwest. It could easily be seen from the rapidly developing center of Philadelphia, about two miles away.[20]

When operating around the clock, tall brick smokestacks belched coal smoke and soot over Brewerytown. Sweetness floated from the malthouse, stench from the stables. Slightly inclining, 29th Street drained sewage from homes and businesses and horse urine, manure, and slop garbage from the many shops lining the canvas awning-covered sidewalks. The whole city could smell the progress from Brewerytown as the number of barrels of lager beer grew into the millions by the end of the 19th century. The income of the Bergdolls rose into the millions along with it.

In 1877, Hexamer Surveys also profiled a Bergdoll and Psotta brewery in Philadelphia's Falls of Schuylkill neighborhood, later known as East Falls. The Schuylkill Falls Park Brewery was probably erected for the 1876 Philadelphia Centennial Exposition, and was located southwest of the Manayunk and Norristown branch of the Philadelphia and Reading, between Indian Queen Lane, Midvale Avenue, and the Schuylkill. It was later discontinued with all brewing focused on the Brewerytown location.

Philadelphia Beer author Rich Wagner determined that this was Bergdoll and Psotta's first large-scale brewery, acquired when they expanded from their Vine Street location. The property, perched above the river and with easy access to the railroad, was the former home of an American founding father and the first Pennsylvania governor, Thomas Mifflin.

Because it contained an elaborate *biergarten* with picnic grounds, a dance floor, a German band stage, and sausage and kraut facilities, the brewery and *biergarten* were active for the millions of people who attended the Centennial Exposition. Steamers would drop them along the river's edge for a short walk to the *biergarten* while others were off-loaded by trains at the Falls station within a stone's throw of the beer taps.

Bergdoll and Psotta's beer production was about 140–160,000 barrels annually when Psotta died while traveling in Europe in 1877.[21] Louis Bergdoll purchased his partner's share in the brewery, renaming it The Louis Bergdoll Brewing Company, for a reported $175,000. From that time onward, it was all Bergdoll beer.[22]

***

---

[20] The description of the Bergdoll Brewery and the Bergdoll mansion in Brewerytown and events at the massive facility are based on multiple newspapers, insurance documents, government schematics, maps, architectural renderings, the National Register of Historic Places, and numerous walking tours of the old brewery buildings and the Bergdoll brewery neighborhood.

[21] Charles Psotta died while visiting with his German family in Badenweiler. His wife Elizabeth traveled to Germany to fetch his body for burial in their Philadelphia cemetery plot.

[22] Alfred Bergdoll's diary suggests that $175,000 was the purchase price awarded to Charles Psotta's widow, Louis' sister, Elizabeth Bergdoll Psotta, but no documents of the transaction are available for confirmation. The sum was equivalent to more than $5.2 million dollars in 2023.

By 1887, the Bergdoll Brewery along North 29th Street between Poplar and Parrish was fully developed and produced 160,000 barrels of beer annually. It was operated by Louis Bergdoll and his son, Louis Bergdoll, and sons-in-law, John J. Alter and Charles F. Schoening. Emma Bergdoll's brother, Charles Barth, was president; Henry Rieger, treasurer; and Albert C. Woerwag, secretary.[23] Then tragedy struck.

Friday morning, July 15, 1887, began like any other day at the grand malt house, the six-story main building for the expansive brewery, when, suddenly, the employees of the second-floor mill were rocked by a massive explosion.[24]

The *Philadelphia Times* reported that it came from one of the grist mills on the same floor. Storage of damp malt produced the explosion in spontaneous combustion so violent that it hurled large pieces of iron manufactured at the nearby Pencoyd Iron Works in every direction.

Vast stores of grain and hops added fuel to the fire which quickly spread. The brewery was equipped with 1,000 feet of 3-inch India rubber water hose to attach to the city's fire plugs at North 29th and Parrish. Employees launched into the firefight in the precious minutes before city firefighters arrived on the scene, said the *Times*. However, by the time the professionals appeared, the main building was in jeopardy of destruction. At that time, it became a question of protecting what was left.

Adjoining the main brewery building was the refrigerator storage house equipped with quantities of liquid ammonia to cool and avoid boiling the hops. Trying to protect this store of chemicals, two firefighters mounted a ladder that quickly collapsed under their weight and hurled them toward the burning building. They escaped unharmed, but the hops, barley, and grains used to make the Bergdoll lager fueled the massive fire. In just two hours, the main five-story building of the renowned Bergdoll Brewery collapsed in a heap of charred beams, bricks, and ashes.

Could the brewery have been saved by the firefighters? It's unlikely. Spontaneous combustion results from massive stores of organic material that, when wet, produces heat and turns into an explosion that results in a fire. However, the focus of the firefighters is called into question in this blaze. The street was not barricaded from intruding spectators, who were more interested in drinking Bergdoll Beer than fighting the fire, until an hour after the flames were ignited. When the Philadelphia fire marshal arrived, he discovered that some of the Bergdoll employees were in a giving spirit and had tapped a few barrels. Said the *Times*, "frequent visits of the firemen to the kegs were retarding their efficiency. Some men hung around the kegs and did not attempt to do their share to put out the blaze."

The fire, and insurance coverage provided the opportunity for the Bergdolls to rebuild. From 1888 to 1890, fire-damaged sections of the brewery were rebuilt

---

[23] In contrast, the former Engel and Wolf brewery, renamed Bergner and Engel, had absorbed other breweries and was producing about 300,000 barrels, Betz and Son about 130,000 barrels, Poth and Sons about 150,000 barrels, and Schmidt and Sons about 100,000 barrels of beer. All together, Philadelphia brewers made the city the second largest beer producer after New York.

[24] The massive brewery fire of 1887 is described in several Philadelphia newspapers.

Copy of a lithograph of the Bergdoll Brewery at the height of its production in the 1880s–1900. The architecture is classic Otto C. Wolf Victorian industrial style. Notice the depiction of an electric cart for hauling beer, an electric car, and the streetcar along North 29th Street. (National Museum of American History)

and other portions were redesigned and upgraded in classic industrial Victorian architecture. The fire recovery and expansion vaulted the brewery into its most productive era with every barrel tapped producing a gusher of cash into Bergdoll bank accounts.

***

As income from the brewery grew, Louis Bergdoll, the elder, continued to invest in Philadelphia commercial and residential real estate, mortgages, stocks and bonds, agriculture products, and resort properties in New Jersey beach communities.

Around 1885, he had picked up a piece of real estate in foreclosure. It was a reach for the Bergdolls. It was located in Somerset, Maryland, at the line with Washington, in the District of Columbia.[25] His ventures were diversified in large and small companies such as Pennsylvania, Baltimore and Ohio, and Philadelphia and Reading railroads, the Philadelphia Bourse, banks, electric companies, granaries and malting companies, fire insurance companies, the Philadelphia Rifle Club, and the majestic Lorraine Hotel on Philadelphia's North Broad Street. A small investment of $2,760 in the Chester Creek Railroad may have assured transportation to his 120-acre farm in Delaware County.

Louis Bergdoll, the elder, also became a philanthropist with his fortune from the brewery. His Sinsheim, Germany biographer, Wiltrud Flothow, details how he traveled throughout Europe, visiting his hometown frequently.

---

[25] The Bergdolls' investment in substantial suburban Washington, D.C. property came at a time when land values around the nation's capital were escalating rapidly. For decades, it would play a significant role in the family's legal and political tangles. It's profiled later in this book.

With 20,000 marks during his stay in 1893, Bergdoll funded a foundation for the poor residents of Sinsheim. The investment paid out about 25,000 marks over four decades until war-related inflation consumed the principal. Showing their gratitude, the town of Sinsheim made Bergdoll an honorary citizen, which occurred at his death in 1894. The Bergdoll family sent the town a copy of Bergdoll's portrait painted for inclusion among the dignitaries whose portraits hung in Philadelphia City Hall.

As a businessman, Louis, the elder, could also be contentious when he believed his efforts were not being rewarded or recognized. As the operator of one of the largest breweries in the region and the owner of dozens of saloons, he opposed the Brook's High License Law of 1887–1888, which imposed a license with multiple regulations on any establishment in Pennsylvania selling alcohol. Its purpose was to reduce the number of free-wheeling saloons that contributed to public drunkenness, regulate wholesale beer distribution, establish taxes, and outlaw the practice of retailers selling or giving beer, wine, or liquor to minors.[26]

Newspapers predicted the law would devastate distilleries, breweries, saloons, and many supporting businesses. It didn't. The only result was a reduction in breweries, from about 130 in 1888 to about 91 two years later. Most brewers who went out of business made fewer than 5,000 barrels yearly.

In March 1889, the elder Louis withdrew from The Brewers' Association of Philadelphia in a legal dispute over how the group used its money. Organized with a similar motive as the Lager Beer Brewers' Association of 1862 (later the United States Brewers' Association) to fight federal taxes, it consisted of the Bergdoll, Baltz, Poth, Betz, and Continental brewing companies, among others. Bergdoll claimed the organization needed to be more effective and able to collect some $40,000 in dues from the member breweries. He wanted his $6,218.94 in contributions to be returned. He won. It was the old man's last major battle before turning complete operating control of the brewery over to his only surviving son.

An extremely energetic businessman, perhaps inspired by the poverty of his youth, Louis Bergdoll is portrayed with a high, wide forehead, broad nose, and thin, undefined lips. Brewery workers often greeted him, dressed in heavy wool suits, walking along North 29th Street from the brewery's Parrish Street offices to his sizeable brick and brownstone accented mansion at Cambridge Street.[27] The house was designed and engineered by Wolf and built between 1883 and 1885.

---

[26] Prior to the Brook's Law, it was common practice for a child to fetch a pail of beer from a saloon and carry it home to a thirsty parent. After the law, enforcement was minimal, and many saloons continued operating without licenses. The Brook's Law also inspired the term "speakeasy" from a Philadelphia minstrel show of 1890 with farcical skits portraying violent police raids of the illegal saloons where patrons were warned to "speak easy" upon entering and exiting. Carncross's shows at the 11th Street Theatre (Opera House) were titled "The Candles" and "Speak Easy."

[27] Louis and Elizabeth Bergdoll's residence within the brewery house was demolished by 1888 upon completion of the grand mansion a few blocks away on North 29th Street.

The Bergdolls' *Rundbogenstil* Germanic Gothic mansion at 929 North 29th Street was still in excellent condition in 2023, despite interior modifications and long periods of neglect.[28] Elevated above the street, it may have been the first free-standing home in Brewerytown. The exterior of bright orange brick is framed by a brownstone-clad foundation, steps, cornices, and a double-columned brownstone portico with a rounded arch that reaches nearly the sidewalk. The property is wrapped with custom-built heavy wrought iron fencing, with each fence balustrade capped with ornamental (iron) hop flowers.

Louis Bergdoll lived in his prominent new mansion for only a brief period. He died in his upstairs bedroom on August 10, 1894, after a long illness from kidney failure. The newspapers reported that the great German beer brewer's only nutrients in his final weeks were raw milk from cows on his farm. His death was attended by his wife, Elizabeth, and family.

The first Bergdoll mansion, 929 North 29th Street, Brewerytown, Philadelphia, pictured in the 1980s in poor condition. It's where the two Louis Bergdolls, father and son, died in 1894 and 1896, overlooking their massive brewery. (Historic American Building Survey, National Archives, and Records Administration)

Upon probate, Louis Bergdoll's estate of brewery stock, real estate, and other investments was valued at more than $4 million.[29] His will of 1894 left the mansion to his wife, Elizabeth C. Woll Bergdoll, for the rest of her life, which ended on April 11, 1895.[30] In her will, the Bergdoll mansion was left to their son, Louis, who lived around the corner with his wife, the former Bergdoll family maid, Emma, in a three-story brick townhouse on Poplar Street.

---

[28] *Rundbogenstil* is a 19th-century historic revival style of architecture combining elements of Byzantine, Romanesque, and Renaissance motifs. Its most distinctive features are round-arched windows and doors.
[29] Louis Bergdoll the elder's $4 million estate was equivalent to $115–$125 million in the 2023 valuation.
[30] Father and son Bergdolls maintained country homes (farms) in Delaware County, Pennsylvania, southwest of Philadelphia. Louis, the elder, built a farm in Chester Township. Louis, the younger, developed his farm (the Bergdoll country estate) in Broomall, Marple Township, the location of many Bergdoll family activities described elsewhere in this book.

The younger Louis wouldn't live in the grand house very long, either. He died intestate on September 9, 1896, at 39.[31] From then on, nearly everything in the young Louis Bergdoll's multi-million dollar estate automatically landed in the lap of his widow, Emma, and their children, including their toddler boy, Grover Cleveland Bergdoll, who was named after the 22nd and 24th President of the United States.[32]

**

Born on October 18, 1893, Grover was the youngest of five children in a family awash in wealth. Emma suffered a critical fall from a stepladder during her second trimester and impaled her arm in a broken glass window while hanging curtains in the parlor of their North 29th Street mansion. When Louis rushed to her rescue, he had to lift her torso to remove her blood-gushing arm from a long shard of glass. She spent the remainder of her pregnancy in bed.

Emma testified that Grover's birth was so tricky that doctors mishandled the fragile infant with long-handled forceps resulting in a bruised skull and a broken arm. Emma was only 34 and wracked with guilt over her baby boy's arm swaddled in a plaster of Paris bandage. It began her lifelong doting on her youngest son.

When grandfather Louis died, Grover and his siblings were left with a sizeable trust to be administered by executors. It would take years to probate the older man's will with a portion of the $4 million in cash, stock, and real estate. Eight months later, when grandmother Elizabeth died in April 1895, she left an estate worth more than $2 million.

While over $160,000 went immediately to several Philadelphia charities such as the German Hospital and St. Joseph's Hospital to fund free beds in memory of Elizabeth's dead children, Charles and George Bergdoll and Elizabeth (Lizzie) Bergdoll Schoening, another $300,000 was directed into investments for the benefit of her daughter, Louise Bergdoll Alter, with the principal to be given to similar charities upon Louise's death. Elizabeth even left $3,000 to the Louis Bergdoll Brewing Company Workingmen's Beneficial Association, a charity helping men who suffered injuries or illness while working at the brewery. Overall, Elizabeth left more than $460,000 to charities. While commendable, it was over half of her $864,000 cash inheritance from her husband's vast estate.

---

[31] While unknown, myocardial infarction (heart attack) and coronary artery disease are the probable causes of death for Louis Bergdoll at the young age of 39.

[32] Records indicate Grover's full name was Grover Cleveland Alfred Bergdoll, a name Emma initially wanted for their firstborn, Louis John Bergdoll. Ironically, President Grover Cleveland also avoided military duty when he was an assistant district attorney in Buffalo, New York. In a procedure legal at the time, he hired a substitute, Great Lakes sailor George Brinski, for $300 when he was drafted into the American Civil War. After surviving the war, Brinski told everyone he received only half the payment.

Elizabeth's generous charitable bequests were initially ruled inoperative by the Philadelphia County Register of Wills for being notarized less than 30 days before her death. However, through an executor, the brewery architect Otto Wolf, heirs Louis and Louise negotiated an agreement with the Orphans Court to probate the will and quickly distribute their mother's estate.

The following May 17, 1896, was nearly two years after the death of the distinguished German brewer, Louis Ludwig Bergdoll, and just over a year from that of his wife, Elizabeth Woll Bergdoll. While many components of Mr. Bergdoll's complicated probate were lingering, the final distribution of Mrs. Bergdoll's $864,000 cash inheritance from her husband's estate was nearly ready when a bombshell headline hit the city papers.

QUESTIONING A WIDOW'S TITLE, crowed the *Philadelphia Times*.[33]

The tall and imposing Bergdoll's Brewerytown mansion at 929 North 29th Street with bedroom windows overlooking the brewery. Out of view in the right of this picture is the elaborate carriage house Emma Bergdoll had built following the death of her husband, Louis. (Historic American Building Survey, National Archives, and Records Administration)

SENSATIONAL EVIDENCE IN THE BERGDOLL ESTATE PROCEEDINGS. HAD A FORMER HUSBAND LIVING. The *Times* called it THE BERGDOLL ESTATE MUDDLE.

The article revealed that Elizabeth Woll Bergdoll had hidden a secret. The executors of the older man's estate had just learned that Elizabeth had been married when she lived in Germany, and they filed a petition for a new accounting of the Bergdoll fortune. The executors, and Louis and Louise, charged that on April 16, 1840, their mother, Elizabeth, was married to Johann Conrad Hepp in Frankenthal, Germany, and that Elizabeth left Hepp in Germany and fled to the United States sometime before October 1, 1849. They charged that Elizabeth married Louis in Philadelphia on October 14, 1849 while she was still married to Hepp. Unable to find his missing wife in Germany, Hepp finally secured a divorce in 1853. By then, Elizabeth had already produced three Bergdoll children.

Despite the challenge over the legality of Elizabeth's union with Louis, in April 1897, the Philadelphia Orphans Court dispersed a sizeable portion of the older

---

[33] The *Philadelphia Times* and *The Times* newspaper nameplates were used interchangeably.

The offices and brewery of the Louis Bergdoll Brewing Company in 1898. (*Philadelphia Pennsylvania, The Book of Its Bourse & Co-operating Bodies*, The Athanaeum of Philadelphia)

man's estate—$282,000 in trust was awarded to his minor grandchildren, Louis, Charles, Elizabeth, Erwin, and Grover, the children of Louis and Emma Bergdoll. $150,000 was provided for his granddaughter, Elizabeth Schoening Rieger. Another granddaughter, Catharine Schoening, received nearly $155,000 in trust. The elder Bergdolls' daughter, Louise Bergdoll Alter, received lifetime use of the elegant home she lived in next door to the Bergdolls' North 29th Street mansion and an annual annuity of $6,000. Another $564,000 was set aside for future determination, pending the legal challenge to Elizabeth's marriage.[34] Because so much time had passed since the death of Mr. Bergdoll, $368,000 in estate income was distributed to guardians of the grandchildren. But that was not the end of it. Since there were so many minor grandchildren, the court retained Bergdoll's real estate holdings and personal estate (stock investments) to produce more income for them in the future.[35]

While there were numerous divisions of the family's wealth, there was certainly enough money. Consider that the youngest child in the Bergdoll clan was Grover, only three when the court dispersed the bulk of his grandfather's multi-million-dollar estate. Little Grover's millionaire grandfather, grandmother, and father had died in those three years since his birth, leaving a tangled web of legal questions, challenges, and probate. And it happened when the brewery was proliferating and producing mountains of cash for the family coffers.

It was undoubtedly not the last call for the young Bergdoll Brewery heirs. Grandmother Elizabeth's undetermined amount of Bergdoll Brewery stock was directed to remain in her estate until Grover turned 21. Income from the shares would be paid to all the Bergdoll grandchildren. The rest of Elizabeth's estate, several hundred

---

[34] It wasn't until late January 1898 that the Philadelphia County Orphans Court determined that Elizabeth's 1849 Pennsylvania marriage to Louis Ludwig Bergdoll was valid. The decision allowed the distribution of Louis' money through Elizabeth's estate to many charities. However, the news was buried in a small column headlined NOTES OF THE COURTS by this time.

[35] One indication of the total amount of money being distributed to the Bergdoll children from their father and grandfather is an 1896 surety bond required before the children's guardian, Emma's brother, Charles Barth, could receive funds into the guardian account. The bond was to be $2 million, twice the amount of inheritance anticipated.

thousand dollars, went to her only surviving son, Louis. His 644 shares of brewery stock would be tied up in litigation over disbursement to Emma or the children.[36]

When Louis Bergdoll died unexpectedly and intestate at 39, his estate was far simpler to settle. Except for the disputed brewery stock inherited from his parents, it all went to his wife, Emma.[37]

Similar to the service for the older man, the funeral was held in the Bergdoll mansion on North 29th Street. The younger Bergdoll's body lay in a "black velvet-covered and white satin-lined casket, in the main reception room, where it was viewed by upwards of 300 friends of the deceased," wrote the *Inquirer*.

Hundreds more people lined both sides of the street, from the mansion down the hill to the brewery. Widow Emma displayed a "large spray of ferns and a sheaf of wheat" while the children placed a rose pillow in the room for their father's eternally resting head.

Employees of the brewery sent "a large scroll of roses, surrounded by soaring doves... and another floral arch with a clock and hands set at noon, with the inscription, The Time Has Come." Following a horse-drawn hearse, a long procession of people in elegant black carriages witnessed his burial at Mt. Vernon Cemetery.[38]

However, it was hardly the younger Bergdoll's time. He was only 39, and after the older man's death, the brewery needed his guiding hand. The Bergdoll Brewery wealth, overflowing with a full head of cash and entering more lucrative years of production and sales, was tapped and poured down through the family to the very youngest of the new generation. Emma became the richest former maid in Philadelphia. Barely out of swaddling clothes, Grover became the wealthiest little boy in Philadelphia. But he had 15 years to wait before gaining total control of his money.[39]

***

In the 1880s and 1890s, the many deaths impacting the Bergdolls had no detrimental effect on the brewery's success. Enormous profits from the brewery, real estate, and securities investments were still pouring into the family's bank accounts. The gains

---

[36] The litigation over the 644 shares of Bergdoll Brewery stock became an issue over who would have voting rights to determine the company's future. Stockholders were trying to keep the Bergdoll children's voting rights away from their mother, Emma.

[37] Died unexpectedly may be an understatement. Shockingly may be more appropriate. When he died, the younger Bergdoll was still investing heavily in brewery upgrades, buying real estate, and expanding his holdings. In January 1894, the Bergdolls began investing in New Jersey vacation resorts with the sheriff's sale purchase of Atlantic City's Hotel Rossmore for $23,781.

[38] Years later, Bergdoll was disinterred and reburied in the large family mausoleum at West Laurel Hill Cemetery across the Schuylkill from Philadelphia, in Lower Merion Township, Pennsylvania.

[39] Louis Bergdoll died without a will, so his estate was not subject to public court-reviewed probate. It all, whatever the amount, went to his wife, Emma.

were so substantial that outside investors tried to get in on the action but were rebuffed by the Bergdolls with cold feet.[40]

A lawsuit against the Bergdolls alleging they failed to follow through on the sale of brewery stock to a British company was brought in 1893 by a broker, Samuel Untermeyer, of New York. The lawsuit is significant primarily because of what Untermeyer revealed in court from his analysis of the Bergdoll books. Aside from substantial benefits provided to each stock owner, he charged that the brewery earned profits of $1,402,712.09 between 1884 and 1888. In 1887 alone, the brewery profited $320,648.63.[41] It was an enormous sum for five families to share. The court case dragged on for years, even after the deaths of Louis, Elizabeth, and their son, Louis.

Even though Untermeyer revised his brewery profit estimates downward to $1,298,150.11 for the same period, the case still had not been decided by 1902. A similar claim against the Bergdoll stockholders was heard in 1891, with a broker claiming $100,000 in lost commission. He charged the Bergdoll group sold his promised stock to other investors, realizing an advantage with a cash infusion into the company of $3.1 million.

A 1979 application to include the Bergdoll Brewery buildings on the National Register of Historic Places called it "one of the most important breweries in the area." It was a significant employer in Philadelphia and fed millions of dollars into the Bergdoll bank accounts until Prohibition shut it down on January 16, 1920.

Alfred Bergdoll recalls his uncle Erwin boasting that the brewery generated a million dollars annually at peak production with a bottling plant as distant as Richmond, Virginia, but it's unclear if that amount represented revenue or profit. Based on the figures in lawsuits, it was probably profit.

By the closing time in 1920, the brewery's bottling plant was at its busiest ever, despite operating for decades without a bottling permit. Blue and clear glass 10- and 12-ounce bottles labeled *THE LOUIS BERGDOLL BREWING CO., PHILA, PA,* were shipped out of the plant in wooden boxes by the tens of thousands.

Bergdoll's "unexcelled Buck Beer" was made from Bavarian hops and Canadian malt and served on tap "at the company's many licensed hotels, saloons, and bottlers." Workers were proud to be part of the prestigious brewery. The millions of dollars from lager flowed for many years.

---

[40] Lawsuits and wills filed by Bergdoll family members and brewery principals provided financial information about the brewery.

[41] Inflation calculations estimate the profit to be equivalent to about $8.2 million in 2023.

CHAPTER TWO

Emma: The Bergdoll Matriarch

Philadelphia, Pennsylvania, 1896–1920

"You would think she was the maid instead of the owner of a brewery," said Harry Feldman about Emma Christina Barth Bergdoll of the Brewerytown neighborhood of Philadelphia. Feldman should know. He kept his eyes and ears open for news of wealthy women who might want to buy what he was selling. Feldman was a Russian Jew who lived two blocks from the German Protestant Bergdolls and sold ladies' dresses in Brewerytown until he moved deeper into the city to run his clothing store. He recalled Emma as an early riser, working in her garden at the North 29th Street Bergdoll mansion in the first decade of the 20th century.

Feldman wondered why the wealthy widow didn't call on him more frequently to adorn herself in his stock of stylish dressing garments. He found it unusual that Emma would often be wrapped in a cheap cotton summer house dress with an apron, planting and watering flowers or pulling weeds. Or, Feldman and the neighbors would see Emma cradling a wicker basket, walking the concrete sidewalk shopping the German markets, heavily laden with rags and tissues folded in her apron tie. She was unusual, they decided.

To Feldman, Emma was the multi-millionaire Bergdoll widow. He didn't know her simple background as the youngest daughter of a German miller.

Two decades into her new life in America, the former immigrant maid in the Bergdoll household inherited a fortune when her husband died unexpectedly at a young age. With the approach of a new century, Emma Christina Barth Bergdoll's life must have felt like three millionaires widowed her. Through the court-ordered distribution of cash, outside stock investments, mansions, farms, vacation real estate, mortgage income, saloons, beer distribution routes, majority stock ownership in the Bergdoll Brewery, and even a medieval castle in Germany, Emma began running her empire from her stately brick mansion on Philadelphia's North 29th Street. She became the queen of Brewerytown.

With the transition from the Bergdoll men to Emma operating the brewery, people lined up outside her door for jobs, advice, hand-outs of food and cash, and personal favors. And she gave to many of them. She avoided the brewery, leaving the daily operation to managers. Emma preferred to work at home through messengers and a private telephone line to the brewery office.

It's where the Bergdoll children learned to get whatever they wanted from their mother.

***

Well into the short-lived Edwardian era, the matriarch of the Philadelphia Bergdoll family and majority owner of the massive brewery was still stuck in the long-ranging Victorian style with her five-gored ankle-length flared skirts with inverted box-pleats and circular flounce. Her shirt-waist blouse was ruffled with great gathers at the bosom, and her dangly underarms were often covered with bishop sleeves. She was heavily laden with wool capes and soft furs in the winter. Unseen beneath the floor-length dresses that dragged on the Brewerytown streets were her thick-soled leather shoes with numerous punched and hooked eyelets laced high around her ankles, the same as her parents' shoes at home in Germany. She seldom wore the removable collar for her blouse because it didn't fit her thick neck. The tines of numerous side combs pinched Emma's full-length coarse hair into a bun that splayed wisps of gray down around the brown skin splotches and moles of her sagging jowls. Darkness semi-circled under her eyes.

Since her husband died, Emma seldom kept a regular schedule. Her mischievous sons, the brewery, the banks, her aged mother, constant calls and correspondence from tenants, saloon keepers, politicians, police, lawyers, German churches and hospitals, and the needy and homeless hounded Emma for decisions and money. With her generous checkbook, she tried to accommodate every one of them.

John F. Smith of West Philadelphia remembers Emma in the early 20th century when his father ran a corner saloon next door to the Smiths' rowhouse, both owned by the Bergdolls. The elder Smith paid rent and split Bergdoll Beer sales proceeds with Emma. One day, Mr. Smith rang up the brewery to ask Emma to send someone over to fix the sagging and rotting boards on the stoop. Later, young John noticed a figure in a worn-out dress and a scarf pulled tight, on hands and knees with a hammer, replacing the steps. He thought it was odd that Ma Bergdoll would send a woman to do the work. Taking a closer look among the planks, hammer, and saw, Smith noticed the workwoman displayed different colored shoes, black and white. He realized that the brewery owner herself had square-head nails dangling between her lips, hammer in hand, performing the carpentry.[1] At the time, Emma was worth several million dollars.

Emma Christina Barth Bergdoll was born on July 27, 1861, in Huffenhardt in the northern part of Baden, Germany, the third child of seven to a grist miller in

---

[1] Harry Feldman and John F. Smith discussed their relationship with Emma with her grandson, Alfred Bergdoll. He wrote of their impressions in his lengthy diary-manuscript in the 1960s.

the Neckar River region.[2] She arrived in New York on December 13, 1880, with her brother, Karl (Charles) Friedrich Barth, in steerage aboard the S.S. *Nederland*, a double-masted steamer of the Red Star Line that plied the Atlantic between Antwerp and New York and Philadelphia.

Soon afterward, the Barth siblings entered the large German community in Philadelphia. Emma immediately found work as a sewing machine operator in a knitting mill, and then as a maid in the Bergdoll home. Charles Barth found a job in the Bergdoll brewery and worked his way up to manager. Both positions were probably arranged because the Barths and Bergdolls were cousins.[3] Within two years and five months, Emma went from cleaning the Bergdolls' large multi-floor apartment in the brewery complex to marrying Louis, the younger, and becoming an American citizen. She was 22. Louis was 26.[4]

Unproved stories within the Bergdoll family suggest that Emma initially intended to marry Louis' older brother, Charles, who died at 28 in 1883. Another unproved tale passed down in the family tells that while working as the family housemaid, Emma became pregnant. When Louis, the elder, discovered this, against his wife's disapproval, he required his son, Louis, to marry the maid. However, Emma and Louis' first child, Louis John Bergdoll, was born on October 9, 1884, well beyond his parents' May 24, 1883 wedding date.[5]

Emma and Louis settled into brewery-owned homes in their neighborhood and then arranged to have Emma's parents emigrate to Philadelphia. Johann Christoph Barth and Margaretha "Minnie" Wilhelmina Doerr Barth arrived with Margaretha's mother, Eva Elizabeth Schneider Doerr, in May 1886.[6]

While Louis immersed himself in the brewery business with his father, Emma produced their five children and gave them nicknames: Louis John Bergdoll (Roos), Karl Charles Alvin Bergdoll (Chess), Elizabeth Bertha Bergdoll (Betty), Erwin Rudolph Bergdoll (Werny), and Grover Cleveland Bergdoll (Groff).

Emma's schooling in Germany is undocumented, but she could read, add, and subtract well in German and English. She understood mortgages, rent, and real

---

[2] Emma's other siblings were Louisa, Alwin, Wilhelmina, and Rudolph, who emigrated to Philadelphia, and Pauline, who remained in Germany.

[3] Charles Barth began with the Bergdoll Brewery, moved to Scranton, Pennsylvania, for the Robinson Brewing Company, and then went back to Philadelphia to work for brewers Rothacker, and Poth and Sons, before rejoining Bergdoll.

[4] Emma Barth and Louis Bergdoll were second cousins. Their common great-grandparents were Jacob Schneider (1772–1842) and Maria Kennen Schneider (1776–1848).

[5] The family tale lacks evidence, but one must consider the possibility of a miscarriage. There is only one record of Louis and Emma's German church marriage ceremony on May 24, 1883. It may have been performed without celebration, partly because Louis' adult siblings, Charles and Elizabeth, died in the same year.

[6] Emma's father, Johann Barth, died in 1902. Her grandmother, Eva Schneider, died in 1903. Emma's mother, Wilhelmina Barth, witnessed Grover's escape and died in 1925.

Emma Christina Barth Bergdoll from a 1927 dime store postcard printed from an 1880s portrait by the Philadelphia artist Augustus Kollner. With her full face accented with makeup, hair in an Edwardian pinless pompadour pulled into a bun, and elegant velvet dress with mink stole, Emma is beautiful and fashionable. Fur shawls, velvet gowns, pearls, and diamond brooches were part of Emma's early life as the wife of a wealthy brewer.

estate in her broken English with a thick German accent. She habitually collected all of them.

Only a few images exist of Emma in her younger years. She must have been appealing at 21, suggested people who commented on Alfred's diary, to attract the son of a wealthy brewer. A 1927 dime store postcard depicting a copy of an undated artist's oil painting shows a beautiful woman tastefully and fashionably dressed.

An 1892 photograph shows Emma, 31, with her daughter, Elizabeth, 4, her mother, Wilhelmina, 53, and her rather dour-looking and aged grandmother, Eva, 74, in a formal pose in Philadelphia. The three women and little Elizabeth are attired in fashionable dresses of the age, with long dark sleeves, snugly buttoned waistlines, tight high collars, and ballooning shoulder sleeves. Emma's dark hair is in a tall bun, and she displays a single large pearl dangling from a gold chain attached to a bosom button. Her protruding chin, round face, and thick neck resemble her mother and grandmother. Young Elizabeth looks just like them, only in miniature form.[7]

In middle age, Emma is intimidating as a short and heavy woman with the circumference of a butcher. She protrudes outward from her breasts with an abdomen resembling a beer barrel's firm oak staves. When she dresses for warmth in her expensive fur coats and stoles and sits, she appears even more enormous, her ample reserves gathering around her waist. Her full-frontal roundness causes Emma to arch her shoulders back and push her square jaw upward, making one think of her

---

[7] Some of the descriptions of Emma Bergdoll are based on Alfred Bergdoll's diary-manuscript. Her family genealogy is available on several genealogical websites. Photographs of Emma at a young age were culled from family members. In contrast, photos used to describe Emma at an older age are readily available from old newspaper records, specifically the Temple University Urban Archives in Philadelphia.

Emma Barth Bergdoll, standing, about 1892, her mother, Margaretha Wilhelmina Doerr Barth (left), her grandmother, Eva Elizabeth Schneider Doerr (right), and her daughter, Elizabeth Bertha Bergdoll (Hall). (Bergdoll Family Collection, Historical Society of Pennsylvania)

as bossy and determined. She is all that, especially with a revolver tucked beneath her apron.[8]

Later in her life, photographed at the many court trials and trips to Washington for Congressional testimony at the U.S. Capitol, Emma was often pictured in stylish black silk suits and dresses with ample but tasteful jewelry choices and heavy-heeled black slip-on shoes. Her outfits were baggy enough to have hidden a small arsenal of weapons if she desired. One photograph taken on a public street shows her carrying a wicker market basket and holding forward a 10-inch kitchen knife.

With the death of her husband, Emma is independently rich in 1900 but lives what she calls a "simple, plain life, doing some of my own work with my own hands rather than aspiring through my wealth to a society that would have been as distasteful to me as I to it." She is a force to be reckoned with in the brewery, her kitchen, the

---

[8] Emma said she always carried a gun after her husband, Louis died "to scare away chicken thieves and others."

A millionaire in court. Emma Bergdoll, January 7, 1920, still dressed in her feathered hat, velvet cape, and warm muffler, was under guard in court at Philadelphia City Hall to answer charges of threatening officers with her pistol. She was later convicted in state and federal court along with her son, Charles, and others, sentenced to prison, but released upon paying substantial fines. Despite her many threats, Emma never fired her gun at anyone. (Temple University Urban Archives)

courtroom, and the halls of Congress. She captures attention with her broad smile too. She has the face of a happy German. But Emma was not a very happy woman for most of her mature years. And that was due to the escapades of her sons.

***

Emma made several trips to Europe with the Bergdoll children, specifically to her homeland in the Baden state in Germany. Her grandson Alfred relates in his diary that she tried to buy a castle on the Rhine River. The transaction was nearing a close until the Russian woman who owned the castle realized that Emma wouldn't be around often enough to care for it. The deal fell through, but Emma would eventually acquire her American castles.

Emma enrolled her children in the Brewerytown Zion German Presbyterian church Sunday school. Still, the boys were often more into trouble than religion. After their confirmations, which included photographic portraits in their best Sunday suits and dress, daughter Elizabeth said she was the only one who continued with Sunday church services. Except for funerals, the Bergdolls did not regularly attend their church. However, the church regularly deposited Emma's generous checks in its accounts.

While the children were young, Emma lived full-time in the Brewerytown mansion. She was deeply involved in the community, shopping among the German merchants and socializing with the neighbors, regardless of class. Within months of Louis' death in 1896, Emma contracted for a large brick and stone stable and carriage house to be built on Cambridge Street around the corner and abutting the mansion's backyard. It would allow her access to transportation without consulting with the men at the brewery where the family carriages and horses were kept. At 28 by 54 feet, the carriage house would be large enough to hold Emma's carriages and horses, feed, hay, and, later, her motor limousines.

For excursions to the Bergdoll farm near Broomall or long carriage rides in nearby Fairmount Park, Emma's coach drivers would hitch up a horse from the stable and whisk Emma along the gravel and cinder roads in the Schuylkill Valley. In March 1911, a favored horse became spooked and charged forward with the driver, Gustave Worker, unable to control the gelding. Emma leaped from her barouche just before it crashed into a fire hydrant, throwing Worker into the razor-sharp cinders. Worker was treated at the German Hospital on the Bergdoll Brewery account, but Emma received doctors' visits at home and took weeks to recover.

In his diary-manuscript, Alfred Bergdoll tells of another coachman briefly employed by Emma in June 1912 and suspected of stealing diamonds from her 29th Street brick mansion. When Homer Cleveland Wiggins, 17, of Wilmington, Delaware, tried to sell the Bergdoll diamonds at a Philadelphia pawnshop, he was confronted and grabbed by police officer Thomas J. Dowling, 24.

Wiggins pulled his .38 automatic and shot officer Dowling at point-blank range in the head, killing him. Dowling, in uniform less than a year, could not reach for his service revolver because he held Wiggins with his right hand. Wiggins briefly escaped before being caught in a nearby warehouse and then beaten by a mob of men. The diamonds were lost.

Tried and sentenced to 20 years in the Eastern Penitentiary, Wiggins and another inmate dismantled their cell door lock.[9] They replaced it with a hand-carved wooden replica made in the prison woodshop, and late on August 21, 1913, they crept out of their cell and scaled the 40-foot stone wall of the Philadelphia prison with a handmade ladder.

Eventually corralled in a Wilmington boarding house, Wiggins got into a shootout with Wilmington police before committing suicide with his gun. Companies Wiggins had robbed, his mother, sister, and others laid claim to cash found on his body and buried in a chicken coop at his mother's home. Emma Bergdoll remained quiet about her former coachman, the cop killer and jewel thief. She never publicly filed for reimbursement of the value of the stolen diamonds.[10]

Emma could handle a team of horses but left the driving to her coachmen. It took years for her to accept the comfort and ease of a car. Only after multiple crashes in her carriages did Emma finally agree to ride in automobiles. Her barouche was dismantled and packed away in the carriage house for decades. She later favored

---

[9] Renamed Eastern State Penitentiary, the 1829 prison-castle is a history museum and infamously held the gangster Al Capone and bank robber Willie Sutton.

[10] The murder of officer Dowling inspired a new regulation requiring Philadelphia police officers to use their left hand to hold prisoners, leaving their right hand free to grab their weapon. Dowling was the 10th officer killed in the line of duty because they used their right hand to grab a suspect.

large, heavy black Hudson limousines, which fit through the carriage house doors with inches to spare.[11]

***

In 2023, the Bergdoll home on North 29th Street appeared as another large brick house in Brewerytown. But, at the time of construction, it was unique. The National Register of Historic Places portrays Bergdoll's North 29th Street mansion as "symmetrical, with a central tower above the entrance. Flat-headed windows under stone moldings light the tower." It describes Wolf's design as an "overlay of bays and window openings that produce a subtle counterplay of Victorian picturesqueness."

The elaborate woodwork, "far richer than the norm of the day, adorns the house's interior, including a central hall that runs the length of the building, subdividing the house roughly into thirds, with rooms on either side."

Portraying the structural cross-in-square pattern, "the second and third-floor rooms radiate from the central stairs with four principal rooms in the corners." These were the bedrooms of the Bergdoll boys, into which Emma forbade the housemaids from entering if they might find evidence of illicit, sexual, and even criminal activity among the boys.[12]

Unfortunately, most of the first-floor woodwork features and the elaborate staircase with "its paired turned balusters rising to the geometric third-floor leaded glass skylight" had been removed by 1984.

Across the shallow rear yard, Wolf later built (for Emma in 1897) a two-story brick carriage house and stable with a tall, round-arched carriage door flanked by a matching entry door and transom light.[13]

The register declares the Bergdoll mansion as:

> [a] rare and important example of Wolf's residential work, his greatest mansion, and his first domestic commission. It is the largest, most visible house in the area and still reflects the early development and lifestyle of the Brewerytown neighborhood. As a collaboration between one of the city's best-known brewers and the country's foremost brewery designer, the Bergdoll house is one of a kind. It is an essential record of the social history of North Philadelphia. It stands today with a remarkable level of architectural integrity and the rich legacy of a well-known Philadelphia family.

---

[11] Emma also kept the family's first automobile in her new carriage house. An early electric car resembling a buggy, Alfred described it with large wheels and narrow, solid rubber tires, a chain drive from the electric motor, and a tiller for a steering wheel. When all the children hopped aboard, Grover, the smallest, had to sit on the battery box, where he often got shocked. It sparked the boys' interest in cars. Alfred said the vintage 1890s electric car was discarded in a barn at the Bergdoll country estate, remaining abandoned well into the 1930s. Its final disposition isn't known.

[12] Emma knew what maids would find in the bedrooms of promiscuous boys. She had been a maid in the Bergdoll household before marrying Louis.

[13] The carriage house was built for Emma in the late 1890s. Previously, the Bergdoll men kept their teams and carriages in the brewery stables and barns and could quickly summon them for transportation around the city.

For more than a decade after their new residence was built, the Bergdolls enjoyed an unobstructed downhill view of their sprawling brewery from the upper floors of the family mansion. The buttonwood trees, a common name for the towering sycamores with their broad leaves and splotchy smooth two-tone gray bark, as familiar as cobblestones in Philadelphia, would later obstruct the view. Many trees planted in the Bergdoll era still towered over the street in 2023. The elder Louis would also develop brick homes along North 29th Street, attached as row homes standard in Philadelphia, and make them available for his brewery managers to lease or buy.

The Bergdoll Beer neighborhood extended from the brewery to saloons to homes and stables, even the dusty baseball diamond across North 29th Street and the railroad tracks. Everyone was connected to and dependent upon Bergdoll Beer for several blocks around.

Next to the Bergdoll brick mansion was Louis and Elizabeth Bergdoll's daughter's house at 935 North 29th Street. Separated by an empty lot, Louise Bergdoll Alter and her husband John Joseph Alter's three-story mansion was built with the same round-arched windows and doors. The exterior was clad in classic brown sandstone from the Hummelstown Brownstone Company in central Pennsylvania. The street façade exhibits the same elegance as the Bergdoll mansion, but it was joined with a much less elegant brick house, which is smaller and, therefore, less prominent. Like its neighbor, the Alters' beautiful mansion was still in excellent condition in 2023.

However, the neighboring house provided refuge for the Bergdoll children, who would run next door to Aunt Louise's place when they wished to escape their mother's demands. The Alters were stockholders in the Bergdoll brewery, and long after the Bergdoll men and John Alter's deaths, Louise and Emma lived side-by-side in their spacious mansions. However, they remained a world apart, adversaries over the Bergdoll business, family affairs, and social standing within Philadelphia's nouveau riche German community.

Despite her wealth and large brood, Emma was never socially accepted into the Bergdoll family by her mother-in-law, Elizabeth Bergdoll, or sister-in-law, Louise Bergdoll Alter. Louise continued living in her brownstone next door, physically close but socially far away.[14]

A family story tells of how Emma's married Austrian house servant disguised herself as a single woman to get the job. When it was discovered that the maid was married, with children, and fearful of losing her job, Emma sat her down and explained her experience joining the Bergdoll family.

Harking to her Barth background, Emma described how she was never good enough for the Bergdoll women, especially after the Bergdoll men died and left the brewery wealth to her and the children. Emma told the maid that her in-laws

---

[14] In 2023, the former Bergdoll and Alter mansions along North 29th Street were separated by a modern four-story black alteration that appears in stark contrast to the side of the Alters' brownstone.

would sometimes place horse manure wrapped in newspapers on the granite steps of her Brewerytown mansion, perhaps as a message that she, Emma, was still the Bergdoll family maid and should clean up the mess.

As a new century began, Emma, known around Philadelphia as "Ma Bergdoll," was the family's grand dame, and she controlled her position with two black leather-bound books buried in her bosom. One listed her mortgages and rents, with amounts payable and due dates. The other contained her checks. Later she included a revolver.

She was conservative in politics but very liberal with her cash, especially within the family. Emma owned dozens of residential and commercial rental properties in Chester, Pennsylvania, where many immigrant laborers toiled in the vast shipyards along the Delaware River. She owned dozens of rowhouses, saloons, and storefronts in North and West Philadelphia and held mortgages and insurance bonds on countless others.

Emma was the mortgagee for the mansions, country estates, and investment properties that her sons Charles, Erwin, and Grover owned. Still, she did not hold financial papers for her son, Louis, or daughter, Elizabeth. She also managed and collected for Grover's dozens of rental units scattered about the Philadelphia area. And she kept hefty balance accounts at notable Philadelphia financial institutions such as the Land Title & Trust Company, Northwestern National Bank, and National Surety Company.

She was open about whom she brought to the business table. She loaned money to Germans, Irishmen, Italians, Jews, African-Americans, farmers, and single women. Her drivers sped her about the city and suburbs, collecting rent and interest, mostly in cash. All of the figures went into her black bosom books.

By 1910, Emma Bergdoll's days of fashionable elegance were in the past. She often wore stained, flowered-print cotton dresses hanging below the rim of the tall, thick wool socks pulled over her kneecaps.

Later in her life, wisps of gray hair escaped her comb-packed bun, and her deep dark eyes darted suspiciously like those of a millionaire waiting to be kidnapped. She was often wary of a salesman, lawyer, detective, or politician waiting to capture her attention and money, but she liked reporters. She knew they were helpful.

When she hooked her arm around the handle of her wicker shopping basket and scoured the open-air markets searching for bargains, Emma sometimes looked like one of the many tired and overworked housemaids of the upscale Brownstone and Victorian residential neighborhoods of early 20th-century Philadelphia.[15]

***

---

[15] Emma Bergdoll was once mistaken for a maid at her home on 29th Street in Philadelphia. It was by a stranger looking for "the owner of the Brewery."

With so many responsibilities—managing the brewery, collecting rent, and running the mansion and country estate—four unsupervised boys caused Emma much trouble.

Following her lead as a gardener, young Charles decided to plant a garden, and, stealing a sack of gold coins from Emma's safe, he buried them in a small plot of dirt behind their house. Discovering her valuable coins missing, Emma confronted the boys. Charles admitted taking them but declared they would soon have more when the garden grew.

In another nerve-wracking incident, the boys accidentally discharged a small keg of gunpowder in the farmhouse attic. Alfred said no one was injured, but there were plenty of fireworks. The boys also built a roller coaster at the Broomall farm, and, after greasing the coaster tracks, their crude car shot off the end and left them with bumps and bruises.

As her oldest son, Louis, matured, he fancied Catholicism and demanded to be sent to a Catholic boarding school. He lasted two weeks before returning home, having had enough of the nuns' strict wrist-slapping regulations. He later enrolled in the University of Pennsylvania (Penn) and became an attorney before settling on a business career.

Astonishingly, each child was given $5,000 for an annual allowance, even at a young age. How the money was dispensed isn't known, but Emma later conceded in court testimony that she felt that $5,000 was appropriate for the children to have spending money. Extra lump sums would be provided for expensive items such as bicycles, motorcycles, automobiles, and airplanes.

Spendthrift young teenager Grover always needed more funds. Turning to his expensive chemistry kits purchased with his allowance, he discovered that he could rub mercury on pennies and pass them off as dimes in a local store owned by a man with poor eyesight. The cheated merchant would have to track down Emma for reimbursement. Because Grover was her youngest child and favorite, he was seldom reprimanded for mischief and petty crimes. Grover graduated from Central High School in Philadelphia and eventually enrolled at Penn but soon dropped out, failing to inform his family.

With disposable income from their allowance, Louis and Charles traveled to Spain at the enticement of an unsolicited invitation that arrived in the mail. The money-making offer was what Alfred called "the Spanish swindle." He said neither Charles nor Louis explained what happened or how much money they lost.[16]

---

[16] In the 19th century, crafty criminals sent letters from Spain to wealthy British and American citizens by accessing public trade directories. A scam that purported a large benefit for the recipient, it often involved enticement by a young attractive woman and a secret stash of money waiting for the person who responded.

At the Brewerytown mansion, Grover used his substantial allowance cash to buy scientific toys. He obtained components for a wireless telegraph system gaining popularity in the German navy, setting up a transmitter and receiver in the carriage house. It's unclear whom he communicated with, but radiotelephony needed to be more exciting for him. He gravitated toward chemistry and engineering.

In 1914, Polish physicist, Marie Curie, gained fame with her experiments with X-ray machines, later used in France during the war. The device had been discovered by German scientist Wilhelm Roentgen only two decades prior, and early misuse resulted in severe burns for patients. Enthralled by science and engineering advances among German nationals and with the money to buy the expensive devices, Grover purchased and installed an X-ray machine among his other costly laboratory equipment in the Brewerytown carriage house. On June 8, 1914, he convinced 13-year-old Joseph Shevlin of Philadelphia to sit for an X-ray of his right arm.

Grover exposed Shevlin's right wrist to third-degree burns requiring multiple medical treatments. Grover later said he learned to operate the machine by reading books. He used it "hundreds of times and never burned anyone else."

Fearful of permanent damage, Shevlin's father sued the Bergdolls for $6,000. When a jury finally returned a verdict more than a year later, the Shevlins got only $620. Grover did not attend the trial. Rather than reprimand Grover, Emma had the expensive X-ray machine destroyed.[17]

The Bergdoll boys weren't the only children who challenged their mother's lax supervision. Elizabeth Bertha Bergdoll turned 21 on May 8, 1909, and immediately gained control of her inherited wealth. It had been professionally invested for over a decade since her grandparents' and father's deaths.

For Emma, daughter Elizabeth had been less troublesome than the boys. Still, within days of collecting her inheritance, she married the family chauffeur, Albert Von Hall, 27, a naturalized American citizen from Hamburg, Germany, who'd been driving the Bergdoll limousines for about a year.[18]

Elizabeth and Albert reportedly grew close when he drove for the family on vacation "down east," Maine, and he was dismissed. Before the marriage, Emma had arranged for Elizabeth to purchase her own home. The Bergdolls' only daughter lived with five women servants in superb comfort in a large three-story stone colonial mansion

---

[17] Joseph Francis Shevlin later became an electrical products salesman. He died in 1958 at the age of 57, not from the effects of the X-rays, but from heart disease. Testimony revealed that Grover also mistreated young neighborhood boys using acid, smoke, physical violence, including a hammer attack, and locking them inside closets of the mansion. It was an abusive characteristic that would also appear later in his life.

[18] Albert Hall's age is estimated. His death certificate states his birth year as 1881 while all other references display 1882.

with a matching carriage house and servants' quarters at the corner of Wynnefield Avenue and Monument Road in Philadelphia.[19]

Elizabeth's May 14, 1909 elopement with her chauffeur was carried in newspapers as far away as New Zealand. Perhaps it was the gossipy scandal of an heiress marrying her driver or the handwritten marriage book notation made by the pastor who married them in the Holmesburg Methodist-Episcopal Church parsonage in front of witnesses described only as "friends."

He wrote, "[the] bride was [the] daughter of Louis Bergdoll, and inherited $2,000,000 from [her] father's estate on reaching her majority, May 8, 1909." Two months later, the *Auckland Star* reported the inheritance amount as merely £50,000. By the following year, Albert Hall, handsome, blue-eyed, brown-haired, and relatively short at 5'6", had been elevated from chauffeur to gentleman real estate investor and developer, selling Bergdoll automobiles and racing Bergdoll cars on tracks around the northeastern United States.

Elizabeth would almost immediately become pregnant with their first child. They named their daughter Elizabeth Emma Hall.[20] Thus, counting Louis John and Florence Bergdoll's son, Louis Jr., born May 1909, the first two children of the new Bergdoll generation were named after Louis and Emma.[21]

***

When the boys' grandfather, Louis, Sr., died in 1894, it took three years to probate the will for his massive personal estate and business assets and complete disbursement to his heirs through the Philadelphia Orphans Court. Not counting the Bergdoll boys' substantial inheritance from their father, who died two years later in 1896, and their shares in Bergdoll Brewery stock and real estate, each of the five Bergdoll grandchildren received $165,467 in 1897 from their grandfather's assets—his cash. Invested with professionals by their guardian and family friend, Judge James E. Romig, the money substantially grew, especially for the youngest, Grover, until it was transferred to each child at age 21.[22]

---

[19] Elizabeth Bergdoll's and Albert Hall's mansion at 4910 Wynnefield Avenue was five suburban blocks from 52nd and Wynnefield Avenue where Emma also purchased a mansion for Grover. Their home later became the Wynnefield Branch of the Settlement Music School, producing famous students such as Chubby Checker, Christian McBride, Kevin Bacon, and Albert Einstein.

[20] Eventually, Albert and Elizabeth Bergdoll Hall would settle into a large stone French colonial mansion along Remington Road in Philadelphia's elegant Main Line suburb, Wynnewood. The Halls developed three contiguous lots there with stone mansions, keeping one for themselves. In 1926 they were surrounded by large estates with names like *Waldeck, Spring Valley, Bailytore, Redleaf, and Clover Hill.*

[21] Elizabeth and Albert Hall also bore a son in 1916 but Charles Hall died at the age of three from poliomyelitis. His death certificate was stamped, *CONTAGIOUS.*

[22] $165,000 in 1897 equals $4.9 million in 2023. Grover's cash inheritance from his grandfather and father was valued at about $825,000 when it was transferred from custodial investments into his personal bank accounts when he turned 21 in 1914. It's the equivalent of $24.9 million in 2023.

The Louis J. Bergdoll Bergson Italianate brownstone mansion at 22nd and Green Streets in Philadelphia. Emma Bergdoll purchased the house for her eldest son, Louis, a pattern of mansion-buying gifts that continued through her youngest child, Grover. This mansion is still standing and is often mistaken for Grover's demolished Wynnefield mansion. (National Archives and Records Administration, Historic American Building Survey, Jack Boucher 1976)

However, the Bergdoll boys began spending their wealth before adulthood through Romig. First, 17-year-old Louis arranged for his mother to buy him a home. And, it was not just any home. Emma Bergdoll, an astute real estate investor, could spot a deal a mile away. Keeping tabs on properties around their Brewerytown–Fairmount neighborhoods, in 1902, she snapped up a massive three-story Italianate brownstone mansion on the northwest corner of 22nd and Green Streets, not far from the brewery.

Situated on the corner lot and high above the street, the cut-stone mid-Victorian mansion appeared from the sidewalk as a castle. Constructed in 1890 for banker and secretary of the Pennsylvania Treasury, William H. Kemble, who lived there for just one year before his death, the National Register of Historic Places describes the mansion façade as "four bays across, with rectangular windows which have carved lintels. Pairs of fluted Corinthian columns flank the main entrance, and the focal point is a carved double-door entrance topped by a balcony. Windows are semi-elliptical, and segmented pediments top some. The second story of the curving bay has a baluster stone balcony. Several bay windows have outstanding stained-glass work."

Inside the mansion, the decorative woodwork was richly carved by European craftsmen of the Victorian style "with evidence of Germanic and Italian influence in the designs." In the master bedroom, "cherubs are the theme echoed in the ceiling painting, mantelpiece carving, and furniture"—all were built for the mansion and included in the sale. Gas sconces and chandeliers adorned the walls and ceilings, and Beaux-Arts sculptures and classic leather-bound books lined the plaster walls hand-stenciled with gold leaf. "The stained-glass windows are reminiscent of the work done by the Tiffany school."[23] The elegant mansion was ideal for a young, wealthy Philadelphia entrepreneur setting his mark on the rapidly growing automotive industry.

---

[23] The Louis J. Bergdoll mansion description is from a 1976 inspection prepared by Lydia Owens and Madeline Cohen of the Philadelphia Office of Historic Preservation. Louis' sons, Louis, Jr. and Wilbur, continued living in the mansion until the early 1990s. In 2023 the elegant mansion appeared from the street, much as it did in 1902. However, it has been sectioned into apartments.

As part of the probate of Louis Bergdoll's large estate, his Broomall farm was listed for sale on April 3, 1902. Containing 66 acres along the north side of West Chester Pike westward up a hill from the Darby Creek valley, the farm was accessible from Philadelphia or West Chester, Pennsylvania, by a trolley line. The farmland was "fertile, watered, and in a high state of cultivation." It was a working dairy farm with a tenant farmer living on the property to perform the daily chores.

The original Bergdoll-built farmhouse was a substantial stone block mansion of three stories, with the top story under a mansard roof and a large central dormer flanked by smaller peaked dormers. A large veranda shielded the front door from the southwestern exposure. For construction, Brandywine valley granite was shipped up the Delaware River from a quarry near Wilmington, Delaware, then carried overland to the Bergdoll farm. Perched farther back on the property stood a barn with stalls for 6 horses, 20 cows, and a hayloft. Additional improvements included a butcher shop-wash house, a long open wagon shed, two chicken houses, and a honey bee shed.

A small orchard on the land, gently sloping to include Darby Creek, grew fruit trees and berry bushes. The creek was dammed with rocks for a large swimming hole in the summer and cutting ice in the winter for use at the Bergdoll city homes and the brewery. Nearby, on the eastern portion of the property, stood the farm's two-story stone tenement house of six rooms, surrounded by three small frame sheds.[24]

The Broomall property was listed for sale as a formality by the Orphans Court of Delaware County, Pennsylvania, in a different disposition to Louis' estate because, located in Marple Township, it was outside the city and county of Philadelphia and the jurisdiction of the Philadelphia Orphans Court.[25] By 2 pm on the date of the sale, Charles bought the entire farm in an arrangement using Emma's cash. He also purchased 88 acres of farmland across the pike.

Later, upon marrying Louise Anna Goetz in 1906, Charles soon grew determined to build a more elegant country home.[26] In 1907, Charles split off a narrow but deep 12-acre parcel on the western portion of the Bergdoll farm property in Broomall and built a three-story stone chateau with a sweeping wraparound veranda of more than 90 feet facing the southwest and set back from the pike across a flat, manicured lawn.

---

[24] After a protracted legal battle over Pennsylvania's use of the law of eminent domain, since 1993, the Bergdoll farm and country estate near Broomall has been consumed by the interchange of West Chester Pike (Route 3) and Interstate 476 (the Blue Route).

[25] It's unclear how and why the farm fell under the jurisdiction of the Orphans Court when Louis Bergdoll died without a will in 1896. Emma apparently funded the property purchase with cash and then split off parcels for her sons either as gifts or sales. The parcels were alternately listed in Emma, Charles, Erwin, and Grover's names over many decades.

[26] Louise Anna Goetz was the daughter of a Bergdoll Brewery foreman. It's presumed that Charles and Louise met and fell in love during the brief time Charles worked at the brewery or brewery social events. They were both young when they married; she was only 17.

The dark gray stone for the mansion was carried in from Charles' quarry near Birdsboro, Pennsylvania, where he and Emma were significant investors.[27] Charles' mansion's massive main entry door was built of hearty dark oak, 4 feet wide, opening to the stone veranda floor and leading to wide stone steps cut into the outer wall.

A heavy red tile mansard roof with a two-story central dormer was flanked by matching stone towers wrapped in curved windows for the southern view. Displayed in the gable end of the central dormer was the date, *AD 1907*.

Beyond the mansion, at the end of a long stone wall and flower bed-lined gravel driveway, sat a sizeable two-story stone carriage house with a classic hip roof, five windows across both floors, and stalls for the horses and the family's elegant carriages and automobiles. A glass greenhouse was positioned to the right of the veranda for those looking at the mansion from the tall stone pillars at West Chester Pike and the "Bergdoll" trolley stop.

Alfred claimed in his diary that the cost of the chateau and carriage house exceeded $200,000.[28] Charles and Louise filled the granite mansion with three children and German servants. Their son was named Charles Alvin, after his father. Their daughters were named Louise Elizabeth and Emma Christina after their mother and grandmother.

In 1909, Emma owned the larger property that backed up to Darby Creek, and, by then, during his racing heyday, Erwin had built an automobile machine shop on this parcel abutting the pike. Later, Emma sold her 54-acre farm to Erwin, and when Charles became estranged from his mother, he sold his adjoining 12-acre chateau property to Emma.

Grover would later purchase Charles' 88-acre lot, including a farmhouse and barn, across West Chester Pike. It must have been unclear for the family to track who owned what farm properties and when.

The Bergdoll boys and their mother enjoyed weekends and long summer months on their neighboring farms until family strife emerged. A tenant farmer and his family tended their livestock, landscaping, greenhouse, and field crops. The entire compound became known as the Bergdoll farm. It served as a place for the family to escape the pressures of city life, the brewery business, their many legal troubles,

---

[27] For many years Charles Bergdoll owned and operated the Birdsboro Stone Company along Sixpenny Creek in Union Township, Berks County, Pennsylvania. A traprock quarry, Birdsboro Stone Company utilized dynamite to blast the diabase, a strong igneous rock, crush it and haul it over the Pennsylvania Railroad for use in road materials and railroad track beds. With Emma and Albert Hall as partners, Charles made handsome profits selling the crushed stone to the state of Pennsylvania and the City of Philadelphia for road construction. Profits from Birdsboro Stone were so plentiful that it took years to notice that a bookkeeper was embezzling thousands of dollars from the company until his arrest in 1913. The former quarry has long been filled with water and was surrounded by Pennsylvania state game lands in 2023.

[28] This value seems particularly high, even for the construction of a stone mansion prior to 1910.

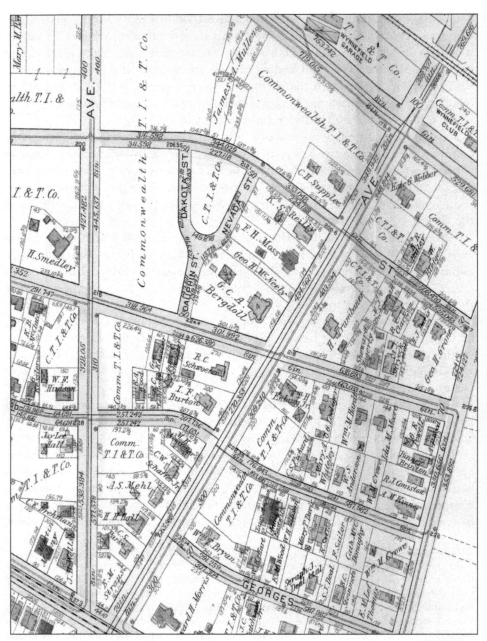

Map showing the location of Grover Bergdoll's Wynnefield mansion. (*Atlas of the City of Philadelphia* (*West Philadelphia*) 1918; Athenaeum of Philadelphia)

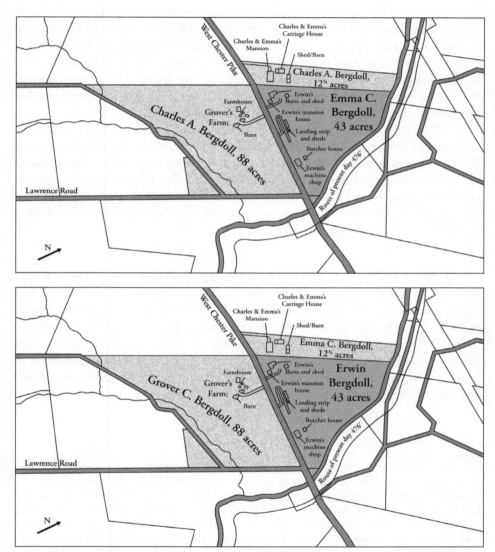

The Bergdoll family farms near Broomall, Pennsylvania. The top map depicts the farms in 1909, and the bottom map shows them in 1929, showing the changes in ownership.

and the prying press.[29] The only son not included in the Broomall farm compound was Louis. He split his time between an Italianate mansion in Philadelphia and an upscale apartment in New York City.

In 1908, Emma expanded her saloon business by building a three-story hotel, bar, and restaurant with Charles as a partner. Named Millbourne Hotel and planned for transient guests, it was located near the terminus of railroads and streetcars that served the southwestern suburbs of Philadelphia. Emma invested $50,000 in the hotel to be operated by Charles, but they failed to win approval for a liquor license. Hoping to recoup her investment, she enlisted managers to run it as a private club for many years until shutting it down for losing money.[30]

In 1907–1908, Emma was at the zenith of running the massive brewery on her account and often used a heavy fist. Loaning Ardmore, Pennsylvania saloon owner William C. Armstrong $15,000 for his Ardmore Hotel, they agreed that he would buy beer only from the Bergdoll Brewery, with one dollar from the seven-dollar cost per barrel going toward repayment of the loan. She sued Armstrong for breach of contract for $1,305.75. The dispute was published in the local papers for all other Bergdoll beer saloon keepers to take notice.

***

While Emma, Charles, and Erwin built or improved their country estates near Broomall in the first decade of the new century, Philadelphia homebuilder and realtor Samuel G. Shoemaker enjoyed some of his most lucrative years developing and selling residential homes in the city's expanding westward neighborhoods.

In 1906 Shoemaker was building a long line of three-story rowhouses on West Girard Avenue between North 38th and 39th Streets, with a primary attraction of facing picturesque Fairmount Park across the avenue. They were selling for $5,500 and $6,000 each.[31]

---

[29] In the end, only Erwin and Grover owned the Bergdoll farm properties with Grover being the last in the family to release ownership when the land was taken by Pennsylvania for Interstate 476.

[30] While the Millbourne club lost money, Emma retained property ownership until she died in 1944. Charles was also an initial investor in the (1919) Philadelphia Ice Palace and Auditorium, which later became the renowned Philadelphia Arena, the early home of the Yale, Princeton, and Penn ice hockey teams. Later, Emma also owned a 10,000-acre forest in Sullivan County, Pennsylvania, and a 132-acre undeveloped plot of land in Somerset, Maryland. The valuable Bergdoll Tract, adjacent to the District of Columbia, led to legal-financial disputes within the family and later became one of the longest-running zoning and development legal battles in the Washington, D.C., region. See Epilogue.

[31] As one of the many rowhouse developers of Philadelphia, Samuel Shoemaker's brick rowhomes on West Girard Avenue in the 2020s are often admired for their original towering architectural beauty and view of West Fairmount Park. However, their maintenance has been lackluster and many of the homes are in a poor state of repair.

With the profits, Shoemaker began constructing a 35-room Gothic stone mansion in the developing Wynnefield neighborhood nearby, taking up the entire northeast corner of 52nd Street and Wynnefield Avenue.

Initially farmland, Wynnefield was matured as a neighborhood by wealthy Jewish, Russian, and German-Americans who could more easily commute to the inner city by recently expanded train and trolley services. It's also where Elizabeth Bergdoll and her chauffeur husband, Albert Hall, settled after their 1909 marriage. Additionally, by 1910, renowned architect Horace Trumbauer lived across the street from Shoemaker.

At four stories tall with a multi-columned, wraparound veranda including a carriage port, Shoemaker's dark gray stone mansion displayed decorative cornices and matching twin towers with curved windows and domes capped by stone finials and iron cresting. Steeply pitched crimson gables peered from the orange ceramic-tiled mansard roof. Oriel bay windows protruded from rounded pavilions on the rear corners. Tall and elaborate brick chimneys stood like sentries on one side of the castle, while a canopy of sprawling trees, tangled bushes, and shrubbery hid the foundation and concave walls of the veranda.

First-to-bloom, Okame cherry trees were abundant. Thick, draping iron chains hung gas chandeliers from the port ceiling, and gas-fueled globes topped a pair of stone driveway entrance columns at the sidewalk. Embedded in the stone above the center of three third-floor window transoms appeared a square block face with large raised lettering and numbers, *AD 1908*, representing the year Shoemaker's Wynnefield mansion was completed.[32]

Alfred Bergdoll said in his diary that it was designed by the same architect who drew the plans for Charles' stone mansion at the family's Broomall farm complex. Still, there is no evidence that neighbor Trumbauer or his many assistants were behind the drawings.[33]

Upon completion of the construction, Shoemaker lived in the dark mansion for several years with his teenage daughter, Florence, his aged father, Nathan, several servants, and boarders until financial problems in the real estate development market caused him to dip into his father's hefty estate before or upon the older man's death in 1913.

---

[32] Similar-sized mansions were scattered through the neighborhood, which is named for Welshman Thomas Wynne, the personal physician to William Penn, and whose 1689 estate, Wynnestay, was just up 52nd Street at Woodbine Avenue.

[33] Except for the year, the stone date stamp at the top of the Wynnefield mansion is identical to the one at Charles' Broomall mansion. Some articles suggest the Broomall and Wynnefield mansions were replicas but their architecture was considerably different. Trumbauer's firm designed some of Shoemaker's premier development properties, including an apartment complex in Philadelphia's Germantown neighborhood at Wayne Avenue and Schoolhouse Lane. The beautiful twin four-story brick buildings were known in 2023 as the Fairfax Apartments of Germantown, designed by Trumbauer's African-American star architect, Julian Abele.

Grover Bergdoll's Wynnefield mansion on the northeast corner of 52nd and Wynnefield Avenue in Philadelphia in the 1920s. Built in 1906 by a developer whose sister accused him of killing their father in the mansion to collect an inheritance, Emma bought the house for Grover at a sheriff's sale. This is where Grover was captured, later escaped, and hid for years on the upper floors while he was a fugitive from justice. The elaborate carriage house is behind the mansion. (Bergdoll Family. Historical Society of Pennsylvania)

Needing more money to cover debts on another property, he turned to Emma Bergdoll with a promissory note for $18,000 secured by the Wynnefield mansion, which he wildly speculated to be worth up to $250,000. Emma's mortgage became a second lien on the Wynnefield property beyond its original $40,000 mortgage to Philadelphia's Land Trust and Title Company.

However, Shoemaker was never able to recover from his debts. In 1914 the stone castle-like structure in Wynnefield was foreclosed upon and put up for sale by the Philadelphia County sheriff in 1915. The price was nowhere near Shoemaker's speculated value of a quarter million dollars.

Perhaps enticed by the proximity of her daughter Elizabeth's mansion down the street, intent upon recovering her loan to the defaulting Shoemaker, and as a gift to her youngest son, Emma opened her checkbook again and bought Shoemaker's troubled and debt-ridden Wynnefield chateau. It became another Bergdoll castle.[34]

---

[34] Details about the evolution of the Bergdolls' Wynnefield mansion are from multiple lawsuits over the builder's bankruptcy and probate records. Descriptions of the mansion are contained in many legal records and photographs from newspaper photographers at the Urban Archives.

Paying the county sheriff $46,850 for the large stone Gothic mansion and carriage house on February 9, 1915, and assuming her $18,000 second mortgage debt, Emma rewarded Grover with his own home for his recent 21st birthday, just as she had purchased elegant homes for Louis, Charles, and Erwin.[35] The only difference was that she planned to live in the Wynnefield mansion with her youngest son.

However, more trouble surfaced within days of moving into their new home. Emma kept a bedroom in her "favorite son's house, on the second floor, separated from [Grover's] bedroom only by a large bathroom," wrote Alfred.

She hired house and garden servants, including Jacob Frederick Miller, a 19-year-old Philadelphia man whose German-born parents had died in Philadelphia years earlier. While Emma may have felt sorry for Miller and hired him for his German heritage, she didn't check his credentials because the self-professed heroin addict was well-known to the Philadelphia police as a robber and burglar and known to carry a gun.

While the police in Trenton, New Jersey, were looking for Miller for a burglary there on February 23, 1915, and while he had been working at the new Bergdoll mansion as a gardener-handyman for just 11 days, he emptied Emma's jewelry box of $1,282 worth of gold, diamond rings, and brooches, including her wedding ring, along with $75 in cash, and two Bergdoll pistols, and ran off with his loot. Emma called the police the next day. It would be the first of many visits by Philadelphia police to the new Bergdoll mansion in Wynnefield.[36]

The same day, the British Admiralty reported that the British steamer *Victoria*, carrying 92 passengers across the English Channel from Boulogne, France, to Folkstone, England, was attacked by a German U-Boat, but escaped. It was the height of the European war, and the official British press report said one torpedo passed just 30 yards off the bow of the *Victoria*. Americans were on board. The United States had not yet been dragged into the war, but anti-German fervor was all over the nation. The newspapers reported that Philadelphia police set their sights on a well-known German-American criminal, Miller, as their thief at the Bergdoll mansion. Detectives were determined to capture him, dead or alive.

When Philadelphia police finally cornered their suspect, known on the streets as Jake "Doggie" Miller, he pulled a gun. He shot and killed police detective James Maneely, the first detective to die in the line of duty in Philadelphia. "Doggie" Miller also shot and wounded detective Harry Tucker and escaped. Three thousand police officers combed the city for the Bergdoll jewelry thief and police killer before

---

[35] Emma said Grover was supposed to repay her for the Wynnefield house, but he never did. Depending on their legal and financial situation, the mansion was alternately listed in Emma's or Grover's names over many years. By 1921, Emma claimed Grover owed her between $128,000 and $141,000 for her investments in the property. Emma preferred the Wynnefield mansion because it afforded more privacy from the press, police, and public.

[36] Details of Emma's servants and their criminal charges are available in newspapers and legal documents. Other descriptions of unusual incidents are available from death certificates and genealogical records.

The spectacular Wynnefield mansion, nicknamed Bergdoll Castle, from the rear. The 1917 Hudson Super Six is parked about where it was in 1920 when Grover escaped. The summer kitchen, far left, is where police intercepted Emma with her gun and gained entrance to find Grover hiding in a window seat, second floor, center. The villa was demolished in the 1940s and replaced by five homes on its subdivided 3-acre corner lot. The only original feature remaining is a concrete driveway ramp from North 52nd Street. (Bergdoll Family Collection)

An architecturally imposing three-story carriage house with 12 dormers and a stately cupola stood behind the Wynnefield mansion. It was used for car storage and domestic staff housing. Behind the garage was a small barn for Emma's cow, which she dutifully hand-milked twice daily. On the left is one of Grover's roadsters. The date on the face of the cupola is 1906. (Bergdoll Family Collection)

capturing him while trying to flee on a Pennsylvania Railroad train. Two months later, Detective Tucker died from his gunshot wound, making him the second Philadelphia detective killed in the line of duty.

In court, Miller confessed to the crimes but claimed self-defense, testifying that detectives Maneely and Tucker allowed him to keep his revolver under questioning in a Philadelphia alley, suggesting they would kill him when he pulled the gun. By the time the case got to trial, Germany had attacked and sunk the British luxury liner *Lusitania* off the coast of Ireland, leading to intense hatred of Germans, especially in cities like Philadelphia. At his murder trial, the jury showed no mercy for Miller. He was sentenced to death in the electric chair.

The execution was carried out with four jolts of 2,000 volts of electricity on July 17, 1916, at the newly built Western Penitentiary of Pennsylvania in Benner.[37] A reporter witness said Miller dropped a crucifix from his clenched fist after the final jolt.

The newspapers said "Doggie" Miller's crime was killing the two Philadelphia detectives. They also reported that it started with Miller stealing jewelry from his sympathetic new patron, Emma Bergdoll, in her new mansion. The publicity about the spectacular crimes began the onslaught of headlines against the Bergdolls for decades.

To make matters worse, the Bergdolls didn't own the new mansion through all the turmoil over the theft, murders, trial, and execution. Because of Shoemaker's legal and financial difficulties, Emma only obtained a clear title to the Wynnefield property when a Pennsylvania Supreme Court ruling in 1917 settled Shoemaker's debts.

Nonetheless, Grover had already moved into the fully furnished chateau. He added his possessions, including more diamond jewelry, his library of collectors' volumes of Dickens' books, and Devon Inn China and Reed and Barton sterling silver flatware fished out of a slop pile by workers at the Broomall farm. He also purchased a nearly new, all-black Lozier roadster that fit nicely into the center bay of the ornate carriage house.[38]

The circus of press and police, the gawking public, local, state, and federal investigators, and lawyers and politicians shifted their focus to Wynnefield too. Emma may have regretted her expensive move. Within a few years, Washington's Alien Property Custodian office would seize the Bergdoll mansion while its heritor, Grover, hid in Germany.

---

[37] In the 2020s called SCI Rockview, the prison opened in 1915 and was the location for Pennsylvania's electric chair, replacing gallows executions in 1913.

[38] The Devon Inn was one of the most elegant hotels along the Pennsylvania Railroad Main Line westward from Philadelphia from the 1880s until 1913. Bergdoll farm workers found the China, and Reed and Barton sterling silver Pointed Antique flatware, in the hotel's food waste fed to their pigs.

CHAPTER THREE

Race Cars and Millions

1904–1916

At the Interstate Fair in Trenton, New Jersey, on the evening of October 2, 1914, driver John "Jack" LeCain, of Cambridge, Massachusetts, held the lead on the second to the last lap of a 25-lap, free-for-all amateur automobile race when the rear axle on his Mercer Special snapped and threw a wheel. His car careened out of control into a tall wooden fence on the width of the track near the massive three-part grandstand structure at the end of the long straightaway.

Designed as a horse-racing venue, the track had a wall in front of the main six-story tall grandstand lined with bales of straw to guide the drivers away from the crowd. However, excited fans mistook the makeshift barrier for safety and crept closer. LeCain's Mercer clipped the bales, sending the roaring machine bowling toward spectators crammed in tight to watch the finish. The chaos led to a trampling stampede among the crowd, injuring many people who fell to suffer from broken bones, cuts, and bruises.

Taking advantage of LeCain's crash, 20-year-old Grover Bergdoll, who had given "a magnificent exhibition of driving" on Trenton's half-mile track, steered his homemade Erwin Special racer around the chaos caused by LeCain's wreck and pushed the accelerator for two more laps.[1] Among the screaming and crying from the anguish of the injured and the cheering for an exciting finish, Grover was about to win when his car burst into flames on the final lap in front of the adrenaline-pumped crowd. Grover braked his new torpedo-shaped racing car to a slow roll, jumped out, and watched the conflagration as firefighters rushed from the green infield to extinguish the inferno, tossing sand from the track into the burning chassis. Another driver barreled past the flaming car to win the race, leaving Grover dejected for so narrowly losing before a local crowd that knew him well.[2]

A week earlier, Grover's black "cigar-shaped racing car" crashed into Frank Calvert's touring car on the tree- and shrub-lined Lancaster Avenue in Haverford,

---

[1] *Trenton Evening Times*, October 3, 1914.

[2] A photograph from 1914 shows Grover's new racing car in front of Erwin's machine shop on West Chester Pike. Painted white at the time with all-black tires, wheels, and spokes, it appeared sleek with the tail shaped into a cone with a sharp point at the end. It was crafted by Erwin to look like a Benz.

Pennsylvania, an affluent leafy suburb of Philadelphia. Grover was racing through the heart of the Main Line, named for the Pennsylvania Railroad tracks westward from the city. Two other people were crammed into the racer's narrow seat: Grover's friends, Kirby Gyles and Charles J. Kraus, Jr. Gyles was thrown and suffered broken ribs. Grover and Kraus were trapped in the car briefly while it caught fire. Pulled from the burning vehicle by another motorist, all three were taken to Bryn Mawr Hospital with burns and other minor injuries. Police officers soon found the injured men at the hospital and took Grover and Kraus to jail. They were immediately out on bail, and Grover used the injuries as a stalling tactic to avoid appearing in court. Reckless and irresponsible driving and crashing were becoming common for Grover Bergdoll, whether on the track or in the public streets.[3]

Four months later, on February 25, 1915, Grover was in another Erwin Special cruising along at about 50 miles per hour on the Vanderbilt Cup practice runs at the San Francisco World's Fair course when he swerved trying to avoid a wire fence strung overnight to keep cows off the plank track. At 5:30 am, with another driver, Ralph DePalma, chasing behind him, Grover was practicing too early. Grover's Philadelphia boyhood companion and mechanic, Thomas E. Furey, who said no one was better at racing than Grover except DePalma, rode in the passenger seat. Furey said they were approaching the track's homestretch "and going pretty fast when I saw the wire stretched across the track. When the machine struck the wire, I ducked under the cowl. The wire cut into the radiator and tank and then caught Grover in the face, badly cutting his face. There was a long, deep gash in his throat right under his chin."

Grover saw the fence when it was too late. "The car plunged... and Bergdoll was thrown into the barbed wire," wrote race reporters at the scene. "His head and face were badly lacerated and cut."

Furey said Grover was bleeding all over the place but that he and track employees got him to "the headquarters and turned him over to a doctor there. They fixed him the best they could, putting 12 stitches in his throat and bandaging up his face." Furey briefly attended to the wrecked race car, and when he returned to Grover, the 21-year-old racer insisted on returning to their hotel and then taking the next train home to Philadelphia. Furey said he was concerned that Grover would fall ill in his condition if he rushed home instead of resting and recovering in California. He and DePalma managed, for a while, to talk Grover out of returning home immediately to allow him time to heal and to provide them time to load onto the train the several cars they had brought along for the races.

"I thought it very dangerous as he might catch a cold or get blood poisoning," declared Furey, with limited knowledge of the cause of either ailment. As Furey and DePalma were tending to the race cars, they discovered, upon returning to their hotel room, that Grover had telegraphed messages home, taken a ferry to

---

[3] The crashed car was an *Erwin Special*. Erwin's son, Louis Erwin Bergdoll, said his father never forgave Grover for crashing his favorite homemade race car.

Oakland and its 16th Street Station, boarded a train, and was traveling eastward. It was a typical Grover reaction: run away at embarrassment and the first sign of defeat.

Grover's 40-horsepower Erwin Special race car, with its low-slung, open seating compartment and pointed tail, was heavily damaged in the dangling wire crash. It had been engineered and assembled at Erwin's machine shop along West Chester Pike on the Bergdoll farm near Philadelphia, from car parts left over from the recently bankrupt Bergdoll Motor Company.

Based on reporters' narratives that he appeared lifeless while unconscious following the accident, rumors surfaced in Philadelphia that Grover had been killed in the San Francisco crash.[4] In the messages he wired home just before he departed the city, Grover wrote to his mother, Emma, "It's all newspaper talk. I'm not hurt. Grover."

Watching from the sidelines was Kraus. If it had been a racing day, he would have been in the car instead of Furey. Sullen when things didn't go his way, Grover didn't formally withdraw from the race, but he maintained a positive stance, if only for his family. The racer's final wire home said, "Have had a little accident. Will not compete in the Grand Prix. Am feeling well."[5]

In May 1915, Grover was at it again with Erwin, train-shipping three homemade race cars, with their signature, Erwin Special stamped over the nose, to Indiana for the Decoration Day weekend Indianapolis 500. But, before the race could begin, mechanical problems set in with their new vehicles. They were forced to withdraw. For the race, the cars were branded as Bergdoll models, one each for Grover, Erwin, and Willie Haupt, to meet the stock production rules of the contest. None got into the race. Only Grover was listed on the paid entrance schedule, but his name did not appear in the race lineup. Such was the auto racing career of the new millionaire daredevil from Philadelphia.[6]

Like the tour to San Francisco, the cost of the Indianapolis trip amounted to hundreds of dollars with no race purse, sponsor, or other benefits to offset the enormous expense. It was simply young Grover recklessly spending his inherited money, trying to make a name for himself and live up to his older brother's success and national fame.[7]

***

---

[4] The Philadelphia *Evening Ledger* of February 25, 1915 reported that Grover "was probably fatally injured."

[5] Kraus was described as "close to Grover as a brother." Erwin never forgave Grover for burning and smashing his homemade race car. He talked about it with family members for many decades thereafter. The scars from Grover's face and neck lacerations would resurface years later on his wanted posters and descriptions.

[6] Ralph DePalma won the Indianapolis 500 in 1915. A few years later, he would show up unannounced in a Philadelphia courtroom to offer moral support to his friend and competitor, Grover.

[7] Grover also entered the 1916 Indianapolis race of 300 miles, along with Stecher, hoping to win the $12,000 purse. Both entered "Erwin" cars but withdrew before the race began.

Erwin Bergdoll and Ike Stecher built an Erwin Special race car at Erwin's machine shop along West Chester Pike at the Bergdoll Farm in Broomall. The race cars were crafted from parts and motors from Bergdoll Motor Company. Stecher is pictured in the car that Grover destroyed in a spectacular crash and fire. Erwin never forgave him. (Bergdoll Family. Historical Society of Pennsylvania)

This Erwin Special is pictured on the smooth driveway leading to the Bergdolls' grand stone mansion in Broomall. Along with Erwin at the wheel is Eugene "Ike" Stecher. Grover took the photograph. (Bergdoll Family)

At 12, Grover became enthralled by racing cars when Louis purchased vehicles for the east coast racing circuit, driving them himself or sponsoring other drivers. Grover also traveled the circuit with his brothers. At 16, Erwin used his inherited money to purchase a Welch roadster and enter races during his summer vacation from high school in Philadelphia. Louis and Erwin caught the automobile racing bug from the first Vanderbilt Cup race on Long Island in 1904. It was sponsored by another millionaire, William K. Vanderbilt, Jr., of New York's renowned Vanderbilt family. Louis envied Vanderbilt for his collection of cars and his celebrity racing lifestyle.

Louis became so enamored with cars and racing (and Vanderbilt's self-titled race) that by 1907, he was planning to build the largest automobile speed track in America on a 223-acre plateau just outside the city limits of Philadelphia near the Bergdoll family's farm and country estate.[8] He wanted a namesake racetrack and race, just like Vanderbilt.

---

[8] Louis proposed building the American Motordrome, a sizeable oval race track with grandstands and a country club on 223 acres of farmland and forest southeast-adjacent to the Delaware County Field Club (Llanerch Country Club). Despite considerable planning and publicity about the track, for which Louis envisioned a race titled the Bergdoll Cup, it was never built. On a plateau bounded by today's Steel Road, Greenview Lane, and Burmont Road, it became a quarry that was later filled to expand the golf course. The Bergdolls' farm lay about two miles westward in Broomall, on land now consumed by the Route 3–West Chester Pike interchange with I-476, commonly known as the Blue Route.

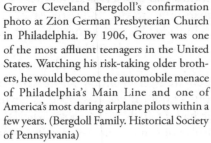

Grover Cleveland Bergdoll's confirmation photo at Zion German Presbyterian Church in Philadelphia. By 1906, Grover was one of the most affluent teenagers in the United States. Watching his risk-taking older brothers, he would become the automobile menace of Philadelphia's Main Line and one of America's most daring airplane pilots within a few years. (Bergdoll Family. Historical Society of Pennsylvania)

Karl Charles Alvin Bergdoll, left, and Louis John Bergdoll as young boys dressed in traditional German costumes and riding boots, about 1892. Within a few years, their inherited fortunes would also go into trust. After their early interest in risky automobile racing, the older Bergdoll boys followed business and legal careers so distinctly different from the younger boys' embarrassing escapades that they would change their names to Brawn and Bergson. (Bergdoll Family, Kathy Bergdoll Brawn Tidball)

As the oldest of the Bergdoll boys, Louis was the first to use his inherited wealth to plunge headlong into the new-moneyed gentlemen's sports—auto racing and aviation—that became popular almost overnight in America in the early 20th century. A tall, slender man with blue eyes, brown hair, an oval face, an engaging smile, and a slight chin, Louis enjoyed patriarch status among his brothers as his interests and actions helped guide their formative years. He was, perhaps, the instigator of Erwin and Grover's speeding habits which gained such notoriety and got them into so much legal trouble.

In what appears to be the first speeding-related traffic infraction for the Bergdoll boys, in July 1906, 16-year-old Erwin was riding with 21-year-old Louis when the elder brother's big touring car hit a woman stepping off a trolley in Philadelphia. Louis was cited for driving too fast and briefly held in jail until he posted a thousand dollars bail. The woman suffered a fractured skull but survived. The experience may have scared Louis into confining his speeding to the racetrack, but it did little to temper the carelessness of Erwin and Grover.

Louis's elegant brownstone on 22nd and Green included an elaborate carriage house facing Mt. Vernon Street with an apartment above for the houseman and chauffeur. Soon after he moved in, the bachelor businessman and lawyer-in-training at the University of Pennsylvania installed an electric elevator in the carriage house to lift his growing collection of limousines, touring cars, and racing automobiles to the second floor.[9]

In 1907, her guardian and brother, Louis, bought 19-year-old Elizabeth Bergdoll a Benz touring car. She would become one of the first women in Philadelphia to own and habitually drive a luxury vehicle. However, the large, heavy machine was too big for Elizabeth to navigate on the city's narrow neighborhood streets, so Louis replaced it with a smaller but no less stylish Welch. He kept the Benz for himself, adding it to his growing fleet.

Also, in 1907, Louis organized the Louis J. Bergdoll Motor Company to assemble and sell automobiles, the most renowned of which was the Bergdoll 30. Building his mansion at the family's country estate in Broomall, Pennsylvania, Charles joined him as a significant shareholder-manager. Later, Erwin invested in the company when it was incorporated and solicited money from others.[10] The Bergdoll Motor Company also produced and operated Philadelphia taxi cabs and bus services.

Louis appeared to be an astute businessman in a growing industry. At 22, he transferred many of his real estate holdings in Philadelphia and its suburbs into the North Broad Street Realty Company, with assets worth $400,000.[11]

The signature auto of the Bergdoll Motor Company was assembled and introduced in July 1910. The Bergdoll 30 was an open-air four-cylinder, 30-horsepower touring car or roadster option, costing $1,500–$2,600. It was described as having a "low, long rakish appearance," although it had 17-inch wood spoke wheels. A runabout model was dubbed Louis J. in a display of vanity; another, Toy Tonneau. They sold for $1,600. The standard colors were Richelieu Blue with turquoise pin striping. The company purchased the chassis and engine parts from suppliers such as Westinghouse engines, Schwarz wheels, and Atwater Kent ignitions, made in Philadelphia. The tires were Continental with either 3½- or 4½-inch width. Bergdoll's workers assembled them into the Bergdoll 30 at its main plant at 31st and Dauphin Streets, smaller factories at North Broad and Wood Streets, and 16th and Callowhill Streets, Philadelphia.[12]

---

[9] The description of Louis Bergdoll's incredible mansion is from the Philadelphia Office of Historic Preservation.

[10] The Bergdoll Motor Company was incorporated in 1912 to raise money from outside stockholders.

[11] Properties included the Eagle Hotel just outside the western boundary of Philadelphia in Haverford Township, Pennsylvania. The large property would factor in the Bergdoll boys' lives as the location of their airstrip, Eagle Field. In 2023, $400,000 would be worth approximately $12 million.

[12] Several car collectors contributed information about the Bergdoll motorcar, and Louis' bankruptcy filings provided a wealth of information about his car company and personal finances.

The Louis J. Bergdoll Motor Company building at 16th and Callowhill Streets in Philadelphia around 1910. The frames, chassis, motors, and other parts for Bergdoll cars were shipped to Philadelphia by train. The classic brick building remained in use for luxury apartments in 2023. (Bergdoll Family)

Where other manufacturers would begin a new line with just a few automobiles, Bergdoll claimed he would build 50 of his 9 models (450 cars) and make them readily available for immediate possession at signing a purchase contract.[13] The Bergdoll Taxi Company used the limousine and town car models.

At North Broad and Wood, Louis kept his office above the Bergdoll showroom. It was the heart of the automobile boom in Philadelphia and the same block as the gleaming new Packard Motor Car building.[14] Bergdoll Motor planned to assemble more than a thousand cars for 1910–1911, at 24 vehicles per week.[15] The company also opened a sales office in Washington, with its first car arriving in the capital in November 1910. To promote the new Bergdoll 30, the company displayed touring

---

[13] Bergdoll motor cars are still held among a handful of collectors in the 2020s.

[14] Later, the Packard Motor Car building became home to the *Philadelphia Record* and the *Evening Bulletin* newspapers and was known as The Press Building.

[15] Most upstart car companies of this era assembled automobiles from parts purchased from suppliers instead of designing their own cars. Therefore, many car brands appeared similar.

A row of new Bergdoll automobiles on display around 1911–1912. The company was owned by Louis Bergdoll with investors such as Emma, Charles, and Erwin, and cars were sold in Philadelphia, Washington, and Trenton, New Jersey. This appears to be a modified runabout branded Louis J. (Spooner & Wells Collection, Detroit Free Library)

models, runabouts, coupes, taxi cabs, and delivery wagons at regional auto shows with Bergdoll plaques behind them. Their company slogan boasted that the cars were "backed by millions"—whether it meant people or dollars wasn't specified. They also arranged for the Bergdoll 30 to be included, with Maxwell, Hudson, Overland, and Reo, in a national endurance test of automobiles best suited to deliver the U.S. Mail. It failed to make the cut.

Despite advertising, racing acclaim, and the renowned Bergdoll name, the cars needed to sell better for Bergdoll Motor Company to be a profitable business. Louis Bergdoll contracted with the Westinghouse Machine Company of East Pittsburgh to produce one thousand gasoline engines for his cars in 1910, at 100 per month. Bergdoll was to pay Westinghouse $210,000 for the motors in "specified installments." Sometime after delivering 550 machines, Westinghouse sued Bergdoll Motor for nonpayment and won with a judgment of $104,000.[16]

Louis hired managers and a renowned mechanic–driver, Willie Haupt, to run the company because Louis often traipsed around the country on a train entering his race cars in the fast-growing sport in New York, South Carolina, Florida, and Illinois. Along with American Locomotive, Berliet, Thomas, and Welch automobile brands,

---

[16] Such lawsuits were common among large industrial contracts. The details of this lawsuit indicate approximately how many Bergdoll cars were built or in a stage of assembly. Because so many unused motors were later found (and stolen from) Erwin's Bergdoll machine shop at the farm in Broomall, the estimate is fewer than 500.

he acquired a Benz dealership and used the fast German cars for racing. However, he would have been better suited to stay home and manage the books because Bergdoll Motor declined into bankruptcy in 1913.

Erwin assumed control of the corporation with assets of slightly more than $100,000 and liabilities of more than $250,000, including debt to Charles' coal company. He obtained the $31,639 worth of unfinished cars, motors, parts, and tools, molding them into the [Erwin] Bergdoll Machine Company in a financial sleight of hand that included transferring the majority of stock to his investor mother and naming friends and acquaintances to the new company's board of directors without their knowledge. Later, a bankruptcy referee chastised Erwin for arranging to pay his creditor brothers but stiffing others. Erwin also tried to carry the original cost of all merchandise, tools, machinery, and equipment to the new corporation without depreciation.

Erwin fitted his new machine shop with the tools and equipment to build his race cars. Most of the car parts remained in the original factory while Louis was still challenged in bankruptcy court well into the 1920s. At the receiver's sale of the Bergdoll Motor Company, it was estimated that the value of nine assembled automobiles, 300 roadster and limousine bodies, 250 frames, 40 motors, dozens of transmissions, 350 radiators, and hundreds of carburetors, wheels, rims, machinery not taken by Erwin, and office furniture was about $150,000. A car company purchased the Bergdoll name in Trenton, New Jersey, which continued assembling cars as Bergdolls for a brief period, but the brand was unsuccessful.

***

Louis' first experience with racing fame came in March 1908 when he won the 150-mile stock chassis class and 125-mile amateur class races in Ormond–Daytona Beach with his #11, 80-horsepower, 2,700-pound Benz racer and George Parker as his rider-mechanic. The Benz was shipped from Germany after racing in the 1907 Kaiserpreis Grand Prix in the Taunus mountains of Hesse. With his "German car," Louis took the lead in the amateur race at the 70-mile mark from an "American car" driven by Sam Stevens, blazing on to win.[17]

Basking in the success of the Florida races, Louis shipped the Benz to Savannah for another run, but it was damaged on the train, and he had to bow out. He entered the Briarcliff, New York race in April 1908 with his powerful Benz, but Parker made a rookie mistake. Despite constant reminders from Louis, the mechanic failed to attach a mailbox to the Benz from which pre-race judges would retrieve and review

---

[17] Newspapers from all over the nation provided descriptions of races involving the Bergdolls. Also, records of early races are now kept online on blogs and websites devoted to historic racing events. The Mercedes Benz Museum in Stuttgart, Germany, was very helpful in describing the Benz racing cars used by the Bergdolls.

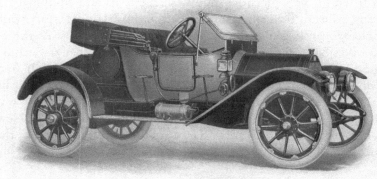

30 H. P. "Louis J" Roadster, Fully Equipped $1500

An unusually handsome two passenger car. Equipped with Quick Detachable Demountable rims, Bosch Easy-starting Magneto, full set of 5 lamps, Prest-O-Lite tank, mohair cape cart top, folding glass windshield, tire irons, horn, tools and trunk. This type of body may also be obtained on our "40" H. P. chassis with a self-starter and complete equipment for $1900.

Two examples of a Bergdoll *Louis J* roadster. The car on the top is parked in front of the Bergdoll brick mansion at 929 North 29th Street. It is a stripped version of a roadster used by Grover to speed around the streets of Philadelphia. A *Louis J* roadster in the Bergdoll Motor Company catalog is on the bottom. From the time each of the Bergdoll children obtained a driver's license, they owned several cars, from racers to roadsters, touring cars to limousines. Elizabeth Bergdoll was reportedly the first woman to drive her own car in Philadelphia. (Bergdoll Family. Chester County Historical Society)

the foreign car specifications, mostly checking the weight. The Benz was disqualified. At about this time, Louis also purchased another powerful Benz intending to take it to Florida in January 1909 to break the 100 miles per hour speed barrier. He intended to set speed records and make a name for himself and his new automobile company. However, this plan was also interrupted by business demands. Despite the disqualification and the failed speed attempt, the publicity and wealth put him on track to become the first national celebrity among the Bergdoll boys. He posed for

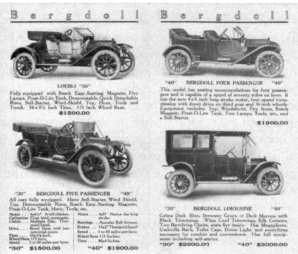

The Louis J. Bergdoll Motor Company offered nine models of the Bergdoll 30 (horsepower) in 1911, from Roadster to Limousine to Town Car, costing $1,600 to $2,600. Its advertisement said the Bergdoll Motor Car was "backed by millions." Later, the company would introduce a Bergdoll 40, but it wouldn't last long. The company declared bankruptcy in 1913. (The *Horseless Age* magazine, 1911)

photographs in the sleek car; when published, they were labeled "the famous No. 11 Benz racer of Ormond and Briarcliff fame, and Mr. L. Bergdoll, owner and driver."

Quietly observing his older brother was Erwin, purchasing or developing the race cars that he hoped, one day, would outrun Louis and his vehicles.

In October 1908, the Bergdoll boys entered the first Fairmount Park Motor Race in Philadelphia. Organized by the Quaker City Motor Club and approved on September 9, 1908, by the Fairmount Park Commission for one race only, the Fairmount Park Motor Race was a 202-mile timed competition around the picturesque rolling hills and flatlands of the largest public park in America.[18] Situated along the Schuylkill and bounded by the Pennsylvania Railroad and the grounds of the 1876 Centennial Exposition, the track also ran through neighborhood streets flanked by brick and stone Victorian mansions and narrow rowhouses. It included a long flat stretch for high speed along the river and heart-stopping curves with a dangerous drop-off under a railroad bridge in a neighborhood frequented by the Bergdoll boys in their fast cars, with nightlife and just across the river from their family's money-producing brewery and *biergarten*.

Philadelphia leaders approved the race to celebrate the city's 225th anniversary during what became known as Founder's Week, October 4–10, 1908. The Philadelphia mayor, John E. Reyburn, also thought the race would showcase sportsmanship and boost the city economically by promoting automobiles. It was ideal for the Bergdoll boys, especially Louis' fledgling car manufacturing and sales business, and as an energy release for the street-racing lust of Erwin and Grover.

"We used to be crazy about the Bergdoll brothers," recalled Virginia Stanton for Alfred Bergdoll's 1960s diary-manuscript, who, at age 71 in 1968, still lived in her family's rowhouse at 52nd and Parkside Avenue. She remembered adoring handsome Erwin and Grover as they frequented a neighborhood confectionery store. "We kids filed in after them, sat at another table, and worshipped them. I used to try to flirt with them," she said. As a 12 year old in 1909, Stanton recalled watching the fast race cars roaring around the sweeping curve on Parkside Avenue between 53rd and 52nd Streets in front of her house. "Every morning before the races (for practice runs), we would hear the cars tearing past the house, and my brothers and I were up early to watch them go around the sharp corner. We used to have crowds of friends come to watch the races and keep score."

Stanton revealed that Erwin was initially the speediest driver of the Bergdoll boys but was shy and "liked to be inconspicuous. Grover liked the attention and got a lot of it," she said. Erwin, known as the "terror of the Main Line," would speed about

---

[18] Consisting of more than two thousand acres, Fairmount Park was split into East and West Park by the Schuylkill. The race was held on the Belmont Plateau and Schuylkill Valley of West Park. Boundaries of the course included West River Drive, Neill Drive, City Avenue, Belmont Avenue, Parkside Avenue, South Concourse Drive and the Grandstand, and the infamous Sweet Briar Curve.

Louis J. Bergdoll (Bergson) raced cars in several states but had limited success. Pictured in 1908 with an Alco, he ran Bergdoll cars and a Benz from the first Benz dealership in the United States. Louis tried to build a massive race track in the countryside west of Philadelphia, but permit applications were denied. (Bergdoll Family Collection)

the city and suburban streets, but after being ticketed many times by local police officers, he "changed his ways."[19] Soon afterward, Grover took over his brother's habit of speeding throughout their community. It would solidify his reputation as the most notorious of the Bergdoll boys.

Louis entered the 1908 Fairmount Park race to drive a 60-horsepower American Locomotive car, while Erwin joined with a 50-horsepower Welch.[20] Billed as the Founder's Week 200-Mile Stock Chassis Road Race in Fairmount Park, the competition was described by Philadelphia newspapers as "the biggest motoring event ever planned in the world."[21] Sixteen drivers and their mechanics were given five days to practice on the course. Warnings were sent out to spectators who might need to be aware of speeding cars through America's most enormous city park. In their 25 trips around the eight-mile track, cars would reach up to 90 miles per hour and often crashed.

As a millionaire and respected local businessman, Louis was foolish to drive his car in the race. However, he felt that racing should include more than just professional drivers. "By having certain classes restricted to amateur drivers," he said, "this system would attract more owners and be a fairer test of real sportsmanship."

---

[19] In a display of more affection toward her youngest son, Emma later said that many of Erwin's driving infractions were blamed on Grover, who didn't deserve it.

[20] The first Fairmount Park Motor Race was limited to American cars only. The Philadelphia Free Library, the Nathan Lazernick collection, and Spooner and Wells display at the Detroit Free Library provided photographs for descriptions of the race cars at the Fairmount Park Motor Races. A few details of the races were compiled from Michael J. Seneca's book, *The Fairmount Park Motor Races*.

[21] Stock chassis described a car purchased from a showroom floor without significant alterations to the engine and body.

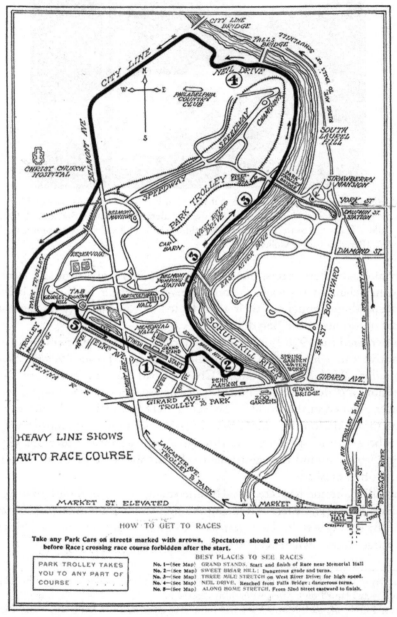

The Fairmount Park Motor Race ran through the largest park in an American city for four years, 1908–1911. Hundreds of thousands would line the course, pumping thousands of dollars into the Philadelphia region. After Erwin won the 1911 race, Park commissioners cut the race from the circuit, saying the Park's charter forbade it. This map comes from a promotional brochure printed by the race directors in 1908. (Quaker City Motor Club)

The *Philadelphia Inquirer*, with a full-page spread on the race, said Louis was "a lover of good sportsmanship, and with his faith in his car, [it's] his chief reason for entering what is looked upon by many as a most hazardous race. [But], he doesn't scare easily." Hazardous may be an understatement. The race cars were deadly.

Riding in open-air compartments, drivers and their mechanics and spectators who gathered along the first race tracks of America were often critically injured or killed during spectacular crashes.

The 1908–1911 races around the dirt, gravel, and cinder-encrusted roads in Fairmount Park were not traditional first-to-the-finish-line-wins races but timed events to reduce the deadly danger of wheel-to-wheel or free-for-all competition.

A few hundred thousand spectators, many traveling to the events in special trains, crowded around the park's curves and straightaways with few safety measures except for bales of hay and straw. The race cars were top-heavy and relatively simple mechanical machines with exposed gears and chains and narrow single-ply tires that often blew, forcing the vehicles out of control. The drivers and mechanics sat high in bench or Bomber seats without rollover protection.[22] The cars were set off at intervals for most of the races, and declaring a winner was based on official timers with their vest watches who logged each racer's speed and time around the track for a cumulative total. The fastest driver of all the laps together was declared the winner. It was common to hear a collective gasp from the grandstand crowd when the timer's fast lap was manually displayed on a massive scoreboard many seconds after the car and driver roared past.

The Fairmount Park races were the most significant spectator events in Philadelphia since the 1876 World's Fair, also held in the park directly behind the grandstands. Crowds watched the races for free along the eight miles of track, 20 to 30 people deep, all craning their necks to view the well-known crash sites. Residents with homes along the course threw parties, including the wealthy family owning Pencoyd Iron Works along the Schuylkill: Isaac, Algernon, and Percival Roberts senior and junior. A VIP invitation to watch the race from the front yard of the original Roberts' vast country estate, known as Pencoyd and Windermere along City Avenue in 1908–1911, afforded unobstructed views along the gradual climb to the Belmont Plateau before the 90-degree turn onto Belmont Avenue. Proceeds from ticket sales for grandstand seats and parking spaces generated more than $15,000 per race and went to fund hospitals. Despite benefiting charities, it was the act of generating income in the public park and the danger along the track that would eventually lead to the demise of the spectacular race.

The Bergdoll boys entered all four Fairmount Park races, beginning in 1908 with Louis and Erwin.[23] Louis had already made a name for himself as a driver in races on South

---

[22] Mechanics were required to ride with the driver for longer races. They watched for competition, monitored gauges, pumped oil and gas for pressure, communicated with the pits via hand signals and signs, changed tires, and relieved exhausted drivers.

[23] Erwin became so engrossed in racing that he dropped out of high school.

Teenager Grover Bergdoll, right, also raced against his older brothers but had marginal success. Here, with his race crew, he watches other drivers on the Fairmount Park Motor Racecourse after his Benz racer broke down. The location appears to be along today's City Avenue separating Philadelphia from its western suburbs. (Bergdoll Family Collection)

Philadelphia's Point Breeze motor track, then with his win at Ormond–Daytona Beach, and in the races in Savannah and Briarcliff.[24] He was compared with fellow millionaire race car owner-drivers Vanderbilt and Harry Payne Whitney. However, Louis was also a pragmatic businessman. Eventually, he would retreat into the racing background while his younger brothers grabbed the wheel and became celebrity champions.

Louis and Erwin were unsuccessful in the 1908 race, so for the 1909 event, the Bergdoll boys ramped up the competition. Louis entered two Thomas racers, one to be driven by himself and the other by Willie Haupt. Erwin entered two Benz racers to be driven by himself and Charles Howard. And the boys' new brother-in-law, Albert P. Hall, entered a Welch. All cars were from Louis' auto dealerships.

The only notable event for the Bergdoll boys in the 1909 race occurred during practice laps when Hall continued speeding through the park after police halted trials for the day. Hall was arrested for the infraction and charged with assaulting bystanders who entered the fray. During the race, competition from professional drivers such as the renowned Barney Oldfield in a Benz proved stiff. Although Oldfield's fast car was disqualified for lack of specifications, the Bergdoll boys failed again to win.

By 1910, Louis was married to Florence Seider and living in the brownstone mansion while starting their family of two boys, Louis, Jr., and Wilbur. Despite his business, he traveled again for more racing and promotion of his car company,

---

[24] The Point Breeze track was on the site of a former horse racing track near today's FDR Park at 26th and Penrose Avenue in South Philadelphia.

as far away as California, where the *Los Angeles Sunday Herald* ridiculed the "sleepy Quaker" for declaring that 60 miles per hour around a scientifically engineered track would become standard for racers. The *Herald* said that racers in Los Angeles were already doing more than 75 miles per hour around their poorly designed track and that Philadelphia racers (and Bergdoll) were "still plodding along on coach time."[25]

However, Louis had a well-formed opinion of the future of racing. He presciently declared to the *Herald*, "I believe that automobile racing is only in its infancy, and if handled properly by the right sort of men, it is sure to become as popular with the sporting public as horse racing, baseball, or college football." Louis also suggested that auto racing was "no more dangerous to life and limb than any other sport." He would soon be proved wrong.

On October 1, 1910, a disastrous and deadly crash occurred at the Vanderbilt Cup race on Long Island, New York. A Marquette Buick driven by Louis Chevrolet crashed into a touring car parked along the racecourse in Hicksville, throwing Chevrolet from the driver's seat and pinning his mechanic, Charles Miller, in the wreckage. Miller was killed. Along with the death of another mechanic in the race and several injuries, it ended the Vanderbilt Cup event on Long Island.[26] Within days, racers moved to Philadelphia and began practicing on the Fairmount Park course.

In the 1910 Fairmount Park race, the Bergdoll boys ramped up their competition again. Erwin entered his 90-horsepower Benz, joined by Hall, practicing for the race in another Benz, and for the first time, by Charles in a third Benz.[27] Louis did not enter the competition to drive but probably sponsored the Benz driven by Haupt. Recalling that her new husband, Albert, had gotten into a trackside brawl the previous year, Elizabeth Bergdoll Hall rode with him around the park roads with impressive practice speed, 8 minutes and 30 seconds. The course record at this time was 7 minutes and 38 seconds. About five thousand spectators watched the trials, always waiting for the crashes.

Because of the publicity of the recent deaths at the Vanderbilt Cup race on Long Island, Philadelphia arranged for three thousand police officers and park guards to keep the anticipated race-day crowd of hundreds of thousands of people safe.

***

---

[25] The Philadelphia race course was described by The *Automobile* magazine in 1911 as "slower because of dangerous curves and grades."

[26] Vanderbilt himself announced the end of the Long Island race—details provided by the Vanderbilt Cup Races blog. Louis Chevrolet co-founded the Chevrolet Motor Car Company, later absorbed by General Motors.

[27] Benz was becoming the preeminent race car of the age, with Barney Oldfield purchasing a 200 HP Benz for racing in 1910. It cost $14,000. The Blitzen Benz or Lightning Benz set speed records at the Brooklands track in Surrey, England, and Daytona Beach with Oldfield and Bob Burman as drivers. Louis had the exclusive Benz dealership in the United States for a time, but neither Louis nor Erwin ever obtained the fastest of the Benz racers.

In 1910, Erwin felt ready for a win with a fast car and many laps of experience on his hometown track. He was still unmarried and living at home with Emma and Grover in their brick Brewerytown mansion while preparing his cars at the Bergdoll automobile dealership on North Broad Street and a nondescript garage in an industrial neighborhood of North Philadelphia. He felt he could take chances in his race cars and was determined to pick up speed and chalk up some victories.

In one trackside scene leading up to the 1910 race, Erwin closely examines his #8 Benz, dressed in cotton coveralls, a cable-knit trapper hat topped by leather goggles, and surrounded by a few dozen men and boys with long, dark wool coats. His admirers wear bowler and flat hats and display short cigars smoking from their clenched teeth. Erwin presented a less polished appearance than his older brothers, Louis and Charles; he was tall and slender but slightly shorter than Louis, with a ruddier complexion than Grover's. Erwin's deep gray eyes were most striking, prominent, and captivating even when covered by the clear oval glass in his racing goggles. He was the handsome and daring millionaire gentleman racer ideal for publicity to sell newspapers. The Philadelphia press and women loved his daring speed, dashing appearance, and bankroll.

Erwin was also shaping up to be a formidable racer. In June 1910, he placed second in the rain-shortened Point Breeze 50-mile race, beaten only by the professional racer Ralph DePalma, in front of a crowd of 15,000 in the massive wooden grandstands of the South Philadelphia track.

On the same day, Erwin won two individual races at the track; a 5-mile event open only to "gentlemen" drivers and a 10-mile event.[28] He did not compete in the free-for-all race, considered the most dangerous, with cars lined up side-by-side and taking off simultaneously. With his victories at Point Breeze, Erwin soon surpassed the celebrity and notoriety of Louis. But he was risking it all by recklessly continuing to speed on local streets.

On June 26, Erwin paid a $350 fine for speeding in the Philadelphia Main Line suburbs. Luckily, the judge did not revoke his driver's license, which would have prohibited Erwin from entering races. Instead, Erwin was told by the judge to wait to drive again in Lower Merion Township until he could prove he was safe. He would prove it to everyone in the next Fairmount Park race.

Meanwhile, at 16 and recently granted his driver's license, Grover tooled around Philadelphia and the Main Line suburbs in a shiny new black Lozier touring car. He, too, was often caught speeding and challenging the local police, but he was still too young to compete in the national races.

As an amateur driver and with Grover helping him in the pits in the 1910 race, newspapers reported that Erwin "time and again flashed by the grandstand in the

---

[28] "Gentlemen driver" was another name for amateurs who received no money or support from a company or sponsor. They paid their own tab.

lead amid a storm of applause." He was ahead by more than three minutes when he was forced to withdraw on lap 16 of the 25-lap race because the oil line to his engine snapped.

Charles never made it beyond the first lap of the only race he started. His poorly attached gas cap was lost, spilling gasoline over his Benz and the track. Not securing the lid was his rookie mistake, and he discontinued the race.

Despite practicing, Albert Hall did not enter. The Benz driven by Haupt dropped out after 20 laps with a stone stuck in the shifting quadrant. The Bergdoll boys and their team would again be denied a victory on their hometown neighborhood track. Unknown to the racing millionaire brothers, they would have only one more chance to race and win in Philadelphia.

Three weeks before the 1911 Fairmount Park race, disaster struck the racing circuit on Saturday, September 16, with a spectacular crash at the New York State Fair in Syracuse. Driver Lee Oldfield blew a tire on his Knox race car while challenging Ralph DePalma on the 43rd lap of the 50-lap race. Oldfield's car crashed through a fence near the grandstands, flipped end over end, throwing Oldfield from his seat and crushing nine spectators to their deaths, including a father and his nine-year-old son.

Syracuse residents and the auto racing community were stunned. It happened in front of the biggest New York State Fair crowd, and President William Howard Taft had just left the fairgrounds on a special train to return to Washington. Oldfield was seriously injured and placed under arrest in his hospital bed to await possible charges. Incredibly, the race was allowed to continue.

Two weeks later, Oldfield arrived in Philadelphia for a week of practice leading to the Fairmount Park race on October 7.[29] He required police protection to keep the angry crowd from accosting him over the fatal crash in Syracuse. Oldfield withdrew from the race as a driver, but his Fiat remained with another driver.

The Bergdoll boys were unfazed by the turmoil and planned to enter three cars in the 1911 race, with 18-year-old Grover preparing to compete on his hometown track for the first time. Twenty-one-year-old Erwin was the first of the boys to enter the race with his 150 HP Benz.[30] Charles and Grover entered Bergdolls from Louis' dealership. It was the first time a Bergdoll brand car would be in the race and a first for Grover. Charles soon withdrew, realizing his Bergdoll 30 did not have the power to compete. Grover's newly assembled Bergdoll 40 was taken on a test run through the city's streets and collided with a trolley, damaging it. He withdrew, then re-entered the race with the same car but never made any practice runs. Newspapers

---

[29] Rain on Saturday, October 7, forced the race's postponement until Monday, October 9.

[30] Erwin's 150 HP Benz was the 1908 model, the predecessor of the legendary 200 HP Lightning Benz, also called the Blitzen Benz. Erwin's car was rated at a maximum speed of 113 mph. The Lighting/Blitzen was at 141 mph.

The most successful racer among the Bergdoll boys was Erwin. He entered the Fairmount Park Motor Race in Philadelphia, the equivalent of today's Grand Prix, each of its four years. He ran a powerful Benz lined up here at the start of the 1911 race as #8. Across the track from #8 is an empty spot where Grover would have lined up if he had not withdrawn his specially built Bergdoll 40 with mechanical problems. It was estimated that 300,000 spectators attended the 1911 race. (Spooner & Wells Collection, Detroit Free Library)

reported that the vehicle had been rushed through the assembly at the Bergdoll plant specifically for Grover for the 1911 contest and displayed many mechanical problems. Grover withdrew again near the end of the week, leaving Erwin the only Bergdoll in the race.[31]

In the 1911 event, Erwin's competing drivers were some of the best contenders on the circuit, and many of them had already competed in that year's inaugural International 500-mile Sweepstakes Race, the first Indianapolis 500: Ralph DePalma, Len Zengle, George Parker, Harry Grant, Louis Disbrow, and Ralph Mulford.

Erwin caught a buzz of excitement when, in a practice lap, he set an unofficial record for the course at 7 minutes and 33 seconds. Erwin reported that his Benz was running well. He had three years of experience on the Philadelphia track, and he could hear the cheers and feel the admiration of his hometown fans.

Finally, one of the Bergdoll boys was in a position to win another big race, and it would be in their backyard.

Preparing for the start in front of a grandstand filled with race fans and draped with American flag bunting, Erwin can be seen in photographs tending to the final details of his Benz. For the first time, he could expertly prep the car in "the factory,"

---

[31] Paragraph compiled from *The Philadelphia Inquirer* and Michael J. Seneca's book, *The Fairmount Park Motor Races*, McFarland & Company, 2003.

Tall and handsome with appealing blue-gray eyes, Erwin Bergdoll became a celebrity at the wheel of his 150-horsepower Benz racer. Despite building his own race cars, Erwin found the most success in races from Florida to Chicago and Philadelphia in his Benz, the precursor to the infamous Blitzen Benz 200-horsepower race car that would later dominate the racing circuit. (Bergdoll Family Collection)

his newly constructed machine shop on the Broomall farm along West Chester Pike he received that year from his mother, Emma.

His #8 Benz race car is lined up inside the track below the grandstands and in front of his fellow Philadelphia beer brewer competitor, John Fred Betz, third in his newly purchased #15 Fiat.[32] Across the track from Betz is an empty space where Grover's #14 Bergdoll 40 would have started had he remained in the race.

The New York Times compiled the lap-by-lap account of the race, noting that Erwin set a new official time record on the first lap with 7 minutes and 34 seconds. Pushing his Benz even faster, Erwin flew around the second lap in an astonishing 7 minutes and 28 seconds, breaking his record and setting the all-time lap record for the course.

Gray, acrid smoke flew from the car's exhaust. Brown dust swirled in circles and floated into the crowd with grit that muddied the spectators' tearing eyes and choked their breathing. Erwin ran so fast in his Benz that he led all but three of the 25 laps. "Speed Boy" Erwin, as the *Times* called him, "drove his car with the daring

---

[32] Like the Bergdolls, Betz was an heir to his family's Philadelphia brewery, John F. Betz & Sons Brewery.

In record time, Erwin Bergdoll won the 1911 Fairmount Park Motor Race in Philadelphia, Pennsylvania, in his #8 Benz racer. It's a feat that remains unbeaten because the famous race was discontinued the following year. Erwin entered several more races over the succeeding years, then retired his championship Benz in his machine shop next to Grover's airplane, where thieves eventually stripped it. (Spooner and Wells Collection, Detroit Free Library)

of a madman." His only competition came from drivers Ralph Mulford and Harry Grant in Loziers, Spence Wishart in a Mercedes, and Len Zengle in a National.[33]

Erwin appeared to command the entire race until lap 17, when he was forced into the pits with a radiator boil-over. However, through a combination of crashes, stalls, and flat tires among the other racers, Erwin finally overcame his opponents and cruised to victory in front of his hometown crowd.

As the big #8 Benz roared down the concourse in front of the grandstand to take the winning flag, a huge cheer rang out from the fans. Finally, after three years of trying several different cars, a Bergdoll had won the Fairmount Park Motor Race! Grover stood in the pits, watching his older brother bask in the winner's glory. How badly he wanted a piece of the action.

"Bergdoll drove a wonderful race," crowed the Philadelphia papers. "One of the greatest road races ever seen in this section." The best time for the big Benz automobile around the 8.1-mile track was 7 minutes and 28 seconds.

Erwin beat the previous year's lap record by 10 seconds. In the win, he topped the course record with a time of 3 hours, 18 minutes, and 41 seconds. His average speed per lap was a whopping 61 miles per hour.

An estimated 300,000–500,000 spectators witnessed the amateur racer on his home track. Hundreds of people were jammed into the wooden grandstands to

---

[33] Harry Grant was later killed in a crash while practicing for the 1915 Astor Cup at the Sheepshead Bay Speedway Track on Long Island.

Erwin Bergdoll is beaming in his wool cap and sweater after winning the 1911 Fairmount Park Motor Race. On the sidelines, Grover watched his brother with envy. Eventually and mysteriously, Erwin's Benz racer and championship trophy were lost from family possession. Their disposition has been the subject of speculation but remains unknown. (Bergdoll Family Collection)

watch their new "Speed Demon," as the *Philadelphia Inquirer* called Erwin, receive the Quaker City Motor Club trophy and two checks, $2,500 for the fastest car in the race and $1,000 for the fastest car in his division.

While famous racer Barney Oldfield reported that it cost Erwin $12,000 to enter and win, Erwin insisted to his family that the cost was about $8,000. Oldfield said Erwin "took more chances, displayed more skill, cut corners with more reckless abandon than the seasoned veterans who opposed him." However, despite his victory and recognition from his fellow racers, Erwin was still the less notable underdog in the family. One newspaper mistakenly reported that Grover won the race.

Following the victory, a photograph shows Erwin relaxing at the leather-bound wheel of his Benz, dressed in a thick, button-down wool sweater and a wool Beanie cap, goggles dangling around his neck, and glancing sideways with his gray eyes. Dozens of men surround him staring into the camera lens. One man has his hand on the steering wheel while another leans to be in the picture with his idol. Erwin's mud-spattered face reveals white circles around his eyes caused by his goggles. The slight grin on Erwin's mouth and his casual poise, right elbow on the seatback, and oily fingers grasping a cleaning rag indicate the confidence of a champion.

The photograph ran in several newspapers and solidified the Bergdoll boys' status as handsome and wealthy celebrity sportsmen, especially among women. It represented the pinnacle of the sporting life for the Bergdoll boys in automobile racing and social standing in Philadelphia. With the publicity of his victory in all the nation's newspapers, Erwin, the amateur champion racer, had become an American hero. For now, Grover remained on the sidelines.

Barney Oldfield praised the Philadelphia race and the expertise of the police in preventing tragedies among the racers and spectators in his newspaper column. He also predicted that the event would continue for many years to come. He was wrong. On May 8, 1912, more interested in preserving their park than attracting money-spending spectators and watching loud, smoky, and dangerous race cars, the Fairmount Park Commission voted to halt the spectacular race. Subsequent legal opinions provided to Philadelphia Mayor Rudolph Blankenburg suggested that park commissioners would be liable for injuries and deaths caused by a private party, the Quaker City Motor Club, leasing the public park for automobile races. They also determined that renting the park and charging for admission and parking cars violated Fairmount Park rules established in 1867. The racing clubs and race fans were highly disappointed. Petitions to revive the race in 1913 failed, so Erwin's records still stand.

Erwin's victory and the termination of the Fairmount Park race led to the beginning of the end of automobile racing for the Bergdoll boys.[34] With a few more runs for Erwin, Grover would push his brothers' racing cars through the end of 1916, when the war suspended American racing.

Over five years, Grover entered 17 races in Benzes, Bergdolls, or Erwin Specials, winning only a few minor contests. While never racing again on the Fairmount Park course, Bergdoll race cars were running at the Belmont Driving Park nearby and other notable tracks around the country, including the disastrous San Francisco Vanderbilt Cup race, the inaugural Astor Cup of October 1915, and the Metropolitan Trophy Race of May 1916 at Sheepshead Bay Speedway Track on Long Island. Under Erwin's supervision, Grover entered an Erwin 40 in the 1916 Long Island race. The boys' longtime Philadelphia companion, mechanic, and Grover's future chauffeur, Ike Stecher, entered an Erwin 40 built especially for the wood-plank oval track.

One of Grover's final races saw him return to the Interstate Fair in Trenton, New Jersey, in September 1916. Despite a muddy path from heavy rain and in front of the most massive final-day crowd of the fair, Grover won the five-mile race, spattered with mud, grease, and oil.

Soon afterward, Grover was denied the renewal of his Pennsylvania driver's license for 1917 because of outstanding and unresolved speeding and crash infractions on the roads of Philadelphia and Pennsylvania's Main Line. From that point onward, Stecher was paid to do the driving.

---

[34] Years later, Erwin's #8 Benz sat as a rusting hulk of a wreck in his machine shop. The disposition of this great race car and his 1911 Quaker City Motor Club trophy were unknown in 2023. A neighbor of Erwin's claimed the trophy was given to an antique automobile museum in Hershey, Pennsylvania, but none of Hershey's antique car museums have a record of it. The 1908 Quaker City Motor Club Founders Cup trophy was auctioned in 2009 for $128,700 plus a significant buyer's premium raising the value to more than $150,000. *Auction News.*

CHAPTER FOUR

Speed Demon Bergdoll

The Main Line, 1911–1914

Soon after midnight on July 7, 1913, Grover Bergdoll walked out as a free man through the heavy iron front gate of the Montgomery County Jail in Norristown, Pennsylvania. He had served two months of a 90-day sentence in cell number 17 in the old part of the jail, which, built of gray fieldstone in 1851, appeared like a medieval castle from the streets of the Borough of Norristown.[1]

When he entered the jail, the youngest Bergdoll boy's weight was 158 pounds. He appeared no less when freed because jailers allowed his mother to supplement their meager jail meals with thick sausage, vinegar potatoes, heavy beef gravy, and pickled sauerkraut dinners.[2]

Grover's stone-walled and barred cell faced a back alley of the dreary jail-castle complex. His solitary existence in his cell resulted from a sparsely populated jail for the Philadelphia suburban county. However, Grover's fellow inmates knew the celebrity automobile speeder and daring aviator was among them. Because of his notoriety and wealth, jail guards awarded him the most attention.[3] Warden Lemuel Roberts reported that Grover was a model prisoner and studious young man for the duration of his sentence.

Despite the dungeon-like surroundings, Grover hadn't shut out the outside world. He received fan mail from people who read the many newspaper articles about

---

[1] Accounts of Grover's and Erwin's traffic infractions, crashes, and escapades with law enforcement on Philadelphia's Main Line are well documented in local and city newspapers around Philadelphia. Court documents provided additional information and confirmations of fines and sentences. Descriptions of the Montgomery County Jail castle-like complex are from my observations during many years of activities in Norristown, the county seat.

[2] Emma had accompanied her son to jail at his 11 am check-in appointment on May 7 and immediately enquired about the meals. Upon hearing that Grover would be served a "chunk of cold ham, potatoes with their jackets on, and a piece of bread for supper that evening," Emma quickly arranged to supplement Grover's menu.

[3] Grover became such a celebrity that Norristown residents would purposely attend the public Sunday religious services at the jail castle, hoping to catch a glimpse of him. Even the choir singers would ask the warden for a chance to visit the infamous speed demon.

Sixteen-year-old Grover Bergdoll with one of his early automobiles. This may have been his first luxury car, a Lozier, in which he was often caught speeding. (Bergdoll Family/Roger Grigson)

his speeding escapades with great interest, including a lovely handwritten note by "Kitty" from West Philadelphia, who lamented that Grover had not written to her when she had scribbled notes to him every other day. Grover told his jail visitors he could occasionally hear the creaking of a wagon or cart passing by his window and the melodious notes from an upright piano in the warden's apartment.

After a multitude of traffic, assault, and gun violations for which the 19-year-old speed demon failed to appear in court, forfeiting bail many times, Grover's final offense stemmed from a severe and near-fatal crash in one of his many cars on Philadelphia's Main Line roadways.[4]

On Saturday night, December 21, 1912, returning from a card party at the Bergdoll country estate in Broomall, Grover was speeding, as usual, along East Lancaster Avenue in the upscale Wynnewood, Montgomery County neighborhood when his Bergdoll 30 collided head-on with a car driven by Walter B. McIlvaine, a local lumber dealer, and carrying a passenger. Grover's car flipped over and smashed into the trunk of a tree, tossing him and four companions, two young men and two young women, over a stone wall and into the front lawn of a mansion estate occupied by Walter and Edith Clothier, lithograph company owners, and heirs to the Strawbridge and Clothier department store fortune. The impact was so severe that the Bergdoll 30's body was sheared from the chassis, driving it some 5 inches into

---

[4] One violation included emptying the cylinder of his revolver to scare a local policeman who jumped onto the running board of Grover's car while he was driving through a Main Line community.

the earth surrounding the concrete sidewalk. McIlvaine's touring car was demolished, scattering wreckage over the avenue and the Clothiers' expertly manicured lawn.

Grover survived unscathed, but one of his passengers was trapped beneath the wrecked car while it caught fire. Fortunately, a Lower Merion Township police officer lived nearby and rushed to help extinguish the fire and save the injured.

Grover quietly disappeared into the darkness of the lush shrubbery. He had recklessly driven without illuminating his headlamps to avoid being identified as he sped through the affluent Main Line community.[5] And his car did not have the proper license plates. Instead, it displayed a 1910 plate on the front chrome guard and a hand-painted license number, *Penna 2-1-7-9-9*, on the back.

Nearby residents roused from their tidy brick, and grey stone Wynnewood mansions hovered about the scene, tending to the injured women who were nervously questioning if the notorious Grover Bergdoll was dead. It tipped off police for a possible cause of the crash. They had previously dealt with Grover and his speeding many times.

The injured from the crash were taken to nearby Bryn Mawr Hospital, where they spent the night or were discharged after treatment. Police did their best to sweep the glass and steel wreckage to the side of the road, where it remained through the night. Grover hid following the crash and boldly returned to the scene carrying a box camera at dawn. While neighbors gawked from a distance, Grover circled the cars clicking photographs, realizing he would need them for evidence in court.

When police closed in, Grover ran again, hiding in an auto repair garage at North 31st and West Dauphin Streets in the Strawberry Mansion section of Philadelphia for several days. Populated with working-class Philadelphians, it was an intimidating part of the city even for Grover, who grew weary of hiding out.

Engaged by no fewer than seven police detectives and numerous badge officers, Grover was arrested and hauled back to the affluent Main Line and a magistrate's court, where he managed his release on $300 cash bail. At the court hearing, crash victims milled about in bloodied bandages while dozens of Main Line residents gathered to hear about the notorious "speed fiend," Bergdoll, and to demand he was taken off the streets. They were not safe in their community, they said, in unison, while Grover and his brother, Erwin, habitually used their local pikes, boulevards, and avenues as their racetrack.

Fresh in the minds of Main Line residents was an incident on November 24, 1911, when Grover and his boyhood friend, Charles J. Kraus, Jr., got into a shootout with a Lower Merion Township policeman. The cop jumped onto the running board of Grover's car and hung on for his life while 18-year-old Grover roared from Ardmore to his country estate near Broomall. Upon stopping his vehicle at the Bergdoll farm in

---

[5] Interestingly, Grover charged that McIlvaine had been driving without lights. In court, McIlvaine and his passenger both insisted that their car had its "oil lamps" illuminated.

Grover and Erwin's companions "Mugsy" Myers, left, and Charles J. Kraus in a Bergdoll racing roadster. Kraus was Grover's sidekick through many infractions with police, including the shootout at the Broomall farm. Later, Kraus served as co-pilot on hundreds of Grover's airplane flights, including his record-setting flights to Atlantic City, New Jersey. Grover took the photograph with one of his professional cameras. (Bergdoll Family, Historical Society of Pennsylvania)

a cloud of dust, the policeman, Ignatius L. Mullen, pushed his revolver into Grover's face. A third person, believed to be Kraus, smacked the policeman with a tire iron or jack handle. Then, the assailant (Kraus) began shooting. Grover dove for his life.

Hiding behind a tree, Officer Mullen shot back and fled the farm property. The entire incident was blamed on Grover, of course. Tried and convicted of assault and battery in Delaware County Court after being found guilty of similar charges in Montgomery County Court, Bergdoll, and Kraus were found guilty and sentenced to minor fines of $300, which Grover immediately paid in cash.[6]

Many people believed Grover got off easy. It was his second assault and battery charge involving Officer Mullen, a frequent adversary.[7] The judge said his court had been appealed to by the authorities and residents of the Main Line to "relieve them of his [Grover's] intolerable speeding" and other crimes. However, he said he spared Grover from jail because he was a student. Grover claimed he was attending the University of Pennsylvania (Penn), a frequent excuse for trying to avoid prison.

In the Bergdoll–McIlvaine crash investigation, police charged Grover with operating his car recklessly and without a proper license.[8] Grover claimed McIlvaine

---

[6] Bergdoll and Kraus were tried and convicted in both jurisdictions because similar crimes occurred while they were driving from Montgomery County into neighboring Delaware County.

[7] Ignatius Loyola Mullen was frequently the Lower Merion Township policeman and detective chasing Grover Bergdoll. He died young, age 46. Severe alcoholism was listed as the primary cause.

[8] From the time Grover first obtained his driver's and owner's licenses, he often was caught and ticketed for speeding through Philadelphia and the Main Line. One of his early street automobiles was painted bright red with a loud horn that Grover often blew when arriving in a neighborhood, too fast. The car was appropriately nicknamed Red Devil or Big Red.

did not have his lamps illuminated while traveling home from a dinner club. Grover's attorneys even tried to claim that McIlvaine had been drinking booze.

Passenger, long-time Bergdoll companion, and automobile mechanic Thomas B. Furey testified that McIlvaine's car "seemed to be zig-zagging" as if the driver were drunk. Irishman Furey, another boyhood friend of Grover's, was seriously injured with a severe concussion and was unconscious for 13 hours. Therefore, authorities didn't believe his testimony, and the drunk driving allegations against prominent citizen McIlvaine failed to stand in court.

McIlvaine retained the legal services of a township commissioner-attorney who charged Grover with assault and battery. Soon after Grover was held for trial on $1,000 bail, a Philadelphia policeman stepped from among the courtroom crowd with a warrant for Grover's arrest on one of his outstanding speeding, assault, and battery with automobile charges in the city, some of which dated from December 1911. Another bond was argued and arranged for $2,000 for both offenses. Then, family fixer Judge James E. Romig pleaded for an overall bail reduction to $1,200 on all charges. The judge demurred until Grover's brother, Louis, the ultimate family fixer, stepped forward and announced that he had arranged with a local bail bondsman to post collateral for Grover's immediate release.

A hush fell over the small courtroom when Lower Merion Township police superintendent James I. Donaghy, the former chief of detectives in Philadelphia, stepped forward to influence and supersede the authority of the local magistrate and admonish the teenage driver, Bergdoll. Casting his arm toward the shoulder-to-shoulder crowd, Donaghy, who knew of Grover as "bright, cheerful, and rational when with his companions but sullen, sarcastic, and wanting to convey the impression he was being persecuted when under arrest," proclaimed, "Grover, there are enough people in this courtroom to put you in prison for a long time. Why can't you drive your vehicle in an orderly manner? Your brother, Erwin, was a speeder and committed many violations, but he has stopped it. Why can't you? I hope this will be a lesson to you!"

Grover smiled and buttoned his coat in a defiant display: his bail had been paid, he was free to go and itching to bolt.

Louis and Judge Romig quickly departed through the crowd of spectators loitering about the sidewalk and street. Grover walked briskly from the court by himself, cranked up another of his automobiles, and "sped off with a roar of his open exhaust." His family wealth and celebrity clout had spared him again.

At court hearings in January and February of 1913, leading up to the trial where Grover would be convicted and sent to jail for three months, it was revealed that Grover had been arrested for driving his mother's two-seater runabout without his license. Additionally, police charged that the car had the wrong license plates.[9]

---

[9] The two-seater runabout may have been Grover's Lozier car but registered in Emma's name.

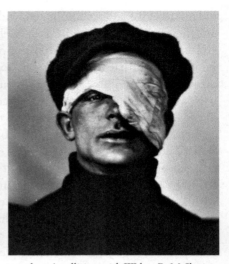

Grover's recklessness was most evident in his frequent car crashes. A collision with Walter B. McIlvaine, a prominent businessman, led to Grover's conviction and 90 days in jail. Grover fled the crash scene but returned the following day to take photographs of his wrecked car and injured passenger, Thomas Furey. (Bergdoll Family Collection)

They also revealed another nine outstanding warrants against Grover. Still, the subsequent legal proceedings were postponed because the magistrate was busy tending to business in his candy store on a Saturday morning.

Emma offered to pay $100,000 cash bail through her attorneys to get Grover out of jail, pending his appeal to the Pennsylvania Superior Court in Pittsburgh. Both efforts failed, and his sentence was upheld in mid-May.

Family fixer and former magistrate Judge Romig, along with Albert Hall, petitioned the sentencing judge to release Grover early so he could take entrance exams at Penn in Philadelphia. The judge denied this request too. Emma's outbursts likely influenced the court decisions in the newspapers. She complained to reporters that police and lawyers "joined hands to harass" her favorite son. Then, foolishly, she threatened them with bodily harm. "If I had a pistol, I would have killed that judge on the bench the day he sent my son to jail for three months," she spouted. As Emma often had a pistol hidden in her bosom, it wasn't an idle threat.

***

On September 25, 1914, Grover was arrested again for reckless driving after another high-speed crash on Lancaster Avenue in Lower Merion Township. He crashed into another car, through a telegraph pole, knocked down a tree, and was taken unconscious to Bryn Mawr Hospital.

Bergdoll cousin Frankie Strohm at the Broomall farm points to a bullet hole in the back of the car that Grover and Charles Kraus used to escape police while speeding through local communities. Grover often took photographs of his many scrapes with the law. (Bergdoll Family Collection)

Passengers Kraus and Charles Gile told police that Grover was "speeding up to 70 miles per hour just before the smashup." In court, Grover agreed to pay for the other car destroyed in the crash and a fine of $25.

Unknown to Grover, the Pennsylvania Department of Highways had decided not to renew his driver's license. It came at the behest of Police Superintendent Donaghy, who gathered hundreds of signatures on a petition against Grover's license renewal application citing the shootout while driving, speeding, spooking a police horse with reckless driving, throwing literature out of his car, and many other violations. Grover, however, insisted to newspaper reporters covering his trials that he would still be able to drive with his "owner's license" issued to owners of automobiles in Pennsylvania. He was confused about the difference between an automobile registration and a driver's license.

CHAPTER FIVE

Airplanes and Millions

1908–1913

Grover Cleveland Bergdoll was no less a menace to the people of Philadelphia and the lush summer playground of its wealthiest residents when he decided to buy the newest sporting machine of affluent Americans, an airplane. And, as he did with his racing automobiles, he gleefully charmed and disrupted the sophisticated lifestyle of the landed gentry of the Main Line with his flying machine.[1]

On Saturday, September 28, 1912, Grover took off from his flying field near the Bergdoll farm in Broomall. He glided through the air in his Wright B Flyer for about 5 miles northward over the green hayfields of the 97-acre Samuel A. Black estate, the 10-acre manicured mansion estate of Charles R. Snowden, the clipped Bryn Mawr Polo Club grounds, and the shiny double rails of the main line of the Pennsylvania Railroad to drop in on the Bryn Mawr Horse Show. It was being staged in a 15-acre dell below the five red-capped spires and semi-circular porch of the elegant granite and wood frame Frank Furness-designed Bryn Mawr Hotel.[2] Grover knew the prestigious horse show was open this early autumn Saturday afternoon because he had buzzed the grounds two days prior and then proudly read about it in the morning papers.

Just as the fashionably dressed Main Line crowd was applauding a rider for winning the cherished prize at the show, the L'Aiglon Challenge Cup, as the *Inquirer* said, "Their cheers and applause were suddenly halted by the whirring of four [sic] motors as Grover C. Bergdoll, the young Philadelphia aviator, in his Wright biplane, soared above the oval."

The spectators craned their necks at the spectacle circling just a few hundred feet above the spires of the hotel. No sooner than Grover banked his plane away from the event, a horse from the Pickering Hunt threw the great Philadelphia and Harvard

---

[1] Grover's flying escapades are described in newspapers, Alfred's diary-manuscript, government documents, and aviation club newsletters. Family photographs of airplanes and Eagle Field helped define the events further. The Smithsonian also provided photographs of Eagle Field, taken by William Sheahan. Details about Grover's flight school in Dayton are attributed to John Carver Edwards' book, *Orville's Aviators*. Additional flying information is from a short biography of Grover by Harold E. Morehouse at the Smithsonian.

[2] The Bryn Mawr Hotel and horse show dell later became The Baldwin Prep School for Girls.

Grover and Erwin Bergdoll on Grover's Wright B Flyer in 1912 at Eagle Field near their farm. Grover gave his brothers airplane rides in 1912, but they later declined as he grew more confident flying under adverse conditions. In this photograph, Grover appears as merely a kid as Erwin, three years older, seems more mature. Grover made 748 successful flights in this airplane, earning him Orville Wright's assessment as one of his best pilots. (Bergdoll Family, Roger Grigson. Chester County Historical Society)

tennis champion and Strawbridge and Clothier department store heir, William J. (Bill) Clothier, Jr., from his saddle. Some blamed it on the airplane piloted by Grover, whom the *Inquirer* called "the Birdman." However, having broken his pelvis during another serious throw from a horse in 1906 and then having gone on to win the U.S. National Men's Singles Tennis Championship soon afterward, Clothier bounced to his feet and remounted his horse.

Grover, the birdman menace, and his Wright B were gone, with another of his hundreds of flights in his logbook, following the glistening railroad tracks eastward toward Philadelphia. Still a teenager, Grover Bergdoll was nearly the only flyer in eastern Pennsylvania and southern New Jersey in 1912 and had the skies to himself. So disrupted by the whirling propellers of Grover's airplane only a few hundred feet above the prestigious horse show ring, the affluent organizers sent Grover free grandstand tickets to the show the following season, hoping he would attend without his noisy airplane.

By October 1912, just a few months into his flying career, Grover was still waiting for his flying certificate from the Aero Club of America.[3] Orville Wright

---

[3] As early as 1912, flight certification from a sanctioned organization was needed to enter international flying competitions. Otherwise, Grover needed no special approval to fly his own airplane. It was unregulated activity.

had promised him that if he passed his flight tests in time, Wright would enter a fast airplane in the International Aviation Meet in Chicago with Grover as the pilot. But, without his certificate, Grover missed the deadline and was forced to close out the 1912 flying season with hundreds of flights but no special awards for competition. He had captured the attention of aviation spectators around Pennsylvania and New Jersey, but other aviators were grabbing national headlines and sizeable prize-winning purses in the favored races. Naturally, Grover wanted part of the action.

Grover and Louis Bergdoll had grown interested in aviation from reading the exciting flight accounts in the first decade of the 20th century of the Wright Brothers and Glenn Curtiss in America, and European aviation pioneer Louis Blériot in France. With their mechanical skill and access to machinery and automotive parts, they built an airplane at the Bergdoll farm with an engine that throbbed so violently that it never got off the ground. Removing the engine, they toyed with it as a glider, instead.

A photograph of the crude aircraft shows Grover sitting in the tubular aviator box, holding levers in his hands while his feet stretch out to large bicycle wheels at the front of the contraption. Extending to each side are monoplane wings of white canvas. Emma said she sewed heavy material for the boys on her industrial sewing machines, a skill learned when she first arrived in America. If there was one in the picture, the engine may have been a Westinghouse cast-off from the Bergdoll automobiles. It's not visible behind the seat, with the propellor at the tail. A vertical post behind the pilot's seat strings a spider's web of bracing wires outward to several locations on the wings and the tail. It is framed with Sitka spruce spars, the solid but flexible wood used by the Wright Brothers on their pioneering flyer of 1903. The loud, smoky, and rickety homemade contraption was only good for scooting on the ground of the Bergdoll farm pastures and photographs with the brothers beaming at the controls. It needed the proper engineering to fly.[4]

The Bergdoll boys, however, did manage to get off the ground. They set up a hot air balloon purchased through the U.S. Mail at the farm. Alfred says, in his diary, that the boys would tether their balloon over hot air rising from a fire pit in the ground. They would sit on a pine board swinging from the bottom, and when the balloon reached a height they dared to go, they would pull a cord weighted above by a brick, opening a hole in the top of the balloon to expel hot air and lower it to the ground. Alfred also claimed the boys would parachute from the balloon with pal Charles Kraus, once landing in a tree, but this seems implausible. It was a great embellishment when Grover described his early adventures to his son.

---

[4] The Bergdoll boys' homemade airplane design appeared similar to a Blériot but matches none of the commercially available airplanes of 1907–1908. It supports the theory that Louis Bergdoll took an early interest in French monoplanes over the American bi-planes of the Wright Brothers.

A family photograph of Grover and Louis' airplane, pictured in front of the Broomall farm sheds with chickens, about 1908. This photograph was rescued from a pile of discarded family documents in the 1940s when Grover and Berta Bergdoll moved to Virginia. (Bergdoll Family, Roger Grigson. Chester County Historical Society)

At about the same time Louis, Charles, and Erwin Bergdoll were racing their sports cars around speed tracks of America in 1906–1907, the Wright Brothers were designing what would become their Wright B Flyer, a biplane with the pilot sitting upright at the front.[5] They revealed the exciting new aircraft to the world by writing a six-page article, with photographs, in *The Century Magazine* in September 1908.

"The ground under you is at first a perfect blur," is how the Wright Brothers described flight in their article. "At the height of one hundred feet, you feel hardly any motion at all, except for the wind which strikes your face." And, especially appealing to a race car driver, "the motor close beside you kept up an almost deafening roar during the whole flight, yet in your excitement, you did not notice it till it stopped!"

Under U.S. Army contract specifications, the Wright Brothers produced an airplane carrying two sitting men, enough fuel for a 125-mile flight, and maintaining a speed of 36–44 miles per hour. However, their first demonstration for the Army Signal Corps, with Orville at the controls and Lt. Thomas E. Selfridge as a passenger, ended in a tragic disaster on September 17, 1908, at Fort Myer, Arlington, Virginia.

The propeller cracked, causing it to hit the rudder wire. The plane went down, and Selfridge was killed. He became the Army's first aviation casualty. Orville Wright was severely injured with a broken leg and ribs and spent months recovering in a hospital.[6]

---

[5] Prior to this event, most of the exciting news about aviation came from the balloon and motorized airship flights, which initially attracted the Bergdolls but proved to be too slow.
[6] From an online article, *The United States Army Buys Its First Aeroplane, 1909*, by National Archives senior archivist Dr. Greg Bradsher, March 19, 2019—Textual Records Division at the National Archives.

In July 1909, Orville tried again with a rebuilt and faster biplane.[7] He flew with a passenger for an hour and 12 minutes, with President William Howard Taft watching the flight from below. The Wrights won the contract to produce Wright B Flyers for the Army. Taking control of the Wright B, the Army organized an aviation school for training pilots at College Park, Maryland.

Similar flight demonstration events were also occurring in Europe, mostly with biplanes, and they glorified the pilots, attracting the attention of wealthy sportsmen. It was big news in American newspapers. Large city dailies, including *The New York Times* and the *Philadelphia Inquirer*, began devoting entire Sunday sections to aviation. Stories and photographs about various biplanes were produced for sportsmen daring enough to fly and who had the money to buy them. For the Bergdoll boys, it juiced their competitive spirit.

On Wednesday, November 3, 1909, Philadelphians awoke to see a large advertisement in the *Inquirer* purchased by Wanamaker's Department Store. It was more like a news article with a photograph of a man behind a one-bottom plow and a team of horses with an airplane flying overhead. But it was a monoplane, not a biplane of the Wright Brothers' design. The ad was intentionally written similarly to an article, in the John Emory Powers simplistic advertising style of the period, in 12-point Caslon text, stating just the facts.

"Everyone knows it's coming. And everybody knows it is Coming to Wanamaker's," the copy blared. "It will land on the steamship Floride that sailed from the other side on October 26." The rest of the half-page ad on the *Inquirer*'s editorial page hawked Wanamaker's tailored suits from $27.50 and $30, Third Floor, Market Street entrance. French flannel nightgowns and silk petticoats for women, Third Floor, North. And silks from China, in the Silk Salon, First Floor.

The Bergdoll boys spied the advertisement but weren't interested in the nightgowns and silks. The impending arrival of a French monoplane at Wanamaker's became the fascination of Philadelphia.

***

Wanamaker's Department Store in Philadelphia in November 1909 was about as exciting a place as one could be in the weeks leading up to Christmas. Construction of a new section of the renowned department store designed by Chicago architect Daniel H. Burnham, built on the site of the existing store in downtown Philadelphia (later known as Center City), would not be completed until 1911. Still, enough of the new 12-story granite Florentine Renaissance building was finished for a grand opening of the Great Christmas Toy Store, First Floor, Chestnut Street entrance.

---

[7] This demonstration plane was known as a Wright Model A. With more revisions, the design became the Wright B Flyer.

Thousands of customers, including the Bergdolls, flocked into the store each season to shop for Christmas and experience Philadelphia holiday traditions.

The wealthy Wanamaker family was high on the social register in Philadelphia, dining and vacationing in Atlantic City with the likes of the Henry Disstons, not the Bergdolls. Rodman Wanamaker, born in New York City, married Fernanda Antonia Henry of Philadelphia and the couple had three children before Fernanda's death at age 36. Depressed, Wanamaker lived in virtual seclusion, mainly in Paris and New York, for the next nine years, managing the satellite stores. He is credited with inspiring American women to view modern French fashion as extraordinary, extravagant, and attainable.

Rodman Wanamaker was also a professional golf sportsman and benefactor of art students worldwide, specifically native American artists in the southwestern United States. While in New York in the spring of 1909, before returning to Europe for a significant social event in his life, he attended the first outdoor "aerial carnival" in North America in the last week of May at North Arlington, New Jersey, a small community a few miles northwest of Manhattan.

Based on the entry list, Wanamaker witnessed some poorly designed biplanes that needed help flying any distance. But, from this early experience of seeing the magic of aviation in France and New Jersey, the frequently ocean-hopping Wanamaker became convinced that airplanes would soon fly across the Atlantic. He grew determined to support an effort to accomplish the feat, initially called "foolhardy" by the Wright Brothers.

Wanamaker returned to Europe that summer for his July 27 London wedding to Violet Douglas Marie Cruger of New York and Paris.[8] While there, it would have been impossible for the newlywed Wanamakers to miss the excitement in the newspapers that a Frenchman, just days earlier, had flown an airplane across the English Channel and landed in Dover.

This signaled a new beginning for Wanamaker, who had been described as retiring and without entertaining at his Philadelphia home since his first wife's death nine years prior. Perhaps energized by his new marriage and a desire to return to his sporting life, he immediately inquired about the best-designed sportsman's airplane he could purchase in France to return to the United States. He was convinced that it was the channel-flying Blériot XI, a monoplane.

Design credit for the 1909 Blériot XI is mainly given to Raymond Saulnier, and it was built by Louis Charles Joseph Blériot. The Frenchman had become internationally famous the instant he touched down on the shores of Dover, after taking off from Los Baraques, near Calais, France, and becoming the first to fly across the 21-mile-wide English Channel.

---

[8] Violet Douglas Marie Cruger had previously been engaged to railroad executive and yachting sportsman, Harold Stirling (Mike) Vanderbilt. Each of the men in her life were worth millions.

Blériot, who looked like a Frenchman with his thick brush of a mustache, wobbly nose, and bushy eyebrows, was in a heated competition for the first channel crossing with a handful of other daring aviators in a variety of airplane designs. The London *Daily Mail* newspaper had posted a $5,000 prize for the first pilot who could do it.

Just days before the July 25 pioneering flight, Blériot caused a sensation by taking two passengers for a ride in another Blériot airplane, the Antoinette XII. Then, in the Blériot XI, he made a 25-mile cross-country flight from Etampes to Chevilly, France, in less than one hour.

It won the French Aero Club's prize of $2,800. With the *Daily Mail* prize up for grabs, Blériot figured he was ready for the Channel. But he needed the weather to cooperate.

Despite a severe leg injury and burns to his body from a crash days earlier, Blériot, 37, rose from bed at 2:30 on the morning of the 25th. Conditions were ideal for a flight in the smaller and lighter Blériot XI with its 25-horsepower, 3-cylinder Anzani engine.[9] Notifying the French torpedo boat destroyer *Escopette*, which had been readied to serve as an escort for his effort, Blériot ditched his crutches and made a short practice run in the XI before dawn. Then, waiting for sunrise, a requirement of the *Daily Mail* prize, he launched the monoplane for the coast.

Only his English crew expected Blériot to appear in his airplane over Dover on July 25. Despite a plan for Dover officials to ring sirens and raise flags warning the public that a flier from France was approaching, Blériot's decision to attempt the 25th was so last-minute that there was no time to sound the alarm. Therefore, only a few people on the English coastline saw the plane arrive from France. Within minutes, however, people were racing toward the meadow to look at the landed monoplane, and some even began tearing pieces from the slightly damaged aircraft for souvenirs.

With Blériot's consent, enterprising Dover officials erected a tent over the plane, posted guards, and charged sixpence admission to see it. The proceeds would go toward a local hospital and the police pension fund. More money would be raised when the Blériot was transported to London for display at the recently opened Selfridges Department Store on the western end of London's "unfashionable" Oxford Street. Capitalizing on a tourist attraction for his new store, Harry Gordon Selfridge was an American who offered to pay Blériot's expenses to remove the plane from Dover. It was described by the British as "characteristic American quickness to seize an opportunity." Not to be outdone, Rodman Wanamaker would soon follow.

Newspapers quickly got the Wright Brothers' opinion on the English Channel flight. Wilbur and Orville were reported calling the feat "remarkable." But they said they were surprised Blériot could accomplish it in his design of an airplane.

---

[9] The Anzani engine was developed by Italian, Alessandro Anzani, with production factories in Italy, France, and England. Anzani lived in France and supervised the ignition and proper fuel-oxygen mixture in the engine on the morning of the Bleriot Channel flight.

Despite numerous accidents in their biplanes, they pointed out the number of crashes involving the monoplane. The Wright Brothers believed their biplane and motor designs were superior to the French monoplane.

Glenn Curtiss, the pioneer aviator from Hammondsport, New York, who sparred in court with the Wright Brothers over aircraft design, called the feat "a splendid performance." He, too, said his biplanes were superior to the Blériot monoplane and that he wished he had done it first.[10]

Reading about the monumental event in their newspapers at home in New York and Philadelphia were the Bergdoll boys. Enjoying their public adulation and press coverage from racing cars, Louis and Grover began to wish for an airplane of their own. Louis, admiring fellow millionaire Wanamaker and his early predictions of flight across the Atlantic, would go for the Blériot monoplane, just as he had admired Vanderbilt in his race cars. Grover would favor the Wright Brothers' biplane. Erwin and Charles showed little interest in aviation.

The first ad in the *Philadelphia Inquirer* teasing that "everyone knows it's coming" was immediately followed by another. On November 12, a smaller display ad appeared as an article but was clearly labeled as an "announcement" and "advertisement." "The Blériot Plane (an exact duplicate) will be on public view tomorrow (Saturday, November 13) in the new Christmas Toy Store," it said. Then, below that copy, "Flying Machines for Sale at Wanamaker's. The Blériot Plane is for Sale – At the Small price of $5000." The advertisement claimed it was the first Blériot monoplane offered in America. Whoever bought it would agree to a week's exhibition at Wanamaker's store in Philadelphia and another week at their store in New York.

The Blériot XI arrived in port in New York on November 6 in a large wooden packing crate. It was accompanied by Edward Robson, who worked with Blériot in his manufacturing shop in France and would reassemble the aircraft in Philadelphia. The container was so long at 25 feet, it had to be shipped south in a Pennsylvania Railroad boxcar and then carried in through the part of Wanamaker's store still under construction. Robson directed the assembly, and then Wanamaker's workers hoisted the monoplane to suspend from the unfinished ceiling in the store's Grand Court. For Philadelphians eager to see the aircraft, the ad said the stairs into the store at Chestnut Street would lead directly to the "airship" in the Toy Store.

On Saturday morning, the opening day of the new Wanamaker's Toy Store, another ad in the morning papers aimed directly at children (through their parents). "Like a huge bird, the Blériot Aeroplane is suspended from the ceiling in the toy store, giving added interest to the opening." It called the entrance to the Toy Store

---

[10] In August 1909, Glenn Curtiss won the International Cup of Aviation, better known as the Gordon Bennett Cup, when he smashed the speed record at the Rheims, France, air show covering 12 miles of flight in just under 16 minutes. He flew a biplane with a design remarkably similar to the Wright Brothers. He beat Blériot, who also set a record for a single lap, by five seconds.

"Flying Machine Avenue." "Bring your parents with you," it declared. "You are going to tell your children and grandchildren that you saw the first airship placed on sale at Wanamaker's in Philadelphia in 1909."

The Wanamaker's display (and the opening of the new Toy Store) resulted in massive crowds at the new store in the weeks leading up to Thanksgiving and Christmas. Family patriarch John Wanamaker, who knew something about promotion, must have been proud of his normally bookish and restrained son for causing such a commotion at the Philadelphia store. Rodman Wanamaker had recently joined the Aero Club of France with profound notions about aviation. Before his summer 1909 trip to Europe and second wedding, he joined the Aero Club of America. Louis Bergdoll would join too.

On Sunday morning, December 12, 1909, a full-page feature section in the *Philadelphia Inquirer* headlined "In Aeronautic Sphere" explained Louis Bergdoll's purchase of the Blériot XI that caused such excitement at Wanamaker's. With pictures of a Blériot in flight and the dapper young Bergdoll in a suit, Brook I collar, and a newsboy cap, the article said the "Blériot machine will really fly." It claimed that Philadelphia had become "the first city in the country to boast a monoplane... owned by an amateur sportsman for sport's sake only." The article described him as "Corinthian."[11] The rapidly ascending oldest Bergdoll boy loved it.

Louis told the newspapers that he planned to study the Blériot and then lay out a field for "an aerodrome within easy reach of the city and a clear space for practice flights." Upon closing the fantastic exhibit at Wanamaker's, Bergdoll paid $5,000 for the airplane, then had it dismantled, repacked in the shipping crate, carried to the elaborate carriage house behind his Italianate mansion at 22nd and Green Streets, and reassembled.

In a news column adjacent to the Bergdoll Blériot-purchase feature story, a report appeared that local fledgling aviators were expanding and opening their Aero Club of Philadelphia to membership from more than 30 communities in eastern Pennsylvania. They would call it the Aero Club of Pennsylvania. Already established at the Philadelphia Motor Drome Association airfield in Clementon, New Jersey, the early Aero Club of Philadelphia was mainly restricted to balloon flying until Bergdoll, Wanamaker, Edward J. Augsberger, and another Philadelphia flyer, Hugh L. Willoughby, generated interest in their airplanes.[12]

---

[11] The boast about Bergdoll being the first American sportsman with a monoplane may have been hyperbole. Other newspaper articles of November 1909 listed several wealthy American sportsmen who were buying or building their own airplanes. Three of them were listed as owning Blériots or having contracts to purchase Blériots when they were built in France. Bergdoll, however, may have beaten them all, becoming the first to buy and take delivery of a Blériot monoplane in America.

[12] Hugh de Laussat Willoughby was another wealthy sportsman aviator of the era who was born near Philadelphia and lived in Brooklyn and Saratoga Springs, New York, and Newport, Rhode Island, where he used a beach as a landing strip. He began flying at age 53 and held several patents on airplane devices.

In January 1910, Louis reportedly traveled to Los Angeles for the premier air show of America, the Dominguez International Air Meet. While he told newspapers that he would take his plane, no records indicate if he brought along his newly acquired Blériot XI.[13] The show was attended by most of the well-known professional and early amateur flyers, except for the Wright Brothers. They were involved in a bitter lawsuit with aviators Glenn Curtiss and Henri Farman over patent infringement on their aileron design.

The meet was almost canceled until a Buffalo judge temporarily suspended an injunction against Curtiss flying his planes with the Wright aileron design. Curtiss attended the meet along with his flying ace, Charles Willard. Also attending the event were Lincoln Beachey, and Louis Paulhan, who arrived in Los Angeles with Blériot monoplanes and were shown in photographs flying them.

Pilot Archibald Hoxsey smashed the altitude record by flying to 11,474 feet and presenting meet judges with his barograph to prove it. Later that year, Hoxsey would give former President Teddy Roosevelt the first presidential airplane ride in his Wright A-B Flyer in St. Louis.[14]

At the Los Angeles meet, a photograph shows the notable aviator attendees gathered around the flying celebrity Curtiss. Louis Bergdoll does not appear to be among them.

In February 1910, Louis was portrayed in *The New York Times,* posing for photographs in his carriage house with the assembled Blériot XI as a sportsman planning to fly if he could establish a flying field in Philadelphia's Fairmount Park, within the 8-mile speed track where the Bergdolls raced their cars. Perhaps getting his mouth in front of his prop, Louis also suggested that Philadelphia host an "aero meet" in the park, and it would be more significant than the the 1909 meet in Rheims, France, and the January meeting in Los Angeles. However, late that month, the Fairmount Park Commission denied his permit to construct a park hangar and landing strip. Commissioners said that if one could have a private "aeroplane house" in the park, others would want one. It prefaced the commission's later decision to halt the famous automobile races in the park.

In June 1910, *The Times* reported that Louis' Blériot XI was "still in the garage" at the rear of his mansion. The snippet of an article was prophetic because, six months after purchasing the plane and announcing in the press that he would soon fly it, Bergdoll and his Blériot XI had still not flown and were being surpassed by many other aviators.

That month, *The Times* and *Chicago Evening Post* offered a $25,000 prize for an air race between New York and Chicago, and the *New York Post* and *St. Louis*

In 1909, he worked alongside Orville Wright, demonstrating the flight of a Wright Brothers biplane for the Army and President Taft.

[13] *The First Air Races.net* and California Center for Military History, Mark J. Denger.

[14] Hoxsey, who worked for the Wright Brothers, was killed in a plane crash on December 31, 1910, while trying to set another altitude record.

Post-Dispatch offered $30,000 for a similar race between their cities. And Clifford B. Harmon, vice president of the Aero Club of America, was trying to goad Louis into representing American Blériot owners in an amateur roundtrip race between New York and Philadelphia, in part because his (Harmon's) Blériot did not have enough engine power for such a long flight.

Louis, of course, didn't take the race bait because he couldn't. His plane had yet to fly in America. Students were even surpassing Louis at his alma mater, Penn. The Philadelphia campus's science and engineering majors constructed the "first practicable aeroplane built by college students." Like a driver's education automobile of later years, it even had duplicate controls for a passenger to learn how to fly[15]

Louis said in July 1910 that he would take his Blériot XI to Clementon, New Jersey, along with other aviators. He was also reported to have a second airplane, which may have referenced the boys' homemade plane that never flew. Aero Club members were building six hangars at the Clementon field, but Bergdoll had none. His architectural rendering of what he had claimed would be the first "aeroplane garage" in America showed a traditional gable roof stone block building with 16 windows and quadruple folding carriage-house doors to accommodate the 24½ feet width of the Blériot's wings.[16]

Louis was celebrated for promoting aviation and having a spectacular airplane in his elegant carriage house, but he had no field, hangar, or anyone to fly it.

Members of the Aero Club also flew balloons and airplanes from the Point Breeze race track in South Philadelphia, where a popular crowd attraction was an airplane racing a car along the way. Among the early and notable events at Point Breeze was a flying exhibition from November 17–24, 1910, except for Sundays.[17] It was illegal to race cars and fly airplanes on the Sabbath.

British aviator Claude Grahame-White and American aviator John Armstrong Drexel of the Philadelphia and London Drexel banking family were flying their imported Blériots at the egg-shaped Point Breeze track and celebrated in the local newspapers read by the Bergdolls. While his plane sat unused, excluded from exciting events with 30,000 spectators attending, Louis Bergdoll would have to be content as a founding member of the Aero Club of Pennsylvania, a group to organize and sanction aviation events to supervise flight training and certification of pilots.

Ironically, Louis, the businessman who drove his race cars, never piloted his Blériot XI. Instead, William Edward (Willie) Haupt of Philadelphia, the 5'3", 135-pound

---

[15] *United Press*, May 1910. From a caption to a newspaper drawing of a photograph.

[16] This hangar would eventually be built at Eagle Field, housing Louis' Blériot XI and Grover's Wright B Flyer.

[17] On opening day of the Point Breeze event, altitude record holder Ralph Johnstone crashed his Wright Flyer in Colorado, killing him instantly. He was in the same type of plane to be later used by Grover.

Louis J. Bergdoll with America's first Blériot airplane, probably in Philadelphia. (Bergdoll Family, Library of Congress)

race car driver and a manager of Bergdoll Motor Company, learned to fly the plane on his own and represented Louis in all public flights of the Blériot XI.

Undaunted by the failed effort to construct a hangar and aerodrome in Fairmount Park, sometime late in 1910, Louis transported the Blériot XI from his Philadelphia carriage house to the Bergdoll farm in Broomall. Studying Louis Blériot himself flying his planes on Long Island, Haupt observed and consulted with Grahame-White and Drexel. Then, from December 1910 through March 1911, he gained the courage to repeatedly lift himself over the Bergdoll farm and practice his flying skill.

Even though the Blériot XI was notoriously difficult to fly, Haupt appeared a natural aviator. Louis took advantage of Haupt's newly learned piloting and, in another case of getting in front of his prop, in March 1911, he made a foolish declaration in the newspapers. He would arrange for Haupt to take off from the deck of a 100-foot motor yacht while it was anchored in the Atlantic Ocean off Stone Harbor, New Jersey, but the spectacular event was scrapped. Louis wanted to show off his plane to fellow Stone Harbor Yacht Club members at their July carnival.[18]

---

[18] No records are available to suggest this feat was accomplished. If it had been achieved, it most likely would have made headlines. The first airplane to launch from a ship had only recently been achieved by the U.S. Navy in November 1910.

In late April 1911, Haupt and Louis again transported the airplane by train, arriving at the Hempstead Plains airfield near Mineola, Long Island, New York. Without announcing to aviators that he knew how to fly the Blériot, the 25-year-old Haupt cranked up the Anzani motor and taxied around and around the field in an amateur display among the less courageous called "cutting the grass." Few paid him any attention.

Then, without warning, Haupt lifted off from the field. After 10 expert laps, he landed softly among the astonished professionally trained flyers. It was the first public flying demonstration for Louis Bergdoll's airplane; the first Blériot purchased in America by an amateur sportsman.

Haupt displayed such proficiency in Louis' Blériot XI that he was hired to fly another Blériot built by the American Aeroplane Company of Garden City, New York. With a 40 horsepower Roberts 4-X motor instead of the 30 horsepower Anzani motor of Louis' plane, Haupt gained more speed with the new Blériot. He was recorded in the *Inquirer* as flying the aircraft at Hempstead Plains from April through July 1911.

Grover was often on these flying trips, a teenager watching from the ground as Haupt and other pilots basked in the glory of daring flights. However, despite the ready availability of the Blériot, Grover was more interested in the Wright Brothers' airplanes. The famous brothers made international headlines again in July 1911 when their sponsored pilot, Harry N. Atwood, flying a Wright Brothers biplane, landed on the grounds of the White House. It was in every newspaper in the country. Grover was hooked.

Orville's Aviators author, John Carver Edwards, suggests in his 2009 book that Grover may also have taught himself to fly his brother's Blériot XI with guidance from Haupt. Still, there is no evidence or researchable records or articles supporting the theory.

The Harold E. Morehouse *Flying Pioneers* biography of Grover also suggests that he learned to fly on Louis' Blériot XI. But it provides no evidence. Perhaps Grover could taxi about in the plane sometime in 1910–1911. Still, if Grover could pilot the Blériot off the ground, no one was around to see it or write about it in the newspapers as they so readily did when he flew his Wright B. Morehouse says Louis gave his plane to Grover in March 1911. Similarly, Edwards reports, "in March 1911, Louis turned his Blériot over to Grover, who continued to refine his airmanship."[19]

These suppositions are contrary to Grover's nature. If he were flying brother Louis' Blériot, Philadelphians would have known about it.

---

[19] In 1910–1911, Grover and his brother, Erwin, focused more on automobile racing than aviation. No evidence can be found that Grover was flying Louis' Blériot in 1910 or 1911, whether a few feet off the ground or high in the air. The smallest of the Blériot airplanes had only enough space and engine power for one person. Despite other pilots of this era learning to fly independently, it appears that Grover did not pilot a plane off the ground at a significant altitude until his formal Wright School of Aviation flight lessons in April 1912.

Young Grover Bergdoll sat in the pilot's wicker seat of his brother Louis' Blériot airplane in 1910, he never flew it. (Bergdoll Family, Roger Grigson)

In August 1911, Atwood was celebrated again for flying his Wright B airplane from St. Louis to eastern New York State. Flying down the Hudson River, he dipped low enough to glide under the central arch of the 1889 Poughkeepsie-Highland Railroad Bridge.[20]

A few days later, he disappointed hundreds of thousands of spectators who had gathered to watch him fly from Governors Island in New York Harbor to Sheepshead Bay in Brooklyn. However, deep mud at his landing location caused him to cancel the flight. Atwood had also intended to enter the Hearst newspaper's $50,000 challenge for the first pilot to fly coast-to-coast in America, but it proved too costly.[21]

At home in Philadelphia, at the Broomall farm, and almost 18, Grover taxied among the chickens in the Bergdoll boys' unflyable homemade plane.

Atwood and other Wright-trained pilots, Calbraith P. Rodgers, and Archibald Freeman, were attaining records and notoriety in their Wright B Flyers that Grover wished to achieve himself. And, even at this early stage of aviation, daring pilots and aviation advocates like Rodman Wanamaker were talking about incredible plans to, one day, fly across the Atlantic Ocean.

Grover ignored Emma's disapproval of flight lessons. Not to be outperformed by his brother, Louis, and Willie Haupt flying Louis' Blériot XI, Grover persuaded

---

[20] Today, the Poughkeepsie-Highland Railroad Bridge is called Walkway over the Hudson.
[21] Pilot Calbraith P. Rodgers achieved the coast-to-coast flight in his Wright B "Vin-Fiz" Flyer, but he missed the October 1, 1911 deadline by a wide margin.

Orville Wright to enroll him in the spring 1912 flight training session at the Wright School of Aviation near Dayton, Ohio. Grover wanted to buy an airplane, but the Wrights had a strict policy: no one could buy their planes without completing their flight school.

The six-week-long spring session learning how to fly the Wright B included Grover, J. William Kabitzke, John G. Klockler, and Charles Wald, with instructor Arthur L. "Al" Welsh. The tuition cost was $250 in advance or $60 per hour. Although Welsh was a daily instructor, the class was billed as "under the personal supervision of Mr. Orville Wright," who assumed complete control of the Wright Company upon the May 30, 1912, death of his brother, Wilbur.[22]

Wald, who had traveled the world for the Army Transport and U.S. Customs Services, became enthralled with aviation in the Philippines in 1905. He read about the Wright Brothers' 1903 Kitty Hawk flights two years after completion. Returning home to New York, he diverted to Dayton and, to his surprise, was immediately befriended by the Wright family.

Wald later watched Wilbur make his historic flight from Governors Island in New York Harbor to (General Ulysses S.) Grant's Tomb in upper Manhattan in September 1909. He traveled to Indianapolis in June 1910 to see the first Wright aviators' flying exhibition. Wald revisited Dayton in 1910 and 1911, photographing the Wright team and their aviation school at the Huffman Prairie field.[23] He kept a diary of the 1912 flight class and detailed notes in his flight log.[24]

Arriving from their Dayton hotel each morning between 5 and 6 am, the eager flight students spent the first several days learning how to inspect all the parts of their trainer, a modified Wright A Flyer, and practicing on the "balancer," a flight simulator the Wrights named Kiwi Bird.

The "balancer" was a Wright B Flyer minus the tail and engine and laid on a cradle.[25] The wait for good flying weather often lasted several days. Therefore, much of the time was spent on the balancer or playing cards in the airplane sheds.

Wald records that his first aerial flight was on April 12, with Welsh as an instructor, which lasted nine minutes. His only reference to Bergdoll is on April 15, after two days of arising at 5 am, driving from their hotel in Dayton to Simms Station, and discovering the wind at Huffman Prairie, a former cattle pasture too strong to fly.

Late in the day on the 15th, however, with the wind still brisk, Wald wrote, "Bergdoll finishes with [a] 10-minute flight in [the] PM." He notes that Orville Wright and Captain (Thomas Scott) Baldwin watched Grover perform this flight

---

[22] Arthur L. Welsh was an early Wright Brothers-trained pilot and a member of the Wright exhibition team before his death in a Wright C biplane in Maryland on June 11, 1912. Wright State University.
[23] Details from Harold E. Morehouse Flying Pioneers Biographies Collection, Smithsonian Institution.
[24] The 1911 Wright School of Aviation class had included notable aviators like Harry N. Atwood, Henry (Hap) Arnold, Welsh, Oscar Brindley, and Calbraith Rodgers.
[25] *Learning to Fly the 1911 Wright Type B Airplane*, by Dr. Richard Stimson.

Grover Bergdoll, 18, right, with Charles Kraus, Jr., center, and Grover's Wright Brothers flight instructor, Arthur L. Welsh, with a Wright B Flyer at Huffman Prairie flying field near Dayton, Ohio, in the spring of 1912. Welsh was killed in a Wright C plane crash in Maryland within weeks of this photograph. Grover and Kraus packed up the Wright B and shipped it home to Philadelphia, where they flew it as an inseparable duo for two years. (Wright State University, Wright Brothers Collection)

which may have been Grover's final check flight. He said the wind was so brisk that day that even the daring aviator, Baldwin, refused the offer of a ride with Orville.[26]

Grover rarely traveled alone, and on the trip to Dayton, his boyhood companion, partner in crime, and mechanic, Charles Kraus, tagged along. A photograph taken by an unidentified photographer (probably Wald) shows Kraus and Bergdoll sitting together on a Wright B (possibly Grover's new airplane) in a pose that would be replicated a year later as they made aviation history in the American Mid-Atlantic region.

Alfred Bergdoll suggests that Grover may have completed his training with a final 10-minute personal flight with Orville Wright, who, Alfred claimed, indicated that Grover knew as much about flying as he (Orville) did.[27]

---

[26] Capt. Thomas Scott Baldwin was a Civil War-orphaned circus performer turned daring balloonist and airplane pilot known for flying under bridges and for the first parachute jump from a balloon. His 1885 jump sounds remarkably similar to Alfred's account of Grover's boasting about the Bergdoll boys parachuting from a balloon. Baldwin's airplanes were named "Red Devil," the same name Grover chose for his first car. National Aviation Hall of Fame.

[27] Whether Orville signed off on Grover's final training flight and the date of Grover's first solo flight is unknown. If Grover had trained himself to fly on Louis' Blériot XI, it might have hastened his lessons with the Wright school. Years later, Orville would describe Grover as one of his best early students.

Then, from April 16–20, Wald completed several flights, again with instructor Welsh riding along, of 17 to 20 minutes each. On April 23, vertical wind current conditions were such that they made more training flights but suffered hard landings in the hummocks of the Ohio prairie. Wald says, "slight improvement at finish. Last landing, cut off power at 100 feet altitude. Welsh thinks no more time necessary. Start for New York [a 24-hour train ride] 8:50 pm."

When Wald completed the spring school session, Grover may have already returned home to Philadelphia from Dayton. Before leaving, however, Grover wrote a check on April 17 for $5,000 to buy Wright B Flyer #13, constructed in January 1912 at the Wright Brothers shop in Dayton.[28] His brother and guardian, Charles, had to approve the expenditure of the funds and do it over their mother's objections.

Kraus and the Wrights' mechanic, Charles Taylor, disassembled the plane by removing the tail structure and sliding it into the aircraft body. They also folded the front section of the skids and the arching footrest into the body of the plane, placed the entire structure into a large wooden crate with reassembly instructions, and shipped it on a boxcar to Philadelphia.

In an unusual obeyance to a summons, Grover had to return home early. He was due in court on April 25 in Philadelphia City Hall, where he accused two police officers of assault and battery with intent to kill him. Grover attended the trial, but the jury didn't believe him. They sided with the police, who said they shot at the tires on Grover's speeding car when he wouldn't stop on command. Grover suffered another conviction and had to pay the fine.

In the late spring of 1912, the Aero Club of Philadelphia shifted its operations from Clementon, New Jersey, to a 24-acre field near the Bergdolls' Broomall farm. The tract was part of Louis and Charles Bergdoll's sizeable real estate holdings between 1907 and 1912. After a slight delay caused by the complicated reassembly of the Wright B and hesitation about flying on his own, in May 1912, Grover used the cow pasture as a takeoff and landing strip.

In June 1912, the former hay lot became Eagle Aviation Field (Eagle Field) in Manoa, Delaware County, Pennsylvania. It was named for the nearby Eagle Hotel, dating on maps to at least 1848 as the Spread-Eagle Hotel and owned in 1912 by Louis and Emma. Grover paid $1,200 to build an airplane hangar with large, wood-frame, folding and sliding doors. They were anchored by wide twin columns of broken ashlar-faced stone blocks on each front corner capped by hip roofs resembling spires. A single windsock pole completed the rather nondescript building. It was

---

[28] A copy of the April 1912 receipt for Grover's purchase of the Wright B Flyer is still in Bergdoll documents stored at the Historical Society of Pennsylvania archives.

Louis John Bergdoll owned the landmark Eagle Hotel at Eagle Road and West Chester Pike, about a mile from the Bergdoll farm and mansions in Broomall, Pennsylvania. Across Eagle Road, Grover purchased a 24-acre hayfield which became Eagle Field. Up to three thousand people would gather around the hotel to watch Grover fly his Wright B airplane and Willie Haupt fly Louis' Blériot airplane. (Haverford Township Historical Society)

large enough to house Grover's Wright B and Louis' Blériot XI. The Aero Club also purchased a Wright B and kept it at Eagle Field for members to fly.[29]

The timing of the establishment of Eagle Field was ideal for Grover. Returning from Dayton and flight school in mid-May 1912 with his new $5,000 Wright B Flyer arriving soon afterward, Grover shipped the plane from the rail freight terminal in Philadelphia to the farm. He reassembled it at Erwin's automobile racing shop. The excitement surrounding the event must have been high, and mechanically minded Erwin, Stecher, and Kraus helped with the reassembly.[30]

---

[29] Upon returning from Ohio with his new airplane, Grover flew from Eagle Field, allowing its use by the Aero Club. In November 1913, he purchased the field from his brother, Charles, for $11,700. However, because he was a minor at the time of purchase, and Charles was his legal guardian, a court later nullified the transaction until Grover turned 21.

[30] The distance from the Bergdoll farm and Erwin's shop to Eagle Field was about a mile.

Where and when Grover first took off with his Wright B Flyer #13 in the farmlands of Delaware County, Pennsylvania, is unknown. Still, the first reference to the young Philadelphia birdman's flying over eastern Pennsylvania appears in the *Inquirer* on May 19, 1912.

The day before the article appeared in the newspaper, Grover is described as making two flights with Charles Kraus and Ike Stecher as passengers, reportedly to qualify for an aviator's license, which he finally achieved on September 16. Stecher and Kraus, who were accustomed to the long levers on the Bergdoll race cars, were both impressed with Grover as he sat in his seat, feet on the torque shaft, and interchangeably pulling and pushing on the release handles to operate the three elevator and warping control levers connected through pulleys by steel cables to the tail of the plane.

With each flight, Grover mastered his ability to control lateral balance by the sideways motion of the lever that would warp the wings' outer rear corners. He would push or pull on another lever to activate the elevator planes in the tail for descending or climbing. He had two methods of turning with his rudder: the main lever, warping the wings for angled turns, and releasing an auxiliary lever for flat arches.

At each lever's base was the torque shaft of steel that could double as a footrest for Grover and his passenger. One woman told of being so excited to climb into a seat next to Grover that he forgot to strap her waistbelt. She was OK when they took off, but when they rapidly descended, she flew off her seat and stood on the footrests until Grover pushed her back down. She said Grover did not forget to fasten himself in his seat, only her.

On the second go-around from the grass field at the Eagle Hotel in the afternoon of May 19, Grover swooped down to within a few feet of the ground. When 2,500 spectators mistook the swoop for a landing and began to cheer, he shot up again, to everyone's delight. It was a spectacular event; for nearly everyone in the crowd, it was the first time they had ever witnessed a flight.

The next day Grover took the proprietor of the Eagle Hotel, William J. Kirk, up in his plane and then Kirk's wife, Sarah. How the couple running the hotel, owned by Louis, had time for their first airplane ride is unexplained. They were busy serving food, drinks, and other services to the hundreds of people drawn to the event. The headline in a local paper said, "Woman Flys (sic) with Grover C. Bergdoll."

On May 26, with another crowd of 2,500 hundred people watching, Grover is described as making several flights in the Wright B from the ground around the Eagle Hotel with passengers Haupt, Stecher, and Kraus. He would lift off and fly westward to Newtown Square and then northward to Wayne, crossing over the spring-green rolling hills of horse farms and country mansions of Philadelphia's wealthiest and most influential families, then follow the Main Line Pennsylvania Railroad tracks eastward to Ardmore, and back southward to the field at the Eagle Hotel.

As he did with speeding automobiles, Grover found himself in trouble with Philadelphia city officials and Pennsylvania pilot licensing officials for repeatedly flying close to the statue of William Penn atop Philadelphia City Hall. They threatened arrest, confiscation of his airplane, and dismissal of his license application. However, Grover continued his antics, using his money and fame to extricate himself from every scrape with the law. (Library of Congress)

The newspaper said he would climb to 2,500 feet in solo flights and perform a spiral descent to the crowd below.[31]

Grover's highly publicized flights didn't go unnoticed, especially among notable Philadelphians. On June 1, he carried Dr. Thomas E. Eldridge, expert balloonist, on a flight from the Eagle Hotel to the lofty stone and brick high-rise buildings of Philadelphia in less than 15 minutes, where he circled the outstretched hand of the William Penn statue high above the relatively new stone City Hall tower three times. Grover dropped off Dr. Eldridge at the Eagle Hotel field, flew a few miles northwest, and scooted low over the Devon Horse Show. Finding the event nearly over, he turned instead to race a Pennsylvania Railroad train from Devon

---

[31] Following the railroad tracks was one of Grover's favorite navigation techniques and he loved to race the trains, always beating them to the next station. It also publicized his daring flights as passengers arrived in Philadelphia spreading the news about the exciting birdman. Even students at Haverford College refer to lazy early summer days on campus along the Main Line railroad tracks as "drowsily watching Bergdoll sail over."

An unabashed self-publicist, Grover cultivated newspaper reporters and photographers who replaced his negative racing image with the glorification of his flying. He hired George Philip Andrews to paint BERGDOLL on the underside of his airplane lest anyone forget who flew overhead in one of the few Wright Brothers airplanes in eastern Pennsylvania and New Jersey. (Bergdoll Family)

the few miles eastward to Villanova. The Wright B Flyer was so much faster than the steam-powered engine that he overshot the destination and circled back only to beat the eastbound Philadelphia train to its stop in Ardmore. Growing bored, Grover turned away and returned to the Eagle Hotel. Passengers on the train held their heads out of the windows, hoping the birdman with his double wings and the roaring engine would reappear.[32]

Through the summer of 1912, Grover regularly flew his Wright B Flyer from Eagle Field as he and the Aero Club gradually installed modern aviation facilities. In his typewritten *Flying Biographies* manuscript, Morehouse says Grover made nearly 200 flights in 1912 and "balloon ascensions from his balloonist, Charles G. Clark."

On July 15, Grover flew over Philadelphia, where hundreds of thousands of people could look up and see what they had been reading about in the city's several daily newspapers. Further, Grover promoted his flight schedule with notifications to the local newspapers and made sure people on the ground knew it was him; he had his name painted on the underside of the Wright B wings.

George Philip Andrews, a talented sign painter from Philadelphia, was called to come to Eagle Field one day in the early summer of 1912, where he lay on the ground beneath the Wright B painting "B-e-r-g-d-o-l-l" on the under planes (wings). Andrews' son, Bennett, later told how Grover rudely started the motor and roared off in the plane three times while the painter lay beneath it, brush in hand. Finally, after the third incident, Mr. Andrews scolded Grover that he'd have to find someone

---

[32] Description in the *Chester Times*, June 3, 1912.

Grover built a modern airplane hangar in 1911–1912 at Eagle Field to house his Wright B and Louis' Blériot, pictured in front. Later, another Wright B airplane owned by the Aero Club of Pennsylvania was kept there too. Hot air balloons were also launched from Eagle Field with spectators gathered around. Grover held on to Eagle Field for decades, eventually selling it for the development of the Manoa Shopping Center. (Bergdoll Family, Historical Society of Pennsylvania)

The earliest known photograph of Grover flying his Wright B airplane over Eagle Field near Philadelphia, Pennsylvania, in the spring of 1912. It was a rare spectacle to see an aircraft at this time, and people flocked from miles around to watch. (Bergdoll Family, Historical Society of Pennsylvania)

else to paint his name if he did it again. Alfred said in his diary, "he [Andrews] was allowed to complete his work."[33]

As a result of all the promotion and publicity, thousands of people made the 9-mile trek by auto and trolley from Philadelphia to the Eagle Hotel for a closer look. Overall, the crowds for the usual weekend flying events were cooperative.

---

[33] A photograph of Grover's Wright B with BERGDOLL painted under the lower wing was used in a newspaper advertising campaign for manufactured homes in the 1980s. "Would you fly in a plane that wasn't built in a factory?" it asked.

However, sometimes people got too close to Grover's takeoffs and landings and had to be shooed away by his many volunteer assistants.

West Chester Pike was topped with gravel, cinders, and dirt, and the trolley stop for the Eagle Hotel was a small guardhouse-type building with a hip roof no taller than the electric trolley car. However, a patron of the hotel, with its three-story rounded gambrel roof and tall-columned front porch overlooking the pike, would have a choice view of the young aviator whirling about the field.

Somehow, Grover avoided the many wires strung from glass insulators on six crossbars for each tall telephone and electricity pole along the pike. However, one problem they could not overcome was the haphazard parking of automobiles around and on the airfield. The problem occurred because drivers traveling to witness Grover's flights would spy the Wright B in the air as they approached the hotel and pull off the road to watch the aerobatics, usually leaving their cars in place.

Cars were scattered in all directions, blocking roads, driveways, farm fields, and the nearby Delaware County Field Club golf course. It became a spectacle, only adding to the allure of the exciting teenage birdman.

Finally, Grover received the accolades he desperately wanted after years of standing in the shadows of his older brothers. Not satisfied with the press accounts of circling the field or buzzing the Main Line social set at the prestigious horse shows, Grover soon set his sights on much more significant aviation accomplishments, flying his plane at higher altitudes and greater distances from home.

And, perhaps, as Rodman Wanamaker prophesied, even flying an airplane across the Atlantic.

CHAPTER SIX

Grover's Historic Flight

Philadelphia, Pennsylvania, 1912–1913

Rising early on August 16, 1912, Grover and Charles Kraus drove the short distance on West Chester Pike from the Broomall farm to the Eagle Hotel. Warming the Wright B Flyer engine, Grover positioned himself in the pilot's seat. At the same time, Kraus made last-minute inspections of the plane's canvas, guide wires, and connections to the warping, rudder, and elevator levers.

At 5:55 am in the cool August dawn temperatures, the pair lifted into the air and turned eastward over the pike for the 69th and Market Streets' Union Station.[1]

Upon reaching downtown Philadelphia and City Hall, Grover climbed the Wright B to more than 800 feet. Then, dropping a bit to about 550 feet, he circled closely around the statue of William Penn atop City Hall. From there, Grover and Kraus could see the Pennsylvania founder's outstretched arm closely, and his gaze pointed toward the Delaware River upon which Penn arrived in 1682.

The roaring of the Wright B's vertical four-cylinder engine caused pedestrians to crane their necks and watch, some in disbelief.

From a summer of press about Grover Bergdoll's new toy, Philadelphians immediately knew the Birdman was flying again.

Then turning eastward again for the ferry terminals along the river, Grover and Kraus were guided by the white spire of Christ Church towering over the grave of America's founding father, Benjamin Franklin. Crossing the wide ship channel with its jostling ferries and many fingers of wharves in a line toward soup-condensing plant #2 of the Joseph Campbell Preserve Company and its neighbor, the Victor Talking Machine Company with its four riverfront smokestacks in Camden, New Jersey, Grover, and Kraus picked up the eastward line of the Philadelphia and Reading Railway, Atlantic City branch, and flew onward toward the rising sun.

Gradually ascending as they cruised at up to 40 miles per hour, by Berlin, New Jersey, their barograph recorded a peak elevation of 8,000 feet. They could see the

---

[1] Description from the *Philadelphia Inquirer*, August 16, 1912.

vast blue of the Atlantic Ocean and the many rivers, inlets, and bays surrounding the New Jersey shoreline communities.

It was a sight few had seen before.

In August, the boys stuffed old newspapers under their wool coats for insulation to stay warm at high elevations. The next day's edition would have their pictures in it. They circled cotton wraps around their pantlegs in a style popular with military uniforms. Their newsboy caps were turned backward so the wind would not catch the bills and blow them into the spinning propellers behind them. They must have felt like Canada geese, rumbling, and jostling among the roar of the engine and the flapping of their heavy canvas planes high above the regenerating growth of southern New Jersey pine forest after years of cutting and burning, fires caused mainly by sparks from the relatively slower train locomotives.

Descending over Ventnor Boat Works on Lakes Bay while approaching Atlantic City and the Thorofare waterway, Grover and Kraus were buffeted by ocean winds they had not previously experienced in the airplane. However, Grover's steady hand on the levers finally brought the duo down to the ground safely at Chelsea Heights in an area known as the Meadows. The landing, said the *Inquirer*, was "two squares north of the Albany Avenue bridge."[2] It was the first airplane flight from Philadelphia to Atlantic City. It took one hour and 23 minutes to fly the 60-mile route.

The newspaper chronicled the daring journey with a photograph of the plane taking off from Eagle Field and an inset photo of Grover and Kraus in their Wright B seats, straddling the tall control levers and steel guide wires, dressed in suits, white shirts, and ties, and with their matching caps. Kraus appears comfortable and relaxed, beaming with a smile. As he often did, Grover sat erect but expressionless with one shoulder cocked toward the camera.

He knew how to take a photograph.

Grover's brother-in-law, Albert Hall, greeted them, arriving from one of the Bergdoll beach properties as arranged by telephone. He drove the boys to his cottage for breakfast with Grover's sister, Elizabeth. If it was a celebration, they made nothing of it.

Grover's airplane attracted much attention as he flew over Pleasantville, toward Atlantic City and its new Million Dollar Pier jutting into the ocean. It wasn't the first time people in the summer beach resort had seen airplanes, but it still drew a crowd of thousands.

Aviator Glenn Curtiss had spearheaded passenger service from the same airfield a year before Grover's landing. Its proximity to water made it ideal for a seaplane base for flights to and from New York City. However, this was still a significant event. Traveling from Philadelphia to Atlantic City took hours by car, ferry, or train with multiple stops.

---

[2] The location for their historic Atlantic City landing was a new airfield opened in 1910, later considered the first airport in America, Bader Field.

It proved that a pilot with an airplane could carry a passenger for great distances and over water to reach a far-flung destination in a fraction of the time.

Attempting to return to Eagle Field the next day was challenging for Grover and the Wright B. He was 19, and with only a few months of experience on the Wright airplane, the unique wind patterns around the Atlantic City and Ventnor shoreline and back bays were so troublesome that he was forced to wait until the cooler air of early evening on August 17 caused the wind to subside. It also required him to leave Kraus' extra weight behind and attempt the flight himself.

The *Inquirer* said the air currents nearly caused the Wright B to overturn and that when Grover finally departed the Chelsea Heights airfield for Philadelphia, it was 6:05 pm. Slowed by a west wind, Grover made it nearly to Berlin, the high point of his previous flight, and was forced by darkness to land in a field of hot-colored blooms on the sprawling Peacock Dahlia Farms. He narrowly missed a telegraph pole when landing.

Hiring men to watch over the airplane, Grover called his brother, Louis, who arrived to pick him up in an automobile. Grover later returned and flew to Eagle Field in the airplane in daylight, said the *Inquirer*'s special report.[3]

Kraus hitched a ride home with Albert Hall. While Grover was already a celebrity in Philadelphia, the incredible flight elevated Kraus to similar status.

During their teenage years, Grover and Charles Kraus were best friends. People described them as being joined at the hip, closer than brothers, running the streets of Philadelphia and the Main Line in Grover's fast cars, on the race track, and in the air with Grover's Wright B.

Charles John Kraus, Jr. was born in Philadelphia on July 29, 1894, to German parents Charles and Caroline Wagner Kraus and baptized at the Bergdoll's Zion German Presbyterian Church as Karl Johann Kraus.

Living in 1910 in a small two-story Flora Street brick rowhouse with his parents and sister, Minnie, just three blocks from the Bergdolls' North 29th Street mansion, Kraus grew up with Grover on the streets of Brewerytown. His father was a cake maker at a local bakery, and from age 15, Kraus worked as a bookkeeper for an electric company and, later, Albert Hall's concrete and plaster company in Grassland, near Eagle Field.

As with his other companions, Grover paid for most of Kraus' travels, including his fare to Dayton, to help collect the Wright B and ship it home to Philadelphia.[4]

---

[3] A "Special to the *Inquirer*" report usually meant that a reporter was not on the scene of an event but, rather, information was transmitted to the newspaper from others who were present. This special report probably came from Grover on a telephone call.

[4] Grassland was a station on the former Philadelphia and Delaware County Railroad in Haverford Township, Pennsylvania. Absorbed by the Pennsylvania Railroad, the line was abandoned, and names like Grassland disappeared.

Unlike Grover, however, Kraus went on to serve in the Army. He mustered at Camp Meade, Maryland, on February 24, 1918, and deployed to the Allied Expeditionary Forces in the 45th Engineers Unit (later, Transportation Corps), arriving in France on July 23, 1918. He saw no battle engagements but worked at railway maintenance operating a team of horses hauling railroad materials on a wagon. He served through promotions from private first class, to wagoner, to sergeant until he was honorably discharged on July 16, 1919.[5]

Throughout Kraus' military service, Grover was hiding from federal agents in the mountains of western Maryland. In 1934, when Grover was hiding in Germany, Kraus applied for veteran's benefits. The final question on his application asked, "Did you ever refuse on conscientious, political, or other grounds to perform [the] full military duty or to render unqualified service?"

Responding, "No," Kraus couldn't help but think of his childhood friend, Grover.[6]

For much of the 1913 flying season, Grover seldom got his airplane into the air, partly because he spent so much time in and out of courtrooms for speeding and assault infractions and then spent two months in the Montgomery County Jail.

Boredom crept upon him in jail, and he dreamed of a new airplane. From his solitary confinement cell, only a year after completing his flight school in Dayton, he wrote a letter to Orville Wright inquiring about the Wright Model R, a smaller and faster airplane nicknamed "Baby Wright" and developed from the Model B.

"I am stuck on the 'Baby' type which you refused to sell," Grover declared to Orville. "Now, if you will decide to part with those two 'babies' which are in the building opposite the (Wright Brothers) shop, can't you make me a price?" Grover wished to buy both the Wrights' Model R airplanes. Not content with the slowness of his Wright B and reading daily in jail newspapers about other aviators moving up to faster aircraft and setting new records, Grover grew determined to achieve more fame. He told Orville he had safely made more than two hundred flights in his Wright B and felt the "Baby type was much easier to handle."

He signed off by suggesting that even though he was in jail, he would "rather [be here] than where poor [Al] Welsh is." His Wright Brothers flight instructor, Welsh, had recently been killed in a crash.

---

[5] Military service records are from Ancestry.com and other genealogy websites.

[6] No evidence of a Charles Kraus–Grover Bergdoll relationship can be found after World War I. However, Kraus remained on friendly terms with Albert Hall and, for a time, was employed by Hall's concrete company as a bookkeeper. Both were involved with real estate and insurance; suspiciously, they traveled together to Havana, Cuba, in the winter of 1926 while Grover was hiding in Germany. Unfortunately, no evidence supports the theory that they met Grover in Cuba. Kraus also remained a close friend to Charles Bergdoll Brawn.

Orville responded by letter on May 19, 1913, saying he would not advise Grover to go for the "Baby" machines. Instead, he recommended the company's new Wright D with a six-cylinder, 60-horsepower engine that could propel the plane up to 67 miles per hour and more than double the climbing speed of the Wright B. He also suggested Grover might be interested in their new hydroplanes (seaplanes). Orville said, "when you are free, we would be glad to have you come to Dayton to see them and the new models." Grover never responded to the offer.

Upon release from jail at midnight July 6–7, Grover was determined to put on another show. Returning to his hangar at Eagle Field within days, he performed a tune-up on the Wright B, reviewing the motor, props, canvas planes, and flight control levers. However, he didn't check the steel guide wires carefully enough, and only because of poor weather conditions did he not take the plane up immediately.

Then, with another examination of the aircraft, Grover noticed that someone had filed through the guide wires on the Wright B while he was in jail, leaving only one strand of steel intact. It would have caused the biplane structure to collapse with the force and pressure of high-altitude flight.

He had the wires replaced. Kraus quickly worked the critical job, and they waited for the weather to improve.

Grover had saved himself from disaster once before attempting to pull out of a dive when his elevator control lever would not respond. A guide wire to the lever had hooked onto a pulley at the location of a splice, and it was stuck. Jostling the control lever in a risky in-flight movement, Grover freed the snag and landed safely. Said Alfred, "he later put friction tape over the area of elevator cable that had caught." As for the filed wires sabotage, Grover considered it a "deliberate attempt on his life."[7]

Finally, on July 13, Kraus convinced Grover that the wind conditions were safe for flying. Some young boys who hung around Eagle Field pushed the plane to the far corner, away from the hangar, and Grover took off with Kraus on board. He intended to fly north to Norristown and circle the jail, putting on a show for the warden and his former inmates. But it was still too windy, and he managed a low three-minute flight around Eagle Field.

In early August 1913, Grover flew around Eagle Field with crowds of more than one thousand people watching the excitement. He raced a car along West Chester Pike and then took Philadelphia aviation enthusiast and photographer William H. Sheahan for several rides. Then, sensing the crowd's admiration, Grover went up alone and performed low-elevation figure eights, a risky maneuver in a Wright B.

---

[7] *Chester Times*, July 16, 1913. Grover never determined who filed through the guide wires on his airplane.

Unknown to him in the air, the Aero Club of Pennsylvania president was watching. Charles P. Wynne declared that Grover took "big chances" with the figure eights and that "he was, by far, the most daring flyer in that part of the country."[8]

Grover told reporters he would adjust the Wright B for longer flights when he landed. He also wanted a faster plane. And then, he declared, he would soon make a long flight from Eagle Field to Atlantic City again.

Grover and Kraus were up early again on Saturday, August 9, 1913. Two short, thin young boys dressed in long-sleeve button-down shirts, caps, and leg wrappings appeared as mere children on an amusement park ride. However, on the morning of their second attempt to fly from Philadelphia to Atlantic City, they could only manage 150 feet off the ground. Grover blamed it on "atmospheric conditions" and stiff wind. Following West Chester Pike until it became Chestnut Street in West Philadelphia, the duo barely made it over a tall gasoline storage tank at 46th Street. Circling back toward Eagle Field, they nearly landed on the roof of the new five-story brick and stone Gothic Revival West Philadelphia High School at 47th and Walnut Streets. They finally managed to land safely at Eagle Field, determined to try again the following day.

The second flight to Atlantic City would have to wait, however. Weather conditions and mechanical problems forced Grover to delay flying until the following weekend when he flew alone instead of taking Kraus.

As he did the year prior, Grover followed landmarks across New Jersey, over the White Horse Pike to Hammonton, where he reached 8,000 feet in elevation. Newspaper reports describe how he circled Ventnor and Atlantic City in the early morning to the delight of tourists below.

Despite changing wind currents from the ocean blowing around the beachfront hotels, Grover landed his Wright B on the sandy beach between Ohio and Indiana Avenues. He was within sight of the summer beach homes of fellow Philadelphia brewer Fred Poth and saw blade manufacturing heir Kate Disston.

Joined by Kraus and another pilot mechanic, George Charles Peddle, who drove a car following the Wright B, Grover had planned to fly four legs on a roundtrip through New Jersey and eastern Pennsylvania. From Atlantic City, he would fly northward to Asbury Park, then to the state capital in Trenton, and finally, back to Eagle Field in Pennsylvania.

Suffering a rare admonishment, Grover was warned by the Atlantic City police chief not to land on the beach again but to use the new airfield across the Thorofare waterway. Surrounded by adoring spectators on the beach, Grover likely smirked at the command. Fewer people saw him land at the airport during his first flight the year prior. He enjoyed the excitement of landing on the firm sand and the adulation of the spectators. He announced a flying exhibition over the beach at 5 pm but,

---

[8] Alfred Bergdoll diary.

later, canceled it. While police officers guarded the biplane on the beach, Grover entertained the reporters with his plans.

He said he would sail on voyage #24 of the R.M.S. *Olympic*, *Titanic's* sister, on August 23 and, upon arrival in France, purchase a new 200-horsepower Deperdussin monoplane, and enter the September 27–29 Gordon Bennett Cup in Rheims, France.[9] He had a written agreement from the airplane's manufacturer to buy one for $10,000, twice what he paid for the pokey Wright B.[10]

From Atlantic City, Grover's planned New Jersey and Pennsylvania roundtrip had to be canceled. Instead, he would fly directly to Eagle Field the following morning. With Peddle and Kraus, he had installed new chains and piston rods on the Wright B and would need to make more adjustments before venturing any farther from Eagle Field.

The following day, August 16, Grover took off from the Atlantic City beach in the Wright B, flying alone. He made a safe departure and gained speed and altitude westward toward Philadelphia until engine difficulties forced him to land early in a field near Hammonton. Throwing a thick canvas over the plane and leaving it, Grover was picked up by Kraus and Peddle, and together, they drove back to Philadelphia.

Whether it was engine trouble or fear of losing his pilot's certificate from the Aero Club, Grover never flew the Wright B back to Eagle Field. Instead, he fetched it with his flatbed truck. Only the week prior, he had received a warning from Aero Club President Wynne not to fly low over the City of Philadelphia again or face suspension of his flight credentials. For his effort to secure a fast Deperdussin and represent American flyers in European competitions, Grover needed the support of the prestigious Aero Club.

Emma and other family members implored him to give up the dangerous sport of flying. His mother offered him a large sum of money to stop flying, and his guardian brother, Charles, initially balked at approving $10,000 for a new plane. But Grover eventually won them over.

After two and a half years and 748 flights without an accident (many simple touch-and-go), in August 1913, Grover hauled his Wright B on his flatbed truck to Erwin's machine shop along West Chester Pike and mothballed it.[11] He was facing another assault trial for attacking a policeman, and he was supposed to enroll in college at Penn to prepare for law school.

---

[9] Formally known as the Gordon Bennett Aviation Trophy, the Cup was a trophy awarded to aviators by *New York Herald* owner, James Gordon Bennett, Jr. The notable races (timed flights) had previously been won by Glenn Curtiss and Claude Grahame-White, among others.

[10] *Philadelphia Inquirer*. August 16, 1913.

[11] Despite mothballing his damaged Wright B in 1913, Grover boldly offered himself and his airplane to the German consulate in Philadelphia in August 1914, following the outbreak of war in Europe. He was curtly told it was not possible.

Instead, he skipped the trial, forfeiting $1,000 bail (paid by Emma), and, with a bench warrant issued for him (again) Grover and Kraus boarded the *Olympic* in New York, and sailed for Europe.[12]

---

[12] Enrolled only briefly at Penn for the first time in 1913, Grover allowed student aviators to use Eagle Field. Notably, upon being elected class vice president, he annoyed Penn officials by printing his newspaper, *Praecursor* (spy), and suggesting that three recent student deaths at Penn resulted from a suicide club. The paper issued puns on the college president and professors, ridiculed church leaders for denouncing tango dancers at Penn, and promised a serial description of his recent "90-day-visit to a two-by-four country jail." The newspaper was banned, and Bergdoll was expelled from Penn for refusing to attend gym classes.

CHAPTER SEVEN

Clipped Wings

September 1913

Onboard the *Titanic*'s sister ship, R.M.S. *Olympic*, 20-year-old Grover Bergdoll carried a check for $10,000. It was twice the amount he'd been reluctantly allowed by his guardian brother, Charles, a year before to pay for his Wright B airplane. But when Grover arrived in Cherbourg, France, and took an express train to Grenelle, near Paris, excited to receive a fast new machine at the Deperdussin airplane factory, he was met with disappointing news.[1]

Grover had been led to believe by Armand Jean Auguste Deperdussin, founder of the Société de Production des Aéroplanes Deperdussin, or SPAD, that he could purchase a Deperdussin Monocoque Racer, initially produced in 1912 by designer Louis Bechereau.[2] The Deperdussin monoplane was the fastest racing airplane globally, winner of Chicago's 1912 Gordon Bennett Cup. With the backing of the Aero Club of America, Grover planned to purchase a new Deperdussin, practice flying it in France, and enter the 1913 Cup at Rheims in late September.[3]

Grover initially believed he would get the plane with a 200-horsepower Gnome rotary engine, but Deperdussin later changed his promise and agreed to deliver an aircraft with a 160-horsepower engine instead. Even with the reduced engine size,

---

[1] The lawsuit filed by Charles Bergdoll against his brother, Grover, to supervise Grover's financial affairs provides valuable information about Grover's effort to purchase a faster and more expensive airplane. Testimony from members of the Aero Club of Pennsylvania affirmed the newspaper reports of Grover traveling to France to buy a Deperdussin airplane. Travel records confirm trips made by Bergdoll, Kraus, the Wanamakers, and others.

[2] The Deperdussin Monocoque utilized a design that integrated the fuselage with the inner structure of the airplane.

[3] Whether the plane promised to Bergdoll was a 1912 or 1913 Deperdussin Monocoque is uncertain. Grover announced to everyone who would listen that he was promised a Deperdussin with a Gnome 160–200 horsepower engine. With his description, the plane would appear to be a 1913 Monocoque.

14 cylinders with 160 horsepower torque required an extremely skilled pilot.[4] The Aero Club of America believed Grover was qualified to fly it.[5]

The airplane design was a departure from the typical appearance of airplanes with rectangular box frames secured by wire bracing. The Deperdussin displayed a smooth and aerodynamic fuselage made of several layers of thin wood. It also included engine cowling and a cone over the nose of the propeller, giving it an even more aerodynamic appearance. With his $10,000 check and mechanic and boyhood friend, Charles Kraus, to help, Grover was eager to buy and get the plane into the air, practicing flights for the Cup.

Although Grover didn't realize it until he arrived at the Deperdussin factory at Grenelle, Armand Deperdussin was in jail. In August 1913, the former cabaret singer and silk salesman turned airplane manufacturer was charged with defrauding banks. He later admitted to producing fake orders for Deperdussin airplanes and forging silk income receipts to gain approval for $6.5 million in loans to help build aircraft and overcome his $7.5 million debt.

Grover and Kraus were told there would be no airplane for them. The three Deperdussin aircraft already produced would be reserved for French and Belgian aviators to enter the Cup. The plane Grover believed had been promised to him went to Frenchman Maurice Lucien Prévost instead.[6]

"Judge my surprise when we reached Paris to find out that the Deperdussin company had given the machine I had contracted for to Prévost," Grover said in dismay to a *New York Herald* reporter. Upon learning what he considered the Deperdussin "double-cross," he said that he tried to buy an airplane from other French companies and a large engine from the Gnome Motor Company. All turned him down. Grover began to believe that a "fix" was on to assure that a French flyer in a French airplane would win the prestigious international Cup in France.[7]

"Finally, I gave up in disgust," Grover declared of his mood and that of his companion, Kraus. "We started for home." Grover ensured the newspaper reporters knew all about the French Deperdussin snub of an American aviator. He declared he would organize with the Aero Club of America to build their racer in the United States.

"Let me tell you something," Grover buttonholed the *Herald* reporter. "Next year, we will be in that race. I am going to take care that my arrangements do not fall through next time."

---

[4] The engine promised was a Gnome 14 Double Lambda utilizing two rows of seven cylinders creating 160 horsepower. In contrast, the engine on Grover's Wright B produced only 30 horsepower with four cylinders.
[5] Aero Club of Pennsylvania President Clarence P. Wynne later testified that Grover was chosen from among a few hundred American pilots to represent the club at the 1913 French race. Grover's selection would have resulted from his pilot skill and daring, but mostly his ability to fund the purchase himself.
[6] Prévost made delightful headlines at the Chicago race in 1912 when he declared that he was looking for an American woman for love. He said he would take her up in his airplane, make love to her in the sky, and then marry her. However, his boasting was all gas. In 1921 he married a French woman instead.
[7] Because of the incident with Grover and another spurned promise of a Deperdussin to 1911 Cup winner Charles Terres Weymann, American racers did not enter the 1913 Gordon Bennett Cup in Rheims.

Leaving Cherbourg for New York on the *Olympic* on September 24, 1913, with a stop in Southampton, England, Grover, and Kraus learned about the September 27 race outcome via the ship's wireless radio, an extra benefit provided to the 513 first-class passengers.[8]

Flying the airplane promised to Grover, Prévost won the Gordon Bennett Cup in Rheims with a world record speed of 124.8 miles per hour. The feat forever embedded Prévost's name in pioneer aviation history. Second place went to a French aviator in a Ponnier airplane, and third and fourth place went to French and Belgian aviators in Deperdussins.

If Grover Cleveland Bergdoll had been able to buy the Deperdussin airplane promised to him, it could have been his name on the prestigious winner's trophy instead of Prévost's.

It may have changed the course of his life.

Also, onboard the *Olympic* with Grover and Kraus, all in first-class cabins, were Rodman Wanamaker and his son, John R. Wanamaker, Jr, boarding the *Titanic*'s twin in Southampton.[9] While there is no evidence that the older Wanamaker and the young Philadelphia flyer met each other in the first-class salons of the four-funneled ship, it would have been impossible for two Philadelphia millionaire celebrity aviation sportsmen to avoid meeting to discuss the Gordon Bennett Cup.

Furthermore, it would have been an ideal opportunity for Grover to hear more 1913 projections by Wanamaker that aviators would, one day, fly across the Atlantic.[10]

In his soon-to-be-finished aviation career, Grover would speak about a future Atlantic crossing as the ultimate goal for sportsmen fliers. Unfortunately for Grover, his damaged, slow, outdated Wright B Flyer was in storage and would remain there for years. Grover would try, but he would never have another airplane.[11]

Arriving in Philadelphia, Grover was about to suffer clipped wings from within his family.

---

[8] The *Olympic* had been re-fitted in early 1913 following the disastrous sinking of its twin ocean liner, *Titanic*.

[9] On the voyage were Edward T. Stotesbury of investment banks Drexel & Company and J.P. Morgan & Company, and his second wife, Eva Cromwell. Although a prominent financier, Stotesbury had little interest in aviation, pursuing and funding the popular Philadelphia sport of rowing instead. The couple became renowned for their spectacular 147-room neo-Georgian Philadelphia suburban mansion, Whitemarsh Hall, more prominent than all of the Bergdoll mansions.

[10] Since there is no way of knowing if Bergdoll and Wanamaker met while onboard the *Olympic* or discussed their mutual interest in aviation, this is theory-based conjecture. In 1913, Wanamaker commissioned the Curtiss Aeroplane Company to build a flying boat for crossing the Atlantic. It was not successful, partly because of the same event that altered Bergdoll's aviation endeavors: war in Europe.

[11] Stung by the Deperdussin affair, Grover and the Aero Club of America secured a promise from Orville Wright to build Grover a Wright biplane racer that he would enter in the 1914 Cup. However, this, too, was halted by the war.

CHAPTER EIGHT

Insane or Just Crazy

Philadelphia, Pennsylvania, 1915

In 1915, Charles took Grover to court. Questioning his brother's sanity, Charles tried to prove that Grover could not handle his affairs, precisely his inherited fortune of nearly a million dollars. The legal challenge would determine if Grover was insane or just crazy.[1]

When Grover turned 21 on October 18, 1914, he claimed control of his inheritance, believed to be more than $850,000.[2] A few days later, on October 25, Grover smashed one of his many high-powered cars and suffered a fractured skull and severe concussion. His brothers and legal protectors claimed it significantly altered his mental capacity.

Before Grover's maturity at 21, his legal infractions had been managed by Judge Romig, and his wealth supervised by a court-appointed guardian, his older brother, Charles. While Charles was required by the Philadelphia Orphans Court to invest, manage, and disburse Grover's money appropriately, Emma often interfered and gave Grover cash or convinced Charles to be more lenient with his control of Grover's purse.

Even Charles took liberties with Grover's money, which was supposed to be securely locked away in investments until he reached maturity. But, as the relationship between Charles and Emma strained and soured over Grover's many legal difficulties, car crashes, daring escapades with and prolific spending on race cars, balloons, and airplanes, reckless use of guns, propensity for astrology, and reneging on financial agreements, the embarrassed Charles, who had become rather conservative in his own economic and social affairs, turned to a new strategy.

"He has purchased numerous automobiles, smashed them up, and bought racing cars. He buys them and leaves them in the shop. He wastes his money recklessly and foolishly and has no respect for the rights of others or himself. He doesn't seem

---

[1] Considerable details in this chapter come from legal documents, testimony in Charles' lawsuit against Grover, and testimony before Congressional committees by federal investigators hunting for Grover. Most of the information was confirmed by newspaper reporters writing articles about the trial.

[2] About $26 million in 2023.

to realize the danger of his actions," Charles claimed. He petitioned the court and tried to have Grover declared incompetent.

The case came up for trial in October 1915.

The shame that Grover (and Erwin) brought on the family was a painful experience for Charles and his older brother, Louis; they both changed their names—Charles in 1916, and Louis in 1919. Charles' last name became Brawn. Louis changed his last name to Bergson.

Charles said, "[We] realized at that time that [we] or any other human being could not live down the bad name that he [Grover] had made and probably would make worse for the name Bergdoll." Charles claimed Grover was not "a man of a normal mind." He said his youngest brother was "irrational" and had a "fondness for violating the law. [He] gives preference to bad advice over good advice. He has very little respect for verbal agreements that he may make and [has] repudiated agreements after agreeing in writing. He has a very poor idea of justice. He is a great believer and student of astrology."[3]

While Emma insisted that medical conditions caused Grover's unusual personality and mental capabilities at birth, Charles, and long-time family fixer Judge Romig blamed Grover's parents and grandfather squarely.[4]

Charles charged in his court filings that Grover's "abnormality" was the result of "[their] mother's neglect in his [Grover's] bringing up due to the death of [their] father when Grover was only a few years old, and [our] mother tried to take care of her household duties in addition to her business affairs which, I'm afraid, were entirely too much for her."

Judge Romig went a step further. Describing himself as Grover's first guardian, informally appointed by Emma (and, on his 1896 deathbed, appointed by Louis to "look out for the boys"), the former court magistrate in Philadelphia described Grover as "erratic, weak-minded, and unreliable." He blamed the parents.

"Grover gets quite a little from his mother," Judge Romig testified. "She's quick-tempered, temperamental, changing from day to day." Romig said before Grover's father's death, he would stop in the Bergdoll brewery to solicit funds from Louis for political activities in Philadelphia. He said he often found the boys' father "sitting with his feet up on the desk looking sickly and fretful, and he could not be induced to be engaged in conversation."

---

[3] With his astrology predilection, Grover followed his mother's lead. Emma made many social, financial, and legal decisions based solely on astrological signs.

[4] Emma blamed her severe injuries and loss of blood during her accident with broken window glass while pregnant with Grover. She also blamed doctors for mishandling Grover's skull and breaking his arm while delivering him with long-handled forceps. Emma doted on Grover, in part, because of several accidents injuring his head and, she claimed, damaging his brain: falling out of a pony cart at age five, a carriage and trolley car crash, a minor airplane crash in 1911, car collisions in 1912 and 1914, and the racing car crash in 1915 that severely scarred his face and neck.

He said Louis would act nervous, just like Grover. Continuing his testimony to federal prosecutors, Romig charged, "I think Grover inherited his nervousness and reticence from his father. His grandfather was [also] very eccentric and erratic. I tell you, gentlemen, it was born in him."

With an order to appear in Orphans Court or lose access to his multiple and flush bank accounts, Grover was punctual and professional this time. Emma, of course, took Grover's side on defense while Charles was joined in his position, to some extent, by their older brother, Louis.

Did Charles fully understand the repercussions of such a public airing of the Bergdolls' dirty laundry? The case became brothers against brother, brothers against mother. And all the Bergdoll baggage and bank accounts spilled out in court and into the press.[5]

In 1915–1916, Charles Bergdoll challenged Grover in court over his younger brother's reckless spending. He lost. Charles changed his name to avoid the Bergdoll notoriety. He sold a farm in Broomall to Grover, who initially tried to avoid the draft with a farmer exemption. Later, recovering from the trauma of his daughter's death from an accidental gunshot wound, Charles sold his Broomall mansion to Emma and moved to California as a rancher and horse breeder. (Bergdoll Family. Kathy Bergdoll Brawn Tidball)

***

With the Bergdoll children's inheritance from their father and grandfather under financial management and investment by court order when they were minors, the children could do little to access the substantial funds except wait for their maturity.

Louis and Charles were the first to reach the age of 21. With a college education and assistance from Emma, they made investments outside of stock in the Bergdoll Brewery, real estate, and other business ventures such as the Bergdoll car company and aggregate mining. But, for the younger children, the Philadelphia Orphans Court took a different path. Louis and Charles had been appointed guardians of

---

[5] Charles legally changed his name to Brawn in 1916 before Grover and Erwin ran from the draft. It was often misspelled in the press and court documents as Braun. Louis changed his name to Bergson in 1919 after his brothers ran from the draft. Despite the name changes, however, they were always described in the press as the Bergdoll brothers who changed their names.

Elizabeth and Grover, respectively; Emma was the guardian of Erwin's inheritance until he turned 21.[6]

At maturity, each Bergdoll child collected between $750,000 and $1 million (more considerable sums for the younger children because of a longer initial investment term), and, aside from immediately marrying the family chauffeur, Elizabeth used some of her inheritance to purchase her large Wynnefield mansion, a farm near Mount Holley, New Jersey, and a summer home in Atlantic City.

With her husband, Albert Hall, Elizabeth invested in stone/concrete materials and residential real estate in the rapidly growing Philadelphia suburban—Main Line housing market.[7] Aside from a few luxury automobiles, her expenditures were not considered reckless and frivolous. Grover and Erwin, on the other hand, were often accused of spending their money foolishly on multiple touring and racing cars, unused farm machinery, first-class travel to races where they would often drop out of competition, machining tools and automobile parts that were usually discarded, aviation balloons, the airplane, Eagle Field and hangar, and underperforming mortgages in slumlord Philadelphia neighborhoods.

Even more confusing, their expenditures and investments were often intertwined with loans and gifts from Emma. She kept crude records, making the affair somewhat unmanageable.

Therefore, along with sensational headlines and editorials in the Philadelphia newspapers portraying Grover as "a public menace" for his preference for speeding his automobiles on neighborhood streets, it was under this scenario that before Grover's maturity, Charles, as his legal guardian, took his brother to court trying to prove that Grover had a mental disorder that caused his reckless behavior and prevented him from adequately managing his money.

However, before their long and protracted civil case in court, Charles and his army of attorneys and private detectives had to find and catch Grover first. Charles hired a pricey team of attorneys well-known in Philadelphia.

Congressman and former Philadelphia County District Attorney George S. Graham was notable for his conviction of the serial killer and con man Henry H. Holmes, who was believed to have murdered anywhere from 20 to 200 people in Chicago, Philadelphia, Toronto, and other cities in the decade of 1890. Holmes had changed his name from Herman W. Mudgett after killing his crime partner in Philadelphia and fleeing to Toronto and Boston, where his infamous killing spree continued.

---

[6] Initially, Judge Romig, the longtime family fixer, had been a guardian for Erwin and Grover.

[7] Elizabeth and Albert Hall owned Hall Concrete Products in the former Grasslands area of the Main Line. They developed new stone mansion homes for sale in the lush neighborhood of Wynnewood, Montgomery County, Pennsylvania. Charles purchased a large stone quarry near Birdsboro, Pennsylvania, the Birdsboro Stone Company, with Emma as treasurer and Albert Hall as secretary.

With district attorney Graham's backing, Philadelphia police detective Frank Geyer cracked the murder case in Toronto and returned his suspect to Philadelphia, where Graham commenced a trial on the single murder charge. Upon conviction, Holmes was hanged at the city prison in 1896.[8] The case's notoriety made Graham's political career move forward to a law professor at Penn and congressman in Washington.

His law partner was former Philadelphia County Sheriff Joseph Gilfillan. In 1915, aside from his Congressional duties, Graham and Gilfillan had been busy defending a Pennsylvania coal and coke company over rebates for railroad shipments of coal and the massive Cramp and Sons Ship and Engine Building Company in a case with the U.S. Navy over building a battleship in their Delaware River shipyard.

Both attorneys realized the Bergdoll case would generate beneficial headlines, and Charles Bergdoll was willing and able to pay their hefty legal fees. They took the case to prove Grover was "insane."[9]

Despite filing a petition on April 28, 1915, for a commission in lunacy to determine Grover's sanity, the attorneys couldn't find him to serve the papers. The case languished through the summer of 1915 while Grover and Erwin strolled around the country to race their cars. Grover also avoided a bench warrant issued in Montgomery County Court in Norristown for speeding and displaying the wrong license plates on his car. Finally, the impasse was resolved.

On October 2, Erwin entered two vehicles in the 350-mile first running of the Astor Cup motor race at the former horse racing track in Sheepshead Bay, Brooklyn, New York. Grover drove his Erwin Special racer, Big Red, from Philadelphia to the track with his mechanic, George C. McDonald. Still, the inaugural race featuring such star drivers as Ralph DePalma, Barney Oldfield, and Louis Chevrolet was rained out.[10]

Returning to Philadelphia, Grover and McDonald entered the fairgrounds race in Trenton on October 6, but it was also rained out. That night they drove Big Red to the Bergdolls' hideaway garage at 31st and Dauphin Streets in the Strawberry Mansion neighborhood of Philadelphia, not far from Grover's Brewerytown boyhood home. Behind locked carriage house doors, they would make minor repairs and adjustments to the racer before returning the following Saturday to Sheepshead Bay for the rescheduled Astor Cup.

---

[8] In 2017, when people alleged that Mudgett-Holmes had escaped the hangman, the University of Pennsylvania Museum of Archaeology and Anthropology exhumed and tested his corpse. They made identification and reburied him. The incredible story gained new interest with author Erik Larson's 2003 book, *The Devil in the White City*.

[9] This wasn't truly an insanity case, in the legal definition, but the term was used to describe the allegations about Grover's mental condition.

[10] Big Red was a Mercedes racer but it was sponsored by Erwin Special or Erwin Motor Company, indicating the Bergdolls paid the sponsor fee. Ike Stecher was entered to drive another Mercedes for Erwin but his car was sponsored by Mercedes.

However, either Charles or the sheriff in Montgomery County had commissioned the Bryant Detective Agency of Philadelphia to track down the Bergdoll fugitive and serve him with the bench warrant from Norristown. With seven detectives in their Maxwell touring cars surrounding the Bergdoll garage, the agency owner Edward Bryant peered through a small pane of glass in the garage window. He spied Grover and McDonald working on Big Red.

"Crank up the engine, George," hollered Grover as he jumped into the driver's seat. Bryant commanded his detectives to leave their Maxwells and break into the garage full force. Within seconds, while Grover revved Big Red's engine, creating a roar and spewing exhaust into the garage bay, Bryant and his men burst inside without opening the carriage doors, the only means of escape. Pouncing on the fugitive in unison with his detectives, Bryant spotted a revolver between the seat cushions and grabbed the weapon while the others tussled with Bergdoll.[11] Grover tried to fight them off, but he was pinned to the driver's seat while Bryant snapped him into handcuffs.

The detectives suffered bumps and bruises but no serious injuries. Then, sandwiched between their burly captors in the back seats of separate Maxwells, Grover and McDonald were hustled to the detective agency office on North Juniper Street, just around the corner from the Philadelphia Court of Common Pleas in the massive City Hall complex.

Bryant served the bench warrant on Grover and placed a second document in his hands. It was the order to appear in court for a sanity hearing on October 18, 1915, his 22nd birthday. Emma was summoned from the mansion in Wynnefield, and when she arrived at the agency, she too was issued a notice to appear on the same day. Emma told reporters who had been tipped off about the arrest, "I'm going to stick by Grover, stick by him through his troubles."

McDonald was released. The detectives took Grover to police in Norristown, where he was advised he could stay in their lockup and sleep on the floor for the night or go to the Montgomery County jail, which resembled a European castle. Since he had spent two months there in 1913, Grover chose the castle.

Grover lied to the reporters scribbling in their notebooks the following day in court. "Now get this right," he demanded, "we intended to race for the Astor Cup at Sheepshead last Saturday. When the race was postponed on account of the weather, we went to Trenton to participate in the races this week. These were postponed, and we came back to Philadelphia to make final arrangements and repairs to our car for the Sheepshead race. When this race was over; we intended coming back and delivering ourselves up at Norristown without the necessity of any police or detectives taking us there."

---

[11] October 1915 *Philadelphia Inquirer* story about the capture of Bergdoll in his race car garage.

Grover was stretching the truth in all directions. And his lying continued when he appeared before the judge on charges of speeding and using the wrong license plate on his car. He claimed that as secretary of Erwin Motor Company, he made a simple mistake among the many license plates he and Erwin had for several vehicles. He was found guilty on reduced charges and fined $100 and court costs. It was just in time; the rescheduled Astor Cup would be run the next day, Saturday, October 9. However, Grover didn't make it back to the race. He withdrew Big Red. Stecher failed to qualify. Norwegian-American Gil Andersen won the first Astor Cup in a Stutz, setting a new speed record of 102.6 miles per hour.

Again, someone else had captured the glory Grover Bergdoll so badly wanted for himself.

With his bench warrant disposed of, Grover returned to his Wynnefield mansion and consulted with his Norristown attorney on his next court case, the sanity and competency hearing in Philadelphia.

Attorney Nicholas H. Larzelere of the distinguished Larzelere family of Jenkintown, Montgomery County, represented him. They had produced district attorneys, sheriffs, and other politicians, and, like attorneys Graham and Gilfillan, Larzelere was expensive.

The seasoned criminal defense lawyer's first move was rather brilliant. On the opening day of the competency hearing, Larzelere had Grover execute a deed of trust, placing his mother and attorney in control of his Wynnefield mansion for five years.

Setting Grover's most significant asset in supervisory authority showed a level of responsibility for the 22-year-old racer and aviator that the court and a jury could not dispute. And Grover was barely 22. The trial began on the morning of his birthday in Courtroom No. 1 of Philadelphia Common Pleas Court in City Hall; the Second Empire gray stone, masonry, and steel seven-story (nine with tower) building suffered through years of political patronage to complete when Grover was just a boy.

Several stories below the statue of William Penn which Grover was so fond of circling, Charles Bergdoll was the first witness to take the stand in Room A, Court No. 1, with Judge William H. Shoemaker, in his first term.

Described in his nephew Alfred's diary as tall and stocky, with dark hair and wearing pince-nez glasses to make his 29 years appear more credible, Charles may have been trying to portray himself as the more mature, sound, and responsible Bergdoll heir while alleging that his youngest brother was nuts.[12] While Grover sat in the well at a large counsel table just feet away from Charles, in the witness box up front, Emma sat behind them, separated by the dark, smooth wooden rail and its swinging doors in the gallery with other spectators who'd packed the ornate and

---

[12] Pince-nez glasses made a person look rather professorial. They included glass frames and a pinching nose bridge without hinges or temples.

tall-ceiling courtroom facing the mammoth judge's wooden bench perched against the front wall of the courtroom. It would be their daily routine for the next 36 court session days.

For his testimony, Charles declared that he believed Grover to be "feeble-minded and mentally defective." He said Grover did not realize any responsibility and that he (Charles) had difficulty acting as Grover's guardian for financial affairs. He continually reprimanded Grover for "squandering his money," but his protests were ignored. Grover would spend what he was given and only ask for more money. Charles said it was customary for each child in the family to receive a $3,000 to $5,000 per year spending allowance. But he noted Grover typically outspent his budget, then borrowed against future allocation, and gave notes as security, which he later declined to honor.

Charles cited examples. When Grover turned 21, he purchased $130,000 worth of Louis Bergdoll Brewing Company stock from his mother, Emma, for $600 per share. He signed a note promising to pay the cost without consulting Charles to determine if he had the funds to make good on his promise. Charles said he only became aware of the transaction when the notes were presented for payment. Charles claimed Grover grossly overpaid his mother because the stock shares were only worth $300. However, Larzelere stifled this argument, showing that Charles had once swapped brewery shares for bonds within the family, realizing $660 per share, more than twice their value.

Charles also charged that Grover was reckless by buying a color printing press for his radical newspaper while a Penn student, condemning Catholics, and philosophizing in obscene verse, eventually leading to Grover leaving the prestigious university. However, it wasn't clear if Charles challenged the indiscretions or the enormous cost of a color printing press.

Charles also claimed that Grover acted irrationally when he contracted to purchase from him (Charles) Eagle Field after spending $1,200 to build a hangar on the former hayfield. The deal included $11,700 cash and a $40,000 mortgage held by Charles for $51,700 for a 24-acre farm field. Despite freely using the flying field and loaning it to fellow pilots while Charles still owned it, Grover was rejected when it was presented for payment through the Philadelphia Orphans Court. Charles had lost this argument, too, when the court ruled that Grover could not be held responsible for the contract because, at the time, he was a minor. Instead of handing over the deed and stopping using the flying field, Grover kept the paperwork and performed in his airplane and hangar as if he owned the property the entire time.

The transaction was problematic because Charles admitted in court that he charged his minor brother's estate, of which he was guardian, more than $2,000 per acre for unimproved farmland. Charles also admitted to borrowing $5,000 from Grover's estate. Grover said Charles "foisted" the property on him and it was not worth it. But he failed to mention that whoever owned the flying field, Grover continued using it as his own and allowed it to be used by the Aero Club of Pennsylvania and aviation students at Penn.[13]

Grover's attorney convinced the jury that Grover paid for his college expenses at Penn, trips to Europe to purchase and race airplanes, and stocked his elaborate library at the Wynnefield mansion with about 500 books from authors like William Shakespeare, Charles Darwin, James Fenimore Cooper, and works of Wadsworth and Longfellow. He pointed out how Grover was elected freshman class vice president and that he possessed and used his color printing press, wireless telegraphy, the X-ray machine, the Wright B airplane, four race cars, and numerous other touring cars, and had invented a device that would make his racers increase their speed to more than 100 miles per hour.[14]

Grover also boasted of achieving more than 500 flights in his airplane as high as 10,000 feet in elevation, the longest being from Eagle Field to Atlantic City. Attorney Larzelere made sure to include the fact for the jury that one of Grover's airplane flights had Charles' wife, Louise Ann Goetz Bergdoll, as a passenger, suggesting that if Charles thought his brother incompetent, why would he (Charles) allow his wife to ride with him? The revelation was another blow to Charles' case. Even in Emma's presence, courtroom spectators withheld their respect for the wealthy older woman and murmured in agreement.[15]

Grover also recounted his most significant expenditure for which Charles was most concerned, the Wynnefield mansion and its dubious path of ownership and title. He said Grover (really Emma) had been prepared to pay up to $50,000 for the 35-room mansion at the auction but got it for $46,000, with $6,000 paid in cash and the remaining $40,000 on a mortgage.

With Charles' attorneys trying to sort out the tangled web of who owed how much to whom, Grover also admitted that his mother owed his estate more than $100,000, but he was uncertain if it could be as much as $200,000.[16] When Grover produced the deed of trust, Graham, with his long and bushy handlebar mustache, challenged Grover that if he was competent to take charge of his vast wealth at such

---

[13] Grover later obtained full title to Eagle Field. Many years later, he would gain an enormous profit when it was sold for real estate development, anchored by the large Manoa Shopping Center.

[14] In October 1915, Grover's four racing cars included two Mercedes with powerful 60 horsepower engines. Known collectively as Big Red for their custom paint, Erwin Motor Company may have had an ownership interest in the cars because Erwin was often listed as a race entrant with Grover, a driver. The invention of a device to make their race cars go faster is unknown. Neither Grover nor Erwin ever applied for a patent on a device to increase speed in their race cars.

[15] Grover miscounted his airplane flights. He achieved an astounding 748 flights in his Wright B Flyer without a severe accident. Many of them, however, were touch-and-go flights. Many other aviators were dead with far fewer flights.

[16] The court later learned that Emma owed Grover's estate more than $240,000.

a young age, why did he place his most valuable property (the Wynnefield mansion) in a deed of trust?

Grover denied that he did it to protect himself from creditors. Following that confusing exchange between Grover and Charles' attorneys, Larzelere scored another win for Grover's defense when he showed that Charles made many mortgage investments with Grover's money without consulting his brother. And then he left a financial tidbit dangling for the jury to ponder. Grover also had to pay his older brother a 2½ percent commission to serve as guardian of his estate.[17]

Since this part of the questioning was about his financial affairs, Grover often answered with "I don't know" or "I'm not sure" and appeared bored and annoyed. But when it came to reciting numbers about his exciting sporting activities, he was precise and interested. Grover testified that he had been in 17 automobile races in the previous four years. Charles' attorneys may not have been well-schooled in the races because they did not ask Grover if he earned or lost money on the expensive ventures. Mostly he lost.

Charles said Grover skipped scheduled meetings to discuss his financial affairs. After agreeing to be examined by three medical specialists of Charles' (psychiatrists), Grover skipped out on those appointments too. Charles' attorneys labeled Grover reckless for burning the Shevlin boy's hand with his X-ray machine.

Other boys (young men in 1915) testified that Grover showed them immoral books and locked them in closets at the Brewerytown mansion. A car insurance claims adjuster testified that he could not process an accident claim on one of Grover's cars because Grover would only communicate through handwritten notes passed through Emma.

Lower Merion Township, Pennsylvania police chief James Donaghy and officer Ignatius Mullen described Grover's many speeding infractions, costly fines, forfeitures, serious crashes, and the gunfight with Mullen after Grover and Charles Kraus raced off to the Bergdoll farm with Mullen straddling the running board of their car. Members of the jury listened intently to the earnest testimony. Still, several merely shook their heads and grew determined that while it showed Grover to be reckless, it fell short of insanity.

Shifting from complicated financial matters to the personal and social aspects of Grover's life, Larzelere explained to the jury that Grover also put his money into a workshop in his home where he studied technology and science and read about it a great deal instead of reading "dime store novels or trashy books." There was more murmuring in the courtroom when Larzelere had to broach the subject and require a blushing Grover to explain that he occasionally would "visit young ladies" but did not ever seek the company of improper women (prostitutes). Despite being the heir

---

[17] Guardianship commissions are standard practice. But when two brothers are involved, and one is loaning the other money, the practice allowed the jury to cast a more suspicious eye toward Charles.

to a brewery fortune, he only "once in a while (drinks) and then only a glass or two of beer."[18] He didn't say which brand.

Grover's mechanics and friends were most excited about being called to testify because they could later read about it in the newspapers. Thomas Furey said, "Instead of being a spendthrift, as Charles alleges, Grover hates to part with even a small amount of money unless convinced that he will receive full value."

Furey said Grover skimped on hotels, choosing lower-class establishments than he could afford. McDonald said that when they competed in New York, Trenton, and Newark races, Grover went for 25-cent meals but occasionally would spring for a 50-cent dinner. Two Wynnefield and West Philadelphia women testified that Grover was like other young men they knew: Katharine Weber told the jury in front of a smilingly approving Grover that "he is a perfect gentleman."

Montgomery County jail warden Lemuel Roberts was complimentary about Grover's behavior when he spent two months in the castle jail in 1913. In another blow to Charles' case claiming insanity, Roberts said Grover instructed other inmates in elementary reading, writing, and arithmetic and had been "a studious young man."

Former Aero Club of Pennsylvania President Clarence Wynn, whose members were still using the Bergdolls' Eagle Field, said Grover was "a very careful and prudent flyer and the possessor of strong and steady nerves." When Gilfillan suggested that flying was "the nerve to take a chance," Wynn discounted the suggestion.

"Steady nerves and a thorough knowledge of mechanics are the principal requisites on the business," he said.

Then a surprise celebrity appeared in Courtroom A to vouch for Grover. Spectators in the gallery's front row leaned forward to the smooth rounded surface of the court's railing. Those in the back kneeled as if praying in church and rested their elbows on the back of the bench seat in front of them to hear better.

The witness, of dark eyes and complexion, in a suit and tie and sporting a brushed pompadour, similar to Grover, said in clear Italian-accented southern California English that Grover had always appeared sane to him, and he was well-liked by the other men in his profession. Still basking in the spotlight after winning the 1915 Indianapolis 500 motor race that spring, he pronounced his formal name while raising his right hand to be sworn in.

Raffaele "Ralph" DePalma was traveling by train from Detroit to New York when he read about Grover's trial in the newspapers. He said he diverted to Philadelphia of his own volition to see if he could help. Grover was no more reckless than other drivers, DePalma declared. However, he also admitted that he borrowed $1,500 from the defendant. But, by then, another admission by another witness of borrowing money from Grover Bergdoll had lost its impact. Spectators said jurors appeared

---

[18] Years later, alcoholic Grover would consume up to a case of mild-tasting and highly carbonated Miller High Life beer and Carling Ale daily.

more impressed by DePalma's celebrity and handsome appearance than his one-time reliance on the defendant for cash on the racing circuit.

Closing out the testimony supporting Grover, with the gallery settling back into their bench seats, three doctors swore he was "of normal mind" and no more unusual than other men his age. Philadelphia neurologist of German origin, Dr. Francis X. Dercum, renowned for treating President Wilson, testified that Grover was "in ordinary health and, without doubt, a normal young man without sign of nervousness." When challenged by Charles' lawyers if an average person would forget on which property he held a $100,000 mortgage, one of the doctors testified that he too had a mortgage against property of a location he didn't know, but it was only $11,000. It sparked a few chuckles from the gallery.

And, with those final few "who cares" comments, Charles' case for a ruling of insanity against his youngest brother appeared full of holes.

After a month of witness testimony, a break for the Thanksgiving holiday, and the usual trial interruptions, it finally came time for case summations on December 8, 1915. Gilfillan represented his team's hundreds of billable hours to Charles' account. He called one of the doctors in Grover's defense a liar or "on the verge of feeble-mindedness himself, due to age." Attacking a doctor for his age may not have impressed the jury. Gilfillan, accustomed to his past authority of the Philadelphia County sheriff, then mellowed a bit. He declared that Grover was not an idiot, but, despite Charles' legal team not presenting its expert medical testimony, Gilfillan claimed that Grover was not normal. He pointed to the deed of trust giving Emma control of Grover's Wynnefield mansion when she already owed him hundreds of thousands of dollars. He claimed that Grover's access to $5,000 annual allowances was "the root of this trouble."

Then, not understanding Emma Bergdoll's propensity for uncontrolled outbursts, the attorney wound up with dramatic flair in front of the jury, reporters, and a packed gallery.

"Where is the mother of this man?" he challenged, certainly realizing that Emma Bergdoll was the overweight woman with her hair in a bun, dressed in outdated heavy clothing, clicking her knitting needles, and frequently sobbing during the lengthy trial. "They do not dare produce her," Gilfillan roared for special effect.

A tense silence filled the courtroom. Reporters recorded that everyone, except Gilfillan, looked toward Emma.

Then, without adjusting her ample skirt or dropping a stitch, Emma hollered in her broad German accent from her bench seat, "Here is his mother! He's a liar!"

Grover's defense team had purposely kept Emma off the witness list. Her propensity for spouting out of control during her courtroom appearances was legendary among reporters, who loved it. When angry, she would break into German during her scolding of attorneys and make threats against judges to a degree where they couldn't truly understand her words. But they understood her tone.

When court bailiffs appeared by her side and demanded she leave the courtroom if she could not control herself, Emma sobbed.

"I know, I know," she cried. "But, he lies, he lies," she burst toward the attorney and former sheriff, Gilfillan. The jury's sympathy for Emma would become apparent when it delivered its verdict on Grover.

Then, in the final moments of the defense, Grover's attorney, Larzelere, described the renowned brothers, Charles, and Grover Bergdoll, facing each other in the court, sitting opposite attorneys' tables with their grieving mother between them in the gallery. Spectators cried as he spoke.

"Think of these two men, the same blood coursing through their veins—brothers, fighting against each other."

Emma sobbed into her white-stained cotton handkerchief in her usual front seat at the rail.

Then, Larzelere delivered a final blow to the jury with his legal analysis of the case.

"If you render a verdict against Grover Bergdoll, you reduce him to a miserable cipher. You indict him forever as a legal imbecile. He cannot marry; his estate will be gone. Then, where will he go? Charles Bergdoll is trying not only to take his brother's money but to ruin him forever. The only designing person to whom Grover Bergdoll fell victim was his guardian and brother."

Again, Courtroom A fell silent.

Judge Shoemaker charged the jury and sent them to deliberate. Incredibly, within 15 minutes they had reached a verdict. They returned to Courtroom A from their jury room just down the corridor and read the verdict to Judge Shoemaker. However, the two warring Bergdolls didn't hear it. They and their legal teams had departed City Hall for refreshments, not expecting such a rapid decision.

The jury declared that Grover Bergdoll was not insane and that he was capable of handling his financial affairs. Charles' expensive effort to continue supervising his youngest brother's finances and clip the source of his social embarrassment was crushed.

CHAPTER NINE

Bergdoll's War

Philadelphia, Pennsylvania, 1917–1919

Grover Bergdoll was taking a chance after ignoring his draft notice. Driving his 1917 Hudson into the city of Philadelphia from the southwest side on September 1, 1917, he crossed over Cobbs Creek, wary of police searching for him. He turned his car left from Baltimore Avenue onto 60th Street when he spied two sisters, Florence, and Viola Rowe, along the street.

Stopping to chat with his friends, he was alarmed at their news.

"Haven't you heard?" they questioned Grover. "The federal agents are looking for you. It's reported in the *Record* that if they catch you, they'll put you in jail for a year."

Grover knew the Rowe sisters from school and their father as a dispatcher for the B & O, the Baltimore and Ohio Railroad. He trusted their warning. Taking them into the Hudson, Grover drove to their home on Hazel Avenue near 60th Street, where they showed him a copy of the *Philadelphia Record* to read the news for himself. They were right. He was a wanted man.

But, of course, he knew that already.

However, Grover did not know that on that same day, September 1, 1917, Philadelphia was staging a farewell parade for 1,500 successfully drafted men and enlistees leaving for training camp, mainly to Camp Meade, Maryland. Philadelphia newspapers said half a million residents lined the city's Broad Street to cheer them on to war. A press photograph shows about one hundred men in their suits, ties, and caps, bags packed, standing in a semi-circle outside a suburban train station, arm-in-arm, smiling, and heads held high, as the first draftees to leave the region for the European war. Many of them would never come back. Grover should have been among them.

"They [the Rowe sisters] told me of the [draft board] threat of a year in jail which had been printed in the papers. I became frightened of the threat and left Philadelphia without going home or seeing my mother," Grover said. From that point onward, Philadelphia's most-wanted draft evader was on the run.

***

Grover Bergdoll with schoolmates Florence and Viola Rowe, the Philadelphia sisters who, on September 1, 1917, warned him about federal agents searching for him for failing to report for the draft. (Bergdoll Family, Historical Society of Pennsylvania)

On April 6, 1917, the United States declared war on Germany. Despite recently being re-elected with a slogan to stay out of the European war, President Woodrow Wilson and his secretary of war, Newton Baker, felt they had no choice because of the recent onslaught of German *Unterseeboot* (U-Boat) attacks on merchant shipping. They chose General John J. Pershing to build an army from the far fewer than 300,000 active and reserve troops already in the ranks.

In contrast, European nations had millions of soldiers from existing military service programs in the war. The United States, always insulated from European conflict by the vast Atlantic Ocean, had no wartime draft or other methods to build an army and supply it with weapons of war. That all changed with the declaration of war and Congressional authorization for three billion dollars to raise an army.

On May 18, 1917, Congress passed the Selective Service Act authorizing 52 states and territories to establish civilian districts and local draft boards to organize and send postal card draft notices to all men between 21 and 30. In the first phase of draft notifications, these men were required to fill out a registration form and return it to their local draft board by June 5.

After road trips throughout the American Midwest in July and August, Grover arrived in Philadelphia that first day of September, claiming he was unaware of what awaited him. Anticipating he would be drafted into the Army later in the year, Grover claimed he took summer trips in his automobile for a vacation to see the country before going to war.[1]

He had registered under the new Selective Service Law, as he was required to do, by June 5, 1917, and received a pale green wallet-sized paper card displaying a reference that he was among about 2,400 men initially called up in his draft district.[2]

He thought he would get a high number and that his turn would not come up until later in the year. However, his draft notice was deposited in his Wynnefield mansion mailbox on Saturday, August 11, 1917. Interestingly, Grover happened to be home that weekend. He then withdrew cash from his Philadelphia banks and fled in his Hudson Super Six.[3]

He remained on the run until returning to the city on September 1 and discovering that the *Philadelphia Record* had scooped the other papers, revealing that Bergdoll had not reported for draft examination when repeatedly called in July and August and was classified as an Army delinquent. The *Record* editor who approved the article was John P. Dwyer, who also served the federal government as a secretary of the U.S. Selective Service, Philadelphia local Draft Board 32 in the city's Overbrook neighborhood, near Bergdoll's mansion. He had signed Grover's draft notice ordering him to appear for the examination.

Another newspaper, the *Evening Public Ledger*, reported on August 23 that Grover's mother dismissed her servants, closed up the Bergdoll Wynnefield mansion, and left the city at 4 am with her chauffeur for the Bergdoll farm in Broomall. The racers and limousines were gone from Grover's elaborate carriage house that summer. Left behind at the Wynnefield mansion, to be fed by the gardener, were two growling and snarling German Shepherd dogs, Kaiser, and Hindenburg.

In another column on the same page, the *Ledger* said that of 28,000 Philadelphia men called up in the first wave of the new draft, 1,500 were slackers who had yet to be reported to the Adjutant General of Pennsylvania in Harrisburg. Many others requested industrial exemptions for their work in factories such as Baldwin Locomotive Works, Remington Arms Company, and Eddystone Ammunition Company.

---

[1] Most of the information in this chapter comes from court testimony and Congressional testimony about Grover's draft-dodging antics. More than one thousand pages of verbatim testimony are provided from the Congressional Record, and scores of pages from Grover's court-martial trial reveal details of how he and Erwin avoided the draft. Many documents were found in the National Archives in St. Louis and had never been accessed by researchers. As a result of queries for this book, this material is now online for everyone to read.

[2] Department of Justice agent in Philadelphia, John J. O'Connor, testified that Grover initially fled to Cuba in April 1917 to avoid being drafted. When Cuba joined the war, the day after the United States, he returned home and fled to the Midwest. No travel documents indicate Bergdoll went to Cuba in 1917 under his own name; only a family photograph marked "Grover on the boat to Cuba."

[3] The amount of money withdrawn was reported to be $105,000.

Grover was also requesting an exemption. He claimed to be a farmer and auto parts manufacturer. Calling himself a farmer was a stretch for Grover. While the family's Broomall country estates were involved with some farming (by a hired man), they were not growing or producing significant crops or products for the market. Alfred confirmed in his diary that many autumns, crops they did manage to get into the ground were never harvested; they were laid to waste in the winter freeze. While Bergdoll cousins from their grandfather's family produced milk on a significant dairy farm near Chester, Pennsylvania, the Bergdoll boys' farmlands in Broomall mainly lay fallow.

The farmer exemption claim becomes transparent with a real estate transaction between Grover and his brother, Charles, on June 2, 1917. It occurred within days of Grover receiving the anticipated June 5th draft questionnaire. From Charles, Grover purchased an 88-acre tract of farmland across

Grover Bergdoll became a fugitive in the fall of 1917 when he failed to report for the U.S. Army draft. A newspaper artist drew his image as a stylishly dressed and handsome young man, making him attractive to men and women readers. While on the run from 1917 to 1918, Grover's West Philadelphia draft board was prosecuted for favoritism. He claimed, with some justifiable evidence, that it processed his draft notice out of order and with errors. Therefore, it took a year and a second draft notice in 1918 to bring formal charges against him. (Historical Society of Pennsylvania)

West Chester Pike in Broomall from the country mansions of his mother, Charles, and Erwin. He paid $43,000 for the property, proving he was willing to spend large sums to stay out of the war.

Along with his castle-like chateau in Wynnefield, Grover now owned a "farm" just as he filled out his draft questionnaire claiming to be exempt from military duty because he was a farmer. Grover may have been harking back to a previous American draft system where exemptions might be granted as personal favors before being called up. However, on May 18, 1917, all of that changed with the passage of the Selective Service Act.

Despite efforts to escape the European conflict, the United States declared war on Germany in early April 1917 after German U-Boats resumed efforts to sink all ships sailing to British and French ports. Later that spring, the war was already close to home, with the tank steamship *Herbert L. Pratt* heavily damaged by a German water mine off Hen and Chicken Shoals near the entrance to Delaware Bay and

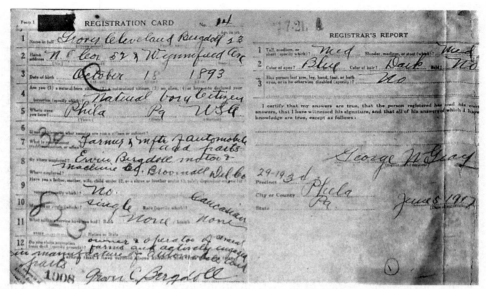

Grover Cleveland Bergdoll's draft registration card for 1917 indicates he requested an exemption as the "owner and operator of several farms and a manufacturer of automobiles and parts." However, he had only recently purchased one non-producing farm and was merely tinkering with his brother Erwin's race cars. (National Archives and Records Administration)

the river for Philadelphia.[4] A German submarine prowled the waters off New Jersey and Delaware and destroyed three other American steamships and three schooners.

Enlisted men were training in camps set up on the vast John Wanamaker estate near Jenkintown, northwest of Philadelphia; students at Temple University and Penn were organizing for training; and Philadelphia city parks were requisitioned for bayonet practice.

Women were organized under the Pennsylvania Women's Division for National Preparedness as nursing aides, soldiers' and sailors' family care, messaging and communications, and clerical service. However, while the Triple Entente powers of Britain, France, and Russia had millions of men fighting against Germany, Austria-Hungary, and Italy, the American military was grossly unprepared to enter the war.

The American Army and National Guard numbered between 200,000 and 300,000 men.[5]

---

[4] Report from the Atlantic Refining Company. *Philadelphia in the World War 1914–1919*. Wynkoop Hallenbeck Crawford Company, 1922.

[5] *American Military History. The US Army in World War I*. Center of Military History, United States Army. Library of Congress. 2005.

Upon declaration of war, the newly imposed Selective Service System supplemented the vast numbers of patriotic American men who were already rushing to recruiting stations to volunteer. And, for the first time, the new draft removed the loophole used during the only previous war draft in the United States, the Civil War, where wealthy draftees could pay $300 for a surrogate to fight for them. It also required all requests for exemptions to be considered after a draftee's initial notification and physical examination, not before. Another significant feature of the new draft system was that while national war policy was governed in Washington, most decisions about drafting men into the Army were left to the local civilian draft boards. In simple terms, the head of a local committee could draw an eligible man in the order he wished. As board secretary, Dwyer, the newspaper editor, who knew all about the previous escapades of the Bergdoll boys, held great authority over the six thousand men in his West Philadelphia Draft Board 32, including Grover Bergdoll.

Additionally, realizing it would take over a month to prepare 30 million draft cards, officers in the Army's Office of Judge Advocate General in Washington risked court martial by printing the questionnaires in advance. As a result, and without penalty, with Congressional passage of the act, questionnaires were immediately received in local draft board offices and mailed to draft-age men (21–30) with orders to return them no later than June 5, 1917.

At age 23, Grover complied. He received his draft questionnaire in early June at his chateau on the northeast corner of 52nd Street and Wynnefield Avenue in Philadelphia. Grover used stylish cursive handwriting for his name, birthdate, nationality, race, occupation, employer, marital status, height, build, hair, and eye color and claimed an exemption to the last question.

He said he was employed by his brother's automobile company, Erwin Machine Co., at the farm in Broomall. He also claimed to be the "owner and operator of a farm" and "actively engaged in [the] manufacture of automobiles and parts." He signed it and mailed it back to Draft Board 32.[6]

One day later, the card landed in a mailbox at Dwyer's fashionable stone twin Victorian home in the tree-lined streets of the Overbrook neighborhood in the far western reaches of Philadelphia. Dwyer commuted by trolley or train to his newspaper editor's office in the center part of the city, but he ran the local draft board from his dining room. He or his chief clerk, Marie Gibbs, made a copy of Grover's questionnaire and assigned him to draft order number 823 and serial number 1008.

The summer of 1917 was quiet for the Bergdolls, but it was busy in Philadelphia and nationwide. Although the war on Germany was declared on April 6, the

---

[6] For many years, Grover kept a 1917 book titled *Manual for Noncommissioned Officers and Privates of Infantry of the Army of the United States*. It was from Gray's Bookstore, Milwaukee, Wisconsin. "Grover C. Bergdoll" was stamped inside. Erwin Bergdoll also filled out his draft questionnaire by the June 5 deadline. His claim for exemption was identical to Grover's: farmer and auto parts manufacturer.

Philadelphia Home Defense Committee had been operating since March 20, and its factories, representing perhaps "the most congested war material producing district in the United States," had been running around the clock since war broke out in Europe in June 1914.[7]

Warships and torpedo boats were being built in Philadelphia-area shipyards. Guns and ammunition were stockpiled in the city and suburban factories. National Guard troops patrolled key bridges and munitions works to thwart subversives. Patriotic rallies were held in public spaces, including Independence Square, to support the war. Anti-war protests and draft-defiance demonstrations were held throughout the city, with people passing out leaflets to convince men to avoid the mandatory draft. Enlistment recruiting stations inside Independence Hall and City Hall were described as carnival-like hawking methods to goad (or shame) men into signing up to fight.

Anti-German sentiment fomented daily through the hot summer since the investigation of an explosion at the Eddystone Ammunition factory south of Philadelphia failed to determine who killed 139 people, maiming more than 100 others. From the blast, body parts were found in the nearby Delaware River. Many victims were young women because the plant advertised for "girls" to do the job. Initially, many people felt that enemy Germans blew up the artillery shell-producing factory, but the tragedy was later determined to have bene caused by a malfunction in electrical equipment.

When the plant was re-opened, hundreds more "girls" applied for the jobs. German applicants were not accepted.

On National Registration Day, June 5, it was estimated that 170,000 Philadelphia men would enroll in the draft. A few days later, former President Theodore Roosevelt declared at the Metropolitan Opera House that a man who won't risk his life in a war should lose his right to vote. On June 25, the Pennsylvania governor named 51 draft boards across the city. Then, from July 20–27, Philadelphia men began watching bulletin boards for their draft numbers, culminating with the first calls and physical examinations of draftees on July 30. Philadelphia's first draft call quota was for 14,245 men. At 23 and single, Grover Bergdoll was among them.

In an essay for *Pennsylvania Magazine of History and Biography*, 2007, author Bill Lynskey writes that Philadelphians were in a "tide of patriotism overtaking a nation about to enter catastrophic world war." They were caught up in the federal government's propaganda campaign to inspire millions of men to join the battle. And what choice? The U.S. Army was so ill-prepared that the federal government even tried to impose drastic censor measures on the press in conjunction with the beginning of its recruitment campaign, but the bill failed to pass Congress.

Another sensitive topic that summer in Philadelphia was the arrest of the editors of a German-language newspaper, *Tageblatt* or daily news, who published the paper

---

[7] *Philadelphia in the World War 1914–1919.*

from offices in the 100 block of North Sixth Street. Owned by the Brewery Workers Union, representing the workers at the Bergdoll Brewery, the newspaper mostly reprinted articles from other German newspapers. Still, when the war began, the reprinted articles took on new meaning in the *Tageblatt.* The broadsheet newspaper was aimed at Philadelphia residents who could speak and read German only. Many of the newspaper's readers lived in Brewerytown.

Emma Bergdoll was a regular reader of the *Tageblatt*, but later, realizing it had become too closely associated with Socialist Party views, she purposely discarded her interest in the German news.

Federal agents felt the *Tageblatt* and its Sunday edition, *Sonntageblatt*, focused too much on pro-German propaganda. Five newspaper employees, including the editors, were charged with making false reports, obstructing the enlistment of men, conspiracy, and treason. It was the first seizure of a German-language newspaper in the United States since the beginning of the war.

News of the arrests in the English-language and highly nationalistic city dailies helped spur more anti-German sentiment. Lynskey's essay explains how nationalist fervor "tried to eradicate outward signs of German culture" right down to renaming Sauerkraut "liberty cabbage." He said Philadelphia schools removed German-language instruction courses and German photographs and articles from textbooks. The world-renowned Philadelphia Orchestra ceased playing German music.[8]

The President Wilson administration organized propaganda campaigns to convince American citizens "to believe their German-American neighbors could be spies and saboteurs." There were reports in the newspapers about Philadelphia residents with German names committing suicide. German butchers reported a significant decline in sales. School children from German families were shunned by their long-time friends and classmates. Even the Pennsylvania Deutsch (Amish) and Mennonites were suspect for their European Swiss-German-Alsace origins.[9]

From June to August 1917, Philadelphia Draft Board 32 officials Dwyer and Gibbs were extremely busy sending draft notifications to men in their neighborhood jurisdiction. Reaching order number 823, they sent a notice to Grover at his Wynnefield mansion to report for a physical examination in three days. Grover likely recognized the draft notice in his mailbox on Sunday, August 12, because the following day, he appeared at his mother's house in Brewerytown.

---

[8] *Pennsylvania History Magazine.* Spring 1996.
[9] In August 1917, a Philadelphia German man, distraught that he no longer heard from his three sons who left their Philadelphia home and joined the German army, took his life by swallowing poison. To assuage some of the anti-German sentiment against the Bergdolls, Emma often publicly announced that she and the brewery were generous buyers of Liberty Bonds used to fund the war. Interestingly, as an indication that Americans were still willing to drink German beer, sales of Bergdoll beer did not suffer a significant decline.

Emma claimed he told her, "he wanted to take his vacation, and he wanted me to fix things for him and that I should go to his house." Grover wanted his mother to retrieve documents from his safe in the Wynnefield mansion that gave her power of attorney over his financial affairs while he was away from home, just as she had done when he took a Cuba trip. It allowed Emma to collect on his mortgages and rent from tenants across the city. She promised she would but could not do it that day. On Monday, August 13, Grover drove his Hudson to at least three of his banks in Philadelphia and withdrew $105,000 in cash.[10] Then, he fled from the city.

Emma believed he had gone to West Virginia, where he liked to be in the wild, open countryside. She arrived at the Wynnefield mansion late in the evening on Monday, August 13, and discovered that Grover was gone. She also found the draft notice in Grover's mailbox where he left it. She knew immediately what it meant. Emma consulted her long-time friend, consultant, and legal advisor, Philadelphia attorney David Clarence Gibboney, who told her to visit Dwyer and report that Grover was on vacation and unreachable..

"I explained to him [Dwyer] that I could not contact [Grover] because he was out in the wilderness. Mr. Dwyer, at that time, said he was satisfied to wait," Emma said.

Emma said she asked Dwyer if she could claim an exemption for Grover, and he told her he would help her fill out the questionnaire. When she returned to Dwyer's home a few days later, he changed his position. Emma said he told her he would "not have anything to do with the matter and would not help me at all."

On August 23, 1917, the *Philadelphia Record,* under the direction of its managing editor, John Dwyer, published exclusive details of Grover's flight based on postcards he sent back to Philadelphia, snubbing his nose at the authorities. Postal cards were received by Naval Coast Reservist Joseph McManus, from Grover, with postmarks in Chicago, the small community of Oak Hill, Illinois, and Chillicothe, Missouri. McManus gave the cards to Dwyer, who made copies, and surrendered them to federal prosecutors.

Dwyer then published the postcards in his newspaper with a highly patriotic editorial saying, "even though bearing the stigma of being posted as a deserter, Grover Cleveland Bergdoll, auto scorcher and aeroplane pilot, is marking the periods of his flight to Mexico by sending postcards to friends in this city." One postcard said, "Our Ford is still plugging away. Will reach the desert in a few days, and then we defy the devil to find us for a year or two."[11] Another card said, "We shipped car home today. We travel by rail now and then by boat. Heading for New Mexico in a few hours."[12]

---

[10] $105,000 is equivalent to about $2.1 million in 2023. However, Emma later testified that Grover took only $6,000 with him, money collected on a mortgage.

[11] It's unclear who was with Grover at this time. He may be referencing his brother, Erwin.

[12] From this, press reports indicated Grover traveled into Mexico too but, unless he entered Mexico illegally, there is no evidence to support the claims.

On Saturday, August 18, an explosive allegation in the Philadelphia *Public Ledger* newspaper suggested that Emma offered Dwyer a $1,000 bribe if he would exempt Grover from Army duty. It caused Dwyer to publish an article in his newspaper, the *Record*, the next day refuting the "sensational story," as he described it. Dwyer said that Emma visited him at his Overbrook home on Friday, August 17, immediately following the local draft board's review of potential exemption candidates. Dwyer told his draft board colleagues within earshot of a *Public Ledger* reporter that Emma begged him for an exemption for Grover. He told Emma that Grover's 10-day limit for claiming an exemption from the local board had expired. Dwyer said he told the *Ledger* reporter that his conversation was in strict confidence and not for publication.

He then relayed "the evident pathetic condition of the devoted mother [Emma], who was opposed to her son entering the Army and cited her statement that she was most anxious that he be exempted from such service, adding that she would be willing to give $1,000 to the Red Cross if he could get out of it." Dwyer said he did not consider Emma's offer a bribe, no matter how his conversation was construed. "She did not create, in my mind, and I am sure did not seek to create, the impression that she was seeking to offer $1,000 for use by the Red Cross as a bribe for the exemption of her son, but rather that she was willing to contribute of her money to the succor of our American soldiers rather than consent to her son taking up arms against her native land."

Dwyer said he told Emma to encourage Grover to come in and serve his country. He suggested to Emma that Grover was "a genius in the handling of automobiles and airships" and that his skills would be put to good use in the Army with the possibility that he would "return to her a hero and wipe out his reputation as a reckless automobile driver." In an opinion article in his newspaper, Dwyer charged that his competitor newspaper, the *Public Ledger*, was "grossly deceived in printing the story… and should immediately correct the false impression of the publication." It didn't.

The *Public Ledger* and its companion newspaper, the *Evening Ledger*, continued publishing stories about draftees taking extreme measures, such as cutting off their fingers with an axe and losing weight to achieve exemptions. Names and addresses of the men reporting for service were printed, along with those who managed to win exemptions and the reasons for the exemptions.[13] Nothing was off limits.

Additionally, unknown to the public, Grover's draft district was being investigated for favoritism and corruption, delaying legal cases like Grover's.

In December 1917, the Bergdolls tried diplomacy from Washington to get relief for Grover. Acting on behalf of the family, it is believed to be Judge Romig who contacted U.S. Congressman from Philadelphia and former City Council Member George W. Edmonds with a plan to offer the federal government the vacant 132-acre

---

[13] Newspapers often printed long public lists because, in most cases, they were paid to do so.

Bergdoll property in Somerset, Maryland (at the Washington district boundary with Somerset and Chevy Chase) for use as military barracks or housing for civilian government workers needed for the war.[14] Naturally, it went without saying that the delicate free offering of prime real estate owned by the Bergdolls since the late 1800s would be in exchange for leniency for Grover.

Emma claimed the government considered the offer for a while but declined.

Federal agents put pressure on Louis Bergdoll too. Still smarting over financial losses at his Bergdoll car company, Louis was accused of "German activities" in December 1917 during a squabble over providing heat in his rented factory building at 16th and Callowhill Streets in Philadelphia for a tenant company with a government contract to manufacture khaki and olive drab fabrics for use in Army uniforms.

Louis' General Realty Company was being miserly on burning coal to fire the steam boilers sending heat to the factory floor radiators. The workers were cold in the 60-degree factory and couldn't finger their cutting shears. They had to be sent home, and, as a result, the company could not fulfill its government contract. Federal agents sent their investigative report to Philadelphia U.S. Attorney Francis Fisher Kane, who held a meeting with Louis, both fully aware that his brother, Grover, was the government's number one fugitive.

Louis reportedly declared firmly to Kane that the problem was a dispute over slower-than-usual coal deliveries to his building, possibly because his name was Bergdoll. He said he would do everything he could to rectify the problem, and he resented the accusation of supporting "German activities."[15]

Louis didn't hold back any of his animosity against his family. He told Kane that he "was not pro-German; he was not in his mother's class, nor in the class of his brother, Grover."

When the federal agents visited the coal company, the Bergdoll bins were filled, and the heat was turned up. The incident was not publicized in the press but was quietly shelved and only much later revealed in federal investigation documents.[16] It was, perhaps, a method of keeping Louis, always considered the most cooperative of the Bergdoll boys, in the government's good graces.

Also, on behalf of the family, Judge Romig contacted another Philadelphia congressman, George S. Graham, a criminal defense lawyer from the University of Pennsylvania law school and former district attorney of Philadelphia County. Graham communicated directly with officials from Draft Board 32, wishing to negotiate

---

[14] The Bergdolls' Somerset-Friendship Village tract along Wisconsin Avenue is today occupied by a large high-rise condominium complex and parkland. The Epilogue provides more details about how the Bergdolls used this valuable and controversial property.

[15] Louis Bergdoll changed his name to Bergson a year and a half later, in 1919.

[16] The Louis Bergdoll coal incident has long been hidden. It was uncovered during the lengthy research phase for this book.

terms for Grover's surrender. He also tried to enlist the U.S. Army Provost Marshal and General Enoch H. Crowder to negotiate terms.

However, General Crowder, very familiar with the new draft law because he wrote it, referred the congressman back to the local board. Under normal circumstances, these communications would likely have been kept private. Still, since Dwyer was both the provincial draft board secretary and editor of the *Record,* the quiet diplomacy went public. On January 1, 1918, the *Record* published a sneering exclusive article about how Grover wished to compromise and return home.

> Grover Cleveland Bergdoll, speed fiend, cop beater, and draft dodger, does not apparently like the Mexico climate at this season of the year. He wants to return to Philadelphia, but he does not like to make the trip back unless assured in advance that a firing squad at sunrise or a long term in jail are not among the possibilities of any reception committee program that may be arranged for him.[17]

Dwyer later testified that while he was the editor of the *Record,* he "wasn't doing much work on it at the time. I was on the draft board." Dwyer was not questioned about how the news of Grover's enlistment of the Philadelphia congressman to negotiate surrender got exclusively into the *Record.* However, Dwyer readily admitted that his reporter consulted with him and then wrote in the paper that if Bergdoll returned to Philadelphia, he might be shot.[18]

Grover later tried to explain his flight from Philadelphia in a letter to the *Public Ledger* newspaper dated July 8, 1918. He had just learned of his mother's arrest for aiding and abetting his draft evasion.[19]

"When I first left Philadelphia on the trip, I intended purchasing a ranch out west," he said, trying to explain the significant withdrawal of cash from his banks. However, he did not buy a ranch, justifying how he managed to remain on the run for so long without the alleged financial assistance from his mother. Grover said he ran because of Dwyer's threats to put him in jail for a year. He said he was ready to return if prosecutors would promise to allow him to "enlist in the Aviation Corps as a flying instructor."[20]

---

[17] Reports in the *Record* that Grover was in Mexico were incorrect. The reporter may have mistaken New Mexico for Mexico.

[18] It should be noted that the offer of free land near Washington, D.C., in exchange for leniency for Grover, was not reported in the newspapers, perhaps because Dwyer was not involved in the brief negotiations. The offer came out later in testimony from Emma Bergdoll and Judge Romig.

[19] On July 1, 1918, Emma and Charles Bergdoll, Judge Romig, former brewery bookkeeper Harry Schuh, and former Bergdoll car salesman Albert Mitchell were charged with aiding and abetting Grover for draft evasion. They were convicted and sentenced to the federal penitentiary in Atlanta with a stipulation that paying fines would suspend the prison sentences. Charles Bergdoll-Brawn wrote a check on behalf of Emma, paying $23,000 in fines for all of them.

[20] The U.S. Army had not yet progressed significantly with aviation recruitment efforts. Instead, it initially focused on what it needed most for war being fought in the trenches of France: infantry.

He called the newspaper's description of him as "pro-German" an "infamous lie and a rank falsehood." Federal investigators later determined the letter was mailed from westbound train number 3 of the Erie Railroad between Jersey City, New Jersey, and Salamanca, New York, on July 8. However, they suspected that Grover was long gone in another direction. They believed he had a friend or acquaintance post the letter along the route. Placed in a canvas mailbag known as a catcher pouch and snared by an eastbound train, it would have returned to New York and Philadelphia, where it was delivered to the newspaper office days later.

While federal prosecutors renewed their nationwide search for Grover in response to the taunting letter, Emma tried to entice her wayward son to return home.[21] She was out on bail on the charge of helping Grover escape, and she placed a newspaper ad.

> Grover C.A. Bergdoll, you are not a deserter. Come back immediately, or other desertion proceedings will be taken. Letter received. They are not used by Counsel's advice. Telephone me as soon as you read this. Your mother, Emma C. Bergdoll.[22]

In her correspondence, Emma wasn't concerned about revealing confidential information about Grover to the federal agents; she claimed they were opening and reading all her telegrams and letters.[23]

Emma had tried to explain Grover's failure to report for the draft examination. In the spring of 1918, she wrote to the adjutant general of Pennsylvania that he was on a motor trip to the Midwest when the draft notice appeared in their mailbox, ordering him for examination "the following day."[24]

Emma said she immediately went to see Dwyer at the local draft board but that he was "very nasty about it and refused to allow me to file an application for deferred classification, pending [Grover's] return." She claimed Grover owned or leased "a number of farms" and that their cultivation suffered due to his absence. She hinted at a conflict of interest by Dwyer by "making a fuss about it in the newspapers" and suggesting that the draft board was "more anxious to secure publicity for themselves than to help a person get justice."[25]

The adjutant general's office replied with a short paragraph referring Emma back to local Draft Board 32 for all decisions concerning Grover. Then, Emma wrote to

---

[21] The nationwide search included thousands of members of the American Protective League, a quarter-million private citizens who helped federal authorities round up German sympathizers and hunt for draft dodgers.

[22] The middle initial A denoted Grover's seldom used second middle name, Alfred.

[23] Federal agents testified they were, in fact, intercepting the Bergdolls' mail in an effort to determine Grover's position. Each time their effort failed.

[24] Draft District Board 2 (containing local Draft Board 32) took months before notifying the adjutant general in Pennsylvania that Grover, and more than 1,800 other men, did not report for examination in August 1917. Members of the District Board were investigated, indicted, and removed from their jobs.

[25] Emma even suggested the Eagle airfield was fallow without cultivation of corn and beans. It typically was left as grass for harvesting hay and to keep it suitable for takeoffs and landings.

Selective Service Headquarters in Pennsylvania declaring that she believed military regulations prohibited drafting former convicts, which described Grover's many automobile and assault infractions. Emma got a reply to this letter too. It spelled out the potential exemptions and military classifications, with Class V describing draftees with criminal convictions. Grover initially fell into Class I as a single man of the proper age. Under Class V, he could apply for exemption only if he had been convicted of a crime designated as treason or felony or an "infamous" crime. But he still had to follow the standard reporting regulations to be considered for exemption.

Class V also provided an exemption if Grover were a licensed pilot "actually employed in pursuing his vocation." Grover didn't qualify for this exemption since his airplane was damaged, unflyable, and stored on a trailer in Erwin's machine shop at the Broomall farm.

Furthermore, all exemption decisions were left to the local draft boards or decided upon appeal by regional and state officials. Emma's pleadings were useless. Dwyer was determined to have Grover inducted into the Army or, at least, follow the federal regulations and report for examination when ordered.

Failing to find mercy at the state level, Emma returned to Dwyer and the local draft board. She pleaded with him to give Grover time to return home and enter an aviation wing of the military.

The dispute grew personal, public, and ugly.

"Then, they put it in the newspapers that he was going to be shot at first sight," Emma said. She tried to persuade Grover to return home to answer the questionnaire, but he refused. "All the time, I try to bring him back, but he is like a little baby—he won't come," Emma sobbed. Some reporters on the Emma Bergdoll beat couldn't help but feel sorry for the old lady.

Repentant or not, stories about her protests and accusations were top sellers in their newspapers, and they printed every word and description.

Also, during the summer of 1918, while Grover was hiding in Maryland and traveling about the country avoiding the draft, clumsily trying to negotiate a reprieve if only he would be allowed to enter the service as an aviation consultant and pilot trainer, another Philadelphia pilot excelled at joining the Aviation Corps properly.

Philadelphia Army Lt. Jonathan D. Este became the first American pilot to fly an airplane assembled in France with a Liberty engine built in the United States. The affluent Este from West Philadelphia was a member of the Philadelphia Racquet and Country Clubs and the Princeton Club. Although beyond the initial draft age, Lt. Este enlisted for training at the Curtis Aviation School in Newport News, Virginia. Upon arrival in France, he worked to train and organize fellow American aviation forces.

It's precisely what Grover claimed he wanted to do and should have done if only he would report to his draft board to be examined.

On July 15, 1918, during a second draft registration period, clerk Gibbs prepared questionnaire number 828 for Grover, addressed to his home at the northeast corner of 52nd and Wynnefield Avenue.[26] In a departure from all other draft notices sent, Dwyer signed and stamped the card himself. Working from Dwyer's home, Gibbs and Dwyer watched the street from a window tucked in the deep wraparound porch of the twin house as Dwyer's son, Paul, 21, dropped the single draft notice into the cast iron mailbox at the corner with the Malvern Avenue trolley loop. Dwyer later testified that Bergdoll's draft notice was handled individually because "it was important."

Paul Dwyer testified that Bergdoll's notice was the only questionnaire mailed that day. He could not recall the recipients' names of all the questionnaires he'd previously dropped into the mailbox in front of his house. It became clear that Dwyer and Gibbs paid particular attention to selecting, composing, and mailing the war draft questionnaire to notable Philadelphia celebrity racer and pilot Grover Bergdoll.

Wynnefield neighborhood mailman Christopher J. Halberstadt said he was told by his supervisor at the Philadelphia West Park postal station to "pay special attention to that mail." He testified that he rang the doorbell of the Bergdoll mansion and handed the draft questionnaire to Emma Bergdoll instead of dropping it into the family's sizeable round-top mailbox mounted on a pedestal just outside the gray stone chateau. The mailman may have been confused about his duty not to read the mail because, in court, he was required to revise his testimony that while he delivered an envelope and placed it in Emma's hands, he could not be sure it contained a draft questionnaire.

"The piece of mail that I delivered was an envelope the size of the usual questionnaire, and I understood it was a questionnaire… we [letter carriers] knew when we handled questionnaires," Halberstadt said.

Gibbs testified in court that Grover's draft order number, 828, was mistakenly issued on the questionnaire she mailed. His actual number, she said, should have been 823 like it was in 1917. A few numbers apart present an insignificant difference when Grover would be called to report for the examination.

Still, it indicates frequently made mistakes at local draft boards, and Bergdoll's attorney seized upon it—to no avail.[27]

While Bergdoll got his second draft notice, another mailman dropped a notice to appear for examination into the small steel mailbox nailed to a porch column of the North 60th Street brick and clapboard rowhouse that was home to Russell C. Gross

---

[26] The year-long delay until Grover's second notice resulted from the corruption uncovered in Draft District 2 and their revisions to notification timelines. The term questionnaire may be inaccurate because the cards were notices to appear for an examination to determine if the selected person was physically fit to be drafted into the Army.

[27] The draft numbers indicate the call order among thousands of draftees in their draft districts. Based on conversations with other draftees in West Philadelphia, Grover said he believed that his number would be in the 24-hundreds, and, therefore, his notice would come much later than the summer of 1917.

and his family. At 25, Gross was single and worked as a clerk for a clothing manu-facturing company in Philadelphia. While Gross lived within the same draft board 32, his notice was one of the hundreds prepared by the part-time clerks hired to process the paperwork. It was not explicitly handled by Dwyer or Gibbs or dropped into the mailbox by Dwyer's son, Paul. It got no special attention whatsoever.

Dwyer may have felt satisfaction when he sent the draft notice to Bergdoll. The newspaper editor who reviewed many articles in his papers about the wealthy celebrity may have held a long-festering vendetta going back to an incident involving Dwyer's young children in the yard of the Bergdoll mansion. The Bergdolls claimed he acted on his simmering grudge when he gained the power of a draft board secretary. Dwyer admitted that he treated Bergdoll differently, saying in court that all 78 draft delinquents in his local board were treated the same in his draft office's private and quiet confines but that in his newspaper, Bergdoll got more publicity than all the others.

John Patrick Dwyer was from north-central Pennsylvania, where he was born in the river city of Lock Haven to parents who were merchants in Renovo, Clinton County. In 1892 he purchased the *Williamsport Republican* newspaper and served as editor. By 1900, Dwyer moved to Philadelphia to become a reporter for the *Philadelphia Record* and the *Philadelphia Press* newspapers.

One of his articles for the *Press* exposed corruption leading to a prominent Philadelphia bank president, insurance broker, and former state senator, John J. Coyle, being indicted on charges of trying to bribe a member of the Pennsylvania legislature.[28] After many years of reporting and editing, Dwyer became managing editor and president of the *Record*, attaining significant wealth and influence as a partner in the newspaper business.[29]

Dwyer was active in civics in his Philadelphia Overbrook neighborhood. His wife, Mary, mother of their five children, died from croupous pneumonia in 1916, leaving Dwyer with four sons and war in Europe sure to snare American soldiers.

In 1917, he was appointed the secretary of Draft Board 32, Overbrook, on a recommendation from Philadelphia Mayor Thomas B. Smith to Pennsylvania Governor Martin G. Brumbaugh. Dwyer had rattled Smith with newspaper articles criticizing his mayoral administration. Dwyer later wrote that Mayor Smith "gave his reason for my selection because he desired to soak me."

---

[28] Coyle was acquitted of the charge in December 1900. Coyle, who lived in a large three-story stone colonial mansion just blocks away from Dwyer's home in Overbrook, later challenged Dwyer for drafting his son-in-law, Charles MacLellan Town. Demanding an exemption as the owner of a coal company, Town was released from duty on appeal to District Board 2. Town's case became part of Dwyer's complaint to Washington about corruption in District Board 2.

[29] The *Record* was owned since 1898 by the Wanamaker family of Philadelphia department store fame and Rodman Wanamaker, who sold the Blériot airplane to Louis Bergdoll. The Record became one of the most successful newspapers in America, with an estimated daily readership of 315,000.

Dwyer's sons served honorably and survived the war on active duty in France or reserve duty in the United States. Because Dwyer operated Draft Board 32 from his Overbrook twin home, two sons were inducted into the Army from their home—the other two enlisted.

Gerald Dwyer arrived in France near the war's end to participate in the Meuse-Argonne offensive on November 1, 1918, just days before the Armistice ended the war on November 11. Frank was wounded during a fight in the Argonne Forest. John served in the Navy in Calais, France. Paul was the son who deposited Grover's 1918 draft notice in the mailbox and entered the service but remained in the U.S. only because of a bout with influenza while training at Army Camp Wadsworth, South Carolina.

Dwyer and his boys were extraordinarily patriotic and even nationalistic about the war and the United States. With his investigative reporter, editor, and publisher experience, Dwyer was meticulous about his new duties as a local draft board secretary. He reported a draft case by letter to President Wilson where he believed a draftee got special dispensation for National Guard duty from his superiors in Philadelphia Draft District 2.

Dwyer told Wilson he thought the members of the district were crooked. He wrote: "A man who had a pull was one of the first men to pass the physical examination in August 1917. More than 250 boys from our district went ahead of him into the Army who should have gone after him. A number of them lie buried in France."

From local Draft Board 32 (his house), Dwyer and his assistants processed 7,587 registrants. Of those, 910 were inducted into military service, including Bergdoll. Dwyer considered himself "loyal to the President and his aides from the beginning.[30]

Sometime earlier in the decade, when Dwyer's children were much younger, an incident may have occurred where Dwyer and Grover crossed paths. Grover's New York attorney, Harry Weinberger, testified before a Senate committee investigating Grover's escape that some of the Dwyer children got into and damaged a cherry tree in the yard of Bergdoll's Wynnefield mansion. Grover became enraged, "spanking" them. When Dwyer got word of it, he became angry and confronted Bergdoll outside the mansion, Weinberger claimed.

"You get off my property, or I'll spank you too," Bergdoll allegedly hollered toward Dwyer.

Weinberger suggested that Dwyer contained his thoughts of revenge for this transgression until he became the local draft board secretary. Weinberger further

---

[30] Dwyer's own words confirm a conflict of interest. Why a newspaper editor was allowed to become a draft board secretary can only be explained by the politics of the era in which it happened. He should have declined the job or recused himself from his newspaper position while he performed his federal duties.

alleged that Dwyer was serving as a draft board secretary for free and lived in a Pennsylvania Railroad-owned home for the sub-rate rental cost of $35 per month.[31]

Weinberger claimed that the notable newspaper editor and draft board secretary acted on his grudge and personally moved Bergdoll's name up the list.[32] Conversely, Bergdoll may have held a grudge against the U.S. Army. In 1916, Bergdoll and fellow Philadelphia Wright B pilot Marshall Earle Reid offered their piloting services to the Army's First Aero Squadron of eight Curtiss JN-3 airplanes called in to assist in The Punitive Expedition, led by Brig. General John J. Pershing chasing Mexican outlaw Francisco "Pancho" Villa into Mexico after he raided Columbus, New Mexico, home to Camp Furlong and the Thirteenth U.S. Cavalry Regiment. While squadron leaders were receptive to Reid's flying expertise and took him in, they turned down Bergdoll because he was German.[33]

At first, Grover tried to say he didn't receive the draft notice in the mail at his Wynnefield Avenue home in July 1918. By regulations, he had 10 days to respond to the message and was required to reply to local Draft Board 32 by July 22. Then he said he could not have personally received the draft notice because he was away from home on an extended summer trip through the Midwest. Perhaps unknown to Grover at this time, his brother, Erwin, was having similar difficulties. Although older, married, and living on his farm, Erwin also got his draft notice.

When Grover returned to the Wynnefield mansion, he claimed he got a telephone call from Dwyer. "[Thomas] Furey answered the phone, and he [Dwyer] said federal agents were after me," recalled Grover. "I made an appointment to meet him [Dwyer] at the *Record* office. I did not keep the appointment because I was afraid [that] he was setting a trap or wanted to get graft out of me. It is my belief that Dwyer would have arranged a soft Army job if I had paid him. I think Dwyer got mad at me when I didn't show up. All I wanted was to wait until Dwyer was out of power. I intended then to surrender."[34]

---

[31] Draft board secretaries initially earned four dollars per day, then were paid by the number of questionnaires filled out. Eventually, they were paid a dollar per hour not to exceed 10 dollars daily. Dwyer claimed the rental value of his twin home was the same as his neighbor, $30, and that he paid it to a subsidiary of the Pennsylvania Railroad.

[32] There is no evidence to corroborate Weinberger's allegation. However, Dwyer did not contest the allegation during his testimony. Furthermore, in the 1939 Court of Appeals decision on Grover's conviction and claim that the statute of limitations had run, federal prosecutors wrote in a brief for the court that Dwyer "had a personal enmity against Bergdoll."

[33] A federal border crossing record for Grover at Eagle Pass, Texas, and Piedras Negras, Mexico, in June 1915 can't be explained unless it was part of an effort to fly for the Army against Pancho Villa. Similarly, Bergdoll claimed he tried to offer his piloting skills to the Army in the European war but was turned down. Marshall Earle Reid, of Irish lineage, was the experienced Wright B pilot and Philadelphia-Baltimore steel wire manufacturer who last flew Bergdoll's Wright B airplane in 1934 in New Jersey.

[34] Dwyer denied ever talking to Grover on the telephone. In another conflict of interest, Dwyer said paid draft board workers prepared more than 6,000 draft cards in a small room next to his editor's office at the *Record* building. It gave the daily newspaper immediate access to the names of draft evaders before they became known to the adjutant general.

Philadelphia Draft Board #32 secretary John Dwyer was also editor of the widely-read *Philadelphia Record*. During court testimony, Dwyer admitted to treating Grover differently than other draftees because of his celebrity status. Furthermore, he did not deny allegations of enacting vengeance against Grover for spanking Dwyer's boys over a damaged cherry tree. Dwyer's newspaper often scooped others on Bergdoll stories because of the editor's unique access to federal draft records. (Historical Society of Pennsylvania)

By July 29, 1918, the Pennsylvania adjutant general's office had been notified of Grover's prolonged failure to obey his draft notices. It sent Grover a letter ordering him to report to their office in Harrisburg by 1 pm on August 8. He would be automatically inducted into the military without a physical exam if he didn't.

Ignoring the direct order from the adjutant general, Grover was, therefore, inducted into the Army on August 8, 1918. However, he was still imagining a pipedream would spare him. He claimed to have been designing a new monoplane (he wasn't), which he said he hoped would be accepted by the Army for use in the war.[35] He and Erwin still expected their motor "inventions" to spare them. Unaware that his own draft problems were about to begin, Erwin weighed in on his brother's flight from the draft. He typed a letter to General Crowder on letterhead from Elizabeth Bergdoll Hall's mansion at 49th and Wynnefield Avenue in Philadelphia but postmarked from his farm in Broomall, sending his message to the general's Washington residence. Still, he did not explain why he sent it there instead of the War Department.

He wrote that he and Grover were "the joint inventors of a new type of carburetor for the automobile and airplane motors." He claimed their invention made improvements to existing carburetors. And then, Erwin suggested he could not patent the new device without Grover present, nor could he divulge the further carburetor details without Grover's consent.

Erwin wanted General Crowder to grant "a temporary exemption of 60 days" on their draft inductions so the carburetor could be patented and its usefulness explained

---

[35] Grover and Erwin produced a homemade airplane at the Bergdoll farm near Broomall long before the war. A family photograph of the homemade plane, which never got off the ground, indicates a design similar to Louis' French Blériot, the most popular monoplane design of the era.

to the National Advisory Board for Aeronautics. He boldly requested that the draft exemption be permanent if the carburetor proved helpful.

General Crowder did not agree to such a delusion. All decisions about draft selection and exemptions, except for appeals, were made at the local draft board level. Again, Erwin and Grover were told that all draftees must answer for examination at their local boards.

Soon afterward, Grover sent his letters to the newspapers. "I made an offer to enlist if they would not prosecute me," he said. "I never saw the questionnaire. I tried to enlist in Dayton, Ohio, at a flying field. I was told I must give my real name. I was afraid to do so for fear of being turned over to Dwyer." Grover also believed that by not keeping his appointment with Dwyer at the *Record*, the draft board secretary had a second reason to enact his Bergdoll revenge. Dwyer, however, later responded.

> The position I occupied as a member of a local draft board came to me unsolicited. The case of Bergdoll is the most notorious of its character growing out of our participation in the great war. The fact that Bergdoll was a deserter from the draft district in which I served during the war [did] not influence me [and] it meant no more to me than any other registrant in our district. I did my whole duty. My four sons who were in the service did theirs. He forced others ahead of their turn into the Army by his desertion.[36]

Immediately upon his August 8 automatic induction, Grover had a federal bounty on his head. The Classification Value Reports Bureau of the Customs Intelligence Service in Washington put out a "lookout" notice, similar to a wanted poster, describing Grover as "five feet four inches tall, 175-pounds, dark hair, a brushed pompadour, scar on his face, and teeth stained by tobacco, and usually wearing brown shoes and clothes," missing for evading the draft. They said he was "flashy and dramatic, a liberal spender, and well supplied with money." In a high-collared white shirt with a dark tie, a photograph showed Grover matching the description with handsome but expressionless features. The confidential memo said he could hide in a wide-ranging area of the Midwest, even in Canada or Mexico.

Grover said that when he left town the second time in his fast new Hudson Super Six in 1918, he had enough money to stay away for 10 years. Some of it may have been gold!

During the summer of 1918, federal agents revealed that Erwin Bergdoll also failed to report for the draft examination and was missing when called up by his local board in Broomall, adjacent to Philadelphia in Delaware County, Pennsylvania, where Erwin lived on his farm next to his brother Charles' country estate.[37]

---

[36] Determining if Bergdoll was a deserter or draft evader became the crux of the decades-long legal case against him.

[37] Charles Bergdoll-Brawn acquired the Broomall country property through his father's estate upon his death in 1896. It is the same property that Charles sold to his mother, Emma, in 1920, and, together with Erwin's farm next door and Grover's farm across West Chester Pike, the properties are

Erwin Bergdoll's 1917 draft card. Like Grover, he listed his occupation as a "farmer & manufacturer of autos & parts for Self and Erwin Motor Machine Co." (National Archives and Records Administration)

At age 26, Erwin claimed exemption from the draft "on the grounds of owning and operating a farm and manufacturing autos and parts." The farm included an old house with a large barn and livestock run-in sheds overlooking Darby Creek, part of their father, Louis Bergdoll's original estate. On his farm, Erwin also operated a business in a machine shop along West Chester Pike called Erwin Motor and Machine or Erwin Bergdoll Machine Company. He and a small band of employees constructed race cars and struggled to continue assembling the Bergdoll brand automobiles acquired after his brother, Louis, declared his Bergdoll auto manufacturing company in Philadelphia bankrupt. From his farmhouse that summer of 1918, Erwin went to his local draft board chairman William Ellis' home the night before he was to be examined and asked to be excused from the draft. He said he "might have to shoot some of his relatives" if he went to fight against the Germans in France.

Additionally, Erwin's wife, Sarah Bolden Parker Bergdoll, wrote a letter to Ellis questioning why her husband was not exempt from the early stages of the draft for

referred to here as the Bergdoll country estate or Bergdoll farm. The West Chester Pike interchange now encompasses the land with Interstate 476 in Delaware County, Pennsylvania.

being married and operating a farm. Ellis replied that Erwin "showed slight knowledge of agriculture and that farming with him seemed but a sideline."[38] Alfred Bergdoll later said of his uncle Erwin that he was no farmer despite having tractors and other farm implements. Alfred noted that Erwin often got excited about cultivating his fields in the spring but never finished the job. Alfred said Erwin's only manual labor was tinkering with cars and piling rocks for a swimming hole in Darby Creek.

When Erwin didn't show up for his draft examination, Ellis reported him to the police and federal authorities, which soon led to a raid on the Bergdoll farm along West Chester Pike. Charles also lived at the family farm estate then and may have distracted the agents while Erwin fled from his farmhouse to the barn. Erwin later testified that he climbed into the rafters of his large barn and hid among the folded and pigeon poop-infested wings of Louis' Blériot airplane while peeking through the cracks in the barn walls at the agents searching his brother's house.[39] The newspaper headlines intensified. Now, both notorious Bergdoll boys were missing from military duty.

The headlines made federal agents in Philadelphia appear foolish for not catching the Bergdolls. They were ordered to send their surveillance of the Bergdoll boys into high gear. First, agent McDevitt personally went to the Wynnefield mansion with five members of the American Protective League and arrested Emma on July 1. The men searched the house but found only letters, postcards, and papers passed between Emma and Grover. It was enough to charge the old lady with conspiracy in Grover's escape. She was held on $10,000 bail.

Then, on July 19, federal investigators in Augusta, Georgia, were advised to be on the lookout for Grover there. Their description of the elusive fugitive was humorous. Five feet four, heavy set, 16 and three-quarters neck collar, broad shoulders, 175 pounds, Teddy Bear fashion brown hair, dark brown eyes, and a passion for brown clothing. They also informed their Georgia agents that Grover wore loud ties, had heavy scars on his face and throat, teeth stained with tobacco, and a chip off his tooth.

The Georgia Bergdoll advisory seemed unusual because the next day and night, July 20, federal agents again surrounded the Wynnefield mansion but reported it was in "total darkness." They scoped out Emma's brick townhouse in Brewerytown, Gibboney's house in Philadelphia, and Albert and Elizabeth Bergdoll Hall's homes in Wynnefield and Mount Holley, New Jersey, where the rural farm property was surrounded by a high fence and signs warning to "Beware of the Dogs." Holding back his Doberman Pinschers, Hall allowed agents to search the farm, but they didn't find Grover or Erwin. They even surveilled one of Grover's attorneys, summering at his

---

[38] From *United Press, The Gettysburg Times.*

[39] Charles Bergdoll-Brawn and his mother, Emma, were charged with aiding and abetting Grover while he was a fugitive.

Erwin Bergdoll's arrest mugshot and the Broomall farmhouse built by the Bergdoll boys' father, Louis. The barn where Erwin hid from federal agents is partially obscured on the right. Erwin would often escape from an upstairs window of the house to the barn when federal agents arrived to search for him. He had a small, hidden, furnished room in the barn, where he stayed for extended periods. (Bergdoll Family)

beach house in New Jersey. They also tracked down Grover's and Erwin's boyhood companion, Stecher, who claimed he hadn't seen Grover in four years.

That night, around 9 pm, federal agent B. J. Cunningham perched himself in the plump cushions of a green wicker chair on the piazza of the Wynnefield mansion. Emma was out on bail from her conspiracy charges, and Erwin's wife, Sarah, who had moved in with Emma for a time, joined him on the porch. In his report, later filed with the U.S. Attorney in Philadelphia, Cunningham wrote of a warm and informative conversation with Emma and Sarah.

"No wonder he does not come home with all these things in the newspapers about him. He is only a boy, and you scared him away," scolded the old lady.

When Sarah was asked when her husband would return, she replied, "When that draft board puts him in his right place. He's a farmer and belongs in another [draft] class."

Emma explained to Cunningham how Erwin bought a tractor and claimed he was raising food for the war effort. "The food we are trying to send overseas," she said, "but the [German] submarine gets it."

Cunningham hinted that the old lady was joyful and talkative, but she shook her head and rolled her eyes at his statements about Grover. Then, he reported, Emma opened up about her childhood in Germany. She claimed she was born in Leipzig, in northeastern Germany. However, Emma was born in Huffenhardt, southwestern Germany, near Mosbach and only 15 miles from Sinsheim, where her husband's father, Louis Bergdoll, was born. With that, Cunningham should have known that Emma was, again, lying under questioning.

Emma also bragged to the federal agent that she was a patriot, no matter where she lived. She helped beat the French, she said, during the Franco-Prussian War of 1870. She carried water in buckets to the German soldiers while she was only nine.

Then, pursuing a discussion about the draft, Cunningham got under Emma's skin. She lamented how the recently installed American draft should follow the methods of Germany and "just call out each class, every man, without picking them out or selecting them." She continued believing that Grover's and Erwin's draft boards had chosen her sons out of order and to be spiteful to the rich and famous Bergdolls.

Emma's conversation with Cunningham sounded like she was pro-German, even though she denied it each time someone in the press or police pointed to her pro-German comments.

Then, she told Cunningham in their cozy piazza chat that her late husband, Louis, was her second cousin. And, closing out their congeniality under the darkness of the warm summer night, Emma, who was becoming known as the Queen of Wynnefield, roared at her final thoughts, "I have to laugh every time I see Queen Victoria's picture. I look so much like her it makes me laugh."

Agent Cunningham had to leave the mansion that night empty-handed again. But, he felt he had made some headway in the federal investigators' relationship with Emma. It may help them, one day, he thought, to track down Grover wherever he was hiding.

***

Celebrity racing champion Erwin and aviation pioneer Grover were just two of 337,649 draft evaders from the Great War. Half of them, or 163,738, were apprehended before July 15, 1919. Approximately 13,000 were released from accusations, leaving about 160,000 men prosecuted and punished for neglecting their duties during the war. Grover Bergdoll was the only one continuously persecuted and prosecuted, while all others were forgiven.[40]

Throughout the summer of 1918, the anti-slacker sentiment was also high in Philadelphia. Spurred by the news of the absent Bergdoll brothers, federal agents began staging "slacker raids" at popular summer venues such as Woodside (amusement) Park and Shibe Park during baseball games and boxing matches. Blocking the exits, police and federal agents accosted young men to produce their green paper wallet cards, proving they had registered for the draft. Those who couldn't show their cards called home for someone to fetch them. They sat in makeshift lockups until they could show the evidence. Similar raids were held in Atlantic City, New York, and even at shift changes among thousands of workers at munitions and

---

[40] Several Great War draft evaders were sentenced to death, but none was executed. Hundreds were sent to prison. All, except for Grover Bergdoll, were forgiven, released, and/or pardoned by 1933.

shipbuilding factories in Philadelphia and Chester, Pennsylvania, Camden, New Jersey, and Wilmington, Delaware.

In September 1918, the five *Tageblatt* employees came up for a trial with the prosecution led by renowned attorney Owen J. Roberts who later became an associate justice of the U.S. Supreme Court. Attorney William A. Gray represented the defendants. He tried to show that the newspaper sided with ordinary Germans, not Kaiser Wilhelm II, the German emperor responsible for the war.

Author Bill Lynskey writes that Roberts successfully proved that the newspaper was pro-German and had edited and republished other German newspaper articles in such a way as to create false reports. By this time, the bodies of American soldiers and sailors were returning home to the Philadelphia seaport and train stations, inciting more anti-German sentiment, described by Lynskey as "rage" and "hysteria."

All five *Tageblatt* defendants were found guilty and sentenced to one to five years in prison. Later appeals to the U.S. Supreme Court upheld the convictions of the editors but reversed convictions for the lesser employees. Then, in a remarkable turn of events, while the federal government continued its decades-long prosecution of the Bergdolls, the late stages of the President Wilson administration issued pardons for the three *Tageblatt* defendants who had their convictions upheld.

Lynskey wrote, "among those recommending clemency was Francis Fisher Kane," the former U.S. attorney for the Eastern District of Pennsylvania who also played a vital role in the lengthy prosecution of the Bergdolls. The instigators of thousands of men who thumbed their noses at the military draft were forgiven, while the most infamous slackers who ran were hunted down forever.[41]

Unsuccessful in gaining exemption from the draft, Erwin initially ran off to Lynchburg, Virginia, to hide from the Pennsylvania federal agents. He managed to stay hidden for several months in Virginia and Maryland, occasionally returning secretly to his farm to visit Sarah.

Then, while Erwin was still on the run, tragedy struck. Lonely Sarah, pictured on the farm as girlish, trim, and fashionable with a round face, firm jaw, punt nose, and attractive eyes, had gone hiking through the woods along Darby Creek one spring evening in a cold downpour searching for her lost pet monkey. She became ill and was taken to Lankenau Hospital near Philadelphia with pneumonia. Although Erwin rushed home, hiding at the farm, he could not visit his wife in the hospital for fear of being captured. She died there on April 21, 1919.

She was only 23.

---

[41] The U.S. Attorney for the eastern district of Pennsylvania, Francis Fisher Kane, who headed the initial Bergdoll draft evading prosecutions, resigned on January 12, 1920, in protest against a national policy of Red Raids where federal agents raided gatherings of Americans suspected of Socialist or Communist activities. Kane called the Red Raid policy "unwise and very apt to result in injustice."

Grover, second from left, and Erwin's wife, Sarah Parker Bergdoll, second from right, along with two unidentified women and Bergdoll companion Thomas Furey, right, with Grover's Hudson Super Six Limousine. (Bergdoll Family Collection)

The influenza epidemic could have caused Sarah's illness. One obituary suggests she was "stricken with the flu" and was five months pregnant when she died. Her funeral was held five blocks from Erwin's boyhood home in Brewerytown, but he could not attend, he arranged for Charles to go in his place. The mourners were surveilled by federal agents looking for Erwin and Grover.

By the time of the tragedy, Charles Bergdoll had changed his name to Brawn.[42] He had foreseen the difficulties his brother, Grover, presented to him since Charles was forced by the Philadelphia Orphans' Court to relinquish his guardianship over Grover in 1914–1915.

Despite living next to Erwin and Sarah, Charles claimed he was estranged from them and had not spoken to Erwin or Grover in years. On the day of Sarah's death, her father, William B. Parker, called and asked Charles to come over to Erwin's farm, where Erwin, from a secret room in the barn, requested Charles attend Sarah's funeral

---

[42] Charles registered for the draft in September 1918 at age 32 as a stone crusher at his Birdsboro (Pennsylvania) Stone Company. Louis registered at the same time at age 33 as a real estate investor living in New York City.

in his absence. Charles claimed this was the extent of their conversation. Still, the truth came out later in court when Charles, Emma, Judge Romig, and two other family friends were convicted of conspiracy for aiding and abetting in Grover's and Erwin's run from the draft. Also, on the day of Sarah's death, Erwin, Charles, and Mr. Parker met with a longtime Bergdoll companion, Fitzhugh Lee Creedon. They discussed and conspired a trip to the south, recommended by Charles, who would stay behind. A fourth person was to accompany them—Grover!

Just shy of his 18th birthday, Creedon spent the night at Erwin's farm, and together, the two men arose the next day at 4:30 am, ate breakfast, and then prepared a car to drive into Philadelphia to pick up Grover and Judge Romig at the Wynnefield mansion. Emma was also there making sandwiches and coffee for the foursome, and by 5:30 am, with Erwin at the wheel, Creedon in the passenger seat, and Grover and Judge Romig in the back seat, they sped off into the emerging dawn.

By late afternoon on April 22, the two draft-dodging fugitive Bergdoll brothers, their trusty advisor, and a family companion arrived at a tent hideout along Antietam Creek near Hagerstown, Maryland. This was where Grover had been hiding intermittently since initially running from the draft in 1917. Back home in Philadelphia, Sarah's body had not yet been prepared for her funeral. Despite his carefree nature and propensity to abandon people and possessions, leaving his wife's corpse behind would haunt Erwin for the rest of his life.

Through the summer of 1919, the draft fugitive Bergdoll boys continually ran from and secretly returned to their homes, able to hide successfully on their farms and in the big stone Wynnefield chateau.

"I slept in the barn almost the entire time so that if anybody came poking around, they wouldn't find me," Erwin boasted. "Once, while I was in the barn, the agents came to raid [Charles'] home, and I watched them. They also came near my place but didn't search the barn very much, or they would have found me."

He claimed, "with the flicker of a smile," to have spent July and August 1919 at his Broomall farm, cutting the hayfields near West Chester Pike, where he could easily have been seen from a passing car or the trolley. If Erwin grew suspicious of another raid on the farm, he might run back to the tent in Maryland for a few weeks.

Grover found the same success hiding in the Wynnefield mansion. He discovered that no one would know he was there if he remained inside and in a large room on the upper floor. Emma lived in the house to present it as being occupied, and for weeks at a time, they remained quietly behind closed doors.

However, the Bergdolls were always hiring and firing servants, or they quit. With employees easily bribed into talking, the word always got out that unusual activities were happening at the mansion. Working on tips, local police, and federal agents spied on the property so frequently that it became a spectacle and tourist attraction. Philadelphians would drive out to the Wynnefield mansion to watch the agents milling about, watching the windows for any sign of Bergdoll. Grover would sometimes stand in dark shadows a few feet inward from an upstairs window overlooking the spectators watching the agents. It was almost laughable. There were so many gawkers on the street that people joked that they could have made money charging admission.

When hiding in the Wynnefield mansion, Grover often slept in rooms on the second or fourth floors with a pistol under his pillow. So nervous was he about being captured while hiding in the chateau that he tied a string across the main staircase and connected one end to a switch that would activate a small bell if anyone tripped the line. Another time, Alfred portrayed Grover sleeping in Erwin's bedroom on the third floor when he heard the locked doorknob jiggle.[43] Creeping out of bed with his loaded pistol, Grover found no one but later noticed crushed ivy branches on the outside walls of the mansion where someone had climbed up and through a window to enter the third-floor hallway.

Such activities often attracted the attention of the neighbors too. On August 21, 1919, while Grover was hiding in the mansion, a neighbor told police he had seen Grover's figure in a window. A few dozen Philadelphia policemen and several federal agents surrounded the house, but they could not enter because they had no search warrant.

A touring car sat in the driveway aiming outward from the carport. At

From 1917 until 1919, Grover and Erwin fled to the mountains of Western Maryland, hiding in a comfortable tent along Antietam Creek west of Hagerstown. Befriended by a local farm family, pictured on a swing the Bergdolls made for the children, Grover and Erwin plied them with $50 and $100 bills to keep their campsite a secret. The tent, hidden behind wooden gates, included cots, a table, chairs, oil lamps, a wood floor, rugs, and a screen door. The campsite became the origin of the Bergdolls' buried gold. (Bergdoll Family, Historical Society of Pennsylvania)

[43] After the death of his wife, Sarah, Erwin often stayed at the Wynnefield mansion, hiding in a large bedroom on the third floor.

7 pm that night, Alfred recounts from newspaper reports, Grover suddenly burst through the main door, jumped into the car, and roared off. The lawmen had no chance of catching him because none had automobiles. Fifteen minutes later, Alfred writes, a Hudson Super Six returned to the Wynnefield mansion, almost tipping over as it swerved into the front lawn to the steps leading up to the wrap-a-round portico. Out jumped tall and slender Erwin to be let into the house with a flung-opened door.

Again, police could not enter because they didn't have a warrant. However, they managed to secure a few cars to be ready for pursuit if necessary. Then, at 10 pm, Erwin ran from the mansion and sped off with the Super Six into West Philadelphia. The officers chased him in a police car, several firing shots wildly into the night, but their driving was no match for the race champion, Erwin, who quickly lost them on the side streets leading westward out of the city.

Then, in another Keystone Cops scenario, Grover roared back into the Wynnefield yard in his touring car and bounded up the steps to the inside of the house. Still waiting for their search warrant, the lawmen, now surrounded by hundreds of spectators, watched the house all night until, finally, at 7 am, they stormed the portico with drawn pistols. Emma met them at the screen door with a gun aimed squarely at federal agents Todd Daniel and Joseph McDevitt.

"I'll shoot the first man who comes into this house without papers," Emma growled. The agents were helpless without a warrant. All they could do was mill about the porch and yard and inspect Grover's car. They spied a long steel pipe inside the vehicle with a lump of lead molded around one end, resembling a crude weapon, according to Alfred.

The federal agents returned to their offices at the grand old Post Office building on Chestnut Street and waited for a warrant to be approved through U.S. Attorney Kane and the federal courts. They told newspaper reporters from the *Record*, conveniently located next door, that they would keep the house surrounded and go in with force if and when they got a warrant.

When the federal men returned to the Wynnefield mansion a few hours later, they tried again to convince Emma to let them in to search for Grover. She still refused, demanding they show a warrant. The old lady kicked a federal marshal's foot out of her door, waved her pistol dangerously, and displayed such a disheveled appearance that they believed she had slept in her clothes, grasping her weapon all night. Barricaded behind the thick oak door of the mansion, Emma could not convince the men to leave the porch, however, and they settled comfortably into wicker chairs and a porch swing, waiting for their search warrant paperwork.

Rumors flew among the spectators watching from the street. Grover had bravely returned home after serving the Army under an assumed name, some wrongly believed. Neighbors claimed he had been home for two weeks. The curious crowd grew so large that people blocked the 52nd Street and Wynnefield Avenue intersection, the main thoroughfare from the western portion of Philadelphia into the vast west Fairmount Park.

Policemen on horses cleared a narrow pathway for cars with gawking drivers to pass through. A few prominent Philadelphians happened on the scene and decided to stay to watch. Among them was the boxing promoter "Diamond Lew" Bailey.

Bergdoll's brother-in-law Albert Hall motored along 52nd Street, noticed the commotion, and asked a boy on the street what was happening.

"Grover Cleveland Bergdoll's in there, and he's liable to shoot all of us full of holes any minute," the boy's high-pitched reply exclaimed. Hall said he was done mixing in with the Bergdoll family affairs. He had been through enough of Grover's escapades with the police and wisely motored on to the nearby mansion he shared with his wife Elizabeth.

From the Wynnefield mansion's porch, reporters quizzed Emma, still positioned behind the partly opened oak door and the closed screen door. She declared to anyone listening that Grover had come home but went out again to meet with his attorney.

"Would you have shot at the police if they tried to force their way in?" they asked. "You bet I would," Emma retorted in her thick German accent. "I know my rights. They cannot come in here without a warrant."

Emma was still smarting from the last time federal agents and police entered her home and searched for Grover with a warrant, not finding him or anything of value to their investigation. She claimed, but was cautious with her wording, that someone stole items from the house at the time. She affirmed with a gun, "If they try to break in now without a search warrant, someone will be killed."

The standoff continued—Emma in the doorway, the officers comfortable in chairs on the large stone porch. Then, at about 2 pm, perhaps warned by her attorney that a search warrant had been approved, Emma declared she would allow agent Daniel and three other men to search the chateau.

Entering through the porch door and into the ornate main hallway of shiny, darkened wood trimming nearly consumed by the massive staircase and a tall grandfather clock on the first stair landing, the men remained under close watch by Emma as they scoured the 35-room mansion from the red tile roof to the bowling alley in the basement. Never releasing the pistol from her hand, Emma even led the federal agents on a tour of all three floors of the carriage house and the chicken coop out back.

Crossing the lawn with the men in tow, Emma called for her dog, Kaiser. Holding the paws of the German Shepherd, she amusingly asked Kaiser, "You're not afraid of the bluecoats, are you?" Then, sullenly, Emma lamented that the other family dog, Hindenburg, had been hit by a car and killed a few days earlier.

Halfway through the search, the federal warrant papers finally arrived at the mansion. The agents, of course, demanded another probe. This time, Emma's chauffeur led them through the maze of stairways, doors, and hallways from the attic bedrooms to the coal chutes beneath the portico. Again, they found nothing and no one. Condensing the newspaper accounts of the event, Alfred wrote that grandmother Emma roared gleefully when the disappointed agents returned to bid her farewell.

Realizing there would be no shootout and no capture of the notorious draft-dodging Bergdolls, the spectators gradually dispersed, save for a few mounted police officers and neighbors still gossiping about what they thought would happen at the mansion. Then Albert Hall arrived at the house, and with help from a companion and the Bergdoll chauffeur, managed to get Grover's car engine started, and the vehicle backed into the carriage house, closing the large wooden doors.

Hall was still involved in Bergdoll family matters, after all. He had arrived from his country home in Mount Holly, New Jersey, and waited at his (and Elizabeth's) nearby mansion for the crowd to disperse before appearing at the Bergdoll chateau. In and out of the house, the men stomped, busily tending to Grover's touring car, consulting with Emma and, reporters noted, a mysterious man in a gray suit. Then, Hall drove away in his roadster while the chauffeur departed in the Bergdolls' touring car, possibly heading off toward Hall's farm in New Jersey and a neighboring federal jurisdiction.

Alfred suggested they managed to sneak Grover into the touring car through a tunnel leading from the mansion to the carriage house.[44]

Later, the defeated and smarting federal agents declared they found the Hudson Super Six used by Erwin to race away from the Wynnefield mansion at his farm near Broomall. They said it had bullet holes in the back of the car. Erwin was not found.

By the weekend of August 23 and 24, calmness had returned to the Wynnefield mansion. The *Inquirer* reported that the grounds were left unguarded, and Emma was gaily picking lima beans with her niece in the garden. Overheard by the reporter, Emma declared, "Groffer, he likes lima beans for supper, *sehr wohl. Sie sind sehr gut.*"

Later in the day, Emma sat on the porch and told the reporter that she only wanted her sons to be treated like the thousands of other American draft dodgers who were being forgiven for their crimes after the war. She said she did not raise her boys to be soldiers. They had gentle souls and could not stand the sight of blood. She suggested they didn't mind being shot at by police in their fleeing cars, but they could never shoot and be shot at in a trench.

"*Ach, Himmel—nein.* Groffer and Erwin, neffer could they do it. Neffer should they fight against good German boys, other mothers' sons. War is all wrong."

Emma railed against the American wartime draft in contrast to her native land, Germany. She said everyone must go to war there, but in the United States, "they pick who they want to go, like my sons, and let others stay." She claimed Erwin's name

---

[44] Reference to a tunnel from the Wynnefield mansion basement to the elaborate carriage house is made a few times in the incredible Bergdoll story but there is no proof that one ever existed. The tunnel story was mostly advanced by patriotic and gun-toting Philadelphia men who organized in an effort to help federal agents capture the Bergdoll boys.

156 • THE BERGDOLL BOYS

was moved up in the draft and that he should have been exempted because he was a farmer. Still grieving over the death of Erwin's wife, Emma "meditatively rubbed the sore ear of her rabbit dog, Kaiser." She had locked up the German Shephard while authorities searched the house, and he had hurt himself trying to break free.

"He wanted his freedom, just like my Groffer," she told the reporter.

Meanwhile, Charles advised Grover and Erwin to give up at the Broomall farm.[45] Instead, three weeks later, in September 1919, as things had cooled from the police search and the waning summer weather, Grover arrived at the farm and picked Erwin up for another trip to their tent hideout in the Maryland mountains. The Bergdoll boys were on the run again.

"While we stayed at Hagerstown, we fished and hunted nearly all the time," Erwin recalled. For several months in late 1919, the Bergdoll boys lived in a large white canvas and wood pole tent with a porch along the banks of Antietam Creek near Keedysville, Maryland. Their tent was complete with a wood plank floor, hooked rugs, a small bureau and washbasin, chairs, a table, lamps, cots for sleeping, and a screen door.

For entertainment, the brothers built a small rope swing for the children who lived on the farm near where they were land-squatting but for which they were paying generously. Their Philadelphia companion and employee, Fitzhugh Lee Creedon, would often stay with them, posing as the camper if someone came nosing around the campsite.

Appearing similar to officers' tents of the American Civil War, photographs taken by Grover show the large 18 by 10 feet tent with taut ropes stretching to steel stakes in the ground and a long canvas porch extending from the main structure. How the rural and remote location south of Hagerstown was chosen isn't known. Still, when Grover and Erwin first arrived to set up the tent, the farm owners along Smoketown Road, Winton, and Otelia Nalley, approached to ask what they were doing. It didn't take long for them to become friendly and acquainted because Grover immediately handed the Nalleys a wad of cash. He told them his name was Knickerbocker, and he would explore Civil War history in the area.

The Nalleys soon invited the Bergdoll boys for dinner in their farmhouse. Winton and Grover became so friendly that they even took a side trip to the nearby Antietam battlefield, where Grover wandered along the sunken road (Bloody Lane) of Sharpsburg, where more than five thousand Union and Confederate troops were killed. He snapped several photographs of the soldiers' monuments with his box camera.[46]

---

[45] In 1919, while Erwin was gone, Sarah's parents remained on the Broomall farm and tried to run it without success. Erwin's machine shop was also empty and abandoned, with Grover's Wright B Flyer sitting on a trailer. Louis' Blériot was also abandoned there, packed in the barn rafters.

[46] The photographs remain part of Alfred Bergdoll's collection at the Historical Society of Pennsylvania in Philadelphia.

Along with meat, eggs, and vegetables from their farm, the Nalleys gave the Bergdolls buggy rides to Boonsboro to catch the trolley into Hagerstown, where they would board a train for Philadelphia and, when needing to escape, points west.

Riding with Nalley allowed Grover to keep his car hidden in the woods or stashed in a garage in Hagerstown. Along with farming, Winton Nalley also worked for the B & O Railroad, Washington County branch. He provided Knickerbocker with train schedules and fetched out-of-town newspapers left aboard the trains, reporting anything suspicious.

When select Bergdoll visitors arrived from Philadelphia, they would check into the Hotel Vivian in downtown Hagerstown, frequently tipping the owner-proprietor, Owen D. Sherley, and his wife, Mary, for meals in their rooms, privacy, and secrecy. The Sherleys, whether they knew the real identity of the men or not, eagerly obliged.

In Hagerstown, the Hotel Vivian was tucked into South Jonathan Street between the tall German Hotel Dagmar and the slightly smaller brick Shockey furniture store. The B & O train depot was convenient across the street. The brick and stone four-story Hotel Vivian called itself "strictly European," containing 36 rooms at a dollar or a dollar and a quarter per day (with a bath). It had bowling alleys and billiard rooms attached. A step lower in class than the elegant Dagmar, the Vivian was frequented by salesmen and showgirls who appeared at the nearby Maryland Theater.

The Bergdoll boys used aliases at the hotel; Grover became James Carson. Erwin became John Roberts or Edward Brown. Judge Romig registered at the hotel as H. Watt. Other alias names were James Smith and Richard Snyder. The hotel clerk said the men checked in and out from July 1918 until late December 1919, claiming they were from Butler, Pennsylvania. They also rented space in the hotel's garage for Grover's car. The men were always suspicious of being identified as the Bergdolls. They never used the elevator, although sometimes their rooms were on the top floor. They settled their room accounts with $100 bills.

Then, as cold weather settled into western Maryland, sometime around Christmas 1919, Grover and Erwin abandoned their tent, paid their hotel tab, and motored home to Philadelphia under the darkness of night. Dropping Erwin at his Broomall farm, Grover stashed his Hudson behind the large doors of the Wynnefield carriage house and hid with Emma in his mansion.

It would be the last Christmas they would celebrate together for years.

Otelia Nalley said Grover left behind the tent and camping furniture and equipment, a wood-chopping ax, a small kerosene can, and a lariat. For many years afterward, Hagerstown residents also believed Grover left behind a fortune in gold buried somewhere in the Maryland mountains. It became the myth of the Bergdoll gold.

CHAPTER TEN

The Bergdoll Casket

Philadelphia, Pennsylvania, 1921

Just picture Company (E)
Right after Germany
Fighting for Liberty
Protecting Gay Paree
We'll get the Kaiser, Rotten Miser
Fill him full of Lead
We'll break his G.D. Head
Pvt. Arthur S. Ruston, Syracuse, NY, A-E-F France, 1918[1]

A long, black Philadelphia and Reading Railroad engine eased into the cavernous shed of the Reading Terminal between Philadelphia's Market and Arch Streets at precisely 10 am on Tuesday, August 30, 1921. It pulled a particular train of cars, and the passengers required no instructions or guidance from a conductor.[2]

They were all silent.

They were dead.

Along with heavy industrial freight from New Jersey and New York and dairy, meat, and produce from the Garden State, the boxcars carried flag-draped pine coffins of 50 American sailors, soldiers, and Marines from the Great War. Traced, documented, and exhumed from French cemeteries by the Army's Graves Registration Service personnel, the coffins had been offloaded from an Army transport ship at Hoboken, New Jersey, and stacked in the boxcars for the rail trip southward to Philadelphia.

The battle for Europe had been over for nearly three years, and finally, these local boys' bodies, disinterred in France, were returning for burial at home. Mothers, fathers, widows, siblings, grandparents, friends, neighbors, officials, police officers,

---

[1] Provided by Ruston's great-grandson, John Rizzo. The poem is from Rustin's diary of his journey through the war and its aftereffects from May 1918 to March 1919.

[2] The description of the body of Private Russell C. Gross returning to the United States is from several newspapers and court testimony and depositions. Gross's personal life details are from Ancestry.com, obituaries, and family records.

firefighters, and dignitaries watched silently. When the train's brakes released their compressed air, the boiler expelled its final cough of steam, and the wailing began.

Several minutes passed before the boxcar doors slid open with a clanking, and the first pine box was carried to the concrete platform. It provided time for Philadelphia's florists to mount small bouquets atop the coffins, sent by an anonymous donor each time a train filled with war dead arrived in the city. Flowers add brightness and color to a tan or brown box and among the mourners' black suits, dresses, and veils, but along with the American flags' red, white, and blue, the colors were lost in the array of 48 stars and 13 stripes.

Wives, mothers, grandmothers, sisters, and daughters buried their heads in their hands or men's chests on the platform, too distraught to look. Seventy-five traffic officers from the Philadelphia Police Department formed a blue line to allow the coffins to be carried off the train with dignity. Still, they found that their most important role was to embrace and comfort the families who broke down at the site of the first flag-draped box.

High above the somber crowd were three-hinged arches holding the roof for the massive space of 267 by 559 feet. The first single-span high-arch train shed in America was built in 1893 in a controversial move by the Philadelphia and Reading Railroad that displaced the favorite street-side Butchers and Farmers Market and the Franklin Market. In a compromise, the railroad offered the market merchants space beneath the new train shed, where they grew by 1921 into the famous Reading Terminal Market with 250 food dealer stalls and 100 farmer stalls. As a result, while the air was silent in the upstairs train shed, crowds of Philadelphians and Pennsylvania farmers were loudly dealing over food and prices and the weather and politics, perhaps oblivious, so long after the war, of the sad occasion above them.

The remains of U.S. Army Private 1st Class Russell Conrad Gross were in the first coffin carried off the train.[3] He was the 11th person to sign up for the draft from his Philadelphia Draft District 2, Local Draft Board 32. He was summoned for examination on September 21, 1917. He carried draft order 845, and Russell Gross went to war only when he did because Grover Bergdoll wouldn't. Since then, Gross was known as Bergdoll's proxy, substitute, and replacement, the brave Philadelphia youth called up when the slacker ran. He took a bullet for Bergdoll, they said.

And he died a hero in the Argonne Forest.[4] Russell Gross was 25 when he became trapped in machine-gun fire in the Meuse-Argonne offensive on October 24, 1918.

---

[3] In some circles in Philadelphia, it was called "the Bergdoll casket with the body of Russell Gross." Newspapers reported the Gross family to be on the platform, but no descriptions of them are available.

[4] Research by the former Russell C. Gross American Legion Post in the Overbrook neighborhood of Philadelphia revealed that Gross was not the next man in line for the draft but, rather, "the first man to die in battle after being called ahead of his turn by the defection of Bergdoll." The next man in line from draft board 32 was draftee 837, Frank Caredydd Williams, who served honorably, survived the war, and died in 1966, the same year as Grover.

Part of Company E, 328th Infantry, 82nd Division, Private Gross was advancing on enemy lines with his automatic rifle team when "utterly disregarding his safety, [he] pushed forward until he was killed by an enemy machine-gun bullet. His example of unselfishness was an inspiration to the other men of his platoon," said a citation by 82nd Division Brigadier General Julian R. Lindsey.[5]

In his last letter home to his parents in their Philadelphia rowhouse, Gross scrawled, "If it's God's will that I come through OK, I can at least feel as though I had done my share for civilization."

At 24, Russell Gross was unmarried and worked as a clerk at Belmont Manufacturing Company in Philadelphia, a woolen mill producing neckwear, hosiery, sweaters, and other knitted garments. However, his registration took some convincing. When the tall, slender, boyish-looking man with black hair and brown eyes was classified under Pignet's formula for physical fitness, he was underweight and unfit for service.[6]

As a young boy, Russell had been raised by his parents, Henry, and Clara, in a simple two-story brick rowhouse between the elaborate grounds of the 1875 Philadelphia Exposition and the Philadelphia Zoo in the East Parkside neighborhood with his brothers Walter and Wesley and a sister, also named Clara. His father worked as a butcher and corner store merchant, and his mother stayed at home raising the children.

The family was first- and second-generation German (Russell's paternal grand-parents were born in Germany), but they had quickly acclimated to American and Philadelphia urban-industrial culture. Sometime after 1911, the family moved farther west in the city to the Carroll Park neighborhood, closer to the elegant homes of the new Philadelphia neighborhoods of Overbrook, Overbrook Farms, and Wynnefield, the site of the Bergdoll mansion at 52nd and Wynnefield Avenue. It placed Gross in the local draft board 32, managed by John Dwyer.

Around the working-class neighborhoods of West Philadelphia, Gross was always known as the "next man in line," the poor rowhouse lad drafted into the war in the rich mansion *Jungling's* place.

Thirteen days after his body arrived by train in Philadelphia, Private Gross was buried in Fernwood Cemetery, East Lansdowne, Pennsylvania, on September 12, 1921. The horse-drawn funeral cortege included his flag-draped casket on a gun carriage through his West Philadelphia community from his funeral at Fletcher Memorial

---

[5] Press reports suggest that Gross was killed by the same German machine gunners who were captured by the hero Medal of Honor recipient, Cpl. Alvin C. York of Tennessee. However, the promoted Sgt. York's heroics occurred on October 8, 1918. Gross was killed on October 24. Incidentally, the war would end 18 days later.

[6] Pignet's formula was used in 1917 to calculate fitness for military service based on height, weight, and chest circumference. But local draft boards were allowed subjectivity to admit those who were slightly under- or overweight and otherwise physically fit.

Church near the home where he was born. It was such a monumental event that all the newspapers carried the story with photographs. Many Army soldiers, Marines, and Navy sailors turned out with gun salutes and flags, marching behind the gun carriage. The funeral procession stopped traffic with mourners and the curious standing four and five deep at the curbs. Gross' remains were laid to rest, where his parents and siblings would later join him. His date of death was misapplied on the Gross family gravestone. It says October 26.

In his memory, the American Legion in Philadelphia's rapidly expanding Overbrook neighborhood renamed its post the Russell C. Gross American Legion Post 562.[7] Years later, in 1934, with endorsement from the post commanders, Gross' mother, Clara, applied for federal pension benefits in her son's name.

While Grover Bergdoll was still on the run and enjoying his endless supply of inherited cash and gold, Gross' mother was awarded $10 per month for 20 months, or a total of $200 in survivor benefits for the loss of her son in the war.

Photographed in front of his row house in Philadelphia, Russell Conrad Gross was often portrayed as the "next man in line" in Grover Bergdoll's draft district. Publicity over Gross' death in the war and his inaccurate portrayal as Grover's replacement fomented more hatred for the draft-dodging Bergdolls. Private Gross served bravely and was posthumously awarded high honors, but another man was drafted before him. (Walter Gross, Pennsylvania Historical and Museum Commission)

[7] The Russell C. Gross American Legion Post 562 was to have been endowed to memorialize Gross beyond the life of the Legion. It ceased operations around 1980.

CHAPTER ELEVEN

Captured

Philadelphia, Pennsylvania, January 1920[1]

Philadelphia police patrolman Charles F. Macready pulled a neighborhood ringer box to check in at the 29th Police District at midnight January 6–7, 1920. Although the veteran police officer's station was at 61st and West Thompson Streets in West Philadelphia, his regular foot patrol shift would extend until 8 am in the upscale Wynnefield neighborhood around Wynnefield Avenue and 63rd Street.

He thought it would be a routine night. Instead, it was the most exciting and adventurous night of his police career.[2]

At 6:45 am, Officer Macready grew suspicious about a large black car with its engine idling parked haphazardly at the intersection of Wynnefield and Bryn Mawr Avenues.[3]

Questioning the driver, Macready discovered that under orders from Philadelphia Department of Justice Special Agent John J. O'Conner, the driver had dropped seven federal agents nearby with a warrant to search the Bergdoll mansion at 52nd and Wynnefield.

The agents had been tipped that Grover had returned home and was hiding in the mansion.[4] Macready immediately hustled up the block to the front of the Bergdoll chateau. He was met by the federal agents milling about the front porch

---

[1] Most of the information in Chapter 12 is from sworn testimony at Grover's first court martial trial. Other descriptions are from first-person accounts of Grover's capture by police officers and federal agents. More details were provided by Grover's first-person account of his capture given to magazine journalist Leighton Blood for *Hearst's International.*

[2] Macready was already viewed as somewhat of a hero. He had given up his secure police job in 1917 to join the Army and resumed his position when the war was over.

[3] During Patrolman Macready's testimony on March 11, 1920, the court reporter wrote "Grinsmore" Avenue for the location of the parked federal car. Still, the recorder likely mistook it for Bryn Mawr Avenue, a prominent intersection one block from the Bergdoll mansion.

[4] While the tip said Grover was hiding in his Wynnefield mansion, it did not reveal that both Grover and Erwin were reunited in the mansion on the night of January 6, 1920, playing cards together in the kitchen. Erwin left late at night to hide in the barn at his farm in Broomall.

with their field supervisor, assistant agent Leo J. Gorman, who loudly argued with Emma behind the heavy oak front door.

The old lady was cinched with a leather gun belt, waving a Colt .38 Special, and threatening to shoot the first man who crossed the threshold. Despite them identifying as federal agents, Emma kept hollering that they were burglars and that she could shoot them if they tried to get in.

Gorman was relieved to see Macready because he formerly lived in the Bergdolls' Brewerytown neighborhood, and Emma knew him by sight. Gorman hoped Macready's appearance would calm the 59-year-old Bergdoll matriarch, but it didn't. She grew more belligerent, scrambling from front to back door, waving the pistol and threatening to shoot.

Realizing the gravity of the rapidly escalating confrontation, Macready ran a short distance to a call box and rang up reinforcements.

Five more police officers arrived at the chateau, joining the federal agents, and positioning themselves at the front and rear doors. They had warrants for the arrest of Grover and Erwin and to search the house. Concurrently, federal agents were at the Bergdoll farm in Broomall, the old brick mansion in Brewerytown, and Albert and Elizabeth Bergdoll Hall's farm in Mount Holley, New Jersey.

By 8 am, seven federal agents and five Philadelphia police officers surrounded the house with several others arriving soon thereafter. They also attracted about 300 spectators to watch the capture of the infamous draft-dodging brothers. Some of them had a rope tied with a noose and were ready to string it to a telegraph pole.

Failing to convince Emma to let them in peacefully, Gorman was about to pry open the back door leading to a summer kitchen porch with an iron crowbar when the old lady hollered, "The first son-of-a-bitch that comes in will be shot."

Gorman backed off, pleading with Emma to recognize Macready, a patrolman she had known for years, and to negotiate for Grover's surrender. She refused.

"I don't care a damn who you are or what officer you have with you; you are not coming in, and the first one who comes in will be shot," she roared.

Philadelphia police officer Thomas J. Carroll joined the federal agents on the front porch, and with agent Adelbert "A. J." Wismer, who had been called up to Philadelphia from Atlanta, they used a mop handle to break a leaded glass panel beside the door.[5] While the panel was too narrow for a man to fit through, Carroll and Wismer could easily reach in to turn the deadbolt lock.

With the revolver in one hand and blackjack in the other, Emma scrambled toward the vestibule, where she momentarily held Carroll on the porch by pointing her gun

---

[5] In his first-person description of the raid, Agent Wismer described Emma's gun as a Colt .45 "with a barrel as big as the end of a beer keg." Wismer described the crowd outside the mansion as numbering one thousand. He also credited another federal agent for wrestling the gun away from Emma, while Philadelphia police credited themselves.

at him. Carroll backed off until Emma spun around to answer the new commotion at the back door. Carroll then managed to reach in and unlock the front door.

Out back, seizing his opportunity after successfully prying open the door to the summer kitchen, Gorman ordered agent L. E. Howe to shoot the lock on the next door leading into the central kitchen of the mansion.

With two blasts from his service revolver, Howe destroyed the lock, and the men rushed inside.

Overwhelmed by the burst of police and agents into the Bergdoll mansion, Emma was quickly subdued. Patrolman Macready grabbed the sizeable old woman around the waist, flipped her gun to an agent, and led her to a chair in the kitchen.

"There was a whole mob shouting at the door," Emma later said. "When I tried to open the door, they fired shots at it, and had it not been that the door was thick, they would have killed me."

Gorman leaned over Emma, read the federal search warrant to her, and shoved a copy into her lap. It declared that the agents could tear the mansion apart, if necessary, to find Grover and Erwin. They asked for Emma's cooperation. Defeated, she led them upstairs, where they began searching the bedrooms.[6] The growing mob of spectators inched closer to the front porch, trying to glimpse what might happen.

Minutes later, Macready was on an upper floor while Carroll and Agent Wismer swept down the broad winding staircase from the third floor, closely examining the ornate curved wood-paneled walls for signs of a door.

Carroll later testified, "I discovered a window seat between the second and third floors. I stood there looking at it for a few seconds, and I didn't think a man could get in there. I lifted the cushion off this window seat and lifted the lid, and it looked to me like a bundle of clothes lying inside the seat box. I put my hand on top of it and felt a hard object slightly moving. I pulled the cover off and found Bergdoll lying in there."

Agent Wismer also claimed a similar experience. "As Carroll and I reached the landing between the second and third floors and raised one of the seats, I saw a Navajo blanket inside move. I pulled back the blanket—and there was Grover Cleveland Bergdoll in person.[7]

Agent Wismer and Officer Carroll held their guns to Bergdoll, ordering him to step out of the window box.

"Don't shoot; I'll come easy," he replied.

Grover stepped out of the box, and the lawmen first noticed how badly the fugitive's dark hair had been clipped, growing back by about an inch. He also displayed about two weeks of beard growth, partially covering the inverted horseshoe scar on his chin.

---

[6] Despite her threats to shoot, Emma never fired her gun.
[7] Who actually made the discovery of Bergdoll in the window seat has been lost to the ever-changing narrative over the next 20 years of the Bergdoll saga.

The Philadelphia police officers who captured Grover in the Wynnefield mansion stairway window box pose with their captive on January 7, 1920. (Bergdoll Family Collection)

Carroll said, "Then, I was forced to put the gun up against his ribs and told him if he didn't put his hands up, I would put him down. He said, all right. I won't try to get away. You got me!"

The Bergdoll family's version of how Grover was captured differs from the story told by any lawman. Many years later, neighborhood residents recalled to Alfred Bergdoll that they were all sitting along the street watching the confrontation and rooting for Grover. They observed Emma hollering and waving her pistol and the lawmen crouching for cover behind the thick stone walls of the porch.

Emma had been awakened by the agents ringing the doorbell and pounding the doors and windows. Alfred wrote about Gorman's actions in his diary-manuscript: "Open the door! We're going to get in if we have to tear down the house."

Angry at being disturbed, Emma waved her pistol and cried out, "The first person who enters will have his brains blown out. You can all go to hell!"

In another version of how Emma was subdued, Alfred writes that agent Howe dove into the old lady's legs when she ran wildly from the front to the back, where she heard the gunshots fired into the house lock on the summer kitchen door. While Macready held her, Alfred explains, Howe wrestled the pistol from her hand.

Alfred offered more of the family version of Emma and Grover's calm and collected nature when they were arrested and captured. Emma led the men through the mansion, searching more than 30 rooms, some trailing well behind her.

Talking loudly, perhaps to cover any noises Grover may make, Emma led them down the stairway between the third and second floors, "on which was a long and built-in cushioned bench." Thinking his mother was alone, Grover lifted the cover to the window seat at this time, "rose up from the storage compartment under the bench and looked straight into the startled face of a policeman."

Alfred said his father related the story of his capture "many times over many years, with no variation." As Grover was led down the stairs, Emma got him a suit, shirt, and collar, which he was allowed to put on.[8]

While holding Grover prisoner, Officer Carroll reportedly described their last encounter many years earlier.

"We're even now, Bergdoll. Maybe you don't remember me, but I remember you. You're the bird who shot at me while I was swimming on your place when I was just a kid."[9]

When pulled from the window box, Grover was dressed in khaki pants and a simple cotton undershirt. Despite pleas by Emma to allow Grover to change his clothes and eat breakfast before leaving the house, the authorities said they wouldn't allow it, except for a warm coat and a hat. During their search, they found several guns and other weapons in the mansion, including a stiletto, a rifle, a shotgun, and "a wicked-looking pistol, a Colt .41 Frontier model."[10]

Aware of the lynching-ready mob with a noose in the front yard, they wanted to quickly get Grover into a car to take him downtown to the Department of Justice field office in the Philadelphia Post Office.[11]

"I thought he should be kept away from a crowd of clamoring workmen on the outside who were trying to get a rope off the telegraph pole. They wanted to string him up," declared Macready.[12]

---

[8] This account is questionable because Grover's lawyers later pressed police and federal agents on why Grover was not allowed to be properly dressed before being taken to court and jail. Photographs show him in a shirt, and jacket, but no collar.

[9] Kids from Philadelphia often went swimming in the dammed portion of Darby Creek on the Bergdolls' Broomall farm. Grover had been accused of firing guns toward them and laughing as the naked boys scrambled out of the creek seeking cover in the woods.

[10] Bergdoll gun descriptions are from a photograph taken at the Philadelphia Police evidence room inside Philadelphia City Hall. Weapons expert Francis Lombardi helped identify the guns from the photograph.

[11] Authorities testified that they also found loaded revolvers, ammunition, Bowie knives, and Maxim silencers on rifles in nearly every mansion room. A press photograph of some of the weapons being cataloged by police appears to show a Lange pistol 08, known as an artillery pistol, two Springfield Trapdoor .45-70 long guns with bayonets, a .22 rifle with a Maxim silencer, a pump action shotgun, the gauge unknown, a pocket Derringer, and an early production Swiss Vetterli rifle. The Colt .41 and Emma's Colt .38 are not pictured.

[12] Patrolman Macready had also seen the fugitive, Grover, at his mansion in the year prior, 1919. Then, when he tried to engage federal agents to burst onto the Wynnefield property to arrest him, Macready says they balked because it was near dusk and warrants were not allowed to be served after dark.

Rarely seen images inside the Wynnefield mansion from 1939. The staircase leading to Grover's window box hiding place, the front door where sidelights were broken by police to get inside, the first-floor sitting room, just off the portico leading to the front door and the carriage house. (Historical Society of Pennsylvania)

The staircase window box where Grover was found hiding on January 7, 1920. These photographs were taken between 1939 and the early 1940s when the mansion was stripped of its elegant woodwork before demolition. Philadelphia police and federal agents claimed discovery of Grover hiding here, a disagreement that was never resolved. (Historical Society of Pennsylvania. Temple University Urban Archives)

Guns were confiscated during Grover's capture at his Wynnefield, Philadelphia mansion on January 7, 1920, and Philadelphia police took silencers for evidence in the Bergdoll trials. Seventy-five years later, the author witnessed police remove 1920s-era guns from the Philadelphia City Hall evidence room for destruction in a Pennsylvania steel mill blast furnace. (Temple University Urban Archives)

Additionally, a newspaper reporter known to the police as "Scoop" questioned if the man pulled from the window box was Bergdoll. Macready was sure he had the right man, but he ordered Bergdoll to remove his hat and turn his head, revealing through his whiskers the long scar from his neck up to the side of his face and the smaller inverted horseshoe scar surrounding his chin dimple.

"I told them that's his identification. That's him."

It's unknown why the federal agents' driver was not on the scene, but a Philadelphia man watching the events unfold from his large car on the street in front of the Bergdoll mansion offered to help.

"Let me haul that slacker to jail," West Philadelphia businessman W. H. Harmon crowed.

The lawmen hustled the handcuffed Bergdoll into the car's back seat and sped off for the Post Office.[13] Harmon wanted to reward the agents with $1,000 for making the arrest. He said he had lost his son and a nephew in the war and suggested they had taken Bergdoll's place.[14]

---

[13] According to Agent Wismer, it was common for federal agents to hire civilian drivers because their local field offices were not supplied with vehicles.

[14] At this time, rumors surfaced that Erwin had been hiding inside the grand piano in the main foyer and escaped when police and agents vacated the house. However, Alfred later dismissed this as fantasy because a man could not have fitted into the piano, especially with the lid closed.

Later that morning, Emma was arrested for aggravated assault and battery with a deadly weapon and the intent to kill. In ceremonial style, federal agents escorted her from the mansion in their top hats and long woolen coats. Philadelphia policemen in their stiff-billed caps, long double-breasted blue coats with brass buttons, and shiny brass badges hustled along the old lady's side, sure to get themselves into the press photographs. Some were grinning.

Emma was dressed in a long ermine-trimmed sealskin coat buttoned up to a fur neck muffler. She sported a simple hat with a few flowers, and hiding her handcuffs was a large ermine hand muffler. With her agent escort and multiple lawmen following her down the steps carrying an arsenal of weapons, the queen of Wynnefield held her muffler out front, arched her back, and in her heavy-laced boots, marched along the stone walk to a waiting automobile.

The hundreds of spectators jeered and cheered at the same time.

Within minutes of her court appearance in City Hall in Philadelphia, Emma tried to pay her $10,000 bail by pulling a wad of cash from the deep recesses of her layers of clothes. Court matrons claimed that when they counted up the money removed from Emma's bosom and stockings, it totaled $28,000. Told she could not pay her own bail with cash, Emma called her son-in-law, Albert Hall, to come with his checkbook. Sitting proudly at the front rail before the city magistrate, Emma reportedly shooed the press photographers to move back a few feet, changing their depth of field, a technique Grover had taught her to appear more attractive in photographs.

"I don't want to look too fat in the pictures," she declared with a bit of charm.

Emma also tried to turn things around in court, and she loudly claimed that police and federal agents stole jewelry and cash from the Wynnefield mansion during their search. She claimed they took a "belt" loaded with jewelry, including an unusual diamond bracelet worth $500 that she often wore wrapped around her wrist like a snake. She also claimed they took a $1,200 diamond ring and $3,000 in cash that she had hidden in an upstairs closet.[15]

To the magistrate, Emma admitted and then contradicted her admission that she waved her pistol at the police and federal agents. It was the same gun she used at the Broomall farm "to scare away chicken thieves and others from the place." She said she "always had a gun about" since her husband died 23 years earlier. She said the police called her "vile names" and that the offensive language was why she waved the gun and threatened to shoot. Conversely, when the police and federal agents told the magistrate of their scuffle with the old lady, they said Emma called them insulting names, not the other way around.

---

[15] Later, Emma said she paid the Burns Detective Agency to recover the "stolen" items, but they were unsuccessful. Police and federal agents insisted that nothing was stolen while searching the mansion.

"The police, they lied like hell," roared Emma. "They said I cursed them, the bastards. I never used bad language at all. Before I could say a bit, they jumped on me, throttled me, and took my revolver. I never had a chance to point my pistol."

Agents for Philadelphia law firms, whose job was to loiter about the courtrooms to pick up clients, were astonished to hear that Emma did not have a lawyer to represent her on the charges. The courtroom crowd was thick with reporters, photographers, and spectators, and soon it became so warm that Emma opened her sealskin coat to reveal that she still wore a belt around her waist holding a leather blackjack. Reporters said that when police swarmed the woman to give up the weapon, she didn't protest.

While booked on the assault and battery charge, Emma was photographed, her foot measured, and her fingerprints inked. She was embarrassed but knew she could walk free by paying the bail. Arriving from his Wynnefield mansion, Hall was delayed long enough that Emma was briefly held in the City Hall jail. In her broken English, she amused her fellow inmates by cursing about her ordeal with the police and federal agents, but the jail matron, Alfred wrote, "was shocked."

After Emma was removed from court, federal agents claimed they found thousands of copies of pro-German propaganda in the Wynnefield mansion titled *The Reconquest of America*. Special agent Todd Daniel described the pamphlet as "one of the rottenest pieces of German propaganda" and "literature to give weak-minded Americans the impression that England is aiming to dominate this country."

While advising a magistrate that his agents confiscated the assortment of knives, shotguns and pistols, and rifles with silencers, Agent Daniel also said Emma claimed Grover took $67,000 with him when he fled nearly two years earlier.[16] He had just $105 on him when he was captured.

While Emma was in court, plans were being made to transport Grover to jail at Castle Williams at Fort Jay on Governors Island in New York Harbor.[17] It was the Army's eastern division of the federal prison at Fort Leavenworth, Kansas. It was also known as the east coast's Alcatraz but would be Grover's new home for only a few months.

Waiting for the 11 am train for New York, other travelers recognized Grover from the intense and nonstop press coverage while evading capture for over two years. Among more "taunts and jeers," as Alfred described them, one man in the train platform crowd ordered Grover to remove his wool olive-drab military-issue top coat given to him only to keep warm.

---

[16] This is another example of the significant disparity in the amount of cash Grover reportedly used to fund his many months on the run until he was captured.

[17] Named Governor's Island when it was reserved for royal governors of New York and their families. Since 1784, it's been spelled without an apostrophe.

"You had a chance to get a whole uniform, and you turned it down," the man scolded. Grover kept the coat on and, surrounded by federal agents John H. Sparks and O'Conner, waited for the train to New York.

Grover remained handcuffed to Sparks, and together they boarded the Pennsylvania Railroad smoker car from Broad Street station in Philadelphia to Penn Station in New York City. While heading to the Battery ferry for the short ride to Governors Island and the Army jail at Castle Williams, Grover and his retinue of federal agents were allowed to stop in a small restaurant near the railroad's Cortlandt Street Ferry Depot in lower Manhattan for lunch.[18]

Followed the entire way, Grover was questioned by a reporter for the *Ledger*. He claimed that while on the run for two years, he had been in Milwaukee, Chicago, Omaha, San Diego, Los Angeles, San Francisco, and many other communities. He claimed he would not have run if he had been allowed to join the Aviation Corps in the Army.

"My god, I'm thankful it's over now. It's been a terrible time. I had about reached the point of giving myself up when they got me this morning," he said.

Grover claimed he arrived at the Wynnefield mansion in his car from Wilmington, Delaware, two days prior. He said that when he heard pounding on the front door, he got out of bed, ran for the stairway window box, and hid. Even Emma didn't know where he had gone.

Apparently in good spirits, despite trying to maneuver a forkful of bratwurst into his mouth while handcuffed to Sparks' wrist, Grover regaled to the reporter how he was ticketed in Illinois while driving his car with the cutout open.[19] He gave the arresting officer his real name, but he was not recognized as the infamous fugitive draft dodger.

"A bunch of hams out there," Grover told the reporter about the police in Peoria.

Grover claimed he spent $12,000–13,000 to remain free, including the cost of a new car when the axle on his first automobile broke, but he wouldn't reveal where or how he got the money. On his way back to Wilmington, Delaware, and Philadelphia, he admitted stopping in Virginia, West Virginia, and Maryland from the west coast. He linked up with Thomas Furey in Baltimore and told him he was going home. He didn't know Furey was cooperating with federal agents after accidentally revealing Grover's plans to a friend at a Christmas party.[20]

---

[18] A simple explanation for this unusual lunch stop could be that they were waiting on the Battery–Governors Island ferry schedule.

[19] A cutout was an after-market valve installed inside a car exhaust pipe connected to a cable that allowed the driver to open the valve and produce a louder sound from the engine.

[20] While some newspapers reported that a girlfriend turned him in, Grover later told magazine writer Leighton Blood that "one of his best friends" betrayed him to the Department of Justice. It was Grover's childhood pal, Furey, while under threat of being charged as an accomplice in the case. While under a similar threat, Creedon was also cooperating by feeding information to the agents about Erwin.

Grover with two guards, Special Agent Sparks and Military Intelligence Captain Jesse B. Cottrell, on the New York City ferry to Castle Williams on January 7, 1920. Grover has cleverly placed his hand close to Sparks' arm, to hide that he's being held prisoner and cuffed. As an amateur photographer, Grover was always aware of impressions in a photograph, and often advised others how to pose. Grover would later use the name Sparks as an alias to illegally return to the United States from hiding in Germany. (Temple University Urban Archives)

In a statement three years later, Grover admitted his foolishness by sending taunting postcards to his pursuers. He said, "The last thing I expected when I went home that time was arrest."

Upon arrival at Castle Williams, the jeering and scowling continued, but this time, it was from the Army staff in charge of the small jail. Grover was formally charged with desertion from the Army. However, he contended, from his brief and incomplete law education at the University of Pennsylvania, he "was adjudged a draft dodger too quickly."

He said that despite his mother's public sentiment, he was not pro-German during the war. He claimed he bought $6,000 in Liberty Bonds and never sought refuge in Mexico. He was adamant that he had "no intention of deserting from the Army." He told the Judge Advocate General officers at Fort Jay that he was on vacation when his draft notice arrived in the mail and that he was labeled a deserter before he returned home. And when he did come home to find out he was wanted and might be shot, he became frightened.

"And then, I decided to beat it."

Grover said he was nearly caught only once on his long run from the law. Leaving his broken-down car in a Milwaukee garage for repairs, he returned to find the name "BERGDOLL" scrawled on the windscreen. When police detectives answered a tip from the garage owner and arrived on the scene, Grover jumped through a window and grabbed a trolley, taking it to the end of the line, where he made his way to the next town, Madison. He bought another car for cash and continued driving westward, "merrily on my way."

**

With Grover in jail, the Army and federal agents re-focused their attention on Erwin. Agent Daniel was quoted saying, "We're sure to get him. If he's wise, he'll comply with his mother's wishes and give himself up." They claimed his arrest would be made within weeks. However, it didn't happen for months until Erwin turned himself in for punishment.

Fitzhugh Lee Creedon, Erwin's friend, and accomplice, said Erwin was hiding in Charles' barn on the day Grover was captured. Late the next night, Erwin uncovered his car from stacks of hay in the barn's haymow and drove into the countryside. A short time afterward, Charles drove Creedon into the country, where they met Erwin. The fugitive and Creedon then went in Erwin's car to Baltimore while Charles returned to his farm. He had given Creedon $1,000 to fund Erwin's escape.

Sleeping for the night in the car, the pair met up with Furey the next day at a Baltimore apartment house. Unknown to the Bergdolls, their longtime friends and employees were cooperating with federal agents. The Irishman and war veteran Furey is the one who tipped them to Grover, hiding in the Wynnefield mansion.[21]

Agent Daniel also claimed that the Department of Justice would also conduct "wholesale raids" on other "slackers" in Philadelphia. Federal forgiveness of war draft dodgers had not yet taken hold in America. Perhaps this was also an attempt to demonstrate to the Bergdoll-consuming public that the feds weren't just picking on the rich Bergdolls but going after everyone who failed to report for duty.[22]

The *Inquirer* wrote about Grover and Erwin escaping the federal agents in the year prior (1919) as they "irritated the redoubtable Todd Daniel [chief federal agent in Philadelphia] and his dauntless band of non-effective sleuths." Of Emma, they said, "stout, whitehaired, sloppily dressed in a wrapper, the widow of the onetime greatest power in Philadelphia's Brewerytown and mother of the draft-ducking brothers, kept the city and federal officers from searching the home for the fugitives by meeting them at the door with a revolver whenever they attempted to enter."

Now, the federal officers had won half the battle. They had Grover in jail and could put him on trial.

---

[21] Furey had been such a close friend to Erwin and Grover since their boyhood days in Brewerytown that Grover once trusted him with $100,000 cash in $1,000 bills for depositing into Grover's bank account. Furey dutifully carried out the task.

[22] To the contrary, Grover was the only draft evader out of 78 in Philadelphia Draft District 2 who was prosecuted. And Grover got more newspaper publicity than all others combined, admitted Draft Board 32 Secretary Dwyer.

CHAPTER TWELVE

A Man Without a Country

Governors Island, New York, March 1920

On the morning after Grover arrived at the Army jail on Governors Island in New York Harbor, he was awakened at 6 am by reveille. He slept in a blue denim jail uniform of blouse-coat and pants with a large #10 painted white on the back of the button-down blouse. He was locked in cell #13 on the third floor of Castle Williams, a circular, three-story thick stone-walled fortification of casemates that held dozens of 10- and 15-inch guns dating to the War of 1812 and the defense of New York Harbor. His cell held a simple steel latticework fold-down cot and thin blue and white striped cotton ticking mattress, a small porcelain lavatory with one spout of cold running water, and a lidless porcelain rim toilet. The only way in and out was through a heavy-hinged door of iron bars. The walls and ceiling were made of sheets of heavily painted steel fastened with carriage bolts at the seams. What little heat there was came through a high wall vent too small for a human to fit.[1] There was no escape.

The cell afforded only a view across a hallway to the courtyard below. Other prisoners were fortunate to view the harbor, the skyline of lower Manhattan, Jersey City, New Jersey, and the Statue of Liberty. Located on the northwestern shore of Governors Island, next to a more extensive hexagonal fortification known as Fort Jay, Castle Williams was designed by a military engineer, Lt. Col. Jonathan Williams, great-nephew of American founding father Benjamin Franklin. After its use as a harbor protectorate diminished, Castle Williams became a Union Army prisoner-of-war camp where some one thousand Confederate troops were crammed into a space designed to hold 150.

---

[1] In the National Archives are several photographs of the inside and outside of Castle Williams on Governors Island, New York Harbor, circa 1930. They depict jail cells and the prison yard where Grover was allowed to exercise. Additionally, several press photographs survive of the Bergdolls at Governors Island, the court-martial trials, and the principals involved. Architectural surveys provided valuable information about the history and layout of Fort Jay, Castle Williams, and the buildings where Grover was court-martialed.

Castle Williams, New York Harbor, in the 1920s. Built between 1807 and 1811, it was part of the defense works to protect New York Harbor during the War of 1812. Its prison dates to the Civil War. The top-floor jail, including Grover's cell #13, was substantially remodeled in the 1930s, before Grover's second stint behind bars there in 1939. (Library of Congress)

By 1895, the imposing structure was one of 10 U.S. Army posts for military prisoners. Steel cells with metal grill prison doors and spiked windows too small for a human body were constructed on the third floor for up to 80 prisoners at a time. Some cells, including number 13 used for Bergdoll, were for solitary confinement. Immediately below the cells, on the second floor, were the guardrooms, washrooms, kitchen, and dining room.[2] The entire structure was nearly a full circle and 210 feet across.

The 8 by 10 feet jail cell was not what the mansion-raised millionaire from Philadelphia was used to, but it may have provided a brief respite from his two years on the run.

***

Meanwhile, back in Philadelphia, arising before dawn on January 8, 1920, Emma milked her cow in the barn behind the carriage house and, with the Wynnefield mansion still under police guard, prepared herself for a trip to New York to visit Grover.

---

[2] Description from *The New York Times*, April 4, 1897, and the U.S. Historical Architectural Building Survey, 1983 Library of Congress. By the time Grover arrived in January 1920, the upper casements had been further altered into jail cells.

She was already out on $10,000 bail on the charges of assault with intent to kill and trying to prevent service of a federal warrant by barring agents from entering the house and waving her loaded revolver at them. She was not charged with having a 3-foot-high stack of German propaganda leaflets scattered about the place.

Taking the morning train from North Philadelphia, Emma arrived on Governors Island with two men (Gibboney and Judge Romig) and a bundle of clothes she hoped to give to Grover.

After breakfast of fried bacon, eggs, toast, and coffee in his cell, Grover was allowed to walk up and down the stairway from the Castle Williams courtyard to the balcony for exercise. It was here where other prisoners first glimpsed their infamous fellow inmate. Newspaper reporters were allowed in the public areas, close enough to shout

A Castle Williams jail cell where Grover and Erwin were held for draft evasion trial. Grover had access to an unlimited supply of cash from Emma, which he spent to gain favors from guards and other prisoners. Here, Grover was read his 1920 court-martial sentence of five years in prison. Afterward, he turned to his fold-down cot and wept. (Library of Congress)

questions to Grover, who refused to answer, saying only that his attorney told him not to talk. He was assigned to Army lawyer Captain Bruce R. Campbell for his military defense. His civilian attorney had yet to be engaged.

Grover was charged with desertion during war, which was punishable by death. To hear the maximum punishment for such a crime must have been frightening. Still, Captain Campbell quickly assured Grover the court-martial judges could issue any sentence they wished, with review from top Army commanders in Washington. He tried to allay Grover's fear that it would be death.

Judge Romig, Gibboney, and Emma initially hired New York attorney Frank A. Spencer, Jr. to represent Grover. Along with his bar credentials, Spencer knew a few things about courts-martial. He trained on field artillery at the remote Stony Point Rifle Range on the eastern shore of Lake Ontario while billeting in the War of 1812-era Madison Barracks in Sackets Harbor. He was charged with being absent without leave from his Army post in 1917, tried at Fort Jay, and acquitted. He survived the deadly field artillery barrage of the Meuse-Argonne campaign in France and returned to New York to practice law. The judge advocates highly respected Spencer as Grover's attorney. Still, his filing for an insanity defense led to the appointment of a medical board of review, and the last thing Grover and Emma wanted was another mental evaluation. Spencer either withdrew or was fired.[3]

Then Emma hired attorney Harry Weinberger, a well-known New York defender of anarchists and radicals. Weinberger was a natural adversary to the government and especially the military. In part, he was disrespected by the Army legal team for his aggressive defense of civil rights and his Jewish heritage.

A scrappy New Yorker since birth in 1886, Weinberger was a short man (at 5'4½", shorter than Grover at 5'6") with a prominent dimple in his square jaw and, by his admission, of the chunky build. Despite the length of his legs, Weinberger had been a championship runner in the mile relay, 100-yard dash, and 440 in his youth. Running and expertly boxing with Irish kids in his East River neighborhoods taught him how to fight a legal adversary in court by never pulling punches and never giving up. At age 12, Weinberger says he tried to enlist in the Army during the Spanish-American war, but they told him to go home. He couldn't even get in as a drummer boy. He later became agnostic and a pacifist, deciding "all war was wrong. War only settled which side was stronger."

Weinberger quit the Republican Party in New York to join the Democrats to support Woodrow Wilson for his promise to keep the United States out of the war. When Wilson turned about, the young lawyer helped organize the National Farmer-Labor Party in July 1920, a few months after he first represented Grover in court. It mounted presidential campaigns but needed to gain more support.

Weinberger was admitted to the bar in 1908 after earning his law degree from New York University by working as a stenographer and studying at night. With borrowed money, he opened his independent law practice. Weinberger advocated civil liberties for Americans and represented aliens, immigrants, anarchists, and radicals, the most infamous of which were Emma Goldman and Alexander Berkman, anarchists convicted of obstructing the military draft in 1917 and deported to Russia.[4] Weinberger says he fought so hard for civil liberties that New York federal Judge Learned Hand jokingly called him Harry "Habeas Corpus" Weinberger.

Longtime Bergdoll family friend David Clarence Gibboney rounded out a defense trio to advise Grover on personal issues and feed Emma vital information while she was writing the checks to pay for the defense team and private investigators. Judge Romig played the role of Emma's escort to and from the Castle Williams jail and the trial.

---

[3] A defense based on insanity would have jeopardized Grover's ability to manage his money. Likely, he and Emma did not want to take this defense path. On January 30, 1920, the same day Spencer filed for an insanity defense, U.S. Attorney General A. Mitchell Palmer arrived in New York, holding meetings with Secret Service and Justice agents. He declined to reveal the purpose of his visit.

[4] Weinberger won a stay for Goldman, but she fled the United States anyway because Berkman was deported. Harry Weinberger Papers, Yale University.

By February 1920, Weinberger satisfied Emma and Grover with another angle of defense. Weinberger knew that claiming insanity would have entered evidence from the 1915 Philadelphia Orphans Court trial when Charles Bergdoll tried and failed to gain control over Grover's inheritance by declaring him mentally insufficient to handle his financial affairs.

Weinberger filed a habeas corpus brief with the federal court in Manhattan, claiming the Army did not have jurisdiction trying the charge of "desertion as a soldier" because Grover had never been inducted into the Army. Weinberger's assigned judge in the argument was none other than Learned Hand, who quashed Habeas Corpus Weinberger, ruling that military court martial was the proper venue to hear the Bergdoll desertion charge because case law proved that a simple mailed notice for examination was enough to be considered induction into the Army.

Philadelphia attorney David Clarence Gibboney, the liquor control advocate, and Bergdoll family fixer, was a long-time aide to Emma Bergdoll. Gibboney is credited with inventing the buried gold scenario to help Grover get released from jail and escape. (Historical Society of Pennsylvania/ *Philadelphia Record*)

Judge Hand went further when pressed for an explanation: "There is nothing to suggest invalidity in the Selective Service regulations. They have been upheld a number of times since the war started." He said the fact that the mailed notice did not reach Bergdoll because he was on vacation holiday was of no consequence.

"The man was merely a morbid coward," Judge Hand dismissed. He said induction into the Army begins when the notice is sent and, therefore, jurisdiction is in the hands of the Army.[5]

The case prosecutor, U.S. Army Colonel Charles C. Cresson, said he believed the federal court filings were an attempt to get bond for Bergdoll, who would skip out and forfeit his bond payment. It may have been part of a plan to escape when Bergdoll was taken from Governors Island into Manhattan for a federal court

---

[5] Judge Learned Hand's admonition appears to undermine Draft Board 32 secretary John Dwyer's continuing involvement with the induction and apprehension process long after he fulfilled his core duty and mailed the examination notices to Grover.

Attorney Harry Weinberger and Grover smartly dressed for court martial trial at Governors Island, New York City, March 1920. Weinberger was a prominent New York civil rights lawyer hired when Grover's first attorney proposed an insanity defense. Pleading insanity would have separated Grover from his fortune. Weinberger, at two inches shorter than Grover, contended that Grover was never inducted into the Army and should be tried in a more lenient civil court. (Temple University Urban Archives)

appearance. Cresson said he was informed by intelligence officer John Sparks, who brought Grover to New York in handcuffs, that Grover told him, "If I could only get bond for one hour, there will be no court martial trial."[6]

By March 1920, Grover and his attorneys settled in for the trial. It was held in a former battery built for the War of 1812 to watch over New York Harbor. It was later transformed into red sandstone and brick military-style buildings named South Battery or Half Moon Battery overlooking the narrow Buttermilk Channel, the waterway separating Governors Island from Brooklyn. Since 1885, the battery housed small low-ceiling rooms for court martial proceedings.

Each day Grover would be led across the vast parade ground from his cell to South Battery and then back to his cell in Castle Williams at the end of the day.

Inside the room where Grover's trial began on Thursday, March 4, 1920, the bailiff arranged dark hardwood tables in a U-shaped pattern so the six judge advocates would sit with their backs to the wall in the curve of the U. Grover, Weinberger, Capt. Campbell, and Judge Romig sat at a small table at one end of the U.

The judge advocates wore olive drab winter wool button-down blouse coats with flap pockets, shoulder straps, and wool riding breeches with spiral puttees and black knee boots, shined smooth. Each wore a service cap with a brown leather bill over his close-cropped hair until seated at the tables when the caps were hung. The only

---

[6] Col. Cresson later wrote that he insisted Grover be handcuffed, never left alone near a window, and constantly guarded by two men. Grover's confinement to the jail in Castle Williams instead of the post guardhouse in Fort Jay indicated a concern for escape because prisoners had previously escaped from the poorly secured guardhouse.

adornments on their uniforms were company insignia on their caps, rank sleeve patches, and collar discs.

All but one wore a short, close-cropped brush mustache.

Grover was allowed to discard the prisoner-numbered denim blouse and baggy trousers he wore in jail and dress smartly for his trial in a thick gray or brown pin-striped and tailored wool three-piece suit with a five-button vest, tie, and Murray Hill celluloid collars, all delivered from the cleaners by Emma. He was slim from eight weeks in jail. His wool trousers were expertly pressed with a crease from the inseam to the cuff. His dark hair was trimmed short, and his mustache was shaved thin and short for a professional and respectful appearance before the tribunal. His race car crash scar made his chin appear like a half-moon protruding bump.

Weinberger also dressed in heavy wool suits for trial, but they seemed unpressed and roomier than Grover's fine tailoring.

The public and press, including Emma and Judge Romig, were provided hard, dark wood and form-fitting fanny chairs just beyond a bar separating them from the court martial. The trial staging, in a room that would later become a basketball court, did not resemble a traditional civilian courtroom with an elevated bench, sidebar, jury box, and witness stand.

Grover's siblings did not attend the trial. Louis lived apart from the family in Manhattan. Still stinging from his 1915 court loss in trying to gain control of Grover's assets, Charles was estranged from Emma and Grover and lived at his Broomall mansion. Elizabeth was with her husband, Albert Hall, mainly at their farm in New Jersey. And Erwin was still on the run between Pennsylvania, West Virginia, Maryland, and Ohio.

Grover was on his own.

***

Philadelphia Department of Justice agent Todd Daniel took advantage of the renewed press interest in Grover's pending trial and issued a warning for Erwin. He said Washington special agent John Joseph O'Connor would remain in Philadelphia to lead the hunt for the draft-dodging automobile racing champion, and it would be wise for Erwin to surrender.

It was still cold in New York in March. Emma was often observed in the court-martial room in thick flowing dresses, scarves, heavy wool overcoats, and her gray hair tucked inside felt hats adorned with flowers and feathers from a bygone era. Her hands were often burrowed into a fox fur muffler. Unwilling to stay in New York hotels, she traveled back to Philadelphia each night on a late train.

Delayed by Weinberger's rejected pleadings, opening statements finally began on Saturday, March 6. However, the opening formalities were overshadowed by the revelation that two Burns Company private detectives were charged the previous day with conspiracy to impede justice by trying to bribe two clerks of Philadelphia

Draft Board #32, Margaret, and Gertrude Ruane, for testimony favorable to Grover. With Captain Campbell's approval, it was later determined that Judge Romig had hired the detectives to gather intelligence on the primary target of Grover's defense, draft board secretary John Dwyer. Emma paid for them.[7]

Then, there was an embarrassing revelation for Romig. Escorting Emma into the court-martial proceedings, Judge Romig was identified by the Hotel Vivian clerk brought to New York from Hagerstown, Maryland, to testify against Grover. She recognized Romig as the man who signed into the hotel on August 1, 1918, under the alias H. Watt, alongside Grover signing in as James Carson.[8]

Soon after prosecutor Cresson made the accusation in court, Romig hurriedly left the room and returned by train to Philadelphia. He had regularly visited Grover in the Castle Williams jail, delivering Philadelphia newspapers and stacks of books and literature about ancient Egyptian history. These details were leaked to the press by jail guards who said Bergdoll read every bit of the newspapers "except the theatrical advertisements." After Romig's embarrassment, however, he laid low, and Emma attended the trial alone. The press reported that she fled the room only once, in tears, when Col. Cresson denounced Grover's desertion as worse than murder.

Weinberger objected to everything in the trial, causing Col. Cresson to call him "a human jackal skulking along the east side of New York, like a Judas Iscariot, to do anything to combat the law for a few pieces of silver." When Weinberger objected to the personal attack, the court overruled it since Cresson did not mention Weinberger by name. Col. Cresson may have overreached a bit, not realizing Weinberger's reputation and abilities as a boxer when he suggested the short-legged civil liberties lawyer "could find me outside anytime on the island after the trial is over."[9] It was all hyperbole. They never came to blows.

Col. Cresson pointed to draft board secretary Dwyer, proclaiming he "gave four sons to the service, and now this man Bergdoll wants to escape his just punishment by the free use of his money." Cresson advised the judge advocates that other draft dodgers had been sentenced to 25 to 40 years in prison. He wanted Bergdoll to get 30.

"He has beaten the law for the last time. Don't let him get away with his crime," the prosecutor demanded. He said Bergdoll's trial was being watched worldwide by people who felt that draft-dodging penalties were only severe against the poor.

---

[7] Prosecution and defense documents were available at the National Archives in St. Louis. One great example is Grover's lengthy hand-written statement that was presented as evidence instead of his testimony. The Harry Weinberger papers at Yale University helped describe Grover's attorney's line of defense, which the federal courts repeatedly struck down.

[8] Judge Romig slid under the veil of attorney-client privilege. He would not be charged in the Bergdoll case until later in 1920.

[9] Col. Cresson later wrote that in his 20 years of experience as a lawyer, "I never saw as much unethical, unprofessional, and reprehensible conduct displayed as was exhibited by the attorneys for the defense."

The case against Grover, however, appeared ironclad from the beginning. One of the first witnesses called by the prosecution was a handwriting expert who testified that Grover's cursive and signature on his 1917 draft registration card matched the many taunting postcards he sent to Dwyer, federal agents, and newspapers. He compared the writing with that on Grover's fat canceled bank checks.

Col. Cresson and his assistants presented to the court martial Grover's prior criminal arrests and convictions for assault and battery, recklessness, attempting to kill a police officer, speeding, property damage, and minor traffic infractions. They also presented a one-page document showing Grover's arrest, trial, and acquittal in Mosbach, Germany, "for enticing a minor [girl]."

The judge advocates analyzed the answers to 27 questions presented to Emma through medical doctors who examined Grover for mental stability. Emma confirmed her significant blood loss during pregnancy for Grover from a plate-glass window accident. Also, when doctors grasped his skull and shoulder with forceps, Grover's arm was broken during delivery. His paternal grandmother was sent to a sanatorium; he often suffered from dizzy spells and had six severe injuries to his skull caused by falling from a pony cart, a carriage–trolley collision, a 1911 airplane accident, car collisions in 1912 and 1914, and the race car crash in San Francisco in 1915, leaving the scars on his scalp, neck, and chin.[10]

The trial court even heard from Grover's childhood companions, who said he would lock them in closets and blow sulfur smoke into them, and he injured them by placing explosive chemicals and mercury on coins.

Despite Emma's many claims that Grover suffered from injury-induced mental issues, the court-martial medical board of doctors declared Grover sane and fit for trial. He was "normal, acceptable physically and mentally" to be a soldier.

Although he had witnesses ready, Grover's military defense attorney, Captain Campbell, focused on Dwyer as the culprit in Bergdoll's complicated case. He suggested a conflict of interest for the editor of an influential newspaper "spreading community vile" against Bergdoll while simultaneously serving as the federal agent inducting him into the regular Army.

Campbell claimed that Dwyer fomented the "vile" with his newspaper, the *Record*, scooping other newspapers with the first stories that Bergdoll failed to appear for an examination and attempting to negotiate with Bergdoll to return to Philadelphia when his only responsibility was to send out draft notices and document them for the state adjutant general in Pennsylvania's capital, Harrisburg.

---

[10] This is the only family reference to an airplane mishap involving Grover. If he was injured in an airplane accident in 1911, it was before acquiring his Wright B Flyer, possibly involving Louis' Blériot or the experimental airplane that the Bergdoll boys built at the Broomall farm and which never got off the ground.

Weinberger continued with a defense position that Grover's notice for examination was not adequately prepared, was improperly authorized by a rubber stamp instead of an ink signature, may have been out of turn, was misnumbered, was knowingly issued when Grover was off traveling around the country and failed to provide the required 10-day period for a response.

From defense notes written in longhand, Weinberger was prepared to cite a previous draft dodger case when an American man obtained a passport from the federal government to move to Brazil as a dealer in cattle hides. After the American consulate in Brazil renewed the man's passport, creating another national document of his new address in Brazil, the man received a war draft notice at his former American address. Without the benefit of time to respond to the mailed examination notice, the man was charged with desertion and listed as a fugitive. However, Weinberger's attempts to demonstrate the shortcomings of the Selective Service Act were futile. The courts previously ruled that a mere notice meant an induction, no matter where you lived or what you were doing. Once inducted, the man whose name appeared on the notice was automatically in the Army, no matter whether he was home to receive the notice or not.

Essentially, the courts ruled that men were inducted even before an examination determined if they were physically or mentally fit to serve in the Army.

Newspapers in New York, Washington, and especially Philadelphia made fun of Grover during the trial, partly because, like Emma, he believed in astrological signs and had a Ouija board in his jail cell. The gossip-leaking Castle Williams jail guards who provided the juicy details to the press were already disgusted with Bergdoll's attitude of entitlement after only a few months on his watch.

In due course of the trial, the writing was on the wall. Grover would not escape with a slap on the wrist this time. However, his lawyers tried to mitigate his sentence, well below the maximum.

Gibboney, the long-time family friend, and fixer, tried the humanity approach. He told the tribunal, "this boy may have acted foolishly, but he meant to be patriotic. The government has utterly failed to make out a case."[11]

Near the end of the trial, Grover's team changed strategy. Weinberger and Campbell consulted with the judge advocates. They decided that instead of presenting a cadre of defense witnesses, including detectives hired to impeach Dwyer, Grover would be allowed to write an explanation for his draft dodging and have it considered by the tribunal as an unsworn statement. Furthermore, it would not subject Grover to cross-examination. Grover and his team then retired to an anteroom of Half Moon Battery, and he wrote ten pages in flowing penmanship detailing why he ran from the draft.

---

[11] Gibboney was part of the defense team, but his role was diminished for his lack of experience in military law.

He blamed John Dwyer.[12]

In accordance with the selective draft law, I registered on June 5, 1917. Sometime in July 1917, a man called me on the telephone [Furey answered the phone] and said that he was Mr. Dwyer, secretary of Local Board No. 32, and that he wished to see me as soon as possible because the Dept. of Justice agents were going to try to catch me without my registration card and he [Dwyer] was of the opinion that the federal agents were out after graft.

I made an appointment to meet Dwyer the next day at the Phila. Record Editor's office as he requested. I did not keep the appointment because, after thinking it over, I came to the conclusion that Mr. Dwyer was either setting some sort of a trap for me or looking for graft himself.

I found out that my draft number was among the 24 hundred numbers drawn from the board at Washington, and as the highest number was 10,000, I knew that approximately ¼ of the whole number of draftees would have to be called before my number came up. And as only a few had been called, I thought I had plenty of time and decided that I could take a few week's tour through the middle west before I went into the Army.

Until this time, I had been constructing a new type of monoplane, which I thought would be accepted as a combat plane by the U.S. government for use in the war. I intended completing this plane after I returned from my automobile trip.

I returned to Philadelphia on the evening of September 1, 1917, and as I turned the corner at 60th and Baltimore Ave., I recognized two girls (Florence Rowe and Viola Rowe) who were friends of mine. I stopped the car, and they asked me where I was going. I told them of my trip and that I was going home. They asked me if I did not know that the federal agents and government men were after me because I failed to report for a physical examination on the day specified. They then told me how Mr. Dwyer had announced in the papers that I would be arrested, thrown into jail, and charged with desertion as soon as I could be found. They told me that they got their information from hearing people talk and also from the newspapers, some of which they still had at their home on Hazel Ave.

I could not fully believe all they told me, so I took them to their home. They showed me a few newspapers, among which was the Philadelphia Record of August 23, 1917, which stated that I failed to report for a physical examination on the day specified and was now classed as a deserter and would be arrested and put in jail as soon as I returned.

I became frightened at Mr. Dwyer's threat and left town without going to my home or seeing my mother or any other relative of mine.

I traveled through the middle-west most of the time. Whenever it was possible in large cities to get the Philadelphia newspapers, I did so in the hope of discovering that the draft board had reconsidered its decision and would allow me time in which to return and report for physical examination, but all the news that I could get was that Mr. Dwyer was determined to put me in jail and have me tried for desertion and would give me no chance to join the Army.

In July 1918, I read in a newspaper that my mother had been arrested on the charge of aiding a deserter, and I wrote a letter to the Philadelphia Public Ledger in which I offered to return and enlist in the aviation corps if the charge of evading the draft and desertion would be withdrawn.

I watched the Philadelphia newspapers for the answer of the draft board. Some days later, an article appeared in which Mr. Dwyer, secretary of Local Board No. 32, and District Attorney (U.S. Attorney) Francis Fisher Kane would not listen to any kind of a proposition from me and were determined to put me in jail as soon as they could lay hands on me. This all happened

---

[12] Grover's court-martial statement is presented here nearly verbatim. It has been edited only for spelling, punctuation, and grammar to make it easier to read.

prior to August 8, 1918, the day of my alleged induction into the Army. When I read this last newspaper article quoting Dwyer and Kane, I again became frightened and withdrew further from Philadelphia. At no time did I see or know of the notice from the Adjutant General's office inducting me into the Army. I never received any notice, questionnaire, or card from either the local, the district board, or the Adjutant General's office.

When I was in Dayton, Ohio, I intended and was anxious to enlist in the aviation corps at Wilbur Wright field on the outskirts of Dayton. Many times I took a number of officers and enlisted men along with me in my car going to and from the aviation field. It was on one of these occasions that I asked an Army captain if a man could enlist under an assumed name, and he told me that any person doing so would be liable to court-martial for fraudulent enlistment. I could not enlist under my correct name as I was afraid that if I did so, I would be turned over immediately to Mr. Dwyer and Local Board No. 32.

I had absolutely no intention of evading the draft or staying out of the Army at any time. If I had such intentions, I would not have registered in the first place. I did my best to comply with the law.

After Mr. Dwyer's threats, I only tried to avoid going to jail. I did not desire to shirk my duty, in fact, I was anxious to get into the aviation corps and still am, but Mr. Dwyer, through his threats, false statements, and his desire to gain publicity, prevented this. I would have enlisted before I was ever called, but I desired to complete and demonstrate the monoplane I was constructing at the time.

It is my honest belief and opinion that Mr. Dwyer of local board No. 32 called me on the phone in July 1917 for the purpose of seeing me and arranging to secure a "soft Job" in the Army (as many other Philadelphians did) if I paid him for it. It is also my opinion that Mr. Dwyer, angered because I ignored him and did not keep the appointment, and knowing that I was in the habit of making frequent auto trips, had me watched, and as soon as he knew I was out of town, sent the notice to my house that I appear for physical examination. As I did not receive the notice, I could not respond in time, and Mr. Dwyer had his chance.

I intended staying away only so long as Mr. Dwyer was in power. After this time, I came back to my house in Philadelphia with the intention of straightening out my personal affairs, regain my health and then surrender voluntarily to the authorities as I expected to get a square deal when Mr. Dwyer was not in the running.

Grover C. Bergdoll.
March 17, 1920.

It appeared that Grover's statement and forgoing defense witnesses were Captain Campbell's decision. He said, "Bergdoll's plight is due to the illegal action of a government agent—John P. Dwyer—who used his position upon a draft board to advance his political position and satisfy ancient grudges. The halo which Mr. Dwyer has bestowed upon himself through his testimony of giving free use of his home for the draft board and of refusing to accept any compensation is somewhat tarnished by the $35 rent he pays for a house with nine rooms and two baths that are furnished him by the Pennsylvania Railroad at a ridiculously low rental. Dwyer waited 20 years to get square with Coyle by trying to force Town, the son-in-law of Coyle, into service. Dwyer's draft board was a newspaper and family board. It's a case of too much Dwyer."[13]

---

[13] Campbell referred to newspaper articles Dwyer wrote two decades earlier, which led to criminal charges against a Pennsylvania banker for bribing a state politician. See Chapter 9.

Dwyer could not respond to Grover's statement and Campbell's accusations in the court martial. Afterward, he wrote his statement for the press.

> I did my whole duty. My four sons, who were in the service, did theirs. The position I occupied as a member of a local draft board came to me unsolicited. The man who suggested me for the place judged me by his own standards and expected me to shirk a disagreeable but necessary public service.
>
> The case of Bergdoll meant no more to me than the case of any other registrant in our district. He forced others ahead of their turn into the army by his desertion. I pity him, but he is even less despicable than others who sought to discredit me after the more than two years of public service to which I devoted, without a cent of compensation, the best efforts of my life—no more than should be expected of any American citizen.
>
> There were over 7000 registrants in our district. More than 1200 of them were in the service of their country.
>
> The neighborhood in which I live and the whole city of Philadelphia, as well as the Pennsylvania county in which I lived the first 25 years of my life, were combed by hirelings to discredit me, and impeach the honest effort I made to do my whole duty. The perjured efforts of hired detectives and the perjured statements of those whose lawless act I had exposed or halted were to be the defense of the deserter. When the round-up came, the hirelings and bribers were afraid to take the witness stand. The deserter stood alone while they ran to cover.

Unlike a civilian court, when the verdict was reached on March 18, the prosecution and defense were not called back to hear it pronounced in open court. Instead, it went directly to Lt. General Robert E. Bullard, Army commander at Governors Island.

General Bullard took 12 days to review the case and gain approval of the verdict from Army officials in Washington. Grover stewed in cell #13, reading his Egyptian history but too nervous to read the newspapers, reported his guards.

However, when the news broke this time, Grover got it before Dwyer's *Record*. Colonel William Weigel of General Bullard's office was charged with going to Grover's cell block at 1 pm on March 30, 1920, calling him to stand at attention at the locked and barred door and reading him the verdict.

Guilty as charged.

Then, Col. Weigel pronounced the sentence: "To be dishonorably discharged from the service, to forfeit all pay and allowances, due or to become due, and to be confined at hard labor, at such place as the reviewing authority may direct, for five (5) years."

***

Four hours later, the bold black banner headline across the front page of the Philadelphia *Evening Public Ledger* blared BERGDOLL GUILTY AND GETS 5 YEARS AT HARD LABOR. The papers flew off the shelves of newsstands all over Philadelphia, New York, and Washington. Inside, the reporter dished the gossip from Grover's jail guards. The convicted war deserter listened to the verdict reading at his cell door and turned in tears to his rumpled fold-down cot. "The slacker slumped in utter collapse and sobbed and whimpered when the verdict was announced," the guards shared gleefully.

Emma got the news at the Wynnefield mansion. Unlike her weeks-long public relations campaign courting reporters camped on her front porch when Grover was on trial, she barred them from the door.

A box with decreasing font sizes inset beneath the headline, typeset in bold black letters but smaller than the banner, said BERGDOLL "MAN WITHOUT A COUNTRY." The dishonorable discharge from the Army carried a penalty of forfeiture of citizenship.[14] Bergdoll cannot again vote unless the President pardons him. Moreover, the slacker loses all civil rights and cannot sue or be sued. Cannot buy or sell a property and has less status as an individual than an emigrant coming to this country."

Losing citizenship rights with the conviction was part of an Army statute dating to 1806. The issue would dog Bergdoll in Philadelphia and Washington and his future home many years later in Virginia.

Captain Campbell knew a guilty verdict was coming, but the five-year sentence may have surprised him. He was expecting more. Weinberger reportedly released a "long impressive whistle" when told of the verdict. He said he would consult with Grover and Emma about an appeal.

The casualty list from these events would mount, as with anything and anybody around Grover Bergdoll. One jail guard at Castle Williams had already been court-martialed for giving favors to Bergdoll in exchange for cash. Other guards wanted him gone from their shifts. They gloated about his sentence of hard labor, which in the Army meant digging ditches, cleaning horse stalls, or working on greasy cars and trucks in the motor pool.

Even before Grover and the world learned the verdict in his court-martial, the new American Legion affirmed its position on the Bergdoll case. Just one year into its founding in Paris in March 1919, the *American Legion Weekly* magazine printed a cover story on Bergdoll titled "The Slacker's Bit."

Congress had only chartered the international veterans' advocacy organization in September 1919, and it was already becoming a force for American military patriotism and soldier support worldwide. With a normal print run of about 350,000 copies, the *Weekly* circulation jumped to 380,000 with the Bergdoll story. The magazine buried a photograph of the dapper-dressed, mustachioed young Bergdoll on the inside pages. It referred to him only once as Grover Cleveland Bergdoll in deference to the late President for whom Bergdoll was named.[15]

An editorial on the cover emphasized that the crime for which "the slimy and traitorous" Bergdoll was being tried was punishable by death; instead, the "national

---

[14] Such a felony conviction, even for desertion by a court martial, forfeits only the rights of citizenship, and not citizenship itself.

[15] President Cleveland, part Philadelphia Quaker, was the conservative Democratic President when Grover was born in 1893. He favored the gold standard, which suited Emma, and his image was on the $1,000 bill, which instilled pride in Grover who often carried them in his purse.

super-slacker" would live. The article was written while the trial verdict was decided on Governors Island. It counted that Bergdoll was only one of 173,911 men who ran from the draft and that "lest we focus too intently… on Bergdoll… he stood not alone. There must be no diminution of effort until the last guilty one" had been sent to prison.

However, the American Legion would hound only Bergdoll for years when others were ignored and set free. The Legion would encourage its members to support every effort to bring Bergdoll home for trial, despite always denying involvement in his pursuit.[16]

At Grover's and Emma's request, Weinberger wrote a letter to General Bullard asking if Grover could serve his five-year sentence at Governors Island and not be sent to the large military prison at Fort Leavenworth. The request was granted, but Weinberger insisted the decision was more influenced by Washington attorney, former U.S. Army Judge Advocate General Samuel T. Ansell, the lawyer whose negotiations with officials up to the White House would get Grover into more trouble than all his other attorneys and fixers combined.

---

[16] The American Legion consistently denied organizing illegal efforts or providing financial support for kidnappers and other bounty hunters who tried to capture Bergdoll for trial.

CHAPTER THIRTEEN

Bribe for Gold

Governors Island, New York, March–May 1920

Grover's journey to walk away from the U.S. Army Atlantic Branch Disciplinary Barracks on Governors Island, becoming a free man, began with a visit to his jail cell by long-time family attorney David Clarence Gibboney.

Initially serving as one of Grover's legal advisors in his court martial, Gibboney had been relegated to a lesser role. However, he was still on Grover's post-conviction visitors' list at the Castle Williams jail, approved by General Peyton C. March, then Army Chief of Staff, and the Judge Advocate General.

Realizing that Grover's conviction for deserting the Army resulted in a five-year prison term, Gibboney had a proposition that might give Grover a break.[1]

"Say, Grover, how would you like to get out of here?" quizzed Gibboney during their conversation in the visitors' room at the jail. He explained to Grover how the Army's Judge Advocate General must review all court-martial proceedings to determine if the procedures followed military law. "Your case has not yet reached the reviewing authority," Gibboney informed Grover just days after his conviction on March 18.[2]

"I knew what was coming," Grover later said. "Money was just shrieking at me."

Then, Gibboney told Grover, "I think that by retaining me, we can get you out. Place this case in my hands, and I am sure we can get you out."

Grover asked to whom "we" referred, but Gibboney would not answer.

Then Grover asked, "How much is all this going to cost me?"

"I think we can get you off for $100,000 cash," replied Gibboney.

"But, I have no money here. What am I supposed to do?" questioned Grover.

---

[1] Despite his five-year sentence, Army officials predicted Grover would be released within 18 months, potentially further reduced to nine months if he performed good behavior.

[2] Trial documents and Congressional testimony provided verbatim accounts of conversations between Grover, his attorneys, friends, and advisors. Ike Stecher's testimony supported claims of other parties about Grover's effort to be released from jail. Judge Romig also testified at length about his involvement with Grover's release. Letters and documents prepared to secure federal permission for Grover's release support the testimony of Grover's cohorts.

Then, Gibboney suggested what he knew would always work. He recommended Grover appeal, through him, to Emma for the cash. However, despite Emma's inclination to help Grover, Gibboney was worried Emma might spill the plan to the authorities.

"Gibboney asked me if I could get any money. I told him I had plenty of money but not in my Fort Jay cell. He then asked if I could get $100,000 cash. I told him I had much more than that buried away. He kept telling me it would cost $100,000 to get my case thrown out on technical grounds and my immediate release. I countered that I would pay up if let out to get the money." [3]

Convinced that either Grover or Emma would contribute the cash, Gibboney put his plot in motion with several trips between Philadelphia, Washington, and New York. However, Grover said he grew suspicious of Gibboney's motives, suggesting the family attorney could "easily skip out of the country and allow me to rot in my cell." Grover said he demanded to see and talk to the men in the War Department who were prepared to sell out for $100,000. Then, in a nearly unbelievable scenario, Grover claimed two top Army generals visited him, on separate occasions, at Castle Williams to work out a verbal agreement to release him on a legal technicality in his court-martial conviction.[4]

Gibboney also began working on another angle to get Grover out of jail. Seizing upon Grover's statement that he had much more money "buried away," Gibboney developed the story that Grover had gold coins buried in the mountains of Western Maryland, near the location of his tent camp and the Hotel Vivian in Hagerstown, where Grover and Erwin hid for months in 1918 and 1919.[5]

During one of his meetings with Grover in jail at Castle Williams, Judge Romig also learned of the plot to get Grover out to fetch gold. In the jail chapel's private meeting room, Grover told Romig that arrangements were being made for him to get out or look for the gold.

"What gold?" asked Romig.

"I have got some gold buried over there," replied Grover.

---

[3] Fort Jay was the 1798 hexagonal stone fort next to Castle Williams and was named at different times after New York Governor John Jay and explorer Christopher Columbus. Grover made his comments to reporter Leighton H. Blood, who organized a trip to Germany, with help from the American Legion, to find Grover, get a story, and convince him to return to the United States to face trial. Blood's three-part article was published in *Hearst's International* magazine in May 1924. It was the only extensive interview with Grover during his entire exile in Europe.

[4] In the thousands of voluminous files in Grover's court martial, no records have ever been produced showing two top Army generals visited Grover at Castle Williams. Furthermore, Grover never publicly named the generals.

[5] It's a theory that Grover made the "buried away" comment offhand and that Gibboney created the buried gold story based on Emma's and Grover's trips to the Treasury to withdraw gold coins.

"Well, now," exclaimed Romig. "Keep me out of any proposition about your gold. How are you going to get out?"

"General Ansell has arranged to get me out on parole to go after the gold," replied Grover.

"What gold?" Romig questioned again.

"The gold I have buried," affirmed Grover, staring directly into Romig's eyes.

Romig thought carefully to himself about Grover's story of gold. He knew, of course that he and Emma had gone twice to the Treasury in Washington and withdrawn gold. But, he was uncertain if Grover had his own stash of gold. Despite knowing that Grover often lied, Judge Romig agreed to tell Emma that Grover was arranging to be let out of jail to fetch his gold. Informed that Grover would "get out" but not aware of a plan for him to escape, Emma worried about how Grover would get back to his Wynnefield mansion when she would be in Philadelphia city court fighting her conspiracy case. So, as she often did in times of need, Emma sent for Stecher, the trusty mechanic and driver who had known the Bergdolls all of his life.

Stecher, who lived with his wife, Frieda, near the Bergdoll farm in Broomall, said a man came to his home from the Eagle Hotel one evening in mid-May with a message that Emma wanted to see him at Grover's mansion at 52nd and Wynnefield. He paid her a visit the next day, May 18, when Emma told him, "Grover is coming out."

Confused because he knew Grover had been convicted of desertion from the Army, Stecher asked what she meant. "He is coming out, and I want you to meet him at the North Philadelphia [train] station tomorrow," Emma said.

Later, under oath, Stecher further explained his conversation with Emma, "she told me to get the car ready, to take the Hudson 7-passenger touring car that belonged to Grover, and go to the North Philadelphia station and that Grover would be on a certain time train." Hardly believing that Grover would be released from jail following his conviction, Stecher followed Emma's orders.

Despite not being driven regularly while Grover was in jail and going through court-martial proceedings in New York, the Hudson had been kept in proper running condition by Stecher himself, who performed the mechanical maintenance on Grover's and Emma's automobiles through his job at an automobile garage across the Schuylkill from the Bergdoll Brewery in Philadelphia.

Parking the car at the train station, Stecher spotted Gibboney and Judge Romig milling about the platform, but instead of joining them, he chose to remain close to the Hudson. It was still morning, and the station was bustling with passengers and merchants. In the distance, Stecher could see a Pennsylvania Railroad engine pulling into the station from the north and New York City.

Inside one of the passenger cars sat Grover, dressed in an olive drab Army uniform with insignia of the 23rd Infantry Regiment. He wore a felt campaign hat with blue cord, canvas leggings, and russet Army shoes. It made him appear as if he was a soldier in the Army.

What few people realized at this moment was that Grover's release was based on a wild story of buried gold, tens of thousands of Bergdoll dollars in cash paid and promised to influential politicians and attorneys with close friends strung to Washington, and the President's cabinet in the White House.

Letters had been written and telephone calls made between long-time friends and co-workers in the Army, state and federal government, and the courts. In a flurry of confusion and misunderstandings between upper- and lower-ranking officers in the Army and the judge advocate general's office, orders were granted to release Grover for the gold hunt without the slightest detail on how they should be carried out or confirmation that the gold existed.

The orders were so lax that they didn't even include instructions to use handcuffs to hold the convicted felon, Bergdoll, a shovel to dig up the gold, or a container to put it in.

Instead, two uninformed and ignorant noncommissioned Army officer guards were assigned to use their prisoner's money and take him out of jail to his home city, where they were to turn him over to a civilian nobody knew and to whom the military guards were to submit for further orders.

It was the perfect opportunity for Grover to escape. But nobody saw it coming.

CHAPTER FOURTEEN

Escape

May–July 1920

In the early afternoon of May 20, 1920, Ike Stecher waited with the Hudson Super Six at the North Philadelphia station of the Pennsylvania Railroad. The station, in the Fairhill neighborhood of Philadelphia and formerly the sprawling estate of the wealthy Quaker merchant, slave trader, and 1724 Philadelphia mayor Isaac Norris, was convenient for travelers between New York City and the rapidly developing townships and boroughs west of the city, allowing them to avoid the larger and more crowded Broad Street Station downtown, farther south and east.

North Philadelphia grew from the gentlemen's estates of Fairhill in the early 1800s to heavily working-class brick rowhouse neighborhoods embedded within munitions factories, textile mills, freight terminals, railroad shops, saloons, horse stables, and automobile garages. Formerly known as Germantown Junction, the train station was convenient to the Bergdoll mansions.[1]

Choosing to remain just outside the subsurface entry level of the station, closer to the Hudson, Stecher watched for Grover by looking up the staircase to the station's vast two-story main waiting room with its "curving hammer-beam framing of the roof, giving an open and airy feeling," Made of brick in 1901 and enlarged by 1915, "the station resembled a French chateau with a steep hipped roof covered in fish scale slate shingles, dormers, and decorative elements executed in creamy white glazed terracotta. Based on 16th Century models found in the Loire Valley of France, the building would have been more at home stylistically in New York City than Philadelphia."[2]

Alighting from the train at North Philadelphia, Grover said Gibboney was the first to meet him and his Army guards. As agreed, Gibboney immediately showed them his letter from barracks commander, Col. John Hunt, matching theirs, allowing Grover to leave his jail cell at Governor's Island to search for gold. Satisfied with the proper authority, Army guards Sergeants John O'Hare and Calvin York allowed Grover to

---

[1] Germantown Junction was named for the Pennsylvania Railroad (PRR) intersection with the Philadelphia, Germantown, and Chestnut Hill Railroad. Amtrak: *The Great American Stations*.
[2] Description based on Amtrak's series, *The Great American Stations*.

command the group, heading them toward the familiar stairs and the waiting car that Grover knew about and they didn't.

"When I saw Grover coming down the stairs in a doughboy's uniform," Stecher explained, "I hailed him and said, 'Where did you get that uniform? You're not a soldier. You're a prisoner. You sure got a nerve.'"

Grover waved him off, fully aware that Stecher had served as a first sergeant for 12 years in the Pennsylvania National Guard. Stecher knew the regulations about uniforms.

Then, in a conspiracy through glances and motions toward Stecher, piling into the Hudson, Grover immediately changed the itinerary from driving to the hills of Maryland to search for gold to going to his mansion at 52nd and Wynnefield.

They convinced the sergeants, riding in the back, there was a severe knock in the engine of the Hudson, which required servicing. Detouring toward the mansion, which Grover had not seen in four months, they first dropped Gibboney off in North Philadelphia, proceeded to Fairmount Park and the Wynnefield neighborhood, and drove into the backyard of Grover's mansion and the carriage house so the car could be fixed.

When they arrived at midmorning, no one was home except for Emma's aged mother, and Grover's maternal grandmother, Wilhelmina Barth, who, despite having her own comfortable home in the Wissahickon Valley nearby provided by Emma, also lived in Grover's mansion.[3] She could only explain that Emma had gone to court and that Stecher's wife, Frieda, was scheduled to come later in the day to cook their meals. The sergeants guarding Grover didn't realize that special arrangements had been made for his coming home event.

They were easily hoodwinked.

Without Gibboney to guide them, as were their Army orders, Grover took control of the schedule for his guards. He proposed they all go out for a ride around town. Still, the sergeants went along, knowing they were forbidden from deviating from their original intentions to travel to Western Maryland to search for gold. They drove in the Hudson through the vast Fairmount Park and then into the countryside surrounding the Bergdoll farm west of Philadelphia. There was no reason for this side trip in a car that was supposed to be running poorly, with a knocking engine. Perhaps Grover was scouting locations to hide near the farm. Upon returning to the mansion, Grover slipped Stecher a note that nearly floored the taller, stout German.[4]

"I'm going to beat it, and I want you to go with me," Grover's note said in his expert cursive handwriting.

---

[3] Army Sergeants O'Hare and York were expressly forbidden from allowing Grover to stop at his mansion while the party was traveling to Maryland to fetch the hidden gold. Whether gullible about the engine knock or charmed by Grover's celebrity and wealth, the guards succumbed to his wishes.
[4] Stecher's testimony of fleeing Philadelphia differs from Grover's explanation in Chapter One. Grover lied to journalist Blood about the escape, and Stecher told his story under oath in a courtroom.

The Wynnefield mansion on the day of Grover's escape in May 1920. Police and gawkers surround the property, awaiting a glimpse of the infamous fugitive. However, by the time this photograph was taken, Grover had fled toward the border with Canada. (Temple University Urban Archives)

"I nearly dropped dead and snook away so the sergeants would not see the note. I was then seriously thinking about sneaking away to get out of the business, but, somehow or other, I did not do it, and I thought possibly I could talk him out of it," Stecher said.

Stecher consulted with Emma. He thought of what might happen to his wife, Frieda, working in the kitchen as a paid servant, uninformed of Grover's plan. He couldn't have thought too hard because Stecher decided to stay and help Grover at some point. He went into the kitchen at the back of the mansion to advise his wife.

"You get out of here because I don't want you to get into this muddle if anything happens. Don't say anything," he told Frieda. Frieda agreed and drove Stecher's car to their home along Darby Creek near the Bergdoll farm. She never imagined seeing her husband just one more time over the next few years, and only for minutes.

"I got a chance to talk to Grover," Stecher later told investigators. Sneaking away from Sergeants O'Hare and York while they were occupied playing pool, Stecher said he tried to convince Grover that escaping was a bad idea, "I told him not to do it, and he said, 'To hell with them. I'm going to beat it. They are trying to frame me up for graft.'"

"I was like a fish out of water and did not know what to do," Stecher said. "That night, we went down to the Gayety; Romig, the sergeants, myself, and Grover, of course. He wanted to go that night, but I always thought I could change his mind. I kept telling him I was not going to do it."

Grover demurred at escaping that night. He said the sergeants left their service revolvers in the mansion when they went to the Gayety, indicating the men were comfortable and not worried about losing their prisoner. Or, they were mentally overpowered by Grover's wealth, demands, and celebrity.[5] And, upon returning to the mansion, they were plied with liquor—top-shelf gin.

"The sergeants like their booze and called for more," Grover explained. "I got it for them."

The men remained in the billiard room until the early morning hours, drinking gin until they were drunk.[6] Emma was also in the mansion that night, along with her mother, who was hard of hearing but could see just fine, and they went to bed early.

"When I turned in at three o'clock in the morning," Grover said about his Army guards, "one of them was playing the electric piano, and the other was dead to the world."

Sgt. O'Hare took a bed in the same second-floor bedroom as Grover to ensure his prisoner did not run off in the night. Sgt. York and Stecher retired to separate bedrooms on the third floor. They all slept late the following day, and by not arising and setting off on the gold hunt, they violated the terms of Grover's release again.

"Gibboney called up, and we told him we were going to take it easy and not start on the hunt for my 'pot-o-gold' for another twenty-four hours," Grover said. "The sergeants started drinking again."

No one made attempts to fix the car. No one discussed a plan for driving to Maryland. And no one notified Governors Island that they were in Philadelphia, where they were not supposed to be.

Late on the morning of May 21, nursing hangovers from the gin, Grover, Stecher, O'Hare, and York gathered in the kitchen for breakfast with Emma.[7] Stecher managed to steal away for a few moments with Emma, where she said, "For Christ's sake, go with him. If you don't, he's going to shoot one of those fellows." "I didn't think Grover was armed," Stecher said. "But I knew he had weapons around the house." [8]

"We had dinner [lunch] later that day, and I went upstairs to the pool room to play, and I was thinking about how he would change his mind or that I could

---

[5] The Army investigation later revealed that Sergeants O'Hare and York were not trained as military police, broke several Army regulations, and did not search the Bergdoll mansion for weapons when they arrived. They had little to no experience guarding a convicted prisoner with access to a large cache of money.

[6] All drank gin except O'Hare, who said he had not touched a drop of alcohol for years.

[7] Emma left the mansion after breakfast to appear in city court later that day to answer charges of helping Grover avoid the draft.

[8] Later, it was revealed that there were 11 "riot guns" in the house, along with shotguns and "ammunition enough to withstand a siege." Police had already confiscated numerous guns from the house when Grover was arrested. Who replenished the gun supply while Grover was in jail at Castle Williams is not known.

convince him not to go," recalled Stecher. "Then, Grover told me to go down and get the car ready."

The telephone rang in the mansion sometime in the 2 pm hour. The Bergdolls had a telephone on the ground floor and an extension on the second floor, in a small anteroom between Grover's and Emma's bedrooms. One had to walk through a water closet and into the antechamber to reach the upstairs telephone. From here, a narrow stairway led down into the dining room at the rear of the house, near the kitchen. The back stairway was designed for use by servants.

As the telephone clanged, Grover exited the billiard room, crossed the hallway into his bedroom, entered the water closet, and then the anteroom, leaving the sergeants in the billiard room knocking balls around the pool table. Faking a telephone conversation for a moment, Grover then laid down the receiver and walked down the stairs to the dining room. There, he blurted goodbye to his grandmother sitting in front of the large dining room bay window, grabbed a prepared bundle, and walked calmly into the central kitchen, through the heavy wooden door into the summer kitchen, and out of the mansion through the back door leading to the carriage house. The same set of doors police and federal agents had blasted open with gunfire when they captured him five months earlier. The sergeants, and Romig, were still upstairs sipping gin and cracking billiard balls on the table slate.

In the driveway between the summer kitchen back porch, and the carriage house, Stecher sat in the driver's seat of the Hudson Super Six, with the motor idling smoothly. There was no knocking sound coming from the car. It was full of gasoline and oil, ready to go.

Stecher knew Grover would come out the back door because the side door, although closer to the bottom of the servants' stairs and emptying onto the wrap-around terrace, had an unusual step and was seldom used. Within minutes of Stecher getting the car out of its carriage bay, Grover had emerged through the screen door, still in his denim prison uniform, number 10 on the arm, a campaign hat, canvas leggings, and tan Army shoes with the bundle under his arm. As Grover stepped into the car, Stecher grew nervous and immediately tried talking Grover out of running from his Army guards.

"I don't care," bellowed Grover over the purring of the Hudson's engine. "I'm going to show somebody up. They want $100,000 from me, and I won't give it to them."

Realizing his efforts were useless, Stecher released the brake and, steering between the stone columns of the narrow porte-cochere, exited the driveway with Grover gripping the bundle on his lap. Stecher could see that it contained street clothes and guns.

"He always impressed me with the idea that they were trying to get money out of him, and I didn't know what to do," Stecher later told investigators. Turning the Hudson westward on 52nd Street, he drove to the Lincoln Highway and headed south toward Maryland, where Grover had run from the draft a few years before.[9]

Stecher drove for a few minutes before realizing that his wife, Frieda, would need money if they ran off together. Arriving at his house near the Bergdoll farm at West Chester Pike and Darby Creek, Stecher was startled to realize an old family friend, "a copper," as he called him, was in the kitchen talking with Frieda. Leaving Grover alone in the Hudson and pretending he needed a cap before driving to an appointment to look at a car for sale in nearby Bryn Mawr, Pennsylvania, Stecher talked for a few minutes with his "copper" friend and winked at Frieda to meet him at the door where he handed her a $1,000 bill, provided by Grover.

Leaving his wife behind, Stecher drove the Hudson southwest on Baltimore Pike while Grover changed his clothes and tossed his Army uniform out of the window. "First went the hat," he said, to leave clues to a southern escape route toward Washington. "Then the blouse and shirt. I tossed them overboard as we raced along. Last of all went the shoes."

Size seven and a half: Grover did not have a large foot.

"They were brand new issue dress shoes," said Stecher, the minimally paid auto mechanic, about his wealthy friend and now a fellow fugitive. "Never been worn before until issued to Grover. It seemed a shame to throw them away. I wanted him to keep them, but we had to toss them off just the same."

With the uniform scattered along the southern road to Washington and Grover now wearing civilian clothes, the two escapees arrived in Bel Air, Maryland, before turning west and driving through the night, stopping in Pittsburgh the following day. They were eager to determine if they were being hunted.

"We bought a paper there, but I don't think there was any news in it. I do remember there was some talk about a revolution in Mexico, and then Grover said we could not go to Mexico.[10] I kept suggesting that we go back, but he refused."

Onward they drove in the Hudson with the risk of being pulled over growing by the minute. Their car and its license plate, Pennsylvania 8-5-4-7-8, were being hunted. They took turns at the wheel through Dayton, Ohio, and New Castle, Indiana, where they stole license plates from a Maxwell car at the East Side Garage and put them on the Hudson, then to Indianapolis, where, years earlier, Grover tried to compete in the 5th International 500-Mile Sweepstakes Race, on to Hammond, Illinois, and later, bypassing Chicago, north to Milwaukee where they stayed for three nights, changing hotels each morning.[11]

---

[9] Descriptions of Grover's and Stecher's journey to the United States–Canada border came from their statements and investigation reports filed by federal agents who were hunting for them. Several investigative documents portray the fugitives' escape, later confirmed by court testimony.

[10] The newspapers were full of news about the murder of Mexican President Venustiano Carranza on May 20–21, 1920.

[11] Grover said, in a first-person article for *Hearst's International* magazine, they found his picture and an article about his escape in the newspapers purchased in Pittsburgh. However, he either embellished the story or was mistaken because news of the escape did not spread widely until later that day, May 22.

"We went around to the moving pictures and theaters every night," Stecher said. "I still argued with him about going back, but he suggested we go to Canada."

By this time, the War Department sent notices to key cities across the Midwest for police to look out for Grover and Stecher. The notice, similar to a wanted poster, focused on Grover.

> Twenty-eight years old; 5 feet 4 inches tall; 175 pounds, heavy build; broad, square shoulders; dark brown hair, brushed back from the forehead; dark brown eyes; good teeth, much stained from tobacco; scars on neck and throat; is a member of a wealthy Philadelphia family and has traveled extensively.
>
> Constantly on the move and probably accompanied by male companions. Expert automobile driver and delights in exploiting his ability. Flighty and dramatic. Liberal spender and well supplied with money. When last seen was in a Hudson super-six automobile, Pennsylvania license 85-478, accompanied by chauffeur.
>
> If located, arrest and notify nearest military post, agents of Department of Justice, or local police authorities, and the military intelligence division.
>
> War Department, Washington, D.C.

In Milwaukee, Grover and Stecher discovered from the newspapers that they were being hunted and that people reported seeing them in several states, including the Midwest. Driving north beyond Oshkosh and Green Bay, Wisconsin, they inquired about the conditions of the roads around Lake Superior, where Stecher thought it best to make a border crossing at the St. Mary's River and Sault Ste. Marie, Michigan. Told the roads were not in the best condition for an automobile, they diverted westward to Minneapolis, where it had not been mentioned in the newspapers that Grover was seen, and then north toward Canada, finally stopping in the railroad junction hamlet of Noyes, Minnesota, situated on the flat prairie along the Red River a few hundred feet from the boundary line.

Here, they had no choice but to stop. Neither man had a passport, and with an automobile, the only way to cross the border into Emerson, Manitoba, was to check into the customs office in the Great Northern Railway Depot in Noyes.

A Scotsman railway agent, William F. MacKay, operated the checkpoint by himself with inspections consisting mainly of freight trains with one or two passenger cars from the Great Northern or its competitor, the Minneapolis, St. Paul, and Sault Ste. Marie Railway (Soo Line), passing through to Winnipeg, Manitoba, Canada, 70 miles north. Grover and Stecher realized they had to be cautious at the small junction of only a few inhabitants. They were fugitives with their Hudson displaying stolen Indiana license plates, number *6-1-5-7-7* on the front and number *6-1-5-7-8* on the rear. They were hopeful of getting the car across the line.[12]

After scoping out the depot and customs office, which contained a holding cell, Grover and Stecher doubled back for two miles to the slightly larger community of St. Vincent, abutting the North Dakota state line and the more populated town of Pembina. There, they found an automobile service garage with a native-American man

---

[12] MacKay was employed by the railroad and served concurrently as the customs agent.

lounging about whom Grover derisively referred to as "a half-breed." Since the garage owner, W. J. Mason, was out of town, the man, Julius Defoe, was easily convinced to allow them to drive the Hudson into the work bay, out of sight.[13] Permission may have involved a fistful of cash because Defoe didn't tell anyone about it, except for Mason, until much later when federal agents came sniffing around St. Vincent.

"We asked the half-breed where we could get some liquor," Grover said to confuse him about who they might be. "He pointed toward the border and told us to take a road that branched off to the left. That road, he said, was not guarded by customs inspectors. He took us for bootleggers."

Leaving the Hudson secreted in the dark garage and walking out of St. Vincent on its gravel roads, Stecher and Grover were intercepted by two men in a Ford automobile who offered a ride. Settling into the rear seat, they thought the men were either revenue agents or bootleggers, but they were eager to get a trip over the border, so they went along. However, instead of turning left toward the unguarded crossing, the driver of the Ford pulled into Noyes, where the two men hopped out and entered the train depot. Stecher described the scene as "a long white house." He and Grover were tense, not understanding what the men were doing. Waiting in the Ford, they could see a sign denoting the boundary with Canada. Afraid of being seen if they ran for it, both men stayed in the car, hoping they wouldn't be caught.

"Stecher and I got our guns ready, for it looked queer," Grover said. "In a few minutes, the men came back out, jumped into the machine, and drove across the border into the village [Emerson, Manitoba]. They had only been registering the car in."[14]

Feeling relieved, Grover and Stecher signed into the only hotel in Emerson using the names George Charles Riggs for Grover and Frank Jeremiah Johnson for Stecher. They began plotting an effort to get the Hudson across the border too. It looked easy when the Ford men did it, but the two fugitives didn't have travel documents and didn't dare enter the depot for inspection by Agent MacKay.

Believing Stecher had a better chance of making it, the following day, Grover sent him walking in an attempt to cross back into Minnesota to get the Hudson out of the St. Vincent garage and drive it across the prairie into Emerson. They were eager to retrieve the Hudson because it contained their clothes and more

---

[13] In 1920, the Noyes, Minnesota railroad junction contained a 30 x 137-foot wood frame depot and a few houses. St. Vincent was only slightly larger, with a dozen homes and a few businesses, including the Mason Garage. Pembina contained dozens of homes and businesses across the Red River, in North Dakota.
[14] Grover carried a .38 caliber revolver in a leather sling and two smaller handguns that would easily fit in his pockets. He also carried a knife. About this time, Grover also gave a letter, addressed to his mother, to a German man, Martin Scheuch, traveling from Weingarten, Germany, crossing the border from Manitoba into Minnesota. The letter requested Emma wire $5,000 for Grover's travel expenses to a predetermined location. The letter was intercepted by a customs agent who searched Scheuch at the depot.

guns.[15] However, while trying to walk into the United States, Stecher was stopped, questioned, and turned away at what he called the "little white house" staffed by a Canadian customs agent in Emerson.

"They asked me who I was, and I told them I was from the United States. They said I had no business there, and I said that I could not help that. I was then sent to the immigration officer, but, luckily, he was not at home, so I snook away," he recounted.

Stecher then returned to the Emerson hotel and Grover. Realizing they might be discovered, they attempted to get on the next train headed north for Winnipeg. Finding the last train had only recently departed and another wouldn't arrive at the depot until the next day, Grover and Stecher began walking north. After about 11 miles, they came to the town of Letellier, another small crossroads community on the railroad. They determined the train had stopped in Letellier, then departed and was ahead of them, but if they could move fast, they could catch it because the many stops on the railroad required time to unload or load freight while passengers waited.

In Letellier, they found a man willing to drive them toward Winnipeg to catch the train, which, he knew, would make an extended stop at a rail junction in Morris for loading agriculture products and aggregate. And, to build speed, their hired driver stretched back the folding top of his car and set off in a straight line across the prairie, avoiding the slower, pockmarked gravel road. Dust might have flown if it had been winter, but in May, the greening prairie path gave the car traction as they sped northward along the meandering Red River. The two Americans hung on for the speedy ride with their Canadian driver determined to catch the train.

Dropping the fugitives at a small depot south of Winnipeg, their driver returned across the prairie to Letellier. Grover and Stecher hopped on the train, riding into the city where they hoped to obtain documents and head east. The Hudson remained in the dark garage in St. Vincent. It would later be used as evidence against them.

Riding the train northward toward Winnipeg, Grover and Stecher felt relieved to be across the border. Stecher gave up trying to convince Grover to go back home. He was too deep in the fugitive running game and knew they would only get back across the boundary with papers. They didn't realize that Canadian and American customs inspectors were already talking to each other about the unusual characters at the border towns of St. Vincent, Noyes, and Emerson.

Acting on a tip from his neighbors on Sixth Street in St. Vincent, deputy customs inspector James A. Noyes sent a telegram to federal agents in Duluth with a description of the Hudson stored in Mason's garage and the American who tried

---

[15] Later, when searching the car, federal agents found a loaded Colt .38 and a Lugar .32 with a 16-inch barrel. They also found a suitcase with a brown, pinstripe, heavyweight wool suit from Wiener Bros., Pittsburgh. Inside the suit coat pocket was sewn a name tag for J. C. Carson, Grover's alias while hiding for the previous two years in the mountains of Maryland. Agents confirmed the car's ownership by pouring gasoline on the stamped engine number, 18387, and rubbing it clean to determine that it had not been altered.

to walk across the border without papers. With the advice in a return wire, Noyes arranged for two local constables, Wallace Cameron and Milton Russell, to watch the Hudson. They ordered Mason to remove the car's carburetor so it couldn't be driven.

By the time Grover and Stecher arrived in Winnipeg, federal agents already suspected their escape route.

In Winnipeg, the eastern fugitives, accustomed to city life in Philadelphia, got a taste of a western city on the high plains of Canada. Checking into the upscale Empire Hotel next to Winnipeg's Union Station and the main line of the Canadian Northern Railway, Grover and Stecher were located convenient to the Great Northern ticket office from where, as Riggs and Johnson, they could obtain travel documents and purchase steamship passage for Europe.

The two Philadelphians found Canada's Gateway to the West on June 1, 1920, still in recovery from the massive Winnipeg General Strike a year earlier. The post-war recession following years of prosperity in cattle and grains, the influx of thousands of immigrants lured by railroads, labor union leaders, and inadequate industrial working conditions led to more than 30,000 Winnipeggers walking away from their jobs in protest. The strike was resolved when several people were killed while Royal Canadian Mounties stormed a crowd of protesters. They went back to work, but it took years for the city to recover from the financial impact of the strike.

None of that mattered much to Grover and Stecher, of course. Grover's endless supply of money fueled them; some of it was sent to him by Emma replying to Grover's coded letters for cash. At their disposal was shopping at Eaton's Department Store for clothes and sundries to replace those they'd left behind in the Hudson. They could easily travel about the city by trolley and blend in with the crowds of people without suspicion of being notorious fugitives. They kept off the streets as much as possible but attended vaudeville performances and picture shows. They dined in some of Winnipeg's elegant restaurants in hotels built as monuments to the great railroads.

One evening, over dinner at the five-story red brick and stone Royal Alexandra Hotel, along Higgins Avenue, decorated with cherubs, lion head sculptures, and faux cast-iron balconies, owned by and attached to the Canadian Pacific Railway Depot, Grover became a bit too friendly with a man showing off his American Legion button.

Grover asked to take it to show Stecher. When he didn't return it, the man reported the incident to American Consul General Joseph Britton, claiming he was sure it was the notorious draft-dodging American fugitive, Bergdoll. The consulate reported the theft to the local Canadian constable, who said he'd read about Bergdoll in the papers. But he did nothing. He first wanted notification from U.S. authorities in Washington before he would open an investigation. It was just one in a long list of narrow escapes for Grover.

In Winnipeg, Grover scouted steamship agencies at the railroad ticket offices. Each time an agent informed him that to buy a passage abroad, he would need a birth certificate to process a passport to buy a steamship ticket. Frustrated and deciding to take a risk, he settled on Great Northern ticket agent Arthur L. Johnston, who, along with his modest salary, could pocket a small commission on each fare sold. But, in a mid-continent city like Winnipeg, Johnston didn't earn many commissions. When Grover arrived in Union Station looking for documents and passage, Johnston, 27, may have seized the opportunity to make some easy cash.

Grover told Johnston that he and Stecher were from western Canada and had come to Winnipeg to get steamship tickets but didn't have identification. When told he needed someone to vouch for their identities, Grover pleaded that he didn't have the money to send someone to travel across the country.

"OK, I can fix that up," replied Johnston, according to Grover. "All you do is fill out this blank page stating where you were born and answering the rest of the questions. Then, you'll have to have some bank president or public official swear that he has known you for twenty years and that you were born in Canada." Grover, realizing he could never find someone to claim he'd lived in Canada for 20 years, turned on his charm.

He reached into his pocket.

Johnston replied that he just happened to know the president of the Royal Bank of Canada, Winnipeg branch, whose office was a few doors from the ticket station. Johnston said that he could fill out the papers and make the arrangements. Grover readily agreed and made the deal in the flash of his hand filled with cash.

Johnston held an account in the Royal Bank. On the same day of Grover's inquiry, Johnston deposited $390.82 into his account. U.S. federal agents later determined it was an unprecedented amount for Johnston and the only deposit he made that month.[16]

Upon leaving the Great Northern ticket office, Grover bought a large map of Western Canada, and together, he and Stecher walked the block from Union Station to their room at the Empire Hotel.

"That night, we picked out a couple of little towns where we figured no birth records would have been kept thirty years ago and made out the blanks," Grover said. They filled out their names as George Charles Riggs and Frank Jeremiah Johnson.

Returning to the ticket office the following day, June 2, Johnston, the ticket agent with a more substantial bank account, arranged for the passport applications with photographs to be taken to the Portage Avenue branch of the Royal Bank of Canada and the president, F. W. Doherty.

"The president swore to the passport applications, stating that he had known Stecher and me for 20 years and that we were both honorable and highly respected citizens of the Dominion of Canada," Grover boasted.

---

[16] In 1920, experienced railway station clerks made about four dollars a day, plus commissions. Despite the odd amount of $390.82, it's believed that Grover paid Johnston $400 cash to expedite the paperwork for two passports.

This was Grover and Stecher's first time in Canada. Their ease in gaining British–Canadian passports underscored the lax immigration regulations in the self-governed dominion of the British Empire.

Again, using his massive cash reserve, Grover bribed an official into giving him what he needed to remain free.

Canadian immigration laws require that a person making a passport application must provide proof of citizenship with a birth certificate. However, much of Canada was rural and without structured local government in the second decade of the 20th century. Exceptions were made for people born in rural areas and often at home, without proper recordings of vital statistics. In these cases, travelers were required to provide documents such as bank books, bank cheques, signed letters with letterheads, and other official documents containing their names and addresses. The documents were to be presented to a notary who would vouch for Canadian citizenship. Johnston, however, was bypassing the regulations and submitting his clients' paperwork to Doherty, who often signed off on 15 applications at a time without seeing the applicants in person, taking Johnston's word that they were legitimate.[17]

And, in the case of Grover and Stecher, it wasn't Johnston who did it at all. A young clerk in the Great Northern ticket office, 20-year-old Harold Bishop, did the clerical work for Johnston. Bishop said he alone took the George Riggs and Frank Johnson passport applications to Doherty, who signed them with several others. Doherty said he remembers the two forms because Riggs and Johnson identified their occupations as "agriculturists." In all similar applications, he said, people called themselves "farmers." Doherty said they were also memorable because it was the only time he simultaneously approved applications for two unrelated men.

Bishop returned the papers to the ticket office, and Johnston forwarded them on the next train to Ottawa for approval. The two new Canadians never saw the bank president's signature, nor did the banker ever see the imposters in person.

While waiting in Winnipeg for their travel documents to be returned from Ottawa, Grover and Stecher took no chances of being followed or captured, but they had a few close calls. Moving from the Empire uptown to the more luxurious Royal Alex with its convenient corridors leading directly into the Canadian Pacific Depot, Grover and Stecher, going by the names Riggs and Johnson, were assured a convenient and rapid departure if they suspected anyone on their trail. And, to be safe, they alternated between the luxury of the Royal Alex and the Empire and the austerity of the Hotel Wolseley across Higgins Avenue from the Canadian Pacific Depot.

---

[17] After the Bergdoll and Stecher affair and demands from His Majesty's government in Ottawa, Johnston's supervisor ordered him to change his practices and process all non-certificated births with notary signatures only.

Realizing their papers would take a few weeks to arrive from Ottawa, Grover established his temporary address at the Wolseley and sent two letters, a few weeks apart, to the Mason Garage in St. Vincent. One letter advised Mason that Grover had been granted permission by Defoe to store the car in the garage, including a cash payment. The second letter requested Mason ship the Hudson on a train to Philadelphia, specifically to Judge Romig in Hillside Station, (Roslyn) Pennsylvania, a Philadelphia suburb.

Federal agents later confiscated both letters containing George Riggs' signature. They would hold them for evidence.

By June 24, passports for George C. Riggs and Frank J. Johnson arrived from Ottawa at the Great Northern Railway ticket office at Union Station. It was customary to have them returned to the ticket office to ensure the prospective traveler purchased steamship tickets from Great Northern and not from another agency, thus securing commissions for the depot and the agent.

"Every day, we would go around to the steamship office," Grover said. "There was a big plate-glass window in this building, and we would stand across the street to see if anyone in the place might be a detective. If the coast was clear, we would go in."

Grover paid cash for saloon passage on the Canadian Pacific Ocean Services Steamship Line vessel, S.S. *Victorian*, a 520-feet, single-funnel, triple-screw, steam turbine ship of three decks sailing from Montreal with a top speed of 18 knots to Liverpool, England.

The departure time and date were scheduled for 9 am, Wednesday, July 7, 1920.

The first-class saloon accommodations on the *Victorian* cost $200 per passenger plus five dollars in war tax. A 5 percent commission or 10 dollars went to Great Northern, which the agent, Arthur Johnston, shared with the company. On June 24, three weeks after crossing the border and arriving in Winnipeg, ticket number 84409 was issued to Johnson (Stecher) for stateroom #125, K Deck. Ticket number 84410 was issued to Riggs (Grover) for the same stateroom. Passports and steamship passage in hand, the two Philadelphia fugitives cautiously returned to their hotel to pack their belongings.

"That night, we beat it for Montreal," said Grover.

Over several days on the Canadian Pacific train from Winnipeg across the top of Lake Superior and through the Muskoka Lakes of Ontario, Grover and Stecher relaxed and dined in first-class luxury cars. Grover stayed in his cabin for much of the trip, studying travel brochures and mechanical engineering books he purchased in Winnipeg.

About to arrive in Montreal at the great Romanesque Revival Windsor Street Station, they realized the next challenge to flee North America was to obtain visas. Uncertain if they wanted to travel to Germany or Sweden, they decided to obtain permits for both countries.

In Montreal in 1920, the Swiss consul provided German visas for Canadian travelers because Germany still needed to reestablish a consulate in Canada following the war. Obtaining permits for Sweden took more work. Again, Grover relied on his charm.

When he told a false story that he wished to visit his grandfather in Stockholm, the consulate clerk demanded his grandfather's street address. Grover presented an excuse for not remembering but returned later with a street name in Stockholm found at the American Express office in Montreal. He added a house number, and, to his surprise, the clerk declared he knew where it was and issued the visas.[18]

Waiting in Montreal for the arrival of the *Victorian*, Grover made another slip-up, which provided American authorities another link to his escape trail.

"I wrote to Judge Romig to get my car," Grover said—it was still in the garage at the Minnesota-Canadian border. The letter went to San Francisco and then to Philadelphia. "When it fell into the hands of the Department of Justice, we were abroad, but it allowed them to trace our movements in Canada."[19]

In Liverpool, Grover and Stecher boarded a special train for *Victorian* travelers, which carried them into London at Euston Station, with its majestic Roman arch entrance. The mission to secure additional travel papers continued with a German visa stamp on their passports. Finally, feeling relieved they had successfully escaped North America, Grover and Stecher set off on a ferry across the English Channel to Holland, then by train across the Netherlands, stopping for customs inspection in Emerich, Germany.

Grover slipped up again, and it could have cost their freedom.

"I had a lot of American money on me, and I was declaring it," Grover explained. "The baggage was all examined, and the train whistled to go ahead. The customs agent was still counting my American dollars. The train started away. But, Stecher pulled the emergency alarm signal and stopped the train. I jumped on board, fixed the conductor, and we were in safety at last."

Grover's money again bailed them out of a tight spot that could have exposed their true identities. The next day they arrived at the Bergdolls' ancestral home, Eberbach, on the river Neckar in Baden, the southwest portion of Germany along the border with France. They checked into Bohrmann's Krone-Post Hotel overlooking the river and stashed their extra guns in their room. They would need them when federal agents came hunting.

Security was guaranteed. Grover's first cousin and her husband owned the hotel.

---

[18] Reporter Leighton Blood wrote that during German and American intelligence investigations of Bergdoll they discovered that his true lineage was Swedish, not German. Blood said the Bergdoll family denied it.

[19] Federal agents were confiscating suspicious mail sent to key Bergdoll allies, including Judge Romig.

CHAPTER FIFTEEN

Congressional Investigation

Washington, D.C., April–July 1921

In the afternoon session of a Congressional hearing in Washington investigating Grover's escape from Army guards, Kentucky Congressman Ben Johnson pulled a pistol from his pants pocket to take a shot at Charles Bergdoll-Brawn, sitting a few feet away at the witness table.[1]

Fortunately, Johnson was stopped by his wife, who grabbed his pistol hand and held it with the gun barrel pointed toward the hearing room floor. It was an incredible scene and a remarkable feat for Mrs. Johnson. Her husband was a strapping man at 6'3" and a dead shot from his game-hunting youth in the central Kentucky forest where Abraham Lincoln was born.

Ben Johnson was known to be reckless and argumentative. He had already tried to have Emma Bergdoll held in contempt of Congress for not satisfactorily answering his barrage of questions. He probably would have killed Charles with a pistol shot at such close range if he hadn't been stopped.

Charles didn't flinch. He stared at Johnson with steel eyes.

It happened on July 23, 1921. Charles traveled from Philadelphia to Washington by train and, with a calm demeanor in the stifling Capitol hearing room, fielded questions about Grover, from whom he had been estranged since he tried and failed to gain control of his brother's inheritance six years earlier. The summer session was a resumption of hearings that had been completed—until the special committee investigating Grover's escape learned of a letter Grover had written to Emma from Germany, claiming he had paid his Army-appointed defense attorney, Captain Bruce Campbell, a significant bribe to take his case to "higher ups" in Washington and win Grover's release. Emma was in the hearing room that dramatic day and was scheduled to testify next.

The committee consisted of five members of Congress, their staff, and about 50 women who happened to be in the hearing for observation, including Johnson's wife,

---

[1] A stenographer records Congressional committee hearings verbatim. The events surrounding Congressman Ben Johnson pulling his pistol on Charles Bergdoll are from both a newspaper account and the record.

Annie. A reporter from *The New York Times* was also in the hearing room. According to his dispatch and the Congressional Record, the near shooting occurred about an hour into Johnson's questioning of Charles. Johnson was trying to ascertain a rather mundane circumstance: how Charles' wife, Louise, could be reached by her husband when she was traveling to the Bergdoll-Brawn family camp in Pennsylvania's Pocono Mountains.

"You're trying to evade my question," snapped Johnson.

"I am not trying to evade your question," replied a calm and subdued Charles.

"You are! Why can't you come here and tell the truth?" shouted Johnson from his seat on the hearing platform, shaking his index finger at Bergdoll-Brawn, seated at a desk on the hearing floor.

"I am telling the truth," Charles replied again calmly.

Johnson grew white and shouted, "You know you're not."

At that, raising his voice for the first time, Charles bellowed, "You're a liar!"

"I can't stand this," blurted Johnson, scrambling to stand. And he reached into his pants pocket for his pistol.

Annie Johnson, who knew her husband always carried a gun, was at his side in the chamber. She grabbed his arm while committee chairman John Peters grabbed it too. A Marine Corps officer leaned over to stand guard while Mrs. Johnson held her husband's pistol arm.

"Ben, Ben, don't," she pleaded.

"Let me go. Let me get at that dirty flag-hating bastard," shouted Johnson to his wife.

Chairman Peters ordered the house sergeant at arms to remove Charles, who had remained calm and unflinching in his seat. He was led from the hearing room and was on his way to Union Station to catch a northbound Philadelphia train before Johnson was allowed to leave the room with a small entourage.

The hearing was adjourned.

When Johnson walked from the room with his wife still holding his pistol arm, he declared, "I would have killed him in a second if I had not been held back."

A supporter followed Johnson from the room and claimed, "If he doesn't want to kill him, I will."[2] Only by the circumstance of Annie Johnson grabbing her husband's arm was Charles able to avoid another disastrous situation for the Bergdolls. Johnson would probably have carried out his threat.

Johnson's father, a veteran of bare-knuckle politics from Bardstown, Kentucky, had been a state senator and lieutenant governor. His mother had been on the

---

[2] From *The New York Times* and the Congressional Record, July 23, 1921. Later in 1921, a burglar broke into Johnson's Washington office and stole a trunk of papers about the Bergdoll investigation. Johnson insisted it was an inside job by someone wanting to get rid of damaging Army or Bergdoll evidence. The crime was never solved.

committee that chose the design for the Confederate flag. Kentucky historians wrote of Johnson, "His early life included several shooting frays… a hunting trip with Jesse James [the train and bank robber], and numerous political quarrels. A pistol remained a part of his daily attire throughout his life."[3]

The awkward incident delayed Emma's testimony. She would return the following Monday.[4]

The House committee investigating Grover's escape had already written its report. Still, with the new revelation, it was re-convened in mid-July 1921 when it received word from Department of Justice investigators in Philadelphia that Grover sent a letter from Germany to his mother claiming he had paid a bribe to his Army-appointed defense attorney, Captain Campbell. Despite the committee being warned in May by the U.S. Attorney in Philadelphia, Charles D. McAvoy, that Grover often lied about paying bribes to gain freedom, the chairman called the members back to the hearing room for more questions.

In Grover's letter to Emma from Germany, he ridiculed the Alien Property Custodian's seizure of his assets, claimed three nations were offering him citizenship and asylum, and that the federal agents were "starting something they couldn't finish."

> We made the Americans look like a bunch of boobs before the whole world. They are all laughing at them. You certainly did tell it to the investigators down at Washington, and you deserve credit. Why did you not tell them of the $5,000 which we gave Campbell up at Governors Island? If you did not, I would advise you to make it public, so that the grafters will be all exposed. We are writing a book which gives away the whole swindle from beginning to end, and the American public will wake up when they read it in the near future.

Grover never wrote a book about the "whole swindle" nor gave Capt. Campbell $5,000. Emma testified that Campbell was given only about $50 for a jail account from which Grover could purchase razor blades, toothpaste, other toiletries, and a new pair of shoes for his trial.

She also testified that a few hundred dollars were given to Grover's jail mate, Frank E. Speicher, a prisoner freed daily from the Castle Williams jail to travel into Manhattan with the understanding that he would return each evening. The Bergdoll money may have bought his silence. Speicher later told the investigators that Grover would try to escape at his first opportunity, but he never warned their jailers about it.[5]

---

[3] *Boss Ben Johnson, the Highway Commission, and Kentucky Politics, 1927–1937.* James C. Klotter and John W. Muir, The Register of the Kentucky Historical Society. Winter 1986.

[4] The gun-pulling incident inside the U.S. Capitol was the only time a sitting member of Congress tried to kill an American citizen while testifying under subpoena to a Congressional committee. It's an indication of the level of vitriol toward the Bergdoll name during the 1920s. National Register of Historic Places.

[5] The committee later determined that Emma provided $700 to prisoners on Governors Island. In its final report, the committee claimed Grover spent $6,000–7,000 "ingratiating himself" with other prisoners and prison authorities at Governors Island. This was never proven, however. Grover had much more opportunity to escape there than if he had been sent immediately to Fort Leavenworth upon conviction.

When the alleged $5,000 payment to Capt. Campbell became known, the committee called in Campbell, his father, and Emma and Charles for an explanation. Emma testified that she traveled to the Castle Williams jail and gave Grover $5,000 at his request, but she didn't know what he did with it. She said Grover told her that Campbell wanted $100,000 to pay to "higher-ups" in Washington before he could be released. Emma went so far as to claim that while riding the Governors Island ferry with Campbell, he told her he "had given the money [the $50] to the proper person." The press mistakenly reported this amount to be $5,000. In Emma's testimony, it's clear she was referring only to the $50 given to Campbell for Grover's jail toiletries account.

Nonetheless, the Army Military Intelligence Department sent a man to New York to examine Campbell's bank account, shared with his wife, Laura. He returned to the committee, not with copies of the Campbells' bank statements, but with handwritten notes indicating deposits no greater than Campbell's $252.50 monthly Army salary and checks drawn in the range of $7–60.

However, the committee later obtained bank statements showing a $5,037 deposit into Campbell's account. Then, records from a stock investment firm in New York City showed that Campbell deposited $6,500 into an investment account in February 1920, soon after he was appointed Grover's Army attorney. It also discovered that Campbell purchased a new automobile for $1,500 shortly after the alleged Bergdoll bribe.

Campbell was under heavy suspicion by the committee.

Not until the committee heard from the Campbells did the members' suspicion begin to wane.[6] Campbell testified that before his $6,500 stock investment, he and his wife had about $24,000 saved. Campbell's father convincingly testified that his son won $6,000 in "a friendly gambling transaction." Furthermore, Campbell convinced the committee with his reputation and military record. He had been gassed in the war, was in Walter Reed General Hospital near Washington for war-related treatments during earlier sessions of the hearings, and had been called from a military base in Arkansas to appear for the re-convened hearings. While traveling to Washington by train, he had been humiliated by the newspapers' false reports that Emma gave him $5,000. His testimony was described as "rambling and disconnected," but no one contradicted his explanation for the money. Furthermore, in her testimony, Emma contradicted some of the allegations Grover made in his letter. The committee ruled out bribery to any member of the Army or official of the federal government.

It determined that Major Campbell disproved the charges, and he was exonerated.

---

[6] Campbell was a captain during the time he represented Grover in 1920. He was promoted to major prior to his testimony before the House committee in 1921.

The select committee was not so kind to the small cadre of enablers employed by the Bergdolls and the Army commanders who signed off on Grover's release to search for gold. Initially, it investigated to place blame on Major-General Peter C. Harris, adjutant general of the Army, Colonel (later Major) John E. Hunt, commander of the Atlantic Branch Disciplinary Barracks at Governors Island, Judge Romig, Gibboney, and prominent New Jersey lawyer, former New Jersey attorney general, and close friend of President Wilson, John W. Wescott.

In the end, however, the committee laid the most blame for the Bergdoll debacle on Gibboney, Wescott, Hunt, and two others, Washington lawyer and former acting judge advocate general during the war Samuel T. Ansell, and the Army prosecutor Lt. Charles C. Cresson.[7]

***

Soon after Grover's conviction, Gibboney had arranged for Emma to give him $12,500 to hire civilian lawyers for appeals. He hired the Washington law firm of Ansell and Bailey, consisting of Samuel Ansell and partner Edward S. Bailey. With a $5,000 retainer, Ansell, Bailey, and Gibboney initially discussed an appeal on the claims that Grover's Army induction failed to meet the 10 days' notice before becoming effective and where the law was silent on a method of service of a legal notice, personal service was compulsory. The draft board had met neither condition. Gibboney had scant experience in military law, but Ansell and Bailey quickly determined that this line of appeal was not strong enough and would not work. It was abandoned.

With Gibboney, they negotiated and drew two contracts providing fees from $20,000 to $60,000 if they gained Grover's release through whatever means, including clemency and presidential pardon. For an undetermined reason, however, neither of the two contracts was signed, although both Gibboney and Bailey verbally agreed that the second contract was favorable to both parties.

Then, Wescott was brought into the case. The former New Jersey attorney general during the war, Wescott made the Democratic National Convention nominating speeches for President Wilson's two terms in office. Wescott helped elevate Wilson from New Jersey governor to the White House, and the President didn't forget it.

Wescott was a Yale Law School graduate who practiced law in Camden, New Jersey, and lived in a lush neighborhood in Haddonfield. Along with his friendship with President Wilson, he was acquainted with Wilson's secretary of war, Newton Baker, and on friendly terms with Wilson's attorney general from Pennsylvania, Alexander Mitchell Palmer. Wescott's contacts in the Democratic Wilson administration leave no doubt about why he was hired.

---

[7] The Donaldson Report provided more details of the escape fiasco, an investigation completed by Colonel Thomas Q. Donaldson of the U.S. Army Inspector General's office. The report was provided to Congress with testimony from its author.

In his first act aiding the release of Grover, Wescott wrote a legal brief and sent a copy to Secretary Baker.[8] In it, he said, "There is not the slightest doubt in the world but that the war authorities made a mistake. I am enormously interested in the situation and want, if possible, to keep the matter out of the courts."

After retiring from the War Department and returning home to Cleveland, Baker acknowledged Wescott's brief and sent it to the Army's adjutant general. However, he dismissed any "degree of intimacy" between him, Wescott, or any other attorneys working for Bergdoll.

Nonetheless, Wescott's correspondence achieved its goal. The secretary of war sent his legal brief to the Army's adjutant general. It opened the door for Bergdoll's paid civilian advisors to influence military decisions about the fate of the Army's number one draft dodger.

When it was determined that an appeal of Grover's conviction on technical grounds would not work, the investigators determined that Gibboney hatched the scheme for Grover to fetch gold he had buried in the Maryland mountains when he was a fugitive and hiding near Hagerstown. Gibboney told Ansell that Grover had hidden more than $100,000 in gold coins "in a lonely spot somewhere in northern West Virginia, and it was known only to himself."[9]

Realizing he would be sent to serve his five-year sentence in Fort Leavenworth, Kansas prison, Gibboney said Grover wanted to recover the gold and put it in a bank for safekeeping. Ansell, the former acting adjutant general, told Gibboney there was precedent for releasing Army prisoners for personal reasons.[10]

The official investigation report indicates that Ansell, perhaps determined to collect the substantial fee he negotiated with Gibboney, first verbally discussed a conditional release for Grover with the adjutant general, the man in the same position which Ansell had vacated only a few years earlier, Major General Peter C. Harris, on May 10, 1920. Harris said to put it in writing, which Ansell did the following day.

The wheels of Grover's release turned quickly. Harris discussed the release request with the Army chief of staff, Peyton C. March, who said it was OK and that responsibility for prisoners at Governors Island was up to General Harris. With approval from his superior, Harris said he did not deem it necessary to seek further permission from the secretary of war, so Baker was not consulted. Harris' assistant sent a letter to Col. Hunt, commander of the Disciplinary Barracks at Governors

---

[8] Secretary of War Newton Baker was fully aware of the Bergdoll conviction and escape. He ordered an investigation and report to be performed by Colonel Thomas Q. Donaldson of the Army Inspector General's office. The report found a "deliberate plot" to escape among Gibboney, Judge Romig, Emma, Stecher, and Grover.

[9] It was probably Grover who changed the gold burial location to Maryland.

[10] Ansell's unreasonable suggestion was that releases could be granted for wild stories such as searching for buried gold when a limited number of other prisoner releases, under guard, had been allowed for cases of terminal illness among prisoners' close family members.

Island, to arrange for Grover to leave his jail cell to recover his gold temporarily. The conditions were as follows: under armed guard, without handcuffs, with at least one of Grover's attorneys, straight to the location to dig up the gold, then to a bank for deposit, and return to Governors Island. It was "suggested" that an officer accompany the Army guard. All expenses were to be paid by Grover.

The final part of the order was most curious. "You are further instructed to keep the matter strictly confidential and not to divulge the purpose of your expedition," wrote Harris' assistant adjutant general, Colonel Julius A. Penn, over his signature.

Soon after Gibboney and Campbell went to Governors Island to discuss details of Grover's release with Col. Hunt, the conditions began to change. Hunt was a career officer from the United States Military Academy at West Point in charge of the Atlantic Branch prison and took his independent command seriously. He had served in Cuba and the Philippines and was into his second decade as a career officer. However, Hunt had a stain on his record: a court martial for drinking alcohol while on duty in 1905. The infraction would haunt him in the Bergdoll case.

Col. Hunt bristled when other officers tried to tell him how to guard his prisoners. He insisted that the Army prison command was to be independent of the Army general staff under Congressional regulations. He had been in control of the Disciplinary Barracks since August 1918 and shuttled some 4,000 prisoners through his prison in two years, far more than the 500 the island barracks were designed to hold. On the day Grover was released and escaped, more than 700 prisoners were held on Governors Island, many sleeping in tents instead of locked cells.[11]

Col. Hunt was also a stickler for Army rules and regulations. When he was informed that Grover would be coming to Governors Island, he summoned his higher command because the Disciplinary Barracks were for general prisoners, those tried and convicted of a crime. Bergdoll would be a garrison prisoner pending his trial and conviction. The ranking commanders immediately approved the deviation in regulations because they wanted Bergdoll in a secure prison cell.

On the same day as Grover's appearance at Governors Island came the first order meddling with Hunt's command. The adjutant general's office sent a letter to Hunt saying that Bergdoll was not to leave the island without a signed declaration. When he did, "he should be securely guarded and not entrusted to the sole custody of the trial judge advocate, defense counsel, or any other officer." This outside order, Hunt felt, was contrary to his independence. His practice was transporting prisoners on court dates with only a single sentinel carrying a stick.

---

[11] Lt. Frank H. Smith, known among the prisoners as "Hard-Boiled" Smith, was the only other notorious prisoner at Governors Island during Bergdoll's incarceration. Lt. Smith was court-martialed at Fort Jay and sentenced to 18 months in prison for ordering guards under his command at the U.S. Army prison farm number two near Paris, France to beat prisoners. Smith testified in his defense that other prisons were worse.

Several weeks later, Hunt received another letter from a colonel in the Army's general staff saying there should be two guards whenever Bergdoll left the island for a court date. "The commanding general directs that he [Bergdoll] be handcuffed to one sentinel and guarded by another sentinel."

Hunt scoffed at the directive because he believed it was written by Bergdoll's Army prosecutor, Lt. Cresson. Instead of following advice and orders from ranking officers, Hunt relied on Army psychiatrists who examined and determined Bergdoll was not dangerous and would not try to escape. Hunt later testified that he and the psychiatrists felt that placing Bergdoll in handcuffs for an extended time would be inhumane.[12]

Before the expedition was to leave the barracks, Hunt called Grover into his office and asked him specifically where the gold was buried. He wouldn't tell. Hunt allowed Grover to keep the location a secret, even though he was a convicted Army prisoner. He was allowed to travel hundreds of miles to a remote area several days distant from the Disciplinary Barracks on a mission that could easily be seen as a mechanism for escape.

Furthermore, Hunt feared that Grover would be identified when he was out in public. He wanted the expedition to be secret, so he ordered that Grover wear a battalion uniform. But Hunt also sent Grover to Philadelphia, where he was most likely to be identified. The Congressional committee wondered why Hunt didn't send the expedition directly to Maryland from New York via New Jersey or from a train station in Baltimore or Washington where Bergdoll was less apt to be identified.

Hunt, who deplored ranking officers' advice on his prison command, had only a simple explanation. He turned control over to a civilian.

"I made a concession to Gibboney to send the prisoner [Bergdoll] to North Philadelphia and from where they would go by automobile to Hagerstown to search for the gold," he said.[13]

Hunt said he was actively seeking rank and job promotion during the Bergdoll escape and was "practically selected" for command of the Army's prison at Fort Leavenworth.[14] The revelation was an effort to enhance his credibility among the members of Congress.

Congressman Johnson, who knew a thing or two about guns, especially the shooter in his pocket, asked Hunt if he would have trusted the advice of his psychiatrist if

---

[12] Congressman Ben Johnson suggested Hunt's reliance on Army psychiatrists was no better than consulting a Ouija board.

[13] In another incredible admission by Col. Hunt, he told the committee that he was unsure if he ever gave permission for the expedition to stop off at Grover's mansion in Philadelphia instead of going directly from the North Philadelphia train station to Hagerstown.

[14] Col. Hunt never got the Fort Leavenworth command. Instead, he was court martialed and promoted simultaneously, but then acquitted and retired from the Army at the rank of full colonel.

he had known that Grover had an arsenal of more than 30 shotguns, pistols, and rifles, one with a Maxim silencer, in his mansion when he was captured.

Hunt's reply, "Certainly, such information would have had great weight with me if I had heard or known that Bergdoll had an arsenal in his house." Hunt admitted he didn't know much about Bergdoll before he arrived on the island.

Col. Hunt insisted his guard force had been depleted, and he could not afford to lose even one officer to be away from the island to guard the Bergdoll gold expedition. Instead, he chose two noncommissioned sergeants, John O'Hare and Calvin York, to serve as Grover's guards. They were part of a sparse guard unit that Hunt described as "mentally under par." Hunt's orders allowed O'Hare and York to carry pistols but no handcuffs. Transporting a prisoner in bracelets would be too conspicuous, he later said.

Additionally, Grover would not wear his blue denim prisoner outfit with the large white number 10 on the back but, instead, wear a disciplinary battalion uniform which, to civilians, appeared no different than an enlisted man's uniform: olive drab, wrapped leggings, and campaign hat, minus the hat cord identifying an Army unit.

Furthermore, none could agree on which attorney would go with the gold-hunting expedition: Gibboney, Campbell, or Romig. And, to make matters worse, Hunt gave Sgt. O'Hare only minimal information about his mission. O'Hare was told only that he was taking prisoner Bergdoll on the morning train to North Philadelphia. He was asked to read the adjutant general's letter of release conditions (which he didn't understand) and told he would meet Gibboney in North Philadelphia, where O'Hare would confirm the attorney's identity by matching letters of expedition orders, a copy of which Hunt was sending to Gibboney.

Neither O'Hare nor York was told the true mission of the expedition. Hunt thought they were going to Hagerstown to get money from a bank and take it for deposit in a Philadelphia bank. York was only informed of the order the night before they were to leave. Neither carried additional provisions for a multiple-night expedition nor understood anything about digging up gold. They didn't even have a shovel.

Incredibly, they were told to take orders from a civilian when they got to North Philadelphia: Gibboney.

Sergeant O'Hare was in command of the guard. Raised in Brooklyn, New York, he was an Army veteran with about five years of experience running drills with prisoners. But O'Hare had been on only one prisoner transport convoy by train to Fort Leavenworth. He was previously assigned to Fort Myer, Virginia, and had never ridden in an automobile until he got into Grover's Super Six.

O'Hare testified that he was 5'5" and 130 pounds, no physical match for the much heavier Bergdoll and half the size of the tall and stout Stecher. Under committee questioning, O'Hare was incapable of spelling or understanding the definition of certain words in the written order permitting Bergdoll's release. The committee found that he did not have sufficient education and experience to guard a man like Bergdoll.

O'Hare initially met his charge by visiting Grover where he was assigned to work in the prison laundry, organizing uniforms for storage and dispensing to prisoners returning to the regular Army. Therefore, he said, Grover got to pick out his uniform for the expedition, approved by Hunt. Against Hunt's order, however, Grover included a blue hat cord, indicating an infantry unit. It was the first time he'd worn the uniform of the regular Army.

At Governors Island, O'Hare withdrew $15 from Grover's prison account and checked out two pistols for himself and Sgt. York, and, using Grover's money, purchased three passenger tickets for the train to Philadelphia.

He admitted that his ignorance about the expedition resulted from scant orders from Hunt.

"In fact, the only instructions I got from him [Hunt] was to go to North Philadelphia and meet Mr. Gibboney. And right there Mr. Gibboney was to tell me what to do because I have no travel order or further instructions."

O'Hare said Grover was cooperative and quiet on the train down to Philadelphia. He just sat and chewed tobacco. He said Gibboney took command when they arrived in North Philadelphia, with Romig and Stecher also in the Super Six. They almost immediately dropped Gibboney in the city where he said he had to attend Emma's trial for threatening police officers with her gun during Grover's capture. By then, Bergdoll's quietness had sprung to life. He took control of the car, driving the group around Philadelphia's vast Fairmount Park, the site of his teenage racing adventures, and then dropping Judge Romig to catch a train for Emma's court case.[15]

O'Hare said he and York were confused. They thought they might be going to get money from a bank. They thought they might be there for Grover to attend his mother's trial. Then, they thought they might be taking Grover to Washington to visit with Attorney Ansell. They were unsure why they weren't headed to Maryland and the bank. But they never questioned anyone. In fact, with Gibboney and Romig gone, there was no one to ask.

"I knowed about going to Hagerstown and getting money out of one bank and transferring it to another bank at Philadelphia. But, as far as going to dig for gold, I didn't know anything about it," O'Hare said.

O'Hare and York were accustomed to following orders. Without the guidance of Gibboney and Romig, they sat in the back of the Super Six. With Grover at the wheel

---

[15] While Gibboney and Judge Romig claimed they had to represent Emma in her trial for trying to prevent Grover's capture, it may have been a ruse. Gibboney was dropped far from the court, and Emma used a court-appointed attorney, was convicted, and paid a $200 cash fine. Investigators believed that by leaving the expedition, Gibboney and Romig were trying to remove themselves from the planned escape.

and Stecher in the front passenger seat, they were driven all around Philadelphia and into the countryside westward from the city and near the Bergdoll farm in Broomall.

For O'Hare, it was a thrill. His first ride in a car, the canvas top open, the wind blowing in his face, and freedom from the confines of the island military base in New York.

That's when O'Hare and York first heard Grover and Stecher talking about the car "knocking." O'Hare said he was further confused about the description of "knocking." He said, "the machine was running all right. I did not know what they were talking about."

O'Hare also described Emma's return to the Wynnefield mansion from the court. "She ran in, threw her arms around him [Grover], and began kissing him. She commenced telling him about the case, how she beat the case, and telling him how much it cost—$200 and something, to beat the case."

He described for the committee how Grover removed a part from the Super Six engine and put it in his pocket after they drove to the Gayety (burlesque theater) and parked to go inside because he was worried someone would recognize his valued car and steal it. And, O'Hare sorrowfully admitted that they stopped at a saloon on the way back to the Wynnefield mansion to get some liquor, probably gin that York later admitted drinking while playing pool on the third floor of the Bergdoll mansion.

O'Hare said he had Gibboney's telephone number written on a crumpled piece of paper in his pocket and a secret code, "S," for when Gibboney called him at the mansion, but he never did. Even though Gibboney was supposed to remain with Grover at all times, O'Hare never saw Gibboney again until after Grover escaped.

O'Hare confirmed that he slept in the same second-floor bedroom as Grover but that York slept on the third floor alone, across the hall from Stecher. O'Hare said the windows were closed, but the door to his room was not locked. It did not have a key. O'Hare claims he stayed awake most of the night, dozing off a few times. Full of gin, Sgt. York slept soundly.

O'Hare said he had not touched an alcoholic drink in over 20 years.

Despite their admissions for dereliction of duty, O'Hare and York were acquitted in their court-martial trials. Both resumed their Army duties and later retired. However, this would not be the last time they testified against Grover.

***

During the conspiracy and campaign to release Grover for his pot of gold expedition, unknown to Col. Hunt, Major Harris, General March, and even Secretary Baker were details of other warnings (outside the Army) sent by letter to military intelligence officials and Department of Justice agents that Grover would try to escape at his first opportunity.

One of the escape warning letters was sent to a federal agent in Philadelphia by Jacob Strohm, Grover's uncle by marriage to Emma's sister, Wilhelmina Barth Strohm.

The agent read the letter and immediately gave it to his superior, the special agent in charge of the Bergdoll case in Philadelphia, John J. O'Connor.

O'Connor was from Washington, sent to Philadelphia to spearhead the Bergdoll search. His investigative efforts led to the tip that Grover would slip back home for Christmas 1919, staying at the Wynnefield mansion.

Agent O'Connor made a special commission in the autumn of 1919 for Army Air Service Lieutenant George C. McDonald of the Overbrook community of West Philadelphia to go undercover in civilian clothes and find out where Grover was hiding. McDonald was one of a family of nine whose father, George C. McDonald, Sr., died of muscular disease in 1913 while young George was running with Grover as his race car mechanic and flight student. Discovering his friendship with Grover, O'Connor pulled Lt. McDonald off the Army Air Service flight line on Long Island, New York, and sent him to a Christmas party where he knew many of Grover's friends would attend with booze flowing just weeks before the implementation of the Volstead Act.

At the party, McDonald cozied up to a woman known to be one of Grover's girlfriends, her name never revealed. He heard the woman say to a man at the party, "If you see Groff [Grover's family nickname], give him my regards." McDonald then heard the man reply, "Groff is coming home for Christmas."[16]

McDonald's infiltration of Grover's inner circle led directly to the federal agents capturing Grover a few weeks later, on January 7, 1920.

Months later, Lt. McDonald was still detached from his military unit on Long Island and working undercover. In late April 1920, McDonald was sent into Jacob Strohm's saloon at 61st Street and Haverford Avenue in West Philadelphia to confirm the details of Strohm's letter to the federal agent. He learned that Strohm was sincere. Grover was making plans to escape.

The Strohms ran their West Philadelphia corner saloon, barley, and hops store for home beer brewers during Prohibition. They lived in a comfortable stone twin house in Philadelphia's Overbrook community, near McDonald's family home and Grover's Wynnefield mansion. Their proximity allowed the Strohms' daughter, Emma, to sit with her aged grandmother at the Wynnefield mansion when her aunt Emma Bergdoll was out of town on business, specifically on two occasions when Emma Bergdoll and Romig fetched the fortune in gold from the Treasury in Washington. While at the Wynnefield mansion with her grandmother, one day soon after Grover's conviction, Emma Strohm overheard discussions of Grover's escape plan and relayed it to her father.

Jacob Strohm's letter to the Department of Justice agent reported that in return for $10,000, Ansell guaranteed Grover's release on bond by submitting another writ

---

[16] Agent O'Connor did not name the man who revealed Grover's trip home for Christmas. It's believed to be Thomas Furey, friend of both Grover and Erwin, who accidentally revealed the plan.

of habeas corpus to the federal court, allowing Grover to forfeit his bond and escape by fleeing the country. Strohm said it would happen within two weeks.[17]

The letter was received in Philadelphia, and when McDonald's undercover work confirmed the contents, O'Connor sent the intelligence in a letter to Washington on May 3, where through a series of errors and misunderstandings by a junior grade agent, it sat unheeded in the Washington office.

The Congressional committee said the valuable letter was "hidden away in a pigeonhole, never to find its way to Bergdoll's prison."

Grover's cellmate Speicher's warnings about Grover's plan to escape were never heard by Army officials either, because Grover was paying cash for Speicher's daily pleasure trips from his jail cell at Governors Island to Manhattan.

Philadelphia U.S. Attorney McAvoy, who replaced Grover's nemesis, Francis Fisher Kane, was also aware that Grover would try to escape. Many years earlier, as a private attorney, McAvoy represented Grover in a simple speeding case on the Main Line of Philadelphia, and he knew of the Bergdolls' reputation. McAvoy later said, "If we had been notified, he [Bergdoll] would never have gotten out if we could have stopped it."

Neither McAvoy nor the Department of Justice, Military Intelligence, Philadelphia Police detectives, or any other legal authority knew Grover was to be released with two noncommissioned officer guards later described by the committee as "stupid, ignorant, in a strange place, and utterly incompetent" until they heard Bergdoll had escaped.

Committee members were incredulous that Grover commandeered control of his Hudson Super Six when the expedition arrived in Philadelphia. He then drove the car with his guards, knowing they weren't supposed to be joyriding around the city. The committee asked why the two guards were so gullible as to accept Grover and Stecher's story that the car engine "was knocking" when it was fit to be driving all over Philadelphia and twice to the Bergdoll farm community west of Philadelphia.

They asked why, if Grover was to be taken directly to Maryland to hunt for his gold, Stecher's wife, Frieda, was given advance notice to come to the Wynnefield mansion to cook dinner and supper for the expedition. The only deduction was that O'Hare and York weren't intelligent enough to figure that out. And the noncommissioned officer guards were accustomed to taking orders and not being in charge. Blame for sending these guards was rightfully sent up the Army chain of command.

The committee also deduced that Gibboney "was not much of a lawyer, but more of a practical manager for better lawyers." They learned that Gibboney retained Wescott with Emma's $1,000 bill to initiate Grover's release.

---

[17] It was never determined why Strohm turned against his wife's family and revealed Grover's escape plan to federal agents. However, like many other saloon operators, he was selling illegal booze and he could have been cooperating with federal agents in return for lenience.

Wescott wrote a letter to the secretary of war suggesting Bergdoll should be released to fetch his gold. Later, with a letter to the attorney general, Wescott told the nation's top prosecutor to send "his ablest man" to investigate and avoid Gibboney's arrest for conspiracy to help Bergdoll escape. Wescott complained to the attorney general that John Dwyer's newspaper, the *Philadelphia Record,* "had the audacity to involve me in a conspiracy to secure the liberty of Grover." He said Dwyer printed his letter-to-the-editor complaint and a reply which he considered a retraction of the newspaper's allegation that both Wescott and Gibboney were the masterminds of Grover's escape. He said the newspaper also attacked the War Department and that Palmer had "a duty to protect the department and the [Wilson] administration."

Palmer acknowledged Wescott's letter and sent a copy to McAvoy in Philadelphia but left the Bergdoll matter to the War Department.

Incredibly, when Col. Hunt was court-martialed for dereliction of duty, he also admitted disregarding the warnings about Grover's dangerous character and his plan to escape. Hunt said, under oath, "the weight of those two warnings, the legal obligation contained in them, was just about the legal obligations of a communication from the mayor of Timbuctoo."

Hunt was prosecuted by Col. Cresson, the same Army judge advocate who prosecuted Grover. Cresson called Major Amos T. Baker to the stand, one of the Army psychiatrists who examined Grover. Baker said that Bergdoll was not a criminal. He was subnormal but was "not of a criminal or dangerous type." Major Baker said handcuffing Bergdoll "would be humiliating to the prisoner and might suggest to him the possibility of escape." He said, "I do recall Col. Hunt not wishing to humiliate the prisoner by attracting attention to him by sending a superfluous guard or unduly securing him."

During Hunt's trial, Cresson sympathized with Hunt, saying, "it's not a pleasant duty… to ask that a brother officer be punished or be admonished or held guilty of neglect of duty." Before any testimony was given, Cresson denied in court "any idea of there being anything crooked or any collusion on the part of Hunt in this matter, or that any money was used, the only charge in the matter being to imply neglect of duty and failure to take due precautions in the matter."

Cresson didn't consider Hunt's prior court martial for drunkenness. Based on Cresson's statements and the trial record, the committee suggested Hunt's acquittal was a "shocking mockery" of justice.

The committee agreed on the guilt of Hunt, suggesting Grover bought his way out, saying, "when he [Hunt] sent Bergdoll away from the island without handcuffs, without a commissioned officer, without the presence of counsel, without a properly instructed guard, and a suitable guard. He was defiant of orders or corrupt; he was guilty."

But the court martial acquitted him anyway.

The committee was astonished to learn that Major Hunt was promoted to lieutenant colonel between Grover's escape and Hunt's court martial. Then, with a special announcement in court during his trial, Hunt was promoted to full colonel. The promotion, they said, influenced his acquittal.

Soon after his acquittal, however, Colonel Hunt retired from the Army and began collecting a $3,600 annual pension. The committee of Congressmen were so incensed over this development that they considered a plan to retract Hunt's annuity. It went nowhere.[18]

The committee also found that O'Hare failed in his duty by permitting Grover to drive around Philadelphia and buy drinks in a saloon and the Gayety for York (despite Prohibition) and supply York with enough gin at the Wynnefield mansion for him to become drunk and remain in a stupor the following day. O'Hare didn't even provide proper guard at night, sending York to sleep in another room with a bottle of gin while he, O'Hare, slept alone in a bedroom with Grover.

The committee couldn't understand how O'Hare and York could be exonerated when they admitted negligence in performing their duties. The committee sympathized with the noncommissioned officers, saying they were "accustomed to act always under orders, and were practically incapable of independent action."

The committee recommended that the War Department investigate how such acquittals can occur.

The committee also said it found a "lack of efficiency" among government agencies in apprehending Bergdoll after his escape. It referred to the lack of cooperation and coordination between the War Department and the Department of Justice, all to Grover's advantage since he ran from the draft and, in a small measure, leading to his taunting letters and postcards claiming agents were incompetent and would never catch him.

Two of the five select committee members had different opinions in the minority of the committee's overall conclusion. They found a conspiracy to aid Grover's escape existed but only among Gibboney, Emma, Grover, Stecher, and Romig. They blamed General Harris on the military side most but said Hunt was also to blame. Hunt should have advised Harris about three escape warnings and asked if his superior officer wished to modify his prisoner release order. They couldn't understand how the military court could decide to acquit Hunt. They called it a severe reflection of the court-martial system in the Army.

One conclusion of the lengthy investigation revealed an unfortunate scenario.

---

[18] Details from the Select Committee to Investigate the Escape of General Prisoner Grover Cleveland Bergdoll, Sixty-Seventh Congress, May–July 1921.

Romig testified that when Sgt. O'Hare sat down in Grover's mansion and realized the gravity of his legal jeopardy from Bergdoll's escape; he reached for his gun, saying, "he thought he would end it all."

Romig talked him away from the ledge. He said O'Hare exclaimed, "My God, I've been in the Army twenty-five years, and this happens."[19] Fearing his job loss and Army retirement pension, O'Hare asked rhetorically, "What will my poor, poor wife and our children do? What is there left?"

Romig testified, "I believe I prevented the man from committing suicide."[20]

---

[19] O'Hare was approaching 20 years in the Army. On whose error it became 25 is unknown.
[20] Master Sgt. John O'Hare later retired from the Army and lived in New York City.

CHAPTER SIXTEEN

Death of a Bergdoll Fixer

July–December 1920

On the morning of December 29, 1920, the bodies of four American men washed ashore from the southern Gulf of Mexico into a small white sand bay of Playa Punta Xen in the remote plantation region of Campeche, Mexico. Their pockets were empty except for a pair of glasses. No cash. No identification. Only cufflinks and a watch were found in the sand nearby. In time, the rapidly decomposing remains were identified as businessmen from Philadelphia.

One of them was David Clarence Gibboney, Sr., Grover's attorney and the Bergdoll family fixer.[1] Within days began wild speculation that Gibboney had gone to Mexico to see Grover and was murdered. A rumor among the public was that Grover was hiding in Mexico, and Gibboney had gone there to deliver cash and gold.[2]

***

The fact that Gibboney had become infamous in Philadelphia, New York, and Washington as the Bergdoll lawyer and mastermind of Grover's release to fetch a pot of gold was not the only reason his story of Yucatan adventure, sailing, robbery or murder, drowning, or hoax was so captivating to the press. Even before he latched onto Emma Bergdoll's purse snap, Gibboney was already making headlines with notorious campaigns against vice in Philadelphia and New Jersey.

Before 1920, Gibboney promoted an appealing alternative to the pending Prohibition that many people in the liquor and beer industry, including Emma, supported.

David Clarence Gibboney arrived in Pennsylvania from his youth in Iowa to attend the Philadelphia College of Pharmacy. After several years as a drug store

---

[1] The details of Gibboney's trip to Mexico and accidental drowning are from Congressional testimony and investigative reports. The information was supported by travel documents, consulate, and court records on Gibboney's business partner, John Markley. Mortuary and burial records support the investigation report that the men suffered from accidental drowning during a violent storm in the Gulf of Mexico.
[2] Speculation about the Gibboney–Grover Mexico rendezvous was mainly among the uninformed public. Military Intelligence had already confirmed on October 26, 1920, that Grover was hiding in Eberbach, Germany.

clerk, he became the powerful secretary of the Law and Order Society, a privately funded group forcing police and prosecutors to raid and close illegal liquor and beer saloons, gambling houses, and whorehouses in the 1890s. If the police wouldn't act, they raided the illegal establishments themselves. The group was highly effective at shutting down saloons that sold beer on Sundays and allowed kids to fetch a pail or large kettle of lager for their parents at home. While the Law and Order Society focused on the unusual proclivities of these establishments, such as scantily clad dancing women and bloody prize fistfights, their activities later benefited Emma while managing the brewery's hundreds of Bergdoll Beer-sponsored saloons. The Society got rid of her competition.

Gibboney was especially effective with raids on the Manayunk Pool Room, where nearly 100 people were convicted, except for a few released by police after a riot.[3] He also focused on Camden, New Jersey, a ferry ride across the Delaware River from Philadelphia, where the Society rounded up 210 violators in one raid alone.

With these well-publicized raids, Gibboney received death threats almost daily. As a result, he didn't keep a residential address in later years, often sleeping in his office. He preferred hotels, and once in a while, he would stay with the Bergdolls, bunking in an upstairs bedroom at the Wynnefield mansion by himself.

With Prohibition looming, Gibboney was popular among liquor and beer producers for his position that state and commonwealth governments should take over alcohol sales. The producers and retailers felt state control was better than a complete alcohol ban with Prohibition. But like Gibboney's failed run for Philadelphia County district attorney, he could not influence the politicians on booze. Prohibition won.

**

In May 1920, soon after Grover's escape and while the federal grand jury was considering conspiracy charges against Emma, Charles, and the others, Gibboney, still smarting over criticism for orchestrating Grover's release, consulted an attorney in Philadelphia while considering if he should sue Philadelphia newspapers and the Bergdolls for laying blame for Grover's escape at his feet. Gibboney felt he was being pilloried and assailed in the press. He claimed he was being treated in "an outrageous way."[4]

The attorney, James Washington Logue, a former Philadelphia congressman who had dealt with Gibboney for many years over liquor licenses, swiftly declined.

---

[3] Manayunk was a working-class garment mill section of Philadelphia along the Schuylkill and not far from the Bergdoll Brewery and Biergartens. Its mill workers and residents were frequent contributors to and victims of vice.

[4] The revelation that Gibboney was trying to turn on his long, lucrative relationship with Emma Bergdoll is supported by testimony from former Philadelphia Congressman and Attorney James Washington Logue.

Laughing at the proposition made in his Philadelphia office, Logue suggested that Gibboney could not bring a suit against anyone.[5]

Logue knew Gibboney well enough from political campaigns to call him "Gib," and he told him he had been "fooled and tricked" by Bergdoll.[6] In a somewhat scolding manner, Logue told Gibboney he had an "implied duty, if not a direct duty," to speak up if he had any helpful information to the grand jury.[7] Logue said he was emphatic with Gibboney that he would not advise or represent him in any criminal or civil case. He later informed U.S. Attorney McAvoy of their conversation.

Logue said Gibboney revisited him that summer unannounced and at his Merion, Main Line, Pennsylvania home on a rainy and stormy Saturday night where Logue couldn't avoid him or quickly get rid of him as he wished. This time Gibboney brought John Wescott with him. Logue said Gibboney questioned again if Logue would help him sue the Bergdolls and get action against the newspapers.

Logue said, "The proposition was such an insane one that I wouldn't discuss it." But he did. He said Gibboney "appeared to be grieved over the [Bergdoll's] escape. He implied again that Gibboney had been a fool.

"How you could permit this man out of your sight for two minutes, I can't understand. Your conduct is reprehensible," the former congressman told his fellow attorney.

Logue said Wescott tried to engage him to support Gibboney and the brief he had written for Grover's release, but Logue managed to shut down the efforts of both men. He surmised they visited him to plead for help because Logue, as an attorney with many federal cases, was often in touch with the U.S. Attorney in Philadelphia, Department of Justice agents in Washington, the attorney general's office, and cabinet secretaries he had known from his stint as a member of Congress, specifically the Secretary of War.

Gibboney left Logue's home that night without the help he desired. Soon afterward, the grand jury declined to indict him but settled on a censure. The news was carried prominently in the local newspapers causing additional public embarrassment.

Gibboney was still peeved, but he had no choice or recourse but to move on and try to resurrect his soiled reputation and focus on new business ventures.

In 1920, while representing Grover in his court martial case and after years of making legal and financial arrangements for Emma, Gibboney also served as president and legal advisor of the Philadelphia-based Tropical Products Company with henequen hemp, fustic, dogwood, mahogany, cedar, and rubber plantations in

---

[5] Logue was a devout Catholic and president of the Catholic Total Abstinence Union which dealt with Gibboney's Law and Order Society over liquor licenses. He also lost a son to influenza while shipping out to France in the war.

[6] Gibboney once ran for district attorney of Philadelphia but was soundly beaten in the polls.

[7] Gibboney appeared before the grand jury and was later censured by the panel but not charged.

the Yucatan Peninsula of Mexico.[8] Tropical Products was organized to absorb another firm, International Lumber and Development Company, when its principal, John Markley, was convicted of defrauding stockholders, fined $10,000, and sentenced to 15 months in the high stone-walled Eastern State Penitentiary in Philadelphia in 1915.

Gibboney was Markley's, International Lumber's, and Tropical Products' attorney. His counsel partner for the company was John W. Wescott, President Wilson's close friend whose expertly crafted legal brief convinced the Army to let Grover out of jail to search for his pot of gold in the Maryland mountains.

Both men tried and failed to have a Pennsylvania congressman obtain a presidential pardon for the imprisoned Markley. The congressman later became the United States attorney general, A. Mitchell Palmer, the same attorney general in office during Grover's capture, trial, and escape. Their mutual connection was Emma Bergdoll, a "significant" investor in Tropical Products.[9]

By October 1920, headlines about Grover's escape and the trial of Erwin, Emma, and Charles were fading. Gibboney applied for a passport from the State Department to travel to Mexico via Cuba on Tropical Products Company business. Because of his connection to Grover, however, the application was denied. He appealed with the aid of U.S. Attorney McAvoy, who, despite his opposition to Gibboney's role in the Bergdoll debacle, said he vouched to the State Department for Gibboney's travel intentions. The appeal was processed on December 10, and on December 17, one day before Gibboney was to sail for Cuba, his passport was approved.

Gibboney, however, told associates he had a premonition about the trip and didn't want to go.

The mission of the Mexico expedition was two-fold. As president of the new company with a stock valuation of $800,000 that replaced a company entangled in stock fraud, Gibboney, Markley, 72, and Shriver, 67, were to inspect several plantations producing henequen and report back to their new stockholders, including Emma.

Like Markley, Shriver was elderly. He was bald, mustachioed, and slightly built. They were to meet with Markley's son, Lawrence, 36, a mining engineer from Elmhurst, Illinois, living in Mexico since 1919 managing the company's henequen contracts at the plantations, who would lead the tour.

The elder Markley had been to Yucatan and Campeche a few times to handle labor difficulties. Because of the elder Markley's fraud conviction, Gibboney and Shriver were required to go along as president and director of the new company for the second part of their mission, carrying cash and gold to pay the henequen

---

[8] Henequen from the Yucatan made hay-baling twine and mooring lines for ocean-going ships.

[9] It's unknown how much money Emma invested in Tropical Products. Gibboney described it as "significant."

producers who, under a Tropical Products land contract, managed the Mexican workers laboring under harsh conditions for a few centavos a day.[10]

Gibboney, Markley, and Shriver first sailed from New York to Havana on the steamer *Mexico*. Then they sailed to the Yucatan port at Progreso, checking in with immigration and the U.S. Consulate, and, by train, overland to Merida, where they visited and inspected some of their henequen plantations. Then came a journey on the Ferrocarriles Unidos de Yucatan with its Philadelphia-made wood-burning Baldwin locomotives, nicknamed *toros de fuego* (bulls of fire), to Campeche, where the line terminated. The rest of their trip would take them inland to the heavily wooded tropical forest, sparsely populated with dangerous animals such as the northern Mexico jaguar. The men were also aware of the violent war from the Mexican Revolution in the previous decade and Mexican bandits who knew that traveling Americans carried substantial amounts of cash in dollars.

Lawrence Markley chartered a small motor sailboat to make their trip safer, easier, and faster. They continued their voyage down the coast, landing at small seaside villages and then traipsing inland, visiting more henequen plantations. Without graded roads, their only other travel option would have been by mule train or horseback, a challenging journey on meandering paths for older men with limited time. Gibboney was only 52, but he was broad-shouldered, 6'1½" tall, and fair-skinned with light brown hair and blue eyes. He was an office lawyer and businessman not accustomed to arduous wilderness adventures in the hot Mexican sun.

After spending 15 months in Philadelphia's infamous Eastern State Prison and rebuilding his fractured business, an adventure trip to the wild lands of Mexico to see his son must have appealed to Markley. No fitter than Markley or Gibboney, Shriver had previously traveled to Jamaica with his family for a holiday and was aware of the challenges of the climate. Still, as far as can be determined, this was his first trip to Mexico.

Running along the vacant coastline in the chartered sailboat with six Mexican men as their *sergios* and *marineros*, on December 27 they were forced into the small fishing village of Champoton by a violent southwest storm. They waited through the night and, despite warnings by Champoton seafarers that "the storm was making danger for everyone who braved it," they set off again on December 28 southward for Chenkan, the most remote region on their itinerary.

The bodies of eight drowned men, four Mexicans and four Americans, washed ashore in a small hook of a bay just north of Punta Xen on the central Campeche coast. They were removed by mule-drawn carts to the nearest community, Champoton,

---

[10] Gibboney's passport application appeal details his need to go to Yucatan and Campeche, where "payments were required." Additional details are compiled from *All in the Family: Railroads and Henequen Monoculture in Porfirian Yucatan*. Allen Wells, Hispanic American Historical Review, 1992, Duke University Press.

examined closely, and then buried in the fishing village's small cemetery overlooking the gulf. It was determined that Gibboney and his Philadelphia and Chicago business associates, John R. Markley, Lawrence Markley, and Frank W. Shriver, had been in the motor sailboat that capsized in a violent storm the previous day. Based on the size of the craft, it was probably grossly overloaded. An investigation headed by the governor of Campeche relied on two other Mexican men who survived on board the boat. Not much is known about the two survivors, but they were able to report their tragedy, and the news was carried by a messenger on horseback about 40 miles north to Campeche.

The U.S. Consulate in Progreso forwarded the news by telegraph to Philadelphia and Elmhurst, Illinois, where families of the men were notified of the disaster by December 30. Gibboney's wife, Ella, their daughter, and son, David Clarence, Jr., lived in Cambridge, Massachusetts, where

Gibboney's small chartered boat, left, capsized in the Bay of Campeche, causing his suspicious and untimely death. The press and public incorrectly speculated Gibboney was in Mexico carrying cash and gold to Grover. Grover would claim Gibboney was still alive and hiding in Mexico two years after his body had been returned to Philadelphia and buried. (Historical Society of Pennsylvania/ *Philadelphia Record*/ Lawrence P. Sharples Photo)

daughter Louise May Gibboney was attending college. Mrs. Gibboney was reported to be "prostrate" with the news of her husband's death.

Despite Mexican and American officials identifying the bodies and issuing death certificates, and witness accounts of the scene from the son of a Philadelphia-area multi-millionaire inventor who was on business in Campeche during the tragedy, speculation in the press and the public began to drift toward robbery and murder, or another Bergdoll hoax.[11]

Telegrams sent to the American consul in Progreso from Tropical Products' Champoton employees speculated that the men had been robbed of the cash and

---

[11] Lawrence P. Sharples, son of Philip M. Sharples of West Chester, Pennsylvania, the incredibly rich inventor of the centrifugal milk cream separator, was on holiday in Mexico then and gathered information about the tragedy among his fellow Philadelphia-area businessmen. A highly reputable man, he vouched for the accuracy of the Mexican authorities' information that the men were dead and identified correctly.

gold they were carrying to pay the henequen farmers and then murdered. Because it was issued to the consul, the telegram report entered the newspapers on January 31, 1921.

Around the same time, Washington's House Military Affairs committee received an anonymous letter with a Philadelphia postal cancelation stamp while members contemplated an investigation into Grover's escape. The letter suggested Gibboney had fled to Mexico with Bergdoll's cash and gold, was still alive, and was hiding there. House committee members became even more suspicious when several life insurance companies withheld about $37,000 due to the Gibboney heirs, claiming they needed more proof that the highly insured Gibboney was dead.

Playing in the newspapers, the controversy prompted Gibboney's survivors to issue a statement. In it, because his mother was inconsolable, Gibboney, Jr. wrote:

> I seriously question the sincerity of any government representative who says he is suspicious of the tragedy which overtook my father. Only a coward would want to bask in the political sunlight created by vague insinuations about a dead man who could not make a reply. The implication that my father is hiding in Mexico was known to be groundless when made, or else was the result of failure to investigate the facts surrounding his death in the slightest degree.

Still, in the spring of 1921, few believed the great Gibboney could be dead. His body was shipped home for final identification through his dental work. It enabled Ella and their children to collect substantial life insurance benefits. He was buried at Arlington Cemetery in Drexel Hill, Pennsylvania.[12]

Gibboney, for years, had been Emma's lawyer, family fixer, and advisor. She paid him well, loaned him money, and invested in his business ventures. They were friends and sometimes social companions, but nothing more.

With his death, Emma lost one of the two men she could call at a moment's notice, day or night, to tend to a family business or legal problem. Her decisions were often her own from that point onward, and they got her into much more trouble.

Even from his hiding place in Eberbach, Germany, Grover knew that Gibboney had consulted an attorney to file suit against the Philadelphia newspapers and the Bergdolls, and it roiled him. Then, adding fuel to the fire, Grover made things worse for the still-simmering Gibboney rumors when, two years after the attorney's death, he made the wildly unfounded accusation in his interview with magazine journalist Leighton Blood that Gibboney was still alive and well in Mexico.

Grover desecrated the memory of the man who had gotten him out of jail and turned a blind eye, providing the opportunity for escape.

---

[12] Incredibly, the two Philadelphia mortuary men sent to Campeche in March 1921 to disinter and return the bodies of Gibboney and Shriver were also caught in an eight-hour violent storm with the men's bodies on board their boat. Gibboney's eyeglasses were still in his pocket, but a substantial amount of cash was missing from his money belt. *Philadelphia Inquirer*, April 12, 1921.

"You know, Gibboney was supposed to have drowned while fishing in the Gulf of Mexico," Grover said. "I know for a fact that he's hiding in Mexico, and give me a week there, and I'll turn him up."

"I know where he is," Grover bragged with complete ignorance from five thousand miles away in Germany. "And I'll be only too glad to see him brought to justice."

***

Emma's longtime advisor and fixer's death closed a disastrous year for the Bergdoll family. Grover had been captured, tried, convicted, released to search for gold, and had escaped. Prohibition shut down the Bergdoll Brewery, the family's cash-flowing spigot. Income from their hundreds of saloons dried up, despite serving "near-beer" and home brewing kits. Emma was convicted of threatening police and federal agents with a gun during Grover's capture. In Grover's escape, she and Charles, Grover, Erwin, Stecher, and Judge Romig were indicted by a federal grand jury. Those who were tried were convicted. The same grand jury censured Gibboney for "gross carelessness," leading to bickering among the Bergdolls and callous blame by the press and public. And finally, after two years on the run, Erwin decided to surrender and face charges of desertion.

Unlike Grover, he walked unannounced into the Disciplinary Barracks at Governors Island and gave himself up on July 21, 1920. Erwin's arrival was so surprising that Army officials had to halt their court martial of Col. John Hunt in Grover's escape to conduct Erwin's arraignment immediately. They made sure the Army guards put him in handcuffs.

Tired of being on the run, he called his father-in-law, William Parker, who was occasionally staying at Erwin's Broomall farm despite the death of his daughter, Sarah Parker Bergdoll, in 1919. Erwin suggested that Mr. Parker notify Charles and Judge Romig to arrange his surrender. Together, all three men boarded a train at Philadelphia, rode to New York, obtained government passes for the ferry, and without being recognized by anyone in public, made the 10-minute crossing to Governors Island. Alerted from the Manhattan Battery ferry dock of the notorious visitor, Judge Advocate Prosecutor Col. Cresson and three guards met Erwin, Charles, and Judge Romig on the Fort Jay parade ground.

"Do you want a civilian lawyer?" Cresson asked his new prisoner.

"No," Erwin replied. "I want to get it over as soon as possible. I'm tired of running around the country. I always knew they wanted me."

Erwin was led into Castle Williams and the same upper floor of steel-walled jail cells from which Grover was released before he escaped. Charles and Judge Romig returned to Philadelphia. They had been trying to convince Erwin to surrender since April 1919, just days after the death of Sarah.

Erwin's court-martial trial in August 1920 followed a similar path to Grover's. Local draft board officials from Broomall were brought to New York to describe how they

While Grover was on trial for draft evasion in 1920, Emma Bergdoll appeared regularly in court, facing conspiracy charges and threatening officers with a gun. She always traveled to court in Philadelphia with a hired companion carrying a small black valise containing $10,000 cash for bail. (Temple University Urban Archives)

sent Erwin's draft notice to the farm and how Erwin and Sarah insisted he was placed in the wrong callup category because he was married and a farmer. Erwin's draft board secretary testified that Erwin told him he didn't want to go to war because "I might have to shoot relatives on the other side."

When challenged about Erwin's status as a farmer, the draft board responded that Erwin showed only "slight knowledge of agriculture." Farming was "a sideline."

Federal agents involved in the hunt for Erwin felt sympathy for him; for Grover, they did not. Federal prosecutor McAvoy said Erwin seemed more sincere about his opposition to the war (he was pro-German). Unlike Grover, he stayed away quietly, without sending taunting letters and postcards to newspapers and the men charged with hunting him down.

Erwin was convicted and sentenced to four years in prison at Leavenworth. He was returned to Philadelphia a few weeks later as a witness in the federal conspiracy trial for Emma, Charles, Judge Romig, and the others charged with helping him and Grover run from the draft.

This time, Army guards were ordered to take no chances with an infamous Bergdoll being released for a cross-country trip. Along with two noncommissioned officers as armed guards, Erwin traveled back to Philadelphia in shackles and handcuffs, supervised by Adjutant Julius A. Penn. He was locked in a cell at the Frankford Arsenal in Philadelphia, and his two guards stayed in the cell with him each night.

At the conspiracy trial in the federal building and post office at Ninth and Chestnut Streets in Philadelphia, Erwin was allowed to testify from the courtroom witness box without handcuffs but with two armed guards surrounding him. He absolved his mother, brother, and even the automobile broker charged with providing him a new car.

He did make the federal agents appear foolish, however, when he testified that he hid in the old barn at the Bergdolls' Broomall farm and, peeking through cracks in the barn boards, watched the agents searching his farmhouse and machine shop, Charles' mansion and carriage house, and the outbuildings on the property, but never coming inside the derelict barn with Louis' pigeon-pooped Blériot airplane hanging in the rafters.

Erwin said he often slept in the hay mow of the dirty old barn, fearing the agents would return at night. They didn't.

During the trial, Erwin told his mother he would gladly return to Leavenworth. He told Emma that the Frankford Arsenal jail was uncomfortable and had lousy food. At Leavenworth, Erwin worked in the machine shop, which he liked, slept on a soft bed, and received quality food with a chance to return for second and third helpings. He was eager to serve his sentence and move on with his life.

Emma and the others were convicted of conspiracy, and their suspended sentences were eventually reduced to hefty fines. Emma and Charles later made the payments for everyone and were free to go. Emma charged through the federal building hallways trailing a line of scribbling reporters around her like a Washington politician. She reserved her criticism for Col. Cresson, calling him a liar for convicting her second son of desertion weeks earlier.

"He's a hog, eh," Emma called out. "And now I'm going shopping."

CHAPTER SEVENTEEN

Kidnap on the Hochzeitsfeier

Eberbach, Germany, 1921

The first kidnapping attempt on Grover Bergdoll occurred in January 1921, a full year after he was captured at gunpoint from the window box at his Wynnefield mansion. It was a disastrous shooting involving two U.S. Army officer detectives who claimed their superiors at Army headquarters in Coblenz authorized them to undertake a daring raid into unoccupied German territory and grab Bergdoll.[1] The secret plot ended horribly, and the officers had to be rescued from German captivity through sensitive diplomacy ordered by Washington.

What no one knew at the time was that a third U.S. Army detective was also surveilling Grover in Eberbach and watching the near-deadly shootout. His orders prevented him from jumping in to help.

He kept it a secret for almost two decades.

***

Grover and Stecher had their first scrape with the German police in October 1920. An American Army officer in Coblenz convinced German officials in Berlin to issue a murder warrant for Grover and Stecher and send it to Baden state prosecutors in Eberbach. Whom they murdered was never revealed. Tipped off to the pending warrant, Grover and Stecher fled to Switzerland in their car for two weeks. Grover's Eberbach lawyer, Karl Zeiss, convinced German authorities to quash the bogus warrant and discipline the federal official in Berlin who signed off on it. It was the first of several legal cases Attorney Zeiss would perform for Grover. He became Bergdoll's full-time attorney in Germany as the Army advanced its effort to capture Grover in his relative haven of unoccupied Baden.

Just as West Philadelphia draft board secretary John Dwyer had ramped up his machine to get Bergdoll in 1917 and 1918, the American Legion and other veterans' support groups focused nearly all of their considerable political influence on capturing Bergdoll from 1920 onward. These efforts also attracted criticism. As stated in *The Boston Sunday Globe* in May 1921, under a headline, BERGDOLL WILL

---

[1] The spelling of Coblenz was changed to Koblenz in 1926.

SMILE AS HE SITS IN GERMANY PERUSING ACCOUNTS OF OUR CONGRESSIONAL INVESTIGATION, "The War Department undertakes to publish a list of several thousand 'slackers'—and the country is lukewarm on the subject, for fear injustice will be done. The War Department allows one slacker to escape—and the country is so indignant that Congress is now investigating. Who was to blame for Bergdoll's escape?"

More importantly, at this time, who was going to capture Bergdoll? Just as Philadelphia police and federal agents repeatedly failed to capture Grover over three years in the United States, detectives and bounty hunters could not catch him for years in Germany.

While hiding in Eberbach, Grover and Stecher agreed to use their bright red touring car (also nicknamed Big Red) to drive a young Eberbach couple to and from their wedding in Neckarwimmersbach, across the Neckar River.[2]

On the evening of January 22, 1921, with Grover behind the wheel of the long, sleek crimson Benz with its rounded fenders, chrome headlamps, and dual horns in front of its plow-shaped radiator grill, he and Stecher drove from the Neckarwimmersbach wedding site to the Krone-Post Hotel to celebrate with the wedding party and wait for a friend arriving on the evening train. With the car's canvas top up against the cool January air, Grover drove the wedding party to the train station. Suddenly, they were accosted by two men who ran up to Big Red, pointing an Army-issued automatic pistol at Grover and hollering, "Throw up your hands; you're under arrest." Acting quickly and fearlessly, Grover swung his right hand, trying to smack the gun down, and sped off in his car with Stecher aiming toward but not shooting the assailants. The bride and groom, and other members of the party, were in the rear seats. At least two shots were fired, and bridesmaid Lina Rupp, 22, of Heidelberg, was hit in the hand.[3] Another bullet punctured a tire on Big Red.

What happened next was all very fast. The story went that people rushed in to grab the shooter and his weapon immediately after the gun went off. The second man was caught when he jumped on the departing train and was pulled off before it gained too much speed. Their four German accomplices were surrounded, trying to get away in an old war surplus taxi ambulance, and all were held until Eberbach police arrived. Within a few months, however, this story would change.

Until their trial on March 21, when the truth came out, all six kidnapping suspects, including the two Army officers, were held in German jails with little access

---

[2] Alfred Bergdoll suggests that Big Red was one of two Benz touring cars that Grover kept in the Hotel Krone-Post garage in Eberbach. Both Grover and Stecher had extended family in Eberbach. Press reports indicated that the wedding party included relatives.

[3] An Army investigation of the events determined that Lina Rupp had her hand behind Grover's shoulder. The bullet hit her hand and was deflected enough to graze Grover's shoulder, piercing only the fabric of his coat. It was a near hit on Grover, but it missed.

to the outside world. Grover and Stecher remained free and fled into the German countryside in Big Red.

One of the men with guns was identified as U.S. Army Sergeant Charles Otto Naef, 27, born in Milan, Italy, in 1893 to a German-speaking Swiss father and an Italian mother.[4] As 18-year-old Carlo Naef, he left Milan for France and emigrated alone to the United States in January 1912 with $50 in his purse. He joined the merchant marine before enlisting in the Army in August 1914 in the 2nd Cavalry at Fort Slocum, David's Island, New York. Interestingly, Private Naef deserted his post at Fort Ethan Allen, Vermont, on May 19, 1915, and fled to Canada for five months. He was captured by an American immigration agent in Montreal and returned to military control at Rouse's Point, New York, and then the nearby Plattsburgh Army barracks on October 25. He was jailed in the Army brig and sentenced to several months of hard labor before returning to duty at Ethan Allen's mess hall.

Then, as mess sergeant, Naef was deployed to France in the 76th Field Artillery in April 1918. He was a fortunate survivor of battle and gas in the summer of 1918, and, upon discharge from the Army at the end of the war, Naef returned to New York City in 1918–1919, where he lived in an old, run-down federal-style rooming house at 51 St. Mark's Place on New York's Lower East Side.

Life in that neighborhood may have strongly ignited his patriotic feelings toward his new homeland.

By then, the former Little Germany community around St. Mark's Place between First and Second Avenues in New York had become a melting pot of European immigrants. It had been the scene of protesting the war draft in 1917. It was well-known for its anti-establishment school organized by the Russian socialists and anarchists Alexander Berkman and Emma Goldman, both of whom were represented in their anti-draft protesting by the man who would later become Bergdoll's long-time attorney, Harry Weinberger.

In 1919, Naef's beliefs contradicted many of his ultra-liberal New York neighbors. He re-enlisted in the Army. He may have begun petitioning through the Army court for citizenship because "naturalization—Army Court" is noted on his re-enlistment records. Despite his lack of experience in law enforcement, Naef was assigned as a sergeant to the Provisional Military Police for the American Forces in Germany (A.F.I.G.) at Coblenz. His status was that of a civilian police detective working with the U.S. Department of Justice. Before reporting to Coblenz, perhaps beginning a mission to track Bergdoll, Naef, with the ability to dress in civilian clothing to perform surveillance, was moved from New York to an American city where he'd never lived or visited his entire life: Philadelphia. He spent several months working

---

[4] Court testimony records indicate Naef's birth in Milan, Italy. Naef repeatedly wrote in his military and travel records that he was born in Switzerland.

from a rooming house in the 1800 block of Arch Street in Philadelphia before moving to Coblenz and American Army headquarters in Germany by March 1920.[5]

Naef's subordinate for the Bergdoll job was Army Technical Sergeant Frank Zimmer, 361st Infantry, of Wheatridge, Colorado, near Denver. Zimmer, also 27, joined the Army through the Colorado National Guard during the conflict with Mexico in 1916. He fought in three battles during the war and then joined the Provisional Military Police at Coblenz as a detective in 1920. Naef said he brought Zimmer on the Bergdoll kidnapping caper so that if something happened to him, Zimmer could alert the military police at Coblenz. Their four German accomplices were brought along for muscle power. One was responsible for tipping Naef that Bergdoll was hiding in Eberbach, Baden, but in the unoccupied territory where the American Army and detectives for military intelligence could not conduct official business without authorization from the Germans.

However, Naef and Zimmer were mistakenly authorized by Army headquarters at Coblenz, specifically the commanding general's chief of staff, to enter the unoccupied zone to make arrests. The mistaken authorization was "contrary to the instructions of the commanding general," reported an Army investigation. Furthermore, Naef and Zimmer failed to gain permission from the Germans in Baden for cooperation in their sovereign zone.

They went renegade, thinking they could capture Bergdoll at will. The kidnapping attempt embarrassed the highly respected A.F.I.G. commander, General Henry T. Allen, who prided himself on being fair and honest with his German counterparts, because it occurred in Baden where, under the terms of the armistice ending the war, Americans had no jurisdiction. It created an international incident and led to the American Legion's direct and long-lasting intervention in the Bergdoll affair.

Separate investigations of the Eberbach train station incident by Baden state officials and the Army revealed that Detective Naef ran up to Big Red and grabbed Grover by the coat, declaring that he was under arrest. Zimmer stood behind Naef, pointing his gun in Grover's face. When Grover tried to push Zimmer's gun away, he hit Naef in the face instead, "using at the same time insulting language," declared a synopsis by the U.S. State Department. When Naef fired his gun, the first shot "went wild," as Grover called it, and punched out a tire on Big Red. The second shot hit Fräulein Rupp, "causing permanent injury and impaired efficiency," according to American and German doctors who examined

---

[5] Sgt. Naef's travels and postings are based on military and immigration records and federal census reports. In theory, Naef likely moved to Philadelphia for several months for detective training and to gather background intelligence on Bergdoll. By the time he joined military intelligence, he was a civilian working undercover.

her left hand. She was described in American documents as a farm worker. The bride and groom were not hurt.[6]

Naef and Zimmer were immediately arrested and jailed.

When Eberbachers discovered that the Army of Occupation officers orchestrated the kidnapping attempt on Bergdoll and the wounding of a bridesmaid, they were described as "indignant and highly wrought up over the affair." It led to strict security measures in the small community of Eberbach, where gun violence was unusual.

Grover went out of sight for weeks, warned by Eberbach police to lay low. He spent considerable time on his hunting leases in the country, staying in a lodge provided by a German friend. He also upgraded his security with two .32 caliber Sauer semi-automatic pistols and was always in Stecher's company. He surfaced when his paid henchmen warned him that an aggressive *Chicago Tribune* reporter was sending a dispatch to Chicago using the telegraph office in Eberbach.

The reporter said he was forced to go to Heidelberg to file his stories because, within a half hour of using the Eberbach telegraph office, Grover appeared with a copy of the un-transmitted article in his hand demanding clarifications. The reporter said Grover was the hero of Germany with "fists full of thousand-dollar bills, a mouthful of chewing tobacco, and a brand-new racing automobile. He now owns the town. He has his own detective system and controls the local press, post office, and pulpit." He said Grover had a "spy system" reporting on people arriving in Eberbach by car and train. He said Grover claimed support from both sides of the political spectrum in Germany because his grandfather, Louis Bergdoll, was "a revolutionist in 1848" and because he, Grover, refused to fight against his German ancestors. Grover also received congratulatory letters from the United States for putting down the kidnapping attempt. He would receive more support letters when the case went to trial.

Although Grover's paid spy system was elaborate and loyal to its benefactor, it missed a third man from the U.S. Army living in Eberbach and reporting back to Coblenz on Bergdoll's activities.

After the war, Carl Walter Alfred Lehmann worked undercover for the European section of the U.S. Military Intelligence Division in Germany, known as G-2. Consisting of officers and civilians, G-2 performed various duties, including surveillance and detention of deserters, photographic and map interpretation, communications interception, prisoner-of-war interrogations, and combat, political, and economic intelligence. It even published the Army's newspaper in France, *Stars and Stripes*, during the war.[7]

---

[6] Naef admitted that he shot his gun at Grover's car, Big Red, in an attempt to stop it from getting away. He said the second shot that hit Fräulein Rupp in her hand was an accident. The court didn't agree with his explanation.

[7] Military Intelligence, Center of Military History, United States Army, 1998.

Lehmann emigrated to the United States in 1911, but in 1920 he still needed to become a naturalized citizen. Born in Dresden, Germany, and fluent in German, upon arrival at Coblenz for G-2, he was ordered to register with the Germans in unoccupied Baden using his German citizenship papers. It was the perfect cover for spying on Bergdoll.

During the war, Lehmann served in the regular Army in France with engineering units, a typical recruiting source for intelligence work. His G-2 predecessor surveilling Bergdoll had been recalled when the Baden Germans learned from his carelessly filed papers that he was an American detective. They tipped Bergdoll to his true identity, and it was suggested that he, too, joined the men on Bergdoll's payroll.

With better cover as a German-speaking citizen, Lehmann was sent to Eberbach to spy on Grover and induce him to enter the occupied zone where he could be arrested. Still, his orders said he was never to attempt to capture Bergdoll by force.

At 32, Lehmann passed himself off as a German aluminum salesman, complete with samples in a cardboard suitcase, sleeping and dining in the same hotel as Grover, even sharing his dinner table at the Krone-Post. His training as a steward at the prestigious Peninsula Hotel in San Mateo, California, gave him the polite manners and patience to watch Grover quietly and unobtrusively in a small community like Eberbach.

Lehmann claimed he heard Grover saying, "To hell with [President] Wilson" during his meetings with Bergdoll. "To hell with the United States. I never want to see that country again."

Everything Lehmann learned; he reported back to Coblenz. It was helping the Army devise a plan to capture their most-wanted fugitive.

Lehmann drove an unmarked Army Cadillac and parked it where he was sure Grover would notice it, in front of the Krone-Post. Somewhat suspicious, Grover sent a man to the street to inquire if the Cadillac was for sale. Lehmann said no but that he had a friend in Ludwigshafen (in the French zone) who would sell him a Cadillac. Trusted as a German, Lehmann arranged for Bergdoll to travel to Ludwigshafen to consider buying the fancy car.[8] This arrangement, Lehmann believed, would have gotten Grover out of the German zone, and allowed Army detectives to arrest him. The meeting was set for two days after the attempted kidnapping. Understandably, Grover did not make the Cadillac-buying trip.

Many years later, after becoming a naturalized American, Lehmann was married and running a tavern and tourist camp in Fairfax County, Virginia, the horse-farm country about 25 miles from Washington, D.C. His patrons were often Washingtonians out for a weekend in the country visiting Civil War battlefield sites and horse farms. This was his quiet retirement vocation. Upon leaving the Army in 1923, however, Lehmann's military intelligence and hotel steward experience gained him a recommendation to work as a butler for a wealthy Washington widower,

---

[8] Grover already owned Big Red, the most expensive and fastest car in the Eberbach region, but he wanted the stylish Cadillac too.

former United States attorney general during the period of Bergdoll's escape, A. Mitchell Palmer.[9] From his remote tourist camp on the Lee Jackson Highway in Centreville, Lehmann traveled to the U.S. Capitol in 1939 to testify about spying on Bergdoll in the early 1920s in Eberbach.

"Naef was dumb," Lehmann told a Military Affairs committee room packed with members of the House of Representatives about his fellow G-2 operative.

"He jumped in front of Bergdoll's car and ordered him to put his hands up. Bergdoll sped away with such force that Naef had to jump out of the way."

Lehmann was at the Eberbach train station the day of the bungled attempted kidnapping in January 1921, standing quietly near the chaotic shooting scene. No one realized who he was, not even Naef and Zimmer. He watched just a few feet away as Naef fired shots at Grover's fleeing car. He saw Lina Rupp grasping her bloodied hand after she had been hit by a bullet from Naef's Army revolver. He watched the "irate" Eberbach police pull Naef and Zimmer off to jail before a mob of angry Eberbachers overcame them.

"About 600 Germans tried to get into the prison when Naef and Zimmer were captured and lynch them" he said.

Lehmann said Bergdoll lied to the Germans about why he was hiding in Eberbach. He learned that Grover gained sympathy among Eberbachers by telling them he was forced into the U.S. Army and sent to France for the war. Grover claimed that as a famous and skilled aviator, he was ordered to fly a plane to Eberbach and bomb his hometown. Grover claimed that when he refused, he was sent back to the United States in chains, where he escaped.[10]

Lehmann also confirmed reports that when Grover returned to Eberbach for Naef and Zimmer's trial, he flew a German flag atop the radiator of Big Red. Lehmann said he also learned the Baden authorities would not give up Bergdoll because he had become a Baden citizen, and it automatically made him a citizen of Germany.[11]

Lehmann said the Naef and Zimmer "unauthorized" kidnap attempt ruined his plan to entice Grover into the occupied zone with an attractive woman to look at a fashionable (Cadillac) car for sale. Lehmann even befriended Stecher's relatives in Baden to gain their trust. He said the failed kidnapping attempt and the arrest of Naef and Zimmer destroyed all hopes of his success in capturing Bergdoll.[12] If he

---

[9] Lehmann's connection to former Attorney General Palmer is an incredible story unto itself.

[10] As if the lie wasn't enough, Eberbach was never Grover's hometown. It was home to his cousin and her husband and he was staying in their hotel.

[11] There is no evidence that Grover ever became a German citizen. His applications for multiple passports under fake names falsely declared he was British-Canadian.

[12] Carl Alfred Walter Lehmann testified before the U.S. House of Representatives Military Affairs committee on a May 1939 Congressman Forest Harness resolution to exclude convicted military deserters from living in the United States. Emma and Berta Bergdoll also testified before the committee. See Chapter 24.

was motivated by a big reward for capturing Bergdoll, Lehmann was not asked or did not volunteer the delicate detail to the members of Congress.

Meanwhile, when the Germans became aware that the reviled Naef and Zimmer were connected to the Army of Occupation at Coblenz, General Allen recognized that he had an "international incident." In his journal, which he compiled in his office or in his five-bedroom, two-bath house, also overlooking the Rhine, he wrote that he immediately apologized to Germany for the actions of Naef and Zimmer.[13] Of his apology message to Herr Karl von Starck, the German commissioner for the Rhineland High Commission, General Allen wrote, "I very deeply regretted the action of my agents of the Department of Criminal Investigation and apologized for both to the [German] Central Government and the Baden authorities."

General Allen said his chief of staff made a mistake, and Naef and Zimmer should not have been allowed to go into Baden and make arrests. They were only allowed to enter unoccupied Germany to "take over offenders... after their arrest by German authorities." General Allen requested that Naef and Zimmer be turned over to him for discipline.

The general soon realized, however, the limitations of Berlin's authority over a state government like Baden. They were powerless. He got no reply. The officers remained in jail.

General Allen further tried to tamp down the growing international incident. He was concerned, he wrote, that "the American Legion may make an issue of it." He issued a press release declaring that Army headquarters at Coblenz was doing everything it could to secure the men's release. However, it was an issue for the Baden judiciary, not the central German government in Berlin. And Baden wanted a trial. He later wrote in his journal that it became apparent that Baden used the incident to exercise its authority with Berlin.

Furthermore, General Allen declined to assign Army attorneys from the judge advocate general's office to represent Naef and Zimmer at their pending trial. Soon, his concern about the involvement of the American Legion came true. A delegation from the Legion in Paris arrived in Coblenz with money to pay defense attorneys and buy tobacco and reading material for the men in their jail cells.

Political matters grew tenser when Naef was allowed to send a telegram to President Harding claiming he was "mistreated in the German jail without help from Coblenz." The President notified the War Department of Naef's missive, and, in turn, it contacted General Allen. The otherwise calm and collected high general must have been annoyed. He sent officers to interrogate Naef and Zimmer in jail, and they reported to Allen that the prisoners were treated well and had no complaints.[14]

---

[13] General Allen's *My Rhineland Journal*, The Riverside Press, Houghton Mifflin Company, 1923. Public Domain.

[14] Details here compiled from a synopsis of the Bergdoll–Naef and Zimmer affair by the Army in Coblenz and archived by the U.S. Army Military History Institute.

Leading up to the trial in March, the international incident that General Allen predicted grew even tenser when the *Chicago Tribune* Paris bureau began front page headlining for the story suggesting Coblenz was doing nothing to free Naef and Zimmer while Bergdoll traveled freely all over Europe. When the *Tribune* trumpeted the story in the United States, it fueled the intervention of the American Legion and patriotic Americans all over the country. General Allen may have been partially to blame. He met with the *Tribune* reporter in his office at Coblenz on February 17 and gave the reporter "all the facts for his personal information, but not for publication."[15]

The *Tribune* ran background stories on Bergdoll's escape with his gold, updating Americans on how the notorious draft dodger "set himself up as a gentleman in Eberbach, where a few Bergdoll dollars could purchase millions of [marks]."[16] Lehmann called it "living like a millionaire in a castle on the Rhine." To Americans reading the articles, it appeared as if the Army in Coblenz bungled opportunities to capture Bergdoll.

As determined by Army investigators, this is essentially what General Allen told the *Tribune* for background. By October 1920, Coblenz realized Grover was living in Eberbach among his German family and friends and operating out of a room at the Hotel Krone-Post, owned by Grover's cousin and her husband, Johanna and Carl Bohrmann. They determined Stecher was almost always with Grover as his driver and protector and lived in Eberbach in a small cottage provided by Bergdoll.

An investigation was assigned to the military intelligence division known as G-2. It notified Baden state authorities that it wanted to arrest Bergdoll and Stecher for desertion and escape violations in the United States. However, Baden replied that "because Grover was never a soldier and did not fall under the purview of the 1918 Armistice Agreement, which said deserters from the Armies of Occupation should be delivered to them by Germans," they wouldn't allow it. The Baden government also said Grover had applied for German citizenship, and they suggested his cause was noble; he didn't want to fight against his family in Germany.

Frustrated with the Baden reply, the War Department appealed to the State Department in Washington to intervene with Berlin. According to the Army investigation, Coblenz declined to intervene when the State Department declined.

Then, at the urging of the Army chief of staff, the intelligence division re-opened the Bergdoll case in December 1920 and assigned the Civilian Detective Naef to the case. The Army synopsis reports that while "working with the Secret Service of the French Army of the Rhine, they planned to entice Bergdoll into the occupied territory," possibly by using attractive German women to lure him on an excursion out of Baden.

---

[15] The *Chicago Tribune* News Service syndicated its Bergdoll stories to hundreds of American newspapers, including *The New York Times*, as did the *Associated Press*. The story caught on like wildfire.

[16] This may have been hyperbole, but inflation in Germany was escalating so rapidly that within months of the trial date, American dollars worth millions of marks were coming true.

The last resort, they said, would be to "shanghai" him (by drugging or use of force). They also clarified that only Germans were to be used in unoccupied zones.

American and French agents regularly spied on Grover in Eberbach, and "the system was working smoothly" for eventual success in capturing him. Then Naef got an exciting tip about Grover and acted upon it unwisely. It significantly undermined the Army's chances of ever enticing Bergdoll into a zone where American detectives could legally capture him.

In mid-March, Grover and Stecher emerged from hiding when the six men were brought up for trial in the Baden courthouse in Mosbach.[17] They drove back into Eberbach in Big Red, flying either a German flag or a pennant with the German national colors, Grover's son, Alfred, wrote in his diary-manuscript. Held in front of a packed gallery, Naef and Zimmer were ridiculed by Eberbachers, who also "hissed" at their American Legion-provided defense attorneys. One of them, Hugo Schrag, said fellow Germans verbally abused him for defending the American officers. Schrag said he was so disgusted by the affair that he later emigrated to the United States.

Army lawyers were on hand, but only to observe. They were not allowed to advise the German lawyers publicly. They reported to their superiors in Coblenz that Bergdoll and Stecher were allowed to insult Naef and Zimmer with support from the jeering crowd.

Charges against the prisoners had been reduced through negotiations between the United States government and Berlin. Most severe was the criminal assumption of state authority and bodily injury to a person. They were not charged with attempted kidnapping because, at the time, the charge only applied to women victims in Germany.

The Army of Occupation at Coblenz sent four officers to the trial, headed by Charles B. Fehrlin of Army Intelligence, to observe the testimony and report back to Coblenz daily. Fehrlin later wrote a multi-part story published in *The Washington Star* in June 1922.

Fehrlin wrote that up to a dozen German bodyguards constantly surrounded Grover and that even the Eberbach, Mosbach, and Baden state police were protecting him from American agents. When Fehrlin rode what he called the "Toonerville Trolley" (train) into Mosbach for the trial, he overheard a German man say, "There go one of them American pigs. We'll show 'em who's boss around this part of the country."

---

[17] Names for Naef and Zimmer were misapplied as Carl and Karl, Neff, Neaf, Neuf, and Franz or Fred Zimmer. Lina Rupp's name was misapplied as Lina Butt and Lena Rudd. In 1926, the U.S. Congress, on recommendation from the Army of Occupation and the State Department, paid Lina Philippine Rupp a $200 indemnity for her injury. Their documentation correctly identified Charles Otto Naef, but he was still incorrectly reported as Carl Neuf in the press. Finally, in 1939, with the issuance of a subpoena, the Army judge advocate general's office corrected the long-misapplied name of Carl Neuf to Charles O. Naef.

He said the Army forbade him from carrying a sidearm, but he secreted a small pistol in his inner pocket and was tempted to use it.

The courtroom was packed with people from all walks of life, including the Baden secretary of state, the attorney general, a representative from the Berlin foreign office, the Berlin Department of Justice, and some other high-ranking Baden state officials. The Baden prosecutor called it the most sensational trial he had ever conducted.

When Grover entered the courtroom, Fehrlin wrote, he wore a blue serge suit cut in German style, had a clipped mustache, and wrinkles on his forehead, and was somewhat bald, nervous, and worried. He continuously opened and closed his hands. "He had more the appearance of a German than an American."

Grover said he wanted to testify in English, but the head judge ruled that he would speak German. Under questioning, Grover said he avoided the draft in the United States because he did not want to fight against Germans who could be his relatives. He told the court he fled to Mexico and the western United States.[18]

After more than 35 witnesses testifying over two days in the Baden Landgericht in Mosbach, Naef and Zimmer were found guilty and sentenced to prison for 15 and six months, respectively, considering time already served. Grover and Stecher were not in the courtroom to hear the verdict. They had gone on another extended road trip in one of Grover's cars, this time eastward from Baden into Bavaria.

Meanwhile, the German trial headlines were matched with more Bergdoll headlines at home in the United States in February and March 1921, this time from Erwin, who had filed a 65-page habeas corpus challenge with the U.S. District Court in Kansas City, Kansas, near where he was in prison for draft evasion at the United States Disciplinary Barracks, Fort Leavenworth. The federal judge promised to rule on the case swiftly because, if he ruled in favor of Erwin Bergdoll's challenge, it would impact tens of thousands of other men who ran when called to war in the draft, including Grover.

Erwin's attorneys, Army Major John Maxwell, former judge advocate general, and a volunteer civilian attorney, J. D. Showalter from Independence, Kansas, filed a brief suggesting all kinds of constitutional challenges about why Erwin was not legally drafted and was improperly court-martialed at Fort Jay, Governors Island, New York, the same place Grover was court-martialed and from where he was turned loose by the Army to fetch his gold.

However, Federal Judge John C. Pollock said the only challenge that mattered for his ruling was whether Erwin and all other men "[became] a member of the Army

---

[18] This is the only time a trip to Mexico is attributed to Grover speaking. All other references to Grover fleeing into Mexico are from reporters or government officials. Grover has only one insignificant border crossing record at Eagle Pass, Texas, and Piedras Negras, Coahuila, Mexico. Nothing else is known about his reported foray into Mexico.

244 • THE BERGDOLL BOYS

the instant [they] registered for the draft." "If he did not," the judge postulated, "the Army has no more jurisdiction over the Bergdoll brothers than it has over this court."

He wanted to have the question decided by March 1. The fact that the trial involving six men who tried to kidnap Grover was unfolding in Germany at the same time was coincidental.

Erwin's attorneys claimed he never received notice at his farm near Broomall, Pennsylvania, to report for military duty because he was not home. They claimed the postcard draft notices sent to him "didn't specify the hour and day or the draft board to which Erwin was to report." They also claimed that a court-martial tribunal lacked jurisdiction because Erwin had not been formally inducted into the Army. Therefore, they argued, Army testimony was inadmissible in the trial that convicted him.[19]

The judge, interpreting the draft law to the letter and probably realizing the difficulty he would cause if he demurred any longer with a ruling, refused Erwin's appeal on April 5. He ruled that a simple postcard sent by a local draft board served as legal notice to appear for a physical examination. Technically, it meant the draftee was already inducted into the military. The ruling would precede Grover's second trial many years later.

In handcuffs and prison garb, tall and lean Erwin, the hero racer, was returned to prison at Fort Leavenworth. He served another 26 months and was released on June 26, 1923, when Grover contemplated returning to Philadelphia to face his crimes.[20]

***

At the trial for Naef and Zimmer, the *Tribune* dispatch from Mosbach said there was so much lying from the witness box in support of Bergdoll, Stecher, and the wedding party that some testimony was thrown out. One of these perjurers, a restaurant waiter from Coblenz, testified that Naef offered him 50,000 German marks to help capture Bergdoll. However, the man was shown to be a cocaine dealer, drunkard, and pimp who said Bergdoll had paid him to say it. When Grover testified, he claimed Zimmer aimed a gun at him, and Naef used his weapon. Zimmer swore in court that he never raised his gun during the melee.

---

[19] Despite the legal denials, Erwin was overheard telling another Army defense attorney that he received the draft notice and that he was tired of "running all around the country."

[20] The 1921 kidnapping story was pieced together using court testimony, newspaper reports, military records, and Congressional investigations. Because Naef and Zimmer were arrested and tried, sworn testimony about their actions and Grover's defense are available in German court and newspaper records. Much was later confirmed by General Henry Allen in his diary, made into a book. And many years later, it was confirmed again by Army Detective Carl Lehmann's Congressional testimony as an eyewitness to the kidnapping attempt and shooting of Rupp, and at Grover's 1939 court-martial trial on Governors Island, Army sergeant Frank Zimmer reappeared to testify about his role in the 1921 kidnapping attempt. He wasn't difficult to find: he was stationed at Fort Jay, Governors Island.

The judge warned Bergdoll about the consequences of violating the German perjury law.[21]

Naef told presiding Judge Kurzmann how Bergdoll sent taunting postcards from Eberbach to prosecutors in the United States suggesting they could not catch him. He sent a picture postcard of Eberbach, showing the Krone-Post along the Neckar, to his old Hotel Vivian owner friend, Owen Sherley, in Hagerstown, Maryland.

"We're doing fine over here," Grover wrote about himself and Stecher on the back of the card. "Regards to your wife and daughter. We sure did fool those poor simps. Hope to see you again when Harding gets in."[22] Some of Grover's postcards were later re-produced by Leighton Blood for his article in *Hearst's International* magazine. Blood, or a magazine graphic artist, circled the location of the Krone-Post in one postcard photograph. It was the equivalent of allowing magazine readers worldwide to zoom in on Grover's German hiding place.

The taunting postcards embarrassed the Army and disgraced the American soldiers who fought in the war, explained Naef. He told Judge Kurzmann and his four associate judges, who made up the jury, that it was his duty to arrest Bergdoll. He had rounded up many American Army deserters with the help of German police and handed them over to military authorities for prosecution. He thought he was authorized to do the same with Bergdoll. The judges disagreed. They said Naef's identification certificate to operate in unoccupied zones was improperly authorized in Coblenz, and the U.S. Army backed the judge's ruling. They said Naef knew there were only charges of desertion and escape against Bergdoll and that he tried to arrest Grover without the cooperation of German police. They called the infractions "a great breach of the law and an invasion of the rights of German authorities."

Naef told a different story of the bungled arrest when he testified before the judges. He said he hatched his plan to "get the fugitive convict Bergdoll," as he frequently called him, only when he learned that Grover was hiding in Eberbach.

On the morning of January 21, at his office in Coblenz, Naef opened a letter sent to him by Johann Gottlieb Keim, 36, of Speyer, a small city on the left bank of the Rhine south of Coblenz. Keim wrote that a French detective, with whom he was on good terms, had shown him a Bergdoll-wanted poster in Speyer and informed him that Grover was a fugitive for robbery and murder and that he was living in Eberbach. Keim, a married man with a significant criminal background but who had worked as a spy for the French police, sent two cohorts, Gustav Fahrenbach, 37, and Philipp Hildenbrand, 31, to Eberbach to spy on Grover and report back to him.

---

[21] Bergdoll was trying to use his money to turn Zimmer against Naef. Based on U.S. State Department reparation agreements with Lina Rupp, it appears that Grover's testimony about Zimmer first pointing his gun was correct.

[22] Grover believed that President Harding would offer amnesty for draft dodgers when he got to the White House in March 1921.

Fahrenbach served in the war with a Bavarian field artillery regiment, and Hildenbrand was a commander of a motorized troop unit; therefore, he was an expert driver with access to a German Army castoff ambulance that he used as a taxi. When the men returned to Speyer and reported their surveillance to Keim, they said they had tracked Grover to Bohrmann's Hotel Krone-Post and learned that he had been sentenced to prison in the United States and that he had a $50,000 bounty on his head.[23] Keim said he dutifully reported this information to his sources in the French police. They insisted they had no interest in capturing Bergdoll, but the American police in Coblenz did.

Then, Keim's French detective friend suggested that Keim send a letter to the American detectives in Coblenz, and he even provided the envelope. In his letter to Detective Naef, Keim didn't reveal where Grover was. He wrote that he wanted to know if he could collect a substantial reward if he managed to get Bergdoll into an occupied zone so American authorities could take him out of Germany.[24]

Upon reading the letter, Naef immediately telegraphed Keim in Speyer and said he would meet him there that evening. Naef rounded up Sgt. Zimmer to go with him. Without a car, they traveled by train south to Speyer.[25]

That evening of January 21, Naef and Zimmer tracked down Keim in Speyer and showed him photographs of criminal suspects in Germany they were trying to arrest. The first photograph was a pass. In the second photograph, Keim fingered the image as Bergdoll, based on the information given to him by Fahrenbach and Hildenbrand.

"Bergdoll is in Eberbach right now," Keim told the detective.

Naef became excited about the prospect of finding Bergdoll. But since it was late in the evening and there were 70 kilometers between Speyer and Eberbach, he realized he would have to wait. He told Keim to meet him in the morning at his hotel, the Wittelsbacher Hof, Speyer, and to bring his friends.

At 9 am the following day, January 22, Keim bid his wife, Elizabetha, farewell at their home in Speyer and met Naef and Zimmer at their hotel. He examined their documents allowing them to operate as detectives outside the Rhineland occupation zone.[26] Keim said he concluded from the records that Naef and Zimmer were approved to search for Bergdoll but not to arrest him. They were to leave an arrest to

---

[23] Carl Bohrmann later testified that he saw the two men, Fahrenbach and Hildenbrand, at his hotel and considered them suspicious. He warned Grover about them.

[24] In 1921, getting Grover to an occupied zone meant crossing the Rhine into either the French or American territories of Germany.

[25] Coblenz had dozens of Cadillac cars and others available for officers, but General Allen had greatly reduced their use for unauthorized activities.

[26] Eberbach is east of the Rhine and outside the American and French occupation zones of 1921.

German police. Keim claimed that Naef contradicted his document interpretation, saying, "It's as good as an arrest warrant." [27]

Over coffee and breakfast sausage with Keim and Zimmer, Naef then spelled out his plan. They would travel from Speyer to Eberbach "and then, with the help of the German police, arrest him [Bergdoll] and take him to the occupied territory."

Eager for the reward, Keim offered that Hildenbrand was an excellent driver from his experience in the war, and he had an old ambulance from the war that he used as a taxi. Keim said they discussed a potential reward, but Naef claimed they did not. Naef, Zimmer, and Keim met Hildenbrand and Fahrenbach at the Speyer bridge over the Rhine. Along with 41-year-old innkeeper Adolf Gustav Steiger, another war veteran, they set off in Hildenbrand's old ambulance taxi for Eberbach. [28]

Keim said they further discussed the reward money while driving along the river Neckar toward Eberbach. Naef, again, said they did not. [29]

With the former Bavarian motorized unit commander, Hildenbrand, behind the wheel of the old ambulance taxi, the six men arrived in Eberbach. They paid an attendant to park their unusual car out of sight in a hotel garage. Steiger and Fahrenbach then prowled the streets asking children if they had seen Bergdoll's car, the unmistakable Big Red. They said the children had seen it and headed toward the train station, a long one-story gallery building of yellow sandstone with "three-story cubic corner pavilions with hipped roofs" on each end, forming a classic H pattern. [30]

Naef claimed he sent Zimmer to alert Eberbach police about their plans, but they seemed uninterested. Naef claimed to have overheard a conversation between the car park attendant and a farmer in which they said the local police were helping Grover stay hidden. It made Naef concerned that Grover might escape to Stuttgart if he did not act immediately. Naef then rode with the Germans in their ambulance taxi from the hotel car park about four blocks and found Grover's car in front of the train station. Zimmer rejoined them.

Naef said he entered the station reception area through the portico, approached Grover on the platform waiting for the train, and, grabbing his coat at the breastplate, hollered, "You're under arrest by the American police."

---

[27] Naef possessed a passport allowing him to travel in the unoccupied zones to surveil criminal suspects and an identification certificate allowing him to arrest robbers and murderers, including Bergdoll, only because he claimed Bergdoll was one of them. The improperly dated certificate did not allow him to arrest Bergdoll on the desertion and escape warrants. Naef said his documents would allow him to "work more easily with German police and avoid political disputes."

[28] It's unclear why they took Steiger along with them. Naef was aware that Grover was an accomplished boxer and that Stecher was a big man who may need to be distracted long enough for them to capture Grover.

[29] All details included here are from Baden district court testimony by Naef, Keim, Hildenbrand, and Bergdoll.

[30] From Zielbahnhof.de description of the Eberbach train station, built in 1879. 2022 Burkhard Thiel.

"Damn the American police," Naef claims that Grover replied, throwing his hand up and striking Naef in the face. Grover then ran to Big Red, where Stecher and the wedding party waited. They drove off at a high rate of speed.

Naef said he fired shots at the car's wheels, one striking bridesmaid Lina Rupp, the other bursting a tire. He said Bergdoll and Stecher escaped before he could get back to the ambulance taxi where Hildenbrand waited for them. Within seconds, the old lumbering vehicle was surrounded by Eberbachers, who took the guns from Naef and Zimmer and held them for police. One of them, a man identified as Karl Dietz, 23, jumped onto the sideboards of the ambulance taxi and hung on until the car stopped.

By this time, Carl Bohrmann arrived at the train station, acting on suspicion about a stranger loitering around his hotel just as he was about to have his evening beer. Recognizing the stranger at the train station, Bohrman alerted a group of Eberbachers, and they cornered Zimmer as he was moving toward the departing train. Zimmer, however, gave up voluntarily, and he was escorted to the police station by Bohrmann and two other men. Zimmer claimed he was running into the village, but his statements did not match those of witnesses who said he appeared to be running for the moving train.

At the police station, the Eberbachers were so excited about the captured Bergdoll kidnappers that the police did not feel safe transferring the suspects to the central jail. Instead, they were kept in an apartment at the police station.[31]

The state trial in Mosbach was a spectacle, with Eberbachers filling the courtroom and mingling among reporters and lawyers in the courthouse. Through testimony to the judges, it was determined that Naef's certificate to operate as a detective in an unoccupied zone was provided to him in error. He made a grave mistake in judgment by firing his gun in the village train station square when it was filled with people. It was a severe encroachment on Baden state authority to act without the approval of the local police. And, they didn't believe Naef when he claimed to have sent Zimmer to alert the Eberbach police.

Keim insisted he did not participate in the kidnap attempt for the reward money. It was his honor to capture a robber murderer as he understood Bergdoll to be. The judge scolded Keim and ordered him never to mention honor again.

Sgt. Zimmer said he had not been in trouble before and followed orders as required because he was still an American Army officer.

Steiger, a cavalry soldier during the war, presented himself in court as the simple operator of a Speyer hotel and claimed that he didn't know where they were going or what they were doing on the trip to Eberbach.

---

[31] Ironically, this same brief security procedure would also be used for suspects during a 1923 kidnapping attempt on Grover.

Hildenbrand claimed to be the least informed, remaining behind the wheel of his ambulance taxi when he heard the gunshots. His car was immediately surrounded. However, he and Fahrenbach couldn't wriggle out of the allegations by feigning ignorance because several witnesses placed them at the Krone-Post surveilling Bergdoll days before the attack.

Grover's brief testimony stuck to the story he'd told all along. He was 27 and had agreed to drive the wedding party from Neckarwimmersbach to the Krone-Post Hotel and then to the Eberbach train station in Big Red. He admitted, however, that he was aware there was a $25,000 bounty for his capture, not the $50,000 portrayed by Keim.

In a fascinating display during the trial, the proceedings moved to the courtyard where Big Red was parked. The judges instructed witnesses to get into the car where they were positioned on the evening of the shooting. Grover stood, one foot on the running board and another just inside the front door. Naef was given the gun he used (without ammunition) and told to show how he fired at Bergdoll.[32]

Fehrlin wrote, "Naef points the pistol directly over the slacker's heart. Then the court's president requests Bergdoll to demonstrate the blow administered that knocked Naef's pistol out of his hand. The slacker makes a blow in an upward direction in such a manner that if the trigger had been pulled, the bullet's course would have been directly into Bergdoll's forehead. Naef smiles and says, had you struck out in this fashion, you would not be alive now, Bergdoll."

Grover said Naef declared, "We've got you, Bergdoll. We're the American police." Grover sped away. "A few seconds later, I heard a shot, and someone in the rear of the car screamed. I looked around and saw that one of the girls in the car was shot in the hand, and blood was flowing profusely. I stopped the car, and we saw that a large crowd had assembled, and the criminals were in their midst."

Fehrlin said he got Grover's testimony only because an interpreter was working for those in the courtroom who could not understand German.

He claimed that Grover shook his fist at Naef and Zimmer, shouting, "You dirty American bums of that Coxey's Army in Coblenz. These people are no fools and will show you that they're bosses around here."[33]

Fehrlin said he feared for his life when German spectators hissed and shouted after Naef's testimony, calling him a "big liar, dirty pig, and ignorant rascal."

The attorney representing Lina Rupp filed documents for her to be paid for her injuries. A doctor testified that the fingers on her left hand were stiff, and she suffered

---

[32] The kidnapping attempt inspired Grover to file for a pistol and ammunition permit in Baden, which was awarded to him on March 26, 1921.

[33] Coxey's Army was a term for unemployment protesters on the U.S. Capitol in Washington, named for Ohio businessman Jacob Coxey advocating government jobs for Americans.

permanent damage.[34] Eberbachers fussed over the payment claim in the gallery, insisting that the American Army should compensate Fräulein Rupp more for her injuries.

Naef got the longest sentence for the illegal assumption of authority as an American detective operating in an unoccupied zone and inflicting bodily injury on Fräulein Rupp. He admitted to firing his weapon but claimed the second shot that hit Rupp was accidental. When the sentences were announced, the audience roared with applause. Fehrlin incorrectly wrote that Bergdoll and his henchmen threw their hats into the air. Bergdoll was already gone from the courtroom.

Fehrlin wrote that a German man commanded him, "You'd better tell your American friends to keep their hands off Bergdoll as long as he remains in Germany, for they might not get away with it as easily as these birds did."

Fehrlin said he and his Army contingent got on the first train back to Coblenz.

The European, British, and American press covered the trial extensively. *The New York Times* and *Chicago Tribune* sent their reporters. The Philadelphia newspapers mainly relied on the *Associated Press* and United News services. Many German newspapers printed the trial testimony nearly verbatim, with many *Zeitungs* filling their pages with long quotations directly from the witness box.

General Allen, briefed on the trial, wrote in his journal that it was a "very impartial and highly indecorous procedure." He immediately sent an emissary to Berlin to remind the central government of their promise to release the prisoners after the trial.

Then, for the first time, on March 26, came the first official intervention from Washington. General Allen received an urgent cable from the War Department.

> The Secretary of War directs that you bring to a conclusion your negotiations for the release of Zimmer and Naef by making a formal application to the proper German authorities for their immediate release. You should impress upon the German Government that the matter is urgent.

General Allen considered that neither the War Department nor the State Department had a direct communication channel with Berlin, or they wouldn't be asking him, a general, to perform diplomatic duties in such a sensitive case. He wrote, "This cable came as a great surprise and, evidently, shows that the Bergdoll case is assuming a strong political phase in the States."

Allen, however, convinced Berlin to act. But they were slow. The delay was caused by the Baden state government demanding 100,000 marks to be paid to Lina Rupp for the injury to her hand.[35]

---

[34] A 1928 photograph of Lina Rupp in Heidelberg, Germany, shows only her left hand without evidence of deformity. I later saw Lina Rupp's name in a long-obscure Congressional Record years after the shooting incident when the federal government finally agreed to pay her for damages. Matching the correct name with genealogy records, I found another photograph of Rupp in which her left hand appears disfigured, possibly from the gunshot wound.

[35] $1,500 is an estimate of the value of 100,000 German marks in the rapidly fluctuating German economy in March, 1921. Because of hyperinflation, several months later the amount would be worthless.

In press reports, the U.S. Foreign Office in Berlin promised a full investigation, despite already knowing the facts of the case. At the same time, Army officials at Coblenz distanced themselves from Naef and Zimmer, suggesting they reported to a different section of the Army, the provost marshal's Department. From his cell, Naef presumed that he and Zimmer were being brushed aside by Coblenz.

During a brief interview at the Mosbach jail, Naef admitted to a reporter that he and Zimmer were "in a tight hole" but had written to General Allen to determine if the Army would help them or if they had been "disowned." Before a German minder abruptly cut off the interview, Naef declared, "As a matter of fact, I got orders to undertake an expedition to capture Bergdoll."

At the time, Grover and Stecher had outstanding arrest warrants from the United States and Canada for escape and aiding and abetting escape, illegal border crossings, and passport forgery, where Great Britain vowed to help its dominion, Canada, capture and prosecute the men. And, of course, Grover was also wanted for his desertion conviction. Because the United States was technically still at war with Germany, there were no extradition agreements. Therefore, efforts to return Bergdoll to America focused on getting him into occupied zones or France or England, where he could be extradited for trial.

Detective Naef, it was said at the trial, had often traveled into unoccupied regions of Germany in 1920 with his superiors' consent to capture American fugitives. And, while Naef often did the capturing, he worked under his superior's understanding that he was taking custody of men whom the Germans arrested. It reassured Naef that he could act independently wherever he might be in Germany.

With the completion of the Baden state criminal trial, American authorities could continue their demand for the clemency of the convicted detectives. The American Legion also appealed from among its many high-level and influential members by adopting "get Bergdoll" resolutions and sending official letters to military and political leaders in their respective states and Washington to return Bergdoll to the United States for trial and prison. Because Naef had been gassed in the war, he also gained the support of the Disabled American Veterans organization, which lobbied Congress to work for his release. They considered Naef an injured war veteran hero.

The pressure from home and in Europe to free Naef and Zimmer and get Bergdoll fell to General Allen. The wheels were already in motion for the prisoners' release when their attorneys missed a March 29 deadline to file appeals with the Baden state court.

Then the American effort to release Naef and Zimmer from jail reached a political settlement in Berlin. While the Baden state government had convicted the two men, the German central government notified General Allen that "the sentences had been remitted pending good behavior." The diplomacy didn't happen out of the kindness of the German's heart. It involved the embarrassing apology from General Allen and his vow to pay Lina Rupp reparations after the men's release. However, there was no admission that the Army of Occupation had supported, orchestrated, or even ordered the kidnapping. It remains a singular allegation from Detective Naef, who felt as if he was abandoned by the Army forever after.

Naef and Zimmer were released from the Mosbach jail at noon on April 2 and they arrived at Army headquarters in Coblenz at 3 am the following day. By daybreak, they were in General Allen's office.[36]

There is no meeting transcript, and General Allen did not describe it in detail. However, a strong rebuke is presumed before Allen quizzed the detectives on what happened and how Bergdoll could be captured. Allen said in his journal that he learned from the boastful men that Lina Rupp's hand was the only thing that saved Bergdoll from taking a direct shot in the shoulder from Naef's Army-issued automatic.

It must have been difficult for General Allen to consider discipline for the men, but for what he could pronounce on one, he could not on the other. Naef was a civilian employee of the Military Intelligence Service, and while he enjoyed Army privileges, it could not discipline him. Zimmer was still a sergeant and would remain in the Army for a long career. General Allen decided the two men had been through enough. No further punishment was given. Their release without serving their sentences amounted to a pardon.

Later that afternoon, General Allen accepted another visit from the American Legion in Paris and Legion members in Coblenz. It's nearly impossible to believe they did not discuss the Bergdoll affair. Still, Allen did not describe their meeting in detail in his journal except to say they pleaded with him for funding to help stranded soldiers who had remained in France and Germany long after the war and who now could not afford return passage home to the United States.

He told them he would investigate a funding source and hoped it would guide and deter the Legion from becoming an enormous political machine.

General Allen met the following week again with German Rhine commissioner von Starck over the still simmering disagreement between Berlin and Baden to pay for Lina Rupp's hand injury. Berlin suggested the Americans would pay the tab because "General Allen is a gentleman and will pay."

The General had no source of funds for reparations for a German civilian. He again suggested Berlin pay the tab, setting off another tense discussion with von Starck. General Allen also said that his position on Bergdoll was made clear to von

---

[36] Some reports suggested Naef and Zimmer were released through a prisoner exchange. However, Carl Lehmann testified they were released through intervention from the American newspaper magnate William Randolph Hearst and his pro-German war reporter, Karl H. von Wiegand. Von Wiegand was the first reporter to introduce Americans to Adolf Hitler in November 1922, calling him the "German Mussolini," with "earmarks of a leader, eyes that spurt fire… and complexion so remarkably delicate that many a woman would be proud to possess it." November 12, 1922, Karl H. von Wiegand for Hearst News Service.

Starck. "There would be no political pleading to bar his surrender." He suggested the deserter be surrendered to the Americans sooner rather than later.

As one of two non-voting German commissioners on the Inter-Allied Rhineland High Commission, Herr von Starck often grated the other members with his brusque and dismissive demeanor. A Coblenz colonel described it as von Starck's "unaccommodating attitude toward malefactors [criminals] and other affairs." Von Starck was accused of vacillating on capturing German criminal suspects who escaped the occupied zone into the unoccupied area where they could be captured only by Germans (who showed little interest). General Allen's intervention once delayed von Starck's removal. But, after a commission hearing, von Starck was forced to resign on May 31, perhaps partly because he failed to understand the American interest and resolve in capturing criminal suspects like Bergdoll.

In September 1921, Detective Naef and his German wife, Minnie, returned to the United States at War Department expense on the Army Transport Service steamer *Cantigny* as an "ex-civilian employee of the A.F.I.G.," along with six other men labeled "destitute ex-soldiers." For them, it appears that General Allen's vow to the American Legion was being fulfilled. The ship arrived at the Army Supply Base in Brooklyn, New York, on September 12, the same day Bergdoll's draft replacement, Private Russell Gross, was buried in Philadelphia. Seven days later, the *Cantigny* sailed up the Hudson River, where it docked at Pier Four in Hoboken, New Jersey, for the remaining passengers to disembark. On September 19, Army personnel off-loaded two thousand caskets containing corpses of American soldiers disinterred from French and Belgian graves.

Naef had failed to capture Bergdoll in Germany and sailed home with dead soldiers who had won the war but lost their lives. His military and detective career was finished.

However, Naef's reward for trying to capture Bergdoll was still due, and his American benefactors didn't forget him. With assistance from the American Legion in New York City, he formally petitioned for naturalization through the State of New York Supreme Court on February 3, 1922. He was married at the time to Minnie K. Naef, from Hennethal, Germany, who obtained her American citizenship through their marriage. They lived in a small apartment on Lincoln Place on Staten Island and then in Queens (through 1930). His citizenship application described him as an honorably discharged soldier, which he was. Naef again listed his birthplace as Winterthur, Switzerland, although he testified in the Baden trial that he was born in Milan.[37]

With vouching signatures by two prominent members of the American Legion in New York who left blank the line on the application for how long they had known

---

[37] Naef may not have known where he was born. His parents likely traveled frequently between his father's home, Winterthur, Switzerland, near Zurich, and his mother's home, Milan, in northern Italy.

Naef, there was no waiting for background checks and processing the application in order of receipt. Naef's citizenship petition was granted the same day.

The Legion rewarded him for his bravery in trying to capture Bergdoll.

Naef eventually took a drastic turn in his life, moved from New York City to the western Catskill mountains of Delaware County in New York State, and changed his occupation from commercial artist, painter, and chauffeur to a farmer. Estranged from Minnie, who moved to the eastern Catskills, Naef lived in the heavily wooded mountains with his much younger companion, Mary Louise Selden, whom he listed as his hired hand, but whom he later married on a small remote farm in Carcass Brook Hollow between the east and west branches of the Delaware River near Harvard, New York. He was issued a subpoena for Grover's 1939 trial at Governor's Island, but there's no evidence he appeared and testified. Because of his age in 1942, 48, Naef was required to register for the second war draft. He wrote on his registration card filed with Draft Board #400 at the First National Bank and Trust Company building in Walton, New York, that he was "permanently disabled from the last war." The detective who chased down and tried to capture Bergdoll alone had no more interest or ability in serving his country. Naef later moved to California, where he died in August 1970 at 77. He was buried at Desert Lawn Mausoleum, Yuma, Arizona.

Sgt. Frank Zimmer remained in the Army in Germany until 1931, when he moved to New York and the following year was joined by his German wife, Ida Fernande Zimmer. They lived at Fort Totten, Queens, New York, and then on Governors Island, where Frank was stationed at Fort Jay, serving as technical and master sergeant through World War II. He was there when Grover was returned to jail in Castle Williams for his second trial in 1939. In September of that year, Zimmer was called to the stand to testify that Grover was the man he and Naef tried to arrest in Germany in 1921. Master Sergeant Zimmer died at 76 at the Presidio of San Francisco on March 27, 1970, and was buried at Fort Logan National Cemetery. Perhaps as a final gesture to his efforts to capture Bergdoll in Germany and, along with Naef, taking the blame for the failure, a significant portion of Zimmer's burial expenses of $1,110.04 were paid by Veterans Services.

The German men in the Bergdoll kidnapping plot, Keim, Fahrenbach, Steiger, and Hildenbrand, were also found guilty and sentenced to five to 11 months with suspensions for time already served in jail while awaiting trial.

Eventually, the four men so misled into trying to reap the Bergdoll reward returned to their homes with nothing.

CHAPTER EIGHTEEN

Kidnap in das Hotel der Krone

Eberbach, Germany, 1923

In the hour approaching midnight on August 10, 1923, Grover bid his German cousin-in-law, Carl Bohrmann, and Stecher, good night and headed for the stairs to his second-floor room in Eberbach's Hotel Krone-Post.[1] He had not been sleeping at his cousin's hotel, his German hideout, of late, warned by Eberbach police that suspicious men or American agents were lurking in the village. One was staying at the Krone-Post, and Bohrmann kept an eye on his activities.[2]

Returning to Eberbach the day prior from a visit with Emma, who had arrived in Heidelberg from Philadelphia in early August, Grover needed rest. His mother had proposed that he return home with her, give himself up voluntarily, possibly accept a reduced sentence for desertion, and recover his confiscated assets. Earlier that evening, Grover sat in his usual corner seat in Bohrmann's private dining room behind the hotel bar and discussed his options with his cousin and Stecher. He had authorized Emma to book passage for him to return to New York, but no final decision about leaving Germany had been made.

While Grover was making his way upstairs, a lone man with a dark Russian complexion quietly walked with a cane out of the hotel café where he had been surveilling Grover for three weeks. From the street, flashing his tubular battery light on and off a few times toward a window on the second floor of the hotel, the Russian then turned and made his way a short distance along the street to the Neckar waterfront, where he got into a large dark Cadillac 7-passenger touring sedan with a canvas top. The car's driver eased it along another few blocks toward the outskirts

---

[1] The Hotel Krone-Post was an ample, three and four-story hip-roofed, two-part building with expansive windows and a few balconies overlooking the Neckar. It flanked the Heidelberg Road and the riverbank of double bulkheads often lined with long skiffs and cargo barges. Stecher lived in a small cabin Grover provided for him nearby in Eberbach.

[2] Although described in the press as Grover's uncle, Carl Heinrich Bohrmann was married to Johanna Heuss Bohrmann, Grover's first cousin. Johanna's mother, Pauline Barth Heuss, and Emma Barth Bergdoll were sisters. Pauline Barth was the only member of their immediate Barth family who remained in Germany.

of the village, pulled over, and stopped with the car pointed toward Hirschhorn and Heidelberg along the Neckar valley. Despite the Cadillac being equipped with a new push-button starter and low on fuel, the driver extinguished the running lights but kept the car's powerful V-8 engine humming.

Grover inserted his key into the lock and turned the knob on his hotel room door. Stepping inside the dark room, he immediately felt arms wrap around his neck in a chokehold. A man with incredible strength threw him onto his side, where he landed on his double bed mattress. He felt another man's hands grappling for his head in such a fluttering commotion that a thumb was shoved into his mouth. Grover chomped down with all the strength of his teeth and jaws. He felt the thumb tip tear away into his mouth and a burst of warm liquid, blood. With a scream of pain, the man with the shorter thumb recoiled. Then Grover felt the unmistakable blow of a blackjack on his skull, but it didn't knock him out. Another blast from the blackjack drew blood from his scalp. Spinning his body around while still bouncing in the chokehold on his bed, Grover reached into his coat pocket and, remarkably, flipped up the safety on his pistol. Pulling out the small weapon, he repeatedly squeezed his trigger finger, and the pistol fired six rapid shots. He heard two thumps as the men who grabbed him fell to the floor. Crouching, he kept his weapon pointed at the men on the floor and backed out of the door toward the dim light from the hallway, smoke wafting from the snub barrel of his gun.

Stecher was the first to reach Grover upon hearing the gunshots. Along with Bohrmann, he found Grover in the hallway, still holding the gun, pointed toward the open door of his room. Blood oozed from beneath the dark hair on Grover's head. With his weapon drawn, Stecher peered into the room, pushed on the wall light switch, and saw two men on the floor. One was wounded and "scared to death," he said. "The other was gasping, dying."

Stecher said he made sure the men could not use their guns against him, and then he comforted the dying man the best he could, giving him a drink of water. Bohrmann tended to the wounded, unconscious man who, he said, "recovered quickly." Bohrmann sent for Eberbach police stationed in their lookout building nearly across the street, who arrived on their bicycles and motorcycles. One officer cradled the dying man in his arms until he drew his last breath. The wounded and scared man was lifted onto Grover's bed, where he bled on the sheets. They called for a doctor to treat his gunshot wounds, causing a broken arm and bleeding from his shoulder. Warned by Grover and Bohrmann that there might be others nearby, Eberbach police officers powered off on motorcycles in search of accomplices and a possible getaway car.

"I just cut loose as you would spray a hose," Grover later told the magazine journalist and American Legion member Leighton Blood for a lengthy first-person article on the dramatic kidnapping attempt in Eberbach. "I heard two bodies fall.

Bohrmann's Hotel Krone-Post in Eberbach, Germany, was Grover's hideout before his marriage to Berta. Two kidnapping attempts were made on Grover in Eberbach, at the train station in 1921 and the hotel in 1923. Both involved shootouts, wounding a young German woman and killing a Swiss kidnapper. The hotel was owned by Grover's cousin, and, along with security guards, it offered him vital protection.

I didn't know how many were in the room or who was outside. I crouched and backed to the door and out." Grover's only injury was a gash in his scalp caused by the blunt force of a lead ball in the blackjack.[3]

From multiple descriptions, he didn't seem rattled about the kidnapping attempt, his head wound, biting off a man's thumb tip, or killing a man and wounding another. Witnesses suggested that he appeared perfectly capable of fighting, defending himself, and expertly handling a gun. However, he tried to remove himself from the grisly scene immediately. Still, the authorities, who had already surmised Grover's self-defense, required him to remain in the hotel for questioning from the Baden state prosecutor in the morning.

Eberbach police identified the men who attacked Grover as Carl Schmidt of Stein and Lausanne, Switzerland, and Ignace Roger Sperber, 25, of Paris, France.

Schmidt was dead. *The New York Times* said he wore a "gunmetal watch, worn brown leather pocketbook, and a document case" in his breast pocket. The case "had a ragged large caliber revolver bullet hole as Bergdoll's deadly fluke shot drove into his abdomen. This bullet also bored through Schmidt's Paris press card with his photograph attached as an editor of *La Vie Parisienne*."[4]

---

[3] Along with the fear of another kidnapping, Grover's head concussion from the blackjack blow caused him to go into deeper seclusion, moving to secret locations across the border in Switzerland for the next several months.

[4] *La Vie Parisienne* magazine was so popular and risqué during the war that American soldiers were ordered not to buy it. Schmidt, who was described as a German and French engineer from Lausanne, Switzerland, may have carried the press pass as cover to enter events in Germany and France as a journalist.

Schmidt had worked as a spy following the war and then as a private detective. Sperber was born in Paris to Romanian parents who were naturalized as French in 1897. During the war, Sperber served in the French regimental artillery through several campaigns and suffered from poison gas. He recorded an exemplary war and military record that filled three pages through reserve duty in 1927. He worked at a car rental agency with his brother-in-law and as a detective. Schmidt and Sperber worked for the Leoni Detective Agency, 89 Rue Ampère in Paris. They were personally chosen for the job by the agency owner, Leon Leoni, to fill a contract for a deep-pocketed client.

At the edge of Eberbach village, motorcycle police pulled over an Army Cadillac and identified the kidnapping accomplices through records in their pockets. The car was surrounded by a small but violent mob of Eberbachers who wanted to string up the three men inside.

From the Cadillac, with Army of Occupation decals on the doors and an American flag standing on the radiator grill, police arrested the driver, U.S. Army Private Eugene Victor Nelson, 29, a farmer's son from the wild lands of Montana, and two other men in the back seat: a Russian, Prince Gregory Gagarin, 28, whose noble family was a casualty of the Russian Revolution, and U.S. Army Reserve Lt. Corliss Hooven Griffis, 28, of Hamilton, Ohio.[5] Pvt. Nelson was dressed in a chauffeur's uniform, Lt. Griffis in civilian clothes, and Prince Gagarin was dressed as a civilian but shabbily for a prince. Griffis and Nelson were quickly separated from the angry mob. The Russian prince had difficulty being led to safety because he was hobbled by an injured knee and carried a cane with only his left hand. Three fingers on his right hand were severely impaired from a bullet wound during his escape from a Bolshevik execution squad during the war.

All three men and their Army-issue Cadillac were taken to the Eberbach police station.[6] Minutes later, the street mob surrounded the jail and "smashed the gate. One woman was wounded in the head with a revolver butt."[7]

---

[5] The many characters involved in this kidnapping attempt were tracked through testimony and military records. This was the first time anyone interested in this story research had followed the history and life of the Russian prince, Gregorii Andreivich Gagarin. Many years later, Gagarin's son revealed his father's life story to a history researcher, Karl D. Qualls, through the Russian Cultural Center of Washington, D.C., and Dickinson College. It nearly matched my research through Grover's legal records but did not include Prince Gagarin's arrest and conviction for the kidnapping attempt.

[6] Few realized the Army kept a fleet of luxury Cadillacs for officers to use during the Army occupation of Germany. Perhaps "misused" is the apt description because General Allen kept track of them near the end of his command, reprimanding those who misused the Cadillacs.

[7] *Chicago Tribune*, August 12, 1923. A syndicated newspaper article described the scene as "extreme Bergdollism," a description used in a few publications for the feelings of Europeans and Americans who supported the Bergdolls running from their military duty. The article said, "the villagers would be willing to give their lifeblood for the American deserter, a local hero."

The police managed to push the crowd back, but they were required to hold the men in an interior apartment of the police station until 4 am, fearing the mob would get to them. Concerned that French operatives would arrive to spring them, the Baden prosecutor secretly moved the men from Eberbach 100 kilometers away to a jail in Wurzberg, in the neighboring state of Bavaria.

Searching the car under its dark blue-painted canvas top, police found two ropes, two pairs of handcuffs, two towels, and two bottles of chloroform. They found and confiscated a battery tube lamp and his cane from Prince Gagarin, which doubled as a big club or a sharp sword. Inside the Cadillac, they found an American officer's post-war uniform issued to Lt. Griffis, military intelligence orders, personal papers, and documents, including Prince Gagarin's written surveillance reports on Grover's Eberbach activities and a sketch of the Krone-Post. They also found a passport for another Army officer who managed the motor pool for the Military Intelligence Division of the Army of Occupation and happened to leave it, along with his wife's documents, in the car. The Cadillac was a staff car marked on the front doors with *U.S.A.* and *For Official Use Only.*[8] On driver Nelson, they found military documents showing that he was in the Army reserve, a member of the American Legion, and assigned as a driver for the Graves Registration Service in Paris.[9]

Also found by Eberbach police were a cake of soap with an impression of a key to Grover's hotel room, steel files for making a duplicate key, the handcrafted key in Schmidt's pocket, two sets of handcuffs on Sperber and Schmidt (made in Waterbury, Connecticut), and coded telegrams between Griffis and Prince Gagarin indicating Griffis was staying in Strasbourg, France. They found on Sperber a list of 22 American Army officers "interested in the Bergdoll case." Sperber later said he kept the list in case of a double-cross where he didn't get paid for the kidnapping. On Griffis, they found telegram codes for unsent messages that Bergdoll had been captured and a letter declaring Griffis' 1922 commission in the Military Intelligence Division.[10]

In Grover's hotel room, Detective Sperber regained consciousness lying in his blood on Grover's bed. While bandaged by the doctor, Eberbach police managed to piece together his story. His participation in the kidnap attempt was evident. He had photographs of Grover and the hotel room's interior in his pockets. And he was missing the tip of his thumb, spit onto the floor from Grover's bloodied mouth.

---

[8] U.S. Army Cadillac description provided by www.LibertyCadillac.com. Despite hundreds of these specially made Army Cadillacs stockpiled for use at Coblenz following the war, only one is known to have survived scrapping.

[9] The Graves Registration Service was an Army department charged with identifying the dead and registering the thousands of unmarked graves of American soldiers killed in France, Germany, and Belgium. Ironically, the first of these units was organized in Bergdoll's hometown of Philadelphia. Members left for Europe from the Army's Casualty Camp on Governor's Island, New York.

[10] Sperber insisted that he and the others were to split a $10,000 reward put up by the American Legion in Paris. Legion officials, however, denied it.

Early that day, Sperber and Schmidt snatched a key to Grover's room from a hook at the hotel check-in desk, pushed it into a bar of soap to make a deep impression, and returned it to the pin. They used a pair of cutters and a file to fashion another key from a thin metal plate, with which they managed to turn the lock on Grover's hotel room door. Their spy, the handsome Prince Gagarin, who shaved off his pencil-thin mustache and sometimes dressed as a woman during his surveillance, told them that Grover would return that evening from visiting his mother, Emma, in Heidelberg; they ducked into his room, locked the door, and lay in wait, Schmidt behind the door, Sperber behind the clothes press.

After a nightcap of beer and wine with Bohrmann in the innkeeper's private dining room behind the bar where Grover regularly held court in Eberbach, Grover crossed the hotel lobby for the stairs. When he entered his room, Schmidt grabbed him in a chokehold and threw him onto his bed, trying to hold a chloroform-soaked hand towel over Grover's face. Sperber said he stood by at first because Schmidt was so strong. He thought his fellow detective could handle the capture himself. Then, Sperber said that his thumb got into Grover's mouth while trying to grab his head while smashing the blackjack ball onto Grover's skull. Even while squealing in pain when Grover bit down hard, Sperber managed to crash the blackjack into his head again. Then, the shots rang out. Sperber said he fell to the floor and didn't remember anything else. When he woke, Sperber was lying on Grover's bed with a man tending to his arm, shoulder wounds, and throbbing thumb. He saw Schmidt appear to be dead on the floor. Then he was confused about the riotous noise from the street below until he realized a crowd of Eberbachers roared with jubilation as they followed police carrying Griffis, Prince Gagarin, and Nelson to the police station.

Grover later gave a similar account of the kidnapping attempt. This one was in a courtroom, under oath, where the chronic liar was more likely but not guaranteed to be telling the truth.

Where Grover spent the rest of that dramatic night is unknown. Perhaps in another room or surrounded by his body guards in Bohrmann's private dining room. Still, he likely spent considerable time under questioning by Eberbach police and the state prosecutor the next morning. Although he tried to follow his long habit of fleeing from an authority, he was required by Eberbach police to remain in the village. He was also waiting for his mother, Emma, to arrive from Heidelberg, alerted to the attack by telegraph.

Emma Bergdoll had arrived in Germany in early August on the ocean liner *Seydlitz* with special passport #323857 issued to her by the U.S. State Department in Washington at the recommendation of the Alien Property Custodian, Thomas W. Miller, with the understanding that she would convince Grover to return to the U.S. voluntarily to surrender and face trial. During their reunion in her Heidelberg hotel room, she told Grover that he might have to serve only a partial sentence if he returned. More importantly, Miller would release the federal government's seizure of his assets. If he didn't, his estimated $1-million fortune would be forfeited to help pay American claims against Germany during the war.[11]

In the few brief statements Grover and his cohorts made to a reporter for the *Eberbacher Zeitung* on August 11, they soon roiled the Americans. Grover said he did not regret killing Schmidt, suggesting he would do it again in similar circumstances. However, police interrogation records indicate he regretted the shooting and said it was done in self-defense.

"Did I kill him? Well, I guess I did. I hope I get a shot at a few more American Legioners," he boasted."[12]

When an aggressive *Chicago Tribune* News Service reporter asked if he would return to the United States alone, Grover replied, "They will never get me. I might have returned to America with my mother if they had not tried to get me by force, but now I will never return." The reporter wrote, "Bergdoll is as cocky as ever."

Bohrmann and Grover's guards managed to keep the American press at bay in the days following the shooting, telling them to read Grover's statement in the *Eberbacher*. His comment about hoping to shoot "a few more American Legioners" only exacerbated his already tense relationship with the veterans' organization.[13] It was widely reported that the Legion was behind the kidnap attempt. The national adjutant of the Legion called the allegation "bunk." The reports riled Legion members all over the world.

Furthermore, despite his testimony declaring he gave the dying kidnapper a drink of water, Stecher was described in the early newspaper reports as standing over Schmidt's body in Grover's hotel room and declaring, "*Keine Chance für dich, du verdammt Schwein* (no chance for you, you damned swine)."

Emma boarded a late-morning train from Heidelberg to Eberbach. When the old lady arrived at the Krone-Post, a reporter overheard her comforting Grover, saying, "It's a pity you did not kill the rest of them." Grover further smeared the Army in the one interview he and Emma did perform with the American press on August 12, saying they (the Americans) didn't dare try to kidnap him themselves but, instead, relied on German-Swiss, French, and Russian men to do their dirty work while the Americans, Lt. Griffis, and Pvt. Nelson, remained safe in the Army Cadillac.

"Why don't they allow me to return?" he asked the American reporter rhetorically.

---

[11] Grover claimed he was preparing to return, booking passage with his mother on the September 27 voyage of the *Albert Ballin* steamship sailing from Hamburg. Instead, Emma returned to Philadelphia on the ship alone because of the kidnapping attempt.

[12] A Swiss national working in France, Schmidt was not a member of the American Legion. However, it was widely reported that the plot was hatched by the Legion, reports that were buttressed by Nelson's Legion membership card.

[13] As early as October 1919, the American Legion adopted unanimous resolutions demanding the federal government "redouble its efforts" to capture Grover and Erwin and punish Emma for helping them to run from the draft.

Then, unaware that the American President had died while she was sailing for Europe, Emma chimed in, "I hate Harding. You did good work, Grover."[14] Following their single American press interview over the incident, Grover and Emma did their best to bide the time in Baden while waiting through the legal proceedings.

As the kidnap ringleader, Griffis denied the plot at a preliminary hearing. He claimed that he and Nelson traveled through Eberbach in the Cadillac and got lost in the dark. They stopped to ask directions, and Prince Gagarin volunteered to escort them to Heidelberg. Griffis claimed not to know Schmidt and Sperber. His story changed when he came up for a trial, and he took full responsibility.

Sperber was hospitalized to treat his gunshot wounds and nipped thumb. One bullet was removed from his broken arm, but another in his shoulder remained. He reportedly had difficulty communicating with the medical staff because he spoke German poorly. When it came time for him to leave, he told his hospital nurse that the American Legion from Paris would pick him up and return him to France. Instead, in a remarkable turn of events, Grover showed up at the hospital with his car and three officers from the Eberbach police.

Since Bergdoll was one of only a few in Eberbach who could drive and had a car, the police allowed him to transport Sperber to jail. Some newspapers were misinformed about the incident and suggested that Grover kidnapped Sperber from his hospital bed, but the bandaged Sperber went willingly to the car. One can only imagine his surprise when he saw it was Bergdoll driving.

In another unusual twist to the story of how the Germans succumbed to Grover's generosity, the Baden prosecutor Trautwein, in finally revealing the remote Bavarian location of the jailed prisoners, adjusted his monocle and peered up at a reporter and said with a straight face that when he needed to travel to Wurzberg to question them, he hoped Grover would give him a ride in his car too.

During the trial, Griffis told the panel of judges that he was from Hamilton, Ohio (north of Cincinnati). His father was the treasurer of American Frog and Switch Company, a maker of steel products for railroad track intersections. Some of the company materials, he said in a patronizing manner, were shipped to Germany for rebuilding railroads after the war. He attended college in Oxford, Ohio, home of Miami University, and then briefly attended law school at Columbia University in New York before switching to journalism. When he joined the Army in October 1917 through the Officer Reserve Corps, he was accepted as a member of the highly patriotic organization Empire State Society of the Sons of the American Revolution. His great-great-grandfather, David Griffith, was an

---

[14] Emma was referring to President Warren G. Harding, who died on August 2, 1923, a week prior to the kidnap attempt. As President, Harding refused to release Grover's assets, seized by the federal government on May 27, 1921. His administration declared Grover an enemy of the United States without citizenship. Emma had written to President Harding, as she did Presidents Wilson, Coolidge, Hoover, and Roosevelt, begging for the release of their assets and a pardon for Grover.

American Revolutionary War infantry and artillery private in Pennsylvania from 1776–1780.[15]

Griffis' arrest and jailing surprised his family because he didn't tell them of his mission when he sailed to Europe in May 1923. He did tell a wartime buddy that he "was going to get Bergdoll and bring him back." However, Griffis' mother told reporters her son mentioned in one of his letters sent home that he had become acquainted with a Russian prince named Gagarin.

Instead, Griffis told his family and immigration authorities for his passport application that he worked as a journalist for the New York City-based Bell Syndicate "to obtain feature articles" in France, Germany, Belgium, and Switzerland... all countries in which Bergdoll might be hiding. A photographer for Bell and Griffis' father vouched for him on a document under Bell's letterhead. It said Griffis would "write a series of articles on travel in Europe... in several American newspapers."[16]

Griffis was gassed at the front during the war while serving in the Meuse-Argonne 131st Infantry defensive sector in October 1918. He continued with the American Expeditionary Forces until he was discharged from the Army as a sergeant and sailed home. Upon returning to Europe in 1923, he was promoted to first lieutenant in the Military Intelligence Department Officer's Reserve Corp.

As *The New York Times* described the sensational trial on December 6, 1923, under German court rules, Griffis was the first to testify in his defense. "[Bergdoll] insulted the American nation and Army and, therefore, every single American, living and dead," he said to five judges in black robes, flanked by Baden state police in faded blue, red-trimmed uniforms with spiked helmets and Kaiser mustaches.[17]

Griffis was further described as well-groomed with freshly cut hair and a small trimmed mustache. "A smartly tailored, well-fitting gray sack suit," said *The Times* to illustrate that he was not in a military uniform. The article said, "Sperber wore large round-horn glasses. Gagarin displayed his Asiatic face. Nelson wore an air of utter indifference as if all the business did not concern him."

Griffis explained how he returned to France representing the American Legion to help organize the American cemetery for Meuse-Argonne war dead at Romagne-sous-Montfaucon. He even made a speech at the event.[18] The Baden judges were

---

[15] As Griffis' name was misspelled frequently during the 1923 Mosbach trial, his Empire State Society of the Sons of the American Revolution lineage path indicates six different spellings of the family name.

[16] If Griffis wrote European travel articles for many American newspapers in 1923, they could not be found. Perhaps his mission was to write a single article about his capture of Bergdoll which would have generated great interest from all American newspapers.

[17] Description from *The New York Times*, December 6, 1923.

[18] The event Griffis described was a ceremony accepting the final plans for constructing the Romagne cemetery visitor's building and staff quarters, replacing crude Army barracks used as YWCA hostess houses. Work began in the late summer of 1923 and continued into 1924. Eventually, the Romagne (Meuse-Argonne) Cemetery became the largest in France, with more than 14,000 graves. Historic American Landscapes Survey, Library of Congress.

sympathetic. They had soldiers buried there, too, fallen in the fierce battles of German and French troops in 1914–1915 before the arrival of Americans.

Griffis impressed the judges by describing how he performed honorary work for the U.S. War Department, Office of the Quartermaster General's Graves Registration Service, documenting the remains of American soldiers and disinterring those whose families wished them to be returned to the United States for reburial. He said that when he arrived in France in June 1923, he carried $3,000 in cash. His main objective was to file feature stories for newspapers.

However, when pressed by Chief Judge Kurzmann, Griffis may have slipped a bit in his carefully rehearsed defense of being only a journalist.

"At that time, everybody was talking about Bergdoll in America. Likewise, in American circles in Paris, and, therefore, I gradually got the idea that it was my duty to the many dead whose bodies I had helped to bury to save them from the traitor and deserter, Bergdoll."

The judges' curiosity was aroused when Griffis mentioned his cash. Had the American Legion provided the money to violate German laws and capture Bergdoll? No, replied Griffis, but he said American Army officers, including his superior at the Graves Registration Service in France, knew about his plan to get Bergdoll.

The dapper black-robed Judge Kurzmann leaned forward, inquisitive about American sentiment five years after the war. "Why are Americans so persistent in tracking down Bergdoll when so many other American slackers remain unscathed?" came the translation to his question to Griffis. "Time eliminates everything—even the hatreds of war," the judge suggested.

A German woman translated the answer: "Because Bergdoll made hateful speeches against his native land. Because he held the Army authorities up to scorn and ridicule on postcards he mailed on his flight. Because he broke his word of honor when he was permitted to return home… for his buried treasure, because he misused his money to corrupt poor devils and strip them of their honor," Griffis charged.

His testimony continued, "You don't have any idea of the rage against Bergdoll in America. Time will never eliminate the feelings of Americans in the Bergdoll case."

Griffis said he knew he would have to "disregard" the laws of Germany and France to capture Bergdoll and take him back to the United States. He also admitted that he was informed of a $50,000 bounty for Bergdoll in the United States and that he had read military documents and newspaper articles about a kidnap attempt on Bergdoll in 1921.

"I am guilty of a crime," Griffis admitted. "But the love of my country was greater than any fear of punishment."

Griffis then admitted that the Cadillac in which he hoped to spirit a drugged, gagged, and handcuffed Bergdoll out of Germany and across France to a ship in La Havre was owned by the U.S. Army, thereby indirectly tying it to the kidnapping plot. He insisted that he was authorized to use the car in unoccupied zones of

Germany because, through the Graves Registration Service, the vehicle had been used to collect the bodies of American soldiers in Germany. He drove the car on the same route across France and Germany many times so that border crossing guards would become familiar with its identifiable markings and be less inclined to search the car when he carried Bergdoll. He used the vehicle, he said, because an early plan to fly Bergdoll over France had been scrapped as too risky and impractical.

Griffis said his plan called for Prince Gagarin, whom he met in Paris through his secretary, to spend a few weeks in Eberbach surveilling Bergdoll. Gagarin often made trips to Wiesbaden to visit his wife, Elizabeth Zouraboff Gagarin, and infant son, Gregory, who still lived there because obstetrics and pediatric care for women and children were much cheaper in hyper-inflated Germany. Since Prince Gagarin had no job, they utilized the large Wiesbaden Russian Orthodox Church and community to help the family through difficult times.

Griffis said Gagarin injured his knee on one of these trips and used it as an excuse to check into the Krone-Post for a few weeks of recuperation. Griffis was paying the hotel tab and giving Gagarin extra money to send home to his wife. The prince sometimes walked with a cane; other times, he dressed as a woman, always watching Bergdoll. After Gagarin traveled to Ludwigshafen to give Griffis a written report of Bergdoll's activities in Eberbach and a drawing of the hotel interior, Griffis returned to Paris, where he contracted with the Leoni Detective Agency to hire private detectives to grab the fugitive draft dodger.[19]

Griffis was so organized and confident of his plan that he compiled special telegram codes to inform his friends (22 fellow officers) in Paris of his success. He carried the codes in his pocket for the night he would use them.

Next in their courtroom defense was the handsome, athletic, and mysterious Russian Prince Gagarin, who had recovered from his knee injury but could not correctly use three fingers on his right hand. A Baden newspaper described him as "the most interesting personality of the four men accused."

Everyone at the trial wished to hear more about how he got mixed up with the kidnappers.

Gagarin remained mysterious in jail and at the Mosbach trial because the prosecutor, defense, judges, and the press continuously referred to him only as Prince Gagarin. It confused people because, in Russia, every Gagarin male descended from the House of Gagarin enjoyed the title of Prince. And, despite being scattered by the revolution, there were several of them.

He was Prince Grigorii Andreivich Gagarin, born in Chatellerault, France, in 1895 to Prince Andre Gagarin, a Russian military captain working in France to procure

---

[19] It does not appear that Griffis took his Army Cadillac car into the unoccupied zone of Germany, in Baden, where he was forbidden to use it for anything other than corpse recovery, until the kidnapping plot was underway.

Army supplies, and Princess Marie Obolenski Gagarin.[20] His grandfather, with the same name, was a famous Imperial Academy of Arts artist who decorated the Russian church in Baden-Baden. The family derived from Prince Vladimir Svyatoslavich, the Christianizer of Russia. Until Bolshevik control after the revolution, they maintained a large estate with a three-story castle-like home in Pskov, northern Russia, near the Baltics. Prince Gagarin was slightly wounded in the war and served as a cavalryman in the czar's Hussar guard.

Though he spoke adequate German, Prince Gagarin's testimony was translated to the judges in the Mosbach courtroom. He told them the same story that inspired Griffis to hire him for detective work and surveil Bergdoll.

Leaving the Russian guard, Prince Gagarin returned to his family estate in Pskov in 1917 following the abdication of Czar Nicholas to raise flax. There, he was seized one day in a political attack. He did his best to describe the dreadful incident in German. "*Die Bolschewiki haben meine Burg angegriffen und mich auf den Pskower Friedhof geschleppt, um mich zu erschießen* (The Bolsheviks attacked my castle and dragged me to the Pskov cemetery to shoot me)," he said. The judges must have been enthralled by what he described next. With his thin, lanky physique, dark complexion and hair parted in the middle of his head, thin mustache, and deep voice, Prince Gagarin resembled the great American actor from Philadelphia, John Barrymore, then famous for starring in the 1922 movie *Sherlock Holmes*.

The judges, reporters, Mosbachers, and Eberbachers leaned in to hear a clear interpretation of the prince's deep voice and polished diction.

He told them he attacked the horseman in charge of the squad, and in confusion among three prisoners and seven Bolsheviks, he bolted from their charge, vaulted a stone wall, and escaped with only an explosive bullet shot to his right hand. It forever disfigured and disabled three fingers.

Unable to return to the Gagarin castle, he fought for the White Army against the Bolsheviks. When they were defeated, he worked as a coal shoveler on a steamer across the Black Sea, but the crew mutinied, and they landed in Constantinople (Istanbul), where his brother, Prince Serge, worked in the Russian consulate. From there, he sailed to Malta and became an interpreter for the British. They sent him to Vladivostok in Far Eastern Asia. He lashed himself to the ship mast during a typhoon on the voyage. He said the British were impressed with his interpretation skills, and he met a fellow interpreter at the consulate, his future wife, Elizabeth. The British realized Gagarin's nobility placed him in danger no matter where he was in the new Soviet Union. They sent the prince and Elizabeth to Paris to spare their lives.

Prince Gagarin first found work helping to clear the French battlefields of the dead. It put him in contact with members of the Graves Registration Service and Lt. Griffis.

---

[20] Prince Gagarin and the first man in space, Yuri Gagarin, are not from the same line of Russian Gagarins.

At first, Gagarin said in his testimony, Griffis only told him their mission was to capture "a traitor" in Germany and move him to France and then America. Griffis' promise of 500 francs to him and his wife in Wiesbaden every two weeks motivated him to take the job. And it wasn't difficult. All he had to do was go to Eberbach, find out what Bergdoll was up to, and report back to Griffis.

In July 1923, Prince Gagarin arrived in Eberbach and checked in to the Hotel Krone-Post. While it wasn't unusual for a Russian to travel around Germany in 1923, Carl Bohrmann and Stecher paid immediate attention to the single man who checked in to their hotel without any general intentions. He had the appearance of a spy. Gagarin drank coffee in the hotel café and explained to anyone questioning him that he needed a few weeks of hotel staff pampering to recover from his knee injury. He paid them marks.

Then, much to his surprise, he learned from a chauffeur that Bergdoll was staying in the same hotel. He immediately cabled Griffis that he had fulfilled his mission and would meet him in Ludwigshafen to give him all the details. So as not to raise suspicion, Gagarin then returned to the Krone-Post and continued his recovery (spying).

Schmidt also ventured to Eberbach in his car, keeping a low profile and never coming in close contact with Gagarin. He watched the hotel while Bohrmann watched him.

Then, when Grover returned to Eberbach from his visit with Emma in Heidelberg on August 8, Gagarin and Schmidt drove to the Grand Hotel in Heidelberg on August 9 to collect Sperber, and together, the three men returned to Eberbach. Gagarin resumed his "recovery" post in the Krone-Post café while Schmidt and Sperber skulked around the hotel and tried to stay out of sight. Bohrmann said he saw the men again and became even more suspicious. He warned Grover.

On August 10, the day of the kidnapping attempt, Gagarin said his directions were to tip off Schmidt and Sperber with his battery tube lamp when Grover appeared ready to retire for the night. Then, he was told to meet Griffis in the Cadillac on the edge of the village, where the road leads to Heidelberg.

Answering a few more questions, Gagarin told the judges that he felt guilty for what he'd done and had the "impression that Griffis had acted on behalf of an organization."

It's uncertain if Gagarin had ever met Nelson before the night of the caper when he jumped into the Cadillac with him and Griffis, and they all waited for Schmidt and Sperber to bring them their captive, Bergdoll.

Imagine the surprise of Sgt. Eugene Victor Nelson, sitting at the wheel of the big Cadillac, feeling safe and unapproachable, in a U.S. Army officer's car when suddenly surrounded by police on motorcycles and a scrambling mob of Eberbachers threatening to hang them.

A fair-haired Swedish man born in Chicago but raised on a farm in the middle-of-nowhere Becket, Montana, Private Nelson luckily spent the war in the Motor Transport Corps driving cars like the Cadillac for officers. He married a French woman when the war was over, and in 1919 they moved to Becket in the shadow of a mountain ridge named Old Baldy, where people and entertainment for a social life were sparse.[21] Their address was simply Gene and Juliette Nelson, Becket, Montana.

After several months, Juliette grew bored with her new life on central Montana's broad range, near the Rocky Mountain continental divide where the explorers Lewis and Clark had traveled a century earlier. They drove 30 miles from the Nelson farm to apply for their first civilian passports in Lewistown.

Backtracking Lewis and Clark's journey by train and sailing from New York in December 1920, they arrived back in France to stay with Juliette's parents, whose home had long been the medieval stone-fortified community of Langres, Haute-Marne, a five-hour drive from Paris. Since he was a former Army sergeant and American soldiers lay dead in graves all over central Europe, Gene Nelson had no difficulty finding a driver's job with the Graves Registration Service.[22]

He drove the Army Cadillac all over France and Germany for Lt. Corliss Hooven Griffis.[23]

Just before the trial, Nelson agreed to speak briefly with a reporter from his jail cell. He broke down in tears from the long isolation. "My god," he said, "just let me write to my wife."

Roger Sperber was even less attractive to the Mosbach, Baden court judges, press, and public, cramming into the courtroom for the trial. He was French—the German enemy.

Ignace Roger Sperber had been an artilleryman for France since 1913 in its 37th Regiment, entering the French Army at Seine-et-Oise, Île-de-France. He was a Parisian, but his parents were Romanian. His military record fills an entire handwritten page from 1913 until 1919, then reserves until 1927. And, like many others, he was gassed. After the war, he ran a rental car company with his brother-in-law and worked as a Leoni detective when Griffis came looking for two tough men to capture Bergdoll. He was promised payment for all his expenses and part of the American reward for Bergdoll.

Sperber described the brawl with Bergdoll in his hotel room in great detail. Still, his most significant contribution to prosecutor Trautwein's case was that Griffis told him, "a well-known American organization was financing the affair." He said

---

[21] Old Baldy in Fergus County, Montana, at 8,678 feet. Part of the 1893–1907 Lewis and Clark National Forest.

[22] Nelson once cried hysterically to *The New York Times* reporter Cyril Brown that had he stayed home on the farm in Becket instead of returning to France with his wife, he would never have gotten into the Bergdoll mess.

[23] The Army Cadillac was the preferred car by officers, so much so that occupation commander General Allen had to reprimand them for their "extravagant use" of the cars. Many officers tried to purchase these Cadillacs for their personal use because they were so cheap during the hyper-inflated post-war German economy. Most, however, were scrapped.

he understood there was a $10,000 reward on Bergdoll's head from the American Legion. However, he had never heard of Bergdoll before he was hired for the job. Legion officials in Paris quickly denied Sperber's testimony, saying a wealthy American businessman posted the reward, not the Legion.

Sperber said he enjoyed receiving 100 francs a day, paid by Griffis from his stash of cash, and that he imagined great success emigrating to America as the detective who captured Bergdoll. It was a dream implanted in Sperber's head by Griffis, who claimed they all would be heroes in the United States one day and find great fortune for bringing the evil Bergdoll home to face justice.[24]

Following the proceedings, Grover's Eberbach lawyer, Karl Zeiss, filed claims with the court for expenses he incurred following the fracas in the Krone-Post. He claimed an incredible 600,000 gold marks (about $150,000) or *Schmerzensgeld*. It was to cover Grover's medical expenses, pain, and suffering from the attack. He also listed a one gold mark expense for the six bullets he fired from his pistol, three of which hit and killed the kidnapper, Schmidt. Grover never collected.[25]

Griffis, Sperber, Prince Gagarin, and Nelson were all found guilty of the kidnapping on December 7, 1923. Griffis appealed his 18-month sentence and was not taken to Baden state prison. He remained in the Mosbach jail.

Grover went into deep hiding following the dramatic events of August 1923. The Baden state government even rebuffed reporters who tried to find him. Before the kidnapping attempt, American reporters needed only a German federal visa to enter Baden. Afterward, the state also required a second visa from the Baden government before reporters could disembark their trains, reported the *Chicago Tribune*. Entry into Eberbach, Mosbach, or Heidelberg was verboten unless you first went to Karlsruhe for interrogation by the authorities about why you wanted to visit a Bergdoll hideaway.

The *Tribune* said Baden went so far as to assign plainclothes police officers to watch foreigners (Americans) arriving at train stations and monitor the roads for foreigners in cars. American Legion emissary Leighton Blood wrote of his December 1923 trip to Eberbach to attempt to bring Grover home that when he stepped off the Eberbach train, he "found German gunmen in front of the station watching the train" as security for Grover.

Meanwhile, another Bergdoll was making headlines in Philadelphia, which was the least anyone would have expected from the older brother, Charles. Having already changed his name to Brawn to avoid connections with his notorious family, Charles was charged twice with speeding in his car. On August 13, 1923, while Grover

---

[24] Roger Sperber eventually emigrated to the United States, arriving in 1929.

[25] Grover counted six bullets fired when he wanted compensation but only two when bragging about the killing in a magazine article. Description from the Baden state court records and the *Associated Press*, December, 1923.

and Emma were still grappling with the fallout from the kidnapping attempt and Grover's killing of Schmidt, Philadelphians read in their newspapers about Charles being in high-speed chases with police. Turning off his headlamps to avoid police in Philadelphia's affluent western neighbor, Haverford Township, one night, he eluded one police car. Still, he was snared by another farther along West Chester Pike, the road in front of his Broomall farm. Stories of the minor indiscretions were placed next to the blaring kidnapping headlines about Grover in Germany. In Philadelphia and worldwide, one could not help but be exposed to more bad news about the Bergdolls.

In Germany, the press devoted considerable newspaper space to the Bergdoll saga. Many Germans were sympathetic toward the Bergdolls, partly because they were German and, like them, were constantly persecuted since the war's end. They also felt pride in the Bergdolls because they retained their wealth when Germany and Germans had been stripped of it by the war, hyperinflation, and reparation demands by France, Belgium, and England. The German press also expressed Bergdollism over promises made by the American Army of Occupation during the previous kidnapping attempt on Grover in 1921, where Lina Rupp was shot in her hand. The German federal republic-supporting *Frankfurter Zeitung* editorialized, "American promises… had not been kept. The sum of money promised to the wounded girl had not been paid, nor the promised fee of the doctor who attended the girl."[26]

***

The magazine journalist Leighton Blood, who also worked as a representative of the American Legion in trying to get Grover to come home, said he knew about three kidnapping plots against Bergdoll between 1921 and 1923. Blood reported that Berlin "had issued orders to show me every consideration. The German government is absolutely sick of the whole Bergdoll matter and is delighted to have it ended," he wrote. Blood confirmed that Army officers organized the two kidnapping attempts involving gunfire (and a third attempt was due in the spring of 1924). And for each of them, Grover claimed, he was tipped off by German family, friends, and police that suspicious men were hanging around and planning to grab him.

However, rattled by kidnapping attempts and his dwindling money supply, Grover appeared receptive to Blood's negotiations to take him home.

Leighton Harold Blood was a Bostonian who moved to New York and worked as a journalist for magazines, including *Hearst's International*.[27] He served a year in the first war and became a member of the American Legion, sending him to Germany for the Hearst company to find Bergdoll. The journalist-emissary arrived in Baden in late December 1923 and was met at the Eberbach train station by Stecher, who

---

[26] Compensation for Lina Rupp was finally approved by the U.S. Congress in 1926; $200 indemnity.
[27] Blood had moved into broadcasting with NBC in New York by the second war.

gave him and Otto Tolischus of the Berlin Hearst newspaper bureau a ride the few short blocks to the Krone-Post. Armed men along the streets watched them closely with Bergdoll cash in their pockets.

Blood and Tolischus first met Grover in the hotel garage, "sitting in one of his two high-powered cars with the motor running." Would he come home and face his crime, Blood inquired.

"This is the first time anybody has requested me to return to America," Grover told Blood. "Everyone seemed to want to bring me back by force. I'm ready to go with a reasonable guarantee and take some chances. I believe that when my story is told, I shall be given a square deal."

After multiple meetings in Eberbach to formulate a plan to return to the United States, Blood told Grover he arranged for a special visa through the Foreign Office for Grover to leave Germany without a passport. Grover, however, was concerned about Stecher remaining in Baden. Stecher's wife, Frieda, was with them and could freely travel back to the United States, but Stecher could not. He also needed a special visa.

"I'm sick and tired of Eberbach and want to go back to Philadelphia," said Frieda when informed of the plan to return to the United States. Stecher demurred, however, because he was suspicious of what might happen to Grover.

Blood claimed he knew the details of Grover's plan "to go to court as a witness to prove important charges against [Army] officials in connection with his escape to Germany," but he would not reveal them.

Blood said Grover finally agreed to leave, but he first went to Heidelberg (for extra privacy) to send a telegram to Philadelphia, making formal travel plans. Additionally, Grover had to dispose of his hunting lease agreements around Eberbach and Stecher's living quarters, sell his luxury cars, and make arrangements for his collection of books and scientific equipment, such as microscopes, telescopes, and camera gear, that he could not take out of Germany without paying taxes on them.

Blood believed he had made a deal beneficial to everyone. He would get an incredible exclusive story, the American Legion would proclaim that it legally arranged to get Bergdoll back home to face trial, the U.S. Army would prosecute Grover on his outstanding charges, and Grover would eventually have his confiscated assets returned to him. But, again, Grover got spooked.

Blood's detailed feature article on Grover came out in a three-part series in *Hearst's International* in April 1924, but only after the efforts to bring Grover home for trial failed. It was headlined, BERGDOLL SURRENDERS TO THE AMERICAN LEGION. Blood wrote of Grover's agonizing decision in December 1923 to finally return home and face justice. Blood was assured of the agreement in a hand-written letter from Grover that he could clear up his German affairs and be ready to sail on the *Ballin* on its first westward voyage after January 25, 1924. Blood later published the letter in the magazine. "When everything is arranged, I will come to Berlin about a week or so, before the sailing date," Grover wrote.

Bergdoll Surrenders
to the American Legion

By *Leighton H. Blood*

The age of romance strikes some people as over. The mists of distance lend enchantment to stories of strange happenings. Here we have something in our very midst that stands up with the tales of antiquity. However one feels about Bergdoll's refusal to enter the war, he certainly did stir up a lively existence for himself. When our young contributor, Leighton H. Blood, was chosen by the American Legion to go over and bring Bergdoll home, a notable chapter was added to the tale of adventure. The best of it is in our May number.—*N. H.*

GROVER CLEVELAND BERGDOLL has surrendered to me as a representative of the American Legion. He has made an agreement to go with me to the United States and give himself up to the authorities. If he keeps his agreement, and if the ship does not go down, we should be on the ocean when these lines see the light of day.

It was in Germany that the famous draft-evader gave himself up to the Legion whose agent I am. In making the agreement to go under my protection, he in reality went under the protection not only of the American Legion but also of the State Department.

[column text continues, partially illegible]

This arena posts to the mysterious "pot of gold" used by Bergdoll to hoodwink the authorities. Whether or not the authorities were willing to be hoodwinked is another story. There ought to be something about that in May.

Leighton Blood was a magazine journalist who arranged with the American Legion and the U.S. Department of State to go to Germany in 1923–1924 to convince Grover to surrender. Funded, in part, by William Randolph Hearst for *Hearst's International* Magazine and clandestinely supported by the Legion, the plan nearly succeeded until Grover got spooked over the kidnapping attempt and his fervent belief in astrology. Blood's April 1924 magazine article, further embellishing the myth of the Bergdoll buried gold, was Grover's only first-person account of his draft evasion. (*Hearst's International*, the Hearst Co.)

And, being ever thoughtful, Grover wrote in his closing salutation, "Give my regards to Mr. [Otto] Tolischus [the magazine's European editor]. Yours respectfully, Grover C. Bergdoll."

Blood wrote in his article about Grover's mood. "He has seemed well and happy since his decision was made. He definitely pulled himself together and began disposing of his property."

In the United States, the managing editor of *Hearst's International* announced that Grover had agreed to return home at the invitation of the American Legion. The Legion, stung over accusations that it was behind the two failed kidnapping efforts, said in a statement, "It was time to show the world that it [the Legion] stood for law and order."

Grover laid low in Germany after the intense publicity from the magazine article. He lied or greatly embellished several elements of the story. On the left, Grover is photographing Blood and Stecher near the Krone Post hotel garage in Eberbach, and, right, Blood, Grover, and Stecher in a photograph taken by Blood's editor with Grover's box camera. (Bergdoll Family Collection)

However, Grover reneged on his promise. Missing their departure on the *Ballin*, Blood went so far as to make a reservation for himself and Grover on another ship, the *Deutschland*, leaving Hamburg on March 27, 1924.

Blood said the terms he negotiated with Grover were simple.

"He must serve his sentence. The American Legion is not so much interested in Bergdoll as in the men who helped him escape from America. Let's bring Bergdoll back and have him make a clean break and tell who the enemies in our own camp are. Then let him do his bit in prison. After that, give him his money and let him go his way."

Instead, Blood traveled home to the United States alone. In his *Deutschland* cabin, awaiting his April 6 arrival in New York, he tapped away on his portable typewriter, preparing his feature article on Grover. In it, he wrote that Grover had shown him his pistol.

"On it were three notches, denoting three dead men. One of these was the ill-fated Schmidt, who died in the Griffis fiasco."[28]

---

[28] While Blood reported Grover's pistol as an FN Browning 1910 with three notches, a Sauer Model 1913 owned by Grover in 1923 is still in family possession and displays two notches on the grip. Therefore, it's uncertain which gun Grover used to defend himself during the kidnapping attempt.

CHAPTER NINETEEN

Bergdollism

Philadelphia, Pennsylvania, and Baden, Germany, 1920–1925[1]

When Grover's plans to return home with his mother and American Legion emissary Leighton Blood collapsed in 1923 and 1924, he didn't give up. On April 5, 1924, the still rich, single, bored, and lonely fugitive set up his typewriter in his room at the Krone-Post in Eberbach and wrote a letter to U.S. Consul General Frederick T. F. Dumont at Frankfurt am Main.[2] He told Dumont he was writing to him instead of the consul in the Baden district, Maxwell K. Moorhead, because he didn't trust the fellow Pennsylvanian from Pittsburgh and thought Moorhead was "incompetent, un-American, unfair, and pro-French."[3]

"A serious friend of my mother has spoken to me that you are an official of the highest type," Grover began his letter to Dumont with a heading identifying his return address as "C. Bohrmann's Hotel Krone-Post" in Eberbach. He asked Dumont to take up with the State Department "the subject of my return and unconditional surrender… under my constitutional rights as a citizen of the United States." But then he attached conditions. Grover said he wished the conditions to set aside his court martial and sentence as a deserter from the Army, suggesting, "I have never been, at any time, a soldier in the U.S. Army, nor have I ever been inducted or sworn into the Army." He said his court martial was "irregular and without jurisdiction." He said he would agree to plead guilty to draft evasion and serve its maximum penalty in federal prison. His last request was most unusual for a man who loved publicity.

He requested to "be allowed to return and surrender… in a dignified fashion without special newspaper notoriety, brass bands, moving picture or grandstand exhibits."

---

[1] Bergdollism is a term displayed in newspapers covering the German and American feelings about Grover Bergdoll following the two kidnapping attempts.

[2] Grover may have had help writing the letter from his attorney because it was filled with legalese about the conditions of his attempt to surrender.

[3] Moorhead's family owned a cottage at the South Fork Fishing and Hunting Club on Lake Conemaugh near Johnstown, Pennsylvania, the origin of the infamous and deadly Johnstown Flood of 1889.

Of course, his proposal was ignored. It was forwarded to the State Department in Washington, but by law, it could not consider Bergdoll's request. By receiving his draft notice to appear for an examination, the federal courts had already determined that Grover and all other draftees who received similar summons were already in the Army. The decision was reinforced in a court ruling in Erwin's habeas corpus appeal in 1921.

The public, of course, never got a chance to see this part of Grover's attempt at negotiations to return home and surrender. His letter was not revealed until many years later, during a 1939 trial for desertion and escape. Since then, it's been hidden in a folder in the United States National Archives in St. Louis, Missouri. Suppose Americans knew that Grover was willing to voluntarily return and surrender as early as 1923 and 1924 under conditions granted to other draft dodgers. Would there have continued to be so much animosity toward him? And would that have changed the course of future events? We can only speculate. But one thing is for sure: Europeans, most notably Germans, had already moved on from the Bergdoll persecution.

Anti-Bergdoll fervor would continue for another 20 years in the United States. Still, gradually, as Americans took stock of the mistakes made in the Great War, many people's feelings toward draft evaders from a war between Europeans began to change.

Unrecognized by the local authorities and the press in the early 1920s, many Philadelphians displayed their first ideology of Bergdollism. They loved Bergdoll beer for the mild, smooth taste of its lager. They envied Emma for her wealth and admired her for her tough earthiness. Gentlemen admired Louis and Charles for their business acumen in automobiles, airplanes, racing development, and their taste in fine architecture. Women adored Erwin and Grover's handsome athleticism and attractive looks on the race track and for their daring flight. Working women admired Elizabeth for daring to become the first woman to drive a car in Philadelphia, snubbing high society rules, and eloping with her chauffeur. And many people quietly and privately applauded Grover for beating the American draft when so many other boys were killed needlessly in the war.

Still, nationalism remained strong in America three years after the war. But in Europe, the feeling of Bergdollism amounted to a sense of pride that someone had beaten a tremendous military-political machine in the United States, and it happened to be a man of German heritage.

From 1921–1923, it was as easy for German sentiment to turn toward American draft dodger and habitual liar Bergdoll as to the rising popularity of the National Socialist German Workers' Party, the Nazis. In Eberbach, a small town of five to eight thousand inhabitants, depending upon how distant from the town center one counted, Grover was perceived as a gentleman who always disbursed cash to the locals in return for favors and protection. He bought meals and drinks for Eberbachers at local restaurants and saloons and spent freely at the local bookshops, appliance and electrical supply stores, gun shops, and automobile garages. He was one of the few who had a car. He leased hundreds of acres of forest for hunting forays where he was not so interested in shooting stag and waterfowl as he was in treating the local constabulary to a day behind the stock of a long gun.

In return, they looked out for Grover; the police were tipping him to new arrivals of American reporters or suspicious characters who might be bounty hunters. One American reporter said Eberbachers were "ignorant" of the circumstances of Bergdoll's flight from the United States. He said Grover would have been shot if he had fled the Prussian army. The Baden state prosecutor, Trautwein, who handled both kidnapping cases, went so far as to ask an American reporter about all the fuss. "He's only a deserter," he said of Bergdoll.

Eberbachers attributed all the Bergdoll fuss to nosy reporters, detectives, or a "Ku Klux Klanner." During the post-war economic depression and hyperinflation in a great industrial nation, the flip of a gold dollar coin from Grover into a German's hand was a blessing not to be jeopardized by talking freely to American reporters and French detectives.

Additionally, German newspapers reported that when news of a potential deal had been struck in the United States for Bergdoll to return voluntarily and face a reduced sentence and the return of his assets, the American Legion funded the kidnapping events. An article in a Karlsruhe newspaper was especially critical.

"This chauvinistic organization of former front-line soldiers wanted to thwart the deal favorable to Bergdoll by violent kidnapping and extradition." The alleged deal, as reported in the American press and spread by Emma in Germany, which may or may not have been confirmed, was only for Bergdoll to return on his own, not as a captive.

Grover first won the support of the German public when he stood up to the Americans during the first kidnapping effort in Eberbach in 1921. From Germany, sympathy for Bergdoll spread through Europe with Bergdollism. The term first appeared in the *Chicago Tribune* to explain how many Germans felt about protecting him from the Americans.

Grover may have displayed too much showmanship in the first full year he hid from the U.S. Army in Germany; he drove Big Red fast all over Baden and Bavaria, eastern Switzerland, Liechtenstein, and western Austria. Reporters claimed he was so free-spirited and free-spending that he impulsively married a restaurant waitress in Austria. He didn't.

He did have warrants for his arrest from three nations, the United States, Canada, and Great Britain. America wanted him for escape and military desertion. Canada and the British wanted him for forging crown passports. This is why he remained mainly in Germany, which still had no extradition agreements with the U.S., France, or Britain, because, five years after the last bullet was fired in battle, it was still in a state of war with the adversary nations.

Grover's safest hideaway remained his family's homeland in Baden, where his German father and grandfather were still idolized for their success, wealth, beer, and charity. If Grover left Germany of his own will, he could quickly be arrested in certain European nations, extradited, and sent to America for trial, conviction, and prison.

By June 1921, however, while Grover felt lofty about beating the kidnapping attempt, he also felt the financial pinch. On May 27, 1921, Vincent A. Carroll, the Philadelphia attorney for the United States Alien Property Custodian, sent a certified letter to Emma advising her that she must vacate the Wynnefield mansion by October 31, 1921. And this date was no Halloween trick or treat. The custodian had confiscated Grover's estimated $749,889.72 in assets, and, at the time, the Wynnefield mansion with a value of $81,000 was in his name. It also seized his Louis J. Bergdoll Brewing Company stock worth $336,000, his Broomall farm and Eagle Field worth $100,000 (purchased from brother Charles in May 1917), his apartments and mortgages payable worth $225,000, and tangible property (cars and airplane) that if sold might generate cash to fuel his flight. The legal action also seized a note payable to Charles Brawn of $15,000. The attachment to Charles was enough, temporarily, to reunite the disenfranchised son with Emma to fight the seizure. The letter described Grover as an "enemy." There was no mention of the gold.

Emma fought the seizure with attorneys in Philadelphia and Washington. In one notable appearance in Equity Court in Washington, as Emma was suing the United States to release the asset seizure, she gained public sympathy when she suffered a mental breakdown in court. Emma had a propensity for talking loudly and disrespectfully in public, and the strict confines of a courtroom did not change her habits. During Charles' hearing to recover rights to collect his $15,000 note, Emma pushed forward and spouted loudly to the judge. When told to shut up, she refused and was fined $50. The bailiff removed Emma from the courtroom, and when she was called back to testify on her attorney's arm, *The Washington Herald* reported, "she was sobbing, and almost hysterical." Even though the judge sympathetically canceled the fine when told that Emma was given such court privileges in Philadelphia, the *Herald* reported that Emma was later observed sitting on the granite steps outside the courthouse where "she sobbed pathetically."

When Americans read about Emma's mental anguish, they couldn't help but feel sorry for the old woman, no matter what they felt about Grover and Erwin.

Many years later, Bergdollism gained more momentum in the United States, despite the refusal of President Roosevelt (and First Lady Eleanor Roosevelt) to address the issue of forgiveness.

In the Philadelphia region by 1930, many people held firmly to their war-era patriotism about how Bergdoll thumbed his nose at the government agents' attempts to capture him. Then came a startling announcement from the man who organized the criminal investigation division for the Department of Justice in Philadelphia and who spearheaded the Philadelphia German *Tageblatt* investigation and managed the federal investigators when Grover was captured in the window box of his Wynnefield mansion.

Frank L. Garbarino left his government post around 1925 and organized a private investigator's office in Atlantic City, New Jersey. In April 1933, as president of the World Association of Detectives working with Philadelphia liquor and beer retailers to control racketeering with the repeal of Prohibition, he turned about on the fugitive he captured and said Grover ought to be forgiven.

He said the government should think of aging Emma, spending time and money hoping her favorite son would be able to return home.

"If he comes back," Garbarino declared, "the sentence of five years should be suspended, and he should be placed on parole in the custody of his mother. The war is over. We have forgiven Germany. Why hold prejudice against an individual? We had thousands [of draft dodgers] during the war, and nothing ever happened to them."[4]

Garbarino said Grover was more of a bad boy than a slacker. He said he and his men thought Grover was more courageous than others.

"The government is to blame. It made a bad boy of him when it labeled him a slacker," Garbarino said.

Continuing his comments about Grover at a time when the press reported on leniency for all other war deserters except for Bergdoll, Garbarino lamented, "times were tense then. The notoriety given to his (Grover's) many daring escapades turned public sentiment against him. He would have served in any capacity other than bearing arms against his kinsmen. Bergdoll said, at the time, he saw no reason why he should shoot his cousins."

Garbarino also provided some inside information from his years as a federal detective. Despite Emma's feigned efforts to get Grover back home, Garbarino declared that Grover remained in Germany at Emma's insistence. She was not comforted by any sense of Bergdollism. Emma feared that if her boy returned home, he might get something worse than prison.

Then, smiling toward an assemblage of newspaper reporters, Garbarino finished his statement. "You know Grover was her favorite son," he said.

Grover tried to exploit Bergdollism in Europe and the Roosevelt administration's frustration with the Nazi military buildup in the 1930s. He typed a letter for Emma

---

[4] While people read newspaper articles about forgiving war deserters, there was no general amnesty following the war. However, about 1,500 draft dodgers who had served their prison terms had their civil rights restored with President Roosevelt's Christmas Proclamation of 1933. This included Erwin since he had served his prison term, but not Grover, who had escaped and remained a fugitive. *The Amnesty Issue: A Historical Perspective*, U.S. Army War College, 1974.

to send to Eleanor Roosevelt in January 1933, begging for a pardon. And he laid on the compliments in his prose as only Grover in the family could do.[5]

"Knowing you to be a woman of great intelligence and justice-loving, I am presenting the case to you so you can put it before your husband," he wrote. Grover's letter, for Emma to send to the Roosevelts, blamed England for his refusal to report for military duty. He reminded the Roosevelts that President Grover Cleveland (his namesake) was a "slacker" during the Civil War. He said Europeans had forgiven their draft dodgers from the world war and that Americans should do the same. He included a legal brief prepared by General Ansell, who wrote the wartime draft legislation claiming Grover was improperly tried for desertion. And then Grover's prose, imitating his poor 72-year-old mother who would not have written such words, grabbed at Eleanor Roosevelt's heartstrings.

"I know that only a mother can understand a mother's love, and I hope you will try and help me get my boy back again."

In the letter, signed by Emma and sent to Mrs. Roosevelt, Emma [Grover] said she had just listened to a radio commentary by Lowell Thomas and that the President and First Lady were "standing the strain of your superhuman work, in great shape. You both must be veritable powerhouses of energy and have steel nerves to keep up such a pace!"

This letter was very unusual in that it suggested a pardon for Grover so Emma could repay a $70,000 loan from the Bergdoll Brewery. She wanted the President to authorize the Alien Property Custodian to release Grover's assets so she could borrow money from Grover, repay the loan and restart the brewery (with the repeal of Prohibition), and "put hundreds of men to work."[6]

The letters, purporting to be written by Emma, were pure nonsense. The fact that they were typewritten in elaborate cohesive sentences by an intelligent American-educated person with vast knowledge of the legal events facing Grover indicates that Grover wrote them himself and had Emma sign them. He hid on the third floor of his Wynnefield mansion in early 1933. He occupied his time listening to Lowell Thomas on the radio and dreaming up concepts of freedom by tip-tapping away on his typewriter, praising the only man who could wheel up to his inkwell, sign an order, and set Bergdoll free.

While Emma kept a large framed photograph of President Roosevelt in the drawer of a table in the Wynnefield mansion parlor nearest the front door for when reporters and photographers were present, she did not speak, write, or even think in

---

[5] I found Grover, Emma, and Berta's typed and handwritten letters at the Roosevelt Library at the Roosevelt homestead estate in the Hudson River valley in Hyde Park, New York.

[6] At this same time, Grover was hiding in his Wynnefield mansion where he told his son, Alfred, that he wished to restart the brewery and become a hero by putting Philadelphia men back to work during the Depression. It was all part of a scheme to gain sympathy for a presidential pardon.

the method of prose that Grover put down on paper for her signature.[7] She wanted everyone to believe she corresponded with Roosevelt, but it mainly was Grover's writing. This became even more evident after Grover returned to Germany in May 1933. He wrote again to President Roosevelt; this time, his letter was referred to the Department of Justice. He appealed to Roosevelt's "Christian spirit," saying that despite being deprived of the rights of American citizenship, "I still feel of myself as an American, and could never swear allegiance to any other country. I always preferred being a man without a country rather than become a citizen of a foreign country."

This letter, sent from Weinsberg in March of 1934, displayed the first hint from Grover that he was concerned about his children being raised in Germany.[8] Berta Bergdoll (Grover's German wife) had checked into a hospital in Heilbronn to await the birth of their son, Erwin Richard Bergdoll. Grover and Alfred did not go with her. Instead, they took Grover's new Hudson Essex-Terraplane automobile shipped to him by brother Erwin (who had a matching car in the United States). They drove south to Bodensee (Lake Constance), where by day, they walked the deserted shores and spent nights in a modest hotel where blinking lights through the windows kept Alfred awake. They returned to Weinsberg only after baby Erwin was born on March 27, 1934.

Then, the Nazi Gestapo appeared at Berta's parents' apartment building in Weinsberg, looking for Grover and Berta.

It happened one day in April or May 1934. Alfred briefly described the Gestapo visit in his diary-manuscript from his father's telling of the events. It was soon after little Erwin's birth, and the infant boy still needed constant care and feeding from Berta. The Gestapo officers told Grover and Berta that they had been denounced as Communist agents by the U.S. Consul at Stuttgart, but, fortunately for the Bergdolls, they did not believe it. Alfred said it led to complaints about a consular official being withdrawn. Grover didn't go much deeper into explaining to his son why Gestapo officers came calling on the most notorious American fugitive hiding in Germany. It was unusual that Alfred used only a few lines of his diary to describe it.

From this point onward, however, it appears the Nazis left Bergdoll alone, partly because, at this time, he was not drawing much publicity, and he was often gone from Baden, secretly living instead in Philadelphia. He was also busy with his typewriter. Emma, and Grover's sister, Elizabeth, called Aunt Betty by the kids, often sent Philadelphia and other East Coast newspapers to Grover in Weinsberg so he

---

[7] This conclusion is drawn from reading thousands of pages of testimony by Emma Bergdoll. Emma's signature on this letter is quite similar to Grover's signature. Alfred said the Roosevelt photograph table later disappeared like many other pieces of fine furniture from the Bergdoll mansions.

[8] Also in March 1934, Grover was buoyed by a letter from the Manoa, Pennsylvania American Legion Post Number 667 pleading with all Legion comrades to forgive Grover "who has done no greater wrong than numerous others to who pardon has been granted." The letter said Grover was not a coward but foolish for leaving and not asking for a pardon at an earlier date.

could keep up with the news on the criticism of his actions and the government's failure to capture him.

He felt compelled to answer his critics and supporters. In July 1934, the *Boston Herald Traveler* published an editorial about the government's inaction and suggested Grover had the foresight to stay out of a war many later realized was futile. They also listed his Weinsberg address, opening a small floodgate of letters to the newspaper and Grover from Americans. One man responded to the editorial that perhaps Grover's reasons for not wanting to go to war were justifiable. He declared that Americans, in 1934, were becoming aware that "had the United States adhered to the essence of the Monroe Doctrine, 78 thousand of America's best manhood would still be lending stronger fiber to our great country instead of fertilizing the fields of a foreign land. Bergdoll has suffered plenty."[9]

Grover claimed he received 87 letters in Weinsberg from the Boston area due to the editorial. He replied to a man in Somerville, Massachusetts, claiming that 86 of the letters he received supported a pardon, while one threatened his life if he returned to the United States. It contained the symbol of the Black Hand, the secret Serbian society that planned the assassination of Archduke Franz Ferdinand. The letter recipient, Henry R. Chetham, whose family arrived in Plymouth, Massachusetts, in 1634 and who served in the U.S. Navy during the war, promptly sent Grover's letter to the Boston newspaper, writing, "I am not of German descent, but I feel that after all these years, Bergdoll deserves a pardon."[10]

Grover also found his supporters in Philadelphia and its suburban Main Line. One man, Isaac R. Pennypacker of Ardmore (Grover's old speeding grounds), a noted historian, magazine, and newspaper journalist, and the brother of former Governor of Pennsylvania Samuel W. Pennypacker, wrote to his former newspaper employer, *The Inquirer*, in July 1934 that President Lincoln and his War Secretary Edwin Stanton arranged for Quakers, Mennonites, and Dunkers to avoid the draft in the Civil War by funding nurses in soldiers' hospitals. "Governmental action in the Civil War, when the nation was in real, not a propagandist danger, appears statesmanlike; the attitude towards the Bergdolls petty," Pennypacker charged.

Pennypacker's comments fell on deaf ears, and he died the following year from a fall that broke his hip and led to a heart attack.

Some of the letters sent to Weinsberg supported both Grover and Emma. They agreed with *The Inquirer*'s stance on leniency. Ida Thoene Pfeil of Camden, New Jersey, who, along with her late newspaper editor husband, was of German descent,

---

[9] The Monroe Doctrine said, in part, that the United States would not get involved in wars between European nations. The War Department counted 116,708 American soldiers killed in the World War from all causes, including disease.

[10] Henry R. Chetham served in the war as chief radioman and electrician first class, U.S. Navy, but under a differently spelled name, Henry Ripley Cheetham. When he died in 1938, he was buried with honors at Arlington National Cemetery. He sometimes went by the first name Harry.

said, "I think as you do. Bergdoll has been punished enough, and my heart goes out to that poor old mother of his. For, after all, he was a victim of venom."

Letters of support probably inspired Grover to continue his letter-writing campaign. In a two-page letter sent by Berta to President Roosevelt but typewritten in Grover's unique prose in December 1936, they proposed the President pardon Grover in return for a "fine" of $100,000 and Grover revealing secret information and "four radical innovations" developed by the German war factories. Grover claimed that he learned of these war machine inventions only because of his "knowledge of mathematics and mechanics." He suggested he had known of new artillery designs increasing shell velocity and range, a new anti-tank weapon, a faster warplane, and "a novel offensive weapon (never before used in war)."

And, if that wasn't enough to ask, Berta (in Grover's typewritten letter) suggested Roosevelt arrange for Grover, and Berta and the children to live in Canada where he could divulge his secret information to the Army while awaiting the President's pardon. In essence, the letter offered $100,000 and Grover as a spy in return for a presidential pardon.

Berta's name was typewritten in the valediction with the return address of the Bergdoll mansion at 52nd and Wynnefield in Philadelphia, but there was no longhand signature. A copy of the letter was sent to the secretary of war while Emma was paying a Washington lawyer $15,000 to convince the secretary to re-open the case with a provision that she would pay for the government's cost of capturing and prosecuting Grover.[11]

None of it worked.

With news of the Nazi gathering in Germany growing almost daily, many worried Americans and even highly patriotic Americans may have considered the risk of taking Grover at his word and giving him a pardon. But President Roosevelt didn't budge.

Despite presidential lenience toward many other draft dodgers, there was no sense of Bergdollism in the White House.

---

[11] It's likely that Grover typed and sent this letter too while he was hiding in the Wynnefield mansion in 1936. Identical letters ended up in the Roosevelt Library and the National Archives in St. Louis.

CHAPTER TWENTY

More Gold

Western Maryland, 1923[1]

Four men from the U.S. Department of Justice arrived in Washington County, Maryland, on August 29, 1923, on a wild gold chase. They converged on the Brownsville-Weverton Road near Weverton, Maryland, between Hagerstown and Harpers Ferry, West Virginia.[2] The area was wooded with tall ridges and deep valleys. The federal men were checking into reports that a county road worker and farmer, Robert "Lee" Houser, 38, of Sample's Manor, Maryland, dug up or uncovered a steel can under a large rock. It was reported to have contained $100,000 in gold certificates and $10,000 in gold coins.

Brownsville-Weverton Road wound through a valley that led northward from the Potomac River at the West Virginia state line to Keedysville, Maryland, and the location of Grover and Erwin's tent hideout on Antietam Creek. It was an ideal location where a fugitive could easily slip between four states—Pennsylvania, Maryland, Virginia, and West Virginia—if needed.

Houser was gone when the agents arrived at his ramshackle farmhouse. Rumors abounded that he had taken the gold to Baltimore for deposit in a bank. The local papers quoted Houser saying, "I'll restore it to him [Bergdoll] or anybody else who can identify it."

Even *The New York Times* jumped on the gold story ascribing a local farm boy, Howard Wheeler, 10, as the first to find the steel "biscuit can" when Houser's pickax revealed it. Young Wheeler told *The Times'* reporter that Houser "tore the box from his hands and made off with it."

Initially, Houser claimed only $10,000 in gold coins, leading many to believe it was long-lost Confederate gold from a paymaster. The Bergdoll gold theory flew through newspaper presses when he revealed $100,000 in gold notes.

---

[1] Details in Chapter 20 are derived from newspaper accounts and Department of Justice investigation records, Congressional testimony, first-person accounts by Grover and Erwin Bergdoll, and allegations by prosecutors in court.

[2] Brownsville-Weverton Road is today's State Highway 858 in a steep valley below Weverton Cliffs. The road is bisected by the Appalachian Trail.

An undated press photograph of the federal agents digging for the gold in the western Maryland mountains based on tips received in Washington. (Temple University Urban Archives)

By the time federal agents arrived in the remote rural area of Maryland, Houser had changed his story a few times from finding the can under a rock to digging it up along the road widening project. The four investigators were sent from Washington, D.C., by the chief of the Department of Justice Bureau of Investigation at the request of the Alien Property Custodian, Thomas Miller.[3]

The newspapers found Hotel Vivian owner Owen Sherley from Hagerstown, who told them the Bergdolls (Grover and Erwin) carried five valises "heavy as lead" and guarded them with revolvers, carrying them away at night.

Houser was caught bragging about the gold while being courted and suckled by the reporters. But, when confronted by investigators, he said the gold story was a hoax. The investigators, however, were coaxed on by their superiors in their Washington offices and didn't give up. They believed Houser changed his story to a hoax to protect the gold. They found an empty tin can but no gold.

In Washington, custodian Miller said, "I'm convinced that Bergdoll buried his pot of gold near Hagerstown, and I'm surely convinced that Houser dug it up. The search for the gold will continue."

Houser was forced to hide. With reporters and agents searching for him, he crawled into the attic of his sister's house and tried to sleep. Rumors were rampant. People

---

[3] In 1927, the Bergdoll-era Alien Property Custodian Thomas W. Miller was convicted of fraud and sentenced to prison for selling German patents. He had also taken a $50,000 bribe from a friend of the U.S. Attorney General for helping a German-owned metals company recover $6 million in seized war assets. He served 18 months and was released on parole in 1928.

thought the Bergdolls, abolitionist John Brown, or a rogue Confederate paymaster had buried the gold. No one ever found it, and interest in Houser eventually faded.

The Houser gold hoax was the third location in western Maryland rumored to be the location for the Bergdolls' pot of gold. One place was along Antietam Creek near their tent site in Keedysville. Another theory gained traction through an *American Legion Weekly* magazine article in July 1920. It said Grover buried his gold in the Conococheague Valley, west of Hagerstown. Locals in the valley said they recalled the initials G. B. and an arrow carved in a large sycamore tree, pointing to the gold's burial location. The magazine printed a photograph of the initials and the arrow. It appeared convincing.

Walter Hose, Jr., 12, lived on his family's farm at the end of the Conococheague Valley and claimed the tree was in a sycamore grove beside a creek and lane leading to their farmhouse. He recalled a man camping near the creek and wrote down the license plate of his Pennsylvania car. The camper became spooked, packed his tent, and left the valley.

The rumors in the Maryland hills were probably fueled by an editorial in the *Philadelphia Inquirer* on June 24, 1920. It said the story of $105,000 in Bergdoll gold originated in the Philadelphia sub-Treasury when a clerk named Alexander, working at the Treasury in Washington, refused to exchange gold for federal reserve notes because of a gold ban during the war.[4] Confusion about the ban continued long after the war was over. Then, clerk William Alexander was ordered by the assistant secretary of the Treasury, R. C. Leffingwell, to pay the gold to Bergdoll based on his legal tender demand notes. The *Inquirer* alleged favoritism for Bergdoll at a time when most everyone could not obtain gold coins from the Treasury in Philadelphia or Washington.

Emma testified that Grover made six trips to Washington in his car to get gold coins from the Treasury, exchanging $25,000 in notes for $150,000 in gold. She also stated that she buried gold on the Broomall farm, commanding her chauffeur to walk off and pick apples while she dug a hole in the ground for the gold. She claimed this happened in the spring… long past apple-picking season in September.

Emma testified that she and Judge Romig were the ones who traveled to Washington on two occasions to get gold. Clerk Alexander said Emma carried Treasury notes in her stockings, reaching for them when approaching the counting tables.

"That was the largest fund in gold that anybody ever came here and got, as far as my knowledge goes," said Alexander.

Judge Romig said the gold was so heavy that he hired a "strange man" hanging around the Treasury building to help him carry the heavy sacks "for a dollar or two."

---

[4] William L. Alexander was a clerk–teller at the Treasury in Washington. He testified that Emma and Judge Romig entered the Treasury cash room in October and November 1919 and exchanged $105,000 in currency, for gold.

Alfred Bergdoll suggested the strange man may have been Grover, along to assure he got his hands on the gold too.

During her testimony, Emma was asked, "Who guarded the gold on the motor trips back to Philadelphia?"

Emma: "I did. I had a pistol in the automobile pocket."

Question: "You were your own guard?"

Emma: "Sure. I was always able to take care of myself."

On their final Washington gold-grabbing trip, Emma and Romig returned to the Wynnefield mansion so late that they left the sacks of gold on the kitchen floor beneath the great table for the night. It was still there in the morning when they got up for breakfast.

Emma also claimed that Grover never got any of the gold she and Judge Romig got from the Treasury.

"It was mine to do with as I pleased," she sniffed "Nobody can find it, and Grover didn't get any of it—not a nickel." When asked where she put her gold, Emma replied, "It's in my possession and buried in the same place I first put it." Emma said the gold was not near Hagerstown, Maryland, as she had never been there.

Because the gold story was so convincing, federal agents were sent to a remote location in West Nottingham Township, Chester County, Pennsylvania, along the Mason-Dixon Line to search for buried Bergdoll gold based on a tip.

All they found was a whisky still.

Additionally, the gold story seemed to be embellished by everyone connected with the Bergdolls.

General Ansell, Grover's paid advisor, said in his letter to General Harris of Governors Island, "He [Grover] now declares that he also hid a second large sum, the remainder of his fortune ($150,000), in a lonely spot on a mountain-side, distance about a day's journey from this city [Washington]; that he placed the gold coin in a metallic container… and hid it in a spot which he alone can identify. Circumstances indicate the truth of his statement."

The Congressional committee investigating the Bergdoll caper didn't believe it. It said, "Somebody conceived the idea of concentrating Gibboney's cunning and energy, Wescott's influence with the administration, and Ansell's standing with the Army officials into one general scheme of defense or escape." It also said:

> It was known to General Ansell that Judge Westcott had put Woodrow Wilson in nomination for the Presidency of the United States, both at Baltimore and four years later at St. Louis, and that Westcott was a personal friend of both the President and the Secretary of War. Knowing that he took particular pains to inject Westcott's name into the letter which he wrote General Harris, then, in his presence, had Westcott write a letter to the Secretary of War on Bergdoll's behalf, based upon Westcott's alleged "enormous interest in the case."

No one knew then how much anyone was being paid for their influence, but it was significant. The lawyers imagined the Bergdoll gold would be their fee. The committee also realized that the amount of gold Emma withdrew was the amount that Grover claimed to have buried in the Maryland mountains, $105,000.

The Congressional committee summed up its conclusions:

> The pot of gold story, which probably started in the imagination of either Bergdoll or Gibboney, acquired momentum when it reached General Harris with the weight of former Brigadier General Ansell, recently from the office of Judge Advocate General, Judge John W. Wescott, one of the most prominent lawyers of the east, who had nominated Mr. Wilson twice for the presidency, and D. Clarence Gibboney, who presented himself a man of high repute in Philadelphia, so impressed General Harris that he asked for it to be put in writing.

In Grover's 1924 Leighton Blood interview in *Hearst's International*, he said, "That pot of gold yarn I told was all the bunk. Everyone seemed to think that because I had money, I was without brains. Because they took me to be foolish, I played the game as they thought I would."

Even Stecher testified at his 1925 trial and again during Grover's 1939 trial that they never traveled to Washington together to get a milk can full of gold. He was guided by a clever attorney, Thomas L. Lynch, who got him off, charging that Emma orchestrated Grover's escape. Stecher said that when they drove away from the Wynnefield mansion in 1920, they went to Bel Air, Maryland, then westward to Pittsburgh, Ohio, Indiana, Illinois, Wisconsin, and then Minnesota, where they crossed into Canada.

They did not go to Washington to fill a milk can with gold.

CHAPTER TWENTY-ONE

Friedel Schmidt

Heidelberg and Eberbach, Germany 1922–1927

Grover first saw 13-year-old Friedel Lucia Elise Schmidt in August 1922 from his car while she was walking along a street in Heidelberg. Using his resources to obtain her address, Grover wrote to her parents, Georg, and Katharina Schmidt, to ask permission to date Friedel, but the mother replied that her daughter "was not yet 14." Infatuated with Friedel, Grover would write home to Emma that they were engaged to be married.

Grover was persistent, however, turning to his portable typewriter to send a two-page letter to Friedel's father.[1] He said he had searched since turning 18 for "a perfect girl, one with a faultless head from a phrenological point of view. To possess Friedl and have her as my best and nearest chum and friend is the bright of my ambition."

The Schmidts insisted that Grover wait five years for their daughter to mature. Grover tried to dissuade them: "Now, after I have found the girl I have sought so long in vain, she seems to be just as far beyond my reach as ever! I do not love Friedl in the way the average man would. I am not a sensual man. If I were, I would have been married long ago... that seems like eternity! It would mean five years of anxious waiting, suffering, and torment, five years of hell to me! I could never endure it; I doubt whether I could hold out a year... my Goddess Friedl."

Grover said in his letter that he would have left Germany in September 1922 if he had not met Friedel in August. "I am not tied to any place in Europe, my relatives here are not real friends of mine, so I can go wherever I wish and when I wish. I have only two real friends in the world, and that is my mother and one of my brothers (Erwin)."

He did not mention Stecher, his loyal friend and bodyguard who left his wife alone in the United States and fled with Grover to Germany. He did not mention his legal difficulties with the U.S. Army either. Grover's following line should have alarmed the Schmidts with its boldness. "If Friedl likes me and you and her mother

---

[1] In Grover's November 17, 1922 letter to Mr. Schmidt, he wrote in English, spelling Friedel's name as Friedl: "I can better express my meanings than if I wrote in German." Letter on file at the German Society of Pennsylvania.

permit me to marry her, I can give you my word of honor that I will not use my right as a husband until she is 17 years of age. What I wish is that she becomes tied and bound to me so as that I can keep her pure and virtuous and watch over her."

Then, Grover suggested that Friedel would become "spoiled hopelessly" while in contact with German boys and girls at her school. He offered to hire private school teachers for her after they were married. Then, he lied, telling the Schmidts he was a graduate of the University of Pennsylvania, a mechanical engineer, and could teach Friedel anything except foreign languages. He further suggested that he and Mr. Schmidt could "be of great usefulness to each other if Friedl wishes it."

In closing his brazen missive, Grover commanded the Schmidts, "Do not force Friedl; Leave her to have her way! I love and worship Friedl's nature and her soul, not her body, although she is very beautiful. It may seem very strange to you, but I assure you, it is the only honest and honorable way!" He signed off, Grover Bergdoll, Hotel Krone-Post, Eberbach/Baden.

Grover's persistence was rewarded, and the parents soon relented. Grover and Friedel became engaged on Christmas Day 1922, with press reports in the United States citing a "letter" from Grover in St. Gall, Switzerland, to an Eberbach relative claiming that the couple was married on January 4, 1923. In it, Grover also claimed that he wished to become a Swiss resident and wait there for amnesty for "political and military offenses" committed in the United States.

The letter from Switzerland and the declaration were found to be false, however. Grover sent a message saying they were only engaged, not married.[2] It undermined Emma's misinformation, too, when she answered the telephone at the Wynnefield mansion in January 1923 and replied to a reporter from the Wilmington, Delaware, *Evening Journal* that Grover "was married in Switzerland to Friedel Schmidt. Good-bye." Emma then hung up the telephone receiver on the reporter.

The relationship between Grover and Friedel Schmidt, born on January 10, 1910, in Alexandria, Egypt, to German parents and raised in Budapest before moving to Heidelberg in 1922, continued with the parents' approval. Court testimony recited almost verbatim in a German newspaper indicated that Grover and Friedel traveled in his Benz automobile through the Black Forest of Baden and into Switzerland for eight days when she was on Easter holiday from school in 1923.[3]

Grover had read about the American novelist Mark Twain and his travels through the Schwarzwald in July 1878 and made several trips into southern Germany. While driving his Benz through the more profound and taller western mountains of the

[2] The contents of the Switzerland "letter" may have been invented by the press to replicate a letter that Grover sent to Emma in Philadelphia informing her that he was engaged to be married.
[3] The alleged victim of Grover's seduction was interchangeably identified by different news services as Liesel Schmidt and Friedel Schmidt. One of Friedel's middle names was Elise, a variant of Liesel. It appears that Friedel Schmidt and her mother were convinced by others to go public with moral allegations against Grover.

former Grand Duchy of Baden, few other vehicles were on the roads, no one knew Grover and Friedel, and they could pass for a married couple on holiday. They collected rocks and frolicked around mineral springs. They gazed at the stars through Grover's telescope at night. The young lovers (ages 14 and 29) stayed in romantic inns around the Titisee for several nights, dining in restaurants and picnicking in the woods along cool water streams teeming with trout.[4]

On this Easter 1923 road trip and other times, Grover is accused of seducing the young girl. He denied it. Later that summer, the difference in age between Grover and Friedel may have taken its toll. Grover cast her aside when he discovered she was also interested in a German boy from her school. He broke off the engagement in August 1923, citing Friedel's "flirtations with a male student at Heidelberg." Documents from court testimony indicate that Friedel and her mother tried convincing Grover to reconsider, but he refused.

Grover later testified that he heard of a Fräulein Schmidt's death in 1925, and, thinking it was Friedel, he went to Heidelberg to pay his respects by visiting her grave. There he discovered the death on March 15, 1925, was that of Friedel's sister, Else.[5] Friedel was still alive and susceptible to the influence of American bounty hunters who were still trying to get Grover, despite two failed kidnappings.

While in Heidelberg, Grover tried to rekindle the relationship with Friedel but was rejected. From that point onward, he tried to put the Schmidts out of his mind.[6]

***

The seduction and morality case against Grover would never have risen to court had it not been for the investigative efforts of a highly nationalistic and wealthy German-American, Robert Paul Sachs, born in Frankfurt, Hesse, who became a naturalized American citizen and considered Philadelphia his home.

Arriving in the United States at 11 with his mother, Elise, and seven siblings from three to 16, Sachs quickly adopted American culture but remained German. He later lived in Oakland, and Fair Oaks, California. As an adult, Sachs made enough money as an advertising salesman and public relations artist for Coast Tire and Rubber Company of Oakland to retire at a young age.[7]

Sachs was an amateur aviator and highly nationalistic for American politics and patriotism. He used his wealth to travel to Europe and pursue Bergdoll.

---

[4] Although viewed as deplorable today, it was not unusual in 1923 for parents of a young teen girl to approve marriage to a much older man.
[5] Else Schmidt died in Heidelberg at age 17 on March 15, 1925.
[6] Court records and research through German ancestry on Ancestry.com and MyHeritage.com revealed the identification of Friedel and Else Schmidt. Details were confirmed by the Robert Paul Sachs investigation documents.
[7] Robert Paul Sachs' life journey was relatively easy to follow. He had one of the most unusual signatures ever portrayed on state and federal documents.

After the war and his lucrative advertising campaigns, such as signing the African-American celebrity pilot, Bessie Coleman, to fly promotional events for Coast Tire, Sachs set his sights on returning Grover to the United States to face trial. Sachs' passport applications indicate he first traveled to Europe in 1920 to explore business opportunities for the William A. Sachs electrical and automobile parts supply company in the Germantown community of Philadelphia, from where he would have been well versed on the Bergdoll legal and family drama.

Then, Sachs made another trip to Europe in 1923 to investigate Grover's secret life in Germany. Sachs presented himself in Europe as a detective with the Alameda County, California sheriff's department, chairman of the League of Friends of Peace in New York and Chicago, and secretary of the American Society for Truth in New York and California.[8] He gathered enough information on Grover and the teenage Friedel Schmidt to convince a prosecutor in Baden to file charges against Grover in February 1926.[9] However, even then, the prosecutor warned the public that he would "proceed cautiously" because the charges were brought by people trying to deport Grover to a country that would extradite him to the United States for trial on the draft-dodging charges.[10]

Grover was arrested at a hotel room in Huffenhardt, Emma's childhood hometown, and formally charged with seduction, corrupting the morals of a child, and passport forgery, and sent to the district jail in Mosbach.[11] But, the description of the multiple allegations by Sachs was much more salacious than the formal charges that were filed. As a committee of the Bar Association of the State of Baden later described it, Grover feared his "economic and moral ruin, deportation to another country, and extradition to America, and possible conviction for desertion, and confiscation of his property." But first, he faced up to 10 years in prison in Germany.

With his mother and other family fixers out of reach, Grover retained his Eberbach lawyer, Karl Zeiss, and a second lawyer from Karlsruhe, Dr. Ludwig Marum, a notable Jewish member of the Reichstag and the liberal Social Democratic Party of Germany. Grover boldly promised to pay them a lot to save his hide.[12] They agreed. It was a wise choice for Grover but a mistake for the attorneys.

The trial was held in a Mosbach courtroom which Grover found very familiar because he'd been involved in two prior trials for his attempted kidnappings. Frau Katharina Schmidt convinced the presiding judge to close the gallery to spectators

---

[8] Neither of these truth and peace organizations are found in historical records.

[9] Sachs told *The New York Times* he posed as a chemistry research student at the University of Heidelberg where Friedel Schmidt studied chemistry.

[10] German extradition policies were long tangled in the lopsided orders of the Treaty of Versailles. Plus, Grover lived in Germany without proper identification and on a fake passport.

[11] Even in custody, German laws protected Grover from extradition and deportation. The local townspeople and police continued protecting him from bounty hunters and the press.

[12] It was later determined that Grover promised a fee of 5,000 reichsmarks for each attorney and a special bonus of $10,000 cash for each.

because of the sensitive sexual details concerning Grover and her young daughter. Still, it was covered extensively by the European and American press. Many witnesses and spectators traveled from Heidelberg and Eberbach to Mosbach by train through the lush farmland of the Neckar River valley.

In the old Mosbach district courthouse surrounded by towering linden trees, Grover's adversary, Sachs, did not attend because he was already back in the United States telling any reporter who would listen that he sent the infamous draft-dodging Bergdoll to trial for molesting a young German girl.

Sachs also claimed that he met with Grover in the Mosbach jail and that Grover told him his hidden loot was the "size of ten cases containing more than $250,000 in gold." Sachs boasted that Grover showed him a chart of the location of the gold, hidden so well that it could only be found using the chart. Sachs also claimed that Grover told him he was a Bolshevist and interested in their movement in Russia, which had peaked with the Russian Revolution in 1922–1923, at the same time when Grover was alleged to have committed his immoral acts on Friedel Schmidt.

"When I saw Bergdoll, he seemed depressed," Sachs told a reporter. "But he maintained his brazen attitude. He's hired famous lawyers to defend him." Sachs said the trial would be heard by the same judge who tried Sperber, Griffis, Nelson, and Prince Gagarin for attempting to kidnap Grover in 1923, hinting that a fix was in. Sachs complained that Grover had comfortable quarters at the Mosbach jail, where the growth of a mustache changed his appearance, and he could roam about the garden with food from a local restaurant. But, he was sure Grover would get six to eight years in prison and then be deported from Germany after serving his sentence. Once deported, Sachs speculated, Grover could be tried for escape and war desertion in the United States.

Sachs could not have been more wrong about Bergdoll's fate.

Grover was indignant when he led the testimony on the witness stand. As reported by the *Associated Press*, Grover was "nervous, and with perspiration streaming down his forehead, [and] bitterly attacked the private detective, Sachs, who had preferred the charges, but who was not present in court." Grover had several relatives and friends testify to his good moral behavior. The prosecutors, however, promised that the court would hear "sensational disclosures by girls ranging in age from 15 to 18 years." It was implied that Grover had been molesting several German girls. However, the teen girl witnesses never appeared.

Grover's defense attorneys spent considerable money on private investigators who claimed that Sachs became friendly with the Schmidt family and convinced them to file the charges, in part because Grover rebuffed Sachs' demands that he return with him to the United States where Sachs would be the hero detective who captured Bergdoll.[13]

---

[13] Sachs claimed he was working on behalf of Emma Bergdoll to get Grover back to the United States.

One issue was the timeline of the alleged seduction of Schmidt. Was the alleged violation before or after the engagement? A psychiatric expert, Professor Hans Gruhle from the University of Heidelberg, testified that Friedel Schmidt was "subnormal mentally and untrustworthy." Friedel, described as "16¼ years old" at the trial, testified with her mother, Katharina. Friedel testified that she was sexually violated in an Eberbach hotel room before the couple's approved engagement. Katharina Schmidt appeared confused and testified that the violation occurred after the couple's engagement.[14]

Grover later told his son Alfred that Friedel sat quietly during the trial and "wagged her bob" while Frau Schmidt sobbed, trying to gain sympathy. However, their story was poorly presented in court. Appearing last on the witness stand, Friedel's testimony was hopeless when she contradicted her mother's story.

Although the trial took eight hours, including a lunch break, Grover was acquitted after the judge and two associates deliberated for 10 minutes. The Baden bar association assessment of the prosecution said Grover "owes a great deal of gratitude for his acquittal to the energetic, aim-conscious and untiring activity" of his attorneys.

Grover told an *Associated Press* reporter in Mosbach, "I'm through with Americans. I have lost all respect for Americans because they have hounded me and, by underhand methods, such as the employment of Sachs, have tried to throw me in jail."

Grover bought beer and wine for the many German trial spectators, police, and court officials at a Mosbach saloon. While celebrating with a glass of Pinot Gris in one hand and Pils in the other, Grover bragged that he would sue Sachs, but he never followed through on the threat, perhaps because his lawyers wouldn't do it. He failed to pay them the promised bonus fees of $10,000 each.[15]

Several years later, the attorneys sued Grover, trying to collect their fees. Their court filings revealed they were as determined as bounty hunters to find him in Germany. At the same time, Grover followed his tried-and-true evasion methods, disappearing in his luxury automobile and living lavishly off his steady stream of cash from the United States, courtesy of Emma.

In his 1926 morality trial court filings, Grover claimed that his American assets were worth $1.4 million and that he was due to receive more money from his father's estate and his mother. His German attorneys took notice. They agreed that if their defense cleared Grover of all charges, including legal work for his effort to become a German citizen and legal issues over his use and possession of a *Stendawerke* pocket

---

[14] Several American news organizations continued to identify Friedel Schmidt as Liesel or Leisel Schmidt mistakenly.

[15] Court records show that Grover stiffed his attorneys for $11,000, including interest. They and their heirs later sued Grover in Germany and New York for the fees on two occasions, 1940–1941 and again in 1955, finally winning a settlement of about $5,000 paid by Grover. Robert Paul Sachs, who never achieved his goal of nailing Grover, ended up as an inmate in the infamous Mendocino State Mental Hospital in California, where he filed for habeas corpus in the courts. He died there in 1964 at the age of 81.

pistol, he would pay them extra. Despite the celebration over winning the morality case, Grover's relationship with the attorneys quickly soured.[16]

While Zeiss was Grover's primary and long-time German attorney, Dr. Marum was also a key figure in Grover's winning defense in the Schmidt criminal charges. Marum was one of the few Jews in the German parliament and an extremely liberal socialist. In 1926, the newly labeled Third Reich was taking notice of the publicity surrounding the controversial German-American draft dodger, Bergdoll, hiding among them and drawing unwanted international attention to what many in Germany (at the time) considered a pending revolution. Grover, who told friends that he liked and respected the German Nazi party, told others that he hated the Nazi totalitarian racism movement but that they represented a path away from the imposed financial restraints of France, Belgium, and England from the European war. It was a classic Grover Cleveland Bergdoll trait.

When the morality acquittal celebration in Mosbach ended, and it ended when Grover stopped paying the saloon tab, attorneys Zeiss and Marum (with Marum's law partner Albert Nachmann) mailed invoices to Grover to collect their fees. However, the invoices were returned from Huffenhardt and Weinsberg with notations that Grover no longer lived at those addresses. Grover was traveling again, and, despite letters and postcards from various locations in Germany, Switzerland, and the Netherlands to Zeiss promising payment of the remaining legal fees plus interest, the attorneys received nothing more in compensation. In Marum's law firm cash book, a clerk recorded that Grover owed Marum about $5,000 and Zeiss about $6,000, with interest compounding.

Collecting their outstanding legal fees proved impossible for Zeiss and Marum as it was for anyone chasing down Grover. With a stack of unpaid invoices, Marum even drove his car to Eberbach, Mosbach, and Obrighaem in the warm summer of 1927 after hearing that Bergdoll might be hiding there. He didn't find him. With tips that Grover drove a black Maybach sedan with the license plate *III D 1218* registered in Berta's father's name, Herr Franck, Nachmann and Zeiss spent two days in September 1927 traveling by car to the villages around Mosbach but did not find Grover either.[17] They sent invoice letters to Herr Franck and Berta Bergdoll in Weinsberg and Emma in Philadelphia but received only a brief correspondence from Herr Franck that Grover "was traveling." They continued their collection efforts, including demands through the German courts. Dr. Marum

---

[16] The case of Grover's German lawyers illustrates Grover's lifelong proclivity to renege on promised legal fees. Legal documents confirming this scenario had been left in the Bergdolls' garage when they fled from Chester County, Pennsylvania, and were saved by the Bergdoll children's former playmate, Roger Grigson.

[17] A photograph of young Berta Bergdoll in a bright sleeveless summer dress posing in front of a shiny black sedan was rescued from Berta's abandoned Chester County, Pennsylvania farmhouse in the 1940s by a neighbor, Roger Grigson. The license plate on the car displays *III D 1218*.

was especially vigilant, sending Grover a personal letter offering a settlement of the fees. "How this is to be done and in what amount—this I would prefer to discuss with you personally," he wrote. "Call me here at Karlsruhe, or we meet at some other place agreeable." Marum never got the call or a meeting with Grover. And he never got the chance to pursue collecting his fees. Finally, in 1932, the lawyers who so expertly extricated Grover from a dire legal situation submitted to a German court to withdraw their active debt collection efforts but, wisely, kept the case open because of an eight percent interest agreement signed by Grover.

It's a good thing they kept their legal options. Much later, in 1940 and 1941, after Grover returned to the United States, he was convicted again of desertion and sentenced to prison. With new collection efforts filed with the Supreme Court of the State of New York, the real reason for the attorneys' debt collection abandonment in 1932 was revealed. They realized what was happening in Germany, and Marum was on the front line of challenging the growing strength of the National Socialist German Workers' Party, the Nazis. The Marum lawyer partners always kept a Bergdoll file in their Karlsruhe office, not because the long-past criminal case was still pending but because the tab had not been fully paid. A similar, nearly duplicate Bergdoll file for attorney Zeiss was kept in his office in Eberbach. They weren't about to let Grover escape without paying his tab.

CHAPTER TWENTY-TWO

Explosive Allegations

Philadelphia, Pennsylvania, 1926

Robert Paul Sachs was mad as a poked hornet when he dictated a 3,500-word letter to the German Society of Pennsylvania president in the summer of 1926.[1]

"I was indeed sorry to learn that your organization has seen fit to expel me as a member just because they do not approve my actions in bringing about the arrest of *Grover Cleveland Bergdoll* in Mosbach, Germany, and I am surprised at the manner in which I was expelled," he wrote. He then had the letter professionally printed for members of the Society to read.

Not long after returning from Germany to Philadelphia, where the newspapers were running sensational stories about Sachs having Grover arrested on morals charges in Mosbach, he was called into the Society's office and told he was expelled from the oldest German-American social organization. Founded in Philadelphia in 1764, the Society was organized to provide German immigrants with legal and financial aid and English language instruction. As a German-American, Sachs said he had been a proud member of the Society, as had his father and brother before him. Sachs' expulsion was the action of a committee, and with his pointed letter, he returned his membership card for cancellation.

"If this had been the action of a society in Eberbach, Germany [where Grover was hiding], I could understand the attitude displayed, but I certainly did not expect it from an organization in my hometown, Philadelphia."

Then Sachs ripped into a long tirade about how he believed his dismissal from the German society had been inspired by the Bergdolls, partly because of their money and influence and because Louis Bergdoll, the elder and younger, had been members and contributors to the prestigious organization of German-Americans. He claimed

---

[1] The Robert Paul Sachs investigation and wild allegations could make a separate dramatic story. Why he used his money to pursue Grover in Europe remains a mystery, unless he was using Emma's money. He was highly nationalistic, spent many years in Philadelphia, and knew how to promote himself and others. His scolding letter to the German Society of Pennsylvania is theatrical but contains many inaccurate statements about Grover's activities in Germany.

that Grover Bergdoll's "henchmen" wrote to the German police denouncing him as a French-American spy "in Germany conspiring against the interests of Germany."

He struggled to understand, he suggested, how the society could side with Bergdoll over him, an upstanding German-American whose father and brother were also members of the Society. Sachs charged that Grover had spent "the last six years as a derelict, a degenerate love pirate, a moral leper, an idle rich parasite, and as aimless human driftwood preyed upon the helpless poor and innocent young [German] girls and school children of both sexes."

Nothing was barred. Sachs told the Society precisely what he learned and believed about Grover's behavior in Germany. Still, neither the Society nor investigators in the United States or Germany could do anything about it. Grover had already been tried and found not guilty of corrupting the morals of a teenage girl.

In his letter, which has been filed away in the Society records since 1926, is the startling revelation that Robert Paul Sachs began his investigation into Grover at the request of Emma. And it's possible that Grover never knew that his mother instigated and possibly paid the amateur pilot, public relations man, and honorary Alameda County, California sheriff's deputy to travel to Europe and find a way for Grover to return home safely to as little legal jeopardy as possible.[2]

Sachs began his Bergdoll investigation before May 1924 when he traveled to Washington to lobby the Department of Justice on behalf of Grover (for Emma). He was there to advocate for the surrender proposal letter sent by Grover to Consul General Dumont in Frankfurt in April 1924. The letter said that Grover would surrender to federal authorities if he were assured a non-military trial without publicity and given protection from newspaper reporters and photographers. The attorney general, Harlan Stone, heard Sachs' appeal, but the proposal went nowhere.

Sachs, who was already nationally renowned for his financially successful public relations campaigns for Coast Tire, said he spent months working for Emma, pleading her case "before the White House, the State Department, the War Department, the American Legion, and the Alien Property Custodian in Washington." Sachs said he arranged a meeting between Emma and the Senate Foreign Relations Committee chairman, Senator William Borah of Idaho. He also claimed to have lobbied many other politicians, lawyers, and other notable influencers to help Emma find a way to get Grover back home with the most negligible legal repercussions possible.

Sachs wrote, "I felt sorry for her as a mother, and because she appealed to me for help because, as she said at the time, she was a poor, sick, persecuted, and a helpless

---

[2] Sachs portrayed himself to the press as a detective and deputy sheriff. In his German Society letter is his lone admission that he was only an "honorary" sheriff's deputy, without the legal authorities of a sworn officer of the law. His detective moniker may have originated when he began investigating and lobbying on behalf of Emma.

widow and could not get a lawyer to help her, since the government sequestered all her money."[3]

Sachs also claimed that while in Europe, he flew from Plymouth, England, to Berlin, Germany, for a meeting with government officials on Emma's behalf that cost him $825. But his efforts failed. He said he did all this without receiving any payment from the Bergdolls.

Then, Sachs revealed that he tried to help Grover personally and became intimately acquainted with the American fugitive living in Germany midway through 1925. Sachs suggested that what he discovered about Grover's behavior in Germany shocked him into having Grover arrested. "I found him a vulgar, unclean political bankrupt and vastly different from the way his mother described him to me, and not worthy of any decent man's or woman's help—or sympathy."

Then, in the letter, Sachs ripped into a litany of immoral and criminal allegations against Grover in Eberbach. He claimed that Grover's aunt kicked him out of her home for allegedly making evil advances toward her teenage daughter.[4] He claimed to have discovered newspaper clippings indicating Grover had been arrested in Friedrichshafen, Germany, using the fake name Freudenberger while entertaining underage girls in his luxury car and restaurants. Sachs claimed that Grover paid midwives for "illegal operations" on teenage girls, thereby causing their deaths from peritonitis. He also made the startling and unsubstantiated allegation that Grover seduced a young girl in grandfather Bergdoll's hometown, Sinsheim, promising to marry her and live together in a Stuttgart castle. Again, without attribution or evidence or names, Sachs claimed that Grover "ruthlessly threw the girl aside after using her—the girl died, and it is common gossip in Sinsheim that she died as the result of an abortion he had some midwife perform on her."

Sachs provided no evidence for his salacious written allegations, and Grover was never charged with anything other than the case involving Friedel Schmidt. Grover claimed that Sachs was working as an agent of other men trying to "get me." Grover heavily criticized Sachs, apparently not realizing that his mother, Emma, had initially engaged the antagonist.

Sachs then claimed he discovered the moral incident involving Friedel Schmidt. He befriended the family and convinced the Schmidts to support his morality charges against Grover. He mistakenly said Friedel was 12 and that Grover's uncle

---

[3] Sachs claims a Bergdoll relative traveled from Eberbach, Germany, to Philadelphia to fetch $6,000 from Emma and return to Germany, delivering the cash to Grover. There are no travel records or family history to support this allegation.

[4] It's likely that Sachs mistook Grover's cousin, Johanna Heuss Bohrmann, for Grover's aunt. Johanna Bohrman was in her 40s in the early 1920s but had a young teenage daughter, Marie, Grover's first cousin, once removed. Grover's aunt Pauline Barth Heuss had been dead since 1900.

informed him of Grover's seduction of the girl.[5] Sachs claimed to have a copy of an engagement announcement to Friedel that Grover paid to insert into an Eberbach newspaper, but he didn't produce it. However, he did produce the letter from Grover to Friedel's father, which won Grover the approval to take Friedel on their Easter holiday trip to the Black Forest. Sachs claimed the only reason Grover was found not guilty of violating Friedel was that Grover paid for the renowned Heidelberg University psychology professor Hans Gruhle to swear that Friedel's testimony was unreliable. Sachs also contended that Grover's attorneys expertly portrayed Grover as a savior for many Germans, claiming he was planning to build a Henry Ford-like automobile manufacturing plant in Baden and put thousands of Germans to work producing affordable cars.[6] It was all a lie. The attorneys, Sachs claimed, suggested Sachs was working for Ford because the American car pioneer feared German automobile competition. However, Sachs failed to mention that the acquittal may have been more influenced by his failure to remain in Germany for Grover's trial. He sailed for New York on March 24, 1926, arriving on April 2. Legally, it's never a good idea for the person filing charges to miss the trial.

Sachs also boldly claimed that he had a letter "not fit for publication," indicating that Grover also wrote to Friedel "in which he confesses his guilt and asks to be forgiven." He did not include it in his submission to the Society, but he said members could see it if interested.

Other allegations made by Sachs against Grover, but that did not rise to a criminal offense, were his habits of entertaining young boys and girls from the Eberbach schools and getting them drunk and his failure to make financial donations to local charities. He claimed that as Coblenz Army of Occupation General Allen collected money from Americans to support destitute German children, Grover "was preying on the very children and women these good-hearted Americans tried to protect." Sachs wrote, "my action in arresting him was only prompted by a high sense of duty as an American citizen."

Sachs said he admired "real, honest, and sincere conscientious objectors" but that Grover was not one of them. As for himself, Sachs missed the war, probably because of his age. He was 36 when it came time to register for the draft in 1917. While he suggested in his letter to the German Society that he served, he didn't. He claimed that he informed his Sacramento County, California draft registration board that he waived "all legal and moral claims for an exemption or deferred classification, putting my services at the disposal of my government in whatever way my government sees fit." He said that after the war, he "devoted most of his

---

[5] There were no Bergdoll uncles in or around Eberbach, only Grover's cousin's husband, Krone-Post hotelier Carl Bohrmann, whom several newspapers also mistakenly identified as Grover's uncle.

[6] The promise of building a car factory in Germany in return for immunity likely came from Grover. He tried the ruse once before, in July 1918, when he said he would build an airplane factory in the United States in return for immunity from desertion. Needless to say, the ploys were not accepted.

time to the interests of German women and children." He described himself as "an aviator and trusting in God." He said that while in Europe (chasing Grover), he was "working to eliminate war psychology among the warring people of the world, and have tried to bring about better relations and understanding."

Grover insisted Sachs was just another quack trying to make himself more famous as the man who brought Bergdoll home to go to prison.[7]

---

[7] Robert Paul Sachs' many serious allegations were discounted with Grover's acquittal. Only later are we able to determine that Sachs misapplied titles to Grover's relatives in Germany, got Friedel Schmidt's age wrong, and offered no evidence for allegations of paid abortions and deaths among teenage girls in Germany attributed to Grover and being arrested for using fake identification. Sachs was later admitted to a psychiatric hospital in California and died while filing legal challenges to get out.

CHAPTER TWENTY-THREE

Berta Bergdoll

1907–1929

In 1926, most Europeans still referred to the second-largest city in Russia as Saint Petersburg, despite its name being changed twice during the Russian Revolution to Petrograd and then Leningrad. It was there on May 13 that Grover arrived with his teenage German fiancée and married her, expanding her long name even further: Bertha Emilie Lydia Helene Franck Bergdoll. It consumed an entire line on the multiple travel documents she displayed many times for travel between Germany and the United States.[1] Aside from Emma, Berta Lydia Bergdoll (as she became known and later spelled her name) would become the most influential woman in Grover's tumultuous life.

Bertha Franck (Berta) may have been an unplanned child. She arrived 18 years after the marriage of her parents, Emanuel Wilhelm Franck, and Katharine Wilhelmine Wellinger Franck, on March 31, 1907, in Weinsberg. Her much older sister Helene became a postal clerk and would later join Berta in Philadelphia. Their brother, Richard, worked as a trainee at Deutsche Bank in Rome before returning home to join the German Army in 1914. Because Berta's siblings were so much older, she lived with her parents as an only child until Grover came along.

Emanuel and Wilhelmine Franck were married in Zwiefalten (50 miles south of Stuttgart), where Richard and Helene were born. Then the family moved to Weinsberg (32 miles north of Stuttgart) sometime around 1903, on the opening of a large psychiatric hospital on the grounds of an old estate property, Manor Weissenhof, in a broad valley of farmland about two miles from the Weinsberg train station.[2]

Emanuel Franck took a job as a resident gardener at the Weinsberg Sanatorium, a sprawling psychiatric hospital community surrounded by a tall stone fence. It utilized horticulture as a calming and soothing therapy for mental illness. Photographs from negative glass plates collected by the sanatorium's first medical director,

---

[1] Marriage and travel records support the travels of Grover and Berta Franck Bergdoll when they lived in Europe, mainly in Germany, with Berta's parents.

[2] Details for Berta's background are in family church records. Vintage photographs of the Weissenhof and its patients show what it looked like when the Francks lived on the grounds.

Dr. Paul Kemmler, show two large, nearly matching four-story classic Bavarian Tudor mansions, Manor Weissenhof, with their steep hip roof dormers peering out to offer "magnificent views of the woody landscape to the southwest, with the romantic Burgruine Weibertreu castle ruins on the hill."[3] They are surrounded by large barn-like structures and equally large stone and brick mansions, all with classic German bright orange tile roofing. The clinic property was circled by a 10-foot-tall stone wall with decorative wooden gates hinged to even taller gate posts with large oil lanterns on top. The glass negatives indicate there may have been guards at the gates with rifles. However, Dr. Kemmler's extensive photograph collection was made from 1908–1915, leading to the Great War. Men in uniforms with weapons may have been part of the wartime security procedures. Less offensive security was provided by "keepers," orderlies in simple uniforms and BDU caps who kept tabs on the inmates and patients throughout the day. Staff members, such as Herr Franck, who worked his way up to head gardener, could come and go as they pleased.

Inside the wall, where inmates and patients were separated by gender, elaborate horticultural gardens crisscrossed by gravel pathways were managed by Herr Franck and tended by a crew of inmates for their curative benefit. Colorful lilies, roses, carnations, German ivy, chamomile, and Baby's Breath choked the formal gardens' pathways, arbors, gazebos, and sitting benches. Long rows of vegetables with thick vines of tomatoes, cucumbers, red onions, beans, squash, German cabbage, sweet corn, and hundreds of hills of potatoes were located just outside the gates with a panoramic view into the valley and Weinsberg below. Along with the sanatorium's lead herdsman of cattle, pigs, sheep, and goats, head gardener Franck provided most of the food for the 550 inhabitants. It was essentially a self-sufficient community.

Dr. Kemmler's photographs show dozens of inmates, patients, and staff, many with listings of their home towns, in various poses, even in bed and bathtubs. Grotesquely, some photographs portray the perfectly shaped brains removed from the skulls of named patients and presumably used for research in programs well beyond the responsibilities of Herr Franck.

The pictures also portray the elaborate architecture of dozens of residential dormitories, staff cottages, elegant administrative housing, clinics, maintenance buildings, and churches. Photographs of residents and performers in *tracht* (regional costumes) portray men dressed in lederhosen and women in dirndls for carnivals at the institution. The women braided their hair into pigtails looped around their ears, a style adopted by Berta and worn well into her adulthood. If the Francks are in any of the more than one thousand photographs from the Kemmler collection, they're not named.

---

[3] Staniewska, A. *Gardens of Historic Mental Health Hospitals and Their Potential Use for Green Therapy Purposes.* Land 2022. Dr. Paul Kemmler Photograph Collection. Land Archive Baden-Wurttemberg

Sometime after 1908 and the birth of Berta at the Weissenhof, an elaborate park of trees, bushes, shrubbery, and flowers landscaping was installed in front of the main administration building of the institution, a task that would have fallen to Herr Franck for supervision among the inmates, patients, and staff. However, from 1914 until 1918, Herr Franck's daily duties in the mosaic of gardens must have been highly challenging. Richard, the Francks' only son, was killed in the early stage of the brutal German invasion of Belgium. French, Russian, and Belgian prisoners of war were incarcerated at the Weissenhof for their labor. Herr Franck was required to supervise the comrades of the enemy soldiers who killed his son in battle.[4]

Berta was only seven when her brother returned home from his Deutsche Bank job in Italy and entered the German Army, despite his parents imploring him to remain in Rome or move to South America to avoid the war. But Richard, at 21, performed his mandatory duty and reported for two years of military service.

With little time spent in infantry training, he was sent to Belgium, where he was killed in the First Battle of Ypres (West Flanders) on October 21, 1914. It was devastating for the Francks, especially young Berta, who lived a somewhat sheltered rural life in and around the sanatorium. The family would later learn that in the weeks of fighting leading up to Richard's death, German soldiers raped and massacred hundreds of Belgian civilians and burned their homes and businesses.

The invasion led to the four-year German occupation of Belgium. Richard's body was believed to be among over 80,000 German soldiers from the First Ypres alone, buried in field cemeteries in West Flanders. There is no evidence that his body was ever returned home.

Emanuel Franck toiled at his respectable civil service job as head gardener inside the sanatorium gates for many years, where the family also lived in a cottage. Berta could leave through the wooden gates and pedal her bicycle to the Weinsberg train station, where she could ride the passenger cars a few miles farther to the larger community of Heilbronn, where she had an apprenticeship.

On one of her forays into the countryside early in 1926, Grover, with his hired German driver (Stecher had returned to Philadelphia to face trial), began stalking the pretty teenage blonde *Fräulein* with his car. One day, driving recklessly, as usual, on the narrow gravel and dirt roads around Weinsberg, Grover nearly hit Berta's bicycle. The incident immediately alerted her to watch out for the large black luxury automobile. Despite Berta repeatedly turning down his clumsy and rude advances, Grover grew determined to get her into his car. Demanding or bribing her address

---

[4] During World War II, the Weissenhof Sanatorium was used by the Nazis as a staging location for psychiatric patients from other hospitals before they were sent out for euthanasia by gas in the Aktion T4 campaign, the despicable attempt to rid Germany of its mentally ill. In 2023, the highly respected Klinikum am Weissenhof included nearly 100 buildings in a 103-acre park-like setting stretching along the Weinsberg valley from the original manor house to a modern teaching hospital for the University of Heidelberg. It still utilized an elaborate therapeutic garden center.

from a ticket agent at the train station, he wrote a letter to Herr Franck asking if he could give Berta rides in his fancy car to and from her apprentice position in Heilbronn.[5] He agreed.

Grover was 32, already plump and softening in his waist and buttocks. Berta was energetic, trim, fit, and eagerly youthful at 18.

It isn't easy to understand why the Francks agreed to their pretty young daughter's relationship with a short, older, scarred, dark-pompadoured, and tooth-stained foreign man with solid demands and rude manners. Slender and appealing with her braided locks, gray-hazel downturned eyes, pale skin, angular jaw, and prominent cheekbones, attractive Berta could easily have been paired with a handsome young German man from the Weinsberg–Heilbronn community. However, Grover was known to spend lavishly, owned an expensive late-model Maybach, and was determined to win Berta's (and her parents') affection. Alfred wrote that his father probably showered Berta and her family with flowers, gifts... and promises.

They traveled extensively throughout Germany and Northern Europe, staying in first-class hotels and inns and dining in fine restaurants on wild game, braised pork with cabbage, *spaetzle* (German dumplings), lamb roast, pork hocks, and rice pudding and streusel. Berta may have abstained from alcohol at such a young age, but Grover drank Pils (pilsner beer) and Riesling or Pinot Gris wine, often with a glass in each hand. Still, they were always on the lookout for federal agents, Army detectives, and bounty hunters.

Grover's temper would often flare, and sometimes the Francks were on the receiving end. On more than one occasion, someone would be threatened with Grover's gun and the withholding of funds, but in time, apologies would be offered, gifts showered and promises made. On one occasion, Alfred wrote, Grover threatened to shoot everyone in the household. Herr Franck went to his bedroom, fetched his old German Army revolver, and said he would "shoot the raving drunk lunatic before he killed or hurt us." Berta and Frau Franck stopped him.

Another time, Grover sent Berta into a butcher shop in Heilbronn to buy pork chops. Grover slapped her hard across the face when she exited the shop without them before she could explain that the butcher was out of chops.

Grover promised to give Herr Franck a fox terrier puppy. Despite the older man reminding his future son-in-law of the pledged gift, he never got his puppy. The Francks should have been more cautious in approving Berta's suitor despite Grover's generosity, wrote Alfred. It was well known that he was a fugitive. He had killed a man who tried to capture him in his Eberbach hotel room, and in another kidnapping attempt, a young bridesmaid in his car was shot in the hand. And he

---

[5] Up until this time, Grover drove red Benz touring cars which attracted much attention. It's believed that Grover's primary car in 1926 was an early black Maybach made in the southern German community of Friedrichshafen.

On their long road, Grover took many photographs with his expensive new Leica 1 (A) 35mm camera. Smitten with Berta and in love, she was often his subject, along with his luxury cars. This appears to be the 1933 Hudson Essex Terraplane that Berta purchased with cash in Philadelphia and arranged for Erwin to ship to Germany. (Bergdoll Family Collection, Chester County Historical Society)

was under investigation for a morality incident in 1923.

***

Attorney Nachmann was working in the Karlsruhe office one day in early March 1933, soon after the Reichstag building fire on February 27 and the resulting Enabling Act giving German Chancellor Adolf Hitler absolute power, when the Nazi secret police raided the office, confiscating their cash receipts book and their Bergdoll file.[6] Because Nachmann's partner, Marum, listed as Grover's leading lawyer from the firm, was Jewish, and a fervent anti-Nazi liberal Social Democrat member of the Reichstag, they took him too. Both the Bergdoll file raid and the kidnapping of Marum were ordered by the fervent Nazi supporter Robert Heinrich Wagner, who was installed as Baden Gauleiter later that month.

First locked up at the Karlsruhe jail for several weeks, on May 16, the opening day of the Nazi parliament, Marum was loaded into an open truck with six other political prisoners and paraded through the Karlsruhe streets for humiliation. It was the first public show of power by the new Gauleiter. A photograph of the prisoner parade spectacle shows the ousted former Baden justice minister, Marum, in his shirt and tie with an overcoat, hatless to his bald head, arms folded, in a prominent backward sitting position in the bed of the truck where most of the people lining Karlsruhe's main street could easily see him and another notable prisoner, former Baden Interior Minister Adam Remmele.[7] Five swastika-banded guards closely surrounded the prisoners, with more

---

[6] Nachmann testified in 1941 about the law firm raid, calling the police Gestapo. However, the Gestapo was not formally organized until April 1933, a month after the raid. It's unknown what became of the law firm's Bergdoll file confiscated by the Nazis. The transcripts of Nachmann's testimony were found at the Bergdoll's abandoned Chester County, Pennsylvania farm in the 1940s and provided for research into this story.

[7] Marum and Remmele were viewed as personal enemies of the Baden Gauleiter, Robert Wagner, on whose order they were arrested and jailed.

in the front of the truck bed as "a howling and hissing mob of spectators met them."[8] Standing in the back of this crowd as the truck paraded through the streets in front of Maurer's music store, specializing in pianos and harmoniums, and people hanging from windows and balconies, was Marum's law partner Nachmann, who would have been arrested, too, if he protested too loudly. He complained but followed his lawyerly advice and laid low. Another witness to the event was Marum's 13-year-old daughter Eva Brigitte Marum. The Nazis would later murder her in the gas chamber.

In the truck, Marum was taken to prison 20 miles north of Karlsruhe at the former 270-acre hunting lodge at Kislau Castle in Bad Schonborn. Kislau was a small prison camp, never holding more than 173 inmates. Still, it became known as a transit station for "Jehovah's Witnesses, homosexuals, and others viewed as undesirables by the Nazis... on their way to Dachau, Sachsenhausen, or Buchenwald."[9] More for his many published anti-Nazi views than his defense of Bergdoll, Marum was strangled there on March 29, 1934, when the camp commandant was on vacation. His was the only death recorded at the camp. Despite a doctor's secret examination of Marum's body proving others had strangled him, his jailers tried to show that he hung himself by the neck from the window bars of his cell, claiming he was depressed.[10]

Marum's wife Johanna published an obituary stating, "In the Kislau concentration camp... my dear husband, father of three beloved children, died." Soon afterward, she fled to France with her two daughters and son. German and Jewish people were considered enemy aliens in France; they were impoverished and could not earn a living wage. The outstanding legal fees owed by Grover to the Marums would have significantly improved their living conditions if not afforded them the immediate financial support to emigrate to the United States and safety.

Throughout this period, although he was a fugitive American living in Germany, Grover would have been aware of the crisis building in his ancestral homeland and the danger presented by the growing German support for the Nazis.[11] Baden, especially around Heidelberg, heavily supported the Nazi party from the early 1930s, partly because of the authoritative power of its Gauleiter, Wagner.

---

[8] *The U.S. Holocaust Memorial Museum Encyclopedia of Camps and Ghettos, 1933–1945. Introduction to the Early Camps.*

[9] Encyclopedia of Camps and Ghettos.

[10] In 1948, the Kislau deputy camp commandant of 1933, Karl Franz Heinrich Sauer, and Paul Heupel, a driver, were sent to prison for Marum's assassination. A third man accused was killed in the war. Today, Dr. Ludwig Marum's memory is celebrated, especially in Karlsruhe, as a martyr and as one of the first outspoken advocates for German democracy and civil rights to challenge the Nazis.

[11] Many years later, Grover told his children that he often socialized in bars with Nazi SS officers and watched Hitler in a parade so close that he could have reached out and touched him. Like many Germans, he may have admired the Nazi party in the early 1930s. Grover's statements following his surrender in 1939 expressed disdain for the Hitler regime.

After a decade of living in poverty in France, Eva Brigitte Marum, her mother, and her sister managed to get exit visas, but Eva was barred from boarding the ship because she was full-term pregnant. After giving birth, she sent her son to a Jewish refugee home. In 1943 she got caught in a German roundup in Marseille and was deported to the Sobibor, Poland, concentration camp organized to experiment with killing Jews in the gas chamber. She was one of its early victims. Some of the Nazis' gas extermination methods originated with inmates from around Germany who were gathered at the Weissenhof Sanatorium.

***

Certain events should have tipped the Francks of Weissenhof to the instability of Grover as a future husband for their daughter. At least once, Berta broke off their planned betrothal and sent her gold ring back to Grover. Alfred wrote that Berta, trying to avoid reconciliation, went to stay with a German family friend who unsuccessfully tried to interest Berta in one of her handsome young sons. One evening, they noticed a strange man watching their house in Erfurt and discovered that Grover had hired a private detective to report to him about Berta's activities. Alfred said that while the woman's son was "tall, blonde, and good-looking, Grover was dark-haired, short, and already chunky." Following the separation, Berta returned home, and after apologies and more gifts, she reunited with Grover.

Grover couldn't get married in Germany because of his illegal immigration status. So, the new couple eloped. They married in Leningrad, described on Berta's 1939 naturalization application as St. Petersburg.[12] A photograph from their wedding trip in Grover's car shows a fit and attractive young Berta sitting in a grass field, pigtails wrapped around her ears, German style, hugging her knees to her chest in a snug tank top short-legged onesie romper. While her faint smile and large, gray-hazel eyes staring into the lens dominate the image, one can't help but notice a gold band and a sparkling diamond on her left-hand ring finger.[13] The diamond ring was described as "a rather large, deep diamond setting on tall platinum prongs that sprout from yellow gold, companion band to a wedding ring of another generation."[14] Emma Bergdoll possessed a substantial collection of jewelry. However, it's not known where Grover got the rings. Because their courtship was relatively brief, it's presumed he purchased the keepsakes himself in Germany. Berta was now Frau Bergdoll, wife

---

[12] Marriage in Russia following the Russian Revolution was easy. The only requirement for simple ceremonies known as "red weddings" was that women sign a statement declaring they were not being coerced into the marriage.

[13] German women typically moved their rings to their right hand after their marriage ceremony.

[14] This report may have misunderstood German customs. Engagement rings were gold bands, while wedding rings were gold and diamonds. However, we don't know if Grover was following German or American customs when he presented Berta with a proposal and the marriage rings.

of the infamous draft dodger, and had little clue what her future held. It was two weeks and four days before her 19th birthday.

It soon became apparent that Grover was always on the run. One night while driving with Berta home to Weinsberg from a club party with some of his old American friends, Grover shoved his .32 Sauer pistol into her hand on the left side of the car as he watched the headlamps of another vehicle, gaining rapidly behind them. Alfred wrote that his father ordered his mother to shoot at the occupants of the approaching car if they came abreast of them, but fortunately, the car turned off before Berta had to make a choice.

Alfred recorded that it was about the time of Grover and Berta's marriage in 1926 that Herr Franck retired from the sanatorium. A reporter searching for

Berta Franck Bergdoll in Germany, wearing her engagement and wedding rings soon after marrying Grover in Russia. (Bergdoll Family, Chester County Historical Society)

Grover in Weinsberg described Herr Franck: "[His] tall, erect bearing unmistakably marks him as a pre-war German officer of the reserve. His attire consists of an old hunting jacket, high leather boots, riding breeches, an old soft hat, and a course walking stick." While the description was accurate, Herr Franck was not an officer in the military reserve. His erect and proud manner derived from decades of working for a government institution, the Weissenhof.

Grover would not have been able to live with Berta and her parents at their state-provided cottage, and the Francks' plans to buy a home were dashed by severe post-war inflation that crippled Germany. They also suffered heavy losses investing in government war bonds. Instead, they moved into an apartment at the former Weinsberg municipal building and district court at 17 Hallerstrasse.

While staying with the Francks in their apartment, Alfred wrote that Grover frequently insulted them with rude table manners and rejected their simple food and homemade wine to favor the expensive items he could buy, such as German sparkling wine. Grover purchased a new car, shipped it from the United States to Germany, registered it in Herr Franck's name with the license plate *III D 1218,* and stored it in a nearby garage. His creditor attorneys reported the large black sedan almost always in Weinsberg, with or without its owner. Perhaps the car was available

The collapsed German economy forced the Francks into a Weinsberg rental apartment in this building upon retirement. They relied on Grover's financial contributions and were forced to accept his strict demands, abusive behavior, and with guns, from which the Francks felt threatened. The building later became the Weinsberg police station. (Bergdoll Family, Chester County Historical Society)

for Herr Franck too. It's also presumed Grover won over his new in-laws by picking up some of the tabs for living expenses, although how much is unknown.

A year into his marriage, Grover came up with a scheme he hoped would redeem his soiled reputation and make him an American hero again.

On June 6, 1927, with great fanfare, two Americans arrived in Germany in a Bellanca airplane, flying from Roosevelt-Curtiss Field on Long Island, New York, and landing in a hayfield in Helfta, near Eisleben, Germany, when they nearly ran out of gas. The incredible feat captured Grover's attention, partly because he had become depressed to read the accounts just weeks earlier of Charles Lindbergh flying solo across the Atlantic and landing in France.[15]

Pilot Clarence Duncan Chamberlain flew the Wright-Bellanca WB-2 named "Miss Columbia" with his passenger, Charles A. Levine, the chairman of the Columbia Aircraft Company, who made a fortune in the junk salvage business.

The president of the company and aircraft designer was Giuseppe Bellanca. Chamberlain could have accomplished Lindbergh's world-renowned flying feat because each pilot accepted the challenge by New York hotelier Raymond Orteig to become the first to fly across the Atlantic to win the $25,000 Orteig Prize. Chamberlain had *Miss Columbia* running like a charm and had set an endurance record in April, flying more than 4,000 miles in circles over Long Island to confirm that he could stay aloft for the distance to Europe.

---

[15] The news about Lindbergh depressed Grover instead of cheering him because the renowned feat is exactly what he wished to do more than a decade earlier.

However, his plan to take off before Lindbergh was held up by a court order from a man challenging Levine over outstanding debts. When the court released the challenge, Lindbergh had already taken off in the Spirit of St. Louis to capture the prize and worldwide fame.

Dispirited but with renewed energy to beat Lindbergh's distance with a navigation setting for Germany, Chamberlain aimed the "Miss Columbia" for the end of the Long Island strip on the morning of June 4 and waited just long enough for Levine to run up to the purring airplane and wish his pilot luck. Instead, without telling his wife, Levine jumped into the Bellanca, and they took off!

When Grover read the news of Chamberlain and Levine landing safely in Germany with a new distance record and with Chamberlain becoming the first pilot to fly a passenger across the Atlantic, he was enchanted. Grover grew more determined to get back in the air. He stopped his car during one of his long trips through the German countryside with a nearly full-term pregnant Berta, and from Hoexter, Westphalia, he telegraphed a message to the *Associated Press* in Berlin. It said, "Will the constructor of the Spirit of St. Louis or the Columbia deliver a plane with a Wright motor in short order? I am anxious to fly from Europe to the American interior until the gasoline gives out, as soon as an airplane can be obtained. No German plane capable of this flight is obtainable at present."

Grover also offered $100,000 to any German company for an airplane capable of flying to New York. An article by the *Universal Press Service* said that while German companies such as Junkers and Dorniers might have been interested in selling an airplane for that price, when they asked Grover to provide his weight—more than 200 pounds—they said no.

When the press asked Lindbergh what he thought of Bergdoll's wish to "rehabilitate himself in the good graces of the nation," Lindbergh replied that flying from Europe to the U.S. is not as easy as it is from the U.S. to Europe.

"Mr. Bergdoll would probably find flying even harder now than it was ten years ago," he said.

Grover had not flown a plane in more than 10 years. And, he certainly would have had a more difficult time handling the larger, faster airplanes than he did with his simple, slow, and forgiving Wright B. One can only imagine how Berta felt as her new husband, without identification or passport, was ostracized in the press with his public effort to find people to let him latch onto their glory by attempting to fly their airplane back to America. Meanwhile, what about Berta? She and Grover were driving from town to town in north central Germany when she should have been relaxing at home and preparing for a baby.

She was weeks away from delivering their first child.

Meanwhile, still basking in celebrity treatment from the European press, Levine and Chamberlain were reunited with their wives in France. Enjoying the limelight,

Levine's wife forgave him for leaving so suddenly without telling her. Levine tried to get Chamberlain to attempt to fly the Bellanca back to the United States, but wisely, the experienced aviator declined. Then, Levine concocted the foolhardy notion of doing it himself, despite having limited piloting skills. Levine managed, however, to get the plane up and over the English Channel, but it took him several near-crash efforts to land safely at Croydon, England. He realized then that "Miss Columbia" must be returned to New York by ship.

When Grover heard about Levine's effort to fly his plane back across the Atlantic, he sat down at his Remington portable typewriter and pounded out a letter that reached Levine as he was leaving for New York.[16] Levine immediately publicized the Bergdoll letter in the press, claiming it was just one of the thousands of offers he received. This letter said,

> Hearty congratulations to you and Chamberlain for your wonderful flight. Should you care to sell or loan me the Columbia, on condition I fly the same from Berlin within a specified time to New York or Philadelphia, or if you do not care to allow me to fly the plane alone, would you be willing to allow me to accompany Chamberlain on a flight to New York. Let me know where I can reach you.

Grover's effort to fly home from his self-imposed exile in Germany was written up worldwide. The press emphasized that "name your own price" appeared several times in the letter. It was desperation. Grover continued his pleadings with Levine well into September 1927 but then gave up on the effort to become a hero again by flying home.

On July 1, 1927, while Grover and Berta were traveling in Germany's Hartz Mountains and avoiding American bounty hunters who might be searching for them, they ducked into the small town of Niedersachswerfen. They placed Berta in the care of a doctor. She delivered their first child, Alfred, a thin baby boy with a light complexion, brown hair, and green eyes who always needed glasses to improve his vision. Alfred was not given a middle name, unlike his parents, who had multiple names. Soon after the birth, Grover and Berta drove home to Weinsberg, where they could find help from Berta's parents in caring for their baby boy.[17]

Later that month, Grover wrote to the American consulate in Stuttgart asking for instructions on returning to the United States. He didn't mention if his plans to return to Philadelphia involved Berta and Alfred.

Back home in Philadelphia, tragedy struck the Bergdoll family farm near Broomall. On a summer afternoon, September 11, 1928, Charles, and Louise Goetz Bergdoll-Brawn's daughter Emma C. Brawn was shot and killed while her brother, Charles,

---

[16] Grover always carried his Remington portable typewriter with him on the road.

[17] While Grover and Berta were traveling or hiding in Germany or Philadelphia, the children stayed with their Franck grandparents for extended periods of time, where they went to school and learned to speak German. Alfred wrote of these times that they didn't miss their parents at all.

Jr., and her boyfriend, Charles Lobb were target shooting. A gunshot wound in Emma's abdomen and left lung caused so much bleeding from her lung that she died soon after the shooting.

Emma was born on the Bergdoll farm on March 21, 1911, and at 17 was still a student in high school. The coroner's report said the kids were playing with a revolver in the hands of another teenager, Charles C. Lobb, when it went off. The owner of the gun was not revealed. The coroner ruled the death accidental. All parties relieved "Lobby" from legal responsibility but an entry written by Louise in the Brawn family bible clearly placed blame. "Will God ever be able to forgive Lobby for his careless act that such a wonderful girl's life should be snuffed out by a bullet from a supposedly empty revolver in the hands of a spoilt unresponsible youth such as he was? His carelessness is no excuse." It was a sorrowful time for Charles and Louise, and it further contributed to their interest in moving away from Philadelphia, the Broomall farm, and the Bergdoll name and reputation. Their beloved daughter Emma had been named in happier family times after her grandmother.

In Heidingsfeld, near Wurzberg, Germany, just weeks later, on October 2, 1928, Berta delivered a baby girl. She and Grover named their second child Emma Lydia Bergdoll. Like their first child, Alfred, Emma was born while Grover and Emma traveled, 65 miles from their home in Weinsberg. Under constant surveillance by American agents, and always fearing another kidnapping attempt, their lives on the run were becoming a matter of routine.

The following spring, Berta made her first trip to the United States and Philadelphia. In his lengthy typewritten and handwritten diary-manuscript, Alfred wrote that Grover persuaded Berta to travel to the United States to join her sister, who was already there. However, immigration records indicate the Franck sisters traveled together, arriving in New York on the steamer *Berlin* on April 13, 1929. Berta was 22 and left her two children, Alfred, and Emma, in Weinsberg with Grover and her parents. Sister Helene was 36 and had no intention of returning to Germany. They both listed their occupations as housekeepers. Traveling under their Franck names to avoid the press, they were met in Philadelphia by a Bergdoll family friend, Emma Price. Berta remained with her luggage at the modest Price home on North Camac Street until nightfall when she was driven to Grover's Wynnefield mansion, where, for the first time, two years after her marriage, Berta met her mother-in-law, Emma.

Berta told Alfred many years later, "When I first came to Wynnefield on a Sunday [night] with Mrs. Price, and Helene opened the door, I was very happy to be with her, but then, in the kitchen, I met Mrs. Bergdoll. I thought she was nice-looking but dirtier than anyone I ever saw before. She showed a bossy nature, even on the first day. She treated Helene like a maid. I did not like my mother-in-law at all at first."[18]

---

[18] To avoid police and the press, Helene may have gone to the Wynnefield mansion ahead of Berta under the guise of a housemaid.

Emma did treat the Franck sisters like maids, even taking them to her Brewerytown mansion to clean the coal-sooty rooms and swab cobwebs. No one lived in the brick house at North 29th Street at this time. Emma had moved to live part-time in Wynnefield since Grover fled and full-time after the senility-complicated death of her mother, Wilhelmina Barth, in June 1925.[19] Alfred wrote that he and his sister, Emma were "perfectly happy" staying with their grandparents. Grover "traveled about alone."

Erwin, who was out of prison by now and living quietly on his Broomall farm, often came by the Wynnefield mansion to help the Franck sisters adjust to life in America and deal with the demands of Emma. He helped them find decent food to eat instead of the "slop" that Emma tried to feed them, took them to the Bergdoll-Brawn farm near Broomall, and got them both in to see his dentist for much-needed dental work that Grover would not allow Berta to have when she was in Germany.

One day, Alfred writes, while Berta and Helene were frolicking and spring cleaning in the Wynnefield garden, a woman beckoned them through the tall iron fence surrounding the three-acre property and tried to hire them as servants at her nearby mansion for $15 a week each. Realizing they were both miserable living with Emma, for a few moments, they entertained the thought of running off to become housemaids in America.

Then reality returned. Grover was hatching a plan to return to Philadelphia.[20] Aside from reuniting with Berta, he wanted to retrieve his gold.

Departing on May 31, 1929, Grover traveled from Germany to Montreal via Liverpool on the elegant new Canadian Pacific Line steamer *Duchess of Bedford* with a fake passport in the name of Joseph Amann. The document listed his age as 38, traveling alone on business in the United States for a few months. The Amann passport said he was born in Hoppetenzell, Germany, leaving his wife, Marie, at home in Radolfzell, a town on Lake Constance in southern Germany near Switzerland. From the port on the Saint Lawrence River, where he arrived on June 7, Grover, as Joseph Amann, planned to go immediately to the Canadian Pacific Railway Windsor Street station in Montreal and board a train for the United States.[21]

Travel records for the St. Albans, Vermont immigration district indicate that Grover crossed the border at Rouse's Point, New York, and continued by train to New York City and then Trenton, New Jersey, where he checked into the elegant

---

[19] On Wilhelmina Barth's 1925 death certificate, Emma and her brother, Charles, indicated they did not know the name of Wilhelmina's father, their maternal grandfather. Although Wilhelmina stayed with Emma, her address was a comfortable three-story brick Victorian house in Philadelphia's leafy Wissahickon Valley. Charles Barth lived just up Sumac Street in another comfortable three-story brick Victorian. Both homes were the results of the largesse from the Bergdoll Brewery.

[20] Helene Franck remained in Philadelphia and eventually married Emil Friedrich Franz Max Dietz, a naturalized American from Dresden, Germany. He helped Helene attain citizenship in 1937.

[21] The fake travel documents were tracked down for Grover's 1939 trial. The Canada incoming passenger list was then flagged with a red code indicating his true identity.

Soon after Berta's first trip to Philadelphia in 1929, Grover followed, traveling on a fake passport, leaving their two children in Germany. Grover uncovered his "buried" gold on this first secret trip home. He hid in his Wynnefield mansion for nearly a year until returning to Germany in 1930 with some of the gold. (Bergdoll Family Collection, Historical Society of Pennsylvania)

12-story art deco Stacy-Trent Hotel with its spacious lobby and marble staircase.[22] While there, he would lay low and scope out his secret arrival in Philadelphia.

However, he made an impression on the restaurant waitress and the bartender. They would remember him.

How or when Grover arrived at the Wynnefield mansion is unknown, but Alfred said he got there "in the dark of night." Constantly wary of police, federal agents, and bounty hunters looking to capture him, Grover remained hidden in the mansion in a second-floor bedroom and the library where he had easy access to the top-floor garrets and their knee wall closet doors, cupboards, and cabinets that could conceal a human. He could survey the streets and the mansion grounds from the top dormer windows while remaining hidden in the dormer recesses.

The upper floor bedrooms were spacious and far enough apart to give Grover and Berta privacy from Emma, whose bedroom was also on the second floor, across the hall from the bathroom and sitting room. Without their children, obligations, or responsibilities in Philadelphia, Grover and Berta lounged away the days while Berta succumbed to Grover's pent-up desires. After being separated for several weeks, the couple resumed their sexual relationship while hiding among the comforts of a sitting room, music room, library, billiard room, full bathroom, several telephones, and a film projector. Emma's kitchen supplied them with food, beer, and wine. Their upstairs *Beischlaf* became an issue several months later.

---

[22] Constructed in 1921 while Grover was hiding in Germany, the "million-dollar" Stacy-Trent Hotel was the in place for politicians and celebrities while in New Jersey's capital for state business or entertainment. Its elegance would have caught Grover's attention when planning his first trip home in nearly a decade.

Sometime in mid-1929, Grover accomplished his other mission in returning to Philadelphia. Using the sharp side of a carpenter's hammer, he clawed at the plaster on the back wall of his second-floor bedroom closet and smashed through the soft wood lathe to reveal his stash of hidden gold. Standing beside him and helping remove the sacks of gold coins were Berta, Helene, and Emma. Together they carried the heavy bags to the music room across the hall from Emma's bedroom and spread them across a large wooden table. Alfred maintains there was about $105,000 in gold coins. The bags of gold remained on the music room table all night. However, $1,000 was missing in the morning when they performed another count. Alfred said that Berta and Helene believed that sometime during the night, the old lady took some gold coins and hid them for herself. Alfred said, "Father must have thought so too, or he would have raised bloody hell."

Alfred said his mother and his Aunt Helene took the sacks of gold and deposited them into Berta's new account at a Philadelphia bank.[23]

It was just in time too. Autumn and the stock market crash of October 1929 were approaching. Alfred said Grover had few stock investments besides his brewery certificates before the collapse.[24] Having his assets in cash and real estate was beneficial later when Grover bought into the depressed market and capitalized on his investments to considerable profits during the long, slow recovery from the Great Depression.[25]

Sometime in early November of that year, Charles Bergdoll-Brawn drove from his farm near Broomall to visit Emma at the Wynnefield mansion. He would have seen Grover hiding on the upper floors, but Alfred didn't mention it in his narration. Charles and Emma had been estranged for years since he changed his name from Bergdoll to Brawn and separated himself from the family. However, unlike Grover, Charles was heavily into the stock market leading up to the crash and was desperate to honor his debts. Alfred wrote that Charles' reason for visiting his mother that November was to borrow $75,000 for a margin call.

"The old lady wrote a check for that amount without turning a hair," Alfred said. "But Uncle Charles was wiped out the next day anyway, and the $75,000 was gone." His losses (along with the death of his daughter, Emma) inspired Charles to

---

[23] In 1939, Albert A. Drucker, the liquidating trustee of Weniger and Company Bank of Philadelphia, stipulated in legal documents that he could testify that Emma and Berta appeared at the bank in late summer or early fall of 1929 and deposited $160,000 in gold coins and currency into the account.

[24] His siblings described Alfred Bergdoll as being an astute investor. His diary-manuscript made it clear that he was presenting an accurate picture of his family's investment gains and losses. He accurately described their losses during the Depression, but, fortunately for the family, they still had plenty of money, especially Grover.

[25] Despite the confiscation of Grover's assets by the Alien Property Custodian, Grover still had access to cash and investments, specifically gold.

transfer the deed to his palatial stone mansion at the farm near Broomall to Emma and move to California to start over.[26]

Back at the Wynnefield mansion, Berta and Grover were insulated from the dire economic conditions gripping the nation. They had access to vast sums of cash but needed Grover to be exonerated to spend it. Emma and, to some extent, Berta helped, collecting the rents and mortgages from those who could still pay. Tenants were unaware of the Bergdoll asset freeze. Those who couldn't pay were often given a free ride in one of the Bergdolls' many properties. For Emma, it was easier than making a fuss over unpaid bills sure to be noticed by the press.

Gone for 10 years, Grover would have recognized only some of his former neighborhoods even if he ventured into the city (and he probably did). Philadelphia was rapidly changing. White Germans were moving to the suburbs with greater use of automobiles. The outer Philadelphia neighborhoods of Germantown, East Falls, Strawberry Mansion, and the Bergdolls' home base, Brewerytown, were becoming heavily populated by African-Americans and Eastern European Jews moving out of the heart of the city.

The Bergdolls' Broomall farm estate was still in the country, but the Main Line community of Ardmore, where Grover so often had been able to speed along its main thoroughfare, Lancaster Avenue, without stopping, was becoming choked with traffic drawn by a new concept in shopping, a mall of interconnected stores built on the grounds of a former grand estate and designed for people arriving and departing in their cars.

Although much of this population transformation in and around Philadelphia was stunted by the Great Depression, if Grover thought Americans' focus on the economy would stop their attention to his draft-dodging past, he was mistaken.

Until late 1929, Berta could travel around Philadelphia while Grover remained hidden in the Wynnefield mansion. Then, Berta also secluded herself in the chateau to prevent neighbors, police, federal agents, and the press from discovering she was expecting a baby.

By whom did she become pregnant if her husband were hiding in Germany, they would ask? If a doctor saw her, it was a discreet house call because her pregnancy remained a secret. Rushed off to Europe in the final weeks of her third trimester, Berta was aboard the steamer S.S. *Berlin* sailing between Southampton and Bremerhaven on

---

[26] Accounts differ on the extent of Charles' losses in the market crash and its impact on his finances, but he could not have suffered too greatly. He retained ownership and income from the Birdsboro Stone quarry in Pennsylvania. He purchased 44 acres of land in Vista, California, that he developed into citrus and avocado orchards from the former Buena Vista Ranch north of San Diego. *Villa Vista Estate History* records that Charles and Louise and Charles Alvin Brawn, Jr. arrived with a trainload of furniture from the Broomall farm in January 1930. They expanded their ranch to 150 acres but later moved to another part of San Diego County, where Charles raised thoroughbred horses.

Berta Bergdoll made several Atlantic crossings in the 1930s with and without the Bergdoll children. They had German citizenship and could stay in the United States on limited visas. During one of her return trips to Germany, she delivered their daughter, Mina, aboard a ship in the North Sea. She also traveled to fetch cash needed to sustain their lives in Germany. (Temple University Urban Archives)

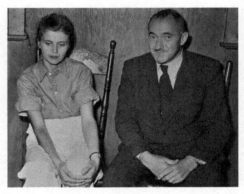

The Francks often cared for the Bergdoll children for months or a year at a time when Grover and Berta traveled in Europe or hid in the United States. Alfred Bergdoll said the children were always happiest with their grandparents and when their father was not around. The Francks with Berta and the children in Germany, and Berta and Grover. (Bergdoll Family Collection)

March 8, 1930, when she delivered her third child, Wilhelmina, nicknamed "Mina."[27] However, Berta managed to do it quietly, and the mother and infant daughter arrived in Weinsberg without incident to rejoin the other children, Alfred and Emma, and the elder Francks.

Less than two weeks later, on March 21, the *Associated Press* published a story about the fugitive Bergdoll living a quiet family life in Weinsberg "in search of a cure for shattered nerves." It said the couple's two children "live in virtual seclusion… and [are] guarded with such secrecy that villagers don't know if they're boys or girls." The "only outsider the Francks receive," the article said, was Emma Bergdoll, "who supports her son and his family."

When the article was written, the reporter could not have known that Berta had just delivered their third child, conceived in Philadelphia, while Grover was still hiding on the upper floors of his Wynnefield mansion.[28]

It was just the first of two long periods of hiding in Philadelphia as federal agents continually bungled their search for Grover, thinking he was still in Germany.

---

[27] Mina Bergdoll's birth location at sea is recorded on Berta's travel documents in latitude and longitude, placing it about 20 miles off the East Frisian Island of Borkum in the North Sea. Reference to Mina's birth "while returning home from visiting her husband" is also recorded by longhand in 1930 in the Franck family sheet at their Weinsberg church. Such records would not have been available to detectives and bounty hunters searching for Grover in 1930.

[28] It was three years before Grover would see his youngest daughter, Mina. He remained in his Wynnefield mansion until he returned to Germany in May 1933.

CHAPTER TWENTY-FOUR

Wreck in the Machine Shop

Camden Central Airport, New Jersey, November 1934

Dressed in a business suit and tie beneath his white mechanic's jumpsuit, leather gloves, backward baseball cap, and goggles strapped around his forehead, Arthur E. Arrowsmith sat in the pilot's seat and pushed and pulled the control levers on Grover Bergdoll's 1911 Wright B Flyer. Surrounding Arrowsmith, a transport airline pilot and vocational school aeronautics instructor in New Jersey, several students and school officials watched with approval as the fluctuating levers and spring-loaded foot pedals connected by the sash and roller chains appeared to activate the motor, elevator, and rudder components responsively. As the lever movement splayed the twin rudders back and forth, the tail number 1-4-3-3-7 flashed in and out of view.[1] It displayed the first federal registration of the 13th Wright B Flyer mass-manufactured in the Wright Brothers' Dayton, Ohio factory in 1911–1912 for young Grover Bergdoll.

Students in the Camden County, New Jersey Vocational School Aeronautical Mechanics class spun the twin laminated clear spruce propellers. The airplane's replacement engine puffed and sputtered to life. Arrowsmith gradually pushed the white duck canvas-coated biplane across the grass portion of the field at the Camden Central Airport. Students scattered like children chasing a kite, some guiding the wings with their hands as the plane's bicycle wheels bounced along the field. Arrowsmith taxied and turned, adjusting the plane levers with his flopping arms and wrists and the motor controls with his legs and ankles. He watched for every connection of the wires, cables, chains, and spars that would determine his life or death when and if the plane got into the air.

However, Bergdoll's vintage airplane was not to fly on November 10, 1934; Arrowsmith only tested the recently refurbished airplane's control capabilities. Then, all together, the high school students who had done incredible work making the old rotting and rundown airplane new again, with personal supervision from none other than Orville Wright, pushed the plane beneath the high nose of a twin-engine

---

[1] Film from Fox Movietone News. Copyright University of South Carolina.

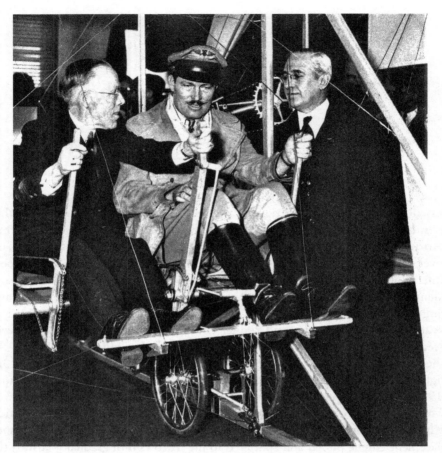

While Grover hid in Germany in 1933, his former flying companion, William H. Sheahan, pictured left on Grover's airplane with stunt pilot Roscoe Turner and engineer Kern Dodge, claimed he exchanged letters with Grover through which the fugitive gave his 1911 Wright B Flyer to Sheahan. Sheahan removed the airplane from storage on the Broomall farm and gave it to the Franklin Institute Science Museum in Philadelphia. (The Franklin Institute)

Douglas DC-3 passenger plane parked at the airport. Along with testing, this was also photography and publicity day. The image spoke a thousand words, with Bergdoll's relic of early aviation a stark contrast to the shiny new prop airliner pointing its nose toward the sky.

Then Arrowsmith, the school teacher, pilot, and engineer, turned Bergdoll's machine over to the veteran Wright B pilot who would take it aloft for the first time in two decades, a former Bergdoll flying companion and fellow Wright B owner, Marshall Earle Reid, also of Philadelphia. Reid, the war veteran who ran a successful welding rod manufacturing company, had flown Bergdoll's plane, but it was years earlier when he was a much younger and more daring man in the infancy of flight.

A single newspaper report in October 1933, without a byline or photographer credit and with numerous misstatements, indicated that Grover's dilapidated Wright B airplane was rotting in storage in Erwin Bergdoll's machine shop at the Broomall farm. After Sheahan removed it from the shop, the aircraft was restored at the Camden County (New Jersey) Vocational School, pictured, with Orville Wright dropping in for a consultation. (The Franklin Institute)

Also dressed in a business suit but without the white jumpsuit, Reid wrapped a white wool scarf around his neck and a knit wool beanie cap with a ball on the top of his head. He, too, approved of the proper functioning of the control levers, planes, and the motor on the refurbished airplane. After checking his wristwatch, Reid and Arrowsmith shut down the engine and set a date for the plane's first public flight since Grover ditched it in brother Erwin's West Chester Pike machine shop in 1913 and fled to Germany.

The flight would be December 17, 1934, at 10:35 am, the exact time of the 31st anniversary of Orville and Wilbur's historic flight at Kitty Hawk. A significant event was being organized for the skies over Philadelphia, spearheaded by the new Franklin Institute science museum for its plunge into the science of aviation. It would be the last time a Wright Brothers airplane with a direct line to their Dayton, Ohio production factory would get into the air.

Still hiding as a fugitive in Germany, Grover was unaware of what was happening with his old airplane at home near Philadelphia. But he would soon read about it in the newspapers his sister, Elizabeth, and mother, Emma sent to him regularly.

How Grover's damaged and dumped 1911 Wright B Flyer got to New Jersey for one final flight in 1934 is an incredible tale that requires questioning the long-presented facts of salvaging the airplane before it was utterly lost to rot and looters. Some of the questions still can't be answered with certainty today.

The final fate of Grover's airplane began 20 years earlier.

During the first week of August 1913, 40-year-old William Henry Sheahan, a superintendent at the American Soda Fountain Company in Philadelphia, showed up along with hundreds of other spectators at Eagle Field west of Philadelphia, where Grover and Charles Kraus were putting on daily shows flying Grover's Wright B. Sheahan carried a Vest Pocket Kodak camera, which attracted Grover's attention. He also wrote aviation news and installed photos in *Aero and Hydro*, an Aero Club of America magazine. Grover loved seeing his name and picture as a daring pilot in magazines and papers.[2]

Feeling confident with his expertise, Grover would turn, swerve, and dip by warping the wings of the Wright B while Sheahan ran back and forth, snapping photographs. Then Grover took Sheahan for a ride. Little did Grover know at the time that taking Sheahan up in his airplane would lead to the long-term preservation of his Wright B, which would become the most original and intact Wright Brothers airplane in the world.[3]

Sheahan, a thin, lanky fellow with a stout nose, had become enthralled with airplanes in 1910 when Wanamaker's Department Store in Philadelphia displayed the Blériot airplane, purchased

Two final flights of Grover's restored Wright B Flyer were made in 1934 by Philadelphia businessman-pilot, Marshall Earle Reid, pictured, a former pilot companion of Grover's at Eagle Field in 1912–1913. The bi-plane was dwarfed by a modern Douglas C-47, and a car clocked the airplane's speed. (The Franklin Institute. Historical Society of Pennsylvania, *Philadelphia Record*)

---

[2] Sheahan reported in *Aero and Hydro* that Grover flew a Wright B on December 28, 1913, during weather so cold he had to put boiling water in the radiator to get the motor started. The Aero Club of Pennsylvania also kept a Wright B at the Bergdoll hangar, probably the airplane in which Marshall Reid flew from Eagle Field in 1912 and 1913. Grover's plane was still damaged, sitting in Erwin's machine shop.

[3] The Wright Brothers' 1903 Kitty Hawk flyer was damaged and rebuilt, diminishing its original parts.

by Louis Bergdoll. Sheahan was born in Maryland but moved to Maine, where he met his future wife, Daisy, and married. They moved to Philadelphia to find work at the soda fountain company. Taking a summer holiday in July 1911, Sheahan witnessed pilot Harry N. Attwood land his Burgess-Wright biplane on the beach in Ocean City, New Jersey. Attwood thought he was landing in nearby Atlantic City during a promotional flight from Boston to Washington with a can of Boston baked beans for President Taft. On the beach with Daisy, Sheahan watched with great interest as Attwood took off from Ocean City for Washington, later landing his plane and the beans on the White House lawn.

The following summer of 1912, all of Philadelphia was buzzed by Grover flying his new Wright B from Eagle Field to the rowhouses of West and North Philadelphia, Camden, and South Philadelphia. Eager to capture the excitement, Sheahan took time off from his job and muscled his way to the front of the crowd at Eagle Field to get a ride with Grover. From this point onward in his life, Sheahan was hooked on aviation.

Two summers of watching, photographing, and riding with Grover in his Wright B over Eagle Field convinced Sheahan to learn how to fly. He was handicapped, however, by growing up in a family of small means and a job that didn't afford him enough income to buy an airplane. He settled for flight lessons and learned how to fly in 1912 and 1913 at the Heinrich School of Aviation Mineola Flying Field, Hempstead Plains, Long Island, New York.[4] He soloed in a biplane like Grover's Wright B for his final test.

Sheahan lived in Philadelphia through the 1920s, during Grover's heavy publicity from fleeing to Germany, the kidnapping attempts, his trial for indecency, efforts to come home, his marriage to Berta, and his legal wranglings with the Alien Property Custodian. All while Grover's Wright B Flyer sat on a trailer at Erwin's machine shop in Broomall. Although he didn't fly much, Sheahan became the first vice president and then treasurer of the Aero Club of Pennsylvania, filing brief reports about pilot achievements in *Aero and Hydro* magazine.

However, by 1930 Sheahan lived in a modest brick rowhouse in Upper Darby, Pennsylvania, not far from Eagle Field and the Bergdoll farm along West Chester Pike. Still plugged into events surrounding the Bergdolls because of his interest in aviation, Sheahan became aware that items were being stolen from the Bergdoll estate by local men who would drive their trucks through the woods in the Darby Creek valley and park in a field at the rear of the machine shop and an adjacent two-story stone storage building containing hundreds of cast-off automobile parts from Erwin's former business of building race cars.

---

[4] Despite learning to fly and soloing in 1913, Sheahan never achieved a pilot's license. Using his photographs and testimony from fellow students as proof of his aviation skill, he was admitted to the Aero Club of Pennsylvania and served as its treasurer for many years. His photographs of early flight were later received by the Smithsonian National Air and Space Museum in Washington, D.C.

While helping themselves to miscellaneous car parts, motors, transmissions, axles, and tools from the storage building, someone also broke into the long, single-story machine shop. They removed and stole the engine, radiator, and part of a control stick from Grover's airplane.[5] They may not have known the historical significance of a vintage race car in the shop.[6] Around Broomall, gossip about looting at the Bergdoll farm began to circulate, despite Erwin still living in his farmhouse and Emma occupying her mansion on the large farm property in the summer.[7]

In 1933, newspapers in Philadelphia reported on the renowned Franklin Institute relocating from South 7th Street to a new Beaux-Arts–Classical Revival building on Benjamin Franklin Parkway at Logan Square. It would house a new concept for science museums, a Hall of Aviation. It would focus on the art and science of developing airplanes and air travel. The Franklin chose a prominent and wealthy Philadelphian to become assistant director and head of the Aviation wing: Charles Townsend Ludington.

A graduate of the prestigious Haverford School, Ludington had been a Navy pilot and flight instructor during the war. He then returned home to his family's magnificent estate, Clovelly, on Philadelphia's Main Line. It was adorned with a large mansion, stables, multi-stall garage, tennis and squash courts, and formal English gardens with an address of Ardmore but located in the more prestigious Gladwyne community. C. Townsend, as he was known, attended the Massachusetts Institute of Technology and Yale University. Originally from New York City and Old Lyme, Connecticut, Ludington's parents relocated to the Philadelphia region when his father, Charles H. Ludington, became an executive with the Curtis Publishing Company of *Saturday Evening Post* and *Ladies Home Journal* prominence.[8] When Ludington's mother and father died in 1922 and 1927, he and his brother, Nicholas, used their substantial gifts and inheritance to invest in the rapidly expanding aviation business.

The Ludington brothers organized Washington Airway Corporation in the mid-1920s. They won early air mail contracts from the U.S. Postal Service, flying mail between New York, Philadelphia, and Washington as one route and New York,

---

[5] The Vertical 4, In-Line 4 Wright B engine stolen from Grover's airplane powered Wright Brothers airplanes until 1912.

[6] The wreck of a race car was Erwin's 1911 Fairmount Park Motor Race championship 150 HP Benz, a 1908 model that preceded the infamous 200 HP Lightning or Blitzen Benz. It's been claimed that the Mercedes Benz museum in Stuttgart purchased Erwin's Benz, but the museum does not have it.

[7] Erwin's machine shop, the storage site for Grover's Wright B Flyer, was somewhat distant and secluded from the farmhouse and stone mansion occupied by Erwin and Emma and another owned by Grover.

[8] The Philadelphia Ludingtons were direct descendants of Revolutionary War Col. Henry Ludington of the Dutchess County, New York militia. On April 26, 1777, Col. Ludington's 16-year-old daughter, Sybil, rode 40 miles through the Hudson Valley frontier, warning that British soldiers were marching on a military post at Danbury, Connecticut. She's celebrated today as the "teenage female Paul Revere." *Sybil Ludington, the Female Paul Revere: The Making of a Revolutionary War Heroine.* Paula D. Hunt. MIT Journals.

Chicago, and Dallas as another. The business, with guaranteed income from the government, was lucrative.

Along with other investors, they purchased land in New Jersey and organized Camden Central Airport as the Philadelphia hub for the air mail route. They also held the mortgage on Hoover Field, their mail transport end line in Arlington, Virginia (Washington).

Their aviation business was considered a regional carrier, of which many across the country focused on government contracts for air mail. Then, efforts to expand the company were stymied by the Post Office's plan to refocus, moving away from regional carriers to a few national airlines that could expand air mail service nationwide. The Ludingtons placed a bid on these new contracts, but even though their request was three times less than a competitor, National Air Transport, they lost the contract. Angered by what he considered an unjust political influence, C. Townsend Ludington tipped off an influential journalist, radio reporter Fulton Lewis, Jr., whose exposé led to an investigation known as the Air Mail Scandal.[9]

Not to be outdone, the Ludington brothers dug deeper into their pockets in 1930 and leased new and faster Stinson tri-motor ten-passenger airplanes to organize the first passenger shuttle service between New York City, Philadelphia, and Washington. Ludington Lines ran "on the hour, every hour." Keeping costs low by using just one pilot, ground signals instead of radio, and cheaper automobile gasoline at cruising altitude, Ludington Lines (New York, Philadelphia, and Washington Airways) flew an average of a thousand passengers weekly. Many first-timers were inspired to fly when Ludington employed famous aviator Amelia Earhart as a vice president to promote the airline. They reported a more than $8,000 profit, unheard of at the time in passenger aviation.[10]

By 1933, however, the Ludingtons realized what other small airlines were encountering simultaneously: earning or maintaining profits was nearly impossible without the air mail contracts. Their primary competitor in the New York to Washington route, the more extensive Eastern Air Transport, added passengers to its mail planes, therefore holding an advantage over the passenger-only Ludington Line; the government

---

[9] Air Mail Scandal investigations led to the exposure of the Postal Service colluding with large airlines for monopolies on airmail, undercutting the small carriers whose air mail bids were much lower. *Airmail and the Evolution of the U.S. Aviation Industry in the 1920s and 1930s.* Grant Cates. Embry-Riddle Aeronautical University.

[10] The Ludingtons also used their family ties in New York and Philadelphia to arrange ticket purchasing at Pennsylvania Railroad ticket counters and allow Ludington busses to pick up railroad passengers. The brothers said they were willing to invest one million dollars in their new passenger airline venture, realizing it would need cash without the benefit of air mail contracts. The total invested, however, was "no amount approaching one-half of this sum." Telegrams of Nicholas and C. Townsend Ludington, *Time Magazine*, September 8, 1930

effectively subsidized Eastern's passenger effort with highly paid air mail contracts. Eventually, the Ludingtons sold out to Eastern in February 1933 for a reported $250,000 and pulled back into their Philadelphia area business investments.[11]

The timing was ideal for The Franklin Institute, organizing its new Hall of Aviation. It named C. Townsend Ludington, assistant director, in charge of the department. His mission: fill the Hall of Aviation with aircraft and other artifacts critical to the early development of the science and art of aviation.

On Sunday, October 8, 1933, as Philadelphians turned to page two of their morning newspaper, *The Philadelphia Inquirer*, they learned what had become of a Bergdoll race car and, more importantly, Grover's infamous Wright B Flyer. *The Inquirer* displayed photographs of two wrecks in an article headlined DELAWARE COUNTY GARAGE SHELTERS GHOSTS OF GROVER BERGDOLL'S DARING. They showed the broken-down and tattered remains of a race car and the airplane, rotting and resting among automobile debris and old tools in Erwin's machine shop at the Bergdoll farm in Broomall.

The vintage 1908 racer was almost unrecognizable.[12] It was sitting on jacks, missing its 875 x 105 Michelin rubber tires from the front wood spoke steel hubs and rims. The motor cowling, radiator, and nose cone were gone, showing large curved exhaust pipes protruding from the four in-line cylinders. One tube was either broken or badly bent. The leather cushions of the two seats were disintegrated, but the side chains from the differential countershafts to the rear wheels were intact. It was a rusting wreck of an original 2,652-pound race car.

Among the chassis of other vehicles, most notably old taxi cabs and buses, sat the Wright B, minus its motor and radiator. Nearby, wooden propellers lay on the floor, and above, the wing canvas was folded in the long angular steel trusses. The floor was scattered with tools, vehicle parts, oil stains, and broken glass. Bird droppings covered everything, including the canvas planes.

The newspaper article mistakenly attributed ownership of the machine shop to Grover, although it was owned by Erwin, who lived nearby in his farmhouse. The report and photographs contain no byline or credit, indicating that they were possibly provided to the newspaper to justify rescuing the airplane. Additionally, the article is produced in such a way as to suggest the writer did not witness the scene or have a knowledgeable source, such as Erwin, who would have explained the provenance

---

[11] In buying Ludington Airlines, Eastern Air Transport acquired Ludington's concept of a fast, no-frills shuttle service. The company later became Eastern Airlines, running a popular shuttle between New York, Philadelphia, and Washington.

[12] The race car pictured is the remains of Erwin's championship 1908 150 HP Benz, in which he won the 1911 Fairmount Park Motor Race. The article said it was one of Grover's cars, Big Red. If Erwin had been there when the photograph was taken, he would have adequately identified the car's provenance.

of the wrecks. The lack of accuracy, attribution, and specific description supports the theory that the writer described the scene from handout photographs.[13]

Only weeks away, the 30th anniversary of the Wright Brothers' first flight at Kitty Hawk, North Carolina, was approaching with a celebration event organized by the Institute. Orville Wright and Amelia Earhart were scheduled to attend. The new Franklin Institute wished to celebrate the Wright Brothers' accomplishments in a big way. One way they could do it was to obtain an original Wright B Flyer for display at the new museum, with its more prominent space. The executives at the Franklin were undoubtedly aware of the October newspaper article displaying Grover's rotting Wright B Flyer in Erwin's machine shop, as was C. Townsend Ludington and Grover's old flying companion, William Sheahan. This may have been the revelation that prompted them to act and save the airplane.

The Wright Brothers' relationship with the Franklin Institute dates back to 1914 when the museum awarded Orville Wright the Elliott Cresson Gold Medal for his and his brother's innovation in the "science and art of aviation."[14] Orville attended the ceremony but did not give a speech. In 1925 the Franklin awarded Orville the John Scott Medal. He appeared in person again at the Franklin in 1928 to honor his friend, Charles Lawrance, receiving the Cresson medal.[15]

In December 1933, Wright attended the 30th-anniversary ceremony of flight at the new Franklin Institute and was taken on a brief tour of the Aeronautical Mechanics workshop at the Camden County Vocational School. He told the instructor, Arrowsmith, and his students that he would advise them on their year-long restoration project of Bergdoll's airplane. It's presumed that the Franklin, or wealthy benefactors such as Ludington, in conjunction with his appointment as assistant director at the Franklin, may have organized funding for the restoration project, an even more difficult venture during the Depression.[16]

Wright and Earhart were the toast of the new Franklin dedication event on December 17, 1933. Wright wore gray slacks, a tie, a wingtip collar white shirt, and tails on his black coat. He did not speak at the event or dinner gathering the night

---

[13] The machine shop entrance was within a few feet of West Chester Pike and easily accessible. Erwin's farmhouse was several hundred feet farther along and set back from the road. The photographs are high quality for 1933, indicating a measure of professionalism. Conjecture suggests William Sheahan as the potential photographer who may have tipped *The Inquirer* to the wrecks and provided the photographs. At the time of this newspaper article, Grover was in Germany, arriving there in May 1933 after spending almost four years hiding at his Wynnefield mansion in Philadelphia.

[14] Wilbur Wright died from typhoid fever in 1912.

[15] Charles L. Lawrance was an engineer who designed the air-cooled Wright J-5 Whirlwind radial engines that Charles Lindbergh and Amelia Earhart used on their record-setting airplanes.

[16] Several years later, Orville Wright suggested the U.S. government singled out Bergdoll for persecution because he was rich and made fools of investigators trying to catch him. He suggested Bergdoll had suffered enough when other draft dodgers from the first war had been forgiven. His opinion was not accepted in the United States.

before at the Bellevue-Stratford Hotel.[17] Amelia Earhart Putnam also dressed for the occasion elegantly in slacks, a blouse, a white waistcoat, and heels. The two pioneer fliers are pictured beneath the airplane Earhart-Putnam flew across the Atlantic alone. She was the keynote speaker, surrounded by Franklin scientists, researchers, students, and fliers of all kinds.

While many others also gave speeches about the future of aviation, nothing was recorded as being spoken about the recent acquisition and pending restoration of Grover's Wright B.[18]

With successive and sponsored visits to Philadelphia, Orville Wright developed a close relationship with the Franklin Institute, partly because it courted his favor at a time when Wright was in a protracted dispute with the United States National Museum at the Smithsonian Institution in Washington for its misguided recognition of the early flight accomplishments of its secretary, Samuel P. Langley, over the genuine first flight accomplishments of the Wright Brothers and their first flyer, the Kitty Hawk.

In 1928, several newspapers reported that Orville's trip to Philadelphia was to survey the site of the new Franklin as a potential repository for the Kitty Hawk, which, as a result of the Smithsonian dispute, he had loaned to the Science Museum in South Kensington, London but which Wright wished to return to the United States. Wright told Philadelphia Chamber of Commerce dinner guests on May 16, 1928, that he would consider donating the Kitty Hawk to the new Franklin for a permanent display. The Franklin was delighted and further organized plans for the Hall of Aviation.

When the December 17, 1933, Franklin Institute dedication event made big news in Philadelphia and Washington, describing how the Franklin was courting Wright and the Kitty Hawk, it may have inspired the Smithsonian into action. It had a Wright Brothers display but no airplane.

Two days later, the Smithsonian announced on December 19 that it had requested Charles Lindbergh mediate its dispute with Wright to return the Kitty Hawk to the United States for installation in Washington. Following protracted negotiations with the Smithsonian for their agreement to portray the Wrights and the Kitty Hawk as the first in flight over Langley, Wright arranged in his will for his executors to send the Kitty Hawk to the Smithsonian for one dollar.[19] Perhaps as a consolation for

---

[17] Wright was notoriously shy about speeches. The *United Press* said he had a throat infection at the dedication event.

[18] Why the exciting Wright B restoration project was not mentioned publicly for the Philadelphia press at such a notable event is mysteriously unknown.

[19] The airplane, Kitty Hawk, was not returned to the United States until long after World War II, in December 1948.

losing out on the Kitty Hawk, the small metal airfoils and notebooks used in the Wrights' wind-tunnel research were donated to the Franklin Institute.[20]

On December 3, 1933, a vehicle with towing capabilities pulled up to Erwin Bergdoll's old machine shop at the Bergdoll farm. It was 20 years since Grover had dumped his flight-damaged airplane in the shop from his flatbed truck and positioned it on an extended trailer.

The contents of the building were somewhat abandoned as Erwin had long ago given up working in the shop. Several men went inside, stabilized the trailer, aired the tires, and checked the hold-down ropes and chains on the folded Wright B airplane. They pulled the bird poop-stained canvas from the ceiling trusses and tied them to the trailer. Then, they slowly and carefully removed the old Wright B through the front carriage doors and onto the road between West Chester and Philadelphia.[21] It would have been so startling that anyone passing on the trolley may have questioned if they witnessed a rescue or a theft.

Surely someone in the Bergdoll family understood what these men were doing. However, the circumstances leading up to this event were not described in family history until long after, sparingly and without specific details.[22] It's unknown who the men were or who from the Bergdoll family may have been present to approve or sign off on their airplane acquisition. Grover was still hiding in Weinsberg, Germany. If Erwin agreed to pull the old airplane out of his machine shop, he never told anyone about it. And, because he didn't own it, Erwin could not have given away his brother's airplane.

The men taking the relic considered it a rescue. While the Wright B aircraft's structure was intact, the rubberized canvas planes (wings) were described as only somewhat salvageable. The trailer and airplane were towed eastward on West Chester Pike to Philadelphia, over the Delaware River Bridge (Ben Franklin Bridge), and to the recently opened Camden County, New Jersey Vocational School in Pennsauken Township, adjacent to the Ludingtons' Camden Central Airport.[23]

The heap of the tattered canvas, wires, cables, struts and slats, twin propellers, bicycle wheels, skids, and empty space over the airplane motor mounts was delivered to the

---

[20] Orville Wright's will is dated June 21, 1937, and President Roosevelt publicized the agreement in 1943. Wright died in Dayton, Ohio, on January 30, 1948. Therefore, the Franklin already had Grover's Wright B Flyer on display when Wright decided the Smithsonian was his choice for the Kitty Hawk. His will stipulated that it forever be described as the first in flight.

[21] Similar salvage events would occur at the Bergdoll farm three decades later when others arrived to rescue Louis Bergdoll's 1910 Blériot airplane and Emma Bergdoll's broken-down Hudson limousine.

[22] In his 1960s diary-manuscript, Alfred Bergdoll wrote, without attribution, "father gave his Wright plane to the Franklin Institute." However, Alfred was unsure if it had been stored "at father's old flying field" or "Uncle Erwin's barn." Alfred didn't understand much about the disposition of Grover's Wright B.

[23] Despite chronicling nearly all other facets of the Wright B's restoration, no comments, documents, or photographs depict who removed Bergdoll's airplane or who carried it to New Jersey.

76-member Aircraft Mechanics and Aeronautics course and instructor, Arrowsmith.[24] Faintly visible on the underside of the lower wing canvas, students from the school could make out the name Bergdoll painted in large black letters from tip to tip.

The high school students had experience in aircraft woodwork and framework, cabling and spars, and engine maintenance. Still, from the Wright Brothers' detailed instructions, they would first have to determine how to properly unfold the vintage Wright B and stand it on the bicycle wheels in their classroom garage.

It was an exciting event for the boys (and some girls) in the three-year-old vocational school—nearly as exciting, according to students, as the 1933 decision by New Jersey to allow the sale of beer and other alcoholic beverages on Sunday. And the publicity surrounding the celebrated airplane being entrusted to the school students significantly boosted continued state funding for vocational schools, threatened with closure at the end of the term because of the financial constraints of the Depression.

Perhaps unrealized at the time was the school's unique relationship with Camden Central Airport, its owners, and the Franklin Institute. They were congruous, all supporting each other to restore the airplane, including the unknown expense.

Alternating between jobs, aeronautics course instructor Arrowsmith was also employed as a reserve transport pilot and ground supervisor at Camden Central Airport in 1933, at the peak of Ludington Airlines' operations.[25] He lived with his wife in a brick rowhouse complex of Ludington Apartments on Morse Street, Camden, about a half mile from the vocational school and airport. A Navy veteran from 1904–1914, he served at the war's end with the Mechanized Medical Corps of the American Expeditionary Forces from 1918–1919.

In a local newspaper, Arrowsmith said of the airplane, "It was pretty much a wreck when we got it. We had to rebuild everything, including the engine. Through the efforts of C. Townsend Ludington, the plane has been given to the [Franklin] institute."

However, Ludington passed the credit onto Sheahan but without naming him. Commenting in the *Bulletin* newspaper Ludington said he heard from a friend (Sheahan) that the plane had not been destroyed but was stored in a Bergdoll barn in Philadelphia. His comments closely resembled those of his employee, Arrowsmith. "Through this chap, who is a friend of Bergdoll's, we got in touch with him and secured the plane," Ludington said. "It was pretty much of a wreck after all these years." And then, acknowledging that it was earmarked for the (Franklin Institute) museum, Ludington proclaimed, "neither the fact that it may be the 13th plane ever

---

[24] A replacement motor was obtained from U.S. Marine Corps pilot Alfred A. Cunningham who salvaged it from the Wright B airplane he flew for the Marines. Cunningham intended to use it for a boat but sent it to Philadelphia instead.

[25] Camden Central Airport was also referred to as Ludington Airport. It was developed on land owned by C. Townsend, Nicholas Ludington, and fellow investors. Arrowsmith was one of several men who founded Whander Field in 1927, a grass strip near Leesport, Pennsylvania. He later worked as a transport pilot for aviation companies that eventually became United Airlines.

built by Orville Wright and his brother or that it once belonged to Grover Bergdoll has brought any objections from the museum people."[26]

Arrowsmith and the students were given a deadline of less than one year to prepare the Wright B for the Wright Brothers' 31st anniversary of flight, December 17, 1934.

Orville Wright would not be in Philadelphia for the big event on that upcoming date. Still, Grover's Wright B would fly again, albeit barely off the ground near Philadelphia, celebrating the incredible feat of the Wright Brothers.

Fifty-four aircraft of all shapes and sizes filled the sky that morning for Philadelphia National Aviation Day at precisely 10:35 am, the same time the Wrights made their first flight 31 years earlier. Twenty-two military airplanes flew from Mustin Field at the Philadelphia Naval Base; another 30 planes took off from private airfields; a gas airship joined them from Lakehurst, New Jersey, and a U.S. Coast Guard seaplane from Cape May, New Jersey.

While spectators could watch the airplanes from locations throughout eastern Pennsylvania and southern New Jersey, the biggest and most prestigious crowd was at Camden Central Airport. Reid got Grover's plane off the ground for just two flights before his rough second landing damaged the struts. One of the more popular and widely read newspapers, the *Philadelphia Record,* capped off its coverage with a final line.

"The plane, formerly owned by Grover C. Bergdoll, World War draft dodger, was presented by his family to the Franklin Institute, which sponsored the flight."[27]

---

[26] Sheahan would write in the museum records that Grover Bergdoll gave him the airplane "in acknowledgment sent by letter to Wm. H. Sheahan." Sheahan's statements about Grover presenting his airplane as a gift in writing would be repeated by the museum for decades but later prove to be unfounded. In 2023, the museum acknowledged it has no written documents from Bergdoll presenting the airplane as a gift to anyone.

[27] Alfred and Berta visited the Franklin Institute in 1938, where young Alfred was allowed to sit in the pilot's seat of his father's airplane to imitate Grover's 748 successful flights. He was told his father gave the airplane to the museum, and he believed it for the rest of his life. Alfred said he received a letter from the Franklin in 1968 in which it described Grover's plane as a "treasured exhibit."

CHAPTER TWENTY-FIVE

Hiding in Plain Sight

How America's most notorious war slacker escaped intense scrutiny from the German Nazis is a bewildering mystery. Throughout all the years Grover lived as an American fugitive in Germany, he had little interference from the Nazis as they rose to power. But, it was the impending control of Germany by the Nazi party that eventually caused him to leave.

Grover and Berta were afraid of staying in Germany much longer than 1938 for themselves and their five children, four of whom were born in Germany. By this time, the U.S. secretary of war, the secretary of state, and the American Legion all favored allowing Grover to return to America. They maintained that congressional interest in withdrawing his citizenship and casting him off as a man without a country would prevent him from being punished for his crimes.

In the early 1920s, while in Baden, Grover possessed his fake British passport obtained in Canada in the name of George C. Riggs. He also had a *Fremdenpass* or "stranger's passport" issued by Baden police to non-Germans living in Germany. Interchangeably, these documents allowed him to travel to neighboring countries, quickly crossing the borders in his car.[1] Additionally, Grover was issued a special American citizen passport for travel home in 1924 at the direction of Secretary of State Charles Evans Hughes. It was part of a plan through the American Legion to persuade Bergdoll to return to the United States voluntarily with Legion emissary and *Hearst's International* magazine journalist Leighton Blood. However, the second attempted kidnapping that ended with Grover killing Carl Schmidt spooked him, and Blood returned to the U.S. alone.

Nine years after he fled to Germany, Grover made his first trip home to Philadelphia. But he didn't use his special American passport. On May 28, 1929, Grover traveled to Amsterdam, Holland. His itinerary was confirmed when he bought $1,000 in American Express traveler's checks using a passport issued to Josef Amann, 38, a married "manager" from tiny Hoppetenzell in southern Baden,

---

[1] Grover's annual *Fremdenpass* was discontinued on his renewal attempt in 1938 because he could not determine when he would travel. Berta received a *Fremdenpass* upon her marriage to Grover in 1926.

Germany. From Amsterdam, he traveled to Rotterdam and boarded the S.S. *Dutchess of Bedford*, and, with a stop in Liverpool, crossed the Atlantic to Montreal, Canada, on June 8. Two days later, using cash from his traveler's checks, Grover purchased a British passport as Bennet Nash, born in Alberta on March 13, 1890, using a photograph of himself without a mustache.[2] Then, within days, he boarded the Canadian-Pacific train, traveled south to New York, and transferred to Trenton, New Jersey, and Philadelphia.

During the Bergdoll investigation lull of the early 1930s, lawyers for the Alien Property Custodian turned their attention to the infamous pot of gold. Investigators later revealed that letters were intercepted from Emma's mailbox and the Hagerstown Hotel Vivian clerk. Working secretly in a Washington office, they drew maps based on messages in the letters until they thought they might have discovered a possible location for the buried gold. Vincent Carroll and Thomas Miller from the Alien Property Custodian and Joseph McDevitt from the Philadelphia FBI went to the Maryland mountains to find it.

Carroll said, "It was a cold November day when we set out, guided by the map which we had drawn up from such phrases as 'ten miles out of Hagerstown' and '20 yards from elm.' We were dressed as hunters and carried guns, partly for protection from moonshiners who swarmed in the Maryland hills then. We tramped all day, but nothing seemed to go right, and we didn't even find a rabbit, to say nothing of the gold."

Grover was still living secretly, essentially hiding in plain sight, in the Wynnefield mansion in the early 1930s when his old flying and racing pal Charles Kraus organized an event on August 16, 1931, to celebrate the 18th anniversary of Grover's flight from Philadelphia to Atlantic City. Kraus had earned enough income in the insurance business to charter a ten-passenger plane to re-enact much of the flight when he rode with Grover in 1913 on the Wright B Flyer. Along with Kraus' wife, Madaline, four other couples flew on the plane from Camden Central Airport in New Jersey to Atlantic City and back. The press covered the anniversary event, which described the daring feat of Grover and Kraus almost two decades earlier.

Kraus said that when they flew beyond the beach and over the Atlantic, he was reminded of their malfunctioning gas gauge in 1913 when the Wright B motor quit by running out of gas, but miraculously only when they had returned to the meadows near the Atlantic City airfield. Nosing into a 35-mph wind, Grover glided the Wright B safely to the ground, and excited spectators soon surrounded them. Kraus said they might have set a record for two people in an airplane reaching

---

[2] According to Alfred, Grover said he chose Bennet Nash for one of the stars in the Ursa Major constellation (Big Dipper), Benetnasch, today's Alkaid. He also named his daughter Vega, after the brightest star in the Lyra constellation. Emma trained Grover in astrology. They both made many decisions based on the alignment of the stars.

11,000 feet that day. Kraus said he flew with Grover on 157 of the 748 flights he made without a severe accident.

Reading about Kraus' flight re-enactment in the newspapers reminded Grover that this 1913 adventure was his final flight on the Wright B when he had to ditch the plane in Hammonton, New Jersey while trying to fly home to Eagle Field. Kraus and Albert Hall trucked the aircraft back to the Broomall farm, offloading the Wright B onto a trailer in Erwin's machine shop. It was still there when Grover read the article, hidden in his Wynnefield mansion library.

Kraus mentioned that he hadn't seen or heard from his friend Grover since the war.

Grover remained hidden in his Wynnefield mansion for almost four years, sailing for Germany from New York on May 21, 1933, on the S.S. *Bremen*, booked in first class as Bennet Nash from Buffalo, and last arriving in the United States on May 15. Just weeks before his departure, however, on May 8, Grover and Erwin purchased for about $750 cash each from Philadelphia's Gomery-Schwartz Motor Company, matching black 1933 Hudson Essex-Terraplane automobiles. The car company said Berta arrived with the money to buy Grover's Terraplane while Erwin arranged to ship the car to Germany.[3] Erwin drove his Terraplane to his farm in Broomall.

Not long after Grover returned to Germany in 1933, it was clear that Prohibition would be repealed. His block of 765 stock shares in the Bergdoll Brewery was held and frozen by the Alien Property custodian.[4] Still, nothing was to stop the brewery management from organizing a crew and working to re-open when repeal was scheduled for December 1933. However, Emma declared that only Erwin would join her in the effort and that Louis and Charles were not welcome back into the new brewery venture since they had changed their names, moved from Pennsylvania, and avoided associating with the family. In conjunction with re-opening the brewery, Emma also loudly declared that she would open a Bergdoll Beer saloon in Brewerytown and run it herself, with Erwin's help.[5]

However, the saloon's batwing doors never swung. The brewery was plagued with significant re-opening problems from the spring of 1933. Its managers planned to rehabilitate the brewery equipment from 1932 through repeal when they hoped to resume operations. It was into several delays when on May 14, 1934, brewery manager Albert C. Woerwag, a Bergdoll Brewery executive for more than 41 years, walked into a ground floor brewery office closet, slipped a rope around his neck, attached it to a clothes hook, took a swing, and fired a bullet behind his right ear.

---

[3] While court records revealed a purchase agreement for a Hudson Terraplane automobile and shipping it to Germany for Grover's use, family photographs rescued by Roger Grigson show Berta Bergdoll standing proudly in front of a Terraplane somewhere in Europe. Grover probably took the pictures.
[4] In 1921, accountants valued Grover's 765 shares of Bergdoll Brewery stock at $336,000. In 1933–1934, with a dormant brewery, its value was undetermined but considerably less with the company's liquidation.
[5] Elizabeth was not included in the brewery re-opening efforts, in part because she and Albert Hall suffered substantial investment losses during the Depression.

The German-born Woerwag, who worked as the brewery secretary under the old man, Louis, Emma's husband Louis, and Emma's brother, Charles Barth, had been trying against all odds to get the brewery back online in time for repeal. It was a miserable failure.

Emma was partly to blame. Short on funds for the massive re-opening effort in 1933, the brewery sued Emma and Erwin for $100,000 to repay loans they took from the brewery in 1929 and 1931, putting up their brewery stock as surety. Emma's attorneys won an injunction claiming that the cost of equipment rehabilitation would place an undue burden on the company. It effectively stopped the brewery from reopening. She contended that the brewery managers held a secret auction of the 979 shares of brewery stock she pledged for her loan at a below-value price, $80 per share, and bought the stock themselves. She maintained that her surety stock was worth $400 per share because the brewery was reopening.[6]

The legal delays cost money and a competitive edge for the Bergdoll Brewery. It did not open. It's unknown how much investment Woerwag had in brewery stock, but he may have been facing significant losses as an executive for four decades. He was probably sure he would have been blamed for the great brewery's failure to join the other renowned Philadelphia beer makers returning to the game.

Woerwag left behind his wife and daughter. He was only 67.

Emma had been searching for a solution to resolve her debt to the brewery for about a year since it became known that repeal would become effective at the end of 1933. On March 28, 1933, Emma (or Grover) sent First Lady Eleanor Roosevelt a letter saying, "I hate to annoy you with my troubles, but I feel that only you and your husband can be my saviors, and all my hope and trust rests with you." The letter was typewritten with few errors, and since the dateline was Wynnefield and it occurred before Grover returned to Germany in May 1933, he may have written it.

Emma may have realized her debt to the Bergdoll Brewery would cause problems at re-opening time because she stated this in the letter to Mrs. Roosevelt. "About a year ago, I borrowed $70,000 from the Louis J. Bergdoll Brewery Company (of which I am the largest stock-holder) on a note and gave them most of my stock as collateral. Now that beer is back [it was coming back], they need the cash quickly and threaten to get a judgment against me."

Emma told the First Lady that she owned real estate valued at more than one million dollars but couldn't borrow against it because of her legal troubles with Grover. And then she (he) got to the point of her (his) letter. "Now, if it were possible to have my son Grover pardoned, he would immediately loan me the necessary money, and everything would be in fine shape. But, if it's not possible to do anything for my son Grover, do you think your husband could authorize the Alien Property

---

[6] For years, Emma was the largest shareholder with 1,350 of the 6,000 outstanding shares of Bergdoll Brewery stock. The value fluctuated with Prohibition.

Custodian to loan me some of Grover's cash on first mortgages?" Emma signed the letter, but the prose was all Grover's.[7]

It was just one of the many letters from the Bergdolls that the President and First Lady didn't answer.[8] The President's private secretary, Marguerite "Missy" LeHand, wrote in a note that they were afraid to answer them because it might generate publicity.

There were so many letters from the Bergdolls and others to the Roosevelts about the Bergdolls forwarded to the attorney general that his staff begged to send them to the War Department instead. One letter from a Philadelphia woman to the President's daughter pleaded to placate Emma because Louis Bergdoll had forgiven her $1,000 loan in 1892.

Even Albert Hall sent letters to the Roosevelts asking for a pardon for Grover, and he included a gift of rare foreign stamps, knowing the President was a stamp collector. Hall did this in January 1934 when, because of the Depression, he and Elizabeth lost investments and had to sell many of their assets. Hall wrote in his letter, "Grover was only a boy with too much money, wild as any boy would be with boats, automobiles, aeroplanes, stocks, bonds, and real estate without a father to guide him. He felt like the Lord himself with everybody advising and waiting on him, and what he did thousands of others have done in our time."

Hall asked the President to "give him [Grover] a break in our New Deal, as he hasn't harmed anybody or taken away anything."

For personal references, Hall dropped some big names for the President: Supreme Court Justice Owen J. Roberts of Philadelphia, New York station master for the Pennsylvania Railroad, William H. Egan, FBI Agent Charles McAvoy, and the former congressman and attorney general from Pennsylvania, A. Mitchell Palmer.

In a response from a White House aide, Hall was chastised for what appeared to be a clumsy act of bribery. The foreign stamps were returned.[9]

In February of 1934, from Germany, Grover wrote to the President asking for a pardon. He said he didn't want his children growing up in Germany "where militarism was rampant." He also sent an Easter greeting to the President. The White House staff sent the correspondence to the attorney general.[10]

In Germany, Grover applied for another American passport in October 1934 at the consulate in Stuttgart, stating that he planned to travel to the United States "when he was pardoned." He listed Alfred, Emma, Mina, and Erwin on it, submitting a photo of the kids standing in a row with the girls wearing near-matching dresses, vests, and long blonde pigtails. With a buzzcut head, seven-year-old Alfred holds

---

[7] Re-opening the brewery had been Grover's dream plan for years. He also stated that if pardoned, he would build a housing development on Eagle Field, his former airplane landing strip.

[8] Bergdoll letters in the archives of the Franklin Roosevelt Library, Hyde Park, New York.

[9] In Hall's follow-up letter after a presidential aide returned the stamps, Hall appeared shocked that someone at the White House would consider the stamp gift a bribe for a presidential favor.

[10] Berta wrote multiple letters to the Roosevelts but they came later in the 1930s and 1940s.

Emma and Berta publicly portrayed themselves and the Bergdoll children in the 1930s to gain press sympathy while lobbying President and Mrs. Roosevelt to pardon Grover. Berta was being advised by Philadelphia newspaper features writer Evelyn Shuler in return for access to good stories. Although pardon plea letters piled up in Washington, the efforts were unsuccessful. (Historical Society of Pennsylvania, *Philadelphia Record*)

seven-month-old Erwin and his fluffy diaper like a bag of flour.[11] Grover added 2 inches to his height and wrongly presented his father's death date as 1897. For identification, Grover gave his German driver's license issued in Eberbach in 1922. For his passport photograph, Grover submitted an image of himself in a dark suit, collared shirt, tie, and mustache. His hair was already receding and he was solid but not overweight. The inverted horseshoe-shaped racing car crash scar was still visible on his chin. This was the first indication in the 1930s that Grover wished to come home with or without a pardon voluntarily. The passport was refused.

Then, Berta renewed her *Fremdenpass* on December 15, 1934, and used it to secure a visa on December 21, to enter the United States with the children. She used the

---

[11] Erwin "Bubi" Bergdoll was born in Germany on March 27, 1934, when Grover and Berta lived in Weinsberg.

same photograph for the kids, as did Grover. They arrived in New York on May 2, 1935, and traveled to Philadelphia.

With her, Berta brought exciting news. She was expecting a baby. Grover remained in Germany, but the news of a new baby, Vega, born in September 1935, perhaps inspired another clandestine trip home.

On October 19, 1935, Grover sailed on the S.S. *Empress of Britain* for Quebec, Canada, under the alias Bennet Nash, arriving on October 24. He crossed the Canada–U.S. border five days later at Rouse's Point, New York, using another passport in the name of John Sparks, then laid low in Trenton, New Jersey, before going on to Philadelphia, where he could easily snuggle with his new baby, too young to accidentally reveal that daddy was home.

However, living quietly on the Wynnefield mansion's upper floors, he risked his secret being exposed by the older children, especially seven-year-old Alfred. One night in late 1935, Alfred said he was kept awake by his sisters frolicking in their bedroom. Hollering for them to be quiet, they replied in a sassy manner. Alfred then got out of bed and dropped to the second floor and his mother's bedroom to complain about his noisy sisters.

"Although the room was rather dark," he wrote, "I noticed someone with hairy hands and a large diamond ring on one of the hairy fingers occupying one of the two beds in the room, fast asleep. Mother was in the other bed. She came with me and told Emma and Mina to be quiet and go to sleep. I asked my mother who the other person was in her bedroom, and she replied, Aunt Helene. I accepted the explanation as young children always accept what their parents tell them. I puzzled a bit, trying to identify Aunt Helene with what little I had seen of the person in the bed."

Another time, Alfred was walking home from school when, from a distance, he saw a figure in an upper-floor window of their mansion. As he got closer, he kept his head down but strained his eyes to look upward, sure he was seeing a man in the window. He didn't question his mother because, at this time, Uncle Erwin was also spending a significant amount of time in the Wynnefield mansion.

School report cards presented a problem for Alfred when his parents were so secretive about their lives in Philadelphia. Of course, Grover couldn't sign them, and Berta had adopted her husband's fear of signing anything that included a date. Alfred's solution: he forged his mother's signature on his report card, only later realizing the jeopardy he would have caused if he had forged his father's name instead. He said it was not a good replication with his mother's previous marking period signature above it. When he turned in his report card, the teacher looked at him "with a puzzled expression" but said nothing.

Most people, including the children's teachers, knew life was unusual in the infamous Bergdoll household. However, the Bergdolls' nearest neighbor, Gertrude Sylk, who lived in a three-story brick colonial next door on Wynnefield Avenue, testified in court that neither she nor her husband nor their chauffeur noticed that a man was living there. The Bergdolls' advantage was a dark and gloomy 35-room stone mansion on a three-acre property surrounded by a thick cover of mature sycamore trees and a tall iron fence.

One evening, Alfred walked down the winding staircase from his third-floor bedroom and noticed that the sliding wooden door to the second-floor library next to his mother's bedroom was open when it was typically closed.

"There was a light inside," Alfred recalled many years later. "Opposite the door, next to a window with the shade drawn, sat a man at a small table with a portable typewriter on it, tapping away. He looked at me, smiled, and said, hello."

Alfred said he was "shocked by this unexpected apparition," but he said nothing and continued down the stairs. Finding his mother on the ground floor, she told him he only imagined seeing his father at the typewriter. Alfred didn't think he had that kind of imagination.

Christmas 1935 was also eventful for the children, despite Grover remaining hidden in an upstairs bedroom and the library. Uncle Erwin arrived with many gifts for them, and they received gifts from grandmother Emma and her Barth side of the family. Berta gave Alfred a special present from the upstairs Santa, "a pair of heavy old handcuffs, with two keys. Father always knew what would please children," Alfred wrote. He never determined where Grover got the handcuffs or if they had been used.

During cold weather, when Grover was hiding at Wynnefield, it was easy to remain inside and distant from the children, but when the weather turned warmer, and the mansion windows and doors were opened, it was more challenging to keep a secret. Therefore, the children were often taken to the Broomall farm in the summer, where they could play on multiple properties, including Uncle Erwin's farm.

Alfred wrote about Erwin's unusual fiancé relationship with Emma Strohm, the same Emma Strohm who sat with aged grandmother Barth and, therefore, was Erwin's first cousin. Erwin and Emma kept ducks and chickens at the farm, gifting a rooster to Alfred. Unrestrained in Emma's vintage 1907 farm kitchen, the rooster ate more dog food than grain, lost a leg in one of Emma's rat traps, and then lost its balance on the super-structure of Emma's cast iron coal and wood stove, and fell into a tall pot of boiling soup on the burner lid.

Alfred may have eaten the "chicken" soup, but he didn't find out what happened to his rooster until much later. Emma mumbled something about the rooster, but Uncle Erwin told him what really happened.

One day, Emma Strohm invited the children to her parents' house in the Overbrook community of Philadelphia for a birthday party for Erwin. Alfred says they met the Strohms at their comfortable stone colonial home lined with sycamore trees on the street. They enjoyed dinner and exploding party favors given to them by Mrs. Strohm without knowing that she was their great-aunt. Suddenly Erwin emerged from the Strohms' house, collected the children, and drove them home.

Erwin must have had a delicate conversation with Mr. Strohm about dating his daughter because she and Erwin never married, and Alfred never saw Emma Strohm at Erwin's farm again.[12]

Also, during the mid-1930s, when Grover was hiding in the Wynnefield mansion, Berta became pregnant again. Erwin spent many nights in Wynnefield during the colder months instead of at his farmhouse, where heating and living without electricity were challenging. During these years, Erwin sometimes lived in his barn with a portable stove, bed, and fuel lamps. Living at the farm required more time to travel to his favorite Brewerytown saloons for pinochle with his old neighborhood friends. Grover's Wynnefield mansion was much more comfortable, where Erwin kept his bedroom on the third floor.

When Berta miscarried the baby, her doctor was required to report the incident to local authorities after the child's remains were buried in the Bergdoll family plot in Philadelphia's Mount Vernon Cemetery. Grover immediately moved out for a few months to a hotel in Trenton, New Jersey, and Erwin stopped spending nights at Wynnefield, afraid he'd be blamed as the father. Although few outside the family knew of the pregnancy and miscarriage, no one pieced together a timeline for Berta's gestational period because no investigators asked questions about how Berta became pregnant when her husband was believed to be in Germany.

Because Emma had great difficulty keeping employees at her farm (she was cheap), Erwin became the caretaker of both properties, dynamiting dead trees and burning them with a blowtorch and using his old 1913 Oliver tractor to replace the horse in pulling the gang mowers across the massive front lawns. Emma's horse had gotten loose and was killed by a car on West Chester Pike, resulting in death for the car too. Erwin also started to repaint his old farmhouse, but after one afternoon of scraping yellow paint from the dry clapboards, he gave up, and the job was never finished. Goaded into it by the children, Erwin spent more time at his dammed-up Darby Creek swimming hole than he did working on the house.

However, he enjoyed working in his large vegetable garden. It supplied everyone in the family with potatoes, onions, corn, and squash.

Alfred said the children always liked their Uncle Erwin. He was often aligned with Charles and Louis regarding decisions about the family business and meeting reputable standards and practices. In contrast, Elizabeth, Albert Hall, Grover, and Berta often aligned in opposite ways, mainly when dealing with their mother, Emma, when she repeatedly changed her will. In one session with an estate attorney called to Emma's Broomall farm, she replaced her children in her will with her grandchildren. However, soon enough, it was changed back to her children.

---

[12] Mr. Strohm was the same Jacob Strohm, saloon owner, who wrote a letter to federal agents informing them that fugitive Grover was returning to Philadelphia in 1919–1920.

Eventually, Berta informed the children of a surprise at the Wynnefield mansion. She marched them upstairs to the second-floor library, where Grover was sitting at his typewriter and smiling back at them. They spent the entire evening with their father in the library, opening gifts he gave them. Before bedtime, however, they got a severe lecture about keeping their family secret. They must never mention to anyone that their father was in the house. He said they were not to use the term father or daddy but to call him Yankee Doodle.

From that point onward, Alfred kept secret while joining Grover in his fourth-floor studio equipped with a wood lathe, drill press, printing presses, and a portrait photography studio, complete with a wooden tripod and box camera. There was even a darkroom in the basement, helping Grover occupy his time hiding in the mansion. He kept his photographs hidden lest the secret got out.

Occasionally, Philadelphia police and federal agents would get some tip that Grover was seen around the city. They would stake out the Wynnefield mansion and the Broomall farm with detectives trying to confirm it. Alfred said his father had an expensive pair of high-quality Zeiss binoculars, and he would stand away from an upstairs window and watch the police and agents watching the house. They never tried to come in, however; they needed proof before getting a search warrant.

On one occasion, the family's secret was in danger of being revealed. Emma's housekeeper at Wynnefield may not have seen Grover in the mansion, but she knew she was washing men's clothes and hanging them to dry in the basement instead of on the outdoors clothesline or the porch with the other laundry. She was released from working at Wynnefield but continued at the Broomall farm with extra pay. She mentioned her awareness of another man, besides Erwin, living in the house many years later when Grover was no longer a fugitive.

With the housekeeper gone, Grover took over some of her duties. Alfred reported that his father became a drill sergeant to the children, ordering them to do the dishes, clean the floors, and run the vacuum cleaner in the mansion's many rooms, even requiring them to clean Uncle Erwin's and Aunt Helene's bedrooms. Grover began forcing them to do the laundry the old-fashioned way, with a washboard in a sink, instead of using one of the new electric wringer washing machines.

Without the challenges of a job, hiding in the mansion daily, Grover developed mental fatigue, which Berta described to the kids as "father's moods." Along with their cleaning duties, he forced them to eat piles of food for dinner (lunch) for their health and then resorted to hitting the children with his hand or fist.

"For the first time in our lives, we had the experience of being hit, bashed," Alfred wrote many years later. "All this was so nauseating that it made it very hard for us to eat at all. We never had any appetite."

Eventually, Grover's moods grew so bad that he began physically abusing Berta too. Alfred witnessed an event when the children were doing dishes in the kitchen.

Berta protested Grover's striking young Emma so hard with his fist that she hit the kitchen table and broke her tooth. When Berta continued protesting, Grover punched his wife in the face. Alfred watched his mother hit the floor, "weeping loudly, carrying on." Alfred said Berta's crying on these occasions would cause "Yankee Doodle" to stop harassing the kids, but only for the rest of the day.

Despite his habit of two-fisting with white wine and Pilsner beer while in Germany, Alfred said Grover was drinking "little alcohol then, not even much beer." He said Berta occasionally got him a bottle of Mount Vernon rye whiskey.

What caused his emotional instability and anger that led to physical abuse? Most likely, his out-of-control life: always hiding from the law, his lack of power and control as he was accustomed to in his early years, and his inability to manage his financial affairs or anything else as a virtual prisoner in his own home.

Alfred said the mansion doors were always locked during the day. When the children returned from school, they would stomp at the back door, waiting for their father to sneak from the central kitchen into the summer kitchen porch filled with an enormous ice box, baskets of potatoes and onions, and crouch in the shadows to open the door, always fearful federal agents would be watching from a distance.

Eventually, paranoia overcame him.

A lack of money also caused Grover's anger. He was still highly wealthy, but cash access was difficult when the federal government controlled his assets. So, Grover and Berta announced to the children one day that they were short on cash and needed to borrow money from the kids' bank accounts. Alfred said the money was taken out but never replaced.

However, being short of cash didn't stop Grover from spending as in his early days. Alfred said he "was always ordering, in mother's name, books, tools, instruments, etc."

One way Grover tried to save money was to give Alfred a haircut, cutting with scissors around the outside of a bowl placed on Alfred's head. Uncle Erwin had to recut Alfred's hair later, "normalizing" his appearance.

During these years, Grover was also a dreamer, hiding in the Wynnefield mansion successfully enough that federal agents were not coming around regularly. He wished to be able to go to his 88-acre farm across the West Chester Pike in Broomall from Emma's and Erwin's farms, but he couldn't. Grover boasted to Alfred that one day when the government returned his property rights, he would build an amusement park on the farm and turn it over to Berta's sister, Aunt Helene, and her new husband to operate.

The dreaming continued. Grover wrote a letter to the Philadelphia newspapers and had Berta sign it, claiming that if allowed to "return to the U.S.," he would re-open the Bergdoll Brewery and build new homes at Eagle Field. The proposal got many responses, mainly from people who wanted a job at the brewery.

Alfred said that during this time, his mother rarely disputed Grover and Emma's old-time traditions and mores, such as Emma lengthening the girls' dresses to their ankles and Grover demanding all the children wear old-style German boot-shoes laced up above their ankles.

"She cheerfully agreed with whatever nonsense Yankee Doodle propounded," said Alfred. He added that his mother "was very, very little help to us in coping with Yankee Doodle." [13]

Although the Wynnefield mansion was plenty large for everyone, the close-living circumstances in Grover's house first caused Erwin to leave, and then Emma, both in 1938. Alfred said that when his grandmother moved her plants from the Wynnefield greenhouse to the greenhouse at the Broomall farm, he realized something was amiss. Erwin had already moved to the farm, and Emma had become estranged from Grover and Berta. Leaving most of her furniture behind, she had her other possessions moved to the farm and then herself out of the Wynnefield house she had lived in since buying it for Grover in 1915.[14]

Alfred later determined that Emma's change of address was precipitated by growing erratic financial behavior to the point that Charles returned from California to help better organize her affairs. She was behind in property taxes, and in some cases, by multiple years. She would hire and fire attorneys when they couldn't find results fast enough. She claimed all of her jewelry had been stolen. Moving her away from the cashless Grover seemed to be the best solution.

What Alfred didn't know then was that the federal government had petitioned for the liquidation and forfeiture of Grover's frozen assets and that Berta, on April 25, 1939, petitioned the federal court to appoint a receiver for Emma's estate. Berta's petition claimed that she won a significant judgment against Emma over a $50,000 promissory note from Emma to Grover in 1919 that Grover had signed over to Berta. It also challenged a realignment of Emma's properties, some with mortgages held by Grover's long-ago friend, co-driver and co-pilot, real estate, and insurance businessman Charles Kraus. The petition charged that Emma placed her estate in trust with Charles and Erwin to avoid paying judgments she lost to Berta. As part of the petition, Berta also won a decision against Erwin for a long-ago loan Grover had made to his brother. Berta went so far as to post a Sheriff's Sale sign in front of Erwin's Broomall farm when he wouldn't pay. Alarmed by the sign, Erwin paid the $10,000 loan with interest.

Harry Weinberger was Berta's attorney. Additionally, Weinberger, maintaining that Grover lost only his rights of citizenship when he was convicted and not his citizenship, petitioned the federal government to return Grover's assets because, by law, they could not be seized when Grover was still a citizen. They included 20

---

[13] Physical abuse by Grover on his wife and children is described in Alfred's diary-manuscript in detail and length as such that he wanted it known that he and his mother and siblings suffered from it. Other family members have corroborated Alfred's recollections.

[14] The Wynnefield mansion was in Grover's name at this stage, but the Alien Property Custodian froze the title. Incidentally, Grover never re-paid his mother for the purchase price of the mansion.

real estate plots valued at $146,450, eight mortgages valued at $19,500, securities valued at $7,000, and seized cash held in the U.S. Treasury valued at $318,284.39. Not including Grover's stock in the defunct Bergdoll Brewing Company, the total came to $491,234.39.

Then, lawyers for both Emma and Charles sued Grover seeking a majority of the $491,000 impounded by the federal government. It may have been a simple legal maneuver, however. The flurry of lawsuits delayed the government's forfeiture petition.

Through Weinberger, Berta was rapidly exerting her legal rights as Grover's wife and, perhaps, looking out for the children.[15] Alfred began questioning his mother during this time, afraid he would not be allowed to remain in the United States, which he considered his home. Berta told her son that they could move to Switzerland or Norway. Alfred said she clarified that part of his father's motivation to surrender unconditionally was the "danger of general European war."

Soon after Emma and Erwin moved out of the Wynnefield mansion, Grover moved out too. He left Wynnefield one evening but soon returned, saying, "things did not go right." Alfred said his mother was appalled to see him return so soon. Berta and her sister, Helene, thought they were rid of Grover for a while. Then just as mysteriously, one evening in early autumn 1938, Alfred said Helene drove Grover's suitcases to the new 30th Street train station in Philadelphia and dropped them off. When it became dark, Grover walked out of the Wynnefield mansion too.

He would never see it again.

Grover boarded a night train for New York City but got off in Trenton in case someone got wind of his ticket purchase and was following him. He spent a week in a Trenton hotel and then traveled to New York where, as Canadian Bennet Nash, he sailed for Germany on the S.S. *Europa* on October 7. The reason for his abrupt departure after living in his Wynnefield mansion as a fugitive for three years was probably caused, in part, by the return of brother Charles to help manage Emma's significant affairs and the prospect that Charles might challenge Grover or even turn him in.[16] Instead of facing his brother again, Grover opted to run back to Germany.

Berta and the children remained in Philadelphia until she organized a plan to gain permanent residency in the United States. Since their visitor visas were expiring, Berta hired an immigration attorney for advice. They decided she and the children would sail to Cuba and apply for quota visas as Germans wishing to go to the United States and receive rapid approval. Grover's sister, Elizabeth Hall, went along to help

---

[15] In a countersuit, Emma claimed that she loaned or provided Berta with $600,000 worth of property and stock, which Berta refused to return, including the value of the Wynnefield mansion and the valuable Somerset, Maryland property near Washington, D.C. The $600,000 was approximately the value of Grover's estate.

[16] Charles Bergdoll-Brawn reportedly returned to Philadelphia from California around 1938 to help manage Emma's financial affairs after learning that Emma signed over to Grover and Berta the Somerset, Maryland property. However, Charles claimed he returned home only once, for Emma's funeral.

with the children. However, upon arriving in Havana in October 1938, they were told the quota was filled until the spring of 1939. Many other Germans were vying for quota visas to escape Germany before the war. It's clear that Grover, in Europe, was fully aware of Berta's Cuba travel itinerary because he sent several postcards to her and the children in Cuba from Germany, Switzerland, and the Netherlands.[17]

To Alfred: "I would come down too, but mother would have to ask the Cuban government if they would let me in. Give my greetings to Bubi. Vater."

"I hope you get out in the sun lots so that you will soon look like an Indian. Tell mother to get lots of sun too. With love, Yankee."

To Mina from Switzerland: "Keep in the sun as much as you can stand in bathing suits, and mother too. It will do you all lots of good. Don't let this big lion scare you. Yankee Doodle."

To Berta at the Hotel Plaza, Havana from Stein am Rhein, Switzerland, on the Bodensee: "Dearest Berta, this is the finest little village I ever saw! The land-Jagers [sausages] are just almost three times as big as anywhere else."

To Bubi from Holland: "This will be my last card from Holland. I sent mother four big boxes of all kinds of statues, including your old friend Napolean. Lots of love, Yankee."

Instead of waiting several months for quota visas in Cuba or soaking in the sun as Grover suggested, Berta decided to travel again, receiving transit visas from Cuba to New York and Germany, with enough time for a brief stopover in Philadelphia.

The whole time, traveling on taxis and trains and ships between Philadelphia, New York, Havana, back to New York and Philadelphia, then to New York again and Southampton, and Bremerhaven, Berta was tagged along by five children aged three to 11.

What would she have been thinking, lying awake at night while the exhausted children slept? The Cuba trip was ill-advised and a waste of time and money. What would she do next?

They arrived in Cuxhaven, Germany, on the North Sea, on December 15, 1938, perhaps meeting Grover from the Netherlands, and traveled south to Weinsberg to reunite with Berta's parents.

Lengthy discussions between Berta and Grover and the Francks indeed followed. How could they remain in Germany when war was imminent? There was no more room at the Francks' modest apartment home for more children. The Francks were growing older. The children needed schooling. And Grover was running out of cash, despite Emma constantly refueling his purse.

---

[17] The postcards sent to Berta and the children from Europe to Cuba were available from the Chester County Historical Society in West Chester, Pennsylvania. They were part of the large stash of papers, photographs, and documents rescued from the Bergdoll's Harmony Hill Farm garage by Roger Grigson.

Grover's behavior during this last period of living with Berta's parents was more erratic. One day, Alfred recalled, Grover was raving mad about something, and Herr Franck threatened to call the Gestapo to come to their apartment. Berta had to step in and diffuse the tension. Another time, Grover was waving one of his pistols, and again, Berta calmed things before the Gestapo, or local police had to be called.

Grover would also take the children on long walks with him to escape the confines of the Franck apartment. Grover would often get tipsy in his favorite restaurant from Pilsner beer and brandy, making loud, offensive remarks about the Nazis. Alfred said that on a few occasions, the other customers would "raise their eyebrows" but "were too polite to say anything."

Berta told the children Grover was acting out because he was returning to the United States soon "to face the music."

On March 20, 1939, Grover personally visited the American consul in Stuttgart, Samuel W. Honaker. He said he wanted to obtain a passport, book passage on a ship to New York, and voluntarily surrender, preferably to FBI Special Agent Joseph McDevitt in Philadelphia. He also told Honaker that if he did not find cooperation, he would try to enter the United States "in an irregular manner," provided he found assurance that he would not be prosecuted and deported for an illegal entry.[18]

Grover declared he would surrender when Berta and the kids settled in Philadelphia. He signed the statement for the consul, who immediately transmitted the document to the Department of State in Washington.

Meanwhile, the permanent immigrant visa applications processed for Berta and the children in Cuba were transferred to Germany and issued for travel to the United States in April 1939. As part of her application, Berta had to prove that she had an income to provide for her German children moving to permanent residency in Philadelphia. Based on her 1937 tax documents, she could show an income of $45,710.56 from investments and securities in her name. Income from Grover was not included. The U.S. Alien Property Custodian still held his assets.

Grover accompanied Berta and the children to Hamburg by train. Alfred recalled seeing German soldiers board their train and, watching them arrange their equipment, Grover quipped, "Soon, they'll all be dead." Alfred said that when he was in Germany, Grover "hated the Nazis, but when elsewhere, he often had a favorable opinion of them."[19]

Along with the children, Berta boarded the M.S. *St. Louis* on April 6, 1939, and made their final arrival in New York on the 10th. When they returned to Wynnefield

---

[18] "Irregular manner" meant that Grover would again travel to North America on one of his illegal passports and cross the border from Canada.

[19] Grover obtained a Hitler Youth knife which he gave to his son, Erwin, ignorantly telling his boy in Nazi parlance of the 1930s, "Now you can use this to kill Jews."

in Philadelphia, the press surrounded the mansion, taking photographs of the family eating cold cuts, boiled eggs, and potato salad in the kitchen pantry. Berta told reporters that Grover would be leaving Europe soon. She didn't say anything about how he was nearly out of money.

The press interviewed Emma for her reaction to the news that Grover had agreed to come home. She got a bit carried away and made a grave admission. "The last time I have seen him was when the last child was born." Startled by the timeline, a reporter shot back. "Was Grover home then?"

"Of course, he was here," replied Emma. "It was when Vega was born. He stayed at 52nd and Wynnefield." Realizing she had mistakenly revealed damaging information, Emma refused to discuss anything further with the reporters.

Berta had to refute her mother-in-law's stupid comments with lies to the press. "He wasn't here when Vega was born. He has never seen his youngest child. Do you think he would be so stupid as to try to sneak into this country?" Berta suggested that Emma imagined things. And, for the first time, she wished they could finally move out of the dark, dingy, oversized Wynnefield mansion for a modern house with more privacy.

CHAPTER TWENTY-SIX

Senate Investigation

Washington, D.C., May 24, 1939[1]

Grover's long-trusted Civil Rights Attorney Harry Weinberger traveled to Washington on May 24, 1939, to inform the Senate Military Affairs Committee in a hearing at the U.S. Capitol that Grover was aboard a fast and luxurious German ocean liner and headed home to the United States to surrender.

When the words came out of Weinberger's mouth, Military Intelligence officers, Immigration, the Coast Guard, and the War and State Departments (and press) began scrambling to grab Bergdoll before he was dropped at the pier in New York.

Weinberger brought along Berta and Emma, who testified briefly before the committee of senators. Elizabeth Hall and only two children, Emma and Bubi (Erwin), were also there. They sat quietly on leather-bound wooden chairs before a locked-glass door cabinet in the back of the Senate hearing room next to a white porcelain lavatory with hand towels and a soap holder. Elizabeth and Berta wore stylish heeled shoes, dress, and skirt, and Berta, with her pigtails circling her ears, wearing a polka dot headband and silk lace blouse beneath a dark sweater, sat nearly touching her mother-in-law, Emma, wrapped in heavy wool. For jewelry, Berta displayed her customary German gold band engagement ring, sizeable diamond wedding ring, a simple gold bracelet, a small face gold band watch, and a small gold and diamond encrusted turtle brooch on her blouse.

The kids' feet dangled from the chairs. They were covered above their ankles with dark leather lace-up boot-shoes, required by Grover.

The Senate was considering a House of Representatives resolution, already passed, that was aimed at Grover and would prevent him from entering the country, despite being a citizen of the United States. Weinberger said he didn't even bother objecting to the measure in the House because he thought such an unconstitutional bill didn't have a chance. He was dead wrong.

---

[1] Information compiled by stenographers in the Senate hearings, and Attorney Harry Weinberger's papers were beneficial here. Alfred's recollections of the Senate hearings and photographs of the family in the U.S. Capitol provided a description. The hearing transcript provided dialogue, some of which I've used in this chapter.

The timing for a trip to Washington from Philadelphia could have been better. Weinberger and the Bergdolls needed to be in New York the following day, May 25, to meet Grover at the ship's pier in Brooklyn. They planned to escort him to Governors Island to surrender to the Army Eastern Division Disciplinary Barracks commander, Colonel Converse Lewis. From Weinberger's revelation that Grover would arrive "tomorrow," it didn't take long for the Military Intelligence Division of the Army to receive orders to get into the Atlantic Ocean and intercept the ship before it docked. They wanted Grover off the ship before it came into sight of the Statue of Liberty.

The effort to ban Grover from returning home began in the House of Representatives. Initially, Berta had tipped them off, based on one- or two-sentence postcard missives from Grover (signed Yankee Doodle), that he would arrive in the spring. Then, Berta received a coded telegram from Grover describing the date and vessel he would sail for the United States.[2] She told the press he was coming home and would not use an alias.[3]

The bill's sponsor, Republican Congressman Forest A. Harness of Indiana, suspected he knew why Grover wanted to come home. Another war was coming to Germany.

Congressman Harness introduced House Resolution #6035, which unanimously passed on May 15, 1939. Its title was *Exclusion from the United States of persons who have been convicted of desertion from the military or naval forces of the United States during the time of war.* When it got to the Senate, it was described as a bill saying that any person convicted of desertion in time of war "is giving up all rights and privileges of American citizenship and will not be readmitted to the U.S., either temporarily or permanently, for any purpose."

With the precise wording of the bill, it immediately ran into difficulties getting passed in the Senate. Revoking one's rights and privileges and revoking citizenship are two different concepts. In their cramped corner of the Senate hearing room, the Bergdolls waited while Weinberger and the senators debated the merits of the unusual bill.

Weinberger maintained the Harness Bill was ex post facto, discriminatory, and unconstitutional, arguments he didn't make during House passage because he thought the congressmen would have seen the wisdom in declining an unconstitutional bill. When he heard the bill's language was revised to apply only to Grover, he requested the hearing before the Senate.

Weinberger correctly asserted that the bill "is directed against only one man, 20 years after the offense was committed (ex post facto), who is returning home to go

---

[2] The postcards were saved. The telegrams were not.

[3] This statement turned out to be untrue. Grover had to use an alias just to get on board the vessel without being detained.

On May 24, 1939, as Grover was sailing to the United States, Berta, Emma, and the children testified before the U.S. Senate to block a bill to strip Grover's citizenship. Sitting left to right, in the U.S. Capitol, Elizabeth Bergdoll Hall, Emma Bergdoll, Erwin "Bubi" Bergdoll, Berta, Emma, senators, and Bergdoll's lawyers, Harry and Harold Weinberger. (Historical Society of Pennsylvania, *Philadelphia Record*)

to prison because he desires that his children be brought up under a free government and attend our schools."

Weinberger reminded the senators in 1939 of Grover's aviation and racing prowess 25 years earlier because some debated the bill without fully understanding who he was. Weinberger's explanation that Grover made the first flight from Philadelphia to Atlantic City and offered his aviation expertise to the Army was a revelation to the senators, who were woefully unaware of Grover's dramatic and heroic life before desertion.

"This offer [to join the Aviation Corps] was refused because of the animosity of one man against him," Weinberger declared without mentioning the name of *Philadelphia Record* editor and Draft Board Secretary John Dwyer. He reminded the senators that Dwyer and the draft board chairman went beyond their duties of signing draftees with sensational articles in Dwyer's newspaper and by proclaiming that Grover's offer to return and enter the Army Aviation Corps would be refused.

Even if Grover returned, Dwyer said, he would be jailed instead of allowed to join.[4] He didn't mention that people were suggesting Grover would be shot.

With Berta, Elizabeth, and Emma listening, Weinberger dredged up the old West Philadelphia neighborhood story that when Dwyer's boys damaged Grover's cherry tree, Grover spanked them. Dwyer's revenge, Weinberger claimed, was exacted with the draft.[5]

Weinberger reminded the senators that more than 337,000 men deserted from the Army during the war. At the same time, hundreds of thousands more didn't even register, were classified as delinquent, and their legal cases were handled in the civil courts, not by a court martial. Weinberger's refrain was, "Why single out one man, after 20 years, for additional punishment?"

He presented evidence that even the American Legion, the secretary of war, and the secretary of state were against the bill and wanted Bergdoll to be able to return to take his punishment. He presented newspaper editorials that the legislation "smacks of dictatorship. The House erred in passing the bill, and the Senate should kill it."

Lawyers for the State Department and the attorney general suggested that Bergdoll lost his rights to citizenship with his 1920 conviction but that revoking his citizenship was an issue for the courts, not Congress. Furthermore, Weinberger contended that Secretary of State Charles Evans Hughes had recognized Grover's citizenship when he issued Bergdoll a passport in 1924.[6] Somewhat confused, some of the senators asked, what was the difference between rights of citizenship and citizenship? Weren't they the same thing?

"No," said Weinberger. He reached far back into case law from the Civil War, citing how the loss of the rights of citizenship was similar to a felony conviction where one loses the right to vote and hold public office but not citizenship. Civil War soldiers who ran to Canada, he said, were later allowed to return, serve their sentences, and keep their citizenship. Then Weinberger reached back even further, explaining to the senators that this was the very reason for the War of 1812, the right of an American's voluntary act of expatriation, not something the Congress could impose on a citizen.

---

[4] Dwyer's job was to process registrations and turn them over to the Army adjutant general of Pennsylvania. As a civilian board member, he had no authority to decide about jailing or prosecuting draft dodgers. The civilian draft boards of World War I were so rife with political intervention and mismanagement, World War II significantly revised the draft process.

[5] Testimony indicates that Dwyer was aware of the spanking allegation. He never denied the incident.

[6] Grover's 1924 American passport and a matching passport for Ike Stecher were issued blank with instructions for the American consul in Germany to fill in the blanks when Grover and Stecher prepared to leave Germany. This passport was the basis for attorney Weinberger's long legal argument that Grover never lost his American citizenship.

In a somewhat unusual gesture, the senators called Congressman Harness to testify. He said he wanted the bill to assure that Bergdoll would not enter the country through Canada, Mexico, or Ellis Island in New York and, therefore, could not be deported.

Congressman Harness made a long speech to the senators about why he drafted the bill aimed only at Bergdoll. A war veteran, Harness was a former Indiana state commander of the American Legion and a special prosecutor who went after Chicago utility magnate Samuel Insull during the Depression for the collapse of Insull's holding company wiping out the investments of hundreds of thousands of Americans. When Insull fled to France, Greece, and Turkey to avoid prosecution, Harness was sent to get him, much like special agents were sent to get Bergdoll. But when prosecuted by Harness, Insull was acquitted.

Weinberger hinted that Harness was trying to restore his prosecutorial failure by going after Bergdoll. Harness denied it, calling Bergdoll an "arch-traitor" and suggesting that Berta and the children had no right to apply for citizenship.[7]

Harness brought former Army Military Intelligence Officer Walter Lehmann from his Virginia tourist camp to Washington to testify before the House committee that passed the bill about Bergdoll's actions in Germany. For the senators, Harness quoted Lehmann quoting Bergdoll as saying, "To hell with President Wilson and the United States. I never want to see that country again."

Weinberger claimed Bergdoll never made the statement but, instead, that it came from author Edward Everett Hale's 1863 magazine article, *The Man without a Country*, where fictional Union Army Lt. Philip Nolan renounces his country and is sentenced to spending the rest of his life at sea by saying, "Damn the United States; I wish to never hear about the United States again."

Harness didn't contest Weinberger's assertion because Lehman's testimony was based on his 20-year-old recollection of a newspaper article which may not have been accurate. Harness then looked toward Berta and the children and said that while he sympathized with them, they should not be allowed to enter the United States just because they were afraid of the impending war in Germany.

Harness reminded the senators of Bergdoll's pro-German sympathies, desertion, taunting postcards, and letters, "the cock and bull story about gold buried in Maryland," and his lies about bribery among Army officials which led to lengthy embarrassing investigations, prosecutions, and the end of several officers' careers. He described Bergdoll as "gloating and gangster-like" and suggested he apply for German citizenship.

Then, in a startling comment by a sitting U.S. congressman who already knew about the multitude of Nazi atrocities leading up to 1939, Harness said, "as loathsome and revolting as are the Gestapo methods of Hitler, this might be an occasion where we could almost view them with tolerance."[8]

---

[7] Berta and the children's effort to become permanent citizens was part of the reason Grover was returning to the United States.

[8] This was 1939. A U.S. congressman would unlikely have made the same comment five years later.

Berta and Emma made a few comments, with the children beside them but remaining silent. Berta's English was fractured, and she confused her words, but the senators understood that she wanted her husband to come home and face his punishment.

> Weinberger: "Tell us why Grover wants to come back to this country."
> Berta: "I can tell you he does not want to come back because over there in Germany, he would have to be afraid he have to fight, if there is war, he would not have to fight, he is not a German citizen; he wants to come back because he wants to raise his children like he was raised, happy."[9]
> Weinberger: "Is that the only reason?"
> Berta: "Yes."
> Weinberger: "And he is not coming back because of the Alien Property Custodian having held his money since 1919?"
> Berta: "Absolutely not."
> Weinberger: "You have sufficient means to support yourself and your children?"
> Berta: "Just now, it is as it goes along."

In his closing remarks, Weinberger was not entirely truthful with the senators. He claimed he knew nothing about Grover getting out of jail to search for his gold in Maryland when he did know. Weinberger may have passed the responsibility of Grover's release to attorneys Gibboney, Ansell, and Bailey. Still, over the years, he admitted that he knew Grover was getting out of jail in 1920 to search for gold.

Weinberger cited the overriding questions for the senators to consider before advancing the Harness Bill for votes. Has Congress the power to convert an American-born citizen into an alien for any offense against the United States? And, has Congress enacted any laws depriving an American-born citizen guilty of desertion in time of war, not only of his rights of citizenship but also of his citizenship, thus making him an alien?

Even President Roosevelt was asked what he would do if the Harness Bill were passed in the Senate. Would he veto it? The President did not reply. The Senate did not advance the bill. It failed.

---

[9] Happy may be an understatement. Alfred wrote that he and his siblings were unhappy when Grover was around. "Our life had always been joyous, happy, and carefree, no matter where we were, so long as father was not present."

CHAPTER TWENTY-SEVEN

Surrender

Lower Bay–New York Harbor, May 25, 1939[1]

Two U.S. Army military intelligence officers boarded the 110-foot Coast Guard cutter *Hudson* at Governors Island in New York Harbor on May 25, 1939, and headed south through the Narrows and into the Lower Bay, where they were joined by a patrol boat from the Coast Guard Station Sandy Hook, New Jersey. Side by side, the vessels headed eastward to find a ship from Europe.

Their orders that afternoon in May were to intercept the S.S. *Bremen*. This German twin-funnel steam turbine-powered high-speed ocean liner had blitzed across the Atlantic in five days from Bremerhaven, Germany, making for its pier at the Nord Deutscher Line at 58th Street in Brooklyn. Among the first-class passengers was Bennet Nash, 48, an automobile agent with a British passport from Montreal, but originally from a tiny dot on the map in western Canada: Castor, Alberta, halfway between Edmonton and Calgary. He made the voyage quietly.

A short, squat man with a pudgy face, long round-tipped nose, tiny mustache, bald spot, and a distinctive scar on his chin, Nash was impeccably dressed each day in a dark three-piece suit with a striped tie, a white collared shirt, and heavy black boot-shoes, polished to a shine by the first-class stewards. He was late on the passenger list of the Bremen, his name third from last on a supplementary list. His steward said he spoke to him in German but in English to the ship's officers. Nash spent most of the five-day crossing in his cabin, #270 on the B Deck, designed for two people, at the bar drinking whiskey neat or the first-class reading room with a small black hardcover book up to his face. The book was about engineering and logarithmic tables.

On one of his five days at sea, reportedly on May 24, Bennet Nash stood at the deck railing of the ship, tore apart his passport, and threw it into the Atlantic.

With that simple act, he returned to being Grover Cleveland Bergdoll.

---

[1] Government documents produced for Grover's second court-martial trial at Governors Island helped write this chapter. Also included in this stash of documents from the National Archives in St. Louis are copies of Grover's and Berta's *Fremdenpasses*.

In Washington, as Grover was tossing away his past life, Weinberger told the senators he had arranged for Grover to surrender at Governors Island and take his punishment, whatever it would be. Despite the threat of war by Germany, Weinberger insisted Grover was coming home so his wife and children could become permanent American citizens and return to school in Philadelphia.

"He is also coming back because he wants to see his mother, who is almost 80," Weinberger told the senators in a softening gesture.

That he made the *Bremen* crossing was almost a miracle. Grover relied heavily on astrology and had turned away from the Atlantic crossing earlier that month of May 1939 because his stars didn't quite line up. He wrote about it in a letter to Berta while laying low in Rotterdam.[2]

> Café Restaurant Modern
> May 16, 1939
> Rotterdam, Holland
> Dearest, sweetest, loveliest Berta,
>   I was just about to get on board the steamer "Statendam" for New York this evening between 8 and 10 pm but bought a *New York Herald-Tribune* at 7:30 pm when I read that the House passed the bill against letting me enter, so I did not get on the ship but will go back to Bremen in the morning so that I can telegraph you and Weinberger about what to do.
>   If I had not bought that paper, I would have been on the ship already, so you see what funny things happen in life. It was the first thing I saw, although it was only a small article on the front page, so I thought that is a sign I should stay here and see first what I should do. You see what that bad Saturn can do; he is troubling me something awful at present, and I don't know what the devil to do. You know I wrote several times in the last few weeks that he is in opposition to my sun at present, and he sure is a big bum!
>   Stay there no matter what happens! I told you that several weeks ago, so obey me and do nothing until I write you. This is in case I cannot come over, but if you wire me to come and Weinberger also says so, then I come on the Bremen, which sails on 20th May and gets there on May 27th.
>   So, don't worry. I have some more good ideas which I can not write you about. But I can't put them into practice as long as this bad Saturn is sitting on me. So, lots and lots and lots and lots and a whole lot more love from your own truest and most loving. Be hopeful, and don't worry at all, all will be for the best.
>   Grover.

Late on May 24, Weinberger left the Senate hearing bound for New York to prepare for Grover's arrival. The Bergdolls traveled on the same train as Weinberger but got off in Philadelphia. There, Berta and Elizabeth Hall rested for the night, then got on another train, traveling with only Bubi the following morning, and, rejoining Weinberger in New York, positioned themselves at the Brooklyn pier to await the *Bremen*. Berta carried a wrapped package for Grover, which was later revealed to contain cigars, aspirin, and plugs of Star chewing tobacco.

---

[2] Grover's handwritten letters to Berta at this time were rescued from the Bergdolls' Harmony Hill Farm garage by their neighbor, Roger Grigson, and later given to the Chester County Historical Society, West Chester, Pennsylvania.

They waited. It was the same pier where four years earlier, in 1935, anti-German demonstrators tore the Nazi flag from a ship and threw it overboard. As a result, Adolf Hitler made the Nazi flag equal in status to that of the German Weimar Republic flag, increasing penalties for its desecration.[3]

Somewhere in the Atlantic, as the *Bremen* approached New York, commodore Adolf Ahrens received a radio message that his vessel would be stopped at sea and boarded by the U.S. Coast Guard, Immigration, and Army Military Intelligence. They were searching for and would remove passenger Bergdoll.

The only problem was that the Bremen didn't have a passenger named Bergdoll on its manifest. However, the ship's master was informed that Bergdoll was traveling as Bennet Nash and to keep this news to himself.

Newspaper reporters, who suspected Grover might be on the *Bremen* based on Weinberger's comments in the Senate hearing, sent a message to the approaching ship asking for Grover Bergdoll to be paged on the ship's public address system. When the paging ended, the reporters were told that there was no Bergdoll on board the vessel but that a Mr. Nash would speak for him. Mr. Nash did not come to the radio room to take the call. It was all anyone needed to determine that Grover Bergdoll was arriving as Bennet Nash.

In the midafternoon, the magnificent SS *Bremen* approached New York. Grover had made enough Atlantic crossings to know that ships reduce speed to take on harbor pilots when approaching a port. However, when the *Bremen* stopped short of New York's Lower Bay at the command of the Coast Guard, Grover must have known his time was up. Instead of remaining in the cabin assigned to Bennet Nash and preparing to disembark, he took an engineering book into the cabin-class reading room, settled into a comfortable chair, and buried his face in the pages.

With the bridge pilot's engine order telegraph pulled back to all-stop and extending a long wooden gangway to the cutter below, the *Bremen* sat idle just outside the Lower Bay as military intelligence officers Colonel Frank K. Ross and Captain Edward F. Glavin pulled themselves upward toward the *Bremen* and on board.[4] They were followed by a harbor pilot and about a dozen reporters and photographers. They immediately began a search for Bergdoll. Ross was distinctive and disarming for a military detective. Instead of a uniform, he wore a grey pinstripe suit, white collared

---

[3] The SS *Bremen* once held the Atlantic speed record, and late in 1939, infamously sped from New York back to Europe to avoid being trapped or captured, or torpedoed by British Naval vessels in the early months of World War II. It found a safe port in Russia, but the luxury liner was later burned and scrapped.

[4] The U.S. Coast Guard cutter *Hudson* (WYT-87) was a Calumet class tug boat. It was routinely used for customs boarding operations, ice breaking, and general tug navigation in and around New York Harbor. Just a month before it picked up Bergdoll, the Hudson ferried reporters to meet Col. Charles Lindbergh and actress Barbara Hutton arriving on the SS *Aquitania*.

shirt, striped tie, and a black-banded fedora. He carried a long black wooden cane with a rubber tip in his right hand.[5]

The *Bremen* crew joined in the search by passing around photographs of Grover that were several years old. They were also aware that Grover was traveling as Bennet Nash. But, since he could not be found in the long lines of passport inspections, it took Ross and Glavin half an hour to find their man on the immense ocean liner.

Cutting through the cabin-class reading room with its elegant stuffed chairs and divans, a junior officer of the ship approached a man reading a black hardcover book, holding it close to his face.

"Are you Grover Bergdoll," he asked, sensing a likeness between the man and the photographs.

The man behind the book looked up and smiled.

"Yes, that's my name," he replied.

"Please come with me," the junior officer requested.

Grover followed the man into the passageway and onto the outer deck, where Colonel Ross and Captain Glavin cordially met and placed him under arrest. The military men first searched Grover and found a mother lode, confirming his identity through additional photographs and papers in his pockets. Grover was carrying securities valued at $150,000, a $2,100 traveler's check payable to Berta Bergdoll, and a handful of Dutch gold coins.[6] There was no doubt that Bennet Nash was Grover Bergdoll. Then, Ross and Glavin consented to a brief intervention by a small press gaggle brought along with them on the patrol boat.

The newspaper scribblers and photographers got about three minutes with Bergdoll in the *Bremen* kindergarten surrounded by its miniature furniture, colorful books, rocking racehorse, tricycle, and wheeled dog and bear. It was just time enough for a few questions for the always-eager-to-answer Bergdoll.

Grover spoke in what a steward described as a southern German accent. He said he was not coming home because of the impending war. Poland had just confirmed its refusal to capitulate to Germany's annexation of Danzig and the Polish Corridor. Finland, Norway, and Sweden rejected Germany's nonaggression pact. Grover said he was not afraid of going into the German Army. He was only a conscientious objector, not a deserter. Despite having lived secretly in Philadelphia for seven of his 19 years in self-imposed exile, Grover claimed he was "homesick." He wanted to be with Berta and the kids as they progressed through immigration. He also wanted the kids to return to school in Philadelphia.

---

[5] Col. Frank K. Ross had a long Army career despite an infirmity in his leg that prevented him from fighting in the war in 1918. In May 1939 he was assistant chief of staff for Military Intelligence in the Army's Second Corps Area, headquartered at Governors Island.

[6] The Dutch guilder was worth about $8. Grover's assets were turned over to Berta upon her first visit to see him at Governors Island.

In what appeared to be a coordinated response, Grover's words on the *Bremen* matched those of Weinberger at the Senate hearing.

"How much do you weigh now?" one reporter shouted. This got Grover's attention as he laughed, waved his book, and replied, "I don't know now, but I am much stouter than I was when I went away." He also used his book to shield his face from the photographers' flash, but it didn't do much good.

Grover perked up and offered half a rebuttal when asked about rumors that he had lived in Philadelphia for years of his exile. "That's not so. I have never come back since…" He didn't finish his response.

Ross and Glavin hustled Grover to the gangway. Ross, at 50, was still a slim and young-looking man who, relying on his cane, walked with an uneven gait from what he described as a "crippled leg" on his 1917 draft registration card. He served anyway, rising to detective and assistant chief of staff. Finally, someone in Army Military Intelligence, watching and tracking Bergdoll for 19 years, had captured its number one fugitive slacker.

Nineteen years after Grover's release from Governors Island to search for gold, a new commander of the island military installation in New York Harbor awaited America's number one slacker. Grover was hustled aboard the Coast Guard tug and, at full speed, whisked back through the Narrows into the Upper Bay and deposited at the wharf on Governors Island.

After Grover was removed from the ship, the *Bremen* was allowed to continue into New York's Upper Bay and its pier in Brooklyn. In the ship's passenger manifest, a clerk wrote in long hand, "Grover Cleveland Bergdoll, Alias" above the typewritten name of the third from the last passenger to board the ship, Bennet Nash.

Although he paid for his passage, Grover got into the United States for free. The port head tax for Bennet Nash was not collected. The Treasury confiscated the contents of his baggage: suits and shoes, shirts and ties, cameras, lenses, meters, film, and binoculars, valued at DM1,640.

When Philadelphia reporters heard the news, they called Emma at her Broomall mansion to get her reaction. The old woman cried, but, at her age, she would not go to New York to see her son

"I was hoping he would call me," she said.

While the surrender was flawless, there was confusion among the federal agencies about who would get him. Immigration believed he would land at the *Bremen*'s pier and be taken to Ellis Island for impoundment until his right to return to the United States was determined in Washington. The War Department, through the Army's Military Intelligence Division, trumped the Department of Labor (Immigration), Justice, the FBI, and everyone who wanted a piece of Bergdoll.

Handcuffed to Col. Ross when he got off the tug at Governors Island, as in 1920, Grover met his Army prosecutor, Major Archer L. Lerch, on the fort's parade ground,

On May 25, 1939, an older and heavier Grover was arrested by federal agents before his ship, the *Bremen*, arrived in New York City. It was such a high-profile spectacle; the press accompanied the Coast Guard to capture him. One photograph shows Grover stepping onto the gangway. Military agents surround him. A tall man is obscured behind Grover, but his hat is visible. It's that of a commodore, perhaps the *Bremen*'s master, Adolf Ahrens. (Historical Society of Pennsylvania/*Philadelphia Record*, Temple University Urban Archives)

Marched off to Castle Williams on the island's northwest corner, Grover was jailed with two men serving sentences for mutiny at Fort Sam Houston in Texas. Then he was locked away on the upper floors of the jail complex, in the same cell he occupied in 1920.

The next day at Governors Island, Grover's fingerprints were stained with ink and copied onto two large sheets of identification paper for the first time in his criminal life. They displayed thick and wide prints, all 10 digits. Berta and Weinberger could see Grover when they returned to Governors Island. It was a departure from Army regulations, but even the Army realized they had a notable prisoner. In their brief meeting, under heavily armed guard, Grover pulled off his five-carat diamond ring and gave it to Berta.

The Army grabbed Grover at the first opportunity instead of waiting for immigration because it opposed the legislation being debated in the Senate to ban Bergdoll from the United States. It sent Major General Allen W. Gullion of the Judge Advocate General's Department to explain why. When Grover escaped, he still had four years and 10 months to serve on his 1920 sentence for desertion. The War Department wanted to charge him with escape, conspiracy to escape, and a second desertion. It feared that the statute of limitations might run for additional charges. The War Department was able to locate witnesses, General Gullion said to the Senate committee, and with the extra charges, Grover faced 10 years and 10 months in prison.[7]

---

[7] Even the War Department conceded that if Grover had not escaped in 1920 and was credited with good behavior, his total post-conviction time in prison could have been reduced to as little as nine months!

CHAPTER TWENTY-EIGHT

BenetNasch

Governors Island, New York, September 1939[1]

Some of the most sensational testimony at Grover's escape, desertion, and conspiracy trial in September 1939 was the briefest statement, and it came from his 10-year-old daughter, Emma.

In a new cotton dress, long blonde pigtails, and laced-up boot-shoes, she sat in a simple brown wooden chair on a slightly elevated platform facing 13 officers in Army uniforms sitting 25 feet away behind a row of tables, their backs to a wall. Above them, a glossy white wooden basketball backboard and goal hung bolted close to the wall. This trial, held in the same building on Governors Island as it was in 1920, was in the gymnasium of the base YMCA.

"It was a secret. We weren't to tell anybody about Daddy living at our house. And we never did," Emma answered Harry Weinberger's questions before the row of judge advocates. She told how she, Alfred, Mina, and little Bubi arrived with their mother in Philadelphia from Germany about four years earlier, enrolled in the Mann school in their Wynnefield neighborhood, and that their father arrived sometime later, mysteriously appearing one evening in their mansion library as a complete surprise to them.

Alfred testified the same. Their father mainly stayed on the mansion's upper floors and even helped them with their homework.

Perhaps believing Alfred might answer differently to a judge advocate in full uniform, Lt. Col. Louis C. Wilson asked him directly.

"While your father was in the house, were you ever told not to say anything to your playmates about his being there?"

"Yes," Alfred replied.

"Many times?" inquired Wilson.

"I can't remember just how often," Alfred continued.

Wilson: "Did you ever say anything about this?"

---

[1] The hundreds of pages of documents about the 1939 court-martial trial in the National Archives in St. Louis include testimony from Grover's oldest children. Press photographs at Governors Island were available from newspaper archives kept at Temple University Urban Archives in Philadelphia.

 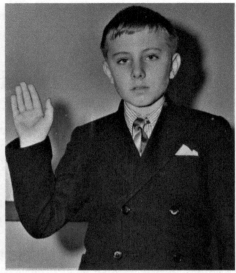

On trial a second time for draft evasion, Grover could not salute the American flag because he was handcuffed to his U.S. Army guards. A key witness in his father's trial, Alfred Bergdoll, 12, demonstrated his oath for press photographers and described how his father hid in their Wynnefield mansion for years. (Historical Society of Pennsylvania, *Philadelphia Record*)

Alfred: "No."

Also dressed in shiny laced-up boot-shoes but with patterned knee-high socks, ballooning knickerbockers, a double-breasted blue flannel jacket, collared shirt, striped tie, and pocket square, 12-year-old Alfred's testimony was convincing. Soon afterward, he stood at attention outside the courtroom and raised his right hand for the press photographers to re-enact his sworn testimony oath.

Establishing that Grover was within the jurisdiction of the United States for several years at a time when he was a fugitive became Weinberger's defense strategy to throw out the escape charge on a statute of limitations. Prosecutor Lerch claimed it didn't matter. He said that even living secretly in the mansion for an extended period as a fugitive put Grover beyond the reach of federal agents, nullifying his rights under the statute.

The public was aghast. How could the nation's number one draft dodger sneak back into the country twice and remain secret in his lavish mansion for years without anyone outside his immediate family knowing about it? And, since the agents were tipped off that Grover might be holed up in the mansion, why didn't they grab him?

Through the summer of 1939, Grover had been prepared for trial with the Army's equivalent of a grand jury. He testified before the Army tribunal that he wouldn't

With an absent father and lenient mother, Alfred Bergdoll's early life was shaped, in part, by his uncle Erwin. Pictured in the wreck of Grover's Hudson Super Six limousine and playing with an airplane at the Wynnefield mansion in 1938–1939, Alfred later became a draft evader himself. (Historical Society of Pennsylvania, *Philadelphia Record*. Temple University Urban Archives)

call witnesses or cross-examine witnesses as part of his defense. And then, rare for Grover, he remained silent.

Prosecutors lined up a list of witnesses for depositions and the trial, including Stecher, who was delayed in the hospital with a broken leg, Sgt. Frank Zimmer, John Dwyer, Sergeants John O'Hare and Calvin York, Military Intelligence Officers Ross and Glavin, and two stewards of the *Bremen* to testify on the ocean liner activities of Grover's alias, Bennet Nash.

Subpoenas were issued to Berta, Emma, Charles, Erwin (if he could be found), Colonel (Major) Hunt, FBI Special Agent Joseph McDevitt, and even the Trenton hotel clerk and a bartender who saw Grover there. Prosecutors tried to serve magazine journalist Leighton Blood, but he couldn't be found.

The summer progressed slowly. During a July 4 visit to her husband in the Castle Williams jail, Berta said she and Grover decided to sell the Wynnefield mansion. Within two days, a large wooden sign appeared on the front lawn. With a crooked S, *Sale* was hand-painted in large print letters on the top of the sign. *Inquire inside* was painted in smaller longhand at the bottom.

The crudely constructed and painted sign, made by Chick, the Bergdolls' gardener, and hastily installed within days of the decision, spoke volumes about Berta's wish to leave the Wynnefield mansion.

While she had been cleaning the dreary old chateau, supervising Chick doing the work, it was still in pathetic condition. Alfred said silk wallpaper was stained and rotting in the parlors, curtains and rugs in every room were dirty and faded, furniture needed repairs and re-upholstery, and much of the plumbing was outdated and needed replacing.

The decorative tile on the front porch where so many police officers, federal agents, and news reporters had camped out was sagging under rotten support beams, requiring anyone who dared walk onto the porch to hug the stone wall. An entire section of the wraparound porch leading to Emma's greenhouse had collapsed and was blocked off only by chipped green wicker porch furniture. All the wood trim on the mansion and carriage house was rotting or needed painting. It would have cost thousands of dollars.

Grover loved the house, and the kids did too, but for Berta, it was dreary and full of bad memories of loneliness, family strife, the gawking public, and Emma. Berta said she and the children would be moving to another location in the Philadelphia area.

She also announced to the press, who came by to see the For Sale sign, that she was expecting another baby, number six.

As the September trial date approached, strict orders were issued about Grover's security, even within the seclusion of Governors Island. His security detail must always be a captain, a sergeant, and a corporal in olive drab uniforms equipped with loaded .45 caliber pistols. Grover must be handcuffed to the corporal while in transit, even inside a car with the windows covered with blankets to prevent people from seeing him and attracting attention. When his handcuffs were removed inside the gymnasium courtroom, the guards were ordered to "keep him constantly under observation and control without interfering with his proper freedom as a prisoner before a court."

Unlike the 1920 trial when Grover and Weinberger, and the trial judges, posed for press photos in and out of the courtroom, posed photographs of Grover were not permitted, but snapshots were allowed. The base commander was taking no chances on another escape.

The trial was so much a spectacle that large tents had to be set up outside the YMCA building for the press and their typewriters. Dedicated telephone and telegraph lines were attached to machines that fed the reporters' copy, and carrier pigeons were used to fly rolls of film across New York Harbor to newspaper offices in Manhattan.

Attending on the first day, September 27, 1939, the same day Poland fell to the Nazis at the beginning of another European war, were Berta and her sister, Helene, Emma and her daughter, Elizabeth, Elizabeth's daughter, Barbara Hall, Charles Kraus' wife, Madaline; and Alfred, Emma, Mina, and Bubi.

Alfred spotted a tall, older heavy man with glasses struggling into the court on crutches. Grover's longtime childhood friend and escape cohort, Stecher, had to be pointed out to Alfred. He had never known or seen him.

Stecher was the first to testify. His crutches lay on the riser next to the witness chair. He said he tried to talk Grover out of running from the Army guards in 1920.

The two had known each other since they were young boys playing on the streets of Brewerytown, and he just went along without any prior planning. He described how they drove to the border with Canada, bought fake passports, and traveled to Montreal, then London, then Germany, where he stayed for five years before returning to the United States, facing trial, and was given a suspended sentence.

Stecher wasn't asked about the infamous Bergdoll gold during the trial, but newspaper reporters did when he was lying in a hospital bed in Philadelphia earlier that year. He claimed the gold withdrawn from the Treasury by Grover, Emma, and Romig was valued at $200,000.

"That money has never been accounted for," Stecher charged. "That amount of gold would weigh about 600 pounds and could not be carried around easily. Grover never had any gold pieces when I was with him."

Stecher did not believe the story about gold buried in the Maryland hills, either.

"Grover wasn't dumb," he said. "He wouldn't have told the authorities the location of the place where he buried it."

Stecher said he had not seen Grover since the day he left him in Germany. His testimony was designed to remove the charge of conspiracy to escape.

Remarkably, Sgt. Frank Zimmer was readily available to testify next. He was still in the Army and stationed at Governors Island in 1939. Zimmer described how he was in Eberbach, Germany, for the first kidnapping attempt on Grover in 1921, and "someone started shooting." He left out the part about Lina Rupp being hit in the hand with a bullet and that his partner, Detective Naef, did the shooting until coaxed into the whole story by Weinberger.

Zimmer admitted that while he was convicted under German law of assuming the duties of an officer, he was granted immunity by the Army and State Department in a deal with the Germans to be released without punishment.

Weinberger hinted at a double standard because Zimmer was testifying against Grover, who was not granted immunity for his offense and released without punishment.

When Grover took the witness chair in his heavy dark wool suit and baggy trousers, he portrayed how he could return to the United States twice, using different aliases to board ships and cross the Canada–United States border by train. Proving that he spent seven years as a fugitive in the United States was designed to run the statute of limitations on his escape charge.

With only a *Fremdenpass* from Germany, Grover had to find a way to travel to the United States under an alias or two. With his Josef Amann passport, he crossed the Atlantic to Canada in 1929. There, he bought another passport in the name of Bennet Nash.

Grover's first trip home, he explained, followed Berta and was for the purpose of retrieving his gold, buried behind the plaster wall of his clothes closet in the second-floor bedroom of the Wynnefield mansion. He said he had Emma deposit the $160,000 in gold in the Philadelphia bank, Weniger and Company, but he was mistaken. It was Berta and her sister Helene who deposited the gold, in Berta's name.

When Grover returned to Germany in 1933 as Bennet Nash, for added secrecy, Erwin drove him to the *Bremen* pier in New York in his new Hudson Terraplane automobile. On the way, they discussed plans for Erwin to ship Grover's matching Terraplane to Germany.

Grover said he returned to the United States in 1935 under multiple aliases because he wanted to see his newborn daughter, Vega, born on September 23, 1935.

For evidence to support Grover's testimony, Weinberger showed the fake passport applications, ship records, and border crossing documents, even testimony from the waitress and bartender of the Stacy-Trent Hotel in Trenton, where Grover laid low for weeks at a time.

The judge advocates reportedly displayed "frozen faces" when Grover admitted to lying in Germany on his 1934 consulate passport application. It was an admission of guilt to civil law.

The evidence presented by Weinberger was overwhelming to prove that Grover had been living secretly in the United States when so many federal agents and police officers were looking for him. The judges were astonished at how he did it. Immigration officials were reported to be "stunned" at so many illegal border crossings using different aliases. It exposed their major flaws in security at the border with Canada. How did he remain hidden for so long, they asked.

Grover explained that he first remained in the Wynnefield mansion's library and bedroom but would move about the house after the kids knew of his presence. When visitors arrived, he would go upstairs to the second-floor library and close the door. When visitors left, he would return to using the entire house. Not even the milkman saw him.

Twice authorities were tipped that Grover might be hiding in the mansion. First, in 1933, police were tipped that Grover was in Philadelphia under the alias of Joseph A. Mann, a version of his alias, Josef Amann. With several pairs of Zeiss binoculars positioned at windows, he watched Philadelphia police watching the house. Still, they never got a warrant, fearing ridicule by the newspapers if they found nothing.

In 1938, Charles tipped the authorities that Grover was hiding in the mansion. Agents claimed that Charles said, "There are too many rooms for you just to go in and find him. The only way to make him come out is to shut off the water, gas, and electricity. Maybe the only way to get him is to tear down the mansion." Alfred doubted that Charles would have said this, but it was never proven.

Despite not being an eyewitness to Grover in the mansion, the Bergdolls' housekeeper testified that she knew another man was in the house besides Erwin by the size 17 collars on the shirts she laundered and hung to dry in the basement, out of the neighbors' sight. Erwin, she said, had a much smaller size 15 neck collar.

Emma's testimony was so confusing that it was thrown out for her poor memory and advanced age. She couldn't remember which years Grover lived at Wynnefield but recalled digging the gold out of the closet wall in 1929. Still believing she would be praised for it, Emma declared she spent about $90,000 of the gold on Liberty bonds. Whose gold was unclear. She could not have spent Grover's gold because it was deposited in Berta's name.[2]

The Weniger and Company bank president testified that Emma often used cash to pay off loans and mortgages, once for a sizeable twin-turret, four-story, cut-stone apartment building at Philadelphia's Broad and Oxford Streets with a large and deep indoor swimming pool lined with Italian tile.

At one point, the court martial moved into an auditorium to view a newsreel of Emma telling reporters she hadn't seen Grover in 17 years. The judges suspected she was not telling the truth in the newsreel either. They discarded her testimony.

Berta and Helene testified about Grover's timeline in the mansion, which matched his testimony and the travel documents. Since multiple subpoenas served on Erwin were not answered, prosecutors wanted him arrested. Neighbors told investigators they had seen Erwin around the Broomall farm during the trial. Finally, both sides agreed to stipulate that Erwin's testimony would corroborate testimony from Berta, Helene, and Grover. They left him alone.

During breaks in the trial, Alfred patrolled around Governors Island and watched the Army band practicing for funeral marches. He was enthralled by the soldiers practicing throwing hand grenades, and he could hear the rat-tat-tat of machine-gun fire at the range in the deep trench of an old moat. He had the run of the Army fort, but he was not allowed near his father's jail cell.

During one break, Alfred saw his father in an anteroom of the gymnasium where reporters sneaked a few questions. Still lying, Grover told them the buried gold story was for real but he would not elaborate. He said fellow passengers on the Atlantic crossings would whisper "Bergdoll, Bergdoll" among themselves whenever he moved around the decks. He also told reporters about watching the federal agents in their car watching the Wynnefield mansion.

"They were always outside my house at 52nd and Wynnefield Avenue. Some of them in cars with their headlights out. Every time they lit a cigarette, I could see their faces. I was watching from the third-floor window with powerful [Zeiss] binoculars," he said before the reporters were shooed away.

Sergeants John O'Hare and Calvin York returned to Governors Island to tell a new crop of judge advocates about Grover's dramatic escape from them in 1920. Both had been prosecuted for dereliction of duty, found not guilty, and were retired, living on their Army pensions.

---

[2] Although Treasury records revealed that Emma had purchased some Liberty bonds, her version of the amounts varied widely and could not be trusted, even in sworn testimony.

Weinberger lost his challenge on the statute of limitations. In his summation, he said, "He [Bergdoll] gave himself up and came back to take his medicine... so he could give his wife a home, and his children an education in the United States. This man should not be punished more than is fair merely because his case has been so publicized. He has already suffered and must spend five years in prison for a youthful folly."

Prosecutor Lerch said, "Bergdoll thumbed his nose at the U.S. Government for nearly 20 years. This case has attracted an undue amount of publicity, so much publicity that it would seem to have been deliberately planned."

The publicity was immense. Alfred said his mother seemed to relish it. She agreed to newsreel and network radio interviews with herself and the children, crying on a national radio show, Vox Pop, which gained her much sympathy. Berta appealed to the American Legion on the program, causing it to demand a response the following week, leading to more publicity. Another interview for NBC Radio at the 1939 World's Fair in New York included little Bubi with the microphone up to his mouth, where a national audience heard him say, "I want my Daddy to come home."

Berta favored a woman reporter with whom she became friendly and who, she believed, wrote favorable articles about her plight. She revealed personal information to Evelyn Shuler, who had a knack for public relations, providing Shuler's newspaper scoops about her pregnancies, her challenges as a single mother, and her plans to sell the Wynnefield mansion and buy a farm in Chester County, Pennsylvania, an agricultural region west of Philadelphia.

Berta also told Shuler of her brother Richard's death in the war.

"He was just 21 and was among the first to be shot. He was killed right after the start of the war in 1914, after less than two weeks of fighting," she said to great sympathy among Americans, especially women.

These articles generated many comments from readers who loathed and supported the Bergdolls. By the end of 1939, however, the scales were gradually tipping in favor of the attractive German woman with a brood of children supporting her jailed husband and vowing to strike out on her own when he went to prison. Alfred believed Shuler's sympathetic articles were responsible for his mother's new public persona. He also believed Shuler helped coach Berta on what to say to other press members, but nothing supports his conjecture.[3] The admiration and sympathy Berta received harkened to the past and the venerated old Bergdoll name returning to support her when she needed it.

---

[3] Evelyn M. Shuler worked as a features reporter from 1922 until 1942 for the Philadelphia *Public Ledger* and *Evening Ledger*. She covered other big stories such as the Lindbergh baby kidnapping, the crash of the Hindenburg, and presidential inaugurations. She later became a public relations executive for Penn Mutual Life Insurance Company.

Grover's trial ended on October 5, 1939, and the judge advocates deliberated for two hours and 15 minutes. They found Grover guilty of escape and desertion but not guilty of conspiracy to desert with Stecher. Their sentence was similar to the sentence in 1920 but, surprisingly, a bit lighter—three years of hard labor. With the nearly five years he still had to serve from the 1920 sentence, he faced about eight years.

Unlike in 1920, when Grover was privately read the verdict in his jail cell, the 1939 verdict was revealed in open court. Grover showed no emotion. Berta wept.

Alfred and Emma were not in the courtroom. They got the news at home in Philadelphia. Alfred later wrote that he only wanted his father to go to prison long enough for him and his siblings not to be bullied or beaten by Grover again. From reporters, Emma got the news by telephone at her Broomall farm.

Grover was returned to his cell to await the formalities, including trial review and approval of the verdict and sentence by Governors Island First Army Commander Lt. General Hugh A. Drum.[4]

Berta was still on a public relations campaign, telling the press she was disappointed in the verdict because Grover "has always been so kind to the children and me."

Weinberger tried his best to appeal the sentence, saying Grover surrendered himself and was not "captured." He also pointed to how hapless federal agents failed the government when they sat and watched after getting tips that Grover was inside his mansion. His effort failed.

Alfred concluded, "Weinberger's brilliant defense almost forced the Army to impose a relatively light sentence."

Four days later, Berta called a taxi cab and checked herself into Lankenau Hospital just outside the western city limits of Philadelphia. At 1 am, she delivered a healthy baby girl. Expecting a boy, she had planned to name the baby Grover. Instead, she wired Grover with the news, and he insisted she should name the baby Berta.

Late in October, Grover and Weinberger were still trying to find a way out of their predicament. Most likely at Grover's insistence, Weinberger wrote to Secretary of War Harry Hines Woodring, claiming Grover had information about advancements in German military equipment; something about interchangeability in German guns and details of a new diesel engine that could make German tanks go faster. Their effort for some kind of government intervention in Grover's case failed. Why Grover waited until after the verdict when the European war was already underway is anyone's guess. This revelation confused Alfred because his father always claimed to be a devout pacifist.

At about the same time, Berta and then Emma began writing regularly to President Roosevelt and the First Lady, requesting an audience and pardon for Grover.

---

[4] Lt. Gen. Drum had risen from the youngest officer in the Army and General Pershing's chief assistant in France to command the First Army headquartered at Governors Island. He was the general for whom Pine Camp was named Camp Drum, then Fort Drum in Northern New York State.

Also, in late October, Berta received checks from the Army paying for their expenses for appearing as witnesses in Grover's trial, including the children. Almost simultaneously, she received word that they won the return of 80 percent of Grover's assets seized or frozen by the Alien Property Custodian. Without the benefit of a court ruling, the attorney general determined that Weinberger had been correct: Grover did not lose his citizenship with conviction, only his citizenship rights. The remaining 20 percent of the seized funds were to go into a special reparations fund for Americans harmed by the war.[5]

Then, as had happened so many times, Grover's relationship with his lawyer, Weinberger, soured. Grover was annoyed that Weinberger had agreed with the government to keep 20 percent of the frozen assets, perhaps as a measure for negotiations. He fired Weinberger, who immediately sued Grover and Berta for his legal fees, claiming he was owed about $60,000. He also sued the Alien Property Custodian, claiming that if the seized funds went directly to Berta, she would flee the country and stiff their creditors. It got ugly, but Weinberger later settled for partial payment, the amount unknown.

On October 17, 1939, a sign appeared on the front lawn of the oversized stone chateau with a wide wraparound porch and 12 acres built in 1907 by Charles and later sold to Emma. The 24-room mansion at the farm in Broomall was for sale for $125,000. Erwin still owned his 54-acre farmhouse, barn, and machine shop next door, and Grover and Berta still owned their ramshackle 88-acre farm across West Chester Pike. The surprise For Sale sign may have inspired cooperation among feuding family members.

The family lawsuits were gradually settled, with Emma's estate put into a trust with her son, Louis Bergdoll Bergson, named the managing trustee. The trust named her five children as the beneficiaries in return for her life use and support to live at her farm in Broomall.

The For Sale sign came down.

One of Louis' first significant moves as managing trustee was to propose selling the valuable Somerset, Maryland, vacant property on the Washington, D.C. line that the Bergdolls had owned since their father was alive in the late 1800s. Its value had skyrocketed, and its location was a temptation for real estate developers, even the federal government. Once trying to use the choice of property as a bargaining chip for a deal with the federal government to forgive Grover's draft evasion, Emma had become the sole owner of the plot when her husband died in 1896.

---

[5] Grover turned down the deal for the return of his seized assets, hired a Washington lawyer to regain the remaining 20 percent, and won. The total amount was about $407,000; $8.6 million in 2023.

The remote farmhouse in Chester County, Pennsylvania offered a separate section, left, for Grover, when he got out of prison. Berta kept horses for the children. When Grover completed his sentence, their life together on the farm turned into family and marital strife with highly abusive behavior from Grover, who began a long spiral into mental illness. (Chester County Historical Society, Historical Society of Pennsylvania)

When Grover was consulted about approving the Washington land sale plan, he forbade it. He thought real estate values would climb higher. Berta had to deliver the bad news to the trust. Louis then sued Berta as manager of Grover's affairs.

When 1939 ended, Berta and the children spent their last Christmas in the dingy old Wynnefield mansion. Despite being listed for sale, there were no takers. Berta wished to buy a farm for her and the children to live on while Grover served his sentence. She harkened back to her youth living on the grounds of the Weissenhof mental hospital in Weinsberg when her father was the head gardener.

Alfred said his mother may have known about raising vegetables in a garden, but she knew little about the agriculture business. However, buy a farm, she did. Just before Valentine's Day, 1940, Berta settled on three contiguous properties consisting of more than 260 acres of forest and fields, with farmhouses and barns on each property between West Chester and Downingtown, Pennsylvania, in Chester County, a rural farming region 30 miles west of Philadelphia. The historical Brandywine Creek flowed through a valley south of the farm, and a smaller stream, Valley Creek, flowed through another valley north of the farm. Because it was on a hill at the top of Skelp Level Road, the property had been named Harmony Hill Farm.

Berta may have bought the farm more for the seclusion it would bring in the woods. There wasn't much open land for cultivation. Alfred called it "as picturesque as New England."

The price for all three parcels was $45,000. Grover approved the expenditure, but the farm was purchased in Berta's name because he was a convicted felon. The children didn't see the farm until they moved in on April 5, 1940.

Their father remained imprisoned at Governors Island but wouldn't stay there much longer.

CHAPTER TWENTY-NINE

Final Flight

Harmony Hill, Pennsylvania–River Edge, Virginia 1941–1966[1]

Berta Bergdoll trudged uphill on a rocky lane beneath heavy limbs from trees that shrouded her farm from Skelp Level Road in East Bradford Township, Chester County, Pennsylvania. It was on the top of a long ridge, and, already in early December 1941, the cold air of approaching winter was creeping into southeastern Pennsylvania. Opening her mailbox along the gravel road, she pulled out a letter she had been expecting. Ripping it open, she read the disheartening news. Parole was denied for her husband, Grover, now held in the federal penitentiary at Fort Leavenworth, Kansas.

Berta may have immediately thought of writing again to President Roosevelt in Washington or Hyde Park, New York, begging to appeal the decision. Before she could organize her thoughts and sit at her typewriter, however, the world changed. Two days after she received the letter from Fort Leavenworth, the Japanese attacked Pearl Harbor.

There would be no sympathy in Washington for draft dodgers.

Grover had been transferred to Fort Leavenworth near the end of 1940 when the Castle Williams prison on Governors Island was closed. In preparation for his first parole hearing in October 1941, three outstanding indictments against him since 1920 were dismissed by the federal court in New York. At Leavenworth, Grover grew comfortable, as had Erwin many years earlier, in a prison cell by himself, with a radio, his books, and regular visits by train from Berta and the children. Despite the long, arduous journey westward, they could see him for only three hours at a time. It inspired Berta's regular correspondence with the Roosevelts—or her one-way letter writing. The Roosevelts didn't reply.

"I am with my children on a Chester County farm, and they all and myself want to be good American citizens, and we are thankful to live in this country, which we love," she wrote of her quest for a presidential pardon for Grover. She explained that

---

[1] This chapter's detail is based on Alfred's diary-manuscript. Only he was old and mature enough to recall the events as he did, and his siblings later confirmed his recollections. Additional information, such as the fire at Louis Bergdoll's mansion, was gleaned from newspapers.

her husband should be home so that Alfred, at age 14, "should have the stronger hand of his father. Thank you with all my heart for anything you can do to help us."

Berta also suggested to the Roosevelts, so wrapped up in American policy and preparation for war, that Grover "would like to build on the Bergdoll property in Washington [Somerset, Maryland], which lies in the defense area, houses for defense workers. And he will do anything to serve his country."[2]

With Grover's 1941 parole rejection, Berta may have realized she was in for a long slog on the Harmony Hill Farm with the children alone. Not that Grover would have been much help, but her dream of a quiet family life on the farm surrounded by cows, pigs, sheep, chickens, and horses was dashed again.

"I can't understand what happened," she told a reporter. "I thought my husband was to be released. Now we are heartbroken. We were all looking forward to having him back for Christmas. The children were making so many plans, but now I have had to say to them he won't be home."

Berta's effort to have Grover released early employed a New York attorney, Joseph C. Thomson, who appealed to the attorney general for a pardon or commutation of Grover's sentence. Thomson wrote to Washington, reminding officials of Grover's accomplishments 25 years earlier and his potential usefulness for the military in the war.

"That prior to 1917, he was an accomplished aviator. In 1914, he was flying his plane. That he was pro-German from 1914–1917, and it was not fear that drove him to violation of the draft laws, but it was his unalterable opposition, at the time, to our war with Germany."[3]

Thomson said Grover would be helpful to the United States during the war because he was well-known in Germany and "could help the German people unshackle themselves from the vicious grip of the Austrian paper hanger [Hitler]."

And, with words that Grover may have written, Thomson stated to the attorney general, "He is ready at this moment to enlist in the Air Corps or any other branch of the Army, Navy, or Marine Corps, to prove his Americanism if released. Mr. Bergdoll is not a coward."

Grover even elicited the help of U.S. Army General Henry H. "Hap" Arnold, a fellow Pennsylvanian raised in the Main Line communities simultaneously with the Bergdolls. As young men, Arnold, and Grover both trained to fly on the Wright

---

[2] Developing the Bergdoll Washington-area property for defense workers was wishful thinking by Berta and Grover. In a settlement agreement giving Grover cash, they had relinquished claim to any portion of Emma's Somerset, Maryland property. It was held in trust, managed by Louis Bergdoll Bergson and attorneys in Washington.

[3] Thomson got Grover's flying years wrong. The Wright B was mothballed in 1913, and Grover never flew again. Grover often told his children about "hob-knobbing" with SS officers in German bars but Thomson's declaration that Grover was pro-German was the first public statement of its kind attributed to Grover.

B airplane in Dayton, Ohio, under the Wright Brothers, but months apart. On a goodwill tour of military bases as chief of the Army Air Corps, General Arnold was in Leavenworth and arranged to see his old friend, Grover. There is no record of Arnold ever supporting Grover's effort at early release, and there is no record of the meeting except for Grover passing along the chance encounter to his son, Alfred.

Grover was 48, growing overweight, and somewhat comfortable in prison. He hadn't been around an airplane in decades and knew nothing of modern technology. No one in Washington considered his "usefulness" in the war whatsoever.

Attorney Thomson was correct, however, with his final statement to the Attorney General. Grover was the only person in prison during the second European war for dodging the draft in the first war.

Meanwhile, Berta and the children hired farmhands to operate Harmony Hill Farm, installing them in cottages on the properties. They purchased a small herd of Guernsey cows, sheep, pigs, chickens, and ducks. The main Pennsylvania stone and wood frame barn was also filled with horses for the farmwork and for Berta and the girls to ride and jump. The classic Pennsylvania farmhouse was small but had a large porch and additions that expanded the interior. Berta spent liberally on a tractor and farm implements for the workers to operate. However, corn, hay, and grain production were complex because there was so much rock, poor soil on the hillside, and limited fertile valley land.[4]

Berta arranged to build a small brick smokehouse where they cured meat from their butchered farm animals. Alfred raised bees and produced honey. Unreasonably, with too much work to handle on Harmony Hill Farm, Berta also purchased another dairy farm nearby in Thorndale, Pennsylvania, and installed another farmer on the property to operate it.

Alfred said Grover, in prison, was aware of the labor requirements and kept sending released Army prisoners to the farm for work. One was an Alaskan Eskimo who began work as a cook for Berta and the children but soon quit, claiming he had contracted syphilis and didn't want to harm the family. Another released prisoner who showed up at Grover's direction was employed as their driver and remained with the family for several years, living in a small cottage on the farm nearby. In the early 1940s, the driver's primary responsibility was to shuttle the children to and from the small Harmony Hill schoolhouse (1st–6th grade) and, later, to public school in West Chester, about six miles away.

Despite recommendations from family and friends that Berta reduce her responsibilities to a hobby farm, she kept expanding Harmony Hill Farm. Alfred said, "for

---

[4] The description of Berta Bergdoll's farm at Harmony Hill, Chester County, Pennsylvania, is mainly based on my personal experience living in Chester County, a few miles away from the farm, for many years. While it's still a rural-suburban area, it was remote and agrarian in the 1940s and 1950s. Several photographs of the farmhouse and the property survive, helping craft the description of Harmony Hill.

some reason, expansion continued, expenditures grew, and control seemed more tenuous. Even the servants in the house increased in number."

Some of Berta's efforts at progress may have been inspired by Grover's long missives from prison. In a hand-written letter to Berta in August 1940, Grover quizzed his wife if she had purchased enough natural fertilizer from the mushroom farmers of southern Chester County for her crops, especially the oats and sugar corn. He encouraged her to build a smokehouse to cure pork after killing their pigs, writing, "You'll get a big kick out of curing and smoking your own bacon and hams."

He suggested Berta buy another horse, with a western saddle and bridle, and to be stern with one of their farmers, who was often getting drunk and not showing up for work. He authorized her purchase of a larger icebox, a luxury for a single woman managing a farm alone with several children. Still, his August 1940 letter gave his wife an awkward compliment while recalling their recent Sunday prison visit with Alfred and Bubi.

> You looked really good today, and you surely look younger every time I see you. Are you putting on a few extra pounds now?

Grover suggested that their next visit would be all business, ordering Berta to cancel the leases on Eagle Field and his 88-acre farm along West Chester Pike in preparation for their sale. He was also interested to hear how she handled their financial settlement over brother Louis' administration of Emma's estate. In the letter, he called his brother by his new name, Bergson, a reference to Louis changing his name to escape Grover's infamy.

Grover also wished to "build those stores and houses on Eagle Field and put hundreds of people to work. But that will have to wait until I can get out," he wrote.

> Do not worry. I will not be absent from you any too long now. Then we will be very happy together, and you will get a chance to reap the rewards which are due to you for your troubles and hard work.

In a shocking revelation, he said he wanted to buy Berta an airplane, a Fairchild M-62 trainer (PT-19), which featured a tandem-seat, open cockpit design. It had been produced for the Army in 1939 as their trainer aircraft and probably caught Grover's attention while reading magazines in prison.[5]

Suggesting he would buy one for Berta, however, was absurd. He asked her if an aviation navigation book had arrived at the farm, and if she would write to the Fairchild aviation company in Hagerstown, Maryland, for literature on the airplane and when they might be able to deliver it. Then, she would have to learn to fly, he suggested. Although Grover still owned the Eagle Flying Field, he had not flown a plane for 27 years.

---

[5] Fairchild built its airplanes at a factory in Grover's old hiding place, Hagerstown, Maryland.

Berta had no training to fly an airplane and less time to think about it.

Grover could lay it on thick with suffocating praise and promises, Alfred suggested, and in this letter, he ended with a salutation of love and kisses to Berta.

> With all the love in the whole universe for the best and dearest angel in all the world; and hundreds of trillions of hugs and kisses for the sweetest and truest wife on earth, I am, as ever always, your own loving husband, Groff.

In the following line, his P.S. inquired about his mother, Emma. Did she get his letter about her 79th birthday?

The farm's dog population rapidly increased at Harmony Hill Farm in 1940. Alfred said that upwards of 25 dogs roamed around the farm properties without consideration for breeding, discipline, or containment. The mixed-breed dogs ranged from St. Bernards to Fox Terriers. When cars or trucks passed along Skelp Level Road in a cloud of dust, the pack of howling and yelping dogs would gallop along for a half mile to the nearest neighbor's farm, the Grigsons', from where teenager Roger Grigson became a regular companion of the Bergdoll children.[6]

Alfred, from his diary-manuscript written years later, appeared to have a grasp of conditions on Harmony Hill in hindsight. He said the Bergdolls' annual income from investments at the time was about $12,000. But, he said, the farm was probably costing them $15,000–$20,000 a year to operate.

To raise cash, Grover agreed from prison to sell two properties, the three-acre Wynnefied property for $20,000 (after demolition) and the hayfield that had been Eagle Field, Grover's airport, for $30,000.[7] Alfred said Grover kept his many run-down rental properties scattered about Philadelphia.

In August 1942, with Grover still in prison, sad news arrived that Louis John Bergdoll Bergson died of a heart attack at his large Italianate mansion at 22nd and Green Streets in Philadelphia. Louis was only 57 and was sipping his daily tonic of tomato juice in front of his bathroom mirror when he dropped to the floor. His wife, Florence, heard the thud and found him dead.

By this time, Louis and Florence retained their New York apartment but lived full-time at their large mansion. Louis' domain was upstairs in the property's elaborate carriage house, with its car elevator. He had been running a Globe Development Laboratories company, although few understood what it was for. It may have been a company (with government contracts) to help keep his sons, Louis, Jr., and Wilbur,

---

[6] The Grigson farm is credited with being the first in Pennsylvania to have a cut-your-own Christmas tree orchard, proving highly successful with Philadelphians who enjoyed a road trip into the country to fetch a Christmas tree.

[7] The Wynnefield mansion had been torn down, with the wrecking company salvaging the stone, lumber, and woodwork for its cost and profit. Eagle Field had sat empty for years and was purchased by developers who later built the Manoa Shopping Center and new homes for Philadelphia's rapidly expanding population.

out of the war. However, the boys had moved on because of their father's strict and "tyrannical behavior" (he timed their walks around the block for precisely 20 minutes).

When Louis died, the mansion interior, with its Tiffany stained-glass windows, was still in superb condition due to Florence Bergson's diligence. However, the exterior was becoming somewhat rundown, like the neighborhood. Louis' old cars remained in the carriage house, a touring car, and a Cadillac limousine from the 1920s. Alongside the vehicles were crates of Marlin lever-action rifles and other long guns Louis purchased on the wholesale market but never removed from their packaging. Upstairs remained his vintage furniture, including oak roll-top desks, a hospital-sized X-ray machine, and a like-new razor blade-cutting machine the size of a car. All were part of Louis' incomplete business ventures. The garage was also packed with machine tools, lathes, and drill presses. After their father was gone, Wilbur and Louis Jr. moved back in with Florence. They continued fulfilling small government engineering contracts, assuring they would not be drafted to serve in the war.

Upon settling Louis' estate (an unknown value), they opened the safe in the mansion to dispose of the contents. Years earlier, Florence's notable pieces of jewelry had turned up missing. Alfred said they found them in the safe where Louis had secretly placed the valuables, locked away from his wife.

Without a ceremony or visits from his family, Louis' remains were cremated and buried in West Laurel Hill Cemetery just outside the city limits of Philadelphia. Later, after Florence, Wilbur, and Louis Jr. died and were interred in the family plot, the name Bergdoll was added to the gravestone, which ultimately read Bergson–Bergdoll, rejoining them with the soiled Bergdoll name.[8]

At the Harmony Hill Farm, Berta and the children were visited regularly by Erwin and his wife, Magdalena "Lena," and Emma, who would dress heavily in her ermine-trimmed cape and shawls when Erwin would drive her out to the farm.

Erwin, Lena, and Berta would often socialize together on reasonable terms without the influence of Grover. On one occasion, Alfred recounts, they attended a farm auction in Pennsylvania's Amish countryside on the Chester–Lancaster County line, where Berta wanted to buy some furniture. When the whole farm came singing from the auctioneer's mouth, Erwin impulsively bought it for $6,000. Reached in Honey Brook Township at the end of a long, private lane, the farm included a relatively small wood frame house, a barn, large fields and woods, and a long, narrow concrete swimming pool fed by a spring. Alfred described it as charming but "way out in the middle of nowhere."

---

[8] In 1989, a fire at the Bergsons' Italianate mansion caused by careless smoking drew Philadelphia police and firefighters. They carried Louis Bergson, Jr., 80, from the house suffering from inhaling smoke. Wilbur, 77, was not injured. A few newspaper lines about the fire and the majestic mansion were outnumbered by background linking the Bergson brothers to the infamous Bergdoll family. It proved that changing their name did nothing to relieve the Bergsons of the notoriety.

It was just what Erwin wanted. The Broomall community around his 66-acre farm and Emma's mansion was becoming developed with homes and would explode with growth a few years later. Alfred said Erwin initially used the Honey Brook farm "to putter around."

On the morning of February 4, 1944, reporters and photographers from Kansas and Missouri milled around the exit gate at Fort Leavenworth prison. They identified Erwin and Berta at the main prison gate, having arrived by train for Grover's release after serving three years and four months (November 8, 1940, to February 4, 1944) in prison. When a short, trim man joined them in a navy-blue suit and overcoat, powder-blue felt hat, and high-top boot-shoes, he told the photographers he was Grover's lawyer. They saved their film and flashbulbs for the pending release of the infamous convict and draft dodger. Berta, Erwin, and Grover's "attorney" got into a taxi and left the prison for Kansas City's Union Station and the train ride back east.[9]

The photographers missed their chance to photograph Grover's first moments of freedom without criminal charges hanging over his head.

The next day, February 5, the Bergdolls' driver, dressed in his black suit and black chauffeur's hat, polished their 1942 Plymouth Woody station wagon, and drove to the Water Street train station in Wilmington, Delaware to await the Baltimore and Ohio train from the south and west. Reporters and photographers mingled at Harmony Hill Farm, where, as the oldest and taking charge, Alfred arranged for the Bergdoll's cook to brew coffee and feed them. They felt invited and welcome. Then, wishing to collect his thoughts about his father returning home from prison after almost four years, 16-year-old Alfred went for a long walk in the woods. He didn't want to be there when Grover arrived.

For his father's reunion with the family, young Erwin hung a photograph on the farmhouse wall depicting the Wynnefield mansion as it was demolished. It included a short poem he wrote.

> It was the biggest house I ever did see.
> For one family.
> But now dead and buried as you see.
> Dear old Wynnefield, how I loved you so.
> The house I did live in but no mo'

After an uneventful arrival at the Wilmington train station, the Bergdolls motored in their chauffeur-driven Plymouth to Harmony Hill Farm just before lunchtime. Grover had never seen it, but upon arrival, before greeting his children, he marched up to the photographers and reporters on the porch and ordered them "off my

---

[9] By 1944, Grover had enough of reporters hounding him for a story. One reporter, Harold M. Slater, rebuffed by Grover and the Leavenworth prison warden to grant an exit interview, asked Missouri Senator Harry S. Truman to intercede. Even the future president could not convince Grover to grant an interview as he was released from prison.

property." Seeing more reporters in the house, one on the telephone, he demanded from anyone within earshot, "get me my rod. Get the hell off my property. I'll give you five minutes to get off."

Alfred returned to the inevitable as the news people ran to their cars and spun the gravel exiting the farm lane onto Skelp Level Road. He realized that his father hadn't changed a bit in prison. He realized that life for him and his siblings was about to become very difficult.[10]

The next day, February 6, 1944, when Grover went to Broomall to visit Emma, he was met by more photographers and reporters on Emma's mansion's long front veranda overlooking the lawn to West Chester Pike. This time, however, with Emma standing nearby and Berta apologizing for Grover's behavior the previous day, Grover was much more cordial.

"I'm glad to be back in Chester County again," he declared. "Away from Kansas." Nearly four years locked away from home may have confused him. At Emma's Broomall mansion, he was standing in Delaware County.

It would be the last time he'd see his mother.

At Harmony Hill Farm, Grover struggled to adjust to a life of relative freedom. He continued wearing his prison-issued suit, and when that wore out, he dressed in military clothing, as he did in prison. He had constantly chewed tobacco, especially cigar nubs, and it ruined his teeth (which had seldom seen a dentist). He then took up smoking pipe tobacco. At the farm, however, he quit smoking altogether.

Grover replaced the bad habit with another: drinking. Beer, at first, and then his favorite, German white wine. Soon enough, Alfred said, Grover discovered how much money was going out for the expenses at Harmony Hill and how little was coming in. There were five farmers, three household servants, and the driver. There was machinery, livestock, feed, fertilizer, seed, fuel, veterinarian expenses, and repairs needed. The farm was bleeding money.

Grover's quiet complaints soon turned to rage. After he loudly insulted the farmers and servants, they all quit. Then, Alfred said, his parents and the kids had to do all the work. Their life was miserable, and the animals and crops began to suffer.

To escape, Alfred would return to the Broomall farm, staying with his grandmother during the height of World War II. After dinner in the old mansion, Erwin would gather the newspapers and, with his father's pince-nez, sit around the table reading the war news from Germany. For Alfred, Erwin would tune Emma's console radio to the short-wave band and listen to Radio Berlin for a different perspective on the war, with the German commentators "poking fun at President Roosevelt and the

---

[10] Alfred said his mother and father, and grandmother, had courted the press for years when trying to gain a pardon for Grover. When reporters were no longer needed, they tossed them off like another piece of their property.

Americans." Events like this probably influenced Alfred's political views, which, later in his life, were highly liberal, bordering on rebellion.

On March 5, 1944, Grover's former attorney, Harry Weinberger, died unexpectedly at his Fifth Avenue home in Manhattan, New York City. He was 58, and the cause was a heart ailment. Alfred said Grover sat in the Harmony Hill Farm kitchen and read the attorney's obituary but made no comment. Despite being fired for representing Grover and Berta, often at great personal expense, Weinberger never held a grudge. Alfred said Weinberger would often send the family candy boxes, but Grover refused to let anyone eat them because "they might be poisoned." Weinberger also sent the family copies of classic literature and the magazine article containing his short autobiography in which "he dealt kindly" with Grover.[11]

Around this time, the Emma Bergdoll trust arranged to sell the three-story Bergdoll brick mansion at 929 North 29th Street in Brewerytown. It was July 7, 1944, and the trustee manager, Louis Bergson, Jr. (by default of his father's death), invited the grandchildren to the mansion to pick out a family artifact.

The old mansion was full of furniture, dishes, and Bergdoll belongings, all dirty and dusty, even the magnificent chandeliers. Alfred remembered seeing dirty dishes in the sink. It appeared as if Emma had just walked away from the mansion years earlier when she moved to Wynnefield and then the Broomall farm, and she probably did.

The Brewerytown house and property sold for $6,500 to a woman who wanted to make it a rooming house. Failing to gain permit approvals, she traded it for a substantial profit to a woman and her son, who planned a funeral parlor. However, the son was drafted into the war, and they changed their plans. The solid old brick mansion, inhabited by the older Bergdoll men briefly, was sold again to become a Baptist church.

If Emma Bergdoll knew that lawyers sold the old Bergdoll brick mansion, she couldn't complain. She was ailing, and on November 27, 1944, she was stricken at home in Broomall and taken to Lankenau Hospital near Philadelphia. Erwin, Lena, Berta, and Elizabeth visited her in the hospital, but Grover did not.[12] Alfred said, "in the hospital, her mind cleared, and she was alert, aware, happy, and knew she was dying."

---

[11] The many press photographs depicting Harry Weinberger as the trusted and wise lawyer representing Grover and Berta, and the children, illustrate the trust and confidence they placed in him for decades. Their soured relationship with Weinberger is an example of how they disposed of close advisors as easily as they discarded beloved properties.

[12] Broomall merchants recalled making deliveries to Emma's mansion in the early 1940s, where she held court in the large kitchen with pots and kettles hanging from the ceiling and chickens having free run of the house. Multiple servants maintained the grounds, barn, carriage house, and cars and cooked on Emma's massive vintage wood-coal stove. She kept dozens of plants and flowers in a cylindrical cut-glass greenhouse on the southwest corner of the long veranda.

On December 4, at 83, the Bergdoll matriarch drew her last breath at 10 am. The cause of death was pneumonia brought on by old age and cardiorenal vascular disease. Her death certificate says she was also "senile." The certificate was signed by the new manager of her trust, Louis Bergdoll Bergson, Jr.

Emma died within a year of her final legal battle with attorneys over outstanding legal fees.

Charles and Louise Bergdoll-Brawn flew in from California for the Oliver Bair Funeral Home funeral at 18th and Chestnut Streets in Philadelphia. Erwin and Lena attended, along with Elizabeth and Albert Hall, Florence Bergdoll Bergson, and Louis' sons, Louis, Jr., and Wilbur.

Berta, Grover, and the older children were ready to go, with the Plymouth Woody warming in the driveway of Harmony Hill Farm, when Grover suddenly announced that they weren't going to Emma's funeral after all. He claimed that driving the 35 miles into Philadelphia was too dangerous because it had been snowing. Appeals from everyone, including Berta, who was pregnant and ready to deliver her baby, and the Irish cook, didn't work. Grover refused to go to his mother's funeral. Alfred said Berta told him late that night that Grover said, "Goodnight, Mother," just before going to bed.

Emma was buried in Mount Vernon Cemetery in Philadelphia next to her husband, Louis. She had outlived him by 48 years.[13]

Emma's obituary, taking up an entire column of a newspaper page, said, "The woman who fought for her sons, her fortune, and her belief that World War was brought about by England and Wall Street, Mrs. Emma Christina Barth Bergdoll, of West Chester Pike, Broomall, died early Monday morning in Lankenau Hospital in Philadelphia."

Somehow the obituary writer included the phrase that Grover "was by her side when death came." He wasn't there for her death or her burial. He did not go to see Emma at the hospital, and he did not attend her funeral.

Sometime after Emma's death, friction mounted between Grover and Erwin, a regular visitor to Harmony Hill Farm. Alfred said that one day when Erwin arrived and knocked on the farmhouse door, Grover quietly got up and slid the lock on the door. Erwin, Lena, and their son, Butsi, turned and left Harmony Hill and never returned.

When it came time for Emma's trust to sell the Broomall mansion next to Erwin's farm, Erwin and Lena packed up their belongings and moved to the Honey Brook farm, more secluded than ever from the entire family and the prying eyes of neighbors who would buy Emma's mansion for apartments.

---

[13] Emma's burial location is misidentified in some records at the Bergdoll mausoleum at West Laurel Hill Cemetery in Bala Cynwyd, Lower Merion Township, Pennsylvania. She and her husband, Louis, were buried at Mount Vernon Cemetery in Philadelphia, and their graves remain there.

The Broomall stone mansion belonging to Charles Bergdoll Brawn, then Emma Bergdoll, and its carriage house around 1944 when it was sold following Emma's death. It eventually became rental units, dubbed Castle Apartments. (Historical Society of Pennsylvania, *Philadelphia Record*)

Meanwhile, Alfred said his father suffered from paranoia and rage, afraid someone was trying to take advantage of him, usually over money. He bore enemies to the point where someone kept tossing nails into the Bergdolls' farm lane off Skelp Level Road. The pins kept piercing tires on the Plymouth and their Hudson. He banished their neighbor, Roger Grigson, from Harmony Hill by "insulting him" so severely that Roger was afraid to approach the Bergdoll children playing baseball in the meadow in case Grover should run him off with a gun.

Grover did use a gun, Alfred said, killing Berta's sizeable black cat that he had given her from a litter of strays at the jail on Governors Island. Alfred said his father may have poisoned one of their many dogs and took several others for a ride in the Plymouth, dumping them miles from home. Only one of them came back. His excuse: he would get them "better dogs." It was becoming clear that Grover had a progressively worsening mental disorder.

One of the many Harmony Hill farm animals mistreated by Grover got revenge. It was their big black horse, Hans. Grover was feeding the horse some grain when he stuck his hand into the feed box, and Hans bit off the tip of Grover's right thumb. It was a severe amputation and bled greatly, but Grover refused to seek medical attention, doctoring it himself with iodine and gauze pads. It was 21 years after Grover bit off the thumb tip of one of his kidnappers in Germany, and he finally realized what it felt like.

Approaching Christmas 1944, the family enjoyed a brief respite from Grover's increasingly erratic bouts with insanity when another baby was born on December 13 at the West Chester Hospital. They named him Grover Franck Bergdoll. Always ready with a nickname, they called him Skipper.

However, by the spring of 1945, Grover's mental and physical abuse became too much. Alfred wrote that Berta took all the other children and moved to a small cottage on one of the adjacent farm tracts she owned and hid from Grover. Alfred stayed with his father at the main farmhouse, where they were heavily burdened as the only ones to tend and feed the livestock. When the girls returned one day to get their horses, it was a good thing they did. Grover had Alfred call the cattle dealer to come pick up all their livestock on the farm, cows, pigs, sheep, chickens, and the remaining horses, paying a pittance of their value.

Soon enough, Grover determined where Berta was hiding from him and cornered her into what Alfred called a "rapprochement." However, Berta's reconciliation was conditional that Grover sign a legal statement promising good behavior and sending the older girls, Emma, and Mina, to boarding school. They enrolled in Oak Grove School, a Quaker institution for girls in Vassalboro, Maine, with brick campus buildings that resembled a Rhine castle.[14]

---

[14] Aside from physical and mental abuse on his family, it's unknown if there were any other reasons for sending Emma and Mina to a Quaker boarding school so far away from home.

Another part of the reconciliation between Grover and Berta was Grover buying Berta several new riding horses. However, one of them got loose and was killed by a train on the nearby Philadelphia to Harrisburg, Pennsylvania, main line tracks.

With the end of World War II, the Bergdolls, like other Americans, felt a rush of excitement and confidence in their future. They sold the small cabin to which Berta had fled amidst marital strife and the land surrounding it, and they sold Berta's other dairy farm in Chester County for a small profit, recorded Alfred. Then, like many Germans from Germany, they became excited about moving the entire family to South America. For a while, they were so interested in joining the Germans migrating to Argentina and Brazil that they sent Alfred alone to New York City, with hotel and train fare, to gather information about the countries from the Argentine consulate.

Then, as soon as that idea soured, they ventured into Virginia's Hunt Country, Blue Ridge Mountains, and Tidewater regions, searching for a new property and another change in their lives. Alfred said the Virginia plan appealed to Grover "because the servants were cheap," but Alfred realized it was simply "the desire to leave for fresh, undefiled territory."

Soon enough, despite the signed legal agreement promising good behavior, marital strife returned to the Bergdoll farm at Harmony Hill. Alfred described a scenario of Berta crawling across the farmhouse's roof to access Grover's locked library window to retrieve stock certificates to fund another escape from her husband's brutality. She took the children to a hotel and then rented a small house in central Chester County near the dairy farm they had recently sold. She sent Alfred to a stock broker with $50,000 worth of Armour and Company certificates for conversion into cash to support their new lives. There was no telephone at their new house, and Grover could not find them for quite some time. Soon, however, fat envelopes arrived at Berta's Downingtown, Pennsylvania, post office box with apologetic letters from Grover begging Berta to come home.

While living alone at Harmony Hill Farm, Grover hired a local German couple as servants. Clement Klein and his wife moved into one of the cottages vacated by the farmers and began keeping house for Grover.[15] While a good cook and handy in the kitchen, Klein had a habit of stocking Grover's refrigerator and pantry with too much food, according to Grover's miserly habits. When Klein presented Grover with a substantial tab at the Downingtown grocery store, Grover allegedly confronted him with a shotgun. "Who do you think I am, Rockefeller," he roared.

When Klein protested, Grover fired him on the spot, not with the gun but with more vitriolic verbal abuse. Klein and his wife and daughter packed up quickly and left Harmony Hill, but their first stop was to file a complaint about Grover's gun threat with police in West Chester.

---

[15] Clement Klein could also have been Clemens Klein, a German national from Philadelphia who had a background of working as a servant for wealthy German families in eastern Pennsylvania.

Berta and the children had returned to Harmony Hill at this juncture. Soon enough, Pennsylvania State Police and a Chester County deputy sheriff arrived to serve Grover with an arrest warrant. He had fled, however, to the small rental house, and they found him there, charged him with assault and battery on Klein, and held him until Berta paid his $2,500 bail. Naturally, it made all the newspapers, and then, everyone realized Grover was up to his old tricks again.

Alfred said it was humbling. "I was walking along the main stem in West Chester when I was shocked by the big black banner headline in the West Chester daily newspaper lying on a newsstand which announced that father had been arrested. I walked on, too embarrassed to look further at the paper or to buy it."

Before the assault and battery case came to trial, however, Klein's former employer stepped forward with exculpatory testimony about Klein. The charges were dismissed. Alfred said his father appeared unfazed about the entire incident.

Renewed press and public interest in the dramatic lives of the Bergdolls may have inspired them to leave Harmony Hill. They soon settled on a 500-acre estate on the flat Tidewater country between Williamsburg and Richmond, Virginia, along the north bank of the James River. It included "a rambling old English style ivy-covered house" built in the 1730s with a wide central hall, multiple dormer windows, and full English basement with brick walls. Set back from Route 5 in Charles City County, the land on upper Virginia Peninsula had been part of a ten-thousand-acre grant by the English crown. It was named River Edge.

Grover and Berta agreed to pay a whopping $100,000 for the property, reduced to $95,000 without the vintage English furniture, a price most local residents considered way too much. Alfred said his parents initially planned to title the property in the children's names, but when that proved impractical, they put in Grover's and Berta's names. Later, Berta would discover that the parcel had only been titled in Grover's name. The whole family moved to River Edge in September 1946.

Leaving Harmony Hill was figuratively in the middle of the night. Alfred said his father locked a sawed-off Browning shotgun and a Mauser military rifle in an upstairs closet. They left behind much of their furniture and boxes and boxes of family documents, photographs, and legal papers in the garage, eventually pillaged and scattered by looters. Roger Grigson later discovered these discarded items when he returned to his neighbors looking for the children.[16]

The setting for River Edge included beautiful low flatlands northward of the James River, where old Route 5 twisted and meandered along an old Indian trail beneath large scarlet oaks, sycamores, sweetbay magnolias, and Virginia pines. A

---

[16] Roger Grigson recovered these abandoned Bergdoll artifacts, organized them, and presented them to the Chester County Historical Society and Downingtown Area Historical Society in West Chester and Downingtown, Pennsylvania. They proved invaluable for research into Grover's legal and financial affairs while he was a fugitive in Germany.

long lane led to the house with multiple peaked dormers, a four-car garage, and implement sheds. Upon moving in, the Bergdolls hired a groundskeeper, housemaids, and a cook. The horses were brought from Harmony Hill, but it took a while to repair the neglected landscaping, even in the horse pastures.

Back in Pennsylvania, Harmony Hill Farm languished. The exorbitant price tag of $65,000 was too high, and no one would buy it. The farm was in Berta's name, but Grover would not approve a sale or agree to rent it. Abandoned, it soon became run down and overrun with wild animals and looters.[17]

At River Edge in the late 1940s, farm workers employed by the Bergdolls planted corn crops and helped install a large vegetable garden, but these were soon abandoned, Alfred said, as too much work for the benefits they produced. Their main farmworker quit when he heard Grover making derogatory remarks about him. Eventually, the fields lay fallow and were overgrown with vines and weeds.

Alfred said his father continued with his cruel treatment of the farm animals,

Like Harmony Hill, River Edge also offered a separate section, left background, where Grover lived a life of alcoholism and paranoia, and more abuse on his wife and children. The family expanded with Katharina (right), and an adoptive son, Buster (left), pictured with Helene, Grover's dog.

to the point of locking the doors and windows of the implement shed, leaving the swallows unable to feed their nesting chicks. Erwin and Alfred had to crawl into a small window to rescue them.

Alfred said his mother made some friends in Charles City County, but his father remained reclusive on the estate, contributing to his growing mania. He also grew more impulsive, once starting a grass fire without considering how fast it would spread, nearly burning the house, and shed. As a result, he suffered blisters on his

---

[17] Many years later, Harmony Hill Farm was purchased by East Bradford Township, Pennsylvania, and turned into a passive park, Harmony Hill Nature Area. Today, the site of the Bergdolls' farmhouse and barn, and the brick smokehouse, are accessible to the public via walking trails that begin at Skelp Level Road and meander into the Valley Creek valley below. The foundations for each structure were still visible in 2023.

sandaled feet. Despite the difficulties of Berta and the children living in one section of the house and Grover in another, the family grew with the last of their natural brood, Katharina, born in 1947 in unusual circumstances. Berta moved to a maternity home in West Chester, Pennsylvania where the baby's delivery was performed by Berta's familiar doctor. Grover then drove them back to Virginia in his new Hudson Commodore, another Super Six.

By 1950, Alfred had enough of life with his parents at River Edge, and he moved to New York City to work a menial job as a clerk, living in a small, inexpensive cold water flat on East 11th Street in Manhattan. His brother Erwin would later join him.

In the summer of 1950, however, the Korean War was developing, and Alfred found his name on the list of young American men being drafted under the updated post-World War II draft law of 1948. Alfred took out his typewriter in August 1950, as his father had done many years earlier. He wrote a letter to the draft board in New York saying, "I will not report for a physical examination on Monday, not on any other day, either! I will refuse to be inducted into the armed forces if an attempt is made to induct me."

With a name like Bergdoll, it didn't take long for federal prosecutors and the Army to hunt for Alfred. He was arrested in New York on December 1 and charged with dodging the draft, just like his father and Uncle Erwin before him. Alfred (probably Berta) hired an attorney, Herman Adlerstein of New York, but, this time, there was no running away or challenging the draft laws as improperly implemented. Alfred pleaded guilty to draft evasion on December 18 and was sentenced to serve five years in federal prison at Lewisburg, Pennsylvania. Adlerstein was quoted in the newspapers, which covered "Bergdoll's boy," extensively, as saying to the judge, "Alfred's father's troubles may have affected this boy's attitude."

Ironically, when Alfred was 12 and Grover was in prison, Berta wrote to her husband about her disciplinary problems with Alfred, otherwise a typical adolescent. Grover's reply suggested sending Alfred to camp to mingle with American boys. "A little military training wouldn't hurt him either."[18] Alfred went to summer camp in New Jersey.

While Alfred was gone from River Edge and serving his prison term, more headlines hit the newspapers about the Bergdolls, but for another unusual reason. On September 1, 1952, Alfred's brother Erwin (Bubi) was on a camping trip in the mountains of northeastern Pennsylvania. Along with Erwin on the camping expedition was Charles P. Van Pelt, 18, of Rosemont, Pennsylvania, Philip Steel, 17, of West Chester, Pennsylvania, the Bergdolls' former Harmony Hill Farm neighbor, Roger Grigson, and,

---

[18] Details of Alfred's draft evasion, arrest, trial, conviction, and prison sentence come from federal records. He omitted his draft evasion and imprisonment from his diary-manuscript, stating only several years of absence from River Edge. Beginning in 1960, Alfred corresponded with the renowned U.S. government official Alger Hiss, convicted of lying about spying for the Soviets. Alfred and Hiss were in prison together at Lewisburg.

in a supervisor capacity, Roger's father, William Herb Grigson, the athletic director at Roxborough High School in Philadelphia's Roxborough neighborhood.

The rain had settled into Cherry Springs State Park in West Branch Township near Coudersport, Pennsylvania, and the boys went to a small airport facility in the park seeking shelter and adventure. Unknown to them, the airport manager stood waiting with a shotgun because burglars had repeatedly broken into the airport facility to steal items. When the boys appeared outside a window at 9 pm, Alfred L. Sallade, 35, recklessly fired his shotgun, killing Van Pelt almost instantly and wounding Bergdoll.[19]

The spectacular incident, reckless but accidental, made national headlines because of the most famous name associated again with gunfire and death, Bergdoll. More attorneys were hired, but the boys were released from any blame. Sallade, the father of three children, was initially charged with first-degree murder and faced the death penalty, but it was later reduced to voluntary manslaughter. He was convicted in 1953 and sentenced to four to eight years for his carelessness.

Alfred was in federal prison in 1952. He could do nothing to help his younger brother through this difficult and emotional time.[20]

Through the 1950s, Grover's mental instability continued as the Bergdoll children matured while living at River Edge. Alfred described his father as increasingly plagued by "delusions and hallucinations." Grover accused a telephone repairman of planting bugs on their phone lines. He accused someone of stealing his valuable horse saddle when he had locked it in a closet, nailed the door shut, and forgot about it. Grover also believed he had contracted syphilis, saw detectives following him, and was being shadowed by pickpockets. Driving home from Richmond one day, Alfred recites how Grover claimed to Katharina and Buster in their Hudson Commodore car that flying saucers were following them, piloted by FBI agents. Katharina said she and Buster just agreed with their father because his comments were "nothing very unusual."

Grover also began the unusual repetitive practice of wiping down his dinner plates and silverware and switching plates of food with the children at the last second before a meal, afraid that Berta was trying to poison him. He placed padlocks on doors to rooms, cabinets, and cupboards, even a chain and padlock around a large chest freezer full of food.

Alfred wrote, "as time went on, father got more and more distrustful of his family." The many padlocks were not enough. Accusing Berta of stealing a $10,000 bill, Grover filled a cigar box with heavy bolts and placed it as a trip device above a

---

[19] Details of Erwin Bergdoll and Roger Grigson's connection to the incident were provided by newspapers and court and prison records for the shooter.

[20] Charles Patterson Van Pelt is memorialized through the Van Pelt Library at the University of Pennsylvania and the Van Pelt Auditorium at the Philadelphia Museum of Art.

locked door in his library. Instead of catching an intruder, he caught himself. The bolts fell onto Grover's head, leaving him and his locked library a bloodied mess from his punctured scalp. Instead of going to a doctor, Berta stitched up the gash.

Alfred said his father's favorite expression was always, "What a mess." One day, Alfred writes, Grover misbehaved severely, and his brother Erwin asked rhetorically, "Shall I go in there and shoot him?"

In the mid-1950s, Grover's legal issues continued. Sued again in 1955 in New York State Supreme Court by his German attorneys and their heirs for his extended unpaid legal fees, Grover finally settled with them for $5,000. It was far less than he had agreed to pay the attorneys who got him out of the moral's allegations brought against him almost 30 years earlier. Paying the settlement and legal fees in the case would not have put Grover in the poor house. Through the 1950s, he was receiving regular distributions from Emma's estate. One check to Grover from Emma's estate was $60,000, and he received several, with the last distribution occurring in 1956. Despite his growing bank and stock portfolio accounts, Grover still pleaded poverty to his family, repeating a motto from grandfather Bergdoll, "shirtsleeves to shirtsleeves in three generations."[21]

Grover's erratic behavior grew. Trying to replicate his youth in Brewerytown when he and his brother had pet bears, Grover bought two black bear cubs through a mail-order service, and the kids named their dog-like pets Blacky and Honey-Bear. Alfred said his father beat the bears with sticks when they wouldn't behave. Blacky died from poisoning by licking flea shampoo from Honey-Bear that Grover had carelessly poured over her body. When Honey-Bear turned on Grover for the stick beatings, Grover shot her with his .44 Magnum revolver. The entire bear incident lasted only four months.

Then Grover got a purebred German Shepherd named Helene. Unable to properly train the dog, Grover kept her tied to a chain or corralled in a kennel, seldom having a moment of freedom to run on the 500-acre secluded property.

Alfred said Grover's animal abuse at River Edge spread to the younger children too, including an adopted son, Buster, who was born in Delaware and survived a tragic car accident in 1950 that killed his parents, distant relatives of the Bergdolls. When four-year-old Buster arrived to live with the Bergdolls, he still had cuts and bruises on his young face from the crash. As he grew older, Alfred relates that Buster became so afraid of Grover that he would hide and have to be talked into coming to the supper table to eat.

---

[21] Emma's estate was distributed by a 1938 deed of trust to Louis, Charles, Erwin, and Elizabeth, or their heirs. The family reached a settlement with Grover in 1940 with $60,000 in cash and 20 percent of the remainder of Emma's estate after distribution to his siblings upon their mother's death. As part of the settlement, Grover also relinquished all claims to a share of Emma's valuable property near Washington, in Somerset, Maryland.

Grover once accused Buster of stealing his driver's license and putting rat poison in his living room. When he ordered Buster to the front lawn, Grover threatened to shoot his adopted son with his gun. Katharina pleaded with her father, saying it was Alfred who placed the rat poison under a cabinet. For standing up to her father, Katharina received her one and only smacking from Grover's backhand. Buster later told his sister the frightening incident was the first time he considered suicide. Then, for about two years, on and off, Grover held Buster from attending school, wanting their adopted son home because, in Grover's fragile mental state of mind, he was afraid of staying at River Edge alone. When Berta arranged for the school principal to come to River Edge to discuss Buster's truancy, Grover allowed Helene, the German Shepherd, to intimidate him so strongly that he left without an agreement.[22]

Alfred said, "Buster had been ordered about, oppressed by father almost every waking minute of the day, except on those rare days when he was allowed to go to school."

Alfred suggested that his mother often went along with the abhorrent behavior of her husband to avoid physical confrontations. Still, she was steadily growing fearful and deeply concerned about how to handle the problem.

While he had times of normalcy, studying astrology, ancient Egyptian history, mathematics, engineering, and bridge building, an issue contributing significantly to Grover's erratic behavior was alcoholism. Miller High Life lager beer became his favorite drug, along with wine and whiskey, sometimes mixed with beer. Alfred said it was not unusual for Grover to drink one or two cases of beer a day, carelessly discarding the clear glass bottles wherever he found them empty.

While drinking heavily, Grover got into automobile crashes. A serious rollover crash in the 1947 Hudson Commodore knocked him out, broke his ribs, and slightly injured his youngest daughter, Katharina. Grover was reportedly traveling up to 100 miles per hour when an overinflated tire exploded. Unconscious, Grover was pulled from the wreckage by prison convicts passing by while working on the road. Carried to a Richmond hospital by the father of Katharina's schoolmate, Grover bled all over the car seat. Returning to River Edge from the hospital in a taxi, Alfred said Grover suffered amnesia and appeared unfazed by the crash or its significance involving himself and his daughter.

In 1959, Grover impulsively accepted an offer to buy his 88-acre farm on the south side of West Chester Pike along Darby Creek in Broomall. He had intermittently listed the property, long since voided of the dilapidated farmhouse and barn, for sale for $100,000 since 1946, but there were no buyers. West Chester Pike had been widened to four lanes in 1954, with Pennsylvania exercising eminent domain

---

[22] Grover avoided prosecution for Buster's long truancy because of political conflict over desegregation efforts in Virginia schools that offered families relief from compulsory education laws.

procedures for about one-third of an acre of Grover's farm, including the old trolley tracks. After legal challenges, Grover finally got a few thousand dollars for it.

In 1959, when he accepted the $100,000 offer, Grover needed Berta's signature to complete the sale. Like her previous negotiations over their marriage, Berta insisted that in return for her signature, Grover would have to stop abusing Buster and let him go to school. Alfred said this measure was his advice to his mother, but Grover refused to go along and declined the sale.

Near the end of 1959, with Grover exhibiting behavior that was "blatantly psychotic," according to Alfred, he and Berta discussed, for the first time, involuntarily committing Grover to a mental hospital. When the adult siblings agreed, Berta and Alfred hired Richmond attorneys to prepare their case. Among all the others, one alarming incident was Grover locking himself inside his library and panicking when he couldn't get out. He tried to shoot the locks off the door with his shotgun, but it was still locked. Alfred had to climb into a window to rescue him.

For commitment, State Police and sheriff's deputies served him papers, effectively an arrest. Alfred said Grover had driven his small Hudson-Nash-American Motors two-door car to the end of the River Edge lane to pick up the younger children from the bus stop. The police met him there and showed the warrant enforcing his travel to Richmond for arraignment in court. First, though, Grover talked the officers into allowing him to drive back to the garage and park his car. While this served to drop the children at the house, another motive was also achieved. Grover had $30,000 in cash on him, and he wanted to lock it in the car. It was later recovered by Alfred and Berta's attorneys and held for safekeeping.

On the way to Richmond and court, Grover must have charmed the police officers because they recommended a reasonable attorney who temporarily got him out of the mental commitment jam. It began a multi-year relationship with Grover's last lawyer in his life, University of Richmond business law professor David Meade White, Jr.

Berta and Alfred's lawyers were authorized to examine Grover's locked quarters at River Edge. Removing the locks from doors, windows, cabinets, drawers, and even the chest freezer, they found weapons, ammunition, and food hordes. Canned and bagged food and hundreds of pounds of frozen food, all locked and hidden away from Berta and the children. They were not starving for lack of food, but it supported Berta's and Alfred's testimony about Grover's senility and psychotic behavior. They also found a trove of financial and legal documents and uncashed dividend checks.

When Grover appeared at his mental capacity hearing in Richmond, the second in his life after Charles Bergdoll's 1915 challenge to Grover's capabilities, Erwin (Bubi) attended and told his brother Alfred that their father "looked like a trapped rat."

David Meade White, Jr., was a crafty and resourceful lawyer with political and legal connections. He understood that if Grover agreed to a marital separation from Berta, he could avoid involuntary mental commitment and live independently. Through negotiations with lawyers from both sides, Grover wisely agreed.

Alfred reported that as part of the separation agreement, Berta got custody of the minor children, with Grover banished from visiting River Edge. Berta was awarded the Tidewater property and Harmony Hill Farm, still in her name, and Grover kept his Broomall farm. Most important for Grover, he would not be sent to a mental hospital. He chose a Richmond hotel instead.

When the lawyers realized the value of properties and securities involved in the agreement and then opened Grover's safe deposit boxes at the Richmond State Planter's Bank containing $120,000 cash and two $10,000 bills, Alfred said the lawyers wanted $15,000 in fees but later raised it to $25,000.

Grover soon tired of living in a hotel and, in 1960, convinced his brother Erwin to let him live at Erwin's farm in Honey Brook, Pennsylvania. Erwin, his wife Lena, and their young children Mercedes and Louis E. Bergdoll (Louis number five in the Bergdoll family) were there. And, at times, Erwin's son Erwin Rudolph Bergdoll, Jr. (Butsi, pronounced Bootsy) would return to Honey Brook, where, according to Alfred, he and his uncle Grover became drinking buddies.

Grover bought Butsi a new car to drive Grover back and forth to Richmond. Grover vowed he would also buy Butsi an airplane, and they would fly back and forth.[23] If Butsi weren't around to drive, Grover would hire a taxi for the 300-mile trip.

Alfred wrote that his father didn't resent being booted from River Edge by Berta and his children; he just moved on with his life. However, it was about this time when Grover created a will, Alfred remembered. It left the bulk of Grover's estate to their youngest child, Katharina, whose age precluded her from playing a role in his departure. The older children, who had conspired to send him away, Alfred claimed, were left $10 each.

On February 12, 1962, Karl Charles Alvin Bergdoll-Brawn died in San Diego, California, at 75. His body was returned to Philadelphia, where he was buried in the Brawn plot next to his daughter, Emma.[24]

Also, in 1962, Grover mainly lived at the William Byrd Hotel in Richmond. Erwin had kicked him out of the Honey Brook farm for insulting comments about Erwin and his family, and providing potentially deadly wild mushrooms to Erwin's and Lena's children.[25] Alfred said he last saw his father in Richmond on Christmas Eve, 1962, during a brief visit with his sister, Katharina.

---

[23] Alfred recorded this revelation in his diary-manuscript. It was all hyperbolic bragging by Grover, however, because he didn't have a pilot's license and hadn't flown an airplane since 1913.

[24] Charles' California obituary does not mention his connection to the Bergdolls. While Alfred's diary-manuscript incorrectly claims Charles died in a mental hospital, Brawn's obituary states, "San Diego hospital." Brawn's grandchildren say Charles had been admitted to a nursing home with vascular disease and died from colon cancer.

[25] The mushroom incident is profiled in the Foreword.

Alfred wrote in his diary-manuscript of the last time he saw his father: "He walked off but watched us until we drove away. It was the last time I saw him. His Christmas must have been sad, alone in the William Byrd Hotel in Richmond."

In February 1963, Richmond police were called when Grover flew into a rage, smashing his hotel room. Then he was found drunk on the street with no memory. Berta was called, and Alfred took the Greyhound bus to Richmond to consult with his mother on what to do with his father. By then, Berta had divorced Grover, stating she feared he would cause her bodily harm. She had no legal recourse. But, with Alfred's help and the police report, they got him checked into Westbrook Sanatorium, a former Virginia plantation rebuilt with grand Victorian mansions and turned into a psychiatric hospital in Richmond. Doctors diagnosed a viral infection in his brain, causing delusions, anger, and rage. He was treated with antibiotics and improved for a while. The hotel did not file charges or costs for the damaged room. Grover had been a loyal paying customer.

Grover's mental disorder was serious, however. Psychiatric experts at the Medical College of Virginia described "bizarre behavior" with "sadistic attitudes toward his children, herding them about with animal shocking devices." They called him paranoid and delusional, shooting locks from doors, and believing that a simple surgery needed to remove an abscess on his neck would leave him dead. Grover finally agreed to the procedure without anesthesia. He thought bellboys at his Richmond hotel were federal agents spying on him. The doctors diagnosed "paranoid delusional thinking" with evidence of organic brain disease.

In April 1963, working with attorney David Meade White, Jr., the Virginia Chancery Court appointed White and Alfred guardians of Grover's estate. Alfred did not find cash through his father's papers, but several stock certificates and his lopsided will were quickly challengeable.

Aside from the stock investments, Grover's most significant asset was the Broomall farm, and Alfred remained resolute. He would not sell the farm because capital gains taxes and state and federal taxes would be enormous. And he felt that the property would increase in value.

While living at Westbrook in June 1963, Grover suffered a minor stroke, partially paralyzing his right side. It slowed him down tremendously. October 18, 1963, marked Grover's 70th birthday. There was no celebration. The rest of 1963 was uneventful for Grover living in Westbrook as the Bergdolls and the nation were overcome with grief over the assassination of President Kennedy.

Then, in February 1964, Grover's German Shepherd dog, Helene, died from old age. She had never acclimated or become friendly and protective of people, as German Shepherds do under normal non-abusive circumstances. Alfred said she was always kept in a pen. The German Shepherd's life was much like Grover's.

Grover probably didn't know his dog had died. He was losing his memory, forgetting the names of his youngest children first. The only memory he retained, however, and resorted to in the form of child talk in German and English, was of his mother, Emma. About the only advantage of his deteriorating mental conditions, Alfred said, was his lost interest in alcoholic beverages, including his daily one bottle of Miller beer, allowed by Westbrook. Instead, he grew fond of sweets, as many dementia patients do. Concurrently with Grover's hospitalization, Erwin's advancing age caused health problems for the other surviving Bergdoll male of his generation. Erwin also resorted to alcohol later in life, as did his son, Erwin, Jr. (Butsi).

Alfred said Butsi called him one day in 1964 in New York to elicit help gaining control of his father's estate, valued at $2 million. Butsi was staying in a New York City Hotel with a man he called his secretary, still driving the car Grover had bought for him. Erwin, Sr., and Lena had gone to live with Lena's family in Haddon Heights, New Jersey, as boarders paying a hefty $300 per week for room and board and caretaker health services for Erwin. Butsi had been waging a legal battle with his father for years. It was coming to a head with attorneys filing lawsuits over the elder Erwin's fortune.

In his downtrodden years, Butsi lived at Erwin's Broomall farm for a while, so desperate that he burned Bergdoll household furniture in the fireplace or woodstove to keep warm. Arriving at the Honey Brook farm one day and finding everyone gone, Erwin, Jr. got into his father's safe and removed securities worth an estimated one-half million dollars. Alfred said his cousin could sell a substantial portion of the securities through an Allentown, Pennsylvania bank because his name was the same as his father's name on the securities. When lawyers for the elder Erwin put a stop order on the securities sales, Erwin, Jr. again challenged his father in court, claiming the securities had been purchased for him.

Alfred said he went with his cousin to court in Camden County, New Jersey but remained an observer because he knew of Butsi's alcoholism and his record of thievery from his father. As a boy, Butsi had discovered a stash of $5,000 worth of silver dollars in Erwin's Broomall farmhouse. When Erwin, Sr., discovered the mostly depleted collection of coins, he hid the rest in his barn. But Butsi found them too and spent every last one.

Erwin Rudolph Bergdoll, Sr., the slim, handsome, and charming championship driver of the 1911 Fairmount Park Motor Race and second most notorious World War I draft dodger, entered Cooper Hospital in Camden for the last time in March 1965. His wife, Lena, and daughter, Evelyn, visited him and found Erwin dead in his bed on March 21 before his nurses realized it. He was 74.

The immediate cause of death was pneumonia brought on by multiple debilitating ailments. Erwin was buried at Harleigh Cemetery, between Collingswood and Camden, New Jersey.[26]

---

[26] Harleigh Cemetery was later renamed Camden County Veterans Cemetery.

By the 1960s, all that remained of Grover's 88-acre Broomall farm were the remnants of old West Chester Pike, center, and scrubland, right. Upon Grover's death, it was sold for $855,000. By 2023, the farm property had become a shopping center anchored by a large grocery store. (Bergdoll Family Collection)

As with Louis', and Emma's deaths, Erwin's obituary mainly focused on the past notoriety of the Bergdolls.

Following Erwin's funeral, disputes over his will began almost immediately. It had been written while Erwin was in the hospital, not long before his death. It left everything to his wife, Lena, and nothing to his children. Alfred believed the will had been arranged and signed hastily without considering taxes. On behalf of Erwin's children, challenges to the will were filed in Pennsylvania and New Jersey. The list of attorneys involved in the legal fight over Erwin's estate would grow to nearly a dozen.

Then, less than a year later, on January 27, 1966, it was time for the ultimate Bergdoll obituary. Grover died at Westbrook Sanatorium in Richmond at 72. Doctors ruled the cause to be bilateral bronchial pneumonia after years of suffering from paranoid illness, chronic brain syndrome and cerebral arteriosclerosis. Alfred was not there at the time—he had never visited his father at the mental hospital—but he recorded in his diary-manuscript that Grover's last word was "Mother."

Along with his cause of death, Grover's doctors opined that Grover was so mentally ill on April 4, 1961 when he revised his will leaving everything to his youngest child, Katharina, that "he did not know the extent of his property, he did not know his rightful heirs, and that he was completely incompetent of making decisions relative to the disposal of his estate."

Grover was buried distant from River Edge, at Heritage Memorial Park Cemetery, in the lower Middle Peninsula, Mathews County, Virginia.[27]

Upon reading Grover's obituary, which appeared in hundreds of newspapers around the world, Vincent J. Tully of Philadelphia, who knew Grover when they were young, wrote to Alfred: "As I write this to you, on my left is a framed picture showing a 110 (150) HP Benz, on its last lap on the way to win the 1911 Fairmount Park race. The driver is Erwin, and at his side is Frank Johnson. Also, there is a snapshot of an aircraft flying over the old Polo Grounds in the same park. It's Grover."

Long after their crimes and dashing from the draft, people still clung to the memory of Grover and Erwin as daring adventurers and champion sportsmen of an earlier era.

In March 1966, Alfred and attorney David Meade White were appointed by Virginia Chancery Court to handle Grover's estate. With a law partner, White presented Alfred with a graduating fee proposal from 10–17½ percent of Grover's gross estate. Alfred said that when he challenged the amount, White agreed to reduce it to 5 percent.

Discussions among the attorneys settling Erwin's estate did not go so smoothly. Alfred described the contentious situation in April 1967 in a Camden, New Jersey courtroom for challenges in New Jersey and Pennsylvania. Alfred said that while Erwin's daughter, Evelyn, arrived in New Jersey in a rented private airplane from Illinois, Butsi drove to Camden from New York City with an attorney who had to pay for the gas. Alfred said Butsi was broke, disheveled, wearing ill-fitting clothing with his dirty pants barely extending to his ankles. He had shaved for court but needed a haircut.

The negotiated settlement provided for Butsi and Evelyn to get $50,000 each in cash and trust and an additional $75,000 each to pay attorneys and end the lawsuits. Erwin's younger children, Mercedes, and Louis, each got $50,000 in trust. Alfred felt that Butsi got more than he deserved because he had already blown through a substantial amount of his father's money. He thought that Evelyn and the younger children "were shorted."

A dozen lawyers in the estate settlement got about $200,000 in fees. The rest of Erwin's $2 million estate went to his wife, Magdalena: about $1.4 million.[28]

One of the lawyers had previously represented Emma's estate. He approached Alfred after the judge approved the settlement agreement and said he had fought

---

[27] Heritage Memorial Park Cemetery is also known Windsor Gardens Cemetery near Dutton and Soles, Virginia.

[28] Alfred Bergdoll's record shows slightly smaller valuations for Erwin's estate settlement. The numbers presented here are gleaned from legal documents and 1967 reporting from the *Associated Press*.

Grover, left, and Berta, holding baby Berta in 1939, right, finally settled lawsuits over Emma's family-guided trust for money that flowed from mother to son and son to mother, unchecked for decades. When Grover's large estate was settled in the 1970s and re-invested to benefit all nine children and Berta, it had grown to about two million dollars. (Historical Society of Pennsylvania/ *Philadelphia Record*)

in France during World War I. He said that when soldiers in his unit read about Grover and Erwin running from the draft, they said, collectively, "Good for them."

In poor health herself, Magdalena Hettmansperger Bergdoll died soon afterward, in 1968. It's presumed that Erwin's estate was further dispersed to his children.

Grover's children were fortunate that their father's final attorney, David Meade White, Jr., properly arranged Grover's will to invest his estate and equal distribution among them. Finally, the locks were removed from Grover's cash hoard, securities, and real estate. Alfred said, "We nursed father's estate along to a reasonably satisfactory realization. Father would have been surprised to see its value. It was divided equally and provided a nice little financial package for each of his children and our mother."

Epilogue

Not long after his father died, Alfred Bergdoll was determined to write the incredible Bergdoll family story. He would call it the *Curse of the Bergdoll Gold*.

Unfortunately, it never got to publication. The unfinished typed and hand-written document is more diary than manuscript, peppered with many illegible notes scribbled in the margins and taking up entire pages added after the typewriting was done.

To gather information about the family in Philadelphia, Alfred and his siblings traveled to their family origins in the United States in 1967–1969 for tours of the many Bergdoll properties. Alfred, Erwin, and Katharina Bergdoll began at the Broomall farm along the West Chester Pike much broader and more traffic-choked than when it was a gravel path lined with a trolley track in their parents' and grandparents' day.

Emma's mansion of granite walls and red tile roof, built by Charles Bergdoll in 1907 on 12 acres of land, was still standing along with the elaborate carriage house, outbuildings, and chicken shed. A large sign in the weed-filled yard said, Castle Apartments.

They walked to Darby Creek and found the remains of Erwin Bergdoll's swimming pool behind the stone and concrete dam he built with the bucket scoop of his 1913 Oliver tractor. For so many summers, the grove around the swimming pool was filled with laughter and socializing among Bergdoll family and friends.

Only the skeleton remained of Erwin's three-story Victorian farmhouse, the original Broomall property developed by their grandfather, Louis Bergdoll, on a hill west of the creek. Erwin bought it in 1911 in preparation for his 1915 marriage to Sarah Parker with 66 acres for $8,000 cash and a $4,000 mortgage. The old yellow barn where Erwin hid from federal agents and Louis stashed his Blériot airplane had fallen in with only the stone foundation and hundreds of slate roof tiles remaining. Erwin's long narrow machine shop, the resting place of Grover's Wright B Flyer, was gone, demolished for the widening of the pike.

Across the highway, there was nothing left to see of their father, Grover's farm, the 88 acres reduced to 75 when they were taken for the wider pike and realignment of Lawrence and Langford Roads.[1]

---

[1] Grover's vacant Broomall farm was finally sold in February 1969 to a real estate development company for $855,000. In 2023, its primary use was for a grocery store shopping center.

Having lived most of their lives in Virginia, Alfred, Erwin, and Katharina could only imagine what it must have been like when their family filled the mansions and grounds and were surrounded by mature trees and landscaping, barns full of livestock, workers, and activity, with race cars in the long driveway and airplanes in the shed … and federal agents spying from the pike.

Later, the three siblings returned to Philadelphia for a tour of the Bergdoll city properties with a longtime family friend, Harry Feldman, who lived near the Bergdolls in Brewerytown and tried to interest Emma to patronize his dress shop. This visit occurred on a Sunday, and in 1968 while meeting Feldman at the Marriott Hotel near the infamous Bergdoll Wynnefield mansion, they could not sip a lager and imagine it was Bergdoll Beer because of Pennsylvania's Blue Laws, prohibiting alcohol on the Sabbath.[2]

First, they toured Brewerytown and the many red brick buildings that made up the renowned Bergdoll Brewery. As luck would have it, they were befriended by a man from inside the old brewery building who gave them pads of paper with the imprint of the Bergdoll Brewery buildings and a trademark, a round disc depicting a griffin "in a standing attitude with its right leg raised and resting upon the side of a beer barrel supported upon the barrel stand." It said, *Old Style Lager, The L.B.B. Co., Philadelphia, PA., Established 1849. Trade Mark.* The pads were left over when the buildings were sold and resold. The kind man even allowed them inside to climb the worn wooden stairs trod by their grandfather and great-grandfather beneath the iron beams and columns, the concrete floor incised with circles for the iron rims of the great oak beer kegs. They could look up to the ceilings designed by the Philadelphia brewery architect Otto Wolf for the tall beer vats as it was being fermented into tasty and foamy Bergdoll lager.

In 2023, the remaining Bergdoll Brewery buildings were used for office space and apartments. The sign of *Bergdoll & Psotta, 1875*, remains inlaid on the brick wall of the main brewery building.

Driving up the slight incline of North 29th Street, they found the old Bergdoll mansion used as a Baptist church. While the mansion was somewhat run down, the heavy iron fence with a decorative hops flower at each balustrade remained firmly intact. Even the horse-hitching post remained. Around the corner on Cambridge Street, the three-story carriage house built by Emma after her husband, Louis, died was used as an automobile repair garage. In the back of the carriage house, high above the grain and hay storage bins, was Emma's four-passenger black barouche, wheels cast aside and its canvas top folded backward. The only reason it remained is that carpenters who rebuilt the large carriage doors for the modern use of the building failed to realize until too late that it would not fit through a smaller

---

[2] Pennsylvania Blue Laws restricting sales of alcohol were enforced for hundreds of years, in part because of the pre-Prohibition influence of such large breweries as the Bergdoll Brewery.

Grover's children, Alfred, Katharina, and Erwin (Bubi) Bergdoll, toured the Broomall farm estate a final time in 1967. Left to right, Katharina Bergdoll standing on the foundation of Erwin Bergdoll's barn, Charles' and later, Emma Bergdoll's mansion, and Alfred and Katharina Bergdoll standing near the door of the remains of their grandfather's, and later, Erwin's farmhouse. Their tour was for research and recollections, some of which were used in this book. (Bergdoll Family Collection, Historical Society of Pennsylvania)

opening. From that point onward, the Bergdoll mansion and carriage house were used for apartments.[3]

Alfred, Erwin, and Katharina also admired the three-story brownstone Louise Bergdoll Alter mansion next door, more elaborate than the Bergdolls' brick mansion and in pristine condition. It had been sold several times without Alter's magnificent antique furniture.

They toured the former Louis Bergdoll Motor Company building at 18th and Callowhill Streets but quickly moved on from the nondescript building, which offered little interest.

---

[3] By 1984, the original Bergdoll mansion was in very poor condition, surrounded by overgrown trees and weeds, and appeared abandoned. In 2023, it was restored with a connecting structure between the house and the carriage house. It was still split into apartments.

They slowed their automobile tour in front of the large Louis Bergdoll brownstone Italianate mansion at 600 North 22nd Street at Green Street but did not get out or enter the property. Louis' sons Louis, Jr. and Wilbur still lived there. The two families had not been on cordial terms for years. In 2023, the splendid Louis Bergdoll mansion, built in 1890 for the Pennsylvania Secretary of the Treasury, was split into apartments but still elegantly appointed and furnished.[4]

Alfred began writing his manuscript and later returned to Philadelphia from his home in New York in 1969 to visit the Bergdoll plots in Philadelphia area cemeteries. He found his grandparents' graves at Mount Vernon Cemetery, the tall stone obelisk topped by an angel with an outstretched right arm. In the center of the stone is a circular carving of leaves around large interlocking decorative letters, LB for Louis Bergdoll. His name is referenced as junior, although the elder Louis Bergdolls did not share common middle names as would a true senior and junior father and son. Because he died unexpectedly and so young, Emma likely chose the obelisk memorial.

Emma's parents, Johann Christoph Barth and Margaretha Wilhelmina Doerr Barth, and her brother, Carl Friedrich "Charles" Barth, are buried at Northwood Cemetery, West Oak Lane, Philadelphia.

Also in Mount Vernon Cemetery, Alfred found the grave of his father's best friend and cohort, co-pilot, and co-racer in youth, Charles Kraus. In his later years, Kraus conducted real estate and insurance business for the Bergdolls and Albert Hall.

A bit farther from the Bergdoll grave, Alfred found a large obelisk, Brawn, surrounded by a low stone wall. It was the final resting place for Charles and Louise Anna Brawn and their daughter Emma C. Brawn, who was accidentally killed by a gunshot on the Broomall farm in 1928. The stone had originally contained the name Bergdoll, but it was recut to install Brawn.

Across the Schuylkill River in Lower Merion Township, Pennsylvania, Alfred visited West Laurel Hill Cemetery and asked the caretaker where to find Lot 318, Montgomery Section.[5]

"Oh, you mean the Bergdoll tomb," the caretaker replied. It was a tourist attraction, even in 1969.

Not far from the cemetery administration building is the large light gray Bergdoll mausoleum, erected by Louise Bergdoll Alter. It stands among other great Philadelphia beer families like the Betz's and Poths. Stained glass windows are on each mausoleum wall, depicting candles burning in them. A concrete walk leads up to the stone block

---

[4] Alfred, Katharina, and Erwin re-visited their Bergson cousins in the early 1970s and were shown great hospitality with a tour of the grand mansion. During this visit, Louis Bergson, Jr. showed them a 1912 telegram from Orville Wright informing Grover that his Wright B Flyer was ready for delivery.
[5] Renamed Laurel Hill West in conjunction with Laurel Hill East across the Schuylkill River and downstream in Philadelphia.

building, with brass and bronze doors. The name Louis Bergdoll Sr is cut into the front of the stone mausoleum below the round dome.[6]

A small bronze plaque on the wall to the right of the door reads: Erected to their memory by Louise Bergdoll Alter, Elizabeth F. Schoening Rieger, Catherine W. Schoening Sauers, Louise Schoening Shmidheiser. A.D. 1915.

The Bergdolls in the West Laurel Hill Cemetery were initially buried at Mount Vernon Cemetery and moved in 1915 at the direction of the elder Bergdolls' sister, Louise Alter. It may have resulted from a schism between Louise Alter and Emma Bergdoll, who lived side-by-side in life but eternally apart in death. A perpetual care trust established by Louise Alter still paid for fresh flowers regularly placed in the tomb.

Also in 1969, Alfred visited his cousins, the Strohms, in their comfortable twin stone home in Philadelphia's Overbrook community. Emma Strohm, Grover's first cousin and Erwin's former fiancé, greeted him warmly. Together, they drove into the Philadelphia suburbs to visit with their aging aunt, Elizabeth "Betty" Bergdoll Hall, the only Bergdoll of her generation surviving. Alfred said Aunt Betty was perfectly groomed and dressed.

"She looked solid, strong, and assured," is how he described Elizabeth Bertha Bergdoll Hall in her 81st year.

They had to drive past the Broomall farms to get to and from Betty's house. Nothing was left to see except Emma's grand mansion, partially obscured from West Chester Pike by thick overgrown trees, vines, and shrubs.

In March 1976, a fire of undetermined origin gutted Emma's abandoned mansion. Photographs taken by local firefighters showed a massive ball of orange fire erupting from atop the stone structure between the matching twin spires. They determined that the fire began in the basement of the vacant house. A stone skeleton façade was all that was left, with the massive stone front porch still intact. High above remained the triangular piece of stone from Charles' quarry inscribed with the date *1907 A.D.* The mansion was a total loss from the fire and had to be demolished.

Many years later, after protracted legal battles between Grover's estate and Pennsylvania and the federal government over the planned construction of the interstate highway bypass around Philadelphia, the West Chester Pike (Route 3) interchange of I-476, locally known as The Blue Route for the blue-penned path of three highway options, cut through the heart of the Bergdolls' Broomall farms.[7]

---

[6] The reference to Sr. was possibly done for clarification .

[7] While Alfred detailed his father's last decade, many of Grover's legal documents produced by his final attorney, David Meade White, Jr, of Richmond, were available for review at the Historical Society of Pennsylvania. They explain Grover's last legal fight, to retain his Broomall farmland or be paid the value he believed it was worth. He lost again. Pennsylvania confiscated 13 acres of the Broomall farm to construct I-476. This time Grover's attorney got paid when he completed his services.

The highway interchange consumed Grover's land and Erwin's farm. Today, tens of thousands of cars and trucks pass through what was then the Bergdoll's fields and side yards overlooking the Darby Creek valley. The front door of Erwin's machine shop sat on what is today the offramp leading to West Chester Pike westward.

Depending upon the time of day, I-476 is either a speedway or clogged with modern automobiles, the same path traveled by Erwin and Grover in their race cars. Occasionally, an airplane will fly overhead following the highway route from the Delaware River inland through Pennsylvania, the same path Grover flew in his Wright B Flyer.

Alfred did not travel farther west to tour the remains of Harmony Hill Farm near Downingtown in Chester County, Pennsylvania, or Erwin's western farm in Honey Brook Township. By then, the abandoned properties had become overgrown and fallen from use. Harmony Hill was later purchased by East Bradford Township and became a passive park with hiking trails leading from Skelp Level Road into the Valley Creek valley below. The trails pass within a few feet of the Bergdolls' farmhouse and barn foundations. A few outbuildings, such as Berta's brick smokehouse, remained for many years. The land still offers privacy and remoteness, the very reason it was chosen as the Bergdolls' retreat.

In 1969, Berta Franck Bergdoll still lived in the Tidewater region of Virginia, but she had sold River Edge. She died on January 2, 2001, at 93, and was buried in a rural community of Virginia's Middle Peninsula overlooking the Chesapeake Bay.

River Edge became run down again and overgrown with weeds for over 30 years, but in 2010, new owners began a complete restoration, consulting with historical preservation experts.

The infamous Wynnefield mansion was long gone by the Bergdoll children's tour of Philadelphia in the late 1960s. The location of Grover's capture and escape and so much drama, the Wynnefield mansion brought out so many emotional memories for Alfred; one reason he may not have wanted to visit the location in the 1960s. Again, because this infamous mansion is gone, the other mansions are often mistaken for Wynnefield. The three-acre lot was subdivided, and multiple homes were built. For many years the old iron fencing remained. Nothing of the mansion where Grover was captured in the window box or where he kept his race cars in the garage is left from when Wynnefield was surrounded by police, federal agents, and scores of gawkers. Neighboring mansions are still there, of course, and just up Wynnefield Avenue is the former Elizabeth and Albert Hall mansion, today's Settlement Music School.

In Delaware County, west of the Philadelphia city limits, the old Eagle Hotel is long gone, replaced by commercial buildings of all shapes and sizes. Across North Eagle Road at Garfield Avenue, the 24-acre Eagle Flying Field site is the modern Manoa Shopping Center with a large grocery store, coffee shops, and various other shops for the dense neighborhood that filled in the flying field in the 1960s and 1970s.

In the early 1940s, a wrecking company demolished the Wynnefield mansion, top, in return for valuable lumber and the ornate woodwork inside. The mansion lot was sold and subdivided into five new home-building lots. The worker is standing in Grover's 1920 window box hiding place. The Broomall mansion, bottom, burned in 1976 and was also demolished. It made way for the West Chester Pike interchange of Interstate 476. (Historical Society of Pennsylvania/*Philadelphia Record*, Temple University Urban Archives)

If Alfred, Erwin, and Katharina had traveled to see the Bergdoll property in Somerset, Maryland, in the late 1960s, they would have found another empty Bergdoll lot that would later be developed into a massive high-rise condominium project and community parkland. While the Emma Bergdoll trust sold the 132 acres of prime Washington-area land in 1946, the first legal roadblocks to its ultimate development were not cleared until 1969.

In the first stage of development approval for "the Bergdoll Tract," the Town of Somerset gained 12 acres of parkland and a swimming pool. They also won a reduction in the height of the future condos and less density. But the development stalled for another 17 years.

Then, in 1987, the Town of Somerset considered de-annexing a portion of the Bergdoll Tract on which the high-rise condominiums would be built. The *Washington Post* reported that Somerset residents were concerned the new "apartment dwellers would not share the interests of the townspeople." Many residents did not want the new condominium owners to outnumber and outvote the existing residents. The town's mostly single-family homeowners also wanted to maintain their bucolic setting near the Friendship Heights subway station and "the chic boutiques of Wisconsin Avenue's so-called Gold Coast." In 1988, the residents of Somerset voted 90 percent in favor of de-annexation. The connection with Bergdoll's controversial past did not influence the vote.

Legal entanglements over the Bergdoll Tract went back as far as 1938 when Emma, having difficulties managing her far-flung properties, had failed to pay the property taxes for years. She turned the Bergdoll Tract and tens of thousands of dollars in securities over to Berta, understanding that Berta would manage the tax issues and sell the securities to pay off the mortgage on a large Philadelphia property. Berta did nothing but hold the paperwork. The only reason the Bergdolls didn't lose the valuable Somerset land for unpaid taxes is that street and utility expansion required taking some of the Bergdoll Tract by eminent domain. Instead of paying the Bergdolls cash for their tiny bits of property, Somerset used the money to satisfy the outstanding taxes.

The entire "what a mess," as Grover often referred to his many tangles, was finally resolved with the creation of the Emma Bergdoll Trust in 1938 and a financial settlement between the trust and Berta and Grover in 1940.

Counting the decades of legal wrangling over the Somerset property between the Bergdolls and the decades of objections over the sale and development of the Bergdoll Tract, it is today, by far, the most protracted battle over residential real estate development in the Washington, D.C. region.

It took over 50 years to clear the Bergdoll Tract from legal challenges until the land was put to its most valuable residential and commercial use.

The high-rise development of condos was named Somerset House. It included three 20-story towers, with the first completed in 1988. The many units sold for $300,000 to $1.4 million in 1987's pre-construction pricing.

Most people today don't realize the immaculate, expertly maintained land for the condos, shops, parks, and swimming pools formerly belonged to the infamous Bergdolls of Philadelphia.

The other Bergdoll artifact missed during the family's tour in the late 1960s sat quietly inside the Franklin Institute science museum along the Benjamin Franklin

Parkway in Philadelphia. Because Alfred went to see his father's Wright B Flyer with his mother in 1938, it's challenging to understand why he and Erwin and Katharina didn't make arrangements in 1969 to view such an essential item in their father's young life, especially since Alfred was preparing to write the family's biography.

Since the Franklin acquired the Wright Brothers Wright B Flyer number 13 in 1933, it either hung from the ceiling or sat on the floor in the museum's Hall of Aviation. For all those years of the exhibit, there was scant information about the airplane, especially its connection to Philadelphia and Grover Bergdoll. It was almost as if the museum curators were afraid to mention that it was owned by the notorious Bergdoll and used to set early aviation records.

In the early 1990s, when I first viewed Grover's Wright B at the Franklin, there was so little information about the airplane's history that it inspired me to look it up in the infant era of the Internet. So did another visitor to the museum around the same time. Writing to the Franklin in April 1993, self-described Wright Brothers enthusiast August E. (Gus) Brunsman said he and his wife, Charlotte, of Kettering, Ohio were historians of the Wright Brothers. The Brunsmans said they "had great difficulty finding any appropriate label explaining the significance and history of your important Model B."

It remained that way for years. With wonderfully displayed exhibits in other parts of its world-renowned museum, the Franklin was remiss about the true story behind its Bergdoll Wright B Flyer for decades. I've always wondered why. The Appendix addresses the provenance of the Franklin's Wright B Flyer.

For his diary-manuscript, Alfred didn't make it to California to see what became of his uncle Charles Bergdoll-Brawn's life, partly because of the travel expense and because the East Coast Bergdolls were estranged from the West Coast Bergdoll-Brawns. Charles and Louise are buried beside their daughter, Emma, at Mount Vernon Cemetery in Philadelphia. The cemetery has suffered financial management problems over many years and has become increasingly overgrown with weeds and brush. It starkly contrasts with the burial site of the elder Bergdolls at West Laurel Hill Cemetery.

Interestingly, Grover's boyhood friend in crime and flying companion Charles Kraus, Jr. remained on friendly terms with the California Bergdoll-Brawns. Kraus spent many years handling their financial, legal, and insurance matters. He handled their burial and estate affairs, beginning with their daughter, Emma Christina Brawn's accidental gunshot death in 1928. As the Brawns' agent, Kraus arranged to pay Charles' funeral and burial cost of $420.60 when Charles died on May 12, 1962.

When the Brawns moved to San Diego County in 1929–1930, they purchased a 44-acre tract of land in Orleavo Heights, Vista, California, subdivided from the historical Buena Vista Rancho for avocado and citrus groves. They contracted with renowned architect Edgar V. Ullrich of La Jolla to build a Spanish Colonial Revival or California Moorish-style home in the shape of an H with "round-topped doors and windows, custom brass hardware, wrought iron railings, patios, and a staircase over the front entrance." According to a survey by the National Register of Historic Places, the 11-room and six-bathroom stucco-walled house also had elements of Mission Revival and is the most historically significant of its kind in the area.

Despite moving to California, Charles and Louise retained ownership and substantial income from their Birdsboro Stone Company in Pennsylvania. Records indicate their Vista home cost about $30,000 to construct, but when the orchards, garages, servants' quarters, and other outbuildings and landscaping were added, the cost rose to about $100,000. The trees alone on the property were magnificent. Avocado, citrus, cypress, eucalyptus, horsetail pine, coral and olive trees, palms, monkey puzzle, and Torrey pines were scattered about the acreage.

When root rot destroyed most of their plantings, Charles and Louise immediately encountered difficulty with the avocado and citrus orchards. They sued the developer of the former Rancho and won because fertile topsoil had been scraped from the surface of their land, rendering it more susceptible to root rot, a common issue in the region. It caused Charles to shift focus, purchase a 100-acre pasture lot and raise thoroughbred horses with two of his Arabians winning national grand and reserve grand champion titles. The Brawns moved twice in San Diego County, settling in Valley Center near Escondido. Charles and Louise maintained a thoroughbred horse farm in Pauma Valley until retirement in 1953.

During the Bergdoll children's late 1960s tours of their family's stomping grounds around Philadelphia, their aunt Elizabeth Bertha Bergdoll Hall was living with her daughter near Newtown Square, Pennsylvania, west of Philadelphia. In a 1968 photograph Alfred and Katharina took with their Aunt Betty, she appears slight in height, no more than 5'2", smartly dressed in an attractive blue dress with pearls, expertly coiffed hair, and wearing rimless eyeglasses. Her expression is stern and resembles Emma and Grover more than Louis, Charles, or Erwin. One can also see hints of her father's likeness.

Elizabeth outlived her husband, Albert Hall, who died at the Masonic Homes Hospital near Elizabethtown, Pennsylvania, in 1964 at 83. Elizabeth, the woman who may have been the first to drive her own car in Philadelphia and who raced around the Fairmount Park track with her husband, died on October 12, 1975, at 87. Elizabeth and Albert are buried near the elder Bergdolls' grand mausoleum at West Laurel Hill Cemetery.

It's clear from his writings that Alfred Bergdoll wished to publish his diary-manuscript and allow people to read his rendition of the incredible story of the Bergdoll family. It's also clear that when a reader gets deep into his account, Alfred holds contempt, disdain, and disgust for his father's actions and his mother's long acceptance of them. In the final decade of Grover's life, however, it's clear from Alfred's description that Alfred and his mother reconciled and worked closely together to manage Grover's mental illness, get him the supervision, and care he needed, and manage his estate for the future benefit of the Bergdoll children.

Alfred never published his story. It was incomplete for publication submission material, missing many names, dates, and details of significant events that were not available to Alfred in pre-Internet days. He expressed frustration with publishers who either didn't want it or demanded a more thorough and professional appearing copy of the manuscript before submission. While reading his 645 pages, many handwritten, it becomes clear that he's trying to set the Bergdoll family record straight. After Alfred completed his writings, in 1970, he admonished a Philadelphia newspaper for misstating that a Bergdoll Motor Company car was built by "infamous Bergdoll draft dodgers." He correctly stated that the Bergdoll car was built by Louis Bergdoll (Bergson), not Grover or Erwin Bergdoll.

Alfred's recollections, however, were most valuable for writing this depiction of the family's story.

Alfred donated his manuscript and many family documents and photographs to the Balch Institute of Philadelphia, which, in turn, donated its materials to the Historical Society of Pennsylvania.

Alfred Bergdoll never married and lived much of his adult life in Virginia and New York City. Alfred and his brother, Erwin, were collectors of underground comic book original artwork, which landed in the Billy Ireland Cartoon Library and Museum in Columbus, Ohio. It's described as "an underground collection beyond compare." When Alfred Bergdoll unexpectedly died of heart disease at 66 in New York in January 1994, his youngest sister, Katharina, assumed management of his estate. She has granted permission to paraphrase, cite, and quote from Alfred's story, *The Curse of the Bergdoll Gold*, for this book.

Additionally, Katharina Bergdoll, Louis Erwin Bergdoll, and Kathy (Bergdoll) Brawn Tidball reviewed and assisted in proofreading this manuscript before publication.

A few final notes on the Bergdoll saga. A few times a year, tours are conducted at the West Laurel Hill Cemetery in Bala Cynwyd, Lower Merion Township, Pennsylvania, with one of the most popular stops in front of the grand Bergdoll mausoleum. There, the tour guides explain the Bergdoll Brewery legacy in Philadelphia. But, when Grover Bergdoll is broached, attention perks up, and guests are intrigued about America's number one draft dodger, escape artist, and gold hunt hoaxer. When the tour ends, this inevitably leads to Internet searches for more information about the Bergdolls. Readers should be cautioned, however: some information found online about the Bergdolls has been stretched, embellished, misunderstood, and misstated for decades. For just one example, at each of the four times I've visited the Louis Bergdoll brownstone mansion in Philadelphia's Fairmount neighborhood, I've heard others on the sidewalk declare, "That's where Grover Bergdoll lived and where he was captured while hiding from the police." The inaccurate detail was printed long ago in a newspaper and, like many others, has been repeated on the Internet.

Also, as a result of misinformation on the Internet, the greatly embellished story of the Bergdoll gold is even more burnished as it travels from newspapers to blogs and social media. As late as 2015, a Pennsylvania newspaper suggested the Bergdoll gold may have been hidden in the Dillingersville train tunnel near Vera Cruz, Pennsylvania. The tunnel carries freight trains under the Pennsylvania Turnpike near Allentown. Another article in *The New York Times* suggested that Bergdoll's gold was hidden in rock in the stone quarry Charles Bergdoll owned near Birdsboro, Pennsylvania. None of this was ever true, but the stories are repeated continuously.

The evidence presented in this story should be understood. No Bergdoll gold is hidden anywhere in the Maryland mountains or Pennsylvania, or anywhere. It's a fact that Grover and Emma withdrew gold coins from the United States Treasury and then hid them behind a plaster wall in Grover's bedroom closet at the Wynnefield mansion. However, the gold was removed by Grover and deposited in a Philadelphia bank by Berta.

Just as you've read here about the family, the Bergdoll gold is simply one hell of a story.

Appendix I

Grover's Wright B Flyer

The Franklin Institute of Philadelphia provided documents and photographs that helped construct the fate of Grover's Wright B flyer. Details on the Ludington family, the Ludington Camden County Airport, and the airline that preceded the renowned Eastern Airlines came from the C. Townsend Ludington papers at the American Heritage Center, University of Wyoming. *The New York Times, Washington Star, Washington Times-Herald,* and *Time* magazine articles confirmed many Ludington documents. Additional information is from the *Philadelphia Inquirer, Philadelphia Record,* and Orville Wright's precisely-worded last will and testament giving the Wright Brothers' Kitty Hawk airplane to the Smithsonian. Long-time Franklin Institute curator John Alviti gave me copies of everything in the museum's Bergdoll Wright B file, including beautiful eight-by-ten-inch photographs taken by museum volunteer William Sheahan in the 1930s.

In 1913, Sheahan also took several photographs of Grover flying his airplane at Eagle Field. They are now at the Smithsonian in Washington. The pictures and Sheahan's unique relationship with Grover probably established his interest in the fate of the old Wright B airplane. A resident of Drexel Hill, not far from the Bergdoll farm, Sheahan would have been aware that the Wright B was rotting in Erwin Bergdoll's machine shop and being looted by thieves in 1933 when he removed the airplane for restoration.

While reading Sheahan's Franklin Institute file notes on the acquisition of Grover's Wright B, I noticed the description would change depending upon where and when it was being made. Multiple statements about the airplane gift were inconsistent. Sheahan or someone else wrote in Franklin Institute records that the airplane had been given to him (Sheahan) in a letter from Grover, then in a wire (telegram) from Grover, then by Grover himself, and then by the Bergdoll family. Sheahan said that he (Sheahan) then gave the airplane to the museum. For decades, this third-party acquisition explanation has been repeated in museum documents and press releases and, therefore, presented as fact in media.

Additionally, in a 1981 book, *Aviation and Pennsylvania,* published by the Franklin Institute Press, it's reported that Sheahan, in 1933, informed Ludington of Grover's airplane in shambles at Erwin's machine shop, not far from Sheahan's home. The book says, "after a short exchange of letters, Bergdoll, who was in exile in Germany, made a gift of the historic craft for display at The Institute." This is the only reference to "letters" as in multiple documents portrayed as gifting the airplane to the Franklin Institute, not to Sheahan "by letter" as is claimed in other documents. Furthermore, Ludington is quoted in the *Bulletin* newspaper as saying the museum acquired the airplane "through this chap, who is a friend of Bergdoll's." Apparently the museum trusted that Sheahan obtained the airplane properly and legally, albeit without a signed transfer document.

It should be noted that no one in the Bergdoll family today believes that Grover gave away his airplane without financial compensation. He was extremely possessive, claimed every cent he believed he was owed, and was tight-fisted with his money, even within his family. Grover limited his life-long companion and bodyguard, Stecher, to twenty-five cents a meal, challenged his butler over modest grocery bills, and went so far as to file for compensation from the U.S. government for the six bullets he fired from his pistol, killing, and wounding the 1923 kidnappers in Germany.

I asked to see the purported airplane gifting letter(s), so I could read it or them, judge Grover's mood, and inspect what he might have written about his predicament of hiding in Germany in 1933 that caused him to give his airplane to Sheahan, a man he hadn't seen in nearly 20 years. After several years of searching, none of the three curators who reviewed the Franklin Institute files could find a letter or any other document from Grover or anyone in the Bergdoll family gifting his airplane to Sheahan or the museum. From the Franklin curators, the conclusion was that an airplane gifting letter does not exist. Seven years of searching and gently, and respectfully prodding the museum to explain how it acquired Grover Bergdoll's airplane finally produced the following statement in April 2023 from Susannah Carroll, Assistant Curator of Collections and Curatorial.

> Though there is overwhelming circumstantial evidence of Mr. Bergdoll's gift of the Wright Model B airplane to The Franklin Institute, at this time, we have not turned up anything signed by Mr. Bergdoll mentioning his gift.
>
> From your own knowledge of Mr. Bergdoll and his background, you should understand why neither he nor The Institute would desire to have anything in writing documenting the oral gift. Bergdoll was still a fugitive and his assets had been and continued to be subject to government seizure.
>
> As you know, his wife, Berta, wrote a letter on November 14, 1943 to Orville Wright referring specifically to the Wright B "which was once his own". Additionally, at no time between 1935 (when the airplane was put on public exhibit) and Mr. Bergdoll's death in 1966 did he, his mother, Emma, or his wife, Berta, ever claim any right to the airplane, that a valid gift had not been made, or request its return.

The museum's statement leads to additional questions. If the airplane was an "oral gift," then why did the museum for decades describe it as a gift in writing? Since the gift in writing had been repeated by the museum on so many documents and press releases, how could it, in 2023, and for the first time, be described as an oral gift? Which is it? Presented by Grover to Sheahan in a letter or given to Sheahan orally in 1933 while Grover was hiding in Germany, four thousand miles from Sheahan in Philadelphia? Why did such a prestigious museum accept a historic and valuable artifact from a fugitive from justice whose assets were under seizure by the federal government, and do so through a third party (Sheahan) with no legal claim to the airplane whatsoever, and without a written and signed ownership transfer document? Why did no one in the Bergdoll family ever claim the airplane, that a valid gift had not been made, or request its return? Was it because the family had a multitude of other legal and financial issues to address? Was it because Grover Bergdoll was a fugitive, a prisoner, and suffered from insanity? Was it because Grover's children were led to believe by the museum that the airplane was a gift from their father? And was it because no one ever asked the museum to show proof that a gift was made in writing?

If the airplane gift was made by letter and it was lost, and the letter's loss could be proved, the benefit of the doubt would go to the museum. However, we should question why such an important document was carelessly handled, unrecorded, misplaced, and lost when many mundane documents have remained intact in the museum's Wright B file for decades. If a letter never existed, it might explain why there are so many mistakes and contradictions in the airplane acquisition timeline documents, including spelling errors in the names of important Franklin officials such as C. Townsend Ludington and William Sheahan. Neither would have misspelled his own name had they been the ones to have written a contemporary account of the acquisition timeline. Therefore, the Franklin report on how it acquired such an important artifact from a man hiding as a fugitive from justice in Germany may have been postdated by someone other than Sheahan and Ludington.

In 2023, I took my research further and arranged a search through the personal papers of Ludington at the American Heritage Center, University of Wyoming, Laramie. While there is a wealth of information in the Ludington papers about his aviation business and connection with the Franklin Institute, there is nothing about such a monumental event as saving the most original Wright B Flyer in American history. Surely, if he was comfortable with the acquisition, Ludington would have recorded his involvement in saving the airplane.

Additionally, and curiously, the only public portrayal of Grover's Wright B airplane rotting away in Erwin Bergdoll's machine shop was in a *Philadelphia Inquirer* article on Sunday morning, October 8, 1933. With two uncredited photographs of the airplane and a race car, and no byline for the article, it appears as if the story was a handout to the newspaper. It incorrectly identifies the building as Grover's "workshop" and misstates the car as Grover's "red racer" when it was Erwin's machine shop and Erwin's championship Benz racer. Based on the many errors in the article and lack of attribution, byline, and photo credit, I've theorized that the article was not written by a reporter who was on the scene, but, rather, by someone in the *Inquirer* newsroom who was given the photographs for publication, possibly as a preamble to buttress a story about rescuing the airplane. While a rescue was vital and valiant at the time, the question remains, was it done properly?

I've consulted with experts on museum curation and antiquities acquisition policies who've said that if they were in a similar predicament of having such a historical and valuable artifact in their possession without a written and signed donation letter, they'd be concerned about their right of clear title. They each expressed concern about the ethics of a third-party donation and acceptance of an artifact that may have been entangled in government seizure regulations at the time. One of them told me that a museum's policy in the absence of a signed gifting document should be to arrange negotiations with the artifact's original source to secure a formal possession agreement and record it for posterity.

Colgate University Director of Museum Studies Professor Elizabeth Marlowe said that a museum finding itself in this position should emphasize transparency about its acquisition. "Create a display telling the whole story of how they assumed the acquisition was made but now they realize ownership [may be] uncertain." Professor Marlow said new ethical standards in the museum profession derived from the 1998 *Washington Principles on Nazi-Confiscated Art* include "the responsibility to thoroughly research provenance and share what they find with the person making the claim."

I believe the Franklin Institute is the best place for the Bergdoll Wright B Flyer and that the Institute has been a responsible caretaker of the airplane for a period approaching 100 years. It is commendable to have saved it from ruination, arranged for funding and restoration three times, and kept it in its true home, Philadelphia. However, the museum's lack of details about the Bergdoll provenance and the airplane's significant contribution to aviation history is regrettable for both the public and the Bergdoll family.

If Grover Bergdoll did not bequeath his airplane to the Franklin Institute, who did? And was it a legal transaction? Could the museum legally take possession of an artifact from someone who didn't own it? Additionally, there is no record of Grover ever challenging the museum's control of his airplane, even after returning to the United States, serving his sentence in prison, and living at Berta's farm in Chester County, Pennsylvania. We don't know if he ever ventured into the museum to see his old airplane, but there is evidence that Berta and Alfred went to see it briefly during a visit to the museum in 1938. Alfred was allowed to sit in his father's airplane. He mentioned it in just a short line in his diary-manuscript. He said the museum officials told him, at the time, it was one of the museum's most important artifacts. Alfred said that he and the other members of the Bergdoll family always believed what they were told, that their father gave his airplane to the museum.

The issue is certainly an ethical, if not legal quandary for the Franklin Institute. In these times of prestigious museums and nations worldwide being forced to acknowledge and relinquish Nazi-pilfered artwork and Egyptian antiquities, the Franklin Institute would continue its tradition as an outstanding science repository through a dialogue with the Bergdoll family for a possession and display agreement satisfactory to both parties.

Appendix II

The Bergdoll Beer Recipe

Charles Barth and his wife, Elizabeth Rebstock Barth, in 1902 with their family. Left to right, the children are Karl, Fritz, Elsa, Alvin (on his mother's lap), and Anna. At this time, Barth was the president and general manager of the Bergdoll Brewery at the height of its production and profits. (Margaret Barth Sutton, Meg Sutton, and Philip Karl Barth)

Sitting at a table just inside the large carriage doors of the 19th-century two-story brick and stone Jack's Firehouse restaurant in the Fairmount neighborhood of Philadelphia, Louis Erwin Bergdoll and I examine the heavy clear glasses of golden pale lager beer placed in front of us for lunch.

"I wish I could taste what Bergdoll Beer was like," lamented Louis, named after his father Erwin, his grandfather Louis, and his great-grandfather, Louis (Ludwig) Bergdoll, founder of the Bergdoll Brewery and its crisp lager beer. Taking a foamy sip from his glass of tap lager, Louis asks rhetorically, "Is this what it was like?"

We swirl our glasses and then gulp our lager after a clinking toast to Bergdoll Beer. Since that afternoon in April 2019 at the former firehouse from where crews were sent to fight the great Bergdoll Brewery fire of 1887, I've wondered if Louis would ever get the chance to sample his family's beer. Until just weeks before the publication of this book, I thought it was impossible. But now, with the July 2023 discovery of an old beer recipe from the turn of the 20th century written on a sheet of notebook paper by none other

The vintage 1900 handwritten recipe for Bergdoll Beer from the company's long-time brewer and general manager, Charles Barth, Emma Barth Bergdoll's brother. While it's impossible to fully replicate Bergdoll Beer with today's ingredients and production equipment, this recipe is as close as we'll ever come to producing the taste of the once-popular lager beer across several Mid-Atlantic American states. (Margaret Barth Sutton, Meg Sutton, and Philip Karl Barth)

than Emma Barth Bergdoll's brother, Karl (Charles) Friedrich Barth (1857–1937), the 30-year brewer and general manager of the great Bergdoll Brewery, I realize it's nearly possible.

Cheers to Louis E. Bergdoll. Your chance to sample your family's beloved lager beer is coming.

In Chapter 1, Philadelphia beer historian Rich Wagner recounts how lager beer in the United States originated in Philadelphia with a Bavarian brewer immigrant, John Wagner (no relation), who smuggled bottom-fermenting yeast into the country after pilfering it from Bavarian monks who had been brewing lager beer since the 1300s. The cleaner-tasting, cold, and less intoxicating lager proved to be much more popular than ale brewed and consumed at room temperature in America before Wagner's introduction of lagering.

Following the lead of other breweries in Philadelphia in the late 1800s, the Bergdoll Brewery produced lager with Charles Barth working as the brewer, collector, superintendent, secretary, treasurer, and then president and general manager of the brewery. Barth knew a thing or two about brewing lager beer, having started brewing with Bergdoll, then going on to work for Robinson Brewery in Scranton, Pennsylvania, and Rothacker, and Poth in Philadelphia, before returning to Bergdoll. Entrusted by Louis Bergdoll and then Emma, Charles Barth ran the brewery during its beer and money-making heyday from 1886 until Prohibition forced it to close in 1920.

Sometime during this period, Charles Barth wrote the recipe portrayed here, and while it's a standard recipe for a small quantity, we presume that he replicated the Bergdoll Beer lager formula of hops, malt, sugar, yeast, and water. The handwritten recipe was presented during a Barth family gathering in Maine following the January 31, 2023, Florida death of Barth's granddaughter, Margaret (Nancy) Barth Sutton, 90. Her daughter, Margaret (Meg) Sutton, provided the beer recipe from family genealogy records, and it was photographed and approved for publication by another of Charles Barth's great-grandchildren, Philip Karl Barth.

On two pages of stationery under the heading, Charles Barth, 260 Sumac Street, Wissahickon, Philadelphia, PA., the beer recipe subtitles are *Cooking, Carbonating,* and *Bottling.* Referencing temperature, Barth emphasizes, "This is important." Upon completion of the beer brewing, he also advises, "It improves with age."

Charles Barth's Beer Recipe

Cooking: Boil package of hops in 3½ gallons of water for 1½ hrs.
Add contents of can of malt, 1½ lbs. sugar, stirring thoroughly until dissolved.
Boil ½ hr. Strain into crock thru heavy muslin and squeeze all the juice from the hops.
Add 3 gallons of boiling water.

Carbonating: Allow mixture to cool to room temperature (This is important)
Dissolve 2/3 of a yeast cake in a cup of warm water and add to liquid in crock, stirring thoroughly.
Cover crock with piece of muslin.
Skim night and morning using a large spoon. When mixture lies flat it is ready for bottling.

Bottling: Use beer bottles. Put ½ teaspoonful sugar in pint bottles.
Syphon off beverage, cork securely. Let bottles stand in the same room for a few days then place in a cool dark room.
Brew is ready for use in one week but it improves with age.

Select Character Biographies

Ansell, Samuel. (1875–1954) Samuel Tilden Ansell was a West Point Military Academy graduate, former Brigadier General, and acting Judge Advocate General in the United States Army during the war. He was awarded the Army Distinguished Service Medal. Upon retirement, he formed the Washington law firm Ansell and Bailey with Col. Edward S. Bailey of Philadelphia. Gen. Ansell died in 1954 at 79 and was buried in the U.S. Military Academy Cemetery at West Point, New York.

Bergdoll, Louis, the elder. (1825–94) Born as Ludwig Bergdoll in Sinsheim, Germany, the grandfather of Louis, Charles, Elizabeth, Erwin, and Grover, and founder of the Bergdoll Brewery was an energetic business builder and housing developer in Philadelphia's Brewerytown neighborhood. It's believed that he never knew that his wife, Elizabeth C. Woll, had a husband in Germany when he married her in the United States. Louis Bergdoll's portrait hung in Philadelphia City Hall and Sinsheim as a financial contributor to the poor in that community.

Bergdoll, Louis, the younger. (1857–96) Named Louis C. without understanding the source of the letter C, the father of the Bergdoll children lived a brief life, dying at the age of 39, probably from heart disease. Louis was head of the brewery for only two years after his father died. He reportedly told his collections assistant, Judge Romig, on his deathbed, to care for his wife, Emma, and the children.

Bergdoll, Emma. (1861–1944) Emma Christina Barth Bergdoll was born in Huffenhardt, Germany, and emigrated to the United States at 19. She worked as a seamstress and then as a servant in the Bergdoll mansion at 929 North 29th Street, Brewerytown, Philadelphia, before marrying Louis C. Bergdoll. Upon her husband's untimely death, Emma inherited a majority stake in the brewery and millions of dollars in cash, securities, and real estate from her husband and his parent's estates. Emma's death in 1944 at 83 was caused by heart disease, pneumonia, and senility.

Bergdoll-Bergson, Louis John, Sr. (1884–1942) The oldest of the five children of Louis C. and Emma Barth Bergdoll, Louis attended the University of Pennsylvania and, with his law degree, practiced law, invested heavily in real estate, and entered the automobile manufacturing businesses with his Bergdoll Motor Company. An early member and co-founder of the Aero Club of Pennsylvania, Louis acquired the first Blériot airplane in the United States but never flew it himself. Louis Bergdoll is also credited in 1907 for having the first Benz dealership in the United States and racing 200-horsepower Benz cars himself. He later changed his name and moved to New York to practice law and escape the notorious headlines of his brothers. Louis married Florence E. Seider, and they had two sons, Louis John Bergdoll Bergson, Jr., and Wilbur Charles Bergdoll Bergson. Louis died at his mansion in Philadelphia on August 2, 1942. His remains were cremated.

Bergdoll, Charles. (1886–1962) Karl Charles Alvin Bergdoll-Brawn's name was often misspelled as Braun. He married Louise Anna Goetz, a daughter of the brewery foreman. Charles built the great Bergdoll castle in Broomall along West Chester Pike but later sold it to his mother. Charles was the long-time owner of the Birdsboro Stone Company, a large, lucrative quarry that provided crushed stone for many asphalt road-building projects in eastern Pennsylvania. Not long after the tragic accidental death of their daughter, Emma, Charles and Louise moved to San Diego County, California, where they remained for the rest of their lives. Charles died in 1962 at 79.

Bergdoll, Elizabeth. (1888–1975) Elizabeth "Betty" Bertha Bergdoll Hall was the only daughter of Louis C. and Emma Barth Bergdoll. Said to have been the first woman in Philadelphia to drive her own car, she caused a social scandal when she married the Bergdoll chauffeur, Albert Hall. Emma arranged for Elizabeth to purchase a mansion in Wynnefield, Philadelphia. She also had a farm near Mount Holley, New Jersey. She raced in automobiles a bit with her husband and brothers. Later, she and Hall invested in real estate development and the cement and aggregate industry but suffered substantial losses during the Great Depression. After Albert died in 1964, Elizabeth lived with her daughter near Philadelphia for many years. She died in West Chester, Pennsylvania, in 1975 at 87 and was buried with her husband at West Laurel Hill Cemetery, Bala Cynwyd, Pennsylvania, but not in the Bergdoll family plot.

Bergdoll, Erwin Rudolph, Sr. (1890–1965) The fourth child of Louis and Emma Barth Bergdoll, Erwin was so interested in cars that he left school early to focus on building race cars. He won the 1911 Fairmount Park Motor Race in Philadelphia with record speed and time around the eight-mile course. He was the only Bergdoll to have entered all four of the prestigious Fairmount Park races. Erwin also ran from the war draft, and his first wife, Sarah Bolden Parker Bergdoll, died of pneumonia while he was hiding as a fugitive. Unlike Grover, Erwin surrendered and served his sentence before returning to his life on the Bergdoll farm. Erwin remarried to Magdalena Louise "Lena" Hettmansperger (1911–1968) in 1949. He died from various medical complications on March 21, 1965. Erwin and Lena named one of their daughters, Mercedes Benz Bergdoll (1953–2014), after his favorite car. Their youngest son, Louis Erwin Bergdoll, participated in the production of this story.

Bergdoll, Grover. (1893–1966) Perhaps suffering from a brain injury at birth and several concussions during his youth, Grover was always described as unusual. Despite the many reported impacts on his brain, Grover was knowledgeable with a firm grasp of complicated mathematics, engineering formulas, chemistry, astronomy and astrology, and history, including ancient Egyptian history. He was often called a coward for running from the draft, but Grover was also recognized for his daring nature with 748 flights in a Wright Brothers airplane without a significant incident and for setting early aviation records in his airplane. His marriage to Berta Franck produced nine surviving children (one adopted), with some conceived while he was hiding in his Philadelphia mansion as a fugitive from justice. After serving his sentence for draft evasion, Grover spiraled down a long road of mental disease and family strife. He died in a Virginia mental hospital at the age of 72.

Bergdoll, Berta. (1907–2001) Berta Emilie Lydia Helene Franck Bergdoll was born at her family's tiny cottage at the Weissenhof Sanatorium in Weinsberg, Germany. She agreed to marry Grover in Russia because she was underage, and he did not have the proper papers to get married in Germany. For many years, Berta lived under Grover's strict guidance, sometimes stingy and often abusive behavior, until their children were stuck in Germany at the start of World War II. Then, Berta became more assertive, gradually taking control of Grover's finances and legal decisions. She prompted his voluntary return to the United States to face trial and prison, purchased their Chester County, Pennsylvania farm, and tried to raise their children in a rural environment away from the glare of the press and the difficulties within the Bergdoll family. Berta later instigated the Bergdolls' move to Virginia and, along with her oldest son, Alfred, arranged for Grover to be institutionalized for mental instability. Berta later moved to the far eastern Tidewater region of Virginia, along the Chesapeake Bay. She died in 2001 and was buried in a small cemetery near Grover.

Bergdoll, Alfred. (1927–94) Alfred Bergdoll was the eldest son of Grover and Berta Franck Bergdoll and the first of their nine children. Born in Germany while Grover and Berta were traveling through the countryside, he lived as a child in Weinsberg, Germany, in his Franck grandparents' apartment. Although highly critical of his father's behavior, Alfred declined to report for the military draft in 1950. He was convicted and sentenced to the same term as his father, five years in prison. Alfred wrote a 465-page manuscript annotated with personal notes replicating a diary about his family and hoped to have it published. Instead, he donated the manuscript and many Bergdoll documents and photographs to historical organizations. Alfred never married and died alone in his New York City apartment in 1994, probably from heart disease. He was 66.

Blood, Leighton. (1896–1961) Leighton Harold Blood was a newspaper-magazine reporter, NBC radio writer, and broadcaster who, as a member of the American

Legion and contracted by *Hearst's International* magazine, went to Germany in 1923–4 to convince Grover to surrender and return to the United States to face trial. Blood's three-part article on Grover, some of it in Grover's first-person prose, is the first and only long-form interview that Grover gave after he became a fugitive. Leighton Blood was an Army veteran of World War I. He died March 29, 1961 and was buried at Long Island National Cemetery in East Farmingdale, New York.

Campbell, Bruce. (1880–1964) Captain Bruce R. Campbell served as Grover's Army defense attorney during his trial for draft evasion in 1920. Wrongfully accused by Grover of accepting a bribe to gain his release from top Army officials in Washington, Campbell was called before a Congressional committee to explain his substantial deposits into his New York bank account. He was cleared of the allegations by Congressional investigators. Lt. Col. Campbell retired from the Army in 1922 and lived in Washington, D.C. He died there at the age of 83. He was buried in Arlington National Cemetery Virginia.

Cresson, Charles. (1874–1949) Col. Charles Clement Cresson, Judge Advocate General, was the Army's chief prosecutor of Grover during his 1920 trial for draft evasion. Cresson was born in Pennsylvania, attended Princeton University and New York University School of Law, and lived most of his life in San Antonio, Texas. He served in both world wars. During the trial, Col. Cresson became so conflicted with Grover's lawyer that he challenged the former boxer, Harry Weinberger, to fight him in the street. The meeting never happened. After a long military and legal career, Col. Cresson died in San Antonio in 1949 at 74. He was buried in Fort Sam Houston National Cemetery, San Antonio, Texas.

Donaldson, Thomas. (1872–1934) A West Point Military Academy graduate, Major General Thomas Quinton Donaldson fought against the Sioux Indians in the late 1800s, with action at Wounded Knee and White Clay Creek. He also served in France during the war. Major General Donaldson reviewed the Bergdoll conviction and escape as inspector general of the U.S. Army. His review and conclusions laying blame for the debacle were submitted to the Army and the United States Congress. He concluded that overall responsibility for the escape lay with the adjutant general of the Army, the man in charge of all branches of the Disciplinary Barracks. Blame was placed on the Governors Island commander and the Army guards in charge of Bergdoll's security. Major General Donaldson died in 1934 at 70 at Long Island Veterans Hospital. He was buried with honors at Arlington National Cemetery, Virginia.

Dwyer, John. (1865–1930) John Patrick Dwyer was the editor of the renowned newspaper, the *Philadelphia Record*. He lived with four sons in Philadelphia's Overbrook neighborhood near Grover's Wynnefield mansion. At conflict with Grover since an incident with the children in the Wynnefield yard, Dwyer was appointed secretary of local Draft Board #32, which encompassed Wynnefield. Whether he exacted revenge by moving Grover's name up in the draft was never proved, but court records indicate that he did pay Grover's draft induction special attention over all others. Additionally, Dwyer instigated and led the public outcry over Grover's draft evasion with exclusive articles in the *Record* deploring Grover's actions. Dwyer was highly patriotic and sent his sons into the Army during the war. All survived. Dwyer died at home in 1930 at 65 while Grover hid in his mansion a few miles away. He was buried near Philadelphia at the Holy Cross Cemetery in Yeadon, Pennsylvania.

Gagarin, Gregory. (1895–1963) Gregory Gagarin was born Russian Prince Grigorii Andreivich Gagarin in Chattelerault, France. A former lieutenant in the Czar's mounted guard (Hussars), Prince Gagarin was wounded in the Russian Revolution and returned to his family's castle in Pskoff to raise flax. Under attack by the Bolsheviks, he managed to escape with a bullet wound to his hand while fleeing, first to the Mediterranean, then to Vladivostok, and finally to Paris to work as an interpreter for the British. He was hired by Lt. Corliss Griffis of the Graves Registration Service to surveil Bergdoll and provided the vital information that Bergdoll was hiding in Eberbach and could be captured. Prince Gagarin eventually emigrated to the United States, where he worked as a horse trainer and riding instructor on Long Island, New York, then in physical education at Penn State University, and later as a stable owner and riding instructor. He died at Chevy Chase, Maryland, in 1963 and was buried in Rock Creek Cemetery.

Gibboney, Clarence. (1868–1920) David Clarence Gibboney was born in Iowa and moved to Philadelphia to attend pharmacy school. He became secretary of the Law and Order Society, which focused on ridding Philadelphia of illegal saloons and excessive alcoholic beverage drinking. He became associated with Emma Bergdoll by shutting down illicit bars that competed with her Bergdoll Beer saloons. He also advocated for government control of liquor sales instead of Prohibition. An attorney who was often described as better at organizing cases for better attorneys, Gibboney ran for Philadelphia County district attorney but lost. He was regularly commissioned to help Emma and the Bergdoll boys in their various legal entanglements and public relations problems. He created the Bergdoll hidden gold scenario, which led to Grover's release from jail to search for the gold. Along with Emma, Gibboney was an investor in Tropical Products, a sisal manufacturing business with plantations in Campeche, Mexico. In December 1920, at 52, Gibboney and three other American businessmen drowned in a boating accident in the Gulf of Mexico. His body was returned to Philadelphia and buried at Arlington Cemetery, Drexel Hill, Pennsylvania.

Griffis, Corliss. (1895–1963) Lt. Corliss Hooven Griffis of Hamilton, Ohio, was the United States Graves Registration Service officer who organized the 1923 kidnapping attempt on Grover at the Hotel Krone-Post in Eberbach, Germany. He was an honorary member of the American Legion sent to France to help inaugurate the Meuse-Argonne American cemetery at Romagne. His nationalistic feelings inspired him to make the kidnapping attempt on Bergdoll. He denied that he did it for the reward. Griffis later became a real estate agent near Cincinnati, Ohio. He died there in 1963 at the age of 67.

Grigson, Roger. (1933–2017) Donald Roger Grigson was a neighbor and childhood friend of Grover and Berta Bergdoll's children in the 1940s at Harmony Hill Farm in Chester County, Pennsylvania. He rescued important Bergdoll family documents and photographs from the Harmony Hill garage when the Bergdolls moved to Virginia, saving them for posterity. They were used for research for this book. Grigson was an avid historian before his death in 2017.

Gross, Russell. (1893–1918) Russell Conrad Gross was the man depicted by the newspapers as the next man in line for war when Grover Bergdoll ran from the draft. Gross was born in Philadelphia and raised in a rowhouse. His father was a butcher, and his mother ran the Gross household. Gross served in France in Company E of the 328th Infantry and was killed in action in October 1918, less than a month before the war was over. It was later determined that Gross was not the true next man in line after Grover, but his story was already in the public spirit as being the rowhouse lad who went to war when the mansion-living Grover would not. The Russell C. Gross American Legion in the Overbrook section of Philadelphia was named in his memory. It later disbanded.

Hall, Albert von. (1881/2–1964) Chauffeur to the Bergdoll family, Albert married Elizabeth Bergdoll in 1909 and moved into real estate investment and development. His lifelong involvement with Bergdoll family affairs included motoring exploits, petitioning for leniency for Grover, and bailing out his mother-in-law. Albert Hall died in Masonic Homes Hospital near Elizabethtown, Pennsylvania, in 1964.

Harris, Peter. (1865–1951) Major General Peter Charles Harris served as adjutant general of the United States Army during Grover's trial in 1920. He was awarded the Distinguished Service Medal in 1919. His only son was killed in France during the war. His brother, William Julius Harris, served as a U.S. senator from Georgia during Congressional investigations calling into question Gen. Harris' decision to release Grover to find his gold. Gen. Harris retired from the Army soon after his trial in 1922. He died in Washington, D.C., in 1951 at 85. He was buried at Princeton Cemetery, Princeton, New Jersey.

Hunt, John. (1874–1951) Colonel John Elliott Hunt was the Atlantic Branch Disciplinary Barracks commander at Governors Island, New York, during Grover's confinement and trial in 1920. Col. Hunt was a West Point graduate and served in the Army in Cuba and the Philippines. He oversaw all the prisoners at Governors Island, landing there from Walter Reed Hospital after being injured in the war. He approved releasing Grover from jail for his gold hunt expedition without question, and assigned two noncommissioned officers for the guard despite the strong suggestion that they be officers. Col. Hunt was court-martialed for dereliction of duty in the Bergdoll escape but acquitted. He was promoted to major during his trial, and the announcement was made in the courtroom. Immediately afterward, in 1920, Major Hunt retired from the Army with a pension. Major Hunt lived in Chevy Chase, Maryland, and died in 1951 at 77. He was buried at Arlington National Cemetery.

Kane, Francis Fisher (1866–1955) Francis Fisher Kane was U.S. attorney in the Philadelphia region, appointed by President Wilson in 1913. He was the chief federal prosecutor through most of Grover's and Erwin's draft evasion activities, overseeing prosecutions through the Department of Justice until he resigned in 1920. Kane was highly liberal and advocated leniency for the Bergdoll boys. He ran as a Democrat for Philadelphia mayor in 1903 but lost to the Republican. He then became the first U.S. attorney for the Eastern District of Pennsylvania. Kane was also a principal founder of the Voluntary Defender Association, a group that provided free legal services to defendants. He also tried in vain to save anarchist murder defendants Sacco and Vanzetti from the death sentence in Massachusetts in 1927. Kane believed they were unfairly tried and found guilty, and 50 years later, Massachusetts agreed. Kane lived in Belmont, Massachusetts, where he died at 88 in 1955.

Kraus, Charles. (1894–1965) Charles John Kraus, Jr. was one of Grover's earliest friends growing up in the Brewerytown neighborhood of Philadelphia. Kraus was involved in many of Grover's driving, speeding, and legal infractions, the one who fired a gun upon a police officer when it was blamed on Grover. Kraus traveled to Ohio to retrieve Grover's Wright B airplane and then flew with Grover from Eagle Field on dozens of flights, including a record flight to Atlantic City, New Jersey. He helped Grover remain safe while in flight. He was with Grover in France when they were trying to purchase a more extensive and faster airplane to set more records. Kraus served in the Army during the first war, driving wagons and trucks in an engineering unit. He worked as an accountant for Albert Hall and Charles Bergdoll-Brawn, settling into the insurance and real estate business. He testified at Grover's 1939 trial for draft evasion and remained on good terms with the other Bergdolls while being estranged from Grover. Charles Kraus died in 1965 in Collingswood, New Jersey, at 70. He and his wife, Magdelena, are buried in Mount Vernon Cemetery in Philadelphia.

Lehmann, Walter. (1888–1948) Carl Alfred Walter Lehmann was born in Dresden, Germany, and served in the United States Army during the war despite his mother still living in Germany. Utilizing Lehmann's German heritage, U.S. Army Military

Intelligence at Coblenz sent him to Eberbach to spy on Grover. He was there watching in 1921 as Naef and Zimmer tried to kidnap Grover from the Eberbach wedding party. Lehmann later became a naturalized American citizen and personal butler for United States Attorney General A. Mitchell Palmer. In 1939, Lehmann testified before a Congressional committee about spying on Grover in Germany in 1921. His testimony was used to craft a bill to prevent Grover from returning to the United States. It was passed in the House but failed in the Senate. Lehmann died in 1948 at 59 and was buried in Sarasota Memorial Park Cemetery in Sarasota, Florida.

McAvoy, Charles. (1877–1937) Charles Dennis McAvoy, Sr. was the U.S. attorney in Philadelphia for the second part of Grover's legal wrangling with the federal government. He succeeded Francis Fisher Kane. McAvoy was appointed by President Wilson and, again, many years later by President Roosevelt. He also served as Roosevelt's campaign chairman in Pennsylvania. McAvoy died from heart disease in Miami Beach, Florida, in 1937 at 59. He was buried in St. Patrick's Cemetery, Norristown, Pennsylvania. His gravestone records his birthdate as 1878.

Naef, Charles. (1893–1970) Charles Otto Naef was a United States Army Intelligence officer who organized the 1921 kidnapping attempt on Grover Bergdoll. Naef was born in Italy but claimed his birth in Switzerland before becoming a naturalized American citizen. He served in the Army before and during the war, deserting his stateside post before returning, serving punishment, and re-enlisting to join the detective division of the Army. Naef was convicted in a German trial of assuming the duties of a German police officer by attempting to capture Grover. His sentence was commuted through negotiations between American and German officials at the highest level. Naef returned to the United States and lived on a small farm in New York's Catskill Mountains for many years before moving to California, where he died in 1970. His remains were installed in Desert Lawn Mausoleum in Yuma, Arizona.

Nelson, Eugene. (1895–1967) Corporal Eugene Victor Nelson drove an Army Cadillac for the 1923 kidnapping attempt on Grover Bergdoll in Eberbach, Germany. He was born in Chicago but lived in a remote region of Montana before the war. After the war, he married a French woman, briefly returning to Becket, Montana. After divorce, Nelson remarried and raised a family, toiling in the iron construction industry in Minnesota. Part of the Army's Graves Registration Service as a driver, Nelson was convicted in Grover's attempted kidnapping; Nelson convinced the German judges that he was an innocent farm boy from Montana and had little knowledge of his superior officer's plans. His sentence was commuted through a German-American settlement. Nelson died in 1967 and was buried in a military grave at Fort Snelling National Cemetery in Minneapolis, Minnesota.

O'Hare, John. Sergeant John O'Hare was the U.S. Army noncommissioned officer in charge of the security detail for Grover when he was released from jail in 1920 to fetch his gold. O'Hare was born in Ireland, emigrated to the United States in 1883, and was naturalized as an American citizen in 1894. He was a career military guard in the Army's 10th Guard Company, Fort Jay, Governors Island, New York. However, he was not knowledgeable about the country, making only one trip with prisoners to Fort Leavenworth, Kansas. His first ride in a car was in Grover's Hudson Super Six. While O'Hare was accused of getting drunk during Grover's escape, it was later determined that he had been sober for decades. O'Hare was court-martialed and acquitted. He later retired and lived in New York City.

Palmer, A. Mitchell (1872–1936) Alexander Mitchell Palmer was a lawyer, member of Congress for eastern Pennsylvania, and U.S. attorney general following World War I. He became notorious for approving the Red Raids in American cities, also known as Palmer Raids. His actions led to the resignation of the U.S. Attorney in Philadelphia, Francis Fisher Kane, at the height of the federal investigation into Grover's escape. Palmer traveled to New York City for a critical meeting with federal agents on the opening day of Grover's draft evasion trial at Governors Island. The trip was portrayed in the press as a public display of support for a court martial of Grover just as he lost an effort to have his case tried in civil court. Palmer also attempted to gain the Democratic nomination for president in 1920. Palmer hired the German-American Army detective Walter Lehmann who spied on Grover while hiding in Eberbach, Germany as his butler at his elegant homes in Washington, Miami Beach, and Stroudsburg, Pennsylvania. Palmer died in Washington following an appendectomy in 1936 at 64. He was buried at Stroudsburg's Society of Friends Cemetery (Laurelwood).

Parker, Sarah Bolden. (1897–1919) Married to Erwin Bergdoll, Sarah was left alone on their Broomall farm while her husband evaded the draft. She died of pneumonia while he was hiding as a fugitive.

Romig, James. (1851–1935) Judge James E. Romig of Reading, Pennsylvania, became associated with the Bergdolls as Louis Bergdoll's (the elder) collector, today's accounts receivable agent. A widower by 1880, he entered politics, became a state representative, and then a magistrate in the Philadelphia city court, adjudicating a variety of minor crimes until he became a full-time advisor and fixer for Emma Bergdoll and her children. Although Romig was never much of a court official, the title "Judge" stuck to him for the rest of his life. With Gibboney, Judge Romig arranged to hire lawyers and other advisors who counseled Emma and Grover on their traffic infractions, saloon and rental businesses, and Grover's conviction for draft evasion. He infamously accompanied Emma to the U.S. Treasury in Washington to withdraw gold. He was disgraced during Grover's first trial for lying about joining the Bergdoll boys at their Maryland hideout to deliver money and was also responsible for trying to gain leniency for Grover by trading federal government use of the

Bergdolls' vacant property near Washington, D.C. Judge Romig retired and died of heart disease at his Roslyn home in January 1935 at 83. He was buried in West Laurel Hill Cemetery, Bala Cynwyd, Pennsylvania.

Sachs, Robert Paul (1882–1964) Robert Paul Sachs was born in Germany and emigrated to the United States in Philadelphia in 1894, where his family joined the German Society of Pennsylvania. Sachs became a naturalized American citizen in 1907 and worked as a vacuum cleaner salesman in advertising, and ran a business providing tools to jewelers and engravers. Around 1920, Sachs moved to Oakland and Fair Oaks, California, where he became the creative genius behind successful advertising campaigns for Coast Tire and Rubber Company of Oakland. Sachs investigated Grover in Germany. Why Sachs returned to the United States before Grover's 1926 criminal trial on the moral allegations inspired by Sachs' investigation remains a mystery. Sachs' absence as the chief accuser was critical in Grover's acquittal. Sachs had returned to California by 1940, living as an unemployed commercial artist in a boarding house in San Francisco. At some stage before 1950, Sachs was institutionalized at the sprawling Mendocino State Mental Hospital in Talmage, California, and died there in 1964 at the age of 81.

Schmidt, Friedel. (1910–90) Friedel Lucia Elise Schmidt was the girl who was the object of Grover Bergdoll's affection in Germany in 1922 and 1923. Tried on a morals charge brought by the American Robert Paul Sachs in 1926, Grover denied seducing the underage Schmidt despite admitting they traveled for weeks together in a romantic journey through the Black Forest. News reports in German, French, and American publications repeatedly confused Friedel Schmidt's name with her sister, Liesel (Else) Schmidt, who died before the trial in 1925. Friedel Schmidt later married and died in Dusseldorf in 1990 at 80.

Schmidt, Carl. (1898–1923) Hermann Karl Heinrich Schmidt was born in Stein, Switzerland, and lived in Lausanne when, as an employee of the Leoni Detective Agency in Paris, he was hired to abduct Grover Bergdoll in Eberbach, Germany for transport across Germany and France to a ship bound for the United States. Not much else is known about Schmidt except that he took three bullets from Bergdoll during the attempted kidnapping and died in Grover's hotel room within minutes. Schmidt's body was later claimed by his brother and returned to Lausanne for burial. He was unrelated to the Heidelberg Schmidts, who were part of the 1926 morals lawsuit against Grover.

Sheahan, William. (1872–1956) William H. Sheahan was born in Maryland but lived until early adulthood in Maine. He took a job at a soda fountain company in Philadelphia and used his interest in photography to gain close access to Grover Bergdoll and Charles Kraus when they were flying Grover's Wright B airplane at Eagle Field in 1912 and 1913. Sheahan took several early photographs of Grover flying in his Wright airplane and the Eagle Field hanger. They were considered significant enough to be placed in the National Air and Space Museum. He also convinced Grover to take him for airplane rides. Sheahan became treasurer of the Aero Club of Pennsylvania and continued submitting articles to *Aero and Hydro*. Sheahan was instrumental in installing Grover's aircraft in the Hall of Aviation. He lived in Upper Darby, Pennsylvania, with his wife, Daisy. He died in 1956 at the age of 84 and was buried in Arlington Cemetery, Drexel Hill, Pennsylvania.

Sperber, Roger. (1897–1956) Ignace Roger Sperber was born in Paris and served in the French Army from 1915–19 during and after the war. He was employed by the Leoni Detective Agency of Paris when he was hired by Lt. Corliss Griffis, along with Carl Schmidt, to capture Grover Bergdoll. Sperber was the man whose thumb tip was bitten off during the hotel room scuffle with Grover that ended with the shooting death of Carl Schmidt. Sperber was wounded with bullets in his arm and shoulder. He was found guilty in the German trial. Sperber's military record indicates he was prosecuted in September and October 1934 for misappropriation of seized objects, convicted by default, and given an undetermined sentence. He traveled to the United States at least twice, married, and had a son. Sperber died in France in 1956.

Stecher, Eugene. (1886–1963) Eugene "Ike" Stecher became a childhood friend of the Bergdoll boys when his father worked in the brewery. Born in Neckarbischofsheim, Baden, Germany, he was a skilled foreign car mechanic and driver. He worked for Louis and Erwin Bergdoll as a mechanic, raced their cars, and served as a mechanic–driver for Emma and Grover. He lived in Philadelphia and near the Bergdoll farm in Broomall. Stecher served honorably as a first sergeant in the Pennsylvania National Guard. Mistakenly entangled with Grover's escape, Stecher was a fugitive for several years with Grover in Germany until he returned to the United States voluntarily to face his crime. He was convicted and sentenced to prison, but the sentence was reduced in return for his testimony against Grover. He did not serve time in prison. His last job was in aviation as a Philadelphia Air Transport Company foreman. Somewhat infirm in his older age due to severe leg injuries, Stecher saw his old friend, Grover, only once since he left him in Germany at the 1939 trial. Stecher died in Philadelphia in 1963 at the age of 76.

Weinberger, Harry. (1886–1944) Harry Weinberger was Grover's long-time American lawyer, defending him for his draft evasion trials in 1920 and 1939. He specialized in First Amendment cases and later focused on copyright issues. Besides Grover and Berta, Weinberger's famous clients included anarchist Emma Goldman and the American playwright Eugene O'Neill. Weinberger notably told a Congressional committee that he was the only lawyer who gained Grover's confidence and trust. Then, not long after Grover went to prison in 1939–40, Weinberger had to sue the Bergdolls to collect his fee. He got only a portion of it. Weinberger died in New York at 58 in 1944.

Wescott, John. (1849–1927) Judge John Wesley Wescott was the attorney general of New Jersey who made both nominating speeches for President Wilson at Democratic National Conventions. Grover's attorneys hired him for his connections with top officials in the White House. As a result, Wescott wrote a letter to Secretary of War Newton Baker in 1920 requesting as a personal favor that he review Grover's conviction and sentence and appealing for Grover's release to search for hidden gold. Wescott died at his home in Haddonfield, New Jersey, in 1927 at 78. He was buried at Harleigh Cemetery (Veterans Cemetery) in Camden, New Jersey, the same resting place as Erwin Bergdoll.

York, Calvin. (1879–1952) Sgt. Calvin York was the subordinate guard assigned to secure Grover when he was released from jail in 1920 to search for gold. York was a noncommissioned officer in the 10th Guard Company at Fort Jay, Governors Island, New York. Originally from Cordell, Tennessee, Sgt. York was accused of imbibing too much alcohol at the Wynnefield mansion when Grover and Stecher plied him with gin. Sgt. York was court-martialed and acquitted. He later retired from the Army and worked for the Borden milk company, living in the Bronx, New York, with his wife and children. York died in 1952 and was buried at Old Saint Raymond's Cemetery in the Bronx.

Zimmer, Frank. (1893–1970) Sergeant Frank Zimmer was from Wheatridge, Colorado, near Denver, born to Belgian parents. He served in both world wars and acted as Lt. Naef's subordinate during the attempted kidnapping of Grover Bergdoll in 1921. Zimmer was convicted, but his sentence was commuted by agreement between the Germans and Americans. He later returned to the United States, where he re-enlisted and served at Governors Island when Grover was returned there to face another trial in 1939. Zimmer retired in 1945 and died in 1970. He was 76. His body was returned to Colorado, where he was buried at Fort Logan Cemetery.

Acknowledgments

A complete story of the Bergdoll Boys would not have been possible without my ability to read and understand Alfred Bergdoll's diary manuscript written in the 1960s and 1970s. Although some of his recollections varied greatly from the official record of the many legal cases, Alfred's manuscript and handwritten diary-style notes were especially beneficial to illustrate the family strife caused by the Bergdoll legal and financial issues. I appreciate the cooperation of the Bergdoll family heirs for allowing me to cite and quote parts of Alfred's recollections in this story.

Alfred left his manuscript to the Balch Institute, which, when it ceased to exist, gave it and many other Bergdoll family documents and photographs to the Historical Society of Pennsylvania. The Society's cooperation with my several visits wading through the Bergdoll collection has been enormous.

With any great volume of research, cross-checking facts with multiple sources is paramount. I've tried to confirm the details of this complicated story with at least two sources, but, in some cases, an exact matching representation was not available. Therefore, any misrepresentations are mine alone.

A personal mention for Bergdoll cousins Katharina Bergdoll, Louis Erwin Bergdoll, and Kathleen Brawn Tidball for their guidance, constructive criticism, and review of the book manuscript. Brookline Books commissioning editor Jennifer Green took an early and keen interest in the story when many others thought it too complicated or that Grover was too reviled to be of interest. Also in Philadelphia (Havertown), Lauren Stead for Marketing of *The Bergdoll Boys*. From Oxford, England, Ruth Sheppard's steady guiding hand perfected the story's pacing, production, and editing, along with Lizzy Hammond and Mette Bundgaard. Also in Oxford, Declan Ingram designed a great book cover that inspires people to open the pages. Many thanks for the proofreading, guidance, advice, and wisdom from my beloved companion, Polly Davis, through many long days of writing, rewriting, and editing the text and photographs. I also thank my children, Grayson, Emery, and Jessie for their patience during my many hours away from them while working on the manuscript. Also, Philip Karl Barth for coordinating the use of genealogy information, documents, and photographs from the Emma and Charles Barth family.

The Chester County Historical Society also contributed many Bergdoll documents and photographs in West Chester, Pennsylvania, and the Downingtown Area

Historical Society in Downingtown, Pennsylvania. The Bergdolls' childhood friend and neighbor, the late Roger Grigson, rescued these artifacts from the Bergdolls' Harmony Hill Farm when they abandoned it in the 1940s. Roger's spouse, Carol Grigson, ensured I had access to all of them.

More documents, records, and confirmations came from the following institutions, repositories, publications, or people interested in the Bergdoll story and may not have been cited in the text. In no particular order:

Franklin Institute Science Museum
German Society of Pennsylvania
Hagley Museum
Haverford Township Historical Society
Free Library of Philadelphia
Library Company of Philadelphia
Clements Library, University of Michigan
Wright State University, Ohio
American Heritage Center, University of Wyoming
Yale University Library
Detroit Free Library
Library of Congress
Stadt Museum, Germany
Heidelberg University
Franklin D. Roosevelt Presidential Library and Museum
National Archives and Records Administration
Congressional Record
National Air and Space Museum
Old Rhinebeck Aerodrome
Penn Pilot
Aero Club of Pennsylvania
Philadelphia City Archives
Temple University Urban Archives
FBI History Files
Center for Jewish History
Landesarchiv Baden-Württemberg, Germany
Newspaper Archive
Newspapers.com
Find A Grave
Ancestry.com
Wikipedia
Governors Island National Monument
Montgomery County, Maryland Historical Society
Town of Somerset, Maryland

Wiltrud Flothow, Germany
Rich Wagner
John Alviti
Susannah Carroll
Philip Karl Barth
Patty Kessler
Nolan Doroski, Albany, New York Public Library
Debbie Harding
Seth Pancoast, Jr.
John Rizzo
Marple Township Historical Society
Delaware County Historical Society
Birdsboro of Yesterday
Bob McNulty, Philadelphia Stories
Canadian Pacific Railway
Hearst Corporation
Karl D. Qualls
Dickinson College
Russian Cultural Center, Washington, D.C.
The New York Times
Times Machine
Philadelphia Inquirer
The Philadelphia Bulletin
The Philadelphia Record
Eberbacher Zeitung
Life Magazine
Time Magazine
American Legion Weekly
Mercedes Benz Museum, Stuttgart
Historical American Building Survey
Fairmount Park Commission
Michael J. Seneca
Roberta E. Dell